D1715898

OLIVER P. MORTON AND THE POLITICS
OF THE CIVIL WAR AND RECONSTRUCTION

Oliver P. Morton, undated carte de visite.

Oliver P. Morton

and the

Politics of the Civil War and Reconstruction

A. James Fuller

The Kent State

University Press

KENT, OHIO

Library of Congress Catalog Card Number 2016054760

ISBN 978-1-60635-310-3

Manufactured in the United States of America

Library of Congress Cataloging-in-Publication Data

Names: Fuller, A. James, author.

Title: Oliver P. Morton and the politics of the Civil War and Reconstruction / A. James Fuller.

Description: Kent, Ohio : The Kent State University Press, 2017. | Includes bibliographical references and index.

Identifiers: LCCN 2016054760 | ISBN 9781606353103 (hardcover : alk. paper) | ISBN 9781631012716 (epdf)

Subjects: LCSH: Morton, Oliver P. (Oliver Perry), 1823-1877. | Governors--Indiana--Biography. | Indiana--Politics and government--1861-1865. | Indiana--History--Civil War, 1861-1865--Biography. | United States--History--Civil War, 1861-1865--Biography. | Legislators--United States--Biography. | Reconstruction (U.S. history, 1865-1877)

Classification: LCC F526.M87 F85 2017 | DDC 328.73/092 [B]--dc23

LC record available at https://lccn.loc.gov/2016054760

21 20 19 18 17   5 4 3 2 1

For my native Hoosiers,
Krista and Carson

Contents

Illustrations

Acknowledgments

IN WRITING THE LIFE OF OLIVER MORTON, I have accumulated many debts to individuals who have helped me throughout the process. Knowing that I cannot thank all of them, and at the risk of failing to acknowledge significant contributions, I humbly hope to express my gratitude to those who guided and encouraged me, corrected some of my errors, and inspired me.

The good people of Centerville, Indiana, have extended their Hoosier hospitality to me on several occasions over the years. I especially thank Ron Morris for his walking tour of the town on a rainy summer day. And I am grateful that he welcomed me into his historic properties—including the Morton House. Jim Resh and Beth Treaster were two among many others who made me feel welcome in Morton's hometown. Centerville has preserved so many historic buildings along Main Street that it allows one to imagine life there during Morton's lifetime.

It is customary and correct that historians and biographers thank librarians and archivists for the help that they provide us. Such professionals have done much to help me with my work on Morton. At the Indiana State Archives, Michael Vetman was always ready to help a scholar working for days on end. Elizabeth Hague and Stephanie Gowler showed me how to use an ultraviolet light to examine what looked like blank pages in a volume of Morton's letter books faded by too many years of storage in a Chicago attic. At the Indiana Historical Society, Paul Brockman, Suzanne Hahn, and Nicole Poletika all greeted me with friendly smiles and happily guided me to the materials I needed. Several dedicated professionals treated me well at the Indiana State Library, and I especially thank Marcia Caudell, Bethany Fiechter, and Brent Abercrombie for assisting me during my many long days spent in the reading room there. Marcia also offered valuable insights into Morton's life, and Brent provided useful information about Daniel D. Pratt as well as his knowledge of many other collections. Among the public historians who have supported me in this project, Pamela Bennett of the Indiana Historical Bureau often encouraged my work along the way.

Editors make the publication of our work possible, and as with archivists, they usually receive a much-deserved expression of gratitude in a book's acknowledgments. Joyce Harrison patiently waited for this biography of Morton through many delays caused by personal circumstances. I thank her and the other professionals at the Kent State University Press for accepting my excuses and making this publication possible.

Several people who should have seen this completed book have passed away since I began to work on it in 2008. Three of my graduate school mentors are now gone, and I regret that I did not finish this biography in time to send them a copy. Jack Temple Kirby, Michael O'Brien, and Andrew R. L. Cayton all shaped my thinking and my work, both during graduate school and in the years after. I can never hope to live up to the examples set by these three men, but I hope that, somehow, my own efforts as a scholar serve as some small part of their legacies.

Friends and colleagues help make writing a less lonely process. At the University of Indianapolis, two of my departmental colleagues, in particular, have always provided a sympathetic ear and sage advice. Larry Sondhaus is a trusted friend with whom I can share the frustrations and joys of research and writing. Ted Frantz helped me with clarifications and suggested useful titles as I tried to comprehend the complexities of Morton's role in the politics of the 1870s.

A number of historians in Indiana and elsewhere have been collegial and supportive of my work. Jenny Weber, Anita Morgan, Doug Gardner, Richard Nation, Thomas Mackey, Glenn Crothers, Chris Phillips, and Anne Marshall all provided comments and criticisms that helped me along the way. Jim Madison encouraged me at several points along the way, and I am grateful for his kind remarks. Eric Sandweiss gave me constructive criticism and useful advice. Mark Summers generously shared sources, and I am indebted to him for his many books that guided me through the twists and turns of the Reconstruction era. Tom Rodgers has shared his research and interpretations with me, sending me copies of conference papers even as his published articles helped me to better understand Indiana politics in the mid-nineteenth century. Nicole Etcheson has become a good friend as well as a clear-eyed critic, and I appreciate that she always employed humor as she prodded me to finish this book. Daniel Stowell shares my interests in Southern history and Southern Baptists as well as a passion for Abraham Lincoln, and he has supported and critiqued my study of Morton from the beginning.

I acknowledge Mike Green's work on Republican ideology during the war in the introduction to this volume, but I must thank him for it here as well. Mike is a longtime friend, but I appreciate his critical eye, and his insightful suggestions forced me to make this a better book. Steve Towne inspired this biography before I knew him, but he has become a good friend as well. His sharp mind and incredible memory embarrass those around him, as we marvel at how he can remember primary sources in many different archives, often citing box and folder numbers as well as specific dates and authors. His criticisms of my rough draft corrected many of my errors and required me to make some difficult decisions about how to explain several important events. He is an accomplished historian as well as an archivist, and Steve's groundbreaking research on the military's investigations of the Copperheads has allowed me to reinterpret Morton in ways that would not otherwise have been possible.

Faith and family provide the firm foundations of my life. Like Morton, my son, Carson, is a native Hoosier who lost his mother at an early age. He has grown up with this book. I started working on it when he was two, and I am proud that his fourth-grade Indiana history project on a famous Hoosier of *his* choice featured none other than the Great War Governor and Reconstruction Senator. My wife, Krista, deserves thanks beyond measure. Even as she worked on her own doctoral dissertation, she took the time to help me with research and editing. She is my best friend and intellectual partner. I am grateful for her mind, her sense of humor, and her love. She brings me joy, and sharing our passion for the past is truly a wonderful experience.

Introduction

Interpreting the "Great War Governor" and
"Reconstruction Senator"

THE HUGE BRONZE STATUE atop the pedestal stands tall beside the Indiana State House, looming over passersby and the steps of the entrance to the capitol building. The statue's main character, affixed between and above two Union soldiers, looks eastward toward Monument Circle and the heart of downtown Indianapolis. The simple inscription visible when looking westward toward the capitol reads "Morton," but the plaque on the other side describes more fully why and how Hoosiers chose to remember their Civil War governor, Oliver P. Morton, when they erected the statue in 1907:

Oliver Perry Morton
Born in Wayne Co. Indiana August 4, 1823.
Died in Indianapolis November 1, 1877.
Aged 54 years 2 months and 25 days.
Admitted to the Bar in 1847.
Served as Governor of Indiana from January 18, 1861, to March 4, 1867.
Served as US Senator from Indiana from March 4, 1867, until his death
    November 1, 1877.
In all ways and at all times the friend of the Union soldier. The friend
    of the country.
The upholder of Abraham Lincoln.
The defender of the flag and the Union of the States. Patriot. Statesman.
Lover of Liberty. Heroic in heart.
Inflexible in purpose and ever to be known in history as
The Great War Governor.

Not far away, on Monument Circle, stands another bronze statue of the Civil War governor. There are others around the state, and many towns in Indiana have streets named after him. One cannot go far in the Hoosier state without encountering Oliver Morton.[1]

Fig. 1. Morton monument, Indiana State Capitol. (Laura Northrup Poland, Reflected Spectrum Photography)

Who was this Morton, this man to whom Indiana has given so much of its public space? I first encountered the many monuments Hoosiers dedicated to their Civil War leader when I moved to the state in 1999 to take a position as a history professor at the University of Indianapolis. Since I was a Civil War scholar, I took notice of the statues and remembered reading something about Morton in the many books I had studied over the years. He had been a ruthless politician who whipped up hysteria about disloyal Democrats, I thought. Then I taught Indiana history and learned more about him. He really was ruthless, it seemed, but maybe he had not been all bad, as he certainly helped the North win the Civil War.

Some years later, having completed my previous research projects, I began to look for a new one. Influenced by Andrew R. L. Cayton, one of my mentors in graduate school, I turned away from my previous interests in Southern history and religious matters. Drew Cayton's study of early Indiana and his groundbreaking view of the regional history of the Midwest made me look closer to home, and I thought I might choose an Indiana topic. Soon I came across an essay in an edited volume, published in 2001, as part of the grand opening celebration of the new facilities of the Indiana Historical Society. The piece, written by an archivist named Stephen E. Towne, was entitled "Scorched Earth or Fertile Ground? Indiana in the Civil War, 1861–1865." Much of the essay focused on the role of Oliver P. Morton, covering what seemed to be an extensive literature that continued to cast Morton either as a great hero of the North or an evil political opportunist who trampled on the rights of citizens to keep power. Towne said that "Morton must be seen as one of the paramount leaders in the North during the rebellion." He argued that "it would be time well spent for scholars to return to the subject of Morton and reexamine his role in light of the growing literature on Northern war politics. . . . Closer scrutiny of Northern war leadership outside the White House would correct the unfortunately distorted, but popular, view of the martyred Lincoln as national savior." He then suggested that "the somewhat unfashionable medium of historical biography can still yield impressive results."[2]

Intrigued, I began to read some of the relevant literature, and at the Thornbrough Lecture at Butler University in November 2007, I spoke to Steve Towne about possibly taking up his challenge by writing a biography of Morton. He was immediately supportive, and I started the project. A few months later, at the 2008 annual meeting of the Indiana Association of Historians, Steve and I established the Civil War Study Group, an informal regional group of scholars who meet yearly for a symposium, and that friendly circle of scholars has nurtured my work ever since. As my research progressed, I began to realize just how significant a project this was. Morton was far more than just Indiana's

Civil War governor. He was a key player in the conflict, to be sure, but he had also served as the state's US senator from 1867–1877, throughout the era of Reconstruction, an aspect of his life that had been largely forgotten. Beyond the richness of his life and career, which makes for a complicated story, the literature is vast and complex, filled with different interpretations and nuances that touch on how one might see and analyze a biographical subject.

Scholars tended to be polarized about Morton, as Towne had explained in his essay, with some seeing him as a great hero and others convinced he was an evil villain. Writers began trying to explain Oliver P. Morton's life and career during his lifetime. Early examples included a campaign biography written in the life-and-letters style of the nineteenth century. First published in 1864 for Morton's reelection as governor, the book by William M. French was expanded slightly and reprinted to support his Senate candidacy in 1866. In keeping with its purpose, it was an exercise in hagiography. An 1876 campaign biography published as a long pamphlet during his bid for the presidential nomination also praised Morton and cast him as a hero.[3]

After his death, the eulogies mostly portrayed Morton as a Union hero, although criticisms often marked the memories of his Democratic foes. The hagiography continued when Charles M. Walker published a short, readable biography in 1879. Walker, the editor of the *Indianapolis Journal*, praised Morton, as one would expect from the newspaper that had so long supported him and often served as his mouthpiece. The nineteenth-century hagiography ignored Morton's faults but correctly explained his role as a war governor and a Radical Republican senator during Reconstruction.[4]

At the end of the nineteenth century, William Dudley Foulke produced his classic biography *Life of Oliver P. Morton*. Published in 1899, that two-volume masterpiece was a sophisticated life-and-letters style of biography that was written with the official sanction of the Morton family. His interpretation was clearly pro-Morton, and it was shaped by Foulke's own career as a Progressive reformer and Republican Party activist.[5] Given access to all available papers (including some that seem not to have survived the past century), Foulke sometimes tended to be too positive, but those who accuse him of hagiography judge him too harshly, as he was quite critical of aspects of Morton's character in his conclusion. In keeping with the life-and-letters style, Foulke included full transcriptions of many primary sources, a fact that continues to make his work valuable to scholars more than a century later.

Later studies also offered mostly positive interpretations of Morton. In 1942 Wood Gray's book on the Copperheads treated Morton fairly, while George Milton's popular history on the disloyal movement published that same year portrayed the governor as one of the most active and able of the Republican political leaders during the war. In these works, Morton's period of one-man rule became a state dictatorship, but his honesty and energetic actions against the traitors made him an admirable hero of the Union. Both authors made factual errors about him in their treatments of the governor, but those mistakes were minor and excusable. Milton, for example, glossed too quickly over the election of 1860 and said that Morton was elected governor rather than taking the time to explain the complicated reality of that election. Gray, meanwhile, said that Morton's name was originally Throckmorton, which conflated the truth with his family's ancestral name change. Such trivial mistakes were not fatal flaws. To be sure, the two writers overstated Morton's role in rooting out the Copperheads, shortchanging in the process the military commanders who led the investigations. But this stemmed from their use of political materials and newspapers rather than analysis of military records. Both Gray and Milton took the Copperhead threat seriously, and this meant that they saw Morton as a strong leader even as they recognized his ruthlessness and were obviously troubled by the way he so quickly thwarted democracy with his executive authority. Such positive assessments leavened with criticism made for honest and balanced accounts that put Morton in a leading role on the Northern home front.[6]

But the late 1940s saw a shift, as scholars began to challenge and overturn the older nationalist view. An important negative portrayal appeared in William B. Hesseltine's 1948 book, *Lincoln and the War Governors,* a classic Progressive study that argued that Lincoln outsmarted and outmaneuvered the Northern governors in order to centralize power in the federal government. In this view, Lincoln saved the Union despite the governors because he was superior to them in intellect and political skill. Hesseltine thought Morton was the most talented of the Republican war governors, but he argued that the Hoosier leader was an opportunist. He also asserted that Morton was an alarmist whose paranoia and tendency to panic offset his energy and tremendous political skills. Thus, in Hesseltine's story, Lincoln patiently calmed Morton down and guided the "hysterical" governor along as he wisely saved the nation.[7]

In his 1949 book, *Indiana Politics during the Civil War,* Kenneth M. Stampp argued that Morton was an ambitious and ruthless opportunist whose great energy and considerable ability allowed him to lead Indiana through the Civil War and help crush the rebellion. Stampp's study was shaped by the Progressive predilection for economic interpretations that emphasized class conflict. Although he recognized Morton's leadership skills, he saw him and other Republicans as ruthless powerbrokers who sided with the capitalists against the agrarians, represented by the Democrats. In Stampp's eyes, Morton would do anything to keep power, and he argued that the governor shifted his political positions in order to maintain his executive position. In Stampp's account, Morton was a humorless dictator who could never forgive an enemy and used his office to crush dissent.[8]

The post–World War II criticism of Morton continued with John D. Barnhart and Donald F. Carmony, who took a negative view in *Indiana from Frontier to Industrial Commonwealth,* a state history published in the mid-1950s that charged the governor with driving loyal Democrats into treason with his ruthless measures. A landmark Progressive study of the Civil War that held to the unfavorable interpretation of Morton was Allan Nevins's multivolume narrative, *The Ordeal of the Union.* Seeing the Hoosier governor as excitable, paranoid, and explosive, Nevins still managed to admit that Morton deserved credit for his energetic leadership. Perhaps the most negative view of Morton as an opportunistic villain came in the work of Frank L. Klement, a historian whose interpretation of the Copperheads dominated the literature for decades. First writing in the era of the McCarthy hearings, he argued that Morton and other Republicans concocted a Copperhead threat in order to win elections and painted the governor as a ruthless dictator who worked closely with his cronies in the military to crush Democratic dissent and maintain their power. Klement's anti-Morton interpretation continued in his later books, published over the next several decades, and the oft-cited Klement thesis became the standard interpretation for scholars of Civil War politics in the North from the 1960s through the 1990s.[9]

Despite the prevalence of Klement's analysis, more balanced accounts of Morton's career came with the so-called revisionist work of the Consensus historians. Emma Lou Thornbrough's *Indiana in the Civil War Era, 1850–1880* saw the governor as an "organizational genius" and praised his leadership of the state during the war. Thornbrough's excellent 1965 book remains the standard study of Indiana in the period for good reason, as she grounded her account in the primary sources and included such a wide range of subjects that she foreshadowed the later turn from political to social and cultural history. But her positive portrayal of Morton was balanced by her acceptance of much of the existing Progressive interpretation of his character and style, as she argued that the "personality and methods of Governor Morton exacerbated the bitterness and fears of his Democratic opponents, and his disregard for constitutional processes alarmed them." In a promising 1968 dissertation that was never published, Lorna Lute Sylvester agreed with the standing view of Morton's personality, but she also tried to overturn much of the negative portrayal of the governor. Sylvester argued that Morton had not fabricated the Copperhead conspiracies, for example, and that the blame for the internal divisions in the state should be placed at the feet of the Democrats, some of whom went beyond loyal opposition to engage in treasonous activities.[10]

Although the next generation of scholars mostly neglected Morton, some New Left historians tended to cast Morton in an even more favorable light. With their emphasis on issues of race, class, and gender, this was not surprising. Writing in the wake of the civil rights movement, such scholars cast Radical Republicans like Morton as heroic figures. Furthermore, many New Left scholars saw the expansion of government power as a positive development, which meant that they excused that aspect of Morton's career as governor. Most New Left historians, however, barely mentioned Morton in their larger studies of the Civil War and Reconstruction. When they did include him, many of their accounts perpetuated the negative assessments of previous scholars, making the meager New Left analysis of Morton somewhat contradictory. One exception came in the state history written by James H. Madison, who saw Morton much more positively as the most significant Hoosier political leader in the nineteenth century. But most New Left scholars ignored Morton and usually hewed to the mistakes of the Klement thesis. Even those who recognized his significance during Reconstruction tended to misread or misunderstand his role.[11]

In the early twenty-first century, new scholarship brought interpretations of Morton full circle, returning in many ways to the view found in Foulke more than a century before. While none of these scholars have studied his career in full, they have seen Morton much more positively and have done much to restore his reputation as a war governor. Nicole Etcheson included Morton in her study of Putnam County, Indiana, and she provided a balanced treatment of him. She portrayed him as manipulative and as a political opportunist, a view that is not untrue, and she rightly saw him as a staunch defender of the Union and unforgiving foe of the rebellion.

Morton was also treated positively in recent reevaluations of the Northern war governors. Best seen as responses to Hesseltine's interpretation more than a half century before, studies by William C. Harris and Stephen D. Engle contended that the state executives played a significant role in the Union victory. Far from being inferior politicians manipulated by the masterful Lincoln, the governors cooperated with the president in ways that not only advanced the cause, but also defended the division of powers between the national and state governments that is so vital to federalism. Although the two scholars did not agree on every point, Harris's brief 2013 book sketched this interpretation that was more fully made in Engle's massive 2016 volume, *Gathering to Save a Nation: Lincoln & the Union's War Governors*. Both books rightly saw Morton as one of the most important of the war governors, but such synthetic works tended to conflate him with other leaders and did not fully assess the ways in which he operated.[12]

Perhaps the best example of the recent restoration of Morton's reputation is found in Stephen E. Towne, *Surveillance and Spies in the Civil War: Exposing*

Confederate Conspiracies in America's Heartland. Towne took the Copperhead threat seriously and corrected the errors of the long-held Klement thesis. In so doing, he put Morton in his proper role as a state leader cooperating closely with the military authorities, showing him to be a receiver and digester of intelligence rather than the mastermind collecting data on his enemies that previous scholars mistakenly saw in their accounts. While Towne's real heroes were army officers like Henry Carrington, Morton also stood tall as a Union protagonist facing off against traitors who planned to murder the governor and overthrow the state government. Towne's groundbreaking interpretation was based firmly on exhaustive research in previously neglected archival collections and deeper exploration of many materials used by earlier scholars. His book was an effective rethinking of the Copperheads and Union actions taken against them, and in overturning the Klement thesis, he offered a much more positive perspective of Governor Morton. But Towne's book was not a biography. Thus, while Morton was a central player in many of the events in *Surveillance and Spies,* most of his work as a war governor did not appear at all in its pages. Nor did Towne's positive portrayal touch on Morton's postwar career. In the end, since the book was not really about Morton, it only began to correct the mistakes of the past.[13]

So I set out to complete the task begun in the recent literature. But this was not as simple as I had hoped it might be. My own political and philosophical inclinations made me quite critical of some of what Morton had done. While I did admire some of what he believed and did, such as his opposition to slavery and strong defense of African American rights, I was troubled by his support for the expansion and centralization of power. Moreover, I did not approve of the ways in which he and other Republicans diminished civil liberties in the name of winning the war. And I did not like many of his party's economic policies during Reconstruction, particularly their support for increased taxation and what we today speak of as corporate welfare. And I disagreed with Morton about the efficacy of government to solve problems. His views were clearly not mine. But should I attack him because I disliked some particular action or another? Would that not be repeating the same old mistake of being too simplistic and one-sided in my analysis? Taking one side or the other did not seem right to me as a biographer, and, furthermore, however I felt about Morton and his actions myself, I recognized that I needed to set aside my own prejudices if I wanted to understand my subject.

Still further, as a professional historian I think it is the responsibility of those who write historical biography to try to analyze the subject in the context of his or her own time, which allows negative as well as positive analysis. Historical biography demands contextual analysis, and that includes recognizing a subject's principles even when a biographer does not agree with those principles. I wanted to write a biography that showed how Morton was complicated and complex, but was that falling into the trap of trying to say that he was both good and bad? Did complexity mean that a scholar had to state the obvious about a biographical subject—that people are complicated—and leave it at that? Especially troubling to me was that these historians all agreed that Morton was a political opportunist and a partisan. I assume that most politicians will be opportunistic and partisan. That is what they do. I do not assume, however, that those are always bad things. Opportunism and partisanship do not necessarily mean that a person has abandoned his or her principles.

Then there were the primary sources. Morton apparently burned his personal papers, so few family letters have survived. But there was still a vast amount of material to use. Without a diary or a collection of revealing letters written to some close confidante, Morton's public papers and speeches provided the biographer the only available window into his mind. What I found seemed remarkably consistent. This was not some mere politician holding his finger to the wind, tacking this way and that in order to win reelection. Even when his positions changed, Morton often seemed to be doing so in ways that could be seen as principled. Perhaps the literature had missed Morton's principles and misunderstood his ideology.

While thinking about how to explain all of this, I read a book offering an interpretation of Republican Party political ideology that seemed to fit Morton almost perfectly. It happened to be written by a good friend, Michael S. Green, whom I had gotten to know when we taught together in Las Vegas, Nevada, in the 1990s. I had bought his 2004 book on political ideology in the Civil War and put it on my shelf after a quick perusal. Now, years later, I turned to it again, and I found exactly what I needed to explain Morton's thought. In his book, Green argued that the Republican Party developed a nationalist ideology of freedom, Union, and power during the Civil War. Dedicated to the doctrines of liberty under the law and the preservation of an indivisible Union, they believed that it was necessary to employ government power to gain and maintain those principles. In an essay published in a collected volume, Green also argued that the same ideology animated Republicans throughout the Reconstruction period. When I added party as a fourth component, the ideology fit Morton like a glove and provided the theoretical framework for this biography.[14]

I argue that Oliver P. Morton consistently held to an ideology of freedom, Union, power, and party throughout his career. In Morton's mind, freedom and Union were cherished principles derived from the Founding Fathers that must be defended by expanding and using the power of the government. To ensure that such power was not abused, it must be controlled by the party best suited to protect the doctrines of liberty and a united country. For Morton, that meant himself and his Republican Party. The four different parts of this foundational ideology served as the primary motivation in his work as a war governor and Reconstruction Senator.[15]

This is an interpretive political biography. This means that it is driven by my interpretation of Morton. In keeping with my training as an intellectual historian, I have constructed a narrative of Morton's career that attempts to explain his actions in light of his ideas as expressed in his public papers and speeches. Because I was trained by the late Michael O'Brien, the stories I tell are anchored in the context of the times in which Morton lived, including the politics, culture, and society of Indiana, the Midwest, and the nation. It is a political biography that focuses on his career. In part, this is because the lack of personal papers prevents me from getting into the social aspects of his life. I do sometimes include personal matters but deal with them primarily only as they intersect with his career as a public man. My interpretation finds Morton to be remarkably consistent in his ideological thinking, and in that sense I challenge the existing literature. Additionally, this book attempts to restore Morton to his proper place as a Radical Republican during Reconstruction by showing how he continued to fight the rebellion in his confrontations with enemies like the Ku Klux Klan and in his championing of civil rights for African Americans. For too long we have remembered the Great War Governor and have forgotten his roles as the Reconstruction Senator and as a Radical Republican who was a national figure during the postwar period.[16]

Driven by my interpretive argument, this book takes up the task of explaining the life and career of the most important Indiana politician in the nineteenth century. Often challenging the interpretations of previous scholars, it offers the first full-length biography of Oliver P. Morton in more than one hundred years. It is a book that admits his mistakes and sees him critically on a number of issues, while fully restoring his reputation as the Great War Governor. It sees him as a flawed man who held consistently to his ideology while living and acting in his own time and place.

In general, the book offers a positive interpretation of a leader committed to his core principles of freedom, Union, power, and party. It is a more favorable view because it measures Morton against his own ideas and principles in the context of his own life and times. In seeking to understand him in such a way, the book sometimes offers explanations that might excuse actions that others have judged more harshly. I think that this stems from the consideration of context, which always makes a character more sympathetic, rather than my own bias. Since I disagree with Morton on many issues, it is my hope that the tension between the subject's and author's principles has helped me to guard against ignoring Morton's mistakes and weaknesses. Throughout the volume, I do not discount his partisanship but try to see it as I think he did, as an important principle rather than as mere politics. In so doing, I hope that I have managed to explain Oliver P. Morton's life while showing him to be an imperfect man operating in his time and place rather than judging him only from the perspective of the twenty-first century.

The book's opening chapter deals with Morton's early life, bringing in more of the context than previous scholars did, including the importance of the National Road in his hometown and the significance of his attendance at Miami University to better explain his personal development. The second chapter shows how Morton broke with the Democrats of his youth on the issue of slavery and became a founding member of Indiana's Republican Party. In the third chapter, on the election of 1860, I turn to the context to offer new insights on how Morton came to be governor just as the Civil War began.

Chapter 4 explains how Morton mobilized Indiana for war and organized the unprecedented expansion of the state government to raise, train, supply, and transport troops. Here he demonstrated his superior skills as an executive and organizer as he worked tirelessly to save the Union. The fifth chapter analyzes the high drama of political warfare, as Morton took on the Democratic majority in the legislature and then embarked on his period of one-man rule, essentially running the state as a dictator. Chapter 6 deals with the questions of dissent and treason, as Morton helped the federal military authorities investigate the Copperheads, who resisted the draft, opposed the war and the expansion of government power, and often sympathized with the Confederacy.

Chapter 7 looks at Morton's role in the transition from war to peace and at how, despite suffering a stroke that left him paralyzed from the waist down, he was elected to the United States Senate. The eighth chapter shows Morton waving the bloody shirt against the Democrats and the rebels of the South, reminding voters about the sacrifices made by Northerners as a means to build support for Radical Reconstruction. Although Democrats used the term *waving the bloody shirt* in a derogatory fashion, I use it in a more positive sense, as it symbolized Morton's view of Reconstruction as a continuation of the war. In chapter 9 I show how the Radical Republican senator became a champion for African Americans, fighting for their civil rights and supporting black officeholders across the South. In return, black Americans embraced him as a beloved friend and became a powerful bloc of support for him in the Republican Party.

The tenth chapter focuses on Morton's loyalty as a Stalwart Republican who supported the administration of Ulysses S. Grant, surveying his life in

Washington society while studying his views on economic and foreign policy and showing how he worked within the organization of his party. Chapter 11 analyzes how he was a serious candidate for the presidency whose campaign was partially derailed by charges of sexual impropriety and concerns about his health. More important, politics had shifted, making Morton seem like an extremist when the majority of voters wanted moderation and reconciliation. Still, he ended up playing a central role in deciding the disputed election of 1876, which sent his friend Rutherford B. Hayes to the White House. Supporting Radical Reconstruction and the rights of African Americans to the bitter end, Morton finally faced the reality of the Compromise of 1877. The different parts of his foundational ideology at last became incompatible; dedication to party and the desire for power demanded that he compromise his beliefs on freedom and equality. Still refusing to yield, he had to come to terms with the tensions between his various cherished principles in the months just before his death, which fittingly symbolized the end of Reconstruction.

The last chapter explores how Morton has been remembered, showing that how the public sees him coincides with society's changing memories of the Civil War. Although most twentieth-century remembrances forgot about Oliver P. Morton's role as a national leader after the war, the many looming statues of him, and the streets named after him, serve as reminders that each new generation reinterprets the significance of Indiana's Great War Governor and Reconstruction Senator, a man who deserves to be remembered across Indiana and the nation.

CHAPTER ONE

A Native Son

ONE DAY IN 1839, a young apprentice sat reading in the drugstore in Center-ville, Indiana, where he worked as an apothecary clerk. The fifteen-year-old boy came to work for Dr. Swain, the druggist, in the fall of 1838, to learn the trade as part of a plan for him to study medicine. He and his family decided that he should become a doctor and learn the apothecary trade in the process rather than continue a formal education, which his father considered an expensive luxury that dishonored young boys who should be working. Trouble soon arose, however, as the apprentice had acquired a strong habit for reading and took every opportunity to stop work and pick up a book. This led to several discussions in which the apothecary complained about the boy's tendency to read instead of doing what his employer paid him to do. That day in 1839, when the druggist went out of the store for a while, the boy quickly quit his duties and began to read. Sometime later Dr. Swain returned, but the clerk was so engrossed in his reading that he did not hear his employer enter. Enraged at his apprentice's continual shirking of duty and lack of respect for his boss, the doctor not only launched into a verbal assault about the young man's bad behavior, he also struck him. The large, strong boy named Oliver P. Morton responded by returning the blow, and he was immediately fired.[1]

Young Morton's reaction could be seen as more than a simple impulse, as it embodied the principles of individualism, a defense of his rights, and a prefer-ence for his own course rather than the traditional authority of his employer in the guild. When his father learned about what had happened, he called a family council, and they decided that the boy's behavior was dishonorable and therefore unacceptable. Here the ethics of individualism clashed with the precepts of honor. The apprentice had defied his master and the son had shamed his father. As punishment, his father sent the young man to his older brother, to work as an apprentice in his hatter's shop for a term of four years. Thus Morton went to work along the National Road, which became Main Street as it passed through Centerville. That event changed Morton's course and led him to the law instead of medicine, only one example of how his experiences growing up as a native son of Indiana shaped his life.[2]

A Life Shaped by Centerville and the National Road

Born on August 4, 1823, in the community of Salisbury, Indiana, Oliver Morton spent many of his formative years in Wayne County, Indiana. The county, situated in east-central Indiana, borders Ohio, and it featured several flourishing towns, including Richmond, Cambridge City, and Centerville. A largely rural county, with plenty of farmers working fertile land along abundant waterways, it was bisected by the National Road. Along that vital artery moved commerce and travelers, ideas and culture. Bringing important aspects of society from the northeastern states to Indiana, the National Road also brought Southerners and elements of their culture. Doing so meant that the road brought together the nation. Growing up in Wayne County, living near and on the National Road, Morton saw firsthand the role of transportation in creating a new, modern style of life in Indiana and the country as a whole. In his early life, he experienced the tensions wrought by shifting notions of ethics and economics, by the merging and conflicting cultures of North and South, East and West. The future nationalist came of age in a milieu created in large part by the National Road.[3]

The National Road was the first infrastructure project in the United States funded and planned by the federal government. Construction on the new highway had begun during the Jefferson administration, although the Democratic-Republicans themselves were divided over the issue of federal funding for the road. Despite political battles fought over the road, by mid-century it had reached Vandalia, Illinois. The building of the thoroughfare in Indiana began in 1829, with sections built both east and west from Indianapolis, and construction in the Hoosier State was largely complete by 1838. Heralded as a path to the west for immigrants, it more often served local and regional purposes, as travelers on the road were far more likely to be regular commuters who used the corridor to conduct business between established centers of commerce. To be sure, the Cumberland Road—as the National Road was often called—connected the East (particularly Virginia, Maryland, and Pennsylvania) with the West (Ohio, Indiana, and Illinois), and immigrants heading westward, often from the South, certainly took the road, especially during periods of increased migration like the California gold rush. But the flow of ideas and culture as well as products and resources along the National Road created a distinctive world in towns like Centerville, Indiana.[4]

The National Road corridor marked a cultural dividing line in the midwestern states. Southern immigrants tended to settle south of the National Road, while those from states in the North were more likely to find homes north of that line. Such divisions played an important part in the history of the state, as politics and culture followed immigration patterns. There, along the National Road, a national culture developed. While it might be too much to say that the road forged the Union, very real connections were formed between East and West, North and South, in places like Wayne County, Indiana.[5]

The East-West connections were clear in Centerville and the surrounding area, as exemplified in the region's architecture. Styles of buildings popular in Pennsylvania were quite common along the National Road. Row houses set gable to gable in Uniontown, Pennsylvania, served as models of style for those in Centerville. Pennsylvania, with its rich German heritage (popularly known as Pennsylvania Dutch), also sent its large barns with their earthen ramps across the Midwest. But North and South also came together in the architecture in Wayne County. Southern barns were as common as German ones, and log cabins, in particular, followed construction styles found in the South rather than in the North. Wagon types, the preference for horses or mules, the raising of cows or hogs—all marked sectional differences but were found jumbled together in the National Road corridor. Such mixing led to blending. Both upland Southerners and settlers from the Middle Atlantic region built two-story homes that were two rooms in length but only one room deep. Slight variations between Pennsylvania and Maryland could be found, but in the Midwest they blended together in what became known as the "I-house," a style most popular in Indiana, Illinois, and, later, Iowa.[6]

Buildings do not a nation make. The people who constructed and used the buildings brought with them their various ideas and all of their cultural baggage. Travelers along the National Road stayed in inns and taverns, brought news from place to place, and carried diseases like cholera when epidemics periodically brought death to many. Wagons, riders, stagecoaches, and even pedestrians created and carried a distinctively national culture along the corridor. Political ideas mingled with religion as politicians and voters met preachers spreading the Gospel during the Second Great Awakening. Religion influenced ethics, as more people came to accept the tenets of individualism, instilling a sense of conscience in their children and coming to rely on that internalized sense of right and wrong rather than the older standards of honor. To be sure, honor persisted, and the two moral and ethical systems were often in tension. Honor demanded behavior that brought respect and avoided shame. It focused on external standards of kinship and community, as people worried about how others viewed them.

Meanwhile, material concerns mattered when the ever-changing methods of capitalism met the local, rural economy as eastern manufacturers distributed their products in stores that sprang up along the highway even as nearby farmers came to sell their goods in the new commercial centers. While capitalism was not new, the growth and impact of the dynamic market economy often conflicted with the older style of capitalist economics. The two existed alongside one another, as the structures of local artisan capitalism, complete with masters, journeymen, and apprentices, continued even as the products of factories came into town by the wagonload. Kinship and community still mattered, but more impersonal relationships came into play as well, as different ideas about money merged in the all-encompassing pursuit of profits. The National Road connected people but also divided them. Ideas were not always accepted, and contention followed. Dangers lurked, as highwaymen lay in wait to rob the unsuspecting, and while real disease spread rapidly from town to town, the threats also came in the form of deeply held differences in beliefs and ideology. The nation that formed and divided along the National Road created a contested space.[7]

One contested idea centered on the road itself. In the course of nineteenth-century politics, different versions of republicanism competed, even as economic liberalism and libertarian sensibilities rose to challenge the vision of a virtuous republic that had motivated earlier generations. This led to new political philosophies and policy changes. The federal project envisioned under Thomas Jefferson had its funding bill vetoed by James Monroe. Sectional interests came into play as federal funding for a Northern highway worried Southern politicians.

Control of and payment for the National Road reached its national glory when John Quincy Adams lived in the White House but shifted to the state governments in the libertarian era of Andrew Jackson. The fights over internal improvements that animated the Second American Party System, with Whigs calling for national funding and factions of Democrats opposing them with a variety of alternatives, eventually gave way to what scholars of the road call the "age of the turnpikes." State governments turned to private companies for help in turning the National Road into toll roads. This move away from federal control reduced costs and ushered in a libertarian era of individualistic laissez-faire capitalism in places like Centerville, but state control also enabled the rise of powerful corporations amid economic consolidation and integration. Ironically, decentralization and local control helped to pave the way for centralization and later renewed federal authority and regulation. But the full implications of all of that lay in the future and during the period when young Oliver Morton looked out upon his world, a world created by the National Road.[8]

Thanks to its location on the road, Centerville became a bustling commercial and cultural center situated between the thriving towns of Richmond to the east and Cambridge City to the west. Already important locally because of the county courthouse, the town soon developed as a major stop on the National Road. Local businessmen built new taverns and inns and enlarged existing ones to accommodate the increased number of travelers. Blacksmiths and wagon shops flourished, as did general stores, stage line offices, and other enterprises along the busy Main Street of town. Centerville entrepreneurs expanded their businesses, and this meant physical enlargement of their buildings. To avoid taxation based on land facing the public street and to deal with the inconveniences caused by the renovations that gobbled up every available square foot along the busy thoroughfare, many businessmen constructed archways in their buildings that allowed access to the back of the property while utilizing as much of the road frontage as possible. These distinctive arches served as entries to yards, gardens, and stables in the rear of homes and shops.

Along Centerville's busy Main Street, gamblers plied their trade in the taverns, where liquor flowed freely. Such leisure activities helped spur reformers to action, as religious and moral activists began pushing for the control of gambling as well as for the popular temperance movement that preceded the later call for prohibition of alcohol. Centerville's cultural life included plays and concerts, as traveling troupes moved along the road and performed wherever they stopped. Evangelists arrived to preach and convert sinners, lawyers argued their cases on court days, politicians came to make their stump speeches, and traveling salesmen offered their wares during brief stays while waiting for the next stagecoach. The community boasted a fine school in the "Wayne County Academy," or "Whitewater Academy," the names by which locals usually referred to the Wayne County Seminary run by Samuel K. Hoshour. By the late 1830s Centerville was a busy destination on the National Road.[9]

While place set one dimension of Oliver P. Morton's context, his family life set another. His father, James T. Morton, hailed from New Jersey, where he was born in 1782 as James Throckmorton. He apparently changed his name to James T. Morton because he was bitter about his brothers cheating him out of his share of his father's estate. He married and started a family, but his wife died, leaving him with two young children. He moved to Ohio, worked on canals, lost at least one fortune, turned to keeping an inn, then became a shoemaker. While living in Cincinnati, he met Sarah Miller, whose parents owned a farm near Springfield (now Springdale), Ohio. James Morton and Sarah married in 1815, and he moved the family to Indiana. The couple settled in Salisbury, Indiana, and James practiced his trade as a shoemaker. He also opened a tavern in what seemed a promising new village that boasted the county courthouse.

The community soon declined, however, and the townspeople left it behind and headed to nearby towns. These emigrants dismantled most of the log buildings and moved them to other locations, but the Morton family stayed in Salisbury and it was there that James and Sarah had their fourth child in August of 1823. His parents had another child after him, but his siblings all died young, leaving the boy with only an older half-brother and half-sister. They named him after a hero of the War of 1812, calling him Oliver Hazard Perry Throck Morton, a name that the young man, later shortened to Oliver P. Morton—encouraged by a law partner who argued that so many initials made it difficult to put his name on a sign.[10]

When Sarah Miller Morton died in 1826, his father decided that the best thing to do was to send three-year-old Oliver to his maternal grandparents, John and Hannah Miller, and their two widowed daughters who lived with them on their Ohio farm. The two widows, Oliver's aunts, agreed to raise the boy and see to his education. Over the course of the next dozen years, Morton and his aunts split time between Ohio and Indiana, the three of them living much of the time with his grandparents but also spending months in a rented home in Centerville, to be closer to Oliver's father. Devout Scottish Presbyterians, the Miller family taught him the catechism and demanded strict adherence to its doctrines and principles. This meant a strict Calvinism, with its emphasis on the sovereignty of God, election, and predestination. While the aunts' views are unrecorded and they probably held to traditional theology, the Second Great Awakening that swept the country wrought changes in the way that evangelical Christians understood themselves and their world. Even strict Calvinists enjoyed the fruits of revivalism as they pitched their doctrine of grace to new converts. Such a theology certainly lent itself to traditional notions of patriarchy and honor, but it also might have served as a springboard for individualistic ideas, complete with a sense of purpose and calling. The methods of revivalism, however, split the Presbyterian Church in the 1830s. Those in the western states like Ohio tended to be more pro-revival and favored innovations in church leadership. They thus became part of the New School, or New Side, versus the Old School/Old Side conservatives who held to more traditional Calvinist doctrines and church governance.

Morton excelled in reciting the catechism to the minister when he came to call upon the family, and his aunts instilled in their nephew a love of reading that began with their rule that he read the Bible through every year. He disliked the fact, however, that they forced him to attend church services on Sunday, as the family took their lunch and made a day of it, sitting on hard wooden pews, listening to long sermons. He later said that those weary Sabbath days made him a nonprofessor in religious matters. Although he always respected the Christian faith, as an adult he refused to embrace it. Perhaps he also found the doctrines of Calvinism too limiting, but he did not say so. Wayne County was home to many Quakers, and Morton knew many members of the Society of Friends. Their individualism and ideas of liberty, equality, and conscience certainly impressed him, and he later counted the Quakers of his hometown among his strongest political supporters. Although he did not admit it in any public way, perhaps he was more inclined to the theology of the Friends. In any case, his embrace of modern ideas could have included at least a partial rejection of the traditional theology of his mother's family. Still, the efforts of his aunts made a lasting impression on him, and he often used biblical passages and references in his work as an attorney and politician. Many Scottish Presbyterians joined the reform movements of the time. This included their opposition to slavery, a position they shared with the Quakers and with Morton. And his later ideas—individualism, ordered liberty, capitalism—all fit comfortably with the Presbyterian and Quaker theologies that he had learned as a child and as a young man.[11]

Beyond their religious training, his family also encouraged Morton's education in other fields. His Aunt Hannah taught school nearby and tutored him at home as well as teaching him in the classroom. He loved to read and a family friend from Centerville, Isaac Burbank, helped to encourage his appetite for books. Burbank, a merchant, often traveled to Cincinnati to buy merchandise for his store in Indiana. He made a habit of stopping to visit the Millers and agreed to buy books for young Morton, who saved all the money he could for such purchases. The boy sometimes stayed up all night reading biographies and works of history. By the time he reached his teen years, Morton was an impressive physical specimen, big and athletic, with a sturdy build. He excelled at sports like running, swimming, and horseback riding. Reserved in manner, he did not stand out as an exceptional student but seemed a rather ordinary small-town boy.

By 1837 James Morton had moved to Centerville, finally giving up on Salisbury. And since Samuel Hoshour had just opened the Wayne County Seminary in town, the family decided that it was time for Oliver Morton to move once and for all back to Indiana and continue his education in the new school. In Centerville he attended Hoshour's school for about a year but did not impress his teacher. Hoshour, a minister in the Christian Church who had served as president of the Northwestern Christian University in Indianapolis, remembered Morton as "a timid and rather verdant-looking youth," whose intellectual abilities were not equal to those of his fellow students. But the schoolmaster recalled that Morton made up for his lack of natural talents with hard work and persistence to maintain a respectable standing in the class ranks. Still, Hoshour said that "if some knowing genius had then suggested to me that the future governor, *par excellence,* of Indiana was then in the group around me, I should probably have sought him in a more bustling form, with brighter eyes and a more marked head, than Oliver's." He remembered that Morton "was a pliant student, always ready to obey" the rules. Despite being unimpressed with his student, the devout Hoshour continued the style of education that the boy's aunts had begun in Ohio.[12]

THE HATTER'S APPRENTICE

Within the year, the Miller family, including Aunt Polly and Aunt Hannah, followed Oliver by moving to Centerville, where his grandfather died on October 12, 1838. Around that same time, his father decided that his son should learn a trade, and he went to work for Dr. Swain at the apothecary shop. There the young man's individualism ran headlong into the traditional social relationships of the older generation. The boy who had readily obeyed the rules in school now began to assert his will. While his father thought a formal education was dishonorable and a waste of time—possibly because his son was not excelling—the boy wanted to continue his studies. James Morton insisted that it was better to learn a trade than keep spending money on school, but his son saw his apprenticeship as a stepping-stone toward a larger professional career. Dr. Swain held to the traditional style of treating his apprentice as a menial, but young Morton thought he could read when he was not busy in the drugstore. While the druggist thought of the boy as a subservient whom he could scold and strike physically, the apprentice thought of himself as an individual deserving of respect as he prepared for more important things. And so tradition met the new modern generation in the Centerville apothecary shop that afternoon in 1839, and the apprentice returned blow for blow. After his altercation with the druggist, Morton took up his four-year punishment in another apprenticeship, working for his older half-brother, William, who owned the hatter's shop along Main Street.[13]

The young apprentice found his brother to be quite like his father, aunts, and Dr. Swain. Thrifty and hardworking, traditional and demanding, William set exacting standards and made his little brother work long hours at his bench. The trade was lucrative in an age when everyone wore hats on a regular basis, but it could be hazardous. The phrase "mad as a hatter" stemmed from the frequency with which hatters suffered from mental illness caused by long exposure to the mercury used in the process of making hats. Some of his friends remembered Morton working at his bench, plucking hair from muskrat skins. Others saw him covered in black dye, working the copper tank in which the

Fig. 2. Centerville, Indiana, row houses. William Morton's home and hatter's shop were in the house with the arch on the right. (Photograph by author)

apprentices heated the dye. His brother's tutelage paid off, and the young man could soon make a hat on his own. But he hated it.

In his spare time, he played various wind instruments, including the flute, in the town band. And he read, passionately consuming every book and news-paper he could buy or borrow. The hatter's apprentice showed little interest in girls and rarely went out with his friends, preferring to spend his time reading. He wanted out of the hatter's shop, and he came to believe that he should pursue a career in the law. But his brother refused to let him out of his apprentice-ship. Finally, with only six months to go before his term expired, Morton won his release by agreeing to give up the set of tools that an apprentice usually received when he finished his training and became a journeyman. This saved his brother the cost of the tools and allowed the young man to pursue a career more to his liking. Using money inherited from his grandfather, Morton set off to college at Miami University in Oxford, Ohio, early in the year of 1843.[14]

Miami University

Founded in 1809 as the second public college in Ohio, Miami University did not open immediately because construction was halted during the War of 1812. After the war ended, political battles further delayed the opening, but Miami finally started to hold classes in 1824. Although it was a state institution, Miami followed the typical pattern for public colleges in the early nineteenth century when it came under the control of Presbyterian ministers, who ran the school as administrators and faculty. Again, his family's faith may have influenced Morton, as he matriculated at what was a de facto Presbyterian university. The school struggled for a period but began to flourish by the late 1830s, reaching an enrollment of 250 students under the leadership of its president, Robert Hamilton Bishop. The college divided over religious matters, with President Bishop joining some professors as pro-revivalist New School clergymen while other faculty members strongly defended the Old School position.[15]

Bishop also promoted antislavery views and racial equality, having organized a Sunday school for black slaves in Lexington, Kentucky, in his earlier years. At a time when doing such meant taking a decidedly controversial antislavery position, he created a chapter of the American Colonization Society on Miami's campus. He invited New School and antislavery speakers to campus while still allowing the conservative Old School and proslavery professors like William H. McGuffey and Albert T. Bledsoe to have their chance to reply. Not all of the Old School faculty supported slavery, but the conservative theological view usually indicated that the man also defended the peculiar institution. Conservatism in religion was often combined with geographic origin, as some of the Old School men came from below the Mason-Dixon Line. Southern professors attracted Southern students, and Miami found itself with a divided faculty and student body when Northern New School and antislavery faculty brought in their student followers, including James G. Birney Jr., the son and namesake of a leading abolitionist. Bishop managed to keep the peace for a long while, but bitterness over theology and slavery brought more controversy and even violent confrontations between students. The conservatives of the Old School and proslavery positions attacked and undermined the aging President Bishop even as the school continued its growth. Miami became the fourth largest college in the United States, attracting students from across the country while keeping theological and political controversies at bay.[16]

But the first president resigned in 1840 because of the ongoing divisions over religion and the politics of slavery. With his resignation, declension began. Bishop returned to teaching as a professor of history and political science, and George Junkin, a Pennsylvania native who had migrated to Virginia, took charge of the school in 1841. Before taking the reins at Miami, Junkin had served as president of Lafayette College in Pennsylvania. He remained as president at the Ohio school until 1844, and Morton's time at Miami coincided with the end of Junkin's tenure. The second president of the college held staunch proslavery views but also supported the Union. Perhaps one sign of his political sympathies was expressed when his daughter later married Thomas J.

"Stonewall" Jackson, with whom the educator formed a friendship that lasted until the military officer joined the Confederacy and Junkin moved back to Pennsylvania. His proslavery, pro-Union views made Junkin something of a moderate politically, but as a college administrator, his ideas hewed to the more traditional side of intellectual conflicts. As president, he proudly defended his conservative ideas in the split between the Old and New Schools of theology, denouncing the innovations of the New School revivalists.

Junkin also carried such ideas into education, where he insisted that the president should be a monarch who ruled an institution with unquestioned authority. His inaugural address set the tone for his presidency with its title, "Obedience to Authority." Convinced that Miami students were too carefree and lax in their ways, Junkin set out to instill discipline with an iron fist, alienating the young men of the student body. He also decided to make the college a truly Presbyterian school and tried to purge the campus of the many Methodists who made up a significant percentage of the students because of their Arminian theology and what he considered crude logic and manners. Junkin also attacked the antislavery men and abolitionists among the faculty and students. His strict rules and strong opinions alienated faculty, students, and local residents alike and he proved so unpopular that graduating students threatened to cut his name from their diplomas. When he returned to Lafayette College in the fall of 1844, Junkin left behind a Miami still deeply divided and suffering from declining enrollments. Among the students who left the school, not to return, was Oliver Morton.[17]

The Hoosier native spent two years in Oxford, and little record of his experience there survived. The college register listed him as an "irregular" student at Miami, which meant that he was not following the prescribed path to graduation. Instead, he chose to take classes in subjects that interested him or that he thought would help him as an attorney. His athletic abilities won him friends, and he awed his fellow students by kicking a ball over the top of the dormitories. His love of music drew him to the college band, but his talent proved insufficient and he did not make the cut. He continued to play the bugle, however, and his performance was so bad that some students supposedly threatened to hang him if he continued to play it. Undeterred, Morton kept trying to play until his roommate, Isaiah Mansur, broke the horn.

Although he did not pursue the regular college course, the young man did well in his classes, especially in mathematics. Morton enthusiastically joined one of the literary societies on campus and participated in the competitions involving the writing and criticizing of essays. He also joined a debating society and won praise for his speaking abilities. These organizations served social as well as intellectual purposes, and he made friends and sharpened his mind in such activities. Morton also studied religion. The Presbyterian faculty insisted that students study orthodox Christianity and apologetics, although they themselves disagreed and fought over theology. Again facing the strong views of devout teachers, Morton chafed under such instruction. But he now asserted his individualism by refusing to study the work of English apologist William Paley, which he had already perused, and the faculty excused him from the assignment when he said that instead of defending Christianity, it would confirm him in unbelief.[18]

No record of Morton's view of the deep divisions at Miami survived. It seems likely that he joined the majority of students in despising President Junkin, especially since the administrator's conservative views varied so much from his own. The bitterness might very well have confirmed his nonprofessing position, as doing so would have allowed him to remain free from the theological controversies between the warring camps of Presbyterians. By the time he arrived in Oxford, Professor Albert T. Bledsoe had left the university, but other proslavery faculty persisted in defending the peculiar institution on campus, and it was improbable that Morton could have avoided the issue entirely. In light of his later public statements against slavery, he probably held such ideas at Miami, but if he argued for them on campus, the record of it was lost. In all likelihood, the divisions played little or no part at all in his subsequent decision to give up his formal education. After all, Junkin left in late 1844, and there was hope that the bitterness of the past could be set aside. Perhaps more important at the time, Morton was out of money. Despite his best efforts to live frugally, he had spent his inheritance and could no longer afford to go to school. So Morton left Miami after two years and returned to Centerville in the spring of 1845 to pursue earnestly both the law and a wife.[19]

CENTERVILLE LAWYER

The twenty-one-year-old man began to study the law in the office of John S. Newman, following the customary path to becoming an attorney. While a few American law schools did exist by the 1840s, most lawyers did not attend a formal legal school. Instead, they studied the law in a form of apprenticeship, guided by a practicing attorney who served as a mentor while the student performed the tasks of a clerk and assistant. Perhaps the leading attorney in Wayne County at the time, Newman took young Morton in and set him to work. With the county courthouse located there, Centerville was home to many attorneys and many law students. The lawyers based in town included George W. Julian (a well-known antislavery activist), James Ray (who became governor), and James Raridan (who served in Congress), as well as half a dozen other prominent attorneys. The law students formed a loose circle of friendly rivals and competed with one another in their reading and progress toward passing the bar. Blackstone's commentaries on the English Common Law and the King James Version of the Bible provided a foundation to which were added a variety of legal treatises and textbooks, as well as whatever copies of legal precedents could be obtained. With only six volumes of the Indiana reports available, Hoosier law students read cases from other states and relied heavily on the textbooks and their own logic for preparation. Morton spent about half of 1845 reading and studying for his chosen profession. That fall he bought books from Newman for $200 and became the older man's junior partner while continuing to study for his eventual admittance to the bar.[20]

But the law shared his time and passion with matters of the heart. While in Oxford, Morton met the sister of a fellow student when she came to visit her brother and attend commencement at Miami. Lucinda Burbank was the daughter of none other than Isaac Burbank, the merchant and family friend who had bought books for Morton when he was a boy. The young woman of nineteen was quiet and reserved, but she attracted the aspiring attorney with her intelligence and refined manners. In the previous half century, social relations in the United States had undergone tremendous changes. The desire for affectionate marriage and modern ideas about family and gender roles brought new rituals of courtship and marriage. But older ways persisted, as paternal authority and the structures of the traditional patriarchal household economy often survived, whether completely intact or in part, alongside the innovations in domestic relationships. Although they left behind no details about their courtship, Oliver Morton said that he fell desperately in love with Lucinda Burbank when he met her at Miami, and he pursued her with purposeful determination. Indeed, some said that his love for her was the reason he left college.[21]

She returned his affections, and they were married in her family's living quarters on the second floor over her father's store in Centerville on May 15, 1845. Eleven months later, she gave birth to the first of five children, a son named John Miller Morton, born in April of 1846. Two daughters followed, only to die young, one before her first birthday, the other at a year and a half. Second son Walter Scott Morton was born in December of 1856 and Oliver Throck Morton arrived in May of 1860. The family left scant evidence of their private affairs and home life, and this was especially true of the couple's early years together. Their living arrangements may have involved staying with her family or renting quarters in Centerville. From 1853 to 1857 they rented a home conveniently located a short walk from the courthouse at the center of town.[22]

Morton began spending more time in that courthouse after his admission to the bar early in 1847. He remained in partnership with Newman until he officially became an attorney; then he formed an association with Charles H. Test, a lawyer widely known for his great sense of humor and practical jokes as well as his legal abilities. The following year, in the summer of 1848, Morton ran for the office of prosecuting attorney. The district in which he sought election encompassed half a dozen counties and the Whig Party dominated it. Morton, an inexperienced young lawyer and a Democrat, had no real chance of winning office. But Test and other advisers encouraged him to run, arguing that the campaign would serve as a form of advertising and allow him to win future clients if not very many votes. It also made him fully aware of what being a Democrat in a Whig district meant. Like many, Morton inherited his political party from his family, and although he shared the views of his Whig neighbors on many political issues, he differed with them on crucial matters. He held to the Jacksonian positions on economic policies in particular, favoring hard money and free trade and opposing Whig proposals for a national bank and high tariffs. And, given his personality, the young lawyer enjoyed being the contrarian who debated the issues against the majority. But most of the voters in his district disagreed with him and did not support the Democrat.

He lost the election and continued his work as a junior partner. His career with Newman and Test really served as an extension of his education, as the senior attorneys handled all of the larger cases and important clients. Morton worked on small matters and with those clients that he could bring in on his own. Being an attorney meant riding the circuit with the judge and other lawyers, holding court in small towns and villages. Property disputes dominated rural Indiana court dockets, and Morton found himself handling many small cases involving mortgages and opinions about surveys and property lines. Farmers sometimes paid him in produce, as when he asked Henry Jarboe to bring him "six or eight bushels" of apples from his orchard as payment for his successful handling of a mortgage case in the fall of 1847.[23]

Morton's personality did not allow him to remain comfortably in a junior position that made him too much like an apprentice. In addition to stirring up bad memories of his apprenticeships as a druggist and hatter, being a junior partner grated against his character. His strong will and sense of individualism chafed at being an inferior of any kind. Not even the easygoing Charles Test could keep the young man happy as a junior partner. In fact, Morton himself did not often make jokes, and those who constantly made fun annoyed him. Ill-suited to being the junior partner in any arrangement, working for the fun-loving, practical-joking Test must have frustrated Morton even more. In the spring of 1849 he broke off his partnership and began to practice alone, and in the fall of 1850 he entered into a new partnership, this time with a junior attorney, Nimrod H. Johnson, with Morton in the senior position more comfortable for him. Johnson, however, became prosecuting attorney while working with Morton. The practice flourished, and within a year or so it stood second only to that of Morton's old partner, John Newman, in the ranks of Centerville law practices. The firm of Morton & Johnson continued until 1852, when the state legislature elected Morton to fill a vacancy as a circuit judge. Indiana's new state constitution, which had taken effect on November 1, 1851, called for the popular election of circuit judges instead of having the legislature choose them. But this was not a regular election because the law called for the legislature to fill vacancies, and the Democratic majority in the General Assembly unanimously elected Morton. He took office in the spring of 1852 and served less than eight months before being defeated in the first popular election of judges, as the Whig candidate easily won the seat. But the brief stint on the bench served the twenty-nine-year-old well, because it allowed him to make connections in Indianapolis and to solidify further his reputation in his home district. He did not like being a judge, as he preferred arguing cases to hearing them, and he happily left the bench.[24]

Morton then decided to go to law school. This seemed an odd choice because of his personal situation. Now almost thirty and married with children, he could return to his law practice and support his family. But he and Johnson had dissolved their partnership, and he and Lucinda had just suffered the loss of their second daughter. Perhaps it seemed that his life was at a crossroads. He believed that more training would make him a more effective attorney, so he left behind his family and moved to Cincinnati to attend law school. While there, he lived in a boarding house with a roommate, Murat Halstead, a young journalist on his way to fame as the editor of the *Cincinnati Commercial* newspaper. After a term of intense study, he returned to his family and practice in Centerville.[25]

There, life changed once again because of the transportation revolution. The railroad came to town in 1853, with the tracks of the Indiana Central Railroad running parallel to the National Road. With the rails that ran from Richmond to Indianapolis only a few hundred feet from Main Street, Centerville now became even more connected to the broader world. Legal business increased alongside transportation, and Morton seized the opportunity. He entered into a new partnership, again with a junior lawyer, John F. Kibbey. A few years younger than Morton, Kibbey shared his affiliation with the Democratic Party, and they had worked together as apprentices in the hatter's shop. In 1851 they had traveled across the counties of southern Indiana for an investor who wanted to buy real estate along the Ohio River. Before Morton's election as judge, Kibbey had studied in his office, and he was now ready to practice. They created the firm of Morton & Kibbey, a partnership that lasted until Morton's election to the governorship in 1860. Kibbey also served as the librarian for the town's circulating library, and the Morton & Kibbey law office not only served as a place to house the books but also became a popular gathering place for the young lawyers and other residents interested in intellectual and literary matters.[26]

The two law partners worked well together, teaming up to apply their individual talents to their casework. Kibbey spent long hours in the office, researching the case, finding precedents, documenting all of the facts. Morton mostly avoided such tasks, but he took up the case when it came time to go to court. The two attorneys often worked together far into the night, as Morton paced about the room, constructing his arguments after reading what Kibbey had compiled. While Morton worked out what he would say, Kibbey took careful notes for the senior lawyer to use in the courtroom. Once there, Morton typically cut through to the very heart of the matter, discarding all that he considered extraneous, and delivered his argument with forceful clarity. He preferred simplicity to flowery language and chose to be direct rather than circuitous in his logic and presentation. Despite his disdain for the tedious office work involved in the profession, Morton enjoyed studying the law and reading on subjects that bore relevance to his case. Morton & Kibbey steadily increased their caseload, and their reputation grew along with the number of cases. Morton won widespread fame when he defended a child murderer and used insanity as a defense. The defendant, Jacob Thompson, had murdered his young son in a horrific way. Convinced that his client suffered from mental illness and that he had not intentionally murdered his child, the lawyer delivered a long and powerful argument that nearly won the jury over. In the end, two jury members refused to accept insanity as a plea and the jury returned a compromise verdict of manslaughter. Rather than facing the death penalty, Thompson received a six-year term in prison.[27]

Lawyers in the mid-nineteenth century handled a wide variety of cases, ranging from minor civil matters to criminal cases like murder. In rural circuits like the one that included Centerville, most cases centered on property or debt and involved very small amounts of money. Morton's legal career now received most of his attention, although forays into politics sometimes distracted him from his profession. He not only worked in the local circuit but also argued nearly eighty cases in the Indiana Supreme Court. He did not enjoy as much success there as he did in the lower courts. Supreme Court arguments required written briefs rather than forceful argument, and appearances before the judges involved answering their questions rather than making a logical case. Morton disliked this style of work and often procrastinated the writing of his argument until the last minute or asked Kibbey to do it for him. The cases at the higher level still involved matters important to rural life, and Morton sometimes had to shepherd arguments about livestock on their way up through the appellate process.

While his record at the higher level was not that impressive, Morton earned a reputation as a good lawyer in the local courts, and his practice flourished.

He also continued to cultivate his social connections. This included membership in the Order of Odd Fellows, which elected him grand master of the Indiana lodge in 1854. The fraternal organization, officially named the Independent Order of Odd Fellows, traced its roots to England. Originally formed by the "odd fellows" in small towns where there were not enough members of any single trade to have guilds, the society came to serve social functions and as a safety net for those in need. The American organization broke away from its English parent in the late eighteenth century, and by the 1850s it was doing mostly charity work. Dedicated to the elevation of the character of all mankind, the benevolent order supported education and provided for widows and orphans. It also served as a networking organization, as it brought together business and professional men for a common charitable cause. Morton enthusiastically participated in the Odd Fellows and gave liberally of his time and money to its work, gaining valuable experience in organizing its activities and making connections across the state. Such relationships added to his thriving practice and won him many friends. In the mid-1850s he began to take on cases for railroad companies and soon became a corporate attorney. Such work meant higher fees, and he soon began to make more money.[28]

His lucrative practice allowed Morton to build a small fortune and to provide a better life for himself and his family. He bought fine clothes and dressed the part of a gentleman lawyer. He acquired other fineries as well and purchased an impressive mansion on Main Street (the National Road) on the western edge of Centerville. Jacob B. Julian, one of the sons of US congressman George Julian, had built the house in 1848. (George Julian and Morton became bitter political enemies when the two men fought for power within the Republican Party, but the elder Julian had earlier encouraged Morton's legal career.) Jacob Julian had known Morton since childhood, and he sold him the house in 1856 for $5,000.

The lawyer moved his family into the home in 1857, and they lived there until they sold it in 1863. The big, two-story house faced the National Road. Inside the front door, one entered a hallway, with the staircase to the left. Across the hall, on the west side of the house and to the right of the front door, were two large rooms, which served as living room and dining room. Doors between them could be opened or closed to allow more space for entertaining. Behind them was the kitchen, in the rear of the house, which faced the National Road. Upstairs were spacious bedrooms, while a room addition on the southwest corner of the house and the basement below provided storage. Despite its size, the house was not ostentatious but was rather a comfortable, stately home worthy of a prominent public man.[29]

Fig. 3. Morton House in Centerville, ca. 1975. (Library of Congress)

In the late 1850s and during his time as governor, Morton often traveled along the National Road or took the train from Indianapolis back home to Centerville. Upon his return home, he often sat on the porch of his fine house and surveyed the view before him. Situated on a knoll just west of town, the house commanded a view of the valley stretching down to Noland's Fork, a large stream flowing through the area. From the porch he could see nearby farms, while the traffic along the National Road passed right by the house. Trains moved along the tracks just a short distance farther to the north, and the hatter's shop and courthouse were just a short walk away. Morton claimed, doubtfully, that he did not think about anything when he sat on his porch but only rested. Even if that dubious statement were true, the view before him served as a reminder of his background. As a youth he had struggled to find his identity while growing up in Centerville, and it was there that his modern individualism had clashed with the traditional ethics of honor. There he had finally thrown off the yoke of apprenticeship placed upon him by his family and an older style of capitalism. In Centerville, too, he had chosen to become an attorney and achieved success as a corporate lawyer. In his hometown he had wooed and wed Lucinda Burbank and started a family.[30]

Morton came from a world created by the National Road that brought together tradition and change, East and West, North and South, in ways that both united and divided a culture and a community. In his early life he saw the birth of modern culture in Centerville. And it was there that a native son of Indiana entered politics and followed the course that led him into a broader world.

CHAPTER TWO

A Rising Republican Star

IN 1854 THE DEMOCRATIC PARTY divided over the issue of the expansion of slavery into new territories, thanks to the introduction and passage of the Kansas-Nebraska Act. This resulted in Oliver Morton choosing to stand on principle and then being driven from the party of his youth. A promising young man with political ambition and potential for statewide office, he refused to bow to the Democratic leaders who made support for the Kansas-Nebraska Act a test of party loyalty. Morton opposed the extension of slavery and also defended his right to disagree with the party leadership. He saw the bill as a violation of the Missouri Compromise and a threat to the Union. In his mind, he was defending the country as well as his own right to freedom of thought. When the state convention endorsed the bill by a large majority, the leadership also pushed through a resolution to expel all of the anti-Nebraska delegates, including four of the nine men representing Wayne County. Accepting the consequences of his principled stand, Morton rose to his feet and walked out of the hall, with his fellow anti-Nebraska delegates in tow. The state Democrats had kicked him out before he could choose to leave.

As the outcasts made their way toward the exit, the crowd of delegates hissed and taunted them, hurling racist epithets at them. As the insults rained down with calls to "Go equalize yourselves with niggers" and "Your heads are getting kinky," one of his friends wanted to respond with curses of his own, but Morton stopped him and said, "No, let us not show them that much respect." The expelled delegates reached the door, where the man who wanted to respond vocally became so angry that he turned and cried out, "Hell dawns upon the Democratic Party from this day onward." Having been forced out of the political organization he had so long supported, the thirty-one-year-old Morton now found himself without a political home. But in the context of the changing times, he soon found a new party, one that he helped to create as he emerged as a rising Republican star.[1]

A Young Democrat

Morton had held fast to the Democratic Party during his early years in politics. The Jacksonian organization lagged behind the Whigs in Wayne County, but usually enjoyed a majority in the state as a whole. James Morton, a lifelong Democrat, had passed his politics along to his son, who rode home from Miami University to cast his first ballot for James K. Polk in the 1844 presidential contest. Young Morton supported territorial expansion and believed strongly in Jacksonian economic policies like hard money, low taxes, state's rights, and free trade. Although no record of his political views from this period have survived, Morton probably encountered the issues on a frequent basis, both in Centerville and Oxford. In his hometown, antislavery men like George Julian held prominent positions, and Henry Clay's visits to the area—including an 1842 sojourn in the home of James Raridan, just across the street from the hatter's shop, before making a speech in nearby Richmond—illustrated how the politics of the Second American Party System were part of life in Morton's world.

The politics of slavery surrounded him at Miami, as the widely despised George Junkin raised the ire of students and faculty with his iron-fisted proslavery views. Morton supported the Compromise of 1850 and hoped it would settle the problem of the territorial expansion of slavery for good. That agreement had nearly died in Washington, DC, but Senator Stephen A. Douglas, an Illinois Democrat, had emerged to manage the various pieces of legislation through the Congress after an attempt to pass the compromise as an omnibus bill had failed. Americans still looked upon compromise as a positive aspect of politics and democratic or republican government. Many of the great statesmen of the early nineteenth century had won their fame as compromisers, with Henry Clay as the most obvious example. But the Kentucky Whig, now an old man, had failed to get the job done in 1850. Instead, the younger Democrat from Illinois took up the mantle of Clay and forged the deal.[2]

In 1850 Morton backed his party and Douglas, and he saw a bright future ahead for the American Democracy (which was the official name of the Democratic Party). He also voted for the new state constitution in 1851, complete with its exclusionary clause that forbade blacks from settling in Indiana. Morton disliked the abolitionists, whom he thought made trouble and divided the country. Fully in agreement with the great statesmen of his youth, he valued the Union above all and preferred to avoid or to compromise on the sectional issues that threatened the nation. Born and raised in the Midwest, Morton had little contact with slavery on a personal level and discounted abolitionist accounts of the institution's brutality as propaganda. He saw the abolitionists as a threat to national unity, and although he had not yet developed the ideology that came to mark his career in later years, he was already putting the Union ahead of all other considerations. Thus, in 1851 he worked hard to defeat George Julian in the antislavery Congressman's run for reelection. Although there had been personal differences between the two Centerville lawyers before, Morton distrusted Julian's radicalism on slavery, and he sought to defeat the abolitionist. At first he tried to get the Democrats to mount a campaign behind a strong opponent to Julian, perhaps himself, and when this failed, he orchestrated a political fusion at the local level and persuaded enough Democrats to support the Whig candidate to deny Julian's return to Washington. The narrow margin of 562 votes, with the victor, Samuel W. Parker, carrying Wayne County by 295 ballots, convinced Julian that Morton was responsible for his defeat, and this served as the foundation for decades of bitterness between the two men. The following year, in 1852, the newly appointed Judge Morton continued his political efforts and campaigned actively in the area for Democratic presidential candidate Franklin Pierce, making speeches on behalf of the victor and other party candidates.[3]

The loyal Democrat finally broke with his party in 1854 over the issue of slavery in the territories. The problem, as Morton saw it at the time, was not slavery itself but its western expansion. Since 1820, the Missouri Compromise stood as the settled law on the subject, but challenges to it had risen in recent years. The Wilmot Proviso attached to the appropriations bill paying for the war with Mexico in 1846 had died in the US Senate, but it called for abolishing slavery in any territory conquered and acquired in the conflict. Then the crisis of 1850 and the resulting deal shifted the ground completely. The Missouri agreement set the 36°30' line as the boundary between slavery and freedom. All territory added to the north of the line would be free, while all to the south of it would be slave. But the vast territories added by the peace settlement following the US-Mexican War upset that arrangement. California soon became eligible for statehood, and while its southern portion lay south of the Missouri Compromise line, it entered the Union as a free state. Furthermore, Congress organized the territories of Utah and New Mexico, from which they later carved those two states as well as Nevada and Arizona, under the rule of popular sovereignty. This meant that future voters there would determine their state's status. Despite all of this, Morton and many others believed that the Missouri Compromise still stood because those territories were farther west and not part of the Louisiana Purchase that was clearly covered by the pact made in 1820. Therefore, many Northern Democrats could support both of the compromises. Then, Senator Stephen A. Douglas of Illinois decided to change the rules for good, hoping to build a transcontinental railroad, preserve the Union, strengthen the Democratic Party, and put himself in the White House.[4]

Douglas claimed that his plan, the Kansas-Nebraska Act of 1854, had nothing to do with slavery but was instead designed to help build a railroad across the country to California and the Pacific Ocean. This would please some of his wealthy Chicago constituents, who stood to reap tremendous profits from investments in such a project and would also bring the support of those voters in the states standing to benefit from a transcontinental line. Organizing the Kansas and Nebraska territories would make a central route to the West more feasible, with governments organized to protect and support the railroad's construction and the settlement that would follow it. With the transcontinental line exacerbating sectional controversies as politicians argued over whether it should take a northern or southern route, Douglas stood to win even more fame as a compromiser and man who got things done, and accomplishing the new railroad to the Pacific would do much to enhance his presidential prospects. Slavery was a secondary matter, Douglas said, one about which he cared little or nothing. But his bill extended the idea of popular sovereignty to the two newly formed territories, both of which were part of the Louisiana Purchase and covered by the Missouri Compromise of 1820.

For many Democrats, especially those in the South, the application of popular sovereignty to the territory of New Mexico in 1850 had already overturned the Missouri Compromise, and they considered the means of deciding the slavery issue by voters on the local level to be democracy in action. That it also fit well under a state's rights interpretation made it constitutionally sound and all the more attractive to Jacksonian Democrats. Douglas hoped to unite his party with the plan and believed it would resolve the problem of the territorial expansion of slavery for good. If it worked, it would also further his presidential ambitions.

In the short term, Kansas-Nebraska brought Douglas much praise from Southerners, just as he had hoped. But it divided Northern Democrats. Many antislavery men in the party, like Morton, saw the Compromise of 1850 as a one-time scheme that did not break the deal made in 1820. But thanks to the maneuvering of politicians, the Kansas-Nebraska Act overturned the Missouri Compromise, not through a settlement forged by statesmen to avert a crisis but through simple legislative action. That the bill became law convinced many of them that their own party was under the control of Southern defenders of slavery. Some Democrats began to talk about the Slave Power, a conspiracy theory that held that evil Southern planters were out to protect and defend their peculiar institution at all costs, including spreading slavery into new territories and even the Northern states. Soon the Democracy began to splinter. While many remained officially within the party but ran as anti-Nebraska Democrats, others decided to bolt the organization or were forced out by the Democratic establishment.[5]

Thus, support for the bill became a test of party loyalty, and like a number of other Northern antislavery Democrats, Oliver Morton failed the test. And by insisting that he follow the official line, the party failed Morton's own test. His views on the issue of slavery matched those of most Hoosier citizens at the time, which meant that he opposed the expansion of the institution to new territories on moral grounds, believing that it was a necessary evil that should be contained until it eventually died out at some point in the future. In the meantime, he accepted it as part of Southern culture and did not speak against the racist views that dominated in many parts of the North, including Indiana. In fact, Morton supported the 1851 state constitution's provision that excluded blacks from settling in Indiana. When the exclusionary clause was put to the voters separately from the rest of the new law code, his vote added to its passage by a majority of about ninety thousand, more than the margin of victory for the widely popular constitution.

Additionally, the young lawyer also complained about the radicalism of the abolitionists, and he opposed them politically. Having almost no experience with slavery himself, it was easy enough for Morton to put the Union and compromise ahead of any moral questions about the peculiar institution. He worked hard to defeat George Julian in the Centerville abolitionist leader's run for reelection, supported the official stand of his party in regard to the Compromise of 1850, and argued that the Missouri Compromise still held. But Douglas's plan for popular sovereignty threatened the compromise and the spirit behind it. By reintroducing the issue of slavery and renewing sectionalism, the scheme also threatened to divide the Democratic Party. As the Kansas-Nebraska bill worked its way through Congress, managed by Douglas in the Senate and Georgia's Alexander Stephens in the House of Representatives, Morton decided that he would try to save his party from itself. He joined fellow antislavery Democrats in speaking out against the bill and calling for its defeat in the House after it passed the Senate in early March of 1854.[6]

That spring was a busy political season, with congressional elections pending in the fall and the Douglas bill wending its way through the process of becoming law. In April, Wayne County Democrats chose Morton to lead their delegation to the May state party convention and passed a resolution supporting him as a candidate for Congress. State elections elsewhere in the North saw the defeat of Democrats over the Nebraska issue and Morton feared that the Democrats would lose their congressional majority in the fall unless they corrected course before passing the new law. So he went early to Indianapolis to meet with state Democratic leaders in hopes of stopping the bill or at least to prevent the Hoosier party organization from endorsing it.

Morton went straight to the top and met with Jesse D. Bright, the powerful US senator who ran the state party with an iron fist and whose proslavery views stemmed, at least in part, from personal interest, as he owned slaves in Kentucky. Not surprisingly, he supported the Kansas-Nebraska bill and was sure that the party was strong enough to carry it forward. A tough politician who had risen through the ranks to being the leader of the well-organized state party machine, Bright refused to listen when Morton warned that passage of the bill would divide the party and bring defeat. Instead, the senator thought that the bill presented an opportunity for him to increase his control over the Indiana party. He feared the growing popularity of his opponents within the Democratic fold, especially their leader, Governor Joseph A. Wright. Using the test of party loyalty on Kansas-Nebraska allowed Bright to make it a way to test loyalty to himself. His intraparty enemies would be forced to choose whether to remain Democrats and accept his leadership or leave the party.[7]

Seeing that Bright would not budge, the young Wayne County politician turned to Joseph E. McDonald, a former congressman who still had an auspicious future in politics. A Methodist whose religious beliefs served as the foundation for his antislavery views, McDonald introduced substitute resolutions opposing an endorsement of the Nebraska bill. But he apparently failed to assure Morton of this and the young lawyer saw himself being backed into a corner politically. Thwarted in his efforts to stop the measure in the convention and realizing that the Democratic leadership insisted on party discipline, Morton declared that he would not be bound by the state organization's endorsement and that, if the bill passed, he would leave the Democrats. Certain that the Kansas-Nebraska bill would bring defeat at the polls and aware that the party leaders would expect him to speak in support of their endorsement of it despite his moral opposition to slavery's extension and his political opposition to the measure, he decided to stand on principle.[8]

Doing so was a politically risky move on his part because Morton was a rising star in the Democratic Party of Indiana. Already considered the party leader in Wayne County at the age of thirty, he was a likely candidate for Congress or a statewide office. Even if he failed to win an election, party loyalty would no doubt bring patronage and appointments like the judgeship he had recently held. Leaving the Democrats would set him adrift politically, as he had opposed the Whigs too long for them to welcome him into their fold and, besides, he disagreed with them on most issues. Third parties like the Free Soil Party were out of the question for a man who detested abolitionists despite his opposition to slavery's expansion into new territory, especially since the Free Soilers were led by his enemy George Julian. The principles on which he refused to yield were more complicated than a moral opposition to slavery. Instead, it was a matter of conscience combined with the party's insistence that its members support the Nebraska bill. He opposed the expansion of slavery and defended his own right to disagree with the party establishment.

Morton still hoped to remain a Democrat, however, as he tried to lead the county organization to repudiate the Nebraska bill and nominate him as a congressional candidate running as an anti-Nebraska Democrat. The county party convention met in late May 1854 in Cambridge City. Morton met with a group of friends the night before the party gathering, and they agreed to support him in the convention. He declared that, if the county party endorsed the Kansas-Nebraska bill, he would officially leave the Democratic Party and would not run for office as an anti-Nebraska candidate. He did not go to the party meeting itself, as his duties as lodge master for the Odd Fellows demanded his attendance at the same time. In light of his political ambitions, choosing to attend the state lodge meeting seemed a strange decision. But he took his responsibilities as the head of the state organization seriously and thought that he had to do his duty. Besides, he had suffered enough humiliation at the hands of his fellow Democrats at the state convention. Instead, he sent a letter expressing his views on the bill and it was read aloud before the vote on endorsement was taken. A fierce political battle followed, but the county organization endorsed the bill by a small margin and Morton left the Democrats for good.[9]

CREATING THE REPUBLICAN PARTY

Cut loose from his political moorings, Morton now had to find a new party with which to affiliate himself if he hoped to keep alive his ambitions for office. He refused to join the Free Soil Party led by George Julian because of his personal disagreements with Julian and his belief that abolitionists were dangerous radicals. The Whigs were not a good choice because of policy differences, his long opposition to them, and the fact that they were also divided over slavery. And, of course, the national Whig Party would soon splinter, and its Hoosier members would find themselves looking for a new home right alongside Oliver Morton and other former Democrats. Another alternative came in the form of the nativist and anti-Catholic American Party, the political organ of the Society of the Star-Spangled Banner whose members were called "Know Nothings" because they always denied knowing anything about the secret organization. But Morton had been a Jacksonian Democrat who supported immigrants and he was ecumenical in his religious toleration. More attractive to him was the possibility of a new Prohibition Party, as a movement was coalescing around support for the "Maine Law" outlawing alcohol. Modeled after the state of

Maine's prohibition code, the movement took temperance from the realm of voluntarism to the legislation of morality. A nondrinker who had defended several of the prohibition activists in court when they were arrested for destroying alcohol while protesting in saloons, Morton found the crusading zeal of the movement intoxicating. He likely did not see the irony of opposing the moral fervor of the abolitionists but liking that of the prohibition activists. The fight against alcohol gained strength as the influence of evangelical Christianity grew across the state. Prohibition enjoyed popular support in Wayne County and was especially strong in Centerville. It appealed to enough Hoosiers that the legislature soon passed a prohibition law only to have it overturned by the state supreme court. Morton clearly supported the Prohibition Party and it needed able leaders, which made it an attractive alternative. But would a single-issue movement be enough to support a political career?[10]

In early July 1854 the Know Nothings attempted to nominate Morton for Congress, but he refused to accept the offer. Within a few weeks, he had begun to help organize a new organization, a coalition of anti-Nebraska Democrats, former Whigs, disaffected Know Nothings and Free Soil members, and many prohibitionists that came to be called the "People's Party" or "Fusion Party." The main issue around which the coalition came together was the Kansas-Nebraska Act, which appealed to the many splinter groups and factions that were seeking a new political home. Morton threw himself into the People's Party and joined his former law partner, Charles Test, on the campaign trail that fall. The two men went to Indianapolis in September and spoke in response to a group of Democrats, including Stephen Douglas and Jesse Bright, who had delivered speeches a couple of weeks earlier. Morton held forth in a long speech that blamed the Slave Power for overturning the Missouri Compromise and argued that a few Northern Democrats—Douglas and Bright—were responsible for allowing that to happen. He thought that Douglas's plan for popular sovereignty was a "preposterous humbug" that allowed Northern Democrats to delude themselves into thinking that settlers in new territories were actually free to decide the question of slavery. Morton called Douglas and his supporters hypocrites, saying that they claimed to hope that slavery would not spread after they had done all that they could to allow it to move westward.

In the October elections, Morton's predictions about the Democrats paying for their support for the Kansas-Nebraska Act came true, and he happily played his part in helping sweep the opposition to victory in nine of the state's eleven congressional races and in overturning the Democracy's majority in the legislature. Although the People's Party was unable to win a majority of the seats in the state assembly, their victory denied the Democrats what had been their traditional control of the body. In the span of just a few months in 1854, Morton went from being a Democrat with a promising future to a political outcast to a highly visible leader of a movement that had swept the fall elections.[11]

He continued working for the People's Party, speaking at various events throughout the rest of the fall, including the People's Jubilee outside the statehouse in November. The following year, he resumed his activities for the new party, traveling widely across the state to speak at local conventions. In addition to speaking, Morton helped build and organize the party at the grassroots level, a matter of significance if the fusion of the different disaffected splinter groups were going to survive. Mentioned as a possible candidate for the state senate in 1855, he joined with other leaders of the movement to broaden their appeal beyond the slavery issue. Morton pushed a prohibition law and compromised with the Know Nothings in the new party by arguing that the Indiana Constitution allowed immigrants to vote too soon because it provided for the franchise after residence of only a year. Becoming a naturalized citizen of the United States required five years, and Morton yielded to the former American Party members in his new coalition by agreeing that the federal restrictions should be adopted for Indiana as well. But he refused to give into the Know Nothings who pushed for anti-Catholic measures and more stringent immigration laws.[12]

Strongest in what is today called the Midwest, People's Party organizations and similar parties with different names had been created across the North in response to the Kansas-Nebraska Act, but there was not yet a national platform, and the state movements developed their own list of policies to support. This meant hammering out compromises between the various factions in the new coalition, and Morton realized that he had to give at least some ground on some issues if he hoped to build a viable party. But there could be no compromise on the essentials. Slavery remained the vital issue for the new party, as settlers poured into Kansas and the proslavery and Free State adherents among them began to fight. With tensions mounting and the border wars along the Kansas and Missouri line looming, Hoosier members of the People's Party appointed delegates to attend a national convention to organize a new antislavery political party to support a candidate in the presidential election. Oliver Morton was one of the delegates from Indiana who traveled to Pittsburgh, Pennsylvania, in February 1856 to participate in the preliminary convention that officially created the Republican Party.[13]

The Pittsburgh convention called for a national convention in June to nominate candidates for the presidential race that fall. It also passed a series of resolutions condemning the extension of slavery, calling for the admission of Kansas as a free state, and urging the defeat of the Democratic administration of Franklin

Pierce that had allowed the Douglas plan for popular sovereignty to go forward. The convention represented the confusing coalition that was becoming the new party, with former Whigs mixing with the former Democrats and former Know Nothings and former Free Soil Party members. Conservatives met with radicals and prohibitionists mingled with nativists while abolitionists marveled that the convention was presided over by Francis P. Blair, a Southern slaveholder and former Democrat who opposed the expansion of slavery.[14]

While the Republicans began their history in Pittsburgh by trying to fuse a party out of confusion, across the state in Philadelphia the American Party nominated former president Millard Fillmore as their candidate for the presidency in 1856. When the Whigs collapsed over slavery in 1854, the American Party had stepped in to fill the void as the opposition to the Democrats. But the nativist party refused to accept delegates from Louisiana because of that state's large Catholic population, and they failed to come to an agreement about the territorial expansion of slavery. Having already lost members to the nascent Republicans, the Know Nothings, who had served as the opposition party for several years in many states, now experienced further division. If the Republican/People's Party/Fusion movement could unite with the nativists or, at least, bring more of them over to the new party, they might become the main opposition.

But that was not yet clear, and in Indiana Morton led those who wanted compromise but resisted making too many concessions to the Know Nothings. His rival, George Julian, denounced the nativists at every turn, making it difficult to unite the Free Soilers and Know Nothings. In the Hoosier State, the secret society of nativists was led by Godlove S. Orth, who had been in the Indiana Senate and had served as acting lieutenant governor as a member of the Whig Party; he would later become a Republican congressman. Another former Whig, the future speaker of the US House of Representatives and Vice President Schuyler Colfax, also worked with the American Party before joining the Republicans. Colfax agreed with Morton that antislavery must be paramount in the new party, but Orth continued to argue that nativism was a strong issue and urged the Republicans to adopt more of the Know Nothing platform when he came over during the fusion of the coalition.[15]

Meanwhile, the Democrats continued to divide. The bolting and expulsion of anti-Nebraska men only deepened the bitter sectional chasm. Northern fears of the Slave Power led many to conclude that Northern Democrats like Stephen Douglas and Jesse Bright were "doughfaces" who had sold out to the South. The term *doughface* stemmed from the words of John Randolph of Roanoke during the sectional crisis surrounding the Missouri Compromise. An eccentric Virginian who carried a riding crop and brought his hunting dogs to the House of Representatives, Randolph had declared that Northern congressmen who voted with the South were weak, half-baked men, who "were scared at their own dough faces." Despite his scornful derision, or perhaps because of it, Randolph and other Southerners knew that they could count on those doughfaces when they defended slavery. Northern Democratic doughface votes were so consistent that conspiracy theorists argued that the Slave Power controlled the country through its dominance of the Democratic Party. Northern Democrats tended to use racism to their political advantage, and some of them, like Bright, were sincerely proslavery, facts that added fuel to the conspiracy theories.[16]

The Slave Power Conspiracy was not simply a manifestation of paranoia, American style, but reflected the long reach of the South in national politics. However outlandish such a theory might have seemed to later generations, it was rational enough to make many Northerners question the motives of those doughface politicians who voted with the South: such worries might deepen the sectional divisions in the Democratic Party and cause more splintering or complete collapse. If the Democrats remained united, North and South, they would likely maintain their domination of national politics and probably return to power in Indiana. Hoosier discontent with the Democracy had led to the opposition sweeping the election of 1854, but if that opposition did not coalesce into a viable political organization, the controversy over the Kansas-Nebraska Act would fade and the Democrats would return. The 1856 election would serve as a test of whether the new Republican Party could unite the various splinter groups from the collapse of the Second American Party System into a real organization that represented true fusion and offered a real alternative to the Democrats. It also seemed likely to test Democratic unity and the power of the slavery issue. If Republicans railing against the Slave Power proved effective, enough voters might turn away from the Democracy to further divide it and open the door for future opposition victories.[17]

The Election of 1856

The election of 1856 confirmed Oliver Morton's place as a leader in the Indiana Republican Party and also secured the new party's role as a viable organization and the opposition to the Democrats at both the state and national levels. By the fall of 1855 many in the People's Party had begun talking about Morton as a possible candidate for governor, but he tried to head off such chatter by publishing a statement in the *Indianapolis Journal* on January 30, 1856, saying that he would not be a candidate. Despite his published protest, the same meeting of the People's Party that made him a delegate to the Pittsburgh convention also passed a resolution supporting him as a candidate for governor. His travels around the state to help organize the new party combined with his prominence as a former Democrat made him an attractive candidate. While the leaders of the other factions in the Republican coalition fought among themselves and held stridently to their views, Morton seemed to be a sound alternative. He had compromised enough to make friends with the former Know Nothings, Free Soilers, and Whigs but had not given up significant ground to any of them. He called for reforming the state's immigration laws while still being pro-immigrant and refusing to take anti-Catholic positions. He denounced the abolitionists as radicals while vigorously taking an antislavery position against the Slave Power and the expansion of slavery. He hinted at his own still-developing nationalism and supported railroads while still maintaining his Jacksonian principles of state's rights and free trade. This was vital in making the new party something more than a rebranding of the Whigs, and Morton's stand for Jacksonian economics helped develop the free-labor ideology around which the Republicans would unite.[18]

Morton stood in the first rank of the former Democrats in the new movement, and this mattered, as the People's Party hoped to attract more disaffected Jacksonians. The other factions seemed sure to vote for the People's/Republican Party because they would have no other choice against the Democrats; Morton, however, might be able to pull ballots from Democratic crossover voters. Young, healthy, with an impressive physique and bearing, already praised as a forceful speaker who cut right through to the heart of the matter, with a character and abilities well suited to an executive, Morton seemed to have all of the qualities needed to make a run for the governor's chair. But other candidates among the People's/Republican Party movement also received support for the nomination.

Especially attractive to many was Henry S. Lane, a former Whig congressman who had joined the Know Nothings when his first party collapsed. Although he opposed the extension of slavery, Lane espoused conservative views on most issues and knew how to play to the racism so prevalent in Indiana's political culture at the time. Such a candidate would attract most of the old Whigs and appeal to conservatives across the various parties and splinter groups unlikely to vote for anyone they considered too radical. Indeed, the desire for a moderate position caused many activists and candidates to refuse to use the name "Republican" for fear it would paint them into a political corner seen as too radical on the issue of slavery. They chose to use the "People's Party" label—although many still called it "Fusion"—for the time being. Morton himself hedged his bets, still calling himself a Democrat on many occasions well after he had publicly taken a stand with the new movement. Lane's prominence as a Whig and a Know Nothing combined with his conservatism to make him a likely choice to head the state ticket for the opposition, whatever name they used. When the former Whig refused to consider the nomination, Morton emerged as the clear choice for what was still officially called the "People's Party," if he chose to accept it.[19]

While Morton remained a possible candidate, the Democrats chose their nominee. On January 8, 1856, the anniversary of Andrew Jackson's victory at the Battle of New Orleans in 1815, the Indiana Democracy held their state convention. They adopted a platform that endorsed the Kansas-Nebraska Act, strongly denounced the Know Nothings (condemning "secret political orders"), supported lenient naturalization laws for immigrants, and opposed prohibition—all issues that clearly defined them against the People's/Republican Party movement. During the convention, the anti-Bright forces led by Governor Wright tried unsuccessfully to remove the senator as party leader. Instead, Bright exercised his power by swinging the Indiana party's support to James Buchanan for president once it became clear that he could not win the nomination himself. Many Hoosier Democrats wanted Stephen Douglas, but Bright would have none of it because the "Little Giant" from Illinois had thwarted his own ambitions when he blocked the Hoosier leader from becoming Franklin Pierce's running mate in 1852.[20]

Wright led the Douglas men in the Indiana party, and the divisions between the factions were deeply personal as well as related to ideological issues like slavery. A devout Methodist whose Christian beliefs animated his political views on reform, Wright was antislavery and supported temperance. Furthermore, his personal charisma and dynamic speaking ability contrasted him with the proslavery, antiprohibitionist Bright, who avoided making speeches in favor of behind-the-scenes manipulation. Democrats could unite in support of state's rights and popular sovereignty, but their own sectional crisis bubbled just beneath the surface and this was expressed in the Bright versus Wright/Douglas battles at the state level. After the purge of the anti-Nebraska men, the remaining antislavery Democrats rallied around Wright and contended that popular sovereignty was actually an antislavery measure because it allowed the voters to prohibit slavery in new states. Bright won the round of the fight at the 1856 state convention and began working at the national level to make Buchanan president.[21]

Amid their infighting, Hoosier Democrats also nominated Lieutenant Governor Ashbel P. Willard for governor. A native New Yorker who had earned a degree at Hamilton College, Willard studied law before moving to Michigan, then to Kentucky, then to Indiana, where he practiced in New Albany. He had worked his way up politically, winning a seat on the city council, then becoming a state legislator and serving as chair of the Ways and Means Committee and, later, Speaker of the Indiana House. In 1852 he won the lieutenant governor's election as Joseph A. Wright's running mate and served as the president of the state senate for four years. Known for being well mannered and charismatic, Willard earned a reputation as an orator during long years on the stump, speaking in support of other candidates, then for himself. Like many of the Democrats in the southern part of Indiana, he preached the doctrines of state's rights and supported the rights of slaveholders, including the Fugitive Slave Act, which had been part of the Compromise of 1850.

Widely unpopular in many areas of the North, the Fugitive Slave Act divided Hoosiers and the state's Democrats, as some railed against it and argued for the rights of individual conscience, while others supported the law and called for its enforcement. In the 1852 election, then, Willard balanced the Democratic ticket, serving as a southern Indiana counterweight to Wright's moderate antislavery position, while his widely discussed imbibing not only caused him to pledge not to drink if elected but also offset Wright's teetotaling. The two men and their party united on most issues, however, and carried the election. By 1856, however, the Democratic division had deepened, and the Wright-led faction that opposed Jesse Bright also turned against Willard. Although he won the nomination, it seemed likely that the right opponent could pull Democrats away from Willard.[22]

Such thinking made the decision quite clear at the People's Party convention on May 1, and they quickly nominated Oliver Morton by acclamation, as no other names were put forward. He responded to the nomination with a speech that boldly called for admitting Kansas as a free state. He said that he did not want to interfere with slavery where it already existed but that he would fight its expansion. With "Bleeding Kansas" capturing the newspaper headlines and the attention of the country, the context seemed perfect for Morton and the People's Party, as they hoped to nationalize the state election and make the expansion of slavery the primary issue. This would unite the Fusion movement that made up the People's Party and would drive the sectional wedge deeper into the Democratic divide. Splitting the proslavery and antislavery factions, the Bright and Wright wings of the state Democracy might well divide their own organization and catapult the new party to power. Morton planned to begin his campaign around the Fourth of July but accepted Willard's invitation to debate him in Centerville in mid-May. The two men took to the stump in what became an extended campaign and argued the issues in towns across the state, foreshadowing the famous Lincoln-Douglas debates two years later.[23]

Fig. 4. Governor Ashbel P. Willard, Morton's Democratic opponent in the election of 1856. (W. H. Bass Photo Company Collection, Indiana Historical Society)

THE WILLARD-MORTON DEBATES

The 1856 race for governor of Indiana pitted two young rising star politicians against one another, as Morton was thirty-two and Willard thirty-five years old during the campaign. They both enjoyed growing fame as speakers, with Willard known for his ability to captivate and rouse his audience, often bringing even his political opponents to their feet to applaud him, while Morton spoke more slowly, without as much emotion, but with force. Everyone agreed that Willard was the better orator, but Morton held his own, and those in the People's Party praised him for appealing to the mind rather than the heart. Democrats found Morton a dull speaker and hailed Willard's graceful skill as complete victory when, in fact, the younger man managed to do well enough to negate any real political advantage to be gained in such debates. Willard was flashy, but he spoke quickly and often left his train of thought behind, wandering off topic to make a side point and never really returning to his main idea. Morton's slower, more methodical style contrasted well with his opponent's forensic manner, and Willard's tendency to presume victory made him seem arrogant.[24]

Physically, Morton was a more commanding presence. He was a large man with a powerful build. His big chest and broad shoulders made him seem huge when standing next to men of average size. Black hair, dark eyes, and high forehead combined in such a way to give him an air of strength and authority. His body was well proportioned, making him tall and broad. His deep, full voice was not loud, but the Centerville lawyer had learned to use it with great skill when speaking. His speaking style was direct, meaning that he often seemed blunt, and his arguments aimed at destroying the logic of his opponent rather than achieving some kind of delicate persuasion. Everyone noticed his strong will and his combative nature. Although he had a fun side and laughed readily during personal conversations, he rarely employed humor in his public speaking. Although he spoke the language of the people of Indiana, he rarely appealed to the emotions, and he avoided telling stories. Instead, he battered his opponents down with direct assaults upon the logic of their arguments. And he always got right to the heart of the matter by sticking to the issues.

"Bleeding Kansas" set the context and became the primary issue of the campaign. In 1852, Joseph A. Wright and his Whig opponent had avoided most national issues and had not debated the Compromise of 1850. They ignored the Fugitive Slave Act, the expansion of slavery, and even prohibition, in favor of a focus on state issues like economics, immigration, and a new state constitution. But the 1856 contest centered on Kansas and the issue of whether or not it would be admitted as a free or slave state. The violence of the border wars between the free-state Jayhawkers and the proslavery Border Ruffians from Missouri divided the country and Indiana along sectional lines. The sack of Lawrence by proslavery forces and the murder of five Southern men by the abolitionist John Brown led to debates in the halls of Congress. When Senator Charles Sumner used provocative language in his speech accusing the South of the "Crime against Kansas," Congressman Preston Brooks later responded by violently caning him in the Senate chamber. Democrats rallied around popular sovereignty and state's rights and blamed the extremist abolitionists, while the People's/Republican Party candidates cried out against the Slave Power, pointing to "Bleeding Kansas" and "Bleeding Sumner" as evidence of the South's dominance. The Democratic candidate for president of the United States, James Buchanan of Pennsylvania, led the way for Northern Democrats by arguing that popular sovereignty was democracy in action and would allow the people of Kansas to determine their future. The first Republican to seek the highest office in the country, John C. Frémont stood on a party platform that called for prohibiting slavery in the territories and for Kansas to be admitted as a free state. He also promoted the free labor ideology that allowed party unity on economic policy.[25]

The 1856 governor's race in Indiana became a venue for arguing about Kansas and slavery. It also became a squabble over which candidate was trying to avoid debating the other. When they debated in Centerville on May 15, Morton surprised everyone by holding his own. Although no one claimed that he had won the debate, the fact that he had not lost badly made it a victory of sorts. After all, most observers expected the eloquent Willard to demolish his opponent. The two met again at Newcastle, Indiana, on June 12, and Morton's supporters claimed a clear victory, arguing that "Willard was completely unhorsed and discomfited." Morton later said that while at Newcastle he invited Willard to debate in July, but the Democrat refused, saying that he might be able to meet in August. But the leading newspaper organ of the Democrats, the *Indiana Sentinel,* said that Willard had won the debate at Newcastle and that Morton had refused to meet him again. Whatever the truth of the disagreement was, the two candidates headed off on separate campaign tours, speaking at various locations throughout the summer.[26]

In late June, while traveling and speaking in southern Indiana, Morton saw more newspaper accounts claiming that he had refused to meet Willard. Incensed, he wrote to Willard and proposed several joint appointments, and he authorized the man who carried his message to arrange the times and places to meet. Willard equivocated in his answer, arguing that he had scheduled speeches until August 9 and could not agree to debate until then. In mid-July the two men met in person to discuss their schedules, but they made no further arrangements. Meanwhile, the People's Party state committee arranged for Morton to speak at numerous locations. Willard tried to blame Morton for the lack of debates and complained about the slate of engagements. The bickering continued, with Morton challenging Willard's assertions. Whatever the reality of the arrangements, it looked like Willard planned to follow Morton around the state and speak right after him on every occasion. The trouble continued when Morton's speaking tour began, as speeches were disrupted by Willard's supporters who then allowed their own man to speak without interruption. Finally, the two candidates returned to joint appointments and, although both still took opportunities to speak alone, they spent most of the late summer and fall debating one another directly.[27]

The debates continued to be something of a stalemate, with Morton doing well enough for his supporters to claim victory, while the Democrats always said that Willard had the best of him. Morton's performance surprised many and brought him national attention. By August the New-York *Daily Tribune* was reporting on the Indiana gubernatorial race and said that "the Republicans have made a strong nomination in the person of Oliver P. Morton, a man of education, of fine personal appearance, in the prime of life, and possessing the physical powers necessary for the labor of a warm campaign. He is an orator, a gentleman, and an honest politician." Morton's confidence grew as he continued to debate Willard, and by fall some of his supporters were predicting that the Republican candidate would carry the northern counties and the National Road corridor and sweep to victory. In September the Holmes County *Republican* saw a landslide coming: "Judge Morton will come from northern Indiana to the National Road with a majority of 30,000 votes." With the People's Party seeming to regain the momentum that had carried it to victory in 1854, the Democrats played the race card. As early as midsummer, both parties began to employ the electioneering tactics of modern politics, focusing on the national issue of slavery and its extension into Kansas. The *Indiana Sentinel,* the leading Democrat newspaper in the state, worried about the Fusionists uniting the Free Soilers and the Nativists and derided their opponents in racist language. "Will Sambo meet Sam halfway and form a coalition against the Democracy? We predict he will and therefore caution Democrats to act accordingly. Already is Abolitionism and Know Nothingism hand in glove in support of the state ticket headed by Oliver P. Morton."[28]

Working hard to keep the focus on slavery, the People's Party held a parade complete with wagon floats that painted the Democrats with the blood spilled in the border wars. As the procession passed by along the streets of Indianapolis, residents of the city could see a float of men dressed as Border Ruffians from Bleeding Kansas, another depicting the infamous caning that led to Bleeding Sumner, and a third with young women wearing hoop skirts in honor of Republican presidential candidate John C. Frémont's lovely wife. The party's national standard-bearer's campaign slogan, "Free Speech, Free Labor, Free Soil, Free Men," borrowed much from the earlier campaigns of the Free Soil Party, but it resonated with many Hoosier voters, and Kansas proved a potent symbol for rousing antislavery sentiment. Desperate to prevent this from splitting their party and losing them the election, the Democrats appealed to racism. They called the People's Party "Black Republicans" and abolitionists and accused them of promoting race mixing and amalgamation. Morton and his supporters, the Willard campaign insisted, aimed at giving blacks full equality, and Democrats held parades of their own, with young girls wearing white carrying banners reading, "Fathers, save us from nigger husbands!"[29]

The Democrats also attempted to further divide the opposition. The Fusion movement represented so many different factions that uniting them into a new party proved difficult. The Know Nothings had mostly joined the People's Party, but some held out, and the American Party ran Millard Fillmore for president. Although most of the nativists supported Morton and the rest of the state ticket of the People's Party, some of them denounced the Fusion movement altogether and some even went over to Willard. Meanwhile, many old Whigs thought Morton too radical in his antislavery position, and their conservatism made them easy prey for Democratic tactics. Joseph A. Wright hoped to be elected to the US Senate and took to the stump in support of many of his allies running for the state legislature. Wright's widely known views as an antislavery man and temperance advocate appealed to many Indiana Whigs, and this caused them to stay home or split their ballots. At the same time, abolitionists and Free Soilers thought Morton too conservative and many of them believed a vote for such a moderate candidate would be a violation of their moral principles. With the Fusionists divided and the racial prejudice of the majority of Hoosier citizens playing a role, the Democrats proved more successful in splitting the People's Party than their opponents did at dividing the Democracy.[30]

When the results finally came in, Oliver Morton received the report in the Cincinnati office of the *Commercial,* a newspaper edited by his old roommate, Murat Halstead. Hearing the final tally, Morton sank down into a chair, unable to bear the weight of the bad news: Willard had won the election with a majority of six thousand votes. Morton's stand against slavery that had caused him to break with the Democrats and help create the Fusion movement that was becoming the Republican Party now seemed like a mistake. Hoosier voters had rejected him and his new party, as the Democrats won control of the state house of representatives and the People's Party held the state senate only by allying with two Know Nothings. Discouraged, Morton turned to Halstead, and told him that he was finished with politics and was going back to his law practice for good. In the aftermath of the election, reports of fraud trickled in and it appeared that the Democrats had used illegal voting to pad their support across Indiana. Although such corruption probably did not turn the election, it added credence to arguments that Morton gave a good showing, for he had performed better at the polls than expected.

The following month, in November, Democrat James Buchanan carried the state by nearly 20,000 votes over Republican John C. Frémont. The November contest demonstrated both the Democracy's strength and Morton's appeal—he had done better than his party's presidential nominee among Hoosier voters. Amid Democratic rejoicing over their victory as Governor Willard and President James Buchanan took office, Morton recovered from the discouragement wrought by defeat. Perhaps he might try his hand in politics again and seek high office. In the meantime, he returned to the law and to the internal maneuvering of what Hoosiers finally began to call the Republican Party. Defeated in 1856, Morton remained a rising Republican star and continued to work in preparation for his shining political moment to come.[31]

CHAPTER THREE

The Election of 1860

OLIVER MORTON'S POLITICAL MOMENT came in the election of 1860 and its aftermath. By then Morton was beginning to develop the nationalist ideology of freedom, Union, and power wielded by his party. This philosophy would animate the rest of his career as he balanced principles with practical and political considerations in the opportunities available at a given time. In the most important election in American history, he played a critical role in forging the Republican victory in Indiana. His performance in 1856 made him a leading contender for the party's nomination for governor in 1860, but his defeat left the door open for others. Furthermore, the context had changed in the course of four years. While slavery remained important, it seemed to demand a different approach than the one Morton had taken earlier. Economic issues claimed a more significant position in the wake of a depression that left many Northerners in dire circumstances. Above all loomed the specter of disunion and civil war, as Southerners threatened secession if the Republicans came to power.

As the election approached, Hoosier Republicans, more united as a party than they had been in 1856, hoped to take control of the state. Once again, many of them preferred the conservative positions of former Whig Henry S. Lane, arguing that he would reassure voters and attract more crossover ballots. But the former Democrats remained solid in their support of Morton, while the Free Soil and Know Nothing components of the party divided between the two men as well. Morton expected the nomination and enjoyed widespread support, but a strong push for Lane made it look like the party would divide. It seemed possible that the new political organization would splinter in Indiana.[1]

Instead, the Republicans concocted a scheme that placed both men in high office. Lane would be the candidate for governor and Morton would run for lieutenant governor. When the Republicans won the election, their majority in the legislature would appoint Lane, the older of the two men, to the US Senate and Morton would succeed him as governor. Morton hesitated at first, arguing that he should be appointed to the Senate, especially if he deferred to Lane in the campaign. Why should he give up the candidacy for governor and not be given the Senate seat? Certainly, many Republicans thought him a likely candidate to replace Democrat Graham N. Fitch in Washington, and there was talk of him doing so even after the election. Morton faced a quandary. He wanted to be loyal to his party, but doing so would require him to humble himself. Although he was a young man, he had never liked being in a secondary or subservient position. And his rapid rise to prominence made him a legitimate candidate. After all, he had already demonstrated his party loyalty with his able but unsuccessful run in 1856. The logic of unifying the party coalition by pairing a former antislavery Democrat with a former conservative Whig made sense, but did age alone mean that Morton should take the secondary place?[2]

As he considered the deal, an old Quaker acquaintance from Wayne County came to Morton and urged him to agree to the scheme, saying, "Oliver, we can't let thee go to the Senate." When Morton asked why not, the Quaker responded, "Because thee is a good man for either of these places, and Henry Lane would make a good Senator but he would not make a good Governor. So he must go to the Senate and thee must stay and be Governor." The Friend's advice made sense. Lane's temperament might make him a better legislator than an executive, and Morton's personality promised to make him a good governor—although his attention to procedure would also allow him to operate in the Senate, where one had to be polite and patient to succeed. At last Morton decided to sacrifice his ego in the name of party loyalty and agreed to the deal. He would do his part to secure the Republican victory and took the second place on the state ticket. He loyally worked for the cause throughout the campaign, and when the Republicans swept the election, the party implemented their prearranged plan. Lane went to the Senate and Morton became governor of Indiana as the sectional crisis spiraled into disunion and civil war.[3]

A Republican Railroad Lawyer

The Republican scheme in 1860 reflected the shifting context of the four years between the presidential elections. During that time, Morton returned to his law practice in Centerville, where he and his family lived in their large house on the western edge of town. His passion for politics meant that he often neglected both his business and his family, but others stepped in to fill the void. His wife, Lucinda, raised their children and directed the household. She was frugal and a skillful financial manager, so her husband left the family largely to her and was able to pay little attention to his private affairs. They had lost both of their daughters, one dying in infancy in 1849 and the other at the age of two in 1852, but their three sons grew to adulthood, and Lucinda took the lead in seeing to their education. The oldest boy, John Miller Morton, attended Miami University in the late 1860s. Like his father, he did not graduate but studied the law. He moved to California, where he was admitted to the bar in San Francisco. After his father's death, he accepted an appointment as the US consul in Hawaii and later returned to California to serve as a surveyor for the Port of San Francisco. He and his wife, Harriet, or Hattie, as the family called her, often invited the widowed Lucinda to come and stay with them and spend time with her grandchildren.[4]

The second son, Walter Scott Morton, named for the great Romantic novelist, went to Westtown School in Chester, Pennsylvania. A Quaker boarding academy founded in 1799, the school taught useful skills like woodworking and bookkeeping as well as the usual basic academic subjects. In 1874, Walter wrote home to his mother telling her about his upcoming end-of-term exams and saying that he was about to give an oration. For his subject he had chosen "The Tariff," although he did not say whether he agreed with his father on the issue. He also pled his case for Lucinda to grant him permission to stay in Chester for a few extra days to spend time with his friends after the term ended for the Christmas and winter break. Young Walter knew his mother well, as he assured her that the extra expense would be minimal, and the appeal to frugality paid off as Lucinda allowed him to delay his trip to meet the family. His own mind must have run to mathematics, because he became an engineer and as an adult practiced his profession in New York. Lucinda's accounting of every penny had clearly made an impression.[5]

Their third son, Oliver T. Morton, or Ollie, as they called him, was considered his father's favorite. Of the three sons, Ollie looked the most like his father and loved to read books. Morton sent his youngest son money to buy gifts and encouraged him to do well in school. In the years after his father died, Ollie went to Oxford University to study. Like most college students, money concerned him, but he assured his mother that he was living quietly within the means provided him. He mentioned that the English thought America was a "money-getting nation" where the people worshiped mammon rather than God. Because of this attitude, Ollie said he did not like going visiting, although he spoke of an invitation to dinner. He defensively wrote that the English were hypocrites who fawned over a rich man, and a man without money was "absolutely beneath consideration." The young man expressed his homesickness and wondered if he would ever see Indianapolis again. He went on to be a successful writer in later years, but in 1881 he told his mother that he was being careful with his finances and would take precautions to avoid debt.

Clearly, Lucinda's frugality had been passed along to the next generation, at least enough so that they told her what she wanted to hear.[6]

Thanks to his law partner, John Kibbey, Morton's legal practice earned him a good living, and his wife's careful management of their finances gave them security and a comfortable life. As always, he let Kibbey tend to the office work and the writing of legal briefs, preferring to show up at the last minute to argue cases in court. There his renowned skills served well in winning decisions for their clients. After the 1856 election, he devoted more time and energy to his practice, and he managed to take on more of the tasks that he had too often left to his partner. Morton now earned substantial fees, especially from railroad cases. His wealth and growing reputation added to his social status. He continued working as a grand master of the Order of Odd Fellows, and he renewed his charity activities with the same zeal and sense of purpose that he gave—temporarily, at least—to his legal business.[7]

But his prominence in the still-forming Republican Party meant that he found plenty of opportunities to continue his political activities. Morton's legal training made him an astute manipulator of procedures, and on his advice the Republicans in the state senate were able to oust a Democrat who still held his seat after being appointed by Governor Wright to serve as a "moral instructor of the penitentiary." The Republicans, in coalition with Know Nothings, held a majority of one in the senate, but they could not remove the violator, who held two offices, because the Democrats could simply bolt the session and deny them a quorum. This tactic allowed the minority to check the power of the majority and was a vital tool provided by the state constitution. Morton studied the situation and suggested to Berry Sulgrove, the editor of the *Indianapolis Journal*, that he advise the Republican chairman of the committee on election, John R. Cravens, that there was a way to remove the double-dipping Democrat. The Democratic minority in the senate often went out into the hallway to convene and caucus among themselves. Morton argued that this was a perfect opportunity for the Republicans to strike because the body was still in session and the majority could quickly pass a motion declaring the violator's senate seat vacant and force him out before the Democrats in the hall knew what was happening. The newspaper editor passed along Morton's idea to Cravens, and the Republican majority carried it out, leaving the out-maneuvered Democrats enraged.[8]

Meanwhile, Morton continued to battle with his Centerville nemesis, George Julian. In the spring of 1858 the Republican state convention elected Morton as the presiding officer, much to the former Free Soiler's chagrin. Julian despised Morton personally, thought him too conservative politically, and still resented that his rival had worked to defeat him for reelection to Congress in

1851. Convinced that Morton was an opportunist who would do whatever was necessary to win, Julian also thought that the former Democrat was too prone to compromise. The abolitionist refused to yield ground, holding to his radical position on liberty and scornfully dismissing anyone who dared to compromise his principles in the name of winning elections. Julian rejected the very idea of compromise with the Know Nothings, bitterly denouncing the nativists, and openly saying that he did not want them in the Republican Party.

And former antislavery Democrats like Morton drew his ire, as Julian thought their moderate stand against the expansion of slavery was one of expedience rather than moral opposition. Even though he opposed Morton's nomination in 1856, Julian did work for his fellow Republican's campaign against Willard. Later, he declared that he was glad that Morton had lost because his campaign was "a combination of weaknesses, instead of a union of forces." He worried that, "had the slippery tactics of our leaders" achieved victory, the cost of winning "would have been far more disastrous in its influence" than was the toll of defeat. He thought the loss in 1856 was a "timely reproof for our unfaithfulness." Instead of fighting a war against slavery, the People's Party had compromised, and the Centerville abolitionist declared that "Fusionism has debauched and defeated us." Now, in March of 1858, Julian and his fellow radicals came to the state convention hoping to change the party platform and make it more abolitionist.[9]

In his role as presiding officer of the convention, Morton faced off against his old political enemy. But his fight with Julian was more than personal, as he thought it foolish to take too strident a view on any issue that might drive away potential supporters. Compromise was expedient and would fuse the new party in a strong alliance even as no one got all that he wanted. He knew that the Republicans could not please everyone and argued that "it is idle to expect that what we do will be what everybody wants. Such a convention was never held. There are diversities of opinion as to the platform and as to the candidates," but Morton hoped that all members could set aside their differences, accept whatever was passed, and support the party.

Compromise had a long tradition in American politics and had marked the Whig Party, especially. Throughout its several decades as the opposition to the Jacksonians, the Whigs had made compromise a principle of statesmanship. The ideology of republicanism that many adhered to in the early nineteenth century held that the American republic aimed at preserving as much individual liberty as possible while still maintaining social order under the law. This idea system called for vigilance against internal threats to liberty and to the republic as well as dangers from outside foreign enemies. The ideology included republican manhood and virtue, in which the true statesman would

Fig. 5. Morton's longtime nemesis, Congressman George W. Julian, Republican, Indiana, after the Civil War. (Library of Congress)

set aside his own interests for the good of the republic. Meanwhile, other Americans held to the ideology of liberalism, which also promoted liberty and hailed the American democratic republic as the bastion of freedom. But liberalism usually emphasized the virtues of individualism and the power of free markets rather than extolling the virtues of sacrificing self-interest for the greater good and praising the principle of compromise. To be sure, many Democrats as well as Whigs accepted the tenets of republicanism and saw themselves as defenders of liberty and the republic when they compromised. But as the decade of the 1850s wore on, compromise seemed less attractive, as political issues came to involve deeply held moral principles. For Julian and others fighting a crusade against slavery, for example, compromise reeked of weakness and selling out one's morality in the name of practical expediency.[10]

Many Republican leaders tried to move to the political center on slavery in the wake of their defeat in 1856. They disagreed with Julian's view that they had been too soft on the issue and, instead, some argued that the party had been too strongly antislavery and should now take a more conservative path forward. Morton agreed generally with this position but still railed against the Slave Power in his opening remarks to the 1858 state convention, noting that President James Buchanan had declared that Kansas was a slave state. Morton argued that, if that were true, then other new territories like Nebraska were also slave. By implication, there could be no free territory in the United States. As the meeting began, Julian quickly called for Hoosier Republicans to reaffirm the 1856 platform upon which Frémont had run for the presidency. That platform denied that Congress or territorial legislatures had the power to legalize slavery in new territories and, instead, said that it was the duty of Congress to prohibit slavery, which it had the authority to do. Morton ruled that Julian's motion was out of order because he had not referred it first to the platform committee. Julian appealed, but Morton's allies moved to table his motion.

The parliamentary wrangling led the abolitionist to deliver a long diatribe in which he said that Morton meant to "gag all opposition" to the more conservative platform that the leadership supported and that Julian called "a milk and water affair." The abolitionist was convinced that party managers rather than the rank and file were scheming to dilute the new organization's opposition to slavery. Angered by his old rival, Morton called one of the convention's vice presidents to take the chair, and he took the floor to do battle with Julian. He argued that the new 1858 platform was essentially the same as the 1856 Philadelphia document that Julian so adamantly wanted to be reaffirmed. Platforms were not sacred writ but rather needed to be updated to fit the changing times and adopted to the particular place in which the party wanted to win elections.

Morton insisted that the 1858 platform agreed with the 1856 one in substance and that that should be enough. He then dismissed Julian with a homespun tale that made his enemy the butt of a joke: "These men who insist on having a platform express to the very letter all that they believe" reminded Morton of "the clergyman who had to have a prayer exactly fitted to the case or he could not pray at all. He was sent for by a family of a man who had been bitten by a rattlesnake and was dying. He examined his prayer-book, but finding no form appropriate to this calamity," the preacher refused to pray and the snake-bit man had to die without the aid of his minister. Morton said that the 1856 platform was designed for that time and place and that the Indiana party should adopt a document that suited them as well. His speech won the debate, Julian's appeal was tabled, and the new platform was adopted.[11]

Despite his opposition to the extension of slavery, Morton still believed in the territorial expansion of the United States. His Jacksonian support for adding land to the growing American empire continued when he became a Republican. Once it became clear that Kansas would finally be admitted as a free state, he began to think about adding more territory to the Union. On one occasion, he discussed his expansionist ideas with John Kibbey while the two men stood in front of a large map that he had hung on the wall of their law office in Centerville. Morton studied northern Mexico and recited the names of the various provinces that bordered the United States. Sure that the issue of slavery in the territories could eventually be resolved peacefully, he wondered what differences would divide the Republicans from the Democrats when that was accomplished. He thought the party "must have a living issue. The Democratic Party has always been the champion of the extension of territory and I think the Republicans ought to be ahead of them in advocating the acquisition of Mexico." His passion for territorial expansion led him to begin working on a speech on the subject to be delivered at some future opportune moment.[12]

The sectional crisis was not resolved peacefully, however, and Morton did not get to give his speech on adding more of Mexico to the United States. Although he would later revive his interest in the West and would travel there on numerous occasions, he had to set aside his imperial dreams of an expanding frontier for the moment. Instead, he worried about the deepening rift between the North and the South. Kansas continued to divide the nation, as the Buchanan administration backed the Lecompton constitution that allowed slavery while the president's opponents cried foul, arguing that Kansas citizens really hoped to make it a free state. Popular sovereignty had failed to solve the territorial expansion of slavery and only made things worse. Then, the Supreme Court issued its ruling in the Dred Scott case, which held that the US Constitution protected the property rights of slaveholders. Chief Justice

Roger Taney also added that blacks were considered inferior and had no rights that the white man was bound to respect.

Southerners rejoiced in their victory while Stephen Douglas realized that his plan to save his party and deliver him the presidency had failed. And it did not resolve the sectional issue. Southerners had loved popular sovereignty in 1854, when it opened the door to new slave states. But now, after Dred Scott, they did not think that slavery could be prohibited. If Douglas held to his position on popular sovereignty, he would lose the South. Meanwhile, Northerners like Morton were appalled and saw the court ruling as further evidence of the Slave Power's control of the country. They feared that, by implication, slavery could be expanded into already-free states. Some abolitionists began to discuss the possibility of secession, with at least some Northern states leaving the Union to form a free republic. Most Northerners still held out hope, arguing that if the Republicans could win enough elections, they could stop the Slave Power and overthrow the dominance of the South.[13]

Indiana Democrats Divide

As it had throughout the 1850s, the sectional divide in Indiana expressed itself in the continuing battle within the Democratic Party between the factions led by Senator Jesse Bright and former governor Joseph A. Wright. Elected to three consecutive terms in the Senate, Bright now exercised a strong grip on the state party. Indeed, many of the divisions in Indiana politics grew out of his service on committees that enabled him to build a political machine based on the control of patronage and important funding for infrastructure projects in the state. A native New Yorker who owned land and slaves in Kentucky, Bright had demonstrated his influence in purging the state party of the anti-Nebraska men in 1854 and in successfully securing the presidency for Buchanan in 1856. His old feud with Stephen Douglas continued, and he reveled in knowing that he had denied the Little Giant the White House by backing Buchanan. He counted many important Indiana leaders among his friends, including Congressman William H. English and Governor Willard. With a loyal cadre to back his play, Bright looked forward to frustrating Douglas and promoting his own ambitions. But his proslavery views and doughface reputation added to the resentment fostered by his ironfisted politics.

The charismatic and dynamic Joseph Wright led the opposition to the senator and joined with Douglas against him. The same old issues still dominated the ongoing struggle: opposing views on slavery combined with personal differences while matters like temperance and moral reform sometimes flared up as well. Wright was a native of Pennsylvania and a Quaker who left the Society

Fig. 6. Senator Jesse D. Bright, Democrat, Indiana. (Library of Congress)

of Friends to join the Methodists. While the two groups shared many theological beliefs, the Methodists were more widely accepted and had become part of the new evangelical establishment. Even as his devout faith continued to spur his bent to reform in his new, mainstream church, Wright had served two terms as governor of Indiana.

A gifted speaker whose independent positions made him a moderate in his party, Wright held to Jacksonian economic positions. Thus, he worked to pay off the state debt, fought against the creation of a state bank, and because he opposed government spending on infrastructure, promoted private investment in the internal improvements needed in Indiana. He pushed for a more equitable tax system, reformed the penal system, and championed the 1851 state constitution. A staunch supporter of the farmers who made up his base constituency and a majority of Indiana citizens, Wright encouraged the development of agricultural science in the state. This included his own studies and publications on various crops and his creation of the State Board of Agriculture, as well as the introduction of county fairs to help farmers learn more about their business. The popular former governor shared the antislavery views of the majority of Hoosiers and proved a formidable foe to Bright within the ranks of the Democratic Party. The two leaders of the sectional factions in the Indiana Democracy were powerful men who stood ready to destroy the other whenever the opportunity presented itself.[14]

The sectional divide in the Indiana party became all the more apparent during Governor Willard's term. Shortly after his electoral victory over Morton in 1856, Willard traveled to Jackson, Mississippi, where he met with that state's legislature and governor. He accepted the invitation to address the legislature and made a proslavery speech, complete with a vow to uphold the Fugitive Slave Act in Indiana and return all runaways to their masters. At a reception at the governor's mansion, Willard proceeded to go back on his campaign pledge to abstinence and entered into a drinking contest with Mississippi's attorney general. The Southerners watched in awe as their representative, a notorious alcoholic, proved unable to match the Hoosier combatant, who drank him

Fig. 7. Governor Joseph A. Wright, Democrat, Indiana. (W. H. Bass Photo Company Collection, Indiana Historical Society)

under the table while still appearing "as cool and clear-headed and as steady on his pins at the close of the banquet as he was at the commencement." The news of Willard's actions in the South spread rapidly across Indiana and contrasted sharply with Wright's moderation as an antislavery and temperance man. In late 1857, Willard supported the Buchanan administration and the proslavery Lecompton constitution in Kansas, although most Indiana Democrats denounced the measure as a fraud and violation of the true spirit of popular sovereignty.[15]

The Bright/Wright factions renewed their battle earlier in 1857 when the legislature elected the state's two US senators. Bright expected to win his third straight term, but the other seat was vacant because the Democrats had managed to prevent the People's Party from appointing one of their own when Lieutenant Governor Willard cast the deciding vote against them and stopped the legislature from electing a senator in a joint session. This allowed the Democrats, who controlled the state senate, to keep the seat vacant. Now, in 1857, Wright hoped to win the vacant seat, but Bright would have none of it and pushed for one of his cronies, Graham N. Fitch. A temporary peace within the Indiana Democracy was made when Bright promised Wright that he would help him get a cabinet post in the Buchanan administration if the former governor would not pursue the Senate. Wright agreed, and Bright had his way, as usual.

Meanwhile, the People's Party members of the legislature turned the tables on the Democrats, and joining with their Know Nothing allies, voted against holding the election in a joint session. But the Democrats went ahead and elected Bright to a third six-year term and Fitch to a four-year term to fill the vacancy. They argued that because there had been a joint session for other matters, they could elect the senators at the same time. The People's Party/ Republicans protested, but Governor Willard, ever loyal to his party and to Bright, commissioned the two men and forwarded the decision to Washington. There the Republicans fought the election and managed to delay Bright's and Fitch's being seated for a year, aided by Stephen Douglas who opposed his old enemy Bright. Eventually, however, the two Democrats officially entered the US Senate. Then Jesse Bright failed to honor his agreement with Wright. Instead of helping him win a spot in the cabinet, he recommended his rival for a foreign diplomatic position. President Buchanan offered and Wright accepted the post of envoy extraordinary and minister plenipotentiary to Prussia. Whatever wounds the broken promise left on Wright would be nursed in Europe. In a shrewd move, Bright had sent his antagonist out of the country, where he was unlikely to lead a rebellion against the senator. Even so, the deep divisions within the Democracy still threatened to destroy it.[16]

The Indiana election in 1858 foreshadowed what was to come two years later. The Democrats teetered on the verge of collapse as they fought over Lecompton and Kansas and their internal factions. And economics returned as an important issue in the wake of the Panic of 1857 and the resulting depression. The Republicans expected to enjoy the typical off-year-election rebound by opposition parties and also gain strength as Lecompton and the economic crisis hurt the Democrats. Refusing to yield to the will of the majority of Hoosiers, Jesse Bright set out to punish all who opposed him. At the January 8, 1858, state convention, he ignored the fact that most of his own party were anti-Lecompton and pro-Douglas. He and his allies tried to defeat all resolutions supporting Douglas, which led to the pro-Douglas faction calling a meeting of their own in February to support their favorite for the presidency in 1860 and insisting that the people of Kansas had a right to vote on their constitution instead of accepting Lecompton. Even with its charismatic leader serving in Prussia, it seemed that the Wright/Douglas faction was about to go into open rebellion against Bright and his cronies. At best, these intraparty battles dampened enthusiasm for Democratic candidates. At worst, they threatened to rip apart the majority party. Bright's post-1856 confidence made him ignore the warning signs and, instead of moderating his actions to assuage feelings and reassure the rank and file, he doubled down on his efforts to purge the party of his opponents and to defeat Douglas.[17] Although the senator suffered a defeat in 1858, he looked forward to crushing his enemies within his party at the next opportunity.

THE PANIC OF 1857

Perhaps the Democrats had grown comfortable with their factional feuding and sectional disagreements. After all, they had survived for several election cycles despite the ongoing turmoil. But the economic crisis following the Panic of 1857 raised the political stakes. Brought on by the failure of the Ohio Life Insurance and Trust Company, the largest Ohio bank, the causes of the panic, like those of other depressions, were actually varied and complex. Many states had adopted so-called "free banking" systems in the wake of Andrew Jackson's "Bank War" and the decentralization of banking that followed. Far from being actual free banking, these new laws established a system of regulation by state governments. The new regulatory system allowed for suspension of specie payments whenever the banks overextended themselves. While this system did allow for the creation of more banks, the "free banking" laws tied the expansion of banknotes and deposits to the amount of state government securities that a bank bought. This set up a pyramid scheme in which banks could overexpand through the purchase of government bonds.

The Ohio bank collapsed when it was discovered that the manager of the New York branch had embezzled large amounts of money. Bank failures had occurred throughout the decade, so this was nothing new; the country had weathered banks going under before. And this crisis, too, might have been limited, but it spread as the failure coincided with other problems. The withdrawal of British investments from US banks combined with the collapse of grain prices following the Crimean War. Peace brought the resumption of European trade, and a bumper crop in the United States meant still lower prices. With Europeans no longer buying Western commodities and prices dropping, the crisis spread to farmers.

Further stress came when the bank failure led to a dramatic drop in railroad stock prices. Speculators began losing money and more banks began to fail. Plans for railroad construction came to a halt, further damaging the farmers, as routes that promised easy access to markets were now uncertain. The loss of a critical gold shipment due to the sinking of the SS *Central America* in a hurricane only added to the difficulty. The Panic of 1857 and the crisis that followed caused the most damage in the North, as Southern states largely escaped the depression, thanks to the strength of the cotton economy. This gave slaveholders confidence that their institutions, including slavery, were better than the free labor system practiced by Northerners. The economic crisis bolstered a Southern sense of superiority. No wonder, then, that James Henry Hammond rose to his feet in the Senate in 1858 and declared, "Cotton is king."[18]

Across the North, the depression wreaked havoc on the economy and society. Leaders in some states, especially New England, declared bank holidays, hoping to prevent more failures. Their efforts fell short, and President Buchanan and his secretary of the treasury, Howell Cobb, pursued a retrenchment policy to head off the crisis created by less revenue and larger government debt. But they did not cut expenditures enough, as revenues proved even smaller than predicted. By May of 1858 the administration was warning Congress of "impending fiscal disaster." Cobb urged more spending cuts to balance the budget and requested that the government borrow $15 million at 6 percent interest, with the bonds to be paid in ten years. This desperate move broke with the traditions of Jacksonian fiscal policy and set off a political storm over economic issues. Some called for using the tariff to ease the crisis, while others insisted that laissez-faire policies must be maintained to ensure a shorter depression. The Republicans generally favored a protectionist tariff, while most Democrats were free traders and some of them supported a free-market approach across the board. Eventually the government authorized $20 million in loans, but Cobb borrowed only half of that amount. The Democrats used the crisis as an opportunity to attack protectionism and passed the Tariff of 1857, which lowered rates to about 20 percent.[19]

Even as the depression deepened, other events attracted attention. Out in the West, the Mormon War, or Utah War, of 1857–1858 caused a stir when the Buchanan administration sent troops into Utah to confront Brigham Young and the Church of Jesus Christ of Latter-Day Saints. Rooted in violent confrontations with non-Mormons traveling through Utah and long-standing resentment against the Mormons and their plans for theocracy and polygamy, the conflict set the context for the Mountain Meadows Massacre in September 1857 that brought the slaughter of travelers in a wagon train. When the US Army expedition reached Salt Lake City, the Mormons blocked their way, but the situation was then peacefully resolved through negotiation. Although politicians tried to make the events fit their own agendas, especially in regard to the tensions between North and South, the LDS Church strongly opposed slavery but supported state's rights, thus defying a neat sectional affinity. Still, the Utah War raised the specter of armed rebellion springing from religious and cultural differences in a fight over local rights versus national authority, all in a western territory.[20]

Religion also related more directly to the economic depression when a revival swept across the North. Although some historians labeled the Revival of 1857–1858 the "Businessman's Revival," the spiritual awakening (like others before and after it) had many roots and complex causes. The evangelical movement began in New York City in the fall of 1857 and spread from there—a different pattern from earlier revivals that started in the countryside and small towns then moved to urban areas. Another difference that marked this revival was that its leaders were not prominent revivalist preachers. Rather, it sprang from prayer meetings led by lay people. Many evangelicals saw the financial panic and depression as a sign of God's judgment upon the nation for its wicked ways. Political corruption, intemperance, and a myriad of other sins joined the long list that always included greed. American avarice caused evangelicals to repeat the oft-quoted scripture passage from 1 Timothy 6:10, "The love of money is the root of all evil." In the North slavery made the list of sins, while Southern Christians added Northern fanaticism to their roster of misdeeds. The sectional rift in the evangelical churches, which had occurred in the 1840s and created separate Southern Baptist and Southern Methodist denominations, continued to deepen. As the depression intensified, many of those who found themselves facing bankruptcy, going out of business, or being unemployed flocked to the religious services held by the evangelical churches. The revival lasted throughout 1858 and followed the typical pattern of revivalism in feeding a new round of growth for the evangelical churches. The Methodists, especially, enjoyed increased numbers in the 1858 revival, particularly in the North, where the Wesleyan doctrine of holiness appealed to those seeking to experience a life free from sin. Such theological beliefs fed impulses for reform that already animated evangelicals hoping to lead converts to Christ and clean up the corruption caused by sin.[21]

The revival came to Indiana as well. In the spring of 1858 Calvin Fletcher, a prominent Indianapolis lawyer and banker and a devout Methodist, reported his attendance at a series of prayer meetings and revival services associated with the broader awakening. He noted that the meetings were conducted with good order and remarked on how the financial crisis provided time for people to attend to their religious state. Fletcher also praised the interdenominational nature of the revival, while an Indianapolis newspaper reported that "the religious revival is gaining strength and interest daily in this city. With very few exceptions, all the churches in the city hold meetings twice a day, and a people's or businessman's meeting, at the hour of noon, is largely attended, with good results." The depression made this possible, and for many Hoosiers "church going is the greatest business of the day, nothing being allowed to interfere with it."[22]

In Indiana, as elsewhere, the Revival of 1857–1858 provided a renewed impulse for social reform. This reinvigorated the temperance movement and antislavery and brought calls for cleaning up the political corruption that marked the Buchanan administration. There were rumors of bribery of congressmen for their votes and strong-armed tactics used in the name of party discipline to get support for the Lecompton constitution. Meanwhile, in Indiana, an ongoing investigation of the state's swamplands program indicated that local and state officials were deeply involved in corruption, as shady real estate deals, embezzlement, and unfulfilled government contracts resulted from the federal government's cession of more than a million acres to state control. While some of the corruption cut across party lines, the most egregious acts were carried out by Democrats supported by Governor Willard. With his proslavery views, intemperate behavior, and corrupt administration, Willard was fast becoming a potent political symbol for the Republicans to use against the Democrats.

While many of the details about corruption were not revealed until later, the scandals that were beginning to break in 1858 were part of the context for the elections that fall. The Republicans narrowly won both houses of the state legislature and took seven of the state's eleven congressional seats. An anti-Lecompton Democrat also won election to Congress and the establishment Democrats won only three seats in the House of Representatives. Although they held on to the statewide offices that were up for election that year, Democratic fortunes in 1858 clearly reversed their victory two years earlier and the stage was nearly set for the 1860 contest that would elect Republicans.[23]

The economic crisis continued well into 1859, and the Republicans tried to push through remedies that appealed especially to voters in the swing states of the North. In Pennsylvania, this meant that Republicans would push for a high tariff. In doing so they hoped, especially, to attract workers and capitalists in the iron industry who demanded higher tariff rates to protect them from foreign competition. Beyond the Keystone State, the Republicans hoped to gain support by advocating for a homestead bill. Favored by some Democrats as well, this legislation granted free land to actual settlers (instead of selling government lands in western territories to speculators), a move that appealed to farmers ruined by the depression and hoping for a fresh start as well as being attractive to out-of-work laborers in urban areas. When Republicans pushed for the protectionist Morrill Tariff and a homestead bill in 1859–1860, the Democrats in Congress postponed the former, while President Buchanan killed the latter with a veto.[24]

While the economic crisis raised new issues, Kansas would not go away. The Republican-controlled Indiana legislature passed a resolution in favor of admitting Kansas under a constitution that agreed with the US Constitution and "without regard to what shall be the opinion of her people on the subject of slavery." Although the language seemed to take a strong antislavery position, because Northerners believed that a majority of Kansans wanted a free state, the resolution amounted to support for popular sovereignty, much to the frustrated rage of George Julian, who denounced the motion as another example of selling out moral principles in the name of expediency. The more conservative approach marked the ways in which many Hoosier Republicans now understood the issue. Watching the events unfold in Kansas convinced them that popular sovereignty could be an effective block to the expansion of slavery, and they now moved to support it as a sound Republican doctrine despite its origins with Douglas. That the move might also appeal to Democrats tired of Jesse Bright and Governor Willard made it all the more appealing in the minds of Hoosier Republicans.[25]

Willard again raised controversy in 1859, but this time in an ironic way. While he was a proslavery man, his brother-in-law, John E. Cook, was an abolitionist who joined John Brown in his raid on Harper's Ferry in October. Captured along with Brown, Willard's brother-in-law faced trial and a death sentence. Cook's actions dishonored and embarrassed his family, but Governor Willard quickly turned to Indiana's Democratic attorney general, the well-known criminal lawyer Daniel W. Voorhees, for help. At the Virginia trial Willard testified on behalf of his brother-in-law and Voorhees offered a vigorous defense, but Cook was convicted and sentenced to death. Willard asked for a pardon from the governor of Virginia, but his plea was denied and Cook was hanged that December.

Ironically, the proslavery governor's actions on behalf of his abolitionist relative bolstered his standing back home in Indiana. Hoosiers admired him for trying to save a family member even as he denounced John Brown's raid. Many Indiana voters feared the Slave Power and opposed the expansion of slavery, but they also feared abolitionist radicalism and thought John Brown's violent acts were extreme and criminal. The 1851 state constitution limited the governor to one four-year term so Willard could not seek reelection, but the Republicans had hoped to make him the face of his party and run against him in the 1860 campaign. The governor leaving office, as well as the Cook trial, weakened the Republicans' ability to use Willard as a negative political symbol.[26]

THE 1860 CAMPAIGN

Indiana's Democrats finally divided completely in 1860. After years of struggling to do so, those who opposed Jesse Bright finally took control of the party away from him. This might have occurred in 1858 had Joseph Wright been present to lead the charge, but his absence in Europe hurt the cause even though the anti-Bright forces managed to thwart the senator's efforts to maintain control and defeat his enemies. Now, in 1860, even with their charismatic leader still serving as a diplomat, the pro-Douglas men moved quickly to win support for the Little Giant for the presidency at the state party convention. As always, Bright fought back hard. He arrived in Indianapolis by train from Washington accompanied by Finley Bigger, a US Treasury employee. His companion was fitting for the occasion, as Bright passed around a lot of cash as well as patronage in trying to stop Douglas and maintain his own control of the party. This time, however, the momentum for Douglas was too great, and the Hoosier senator soon lost the fight, as even many of his stalwart cronies crossed over to support the Little Giant for president.

The party also nominated Wright/Douglas faction men to lead the state ticket, with Thomas A. Hendricks for governor and David Turpie for lieutenant governor. Seeing that the pro-Douglas men had the majority and that he could not defeat them through the regular channels, Bright began meeting with his most loyal supporters and planning to retaliate. Eager to head him off, the pro-Douglas faction tried to make concessions to Bright. They endorsed the 1856 Democratic platform, complete with its support for popular sovereignty, and they also adopted a state platform that accepted the Dred Scott decision. They declared as well their respect for President Buchanan and offered to support him in defending Democratic principles. But such measures were not enough for Bright. He always held a grudge, always sought revenge, and he would make his opponents pay for their rebellion. He soon set off for the national convention at Charleston, ready to do whatever he could to defeat Douglas at the next level.[27]

The Charleston convention split, as the Democrats divided nationally. Bright was on hand, seeking his revenge while wearing a yellow vest that befit his reputation for sartorial splendor. No doubt he played a role, inasmuch as he helped the Southerners choose to break up the party rather than support Douglas. The Little Giant was clearly the favorite, but he failed to win the nomination, and Southern delegates walked out of the convention. The party moved to Baltimore, where its Northern members nominated Douglas for president and Governor Herschel Johnson of Georgia for vice president on a platform supporting popular sovereignty. The Southern Democrats who had bolted in Charleston met on their own in Baltimore and nominated Vice President John C. Breckinridge as their presidential nominee and Senator Joseph Lane of Oregon as his running mate.

Most Indiana Democrats rallied to Douglas, but Senators Bright and Fitch joined Governor Willard and others to work for Breckinridge in the Hoosier state. The threat of division that had loomed so long finally became a reality and the Democrats fell apart, separating along the factional lines that had marked their sectional and personal differences throughout the past decade. Some Indiana Jacksonians blamed the Southerners for the split and quietly hoped for a Republican victory as a means of bringing them to their senses. Others feared for the Union, believing that the election of a Republican president and congressional majority would lead to war between the sections. Bright yearned to defeat Douglas at all costs and to retake control of the Indiana party, but he also sincerely supported Breckinridge and Lane, with whom he agreed on the issues, especially slavery. The Hoosier doughface continued to combine his personal grudges with a decidedly pro-Southern, proslavery ideology. The Breckinridge candidacy brought together Bright's views on the issues with his thirst for revenge and gave him a valid reason to oppose Douglas. That Joe Lane had lived in Indiana before moving to Oregon made it seem likely that he might attract some Hoosier voters. The chances of Breckinridge carrying Indiana remained slim, but Bright's influence and the cultural affinity with the South that existed in much of the state, especially the southern half, made it seem possible that the Kentuckian could win. The Douglas men saw better prospects for their candidate, as the Little Giant enjoyed widespread popularity and his stand on the issues lined up well with the majority of Hoosiers. But the fact that the Democracy had split opened the door for the Republicans to win the state and national elections that fall.[28]

In Indiana the Republicans seemed well situated to carry the state. They had been gaining strength as the Democrats faltered and had taken the state legislature and a majority of the congressional seats in 1858. As long as the party's presidential candidate was not someone believed to be too extreme, they were confident of victory. Another consideration was their nominee for governor. The Republican coalition brought together factions that could easily separate rather than unite behind the party's candidates. While it seemed that some of their constituents had no real alternative, no matter who carried the party's banner, if the candidates proved too divisive those voters would just stay home. The Free Soil wing of the party seemed secure, despite their complaints about the organization selling out on slavery. The truly radical abolitionists would vote for third-party candidates or not vote at all. George Julian and his allies liked to complain, but they would rather vote for a conservative Republican than see the Democrats win. In 1860, Julian tempered his public criticism of compromise and let his party claim the mantle of conservatism. So many Know Nothings had joined the Republicans that they effectively destroyed the American Party. This left the nativists no real place to go besides the Republican Party. Late in the campaign, Know Nothing Richard W. Thompson organized the Constitutional Union Party convention that offered another choice to the nativists, but it was not effective in breaking up the Republican coalition.

That left the former Whigs and former Democrats to be considered. Both preferred one of their own and both had a strong candidate to support for governor of Indiana. With a fight looming between those who wanted Morton and those who liked Henry Lane, it seemed possible that the coalition would splinter. Instead, the Republicans concocted the scheme that ran the two men together with Lane for governor and Morton for lieutenant governor and the agreement that Lane would be elected to the US Senate and Morton would replace him upon his resignation. Lane leading the ticket sent a strong signal that the Republicans would continue to take a more conservative approach on the slavery issue, a move that promised to attract ever more voters in Indiana. With the old Whig combined with the former Democrat, the Republicans presented a mainstream ticket that was designed to reassure voters afraid of radical abolitionists like Julian. When the national convention nominated Abraham Lincoln instead of a more strident antislavery candidate, the stage was set for the election. With their deal in hand and candidates moderate enough for them to claim the conservative position on slavery, Indiana's Republicans began the 1860 campaign with high hopes.[29]

The election in the Hoosier State attracted a lot of attention in 1860. Indiana, along with some other states like Pennsylvania, still held separate October elections for state and congressional offices, while voters cast ballots for the presidency in November. The October elections served as a bellwether for the presidential campaign and were thus closely watched. Moreover, the state had been highly contested in recent elections, with the People's Party winning in 1854, the Democrats returning to the majority and Buchanan carrying the state in 1856, and the Republicans dominating in 1858. The margins of victory had been narrow, meaning that Hoosiers might easily go in a different direction

Fig. 8. Senator Henry S. Lane, Republican, Indiana. (Library of Congress)

the next election. Buchanan had barely gotten 50 percent of the ballots, but the divided opposition—with Know Nothing Millard Fillmore taking some votes from John C. Frémont—made his victory of less than two thousand votes seem more dominant that it really was.

The 1860 presidential election featured four major candidates: Lincoln the Republican, Douglas the Northern Democrat, Breckinridge the Southern Democrat, and John Bell the Constitutional Union candidate. Bell, a former Whig from Tennessee, and his Massachusetts running mate, Edward Everett, held to the old Whig doctrine of compromise. The Constitutional Unionists were popular in the border states of the upper South where fear of a war fought in one's own area made preserving the Constitution and the Union an attractive proposition. For the most part, the presidential race became two elections, with Breckinridge and Bell competing in the South, while Lincoln and Douglas faced off in the North. There were certain exceptions and some attempts at implementing plans for fusion that would give support to the candidate most likely to deny Lincoln the electoral votes he needed.

When Richard Thompson organized the state Constitutional Union Party for Bell, Indiana was one of the few states where all four candidates actually had campaigns. Lincoln and Douglas attracted the most support, but Bright's efforts on behalf of Breckinridge resulted in a concentration of votes in the southern counties of the state while Thompson's late push for Bell meant limited results. Still, that all of the major candidates had active campaigns in the state made it all the more important to watch Indiana. Finally, the state could prove to be the key to a Republican victory. As observers worked out the numbers, if Lincoln could carry Pennsylvania and Indiana, just two out of the five Northern states that Frémont had lost in 1856, he would win the election. Such high stakes made the Indiana election more important than ever.[30]

Oliver Morton took the deal to run for lieutenant governor out of party loyalty, and he dutifully set out on the campaign trail. On March 10, 1860, the Republican candidate for lieutenant governor delivered a speech at Terre Haute that demonstrated his more conservative approach to the election this time around. To be sure, he began with a lengthy discussion of Douglas's idea of popular sovereignty and an insistence that the Democrats were the true sectional party. He made his party's position seem more conservative by arguing that the Republicans were the party that hoped to preserve the Union. They were the ones trying to save the American republic from the radicals in both North and South. He denounced the Dred Scott decision and gave grudging support to the enforcement of the Fugitive Slave Act that he thought deserved to be amended and improved. Morton denied that he was an abolitionist but argued that "I am opposed to the diffusion of slavery. I am in favor of preserving the Territories to freedom, of encouraging, elevating, and protecting free labor," but "with slavery in the several States we have nothing to do, and no right to interfere." He nodded at the Slave Power conspiracy by noting that Northern Democrats now served the interests of the South: "Power has passed from the democratic party in nearly all the Northern States. Its vitality and force are concentrated in the South."[31]

Having spent most of his speech on the issues surrounding slavery and its extension and the nature of the two parties, Morton came at last to the economy. Here he employed Republican strategies created in the wake of the Panic of 1857, as they used economic issues to rally support in certain areas and generally paint their opponents as the enemy of free labor. Democrats responded by arguing that economic woes would follow a Republican victory because that would mean the end of the Union. Douglas and his supporters tried to outmaneuver the Republicans by deflecting criticism on economic issues. They blamed Buchanan and Southern Democrats for the party's failure to pass legislation favored by some Northern voters. In Pennsylvania Douglas the free trader set aside his principles and argued that "a proper tariff" was in order.

When Election Day came, the Republican strategy worked in Pennsylvania, as coal and iron districts abandoned the Democrats. While the tariff was not as important in Indiana, Morton still addressed it when he turned to "Protection to American Industry," arguing that "in collecting the revenues of the nation, the duties upon imports should be so adjusted that adequate protection be afforded to American industry." He tried to preempt Democratic charges of favoritism, cronyism, and the creation of monopolies by saying that "it is not the duty of the government to build up and maintain monopolies at the expense of the body of the nation." Still, he argued, Congress had the constitutional authority to set tariffs for the "just encouragement and protection to the agricultural and manufacturing interests of our country." Although coming at the end of the speech, the tariff still played a part in Morton's appeal to the voters.[32]

He next turned to "the Homestead," another Republican remedy to economic ills that attracted support from across the political spectrum in Indiana. Morton reminded his audience that many political leaders had long argued that federal land should be given to settlers who would build new communities and carve new states out of the territories. The Republican recalled that the previous policy of selling government lands had resulted in widespread speculation, as real estate speculators bought up the land in hopes of making their fortune. This hurt those who really wanted to settle on the new land, as they had to buy it from the speculators at higher prices, "while the poor man has been debarred from a home and from a field for his industry." Morton extolled the virtues of "the hardy pioneers" and argued that the settlers themselves were the ones who built the nation, added new states, and brought wealth and power to the United States. In fact, he thought that the settlers "are public benefactors" and argued that "their homes should be given to them by the nation, upon conditions that they improve them, and thus add to the aggregate of our national prosperity." Finally, anticipating Democratic arguments that the Republicans favored the rich at the expense of the poor, Morton closed his Terre Haute speech by addressing worries about economic inequality: "It is not important that we have very rich men in this country, but it is important that all have homes and competence, and be made to feel that their country is a nursing mother, whose devotion to their interest, and protection of their rights can only be requited by a life of patriotism." Thus, the Republican ideology of free labor combined with economic policy in a call for a Homestead Act.[33]

Therefore, economic issues played a part in the election. Morton and the Republicans interpreted the issues in the same ways that the party did elsewhere. The crisis following the Panic of 1857 brought widespread social unrest. Jacksonian hatred toward banks meant heated verbal onslaughts against the financial institutions, and soon fears about the instability of the nation's financial system led to change. The long-standing Suffolk system of redemption, a free market system of specie redemption created by New England bankers in 1818, came under attack. In the wake of the Panic of 1857, some state legislatures passed laws favoring Boston banks, and many leaders began calling for competition to curb the power and profits of the Suffolk bank. This eventually led to the creation of the Bank for Mutual Redemption in 1858 and the demise of the Suffolk bank, perhaps the most successful free market banking system in history. Now, in 1860, railing against the banks remained a potent part of Democratic rhetoric.

But other economic matters also caused protest. The depression brought unemployment for many Northern workers, and there were strikes, protests, and riots in many Northern cities. Many Southerners saw this turmoil as evidence of the superiority of slavery, and their criticisms of free labor and defense of bondage made them seem callous and eager to spread slavery to the North. Their talk of "wage slavery" and the superior Southern institution fed fears of the Slave Power conspiracy that held that evil Southern planters hoped to not only spread slavery to the North but also to enslave poor whites. Worries that Southerners controlled the national government through their influence in the Democratic Party fueled the growth of the free labor ideology espoused by Republicans.[34]

The Republicans continued to cast themselves as the defenders of free labor in the North, while accusing the Democrats of being the enemies of the working man. In Indiana, Morton argued that his party defended free labor against the encroachment of the Slave Power. This placed the economic crisis within the framework of the Slave Power conspiracy and made the Republicans the defenders of free labor and the liberty of the white working man. In speech after speech, Morton reminded his audience that the Republicans were the true friends of labor. He constantly and consistently unfurled the banner of free labor ideology as he attacked the Democrats and the forces of slavery.

In a speech made in Fort Wayne later in the campaign, the Republican candidate argued that his party's mission was "to prevent the further extension of slavery, and to rescue the government from the corruption and abuses of the party in power." The antislavery position lay at the very heart of the party. But the Republicans also held to their "great central idea . . . the protection, dignity and elevation of free labor." Morton asked who could fail "to see that labor is degraded and put beneath the dignity of free men, when it is performed by slaves?" Consequently, even slavery had to be understood in the terms of a free labor ideology the doctrines of which were made real and concrete by the Panic of 1857. The crux of the matter was the struggle between slavery and free labor. "We believe that slavery is a moral, social, and political evil." Republicans therefore opposed this evil on moral grounds.[35]

But he also said that personal and selfish reasons demanded that they oppose slavery, arguing that "free labor and slave labor will not flourish in the same bed." He appealed to Hoosiers as workingmen, reminding them that "where slave labor strikes its roots deep into the soil of a Territory, free labor will not grow but perish at the threshold." He urged them to realize that they were all directly involved in the great issue of the day, that it struck at their economic well-being as well as their moral sensibilities. If for nothing else, Hoosiers of all parties should oppose slavery for selfish reasons. Morton warned his audience that slavery limited the number of free workers who might live in them. He wondered how any Northern worker could continue to support slavery given such realities and called on them to oppose it for their children's futures if not for their own self-interest.[36]

Even in this Fort Wayne address, which focused primarily on the slavery question, Morton did not just interpret the issues in light of free labor but also found time to take up other economic matters. Much of his speech attacked Stephen Douglas, now the Northern Democratic candidate and the clear rival to Lincoln in Indiana. After blasting away at the Little Giant on slavery, Morton now bombarded him on economic matters. The Republican reminded his audience that "Mr. Douglas has been distinguished throughout his public life as an ultra free trade man. He has upon every occasion denounced protection in every form." But Morton reminded the voters that Douglas no longer held to his principles and flip-flopped on the tariff issue. Now, in a speech in Pennsylvania, "Douglas came out boldly for a protective tariff, declaring that it was the duty of Congress to protect the coal and iron interests of Pennsylvania." Later in the same speech, the candidate for lieutenant governor defended the Republican Party against charges that they had used the Swamp Lands Committee to take good land by fraud. Corruption intertwined with economic matters, and Morton hoped to convince Hoosier voters that the Republicans stood for honest government as well as new economic measures that would protect them from another panic and depression.[37]

Morton closed his campaign speech in Fort Wayne with praise for "Honest Old Abe." Evangelical voters motivated by moral issues liked the label of honesty while those who held to republicanism saw integrity as part of the virtue needed in a true statesman. And character mattered in other ways as well. Among the many attributes that recommended Lincoln to the voters of Indiana, Morton found the chief economic issue of the day: the contest between free labor and slavery. Lincoln's many years of hard, physical labor made him someone to whom farmers and workers could relate on a personal level. Morton argued that, at "a time when free labor and slave labor are brought in conflict face to face," Abe Lincoln was a living "representation of free labor, and what it can do in ennobling and dignifying the human character. His hands, like yours, have been hardened with toil, and his brow has dripped with the perspiration of honest labor." Lincoln already stood tall as a political symbol, and Morton called on his fellow Hoosiers to support him and the Republican Party. He cried out, "If . . . you believe that freedom is better than slavery—that the Territories should be preserved for free men and free labor—that freedom should be national and slavery sectional, then vote the republican ticket." If they did, he assured them that "you will vote your sentiments, and do your duty to your country and your God!" Economic issues embedded in the ideology of free labor not only promised that Republicans would prevent another panic but also meant that Hoosiers must support Lincoln and his party if they hoped to protect their own self-interest, their own way of life, the nation as a whole, and to please the Almighty. According to Morton, God clearly planned to vote Republican.[38]

Keeping the focus on slavery while adopting a more conservative style than he had in 1856, Morton avoided using the racist language that his running mate employed. In some ways, he proved a more effective campaigner than the gubernatorial candidate. Having learned much in his failed campaign in 1856, Morton now trimmed his speeches and molded them to fit his audience. In 1860, this meant portraying the Democrats as the radicals and his own party as the conservatives. Republicans around the nation watched carefully to see if going conservative would work and liked what they saw in both Lane and Morton. A Kansas Republican newspaper observing the Indiana governor's race reprinted a comparison of the candidates using a metallurgical metaphor from the Bible. According to the Republican *Evansville Daily Journal,* Lane was like gold, while Hendricks "is like Silver, with much intrinsic worth, yet has become tarnished by official favoritism and Lecomptonism." The two candidates for lieutenant governor also differed, with the editor saying that Morton "is like the useful and substantial Iron, capable of the most exquisite temper and finish, yet adapted to the sturdy and serviceable purposes of life." But the newspaperman saw David Turpie as "like sounding brass and tinkling cymbal. His words, though musical, have no value in them, only to amuse and divert from the more serious purposes of life." Even in their criticism of the Democratic candidates, Hoosier Republicans tacked conservatively. This meant acknowledging some positive qualities in their opponents, even though they thought the Democrats looked weak compared to Lane and Morton.[39]

As the campaign continued, the Republicans worried about the Democrats stealing the election. Voting irregularities in 1856 and other elections had been uncovered. And the Republicans especially worried about the Irish, who voted overwhelmingly for Democrats. This was not just nativism, as there had been evidence of fraud among the Irish, including the selling and buying of votes and voters casting more than one ballot. But the Know Nothing wing of the Republican Party added prejudice against Roman Catholics to the suspicion of the immigrants. These worries led to the Republicans working harder to prevent and detect cheating at the polls.

On September 11, 1860, Calvin Fletcher accused the Democrats of voter fraud in his diary: "In politics the Republicans are greatly alarmed lest the Democracy will import so largely on them that they will be beat again by the Frauds. The Catholic Irish & Germans indeed most of the Catholics in the U. States go for Douglas. They are Democrats not by choice but from arrangements . . . by the Catholic Bishops . . ." With anti-Catholic nativist fears of a papal plot running through his mind, the Hoosier banker remembered that the Democrats had used immigrants in fraudulent ways before. After previous elections, he had seen reports that Irish workers had voted multiple times for Democratic candidates. Importing voters from other districts to steal elections remained a common practice.[40]

By the end of the month of September 1860, Fletcher worried that the Republicans were committing fraud as well, as he learned of corrupt methods while on a business trip to Morgan County. In that rural county southwest of Indianapolis, he heard that Republican voters were being brought in from other areas to strengthen the party's performance there. Disgusted, Fletcher worried that "the Republicans have determined to act in a defensive & aggressive manner. But it is decidedly wrong & destructive of the purity of the Ballot box." By the following day, he was again concerned about the Democrats using Catholic immigrants to win the election and lamented, "I regret I have lived to see such corruptions."[41]

In addition to fears about corruption in the electoral process, moral and reform issues besides slavery also emerged in the election of 1860. The Republicans rushed to claim the mantle of reform, of course. But the Democratic split meant that Stephen Douglas and his supporters denounced the corruption of Buchanan while simultaneously attacking the Republicans as nativists and zealots bent on legislating morality and depriving law-abiding citizens of their liberty. Southern Democrats also chimed in, laying corruption at the feet of Northern Democrats while also blasting away at Republican extremism. For Breckinridge supporters, the term *Black Republican* meant more than just abolitionism and a desire for racial equality. It meant socialism, free love, women's rights, and other new ideas that would tear at the very fabric of society. But it also meant corruption. All parties, then, cried out against graft and the abuse of power and tried to say that they were the true reformers. In such a context, Abraham Lincoln's appellation "Honest Abe" took on new meaning. The Republicans moved quickly to lay claim to the moral high ground and win the votes of those for whom integrity meant so much. This included, of course, the many Evangelical Christians across the nation. More complicated than a movement spawned by the depression, the Revival of 1857–58 spurred political action on many fronts.[42]

Despite all of these other concerns, slavery remained the central issue. As they always did, the Democrats used racism to rally their support. For example, William H. English, a longtime Democratic congressman, worked on a circular that accused the Republicans of wanting full "equality between negroes and white people." He wrote to an acquaintance in Massachusetts to gather information for his document, asking about what the Republicans in New England thought about a long list of questions. English wanted to know if blacks were allowed to vote, hold office, testify in court, serve on juries, and intermarry with whites. He also asked for his friend to send along any Republican publications that showed that they supported such rights for African Americans. On March 7, 1860, the Republican paper in Terre Haute, the *Wabash Express,* denounced the "ridiculous blunders" that had appeared in the *Evansville Enquirer.* The Democratic paper had claimed that "a negro as black as the ace of spaces aided Mr. Morton in the canvass of 1856." Clearly, the Democrats hoped to use their familiar strategy on race to win over voters.[43]

Meanwhile, the Republicans tried to portray themselves as being more conservative than their Democratic counterparts. In Indiana, at least, it usually meant that the Republicans argued that their party could better defend the antislavery position and the republic than the Democrats. The Republicans contended that, if elected, they would do better than the corrupt, incompetent Democrats when it came to stopping the expansion of slavery into new territories. They claimed that Northern Democrats could not be trusted on the issue, as they had changed their position time and again in opportunistic moves designed to win elections. Further, the Republicans charged their rivals with complicity in the peculiar institution. The Slave Power, they said, controlled the Democratic Party. Hoosier voters could not trust the Democrats to defend free labor and stop the extension of slavery. Whether caused by corruption or conspiracy or incompetence, the Democratic record made it clear that they had failed to do the job on the most vital issue at stake in the 1860 election.[44]

Some Republicans, including Lane, downplayed the slavery issue as a means of seeming more conservative and moderate by avoiding charges of abolitionism. Lane went so far as to make racist statements in his public speeches and question the wisdom of including abolitionists like George Julian in the party. Most of the Republicans outside of the southern counties of the state did not go quite so far. Indeed, instead of avoiding slavery or trying to be more racist than his opponents, Oliver Morton faced the issue head-on, although he was less strident in his language than he had been in 1856.[45]

In his Terre Haute speech early in the campaign, Morton argued that Democrats were actually the radical party, as they had been the ones to overturn the long-standing Missouri Compromise. Here Morton's personal views clearly entered in, as he had been an anti-Nebraska Democrat who left the party over the issue of Douglas's Kansas-Nebraska Act in 1854. He charged that the Democrats were the true sectional party, because Republicans were not even allowed to operate in the Southern states. Morton quickly answered the charges that the Republican Party was "radical, revolutionary, and subversive in its character." He denied this, arguing that "the republican party is the historical and conservative party of the nation." To make his point, Morton defined a conservative as "one who aims to preserve from ruin, innovation, injury, or radical change; one who wishes to maintain an institution or form of government in its present form." By showing that the Republican "policy of opposition to the general diffusion of slavery, the preservation of the Territories to freedom, and the protection and elevation of free labor, is coeval with, or antecedent to, the adoption of our Constitution," Morton argued that he had established that his party was conservative.[46]

If the Republicans were the conservatives by this standard, then "the democratic party will be found to be radical, revolutionary and subversive, departing from its own creed, revolutionizing a long course of judicial decisions, and subverting the practice of the government from the time of its creation." Morton argued that the Democratic Party held to "the new, dangerous, and portentous dogma, that the Constitution, by its own inherent power, establishes slavery in all the Territories, and that there is no power . . . that can exclude it there from." Here he turned the Democratic argument that the Republicans were radical on its head and argued just the opposite. For Morton, claiming the conservative ground meant redefining not his principles, but the definition of conservatism. In 1860, that meant being the party and the candidate best able to save the republic from the radicalism of the Democrats and the Slave Power that controlled them.[47]

Abolitionist radicals also threatened to destroy the republic, and the candidate for lieutenant governor dutifully denounced the violence of John Brown. But the antislavery zealots were not the real culprits in the conflicts of sectionalism. Instead, Morton blamed the controversy over slavery on the Democrats who had repealed the Missouri Compromise. The Kansas-Nebraska Act "found the country at peace, and has left it stained with blood and torn by civil dissensions. It re-opened the slave question in a form most offensive and under circumstances most aggravating to the antislavery sentiment of the North." Far from defending Northern views on antislavery, Stephen Douglas and the Democrats had caused the turmoil and strife that threatened to tear the country apart.[48]

Furthermore, Morton asked, "What is the cause of the hostility pervading the Southern mind toward the people of the North?" He answered his own question: "There are many causes, but the chief one is to be found in the policy of the democratic party." The Democrats had used the slavery issue to their political advantage, but in so doing they had indoctrinated the two sections of the country to distrust and even hate one another. In tying the protection of slavery to themselves only, Democrats made the South suspicious of any other party, as slaveholders feared that Northerners wanted to destroy their institutions. By demonizing Republicans as abolitionists, the Democrats made it impossible for their rivals to even speak or circulate their newspapers in the South. The slavery question had "been invoked and fostered by the democratic party as a source and means of power," while the Republican Party "has not produced this agitation, but has been produced by it. It is the creature rather than the creator. It sprang like a phoenix from the ashes of decayed parties, not as a sword, but as a shield" to protect freedom.[49]

Raising the specter of the Slave Power, Morton argued that the Democratic Party was dedicated to the extension of slavery to all of the states, not just the new territories. Their ultimate goal was to spread slavery to the North. Democrats planned to accomplish this goal by using "the supreme court; an irresponsible tribunal, the members of which hold their offices for life, and who are not elected by nor amenable to the people." Morton complained that for too long the court had served as a Democratic Party retirement home "for broken, spavined and asthmatic politicians." Far from fulfilling the vision of the Founders, who hoped the Supreme Court would be a true final court of appeal that decided great questions of law that arose from the lower courts, the body had "been converted into an engine for the subversion of free institutions and the propagation of human slavery."[50]

The first step in extending slavery across the nation had been the repeal of the Missouri Compromise through the doctrine of popular sovereignty. The second step was the Dred Scott case. Only the Republican Party stood in the breach against the growing Slave Power. Only they could protect Northern free labor from slavery. Only they could save the Union against the tide of revolutionary radicalism promoted by the Democratic Party. Morton asserted that "by republican doctrine, I mean that sentiment which is opposed to the general diffusion of slavery; desires the preservation of the Territories to freedom, and seeks the elevation and protection of free labor." Not only would Republicans best protect voters from economic crisis, they would also defend freedom against the forces of slavery. Democrats could no longer be trusted on the slavery question. As always, Morton stoked fears of the Slave Power as he argued that Democrats had created the problem facing the nation and certainly could not be expected to fix it.[51]

Throughout the campaign, Morton returned to these themes, casting the decision facing Indiana voters as a matter of choosing who could better save the republic, defend free labor, and stop the spread of slavery. Both parties accused the other of being radical while portraying themselves as the true conservatives. The results in 1860 proved that the Republicans were effective in doing this. But the outcome also stemmed from the fact that the Democrats had split and that opened the door for the opposition. Despite his own ideological preferences on the slavery issue, Jesse Bright's attempt to defeat Douglas and regain control of the state Democratic Party by supporting Breckinridge was a major blunder that only added to the Republican momentum. David Turpie, the Democratic candidate for lieutenant governor, blamed Bright for the party's defeat in 1860: "In October we suffered a defeat not unexpected. . . . The majority against us in the state corresponded somewhat with the vote cast for Breckinridge in November. . . . Our discomfiture was principally due to the Breckinridge movement."[52]

When the votes were finally cast in October, Lane defeated Hendricks by more than 9,000 votes and Morton defeated Turpie by more than 10,000. The Republicans also held their majority in both houses of the legislature and also kept their seven congressional seats. In the November presidential election, Lincoln carried the state with a total of more than 139,000 votes, while Douglas received more than 115,000, Breckinridge just over 12,000, and Bell pulled more than 5,000 ballots. In 1857 Jesse Bright had reneged on his deal with Joseph Wright, a decision that deepened the Democratic division, and in 1860–1861 the Republicans followed through on their agreement. After only two days in office, Henry S. Lane was elected to the US Senate by the Republican-controlled legislature, and he resigned as governor. As Lane headed off to Washington to replace Graham Fitch, and as Indiana and the rest of the nation faced the coming of the Civil War, Oliver Morton took the reins of the state government.[53]

CHAPTER FOUR

The War Governor

THE CRISIS OF THE CIVIL WAR prompted government executives like Governor Oliver P. Morton to take unprecedented action and expand their power. In the summer of 1862, Northerners worried about Confederate military offensives. Southern armies on the march northward threatened to invade the North and, perhaps, win the war. As Confederate troops marched into Kentucky, the Union Army officer in the western theater called on nearby state governments for help, asking for desperately needed troops and supplies to repel the invasion. By this time Morton had already raised many regiments of soldiers for the Union cause, and he quickly acted to recruit more men for the looming emergency. He soon discovered that there was no money to pay the cash bounties the government offered to recruits. This meant that many new soldiers refused to sign up or resisted being sent forward to the field because they needed the money to provide for their families while they were gone. Unless he could pay the troops, Morton could not hope to provide the men needed by General Don Carlos Buell, who was facing off against the Confederate army led by General Braxton Bragg and his subordinate, General Kirby Smith.[1]

The governor did not hesitate but immediately took action on his own authority, and using his personal credit, borrowed a total of $500,000 from banks in Indianapolis and Cincinnati to pay the soldiers and get them moving to the front. One Indianapolis banker answered his request by filling a basket with rolls of greenbacks amounting to $30,000. Having acted, Morton then telegraphed the secretary of war, Edwin M. Stanton, saying that he had sent nine regiments to Kentucky on borrowed money. The governor asked for repayment from the War Department, hoping that his personal credit would not be hurt by the situation. Stanton responded, "The most peremptory orders have been given to supply you funds. If it is not done I will dismiss the officer whose neglect occasions the delay, no matter what his rank." The money was sent, and when he repaid the loans, Morton discovered that he had inspired others to patriotism, as the bankers who made the loans to him refused to charge or accept any interest. This incident proved to be only one of many in which Morton exercised his executive powers in new ways and expanded his authority to get things done. And he put his own credit on the line, making a personal sacrifice in order to save the Union. In doing so, he demonstrated what it meant to be a war governor.[2]

Morton's "War Speech"

Morton had made an argument on behalf of the expansion and use of executive power in the days just after the 1860 election, while still the lieutenant governor–elect. Speaking in Indianapolis at a victory celebration on November 22, 1860, he had justified such powers by outlining the cause for which he would fight and expressed in strident terms the ideas that lay at the foundation of his thinking, laying out all of the elements of his nationalist ideology of freedom and Union secured by the power wielded by his party. He argued that the Union could not be broken up, because "a state once admitted into the Union becomes a part of the body of the nation," and the US Constitution provided no means for secession. He insisted that the United States was a nation, consisting of "one mighty people," and said that "we must cling to the idea that we are a nation, one and indivisible," adding that "we are one people, the citizens of a common country, having like institutions and manners, and possessing a common interest in that inheritance of glory so richly provided by our fathers." And the nation stood for freedom. Morton dismissed arguments that the Southern states seceding compared favorably to the American Revolution. How could one compare "our glorious war for independence with a war set on foot to propagate human slavery, to crush out liberty of speech and of the press" and revive the African slave trade? He extolled the virtues of free labor, reminding his audience of that vital Republican ideology, and declared that the newly elected Republicans stood ready to fight to secure the legacy of the American Revolution: "We believe that our principles are those of the constitution of the fathers, and that peace can only be restored and the safety of our institutions restored" by returning to the "just and liberal policy" upon which the republic had been founded.[3]

In his "War Speech" that cold November day, Morton justified the use of executive authority in response to secession, arguing that "In this matter the President has no discretion. He has taken a solemn oath to enforce the laws and preserve order, and to this end he has been made Commander-in-chief of the army and navy." The newly elected lieutenant governor contended that the new president should treat secession as rebellion and force the seceding states back into the Union, clearly stating his position on the matter when he said,

Fig. 9. Governor Oliver P. Morton, ca. 1863. (Library of Congress)

"If South Carolina gets out of the Union, I trust it will be at the point of the bayonet, after our best efforts have failed to compel her to submission to the laws." To allow a peaceable withdrawal from the nation would be to concede rights that did not exist and to fly in the face of history and destiny. Doing so would encourage future secessions and doom the nation. Morton insisted that independence had to be won through blood and struggle rather than through words. He hoped that the United States would not let South Carolina or the other Southern states go, that the government would not "publish to the world that the inheritance our fathers purchased with their blood we have given up to save ours." The Hoosier leader preferred to fight, no matter how long it took. "Seven years is but a day in the life of a nation, and I would rather come out of a struggle at the end of that time, defeated in arms and conceding independence to successful revolution, than to purchase present peace by the concession of a principle that must inevitably explode this nation into small and dishonored fragments." With his fighting words, Morton maintained the nationalist position and hoped that President Lincoln would use his executive authority to crush the rebellion.[4]

Virginia's Peace Convention

When he took office as governor on January 16, 1861, Morton immediately exerted his own executive power on behalf of his cause. With the states of the lower South out of the Union, there were many who still hoped for some sort of peaceful resolution. This was especially true in the upper South and border states, where a war between the sections would be fought. The Virginia legislature called for a peace convention and invited the various states to send commissioners empowered to help prevent a civil war. Morton doubted that any good would come of such a meeting, but he dutifully forwarded the invitation to the Indiana legislature, which passed a resolution authorizing him to appoint five commissioners to attend the convention. The Democrats had hoped to have the legislature appoint the delegates, fearing that Morton would choose only Republicans similar to himself. The majority disagreed, and, sure enough, the governor carefully chose five reliable Republicans, including Caleb B. Smith and Godlove S. Orth.[5]

Before he made his selections official, Morton sent the chosen men a list of questions to determine their exact positions on the situation. He asked them if they favored a constitutional amendment to achieve compromise, if they thought slavery should be recognized as existing in present or future territories, if they believed in granting any more concessions to slavery, and if they were dedicated to maintaining the Constitution and enforcing the laws. The

Fig. 10. President Abraham Lincoln. (Library of Congress)

men all responded, and all answered no to the first three questions and yes to the fourth, showing Morton that he had found his men. Caleb B. Smith, a congressman from Connersville, Indiana, who would soon be appointed as Lincoln's secretary of the interior, also served on a congressional committee that tried to forge a compromise during that secession winter. All such efforts proved to be in vain, as Morton had predicted.[6]

In February the new president visited Indianapolis while making his way to Washington by train. Morton and the Republicans from the state legislature joined a huge crowd in welcoming Lincoln to town and wishing him well as he headed east. The governor made some brief remarks and again stated a nationalist position, arguing that the people would support Lincoln and help

him to save the Union. Though lamenting that the Union seemed about to collapse, he remained confident because he knew that the country's leaders would
ensure "that the precious inheritance" of the American Revolution would not
be lost without a fight. When Morton finished, Lincoln thanked the governor
and the state for the warm welcome and said that the Union needed only the
hearts of people like them to ensure its salvation. He was sure that when the
people "rise in mass in behalf of the Union and the liberties of their country,
truly may it be said 'the gates of hell cannot prevail against them.'" He called
upon the crowd to join him in the coming struggle to "preserve the Union and
liberty." The president closed by saying, "I am but an accidental instrument, to
serve but for a limited time," and he again reminded Hoosiers that it was up
to them to decide whether the Union and freedom would be preserved. The
two Republicans already linked freedom and Union and saw themselves as the
ones needed to wield the power necessary to protect those ideals. Satisfied that
Lincoln agreed with him completely, Morton continued his work in Indiana as
the president traveled on toward Washington and his inauguration.[7]

EXPANDING EXECUTIVE POWER

While most new governors took time to cooperate with their party in the legislature to get things done, Morton moved quickly, counting on the Republican
majority to support what he did to ready the state for the civil war that he was
sure was coming. He set the agenda and led the way, confident that his party
was with him. This would lead to the expansion of power and bring the tradition of a strong governor to Indiana. Hoosiers had tried to avoid putting too
much power in the hands of one man, preferring to divide authority and put
most of it in the legislature. This fit well with Jeffersonian and Jacksonian ideas
of democracy, and although certain men (like Wright, for example) were able
to accomplish a great deal as governor, the office remained more of a symbol
than a real platform for wielding power. Morton used the context of the Civil
War to change the nature of the governorship and centralize power in the office.
He often did so by skirting or even breaking the law, and although many of
the changes did not last beyond his own tenure in office, he set precedents for
the future, and his often-dictatorial use and abuse of executive power showed
how a strong governor could lead his state in a time of crisis.[8]

Finances concerned the new state executive, as Morton discovered that,
as usual, Indiana's budget was a mess. Willard's administration had spent too
much money and borrowed against future revenues. The state government
chronically overdrew on its appropriations and never seemed to make progress
on paying down its debt. Morton came in and found that the treasury had only

about $5,000 on hand, not nearly enough to cover expenses. He reported this to the legislature and recommended a short-term loan from the State Bank or the State Sinking Fund, with repayment coming from collections due to be paid to the state by county governments. Before the legislators could act, the warden of the state prison at Jeffersonville reported a budget shortfall. He demanded $18,000 immediately, saying that if he did not receive the money, he would have to free the prisoners and close the facility. These funds had not been included in the amount that Morton hoped to borrow in the short-term loan, so the state legislature increased the total and recommended getting the money from the Sinking Fund. The state house of representatives quickly passed the bill, but it stalled in the state senate and Morton had to anxiously wait on the vote. He helped work on certain senators, explaining that they faced dire consequences, as another interest payment on the debt was coming due and the state would have to default. Finally, the senators relented and passed the bill, allowing for the short-term loan to carry the government through the short-term crisis.[9]

But the budget shortfall proved to be only the beginning. Charges of fraud against the Willard administration came in the wake of revelations about the mismanagement of money dedicated to the building of a new state prison at Michigan City. A legislative committee implicated Governor Willard, who had died in office, in the corruption, although a Democratic minority opinion disputed this. No matter what the reality was concerning the scandal, Morton had to deal with cost overruns, and he forced a new contract and new board of directors to try to clean up the mess. More significant scams involved the ongoing Swamp Lands scandal, the giant fraud that resulted from the sale of wetlands and the payment of public funds in contracts to drain them and make them tillable. Although mostly carried out by Democrats, the shady land deals and contracts included some Republicans, too, as it seemed that nearly every official with an opportunity to profit in the corruption had done so.

The most notorious deals involved speculators buying thousands of acres of public land for far less than market value, helped along by well-placed friends or relatives, while other illegal acts involved receiving payment for drainage work not done. One of the worst offenders was Michael G. Bright, the brother of Senator Jesse Bright, who obtained huge tracts of land in Newton County. The costs of the scandal kept mounting and hurt the state's already woeful finances. Throughout his tenure as governor, Morton struggled with Indiana's money problems. He repeatedly had to use creative methods—such as using his own credit to pay bounties or pushing for short-term loans to bridge a crisis—to keep the state solvent. He relied on the legislature when he could but used his own authority when he could not, and this would later lead to some of his most egregious abuses of power.[10]

Mobilizing for War

Money mattered a great deal in the spring of 1861 as the new governor tried to get the state ready for the coming civil war. He discovered that the Indiana militia was in no shape to fight. Although a militia act had been passed in 1852, giving the governor more authority over the organization, it had been allowed to lapse and had not been revived. Supposed stockpiles of arms and ammunition no longer existed or were obsolete or in poor condition. Enrollments were spotty, at best, and nonexistent in many areas. Furthermore, when the Republicans in the legislature introduced a new militia bill to allow the governor to reorganize and modernize the state's armed forces, the Democrats refused to support it. Governors Willard and Hammond had appointed the militia officers, a source of patronage for party loyalists who received the title and pay even though the organization barely existed. The Republican majority in the Indiana House passed their new bill, but the Democrats in the Senate bolted the session to deny the majority a quorum. Realizing that the battle would drag out and delay other work, Morton urged his party to compromise, and they agreed not to push their militia bill forward so that the Democrats would return and other bills could be passed.[11]

Although the war had not yet begun, the governor wanted to take preemptive action. But the system and the Democrats stood in his way. In the end, the only thing that Morton was able to do was gather firearms not being used by military companies and distribute them to any volunteers. Otherwise, he would have to work with the existing structure and the many Democrats who held offices around the state. He set to work scouring the state for guns, sending messages to officials in every county asking them to report on how many firearms they had for their militia troops, but he found that there were very few, and most of those he did find were outdated or broken. When the Republicans in the legislature offered a resolution authorizing Morton to fix and modernize whatever weapons were on hand, Democrat Horace Heffren snorted that "I understand that there are thirteen muskets and two rusty horse pistols." Even though both sides agreed that the situation was abysmal, the Democrats refused to pass any legislation to address the lack of guns.[12]

So Morton used his executive power as a remedy to the problem, establishing a style of simultaneous action that he would use repeatedly during the war years. First, he followed the official channels and fired off a steady volley of messages to the federal government demanding guns for the men. Second, using borrowed money, Morton began working to procure the arms himself. He dispatched men to search the country for guns, sending Indianapolis banker Calvin Fletcher and his son Miles on journeys east before finding a

Fig. 11. Robert Dale Owen. (W. H. Bass
Photo Company Collection, Indiana
Historical Society)

more effective agent in Robert Dale
Owen. The Scottish-born Owen was
the son of the socialist Robert Owen,
who had established a communal experiment at New Harmony, Indiana,
in the 1820s. Still a believer in his
father's ideas, Robert Dale Owen had
entered politics, where he learned it
was sometimes necessary to compromise principles in the name of getting
things done. At the start of the war,
he had just returned from serving as
minister to the Kingdom of Naples,
and Morton asked him to work as the
state's procurement agent, a position
he held until 1863.[13]

Owen traveled extensively along
the East Coast and to Europe, and
unlike most other agents for Indiana
and other states, managed to purchase
a large number of firearms. Eventually all state arms purchases went through
Owen and he bought thirty thousand Enfield rifles from England, plus many
other smaller purchases from various sources. He also bought guns from the
federal government, a system that reflected the timeless illogic and inefficiency
of government bureaucracy, as Indiana purchased guns from the federal arsenals
and the federal government eventually reimbursed the state for them. Morton
wanted Indiana to provide ammunition for her soldiers, so he established the
state arsenal. Begun in a blacksmith shop with volunteers from the 11th Indiana
doing the work, the arsenal grew beyond those small-scale operations to become
a viable and profitable source of bullets. Worried about maintaining his control
over the supply of ammunition, Morton refused to relinquish the state arsenal
to the federal authorities and often bickered with the War Department about
keeping it open. Here was an example of where his nationalist beliefs collided
with his own defense of state's rights. Morton argued that the state arsenal was
more effective and showed that it was profitable, but it also came down to his
reluctance to give up the power to control it.[14]

In the weeks after Lincoln's inauguration on March 4, 1861, Morton worked
hard to prepare for what now seemed the inevitable conflict. He traveled to
Washington, DC, and joined other governors in meeting with the new president to offer their counsel. He and Governor Israel Washburn of Maine urged

Lincoln to defend every Southern fort and not give an inch to the rebels. A few days later, Washburn and Morton returned to the White House with two other state executives, Andrew Curtin of Pennsylvania and William Dennison of Ohio. There, worried that the new president was not doing enough, the governors decided to take matters into their own hands. They all agreed that they should call up their militias and begin arming them. Having already begun preparations in Indiana, Morton had his militia organized, and he felt confident that the Hoosier State would be ready when the Union needed her sons to help crush the rebellion.[15]

When the war began with the firing on Fort Sumter on April 12, 1861, President Lincoln responded by calling for volunteers. Upon receiving the call for troops, Morton replied with a telegraph to Lincoln on the morning of April 15, saying, "On behalf of the state of Indiana, I tender to you for the defense of the nation, and to uphold the authority of the government, ten thousand men." The War Department, however, soon issued a quota of troops to be raised in each state, and Indiana's share of men was to be six regiments totaling about 4,600 soldiers. Not wanting to waste the enthusiastic response of Hoosier men to the call for volunteers and confident that the government would soon need more men than they thought, Morton continued to raise troops on his own authority. He recruited five regiments for the state militia for a term of one year's service and had them ready when, sure enough, the War Department needed more men. The governor proved prophetic in his predictions about the coming of the war and how difficult it would be, forecasts that sprang from that aspect of his personality that often led him to seem paranoid. But in 1861, as well as at other times, there was nothing wrong with being paranoid when someone really was carrying out actions against the country. And, of course, one did not need to be a prophet to predict that secession would follow the Republican election and that the government would resist it. In his worries about the numbers of men needed to fight and win the war, however, Morton was ahead of the curve among Northerners, many of whom expected little or no fighting at all in a very short contest.[16]

THE 1861 LEGISLATIVE SPECIAL SESSION

With hostilities begun, Morton called the legislature into special session so that they could help him prepare Indiana for the crisis. When the lawmakers convened on April 24, the governor delivered a message outlining both the seriousness of the situation and his readiness to lead in the fight against the Confederacy. He noted that the conflict had started and argued that this meant that "every man must take his position upon the one side or the other." Morton thus defined patriotism by insisting that there could be no middle ground: either one was loyal to the Union or a friend of the rebels. The governor believed that the Union cause deserved the full support of the state's citizens and called on them to devote themselves to it, giving up their fortunes and their lives if need be. The Union deserved such devotion because "upon the preservation of this government depends our posterity and greatness as a nation, our liberty and happiness as individuals."[17]

He called on elected officials to lead the way and to set aside partisanship by approaching the conflict, "not as politicians, nor as ambitious partisans, but as patriots." The Republican leader declared that "the voice of party should be hushed, and the bitterness that may have sprung out of political contests be at once forgiven and forgotten." He pleaded for unity and cooperation, with everyone coming together in a grand, patriotic era in which there "shall be but one party, and that for our country." Therefore, the man who would make party a vital piece of his political ideology called for the end of partisanship in the name of the Union. He soon organized those who supported the war into the Union Party, which included both Republicans and Democrats, and made it his own. Morton sincerely believed in what he said, as his actions in cooperating with many Democrats who supported the Union cause proved throughout the war.[18]

Morton's message also called on Kentucky to remain in the Union and reject the overtures of the Confederacy. Here, too, he declared that there could be no middle ground, saying that Kentucky's neutrality put the state at odds with the nation and actually helped the rebels. He made it clear that he thought that the Slave Power was at work: the rebels not only wanted to break up the Union, they also sought "the destruction of the democratic principle of government, and the substitution of an aristocracy in its stead." This was not just a war to crush a rebellion, it was a conflict over the very foundational principles of the nation. It was a war to defend freedom and democracy against the machinations of evil aristocrats seeking to impose their tyranny over the entire country. Such high stakes called for action, and Morton asked the legislature to appropriate $1 million for arms and ammunition. He also requested a new militia bill that would allow him to reorganize the existing forces. Beyond those military concerns, the governor wanted a new law "defining and punishing treason against the state," and he hoped to suspend "the collection of debts against those who may be actually employed in the military service of the state or United States." To pay for all of this, he wanted to issue state bonds, and he also asked that "all necessary and proper legislation be had to protect the business, property and citizens of the state" during the war against the rebellion.[19]

In those heady early days of the war, patriotic enthusiasm ran high, and the legislature was almost unanimous in its actions. The lawmakers doubled the appropriation for guns and ammunition to $2 million, provided for state bonds, passed a new law on treason, and created a new militia system that extended Morton's flexibility and control over it. Even most of those Democrats who had urged compromise and peace with the South joined in voting through the new war measures. Only the suspension of debt collection from soldiers failed to pass, and that was because the legislators doubted that such a law was constitutional. The debt suspension bill stirred debate, especially when it was combined with the Felonies Act, a measure that made it illegal to help the Confederacy in any way. This heightened the state's sectional divide, as southern Indiana representatives feared that the government would outlaw the river trade that allowed their constituents to make a living: farmers in southern Indiana sold their goods to Southern markets, using the Ohio River as a conduit to the Mississippi River and New Orleans. On the other hand, the northern part of the state traded with New York via railroads and the Great Lakes system, and their legislators argued that any kind of trade with the South gave aid and comfort to the enemy. The militia bill also caused some controversy, as Democrats said that it gave too much power to the governor, while many Republicans insisted that it did not provide enough authority to be effective.[20]

Beyond those debates, which focused on state economic and governance issues, the only real dissent came from a legislator from Johnson County, a Democrat who worried that Indiana's military preparations were an insult to the patriotism of Kentucky. Although he mostly supported the various new laws, on May 9 the legislator offered a resolution that said that Indiana respected "the sympathies of the border states for the reason that their institutions and interests are kindred with those of the Confederate states and we will recognize a neutral position on their part." Such thoughts had been popular among Democrats throughout the secession winter, but now the man who uttered those words found himself attacked by the rest of the state assembly. A Republican immediately called for a vote to reject the resolution. Sensing the mood, the Johnson County man tried to withdraw his motion but was unanimously voted down. The state house of representatives then voted to reject the resolution recognizing border state neutrality with only one abstention—the man who had offered it. Any kind of sympathy for the South was suspect in the patriotic rush to support the national cause. It seemed that many Hoosiers across the political spectrum now accepted Morton's redefinition of patriotism.[21]

At least one of the bills introduced during the special session went far beyond military matters and tried to define loyalty and citizenship along racial lines. The bill would have made it illegal for any white person who had married a black or mulatto person from testifying in a case to which another white person was a party. When the bill came to a vote, it was announced that the committee had decided that since such marriages were illegal in Indiana and "that any white person who would debase themselves so low as to intermarry with a mulatto or negro, should not be debased any lower by an act of the Legislature." Consequently, the committee recommended that the bill should be indefinitely postponed. But the vote on the bill was taken, and it was defeated by a count of 58–18. When it came back for a third reading, it was tabled, as the House finally decided to follow the committee's advice.[22]

The special session of the legislature also included an attempt to get rid of Senator Jesse Bright. The senator, ever the doughface, had expressed his sympathy for the South during the winter and argued that secession was legal and right. When hostilities began, he staunchly called for peace and expressed his opposition to war. Now his enemies at home moved to destroy him, and on May 23 the House asked for his resignation. Later they declared that Bright was no longer a resident of Indiana because he had moved to his land in Kentucky. Ergo, his enemies claimed that he had forfeited his right to represent it in the national government. A resolution was passed asking the US Senate to declare his seat vacant. Although it would take more than this to remove the powerful senator, he could not hope to stand by his long-held views on slavery, express his friendly feelings for the rebellious South, and protect his personal interests much longer. The winds of war blew against the fortunes of the old powerbroker even as they favored the rise of a new force to replace him. Morton, the new powerbroker, would have his revenge served cold the following winter.[23]

MAKING APPOINTMENTS

Armed with the new laws that gave him expanded authority, the governor continued his work to prepare Indiana for war. The appointment of officers cast doubt on his call for setting aside partisan concerns. The 1852 Militia Act, which gave the governor authority to give commissions to all regimental and company officers, put the responsibility and the power for addressing the need for military leaders in his hands. At the same time, the Lincoln administration had the power to appoint officers of higher rank, and congressional leaders and cabinet members also wielded influence. Of course, such patronage brought out lots of claimants. Letters flooded in, recommending individuals for positions. To help sort it all out, Morton appointed Lew Wallace as adjutant general, a position the Mexican War veteran and son of a former governor held briefly before accepting command of the 11th Indiana regiment. Wallace's posting illustrated an important part of the appointment process: politics. A Democrat until the secession crisis, Wallace switched parties as a demonstration of

Fig. 12. Union general Lew Wallace. (Library of Congress)

his loyalty to the Union. Because so many Democrats opposed the war, the usual political considerations involved in patronage took on the added issue of loyalty.[24]

Other governors and President Lincoln at the national level shared the same problem that Morton faced. On the one hand, they wanted to reward fellow Republicans by giving them the positions they sought. On the other hand, they needed to appoint enough loyal Democrats to secure their support for the war. In keeping with the call to set aside old party divisions that he had made in his message of April 24, the governor soon led the organization of the Union Party, made up of War Democrats and Republicans. Yes, he would set aside the old bitterness between the two parties. But new bitterness arose in the form of redefined patriotism, as only those deemed loyal could join the party in power. Politics mattered, but so too did competence. The practical side of things deserved attention, and Morton quickly appointed officers from those who had experience. Indiana had few West Point graduates and not very many officers with experience, although the governor managed to find some veterans of the Mexican War to commission. The administration trumpeted the names of the Democrats among those made officers, using them as evidence that partisanship had been set aside. The colonel of the 10th Indiana, Lafayette businessman Joseph J. Reynolds, was a Democrat and a West Point graduate. John Love, who became one of the governor's most trusted military aides, was also a Democrat as well as a wealthy real estate and railroad investor. Love later helped John Gatling set up a factory in Indianapolis and invested in the development of the Gatling gun. A West Point graduate who had served in the Mexican War, Love had military training and experience to add to his commitment to the cause. In such cases, Morton preferred competence to party affiliation, but loyalty to the Union was paramount.[25]

Despite his call for unity, Morton remained a partisan politician in the sense that he demanded loyalty to the cause and, over time, to himself. John Love was an example of a Democrat who demonstrated his ability as well as his loyalty to both the Union and to the governor. For Morton, power and party went hand in hand. Only those Democrats who were clearly in support of the war made the governor's list of appointees, and he commissioned more Republicans than Democrats. And no matter which man he appointed, his critics found fault with the decision. They accused Morton of nepotism for his friends and of trying to attach former Democrats to his own power base. Some of the officers he appointed did indeed become loyal supporters of the governor. Alvin P. Hovey, a Mexican War veteran who had not seen action in that conflict, was made colonel of the 24th Indiana Regiment. Like Morton, he was a former Democrat who had joined the Republicans and he became a trusted friend and ally.[26]

Solomon Meredith also switched parties in the 1850s, and having supported Morton politically, he expected a commission. When Morton moved too slowly, Meredith and his friends complained that the governor did not return favors to those who had helped him win the election. Meredith went ahead and started a regiment, recruiting men in eastern Indiana. Eventually he persuaded President Lincoln to intervene on his behalf, and Morton commissioned him a colonel so he could command his regiment. This caused a controversy when George Julian began to criticize Meredith as being inexperienced and uneducated and thus not qualified for a colonelcy. The congressman believed that Meredith had raised troops illegally because he had no authority to recruit them. And he blasted Morton's granting the commission as a political appointment. Such criticism disappeared as the war continued, although Morton helped secure Meredith a promotion to general and he was given command of the Iron Brigade, which he led at the battle of Gettysburg. Later, political infighting among commanders caused Meredith to lose his command for a time, and upon his return, he was wounded. But he did not forget that Julian had criticized him publicly. Morton in his turn continued to support the loyal Meredith, recommending him for promotion to major general late in the war.[27]

While Meredith was a political appointee, others combined military backgrounds with their connections to the governor. Jefferson C. Davis, another man with experience in Mexico, received an appointment to command the 22nd Indiana. A very close friend of Morton's, Davis also proved a capable field commander and may have been the most competent officer the state provided to the Union military. Hovey and Davis had experience to recommend them, but others among Morton's friends received his patronage because of politics alone. Conrad Baker was a lawyer with no military experience at all, but the governor urged him to recruit men for a cavalry regiment. Baker did so and commanded the unit before returning to Indiana, where he worked closely with Morton as a provost marshal and, later, lieutenant governor. Young Benjamin

Fig. 13. Union general Solomon Meredith. (Library of Congress)

Harrison enjoyed the Republican governor's patronage during the war years, and he, too, raised and led a regiment. As Harrison later discovered, however, Morton's friendship could be lost. Walter Q. Gresham also learned a lesson about loyalty to the governor. A Republican leader in the state legislature, he did not curry Morton's favor, and the two men disliked each other. When he applied for a commission in the military, the governor refused to grant it. Gresham was forced to enlist as a private, but he was soon elected by his men to be the captain of their company, and eventually he received his commission as a colonel.[28]

Snubbing Gresham contrasted starkly with the governor's appointment of Horace Heffren, one of the most strident Democratic critics of the Republicans throughout the secession winter. But when the war began, Heffren changed his views and supported the Union cause. He energetically helped pass many of the war measures during the early part of the special session, and Morton rewarded his loyalty with a commission as a major. When Heffren resigned from the legislature to assume his place in the military, the Republicans were outraged, and one of them, Lucius Bingham, even introduced a resolution to censure the governor. Heffren listened to the Republican's tirade against the appointment and Morton, then calmly nipped the move to censure in the bud by suggesting that the accusing legislator would be better off enlisting in the army. In the heat of war fever, that was enough to silence the critics who feared that Morton was using appointments politically. Before the war ended, the governor would have cause to question Heffren's loyalty, but at the outset of the conflict, he appointed the Democrat in the name of bipartisan allegiance to the nation. In the context of the patriotic wave against the rebellion in 1861, the new Union Party in Indiana largely became the party of Morton. As the months went by, loyalty to the Union and loyalty to the governor overlapped and intertwined to the point that it became difficult to separate the two.[29]

Of course, the president held the authority to make many of the appointments and Morton joined other Indiana politicians in asking Lincoln to put their favorite candidates into particular positions. Getting Joseph Reynolds commissioned as a brigadier general illustrated the ways in which Morton operated in such situations. Reynolds had been promoted to brigadier general of state troops after his initial appointment as a colonel. Although the officer had served only a short time, Morton wanted Reynolds commissioned in the federal army because he feared that Indiana would have few generals due to the lack of West Point training in the Hoosier State. On June 3, 1861, the governor telegraphed Lincoln his recommendation that Reynolds be promoted, saying that he was "a man of talents" and of good character. Furthermore, Reynolds was a West Point graduate and had "for some years been an instructor at that institution." All of that combined with his current state rank made him an ideal candidate for a federal promotion.[30]

But the national government moved slowly, and Morton was impatient. On June 7, 1861, he sent another telegram to the president, again recommending Reynolds and asking, "Will he be appointed?" Two days after that, he sent a letter, cosigned with a congressman, that complained that he had "received no answer" to his two recommendation telegrams. Frustrated by the pace of the system, Morton closed his letter by saying, "It would be an appointment eminently fit to be made, and I trust it will be." The president finally agreed and endorsed the promotion on June 12, 1861, noting that Reynolds was "well recommended, particularly by the Governor of Indiana." On July 26, Reynolds finally got his appointment, and the Senate confirmed it on August 3, making the commission retroactive to May 17, 1861.[31]

Sometimes Morton complained about the appointments made by the federal authorities. In the summer of 1861, Lincoln appointed colonels to command three of the six cavalry regiments from Indiana. Incensed that the president had given the commands that would usually be made by the governor of a state, Morton fired off a letter to Lincoln to vent his anger. "I know of no reason making it necessary to take the appointing power from the Executive of the State," he fumed, and worried that it was being done only to him, added, "Such an indignity, as far as I can learn, has not been offered the Governor of any other loyal state."[32]

The commissioning of brigadier generals especially upset the governor, as had been the case with Reynolds. In July of 1861, Morton heard that the president had appointed generals based on recommendations from the Indiana congressional delegation, and he expressed his irritation in another missive to Lincoln. He complained about the men who had been made generals, saying, "I do not know who they are and have not been consulted." He grumbled that "I have had much more to do with the officers than any members of Congress and have had much more responsibility in connection with the organization than any of them and believe I should at least have the chance of being heard before any action is taken."[33]

Appointments illustrated how Morton became frustrated with the president and other federal officials. As he tried to expand and centralize power in his office, Morton often came into conflict with the authority of the national government. His relationship with Washington was a complex and complicated one. On the one hand, he tried to defend state's rights, arguing for local control and competence, especially when it involved him personally keeping command over something. On the other hand, he held to his nationalist ideology and strongly supported the Lincoln administration. He chafed under the inattention of federal officials and often became frustrated with the slowness of the national bureaucracy. Morton also became disgusted with the incompetence of some who held federal office. He often traveled to Washington, DC, and visited government officials in person. He also made trips to New York City to make speeches or to borrow money for the state. And his travels to the front allowed him to see the situation for himself while meeting with military commanders and Indiana soldiers. In practical terms, however, he learned to deal with the federal government in ways that suited him. Other governors complained to the Joint Committee on the Conduct of the War, the congressional group that investigated the government's war efforts, but Morton did not often do so. Chaired by abolitionist Benjamin Wade of Ohio, the committee also included Morton's old enemy, George Julian. That fact, and his own strong relationship with Secretary of War Stanton and others in the Lincoln administration, made it less likely that the Indiana governor would go to the War Committee. Although he often badgered and annoyed bureaucrats, generals, cabinet officers, and the president, he also loyally and ably implemented national policies in the Hoosier State. But he usually did so in ways that helped him further his own power. While he was quick to go around the bureaucracy when he felt it was necessary, he also turned to the federal government for help when he needed it. Like many governors in future years, Morton's executive leadership centered on getting things done in order to deal with real problems in what he thought were practical ways. Governance required pragmatism, a fact that served Morton well, as it lent itself to both his practical nature and his political opportunism.[34]

Politics still demanded his attention, and he traveled to Rockville, Indiana, where he gave a speech on August 3, 1861. The town served as the headquarters for proslavery Democrat John G. Davis, who continually criticized the government and sympathized with the South. The governor and his allies decided to hold a Union meeting there to take the fight to the very heart of this troublesome enemy. Morton defended the war efforts undertaken so far and dismissed Davis's charges that the government was taking on too much debt. The Democrat had criticized Republicans for limiting free speech, and the governor quickly responded by saying that he was a longtime defender of freedom of speech. In the earliest days of the war, he had posted armed guards outside the *Indiana Sentinel* to protect the opposition party's mouthpiece from mob violence after the paper's criticism of the government brought threats from citizens swept up in patriotism and angered by what they thought was treasonous talk. Over time, of course, Morton saw the *Sentinel* become his most consistent and strident source of criticism, and he thought the paper sometimes went too far. Free speech was one thing, but the governor recognized that speech could cross the line into treason. Attacking Davis, Morton denounced the doctrines of state sovereignty and rallied his audience with admonitions to fight to preserve the Union and the government passed down from the Founding Fathers. Learning to be pragmatic as an executive, Morton still clearly saw the ideological divisions that had caused the war.[35]

Defending the State and Saving Kentucky for the Union

By that summer of 1861, Morton's pragmatic sense wore thin in the face of his increasing frustration with the national authorities. He worried about the defense of Indiana and the Midwest as a whole. Convinced that Lincoln and the War Department were neglecting the western theater, he sent a flurry of correspondence to Washington trying to remedy the situation. On August 9, 1861, Morton confidently reported that he could raise 37,000 men in Indiana and offered to lead 10,000 of them into the field himself. He hoped that the president would endorse his plan and make him a major general in order to carry it out. Lincoln ignored his request and had him send his regiments to St. Louis.[36]

Throughout the late summer, Morton continued to send unsolicited advice to the president in what eventually numbered more than sixty letters. In September he offered his plans to send Hoosier troops into Kentucky to help defend the railroad to Louisville, and a short time later he warned that the enemy was about to take Owensboro, Kentucky. He also worried that the Confederates were dangerously close to Evansville, Indiana. He thought that the threat to southern Indiana was the direct result of the federal government neglecting the state's defense and sending Indiana equipment to Union troops elsewhere. The governor's worries led him to telegraph the president, saying, "Southern Indiana is almost defenceless [sic] as the Government has already been advised the state arms having been put into the hands of U. S. troops." Although the constant stream of letters and telegrams must have been annoying, the president reassured the governor and replied with messages that directed Morton to act in accordance with the plans made at the national level.[37]

Worries about Kentucky brought more disagreement between the governor and the national government. The Bluegrass State presented all of the problems of a border state. Kentucky was a slave state but had strong Unionist sympathies. The governor, Beriah Magoffin, was proslavery and pro-Confederate, but he was unable to persuade his state to secede. Instead, Kentucky declared itself neutral and took up an official policy of "armed neutrality." A Union meeting in Louisville defined the policy this way: "We oppose the call of the President for volunteers for the purpose of coercing the seceded states, and we oppose the raising of troops in this state to cooperate with the Southern Confederacy." Supporting neither the Union nor the Confederacy, Kentucky declared "her soil to be sacred from the tread of either." The state government warned both sides to stay out of Kentucky and threatened to join the other side if one or the other did violate its neutrality. While Morton tendered ten thousand men in answer to Lincoln's call to arms, Magoffin responded by saying, "Kentucky will furnish no troops for the wicked purpose of subduing her sister Southern states."[38]

The Kentucky governor invited Morton to "cooperate with me in a proposition to the government at Washington for peace, by the border states, as mediators between the contending parties," but the Indiana governor thought it was a political trap that would force him to stop his preparations for war. Magoffin sent a similar invitation to William Dennison, the governor of Ohio. He hoped that both men would reject his invitation because that would allow him to argue that the North was bent on coercion and did not want peace, strengthening his case for Kentucky's secession. Morton foiled the plan, however, by replying to the invitation, "I will unite in any effort for the restoration of the Union and for peace which shall be constitutional and honorable to Indiana and to the Federal government, and will, if you so appoint, meet you tomorrow at Jeffersonville." Frustrated, Magoffin continued to negotiate for a meeting with both Morton and Dennison. When the time came to actually have the face-to-face conference, however, the Kentucky governor failed to show up, sending a representative instead.[39]

Morton insisted that neutrality was akin to secession and that Kentucky could not carry out such a policy. He watched as the military commanders on both sides carefully avoided violating Kentucky's neutrality while recruiting soldiers in the state. He saw that Magoffin and other pro-Confederate leaders were working for secession but he believed that neutrality also hurt the Union cause. Refusing to allow federal troops to cross the state's borders was treason, an act of rebellion, and Morton urged the national government to put a stop to it by force. He met with Governor Dennison of Ohio and Richard Yates of Illinois, and the three leaders issued a call for the federal government to seize control of Kentucky, especially taking key points along the Ohio River and the railroads. President Lincoln took a more cautious approach and refused to allow Union soldiers to enter the Bluegrass State.[40]

Tensions mounted as Magoffin tried to bait the North into violating neutrality, hoping that it would push Kentucky to secede and join the Confederacy. Throughout the summer of 1861, Morton continued to disagree with the Lincoln administration and argue for the use of force in Kentucky. In the end, the Confederacy took Bowling Green in September, violating the state's neutrality, and allowing Kentucky Unionists to get the upper hand politically. Kentucky stayed in the Union. Kentuckians who supported the Union cause did not forget Morton's work on their behalf, including his efforts to allow Kentucky Unionists to join Indiana regiments, preparing troops to move across the Ohio River if needed, and constantly urging the federal government to act. During Magoffin's term as governor, many Kentucky Unionists referred to Morton as the "Governor of Indiana and Kentucky," an expression of their gratitude for his defense of their interests. Meanwhile, Confederates urged Magoffin to resist the Union and warned him not to take his place in the same "historic niche" as the Indiana governor.[41]

The situation in Kentucky demonstrated how Morton sometimes disagreed with the federal government, despite his nationalist ideology. In September, he forwarded reports from generals in the field to Washington and leaked the information to the newspapers. This helped stir fears of the Confederate incursion into Kentucky, and Morton used the situation to press harder for the administration to pay attention to him. His badgering sometimes caused Lincoln to lose patience and fire back longer explanations of what was going on. On September 26, 1861, the governor griped to the War Department that "my state has done well. Has stripped herself of arms for the Government and the War is now upon her borders. If I have done anything the Government don't like charge it to me & don't let the state suffer. I wish this shown to the President." The president did see the message and responded, "We are supplying all the demands for arms as fast as we can. We expect to order a lot to you to-morrow." Still unhappy, Morton again complained that the national government was ignoring Kentucky: "The difficulty of our situation would be immeasurably increased by the loss of Kentucky. Her central position, the character of her people her power for good or evil almost so make her the turning point of the contest." Urging action, Morton cried that "there is no time to be lost. Every day is an age." He thought that the president failed to understand the gravity of the situation: "Situated where you are, and as you are, I can hardly hope that you will enter fully into the spirit in which I write, but I hope you will give the subject of my despatch [sic] your earnest and immediate attention."[42]

That was too much for Lincoln, who fired back in a letter rather than his usual telegram: "I write this letter because I wish you to believe of us (as we certainly believe of you) that we are doing the very best we can. You do not receive arms from us as fast as you need them; but it is because we have not near enough to meet all the pressing demands; and we are obliged to share around what we have, sending the larger share to the points which appear to need them most." When it came to Kentucky, Lincoln told Morton that "you do not estimate that state as more important than I do; but I am compelled to watch all points." Hurt by Morton's insinuations that he did not understand the situation, the president reminded the governor of where he sat: "While I write this I am, if not in range, at least in hearing of cannon-shot, from an army of enemies more than a hundred thousand strong. I do not expect them to capture this city; but I know they would, if I were to send the men and arms from here, to defend Louisville, of which there is not a single hostile armed soldier within forty miles, nor any force known to be moving upon it from any distance."[43]

Having been scolded by the president, Morton took a week to respond. When he did, he denied that he had done or said anything "for the purpose of weakening your administration in the confidence of the people, but on the contrary have Sought to give it strength in every possible way." The governor defended himself as well as state's rights and federalism: "In this contest the Government is compelled to lean upon the States for its Armies, and in my opinion the hands of these men who labor without ceasing to sustain the Government should be held up and not deposed by indifference to their recommendations or demands." Despite Lincoln's retort the week before, Morton continued to insist that he understood the situation better than the president: "Indiana from [a] geographical position is more deeply interested in Kentucky than any other state, and you cannot understand without being here, the anxiety felt and expressed in regard to Kentucky affairs."[44]

Becoming the Soldiers' Friend

While his worries about Kentucky revealed both Morton's energy and tendency to complain, other examples of his executive style and clashes with the federal government came in his efforts to help Indiana soldiers. More than any other Northern governor, Morton worked tirelessly on the behalf of the men in the ranks, and his efforts earned him their affection and political loyalty as well as the title "The Soldiers' Friend." Throughout the war, he continued to recruit men for the army. Although that job became more difficult over time, he managed it with great skill and effectiveness. In fact, even though Indiana was smaller in population than many other states that sent far fewer troops, she supplied the second largest percentage of men to the Union Army. But his work as war governor meant more than just gathering soldiers for the army. He had to see to the organization, training, equipping, and supplying of the soldiers. Lew Wallace chose the state fairgrounds in Indianapolis as the place to muster the troops, and there he established Camp Morton, named after the governor. Volunteers from around the state came there by train to be made ready for war.

Morton appointed one of his state's precious few West Point graduates, Thomas A. Morris, to serve as quartermaster general for the state, and the two men set to work procuring uniforms, equipment, and supplies. But Morris soon took a field command, and for the rest of the war Morton worked with his successor, J. H. Vajen, and commissary generals Isaiah Mansur and Asahel Stone, to provide what the men needed. The governor pressed the United States quartermaster general, Montgomery C. Meigs, for uniforms for the Indiana soldiers. He authorized his own agents to buy some items, only to discover that it was difficult to obtain reimbursement from the War Department for such purchases. By August of 1861 Morton had decided to ask the federal government to send their own commissary and quartermaster officers to help equip and supply the new regiments in Indiana. When these men arrived, Morton realized that he had given up his direct control over spending and tried to reverse the decision, but it was too late. From that mistake, Morton learned to be more jealous of state's rights. But it did not discourage the governor from acting on behalf of the soldiers. That fall, Morton learned that Hoosiers posted in western Virginia still lacked overcoats as cold weather set in. He went to great lengths to procure thousands of coats and get them to those who needed them, eventually buying 29,000 overcoats on his own authority and drawing the wrath of Quartermaster General Meigs amid a bitter controversy. Even though such efforts often fell short or happened at the glacial pace set by federal government bureaucracy, others noticed Morton's work. His constant stream of letters and telegrams sometimes harassed federal officials, while the men in the ranks expressed their appreciation for their governor's attention to their welfare.[45]

Not everyone praised the governor's efforts to provide coats for the soldiers, however. J. J. Bingham, editor of the *Indiana Sentinel*, accused Morton of fraud, arguing that he overcharged the government for the overcoats and kept the excess money for himself. Bingham included the charges in an editorial lead story about ongoing investigations of war contracts and did not mention the governor by name when he claimed that the coats had cost $7.50 each when they were being sold for $6.50 by the supplier. But he jabbed that "either the parties acting for the government had the wool pulled over their eyes or else somebody made a snug profit of one dollar on each overcoat." The editor of the state's leading Democratic newspaper closed by saying that the investigations would prove interesting and would serve as a true test of patriotism as they revealed who was actually robbing the government and, thus, helping the Confederate cause. Outraged, Morton fired off a letter to Bingham, defending himself and explaining that the coats cost more because they were of better quality. He thought the money well spent if it helped Hoosier soldiers, and he took offense when his loyalty to the Union cause was questioned in such a way.[46]

The governor's actions to supply the troops continued throughout the war. He visited the front on several occasions and sent out agents to keep in contact with the military forces. On the home front, Morton had called for civilians to help with the war effort, and supplies came from across the state. At the outset of the war, he enlisted the help of his wife, Lucinda, who headed a committee of Indianapolis women who wrote to General Lew Wallace asking how they could support the war effort. The governor extolled with pride the efforts of such groups, and he turned again in the fall of 1861 to "the patriotic women of Indiana" with appeals for help. When shortages continued, he saw the need to organize such endeavors in a more permanent way. So, in February of 1862, Morton, like leaders in other Northern states, established the Indiana Sanitary Commission and the General Military Agency. Under the direction of William Hannaman, the Sanitary Commission collected needed items and the Military Agency distributed the supplies to the men at the front. Over the course of the war, auxiliary societies of the Sanitary Commission held sanitary fairs in counties and towns across the state, raising cash to purchase needed military equipment and collecting clothing, food, medical supplies, Bibles, books, tobacco, and alcoholic beverages to be sent to the soldiers.[47]

Here again there was controversy. Soldiers from other states jealously resented Indiana's efforts and complained that Hoosiers were receiving better treatment. To be sure, the Indiana Military Agency distributed supplies to men from other states as well but understandably insisted on taking care of Indiana's own troops first. Some military officers complained that the supplies created discipline problems, and there were perpetual tensions between the state organization and the United States Sanitary Commission, which Congress had established in June 1861. The leaders of the national organization thought that the Indiana agencies should be brought under its authority. Once more, Morton defended state's rights and managed to keep the Indiana Sanitary Commission and the General Military Agency separate and under his control.[48]

The governor also acted on behalf of the wounded. As the war escalated and the battles grew larger, the number of casualties rose dramatically. His authority included appointing surgeons, and Morton constantly searched for doctors to send to care for the rising number of wounded men. After Union forces took Fort Donelson in February of 1862, Morton quickly suggested that the wounded be brought from Tennessee to Indiana for care, with hospitals established at Evansville, New Albany, and Indianapolis. A couple of months later, after the Battle of Shiloh, the governor chartered steamboats—again on his own authority and using his personal credit—to bring home the wounded and then sent sixty doctors, three hundred nurses, and a vast load of medical supplies to the front. When one of the steamers was loaded with wounded men and about ready to pull away from the landing to return, a Kentucky officer approached the captain of the boat and asked that twenty of his own wounded men be taken aboard. The steamboat captain replied that he was supposed to take only Indiana troops. The frustrated army officer who had heard about Morton's work to keep Kentucky in the Union, snapped back, "But, damn it, sir, isn't Morton Governor of Kentucky? If he can care for our state he certainly will protect you in caring for our soldiers." The ship's captain brought the wounded men aboard.[49]

Caring for the wounded continued as the war went on, and Morton's letter books contain many copies of the commissions and appointments of doctors and medical agents. The governor's agents scouted out the conditions at the front after every battle and reported their findings to Indianapolis. Some army commanders appreciated such efforts and were quick to use whatever help Morton could send. Others complained that the agents were nosy and meddlesome and griped that they caused discipline problems. Beyond the wounded, the governor also tried to help soldiers who needed transportation home for furloughs or after they received their discharge from the service. He sometimes intervened when Indiana soldiers faced a court-martial, as he did in 1863 in the case of Frank E. Johnson, a sailor charged with desertion when he got drunk and did not return to his gunboat. When Hoosier men were captured, Morton worked to get them released and tried to get supplies through to the enemy prisons where they were held. He also worried about the conditions of Confederate prisoners, including his overseeing for many months the prison established at Camp Morton in Indianapolis. Sometimes the trainloads of prisoners included so-called contraband, former slaves whose legal status was not determined until after emancipation.[50]

The families of soldiers who marched off to war faced tremendous difficulties, and Morton tried to help them. In mid-nineteenth-century America, society expected men to be the providers for their wives and children. Most Indiana residents lived as farmers, and the men who marched away made up the bulk of the agricultural labor force. While enlistment bounties were intended as a way to help offset the hardships faced by the families at home, the money was not nearly enough to make up for the amount of time the men were gone nor did it prove adequate as prices rose. Women struggled to make ends meet, taking on work previously done by their husbands or moving in with their in-laws or hiring hands when they were available. Some women entered the workforce or started businesses to provide for their families during the war. Governor Morton helped create such opportunities by sending many nurses into the field and by opening the state arsenal, which hired women to make ammunition.[51]

War fever sometimes gripped Indiana women and they responded by urging Morton to take action to save the Union. In the fall of 1861, recruiting efforts flagged even as the Hoosier State continued sending regiments to the front. A shortage of Indiana troops meant that there were not enough men to guard several bridges across the Ohio River to Kentucky, so Ohio soldiers were brought in to secure the bridges. When the news of this spread, groups of women in the southern counties of Indiana formed organizations in river towns like Lawrenceburg to encourage the men of the area to join the army. The women of Lawrenceburg sent word to Morton saying that if there were not enough men, they—the women—were willing to enlist and be given uniforms and guns to perform their duty. While the report probably shamed some of the men in the area and induced them to enlist to defend their honor, the ladies volunteering confirmed the governor's confidence in the capabilities of women. Hearing about the case, *Vanity Fair,* the New York journal, published on November 9, 1861, a full-page cartoon about the incident. The cartoon, titled "Morton Leading on His Gallant Lawrenceburg (IND) Brigade," depicted the governor leading a regiment of uniformed women in an infantry charge under the American flag (see Fig. 14).

While Morton did not actually lead women in combat, many Indiana ladies found other ways to actively support the Union cause. Some Hoosier women served as agents of the Sanitary Commission. One such female agent was Elizabeth E. George of Fort Wayne. In 1862, at the age of sixty, George volunteered to work for the Sanitary Commission, and she was sent to the front to help Indiana soldiers by working in the camps and hospitals. She carried out her duties for three years, "braving all the dangers, privations, and hardships of the camp, the march, and the battlefield, and performing the part of a ministering angel" to the troops. On one occasion, while she worked as a nurse in a field hospital during a battle, an artillery shell landed within a few feet of her. It exploded and killed two men, but she was uninjured and calmly continued nursing the wounded men under her care. She remained on duty even as the war came to a close. Unfortunately, she contracted a fever and died on May 9, 1865. The governor learned the sad news and wrote to her family in Fort Wayne to express his condolences and remember her patriotic service to the Union.[52]

But most Hoosier women stayed on the home front, where their families faced the harsh financial realities created when the primary provider marched off to fight for the Union. In the special session in the spring of 1861, the Indiana legislature passed a law that made the local governments responsible for the care of the military families in their jurisdiction. The law authorized counties and municipal governments to levy a special tax to pay for such efforts. But raising taxes in Indiana proved difficult, as always. In some areas, local officials refused

Fig. 14. "Gov. Morton Leads His Gallant Lawrenceburg Brigade" (*Vanity Fair,* November 9, 1861). (Courtesy of the Indiana State Library) This cartoon captures the sentiment of Northern women shaming men into fighting for the Union cause. It depicts Morton leading a brigade made up of patriotic women who have volunteered to help defend the state against a Confederate invasion. The caption below the illustration quotes a letter from the ladies of Lawrenceburg to Governor Morton: "Now we feel it an everlasting disgrace that our bridges should be guarded by Ohio soldiers when we have so many able-bodied men who should be formed into regiments and prepared for duty. And we must earnestly request you to take some steps to arouse their dormant energies and compel them to act as men, or let us take their places, leaving them to attend to domestic affairs, while we shoulder the guns you so generously sent here, and go forth to assist you in protecting our homes.—Letter from the Ladies of Lawrenceburg to Gov. Morton, of Ohio [sic; Morton was, of course, governor of Indiana]."

to spend public dollars on the effort. Private charities did what they could, but in most cases those benevolent organizations soon turned to the government for help, arguing that the task was simply overwhelming and beyond their capacity to address.[53]

In the face of such hardship, Morton turned his energies to caring for the soldiers' families. In the fall of 1862 he endeared himself to the soldiers when he called for increasing their pay. At the same time he tried to rally private support with a call for the people to help the military families. Even his Thanksgiving Proclamation encouraged Hoosiers to "especially pray that the Divine Will may put into the hearts of the people to provide for and protect the families of our gallant soldiers, and preserve them from all want and neglect." He made similar pleas for private aid again in 1863 and 1864. Despite such appeals, the efforts to help the families proved inadequate. Letters poured in from across the entire state, telling sad stories of deprivations and begging for help.

Without funds to do anything through the state government, the governor continued his efforts to organize and lead private charity. This included working with ministers of various denominations to organize Indiana churches on behalf of the military dependents. After Morton suggested the formation of local committees to raise money and distribute aid to the needy families, many Hoosier communities established soldiers' aid societies. Often borrowing tactics from the Sanitary Commission, these local societies raised funds and collected food, clothing, and firewood to distribute. They sponsored fairs and arranged for regular collection days to promote charitable contributions. The response was quite enthusiastic, perhaps because it allowed noncombatants another means of doing their part for the war effort. Thus, Morton's appeals often fell on patriotic ears. During the war, many praised the private benevolence that did manage to provide much for many soldiers' families. Later observers criticized the government for not doing enough and lamented that the private efforts often fell short and, even at their best, were uneven and sporadic. In 1865 the governor pushed a law through the legislature providing for a state tax to fund local government support for the soldiers' families. While the law came too late to make much difference for most military families, it demonstrated that the Soldiers' Friend was still at work on their behalf. Most of the soldiers appreciated his efforts and did not forget to support him politically.[54]

As a war governor, Morton displayed his innovative approach to executive leadership. His establishment of a state sanitary commission paralleled the national organization and put Indiana ahead of the other Northern states. Likewise, the governor's creation of the state arsenal and refusal to give it up proved to be advantageous. He used his authority, borrowed money, chartered steamboats, enlisted the help of women, and called for actions well ahead of the national trends. He acted quickly and confidently, sometimes beyond the boundaries of the law. Seemingly unafraid of the consequences, Morton tended to be abrasive and even arrogant in his dealings with others. But he got things done. This often meant that he clashed with the War Department and other national government agencies. Having yielded control of the commissary to the federal authorities, the governor became more jealous of his own power and of state's rights. This proved especially beneficial in areas like the sanitary commission and in his control of the state arsenal. His power over such institutions allowed Morton to step in and help the troops when the national government failed to provide needed supplies and equipment. In so doing, Morton joined other Northern governors in helping to maintain federalism even as they helped expand the power of government.[55]

PARTY AND PATRONAGE

In addition to fighting to keep the state arsenal under his own control rather than turn it over to the federal government, Morton often clashed with the national authorities over military and political appointments. He thought that Indiana should have more men in high-ranking positions and worried that the state did not receive its fair share of recognition. Following through on a deal made at the Republican National Convention in Chicago in 1860, President Lincoln appointed Caleb B. Smith secretary of the interior, making him the first Hoosier to hold a cabinet office. But Smith did not have much influence over the president, who made the appointment in the name of political equity rather than any belief that the Indiana man was right for the job. Hoosier Republicans had done a great deal to get Lincoln elected, and putting Smith in the cabinet was a form of payback. The Connersville attorney and congressman had been a Whig when he served in the state legislature in the 1830s and came to know Lincoln when the two served together in Congress in the 1840s. Smith got involved in railroads in the 1850s and became president of the Cincinnati and Chicago Railroad. He returned to politics as a Republican and, along with Henry S. Lane, represented the conservative Whigs, which meant that his appointment brought howls of protest from George Julian.[56]

For Morton, Smith's appointment brought access and a line of patronage, although it had to be used carefully. The new secretary of the interior quickly turned out Democrats in favor of Republicans in his own department. This included positions in the Indiana office. But Morton could not rely too heavily on the cabinet officer for patronage. Although he had recommended Smith to the president, the governor could not ask for too many jobs in Smith's department, and the secretary had to avoid placing too many men from his own state. When Smith resigned in 1862, John P. Usher of Terre Haute replaced him. Like his predecessor, Usher was a former lawyer who had served in the state legislature. He failed in a bid for Congress in 1856 but remained a loyal Republican. Also like Smith, he did not exert much influence in the cabinet, and Lincoln found him unsatisfactory despite keeping him in the post for the remainder of his presidency. Still, having a Hoosier in the cabinet kept open an important line of patronage.[57]

Morton made some mistakes in his appointments, especially in choosing men to oversee the supplying of the troops. At the outset of the war he appointed his good friend and old college roommate Isaiah Mansur to be commissary general. Mansur, a meatpacker and a good Republican, seemed to have some credentials, but the decision resulted from political and personal considerations rather than competence. Morton knew Mansur well and thought he could trust him. The critics soon began to complain about the commissary general's activities and charged him with overcharging for poor quality food. To be sure, in the bewildering rush of war preparation, it proved difficult enough to supply the many thousands of volunteers descending on Indianapolis. The demand for supplies was huge and immediate, and Mansur bought food without any kind of system for establishing prices or ensuring quality. Contracts were given without competition and high prices were paid, mostly to well-placed friends and political connections. Within weeks the flood of complaints began to pour in: the meat was too salty and of poor quality; the dried apples were wormy and the coffee was too weak—some soldiers thought the watery brew was an insult to their manhood and called it "effeminate." The men mustering and training at Camp Morton raised a bitter cry of protest, and during the special session of 1861, Horace Heffren led the legislative demand to investigate Mansur for corruption.[58]

Mansur resigned, but Quartermaster J. H. Vajen also became the target of an investigation. Vajen, an Indianapolis hardware dealer and friend of the governor, struggled to meet the demand for supplies. He, like Mansur, handed out contracts without competition and faced complaints about the poor quality of equipment and clothing that was delivered to the men at Camp Morton. The governor defended his appointee, and Vajen continued in office. But in early 1862 a Congressional committee went to Cincinnati to investigate government contracts and found evidence of corruption in Indiana. The charges seemed to implicate the governor's office as well as the quartermaster general, so Morton moved quickly and invited the committee to Indianapolis, where he threw open the doors of his office and the government's records for them to examine. The inquiry eventually proved that Morton was completely innocent but found Vajen guilty of serious malpractice. Despite his insistence that such problems were caused by the rush to create an army and were beyond his control, Vajen remained an example of Morton's failures.

The governor later admitted that he sometimes fell short of the mark in those early days of the war. "When I first began to make appointments of officers during the war, not understanding the business (it was all new to me), I tried to please everybody and his friends, but I soon found that would not do." He remembered that he had decided to "follow the dictates of my own judgment without fear or favor—that I would do the best I could." Although he knew he might lose friends because of it, he thought he had to do what he thought was right and get to the point where he did not concern himself with such personal feelings. Looking back, he offered a clear-eyed assessment: "I sometimes made mistakes, sometimes I appointed the wrong man," but he was proud that so few of Indiana's officers "disgraced the state, or dishonored their commissions." In hindsight, as well as in the context of the time, the governor's many successful appointments seemed to outweigh his mistakes.[59]

If one judged success in political terms, Morton excelled in using his appointment powers. He built the Union Party carefully, and those who dared to oppose him found that they could not secure positions for themselves or their friends. Fellow Republicans often discovered the power of Morton's wrath, and Walter Gresham was not the only man unable to get what he wanted from the governor. Morton closed the door on Michael C. Garber, the influential editor of the *Madison Daily Courier,* who fought back by turning his publication into a fierce anti-Morton newspaper. John R. Cravens, the president of the state senate and another resident of Madison, Indiana, also became an enemy, although Morton initially gave him a commission and a place on his own staff. But when he suspected that Cravens was supplying Garber with inside information, he promptly dismissed him. Garber and Cravens joined Gresham and Lucius Bingham as the leaders of a group of anti-Morton Republicans from southern Indiana, and they remained among his sharpest critics. And, of course, the governor continued his ongoing feud with George Julian, never forgetting to try to undermine the congressman at election time. But most Indiana Republicans supported Morton, and he returned their loyalty. His growing power allowed him to curry favor with War Democrats as well as members of his own party, and he found that the anti-Bright faction included many willing collaborators. Together they took their revenge on the ironfisted senator.[60]

THE REMOVAL OF JESSE BRIGHT

Jesse Bright's support for the South during the secession crisis angered many of his fellow Hoosiers, and the legislature had expressed those feelings in its special session in 1861. When the legislature asked him to state his views on the war, he remained silent. Instead of speaking out, the senator took up residence at his Kentucky farm, a move that expressed his proslavery/antiwar sympathies and led to complaints about him no longer being a resident of Indiana. Defeated by his Democratic rivals, Bright bitterly watched as the war began and Morton expanded his power. The state senate passed resolutions against him, but the house failed to pass them. Nevertheless, Bright's own words eventually brought his removal. In March 1861, during the secession crisis, he wrote a letter of introduction for a friend who was traveling to the South to sell guns to the Confederacy, and addressed it to "His Excellency, Jefferson Davis, President of the Confederation of States."

The letter was discovered by a detective and delivered to the US Senate in August 1861. It had been written before the war began, but Bright's enemies used it as evidence of treason. The senator and his supporters held that the letter was written before the war and that it was not treasonous. He knew Jefferson Davis from their years of serving together in Washington, and Bright had used the title because that it is what his old friend was currently calling himself. It was a courtesy, not an indication of loyalty. Even the leading Republican newspaper in Indiana, the *Indianapolis Journal,* agreed that the letter was not enough evidence to convict the senator. But the doughface politician could not escape his enemies, and they pushed hard for his removal. Finally, on February 5, 1862, the US Senate voted to expel Bright and vacated his seat. It fell to Governor Morton to choose a successor, and he received many letters recommending many different capable men for the office. There were numerous Republicans with a claim to such a seat, but Morton went in a different direction. He took his revenge on the expelled senator by appointing none other than Bright's longtime foe, Joseph A. Wright. This kept up the appearance of Union Party cooperation, as Wright had recently returned from his post in Prussia and had declared himself a War Democrat. The move also served as an olive branch to those in the Democracy who opposed the governor and thought he appointed too many Republicans. And it added insult to Bright's injury, paying him back for forcing Morton out of the Democratic Party in 1854.[61]

Some Democrats criticized Wright for accepting Morton's appointment, arguing that it was a sign that he had conceded his principles to ally with the governor and the Republicans. The *Indiana Sentinel* denounced the appointment as a calculated move by Morton that was designed to "be most damaging to the Democratic Party" and said that for Wright to accept the appointment showed that he had sold out to the Republicans. The leading Democratic newspaper thought that the price of Wright's appointment was a repudiation of his own party's platform. The paper saw his declaration of support for the war as part of an arrangement with Morton. To many in his own party, Wright had turned traitor. Heaping such abuse on Wright signaled that the spirit of unity that had prevailed from the outset of the war throughout most of the rest of 1861 was fading quickly. Increasingly, the Democrats found fault with the Republican leadership of the war effort. Morton and Lincoln became the targets of harsh criticism as they both centralized power in order to fight the rebellion. Wright had been away too long, it seemed. When he announced his support for the war and accepted the job as senator, he cooperated too closely with Morton and the Republicans for the rest of his party. Indiana Democrats turned away from the "turncoat" Wright and looked to men like Thomas Hendricks and Daniel Voorhees to lead them. The pro-Southern, proslavery Bright was gone, at last. But he was replaced by a new generation of Democrats, men who claimed to support the war while criticizing the Republicans. As Morton increased his power, the Democrats returned to the familiar pattern of American politics, taking up their role as the opposition with great energy, accusing the governor of being a tyrant. When the fortunes of war and national politics changed the context in 1862, it set the stage for the fall elections and a standoff between Morton and his political foes. In the end, the war governor would expand his powers to an even greater extent and demonstrate many of the dictatorial tendencies of which his critics accused him.[62]

CHAPTER FIVE

One-Man Rule

THE WORK CREW USED A HORSE and tackle to move the heavy safe into the second-floor governor's office in September of 1863. Oliver Morton had purchased the vault from the Diebold Banhamm Safe Company in Cincinnati and was having it installed in his office for a purpose. After months of political fighting with the Democrats in the state legislature, the governor had decided to run Indiana on his own rather than capitulate to his foes in the other party. One-man rule meant that he had to be creative in how he governed, and that included finances. Without a budget, Morton could not use the proper, legal channels to pay expenses. Instead of going through the state treasury, he set up a "bureau of finance" in his own office in April of 1863 and charged his trusted secretary and adjutant, W. H. H. Terrell, with the task of single-handedly running Indiana's fiscal operation. Answering only to the governor, Terrell used the safe to deposit money that Morton provided from a variety of sources and took funds from it to pay the bills. Coming up with the money to run the state required ingenuity and maneuvers that took the governor far beyond the bounds of the state constitution. Though willing to stretch or even break the law in the name of the Union cause, Morton still insisted that the money be handled carefully.[1]

He wanted no corruption heaped on top of his frankly illegal moves. If the Union won the war, he would be able to justify his actions, and as long as the books were balanced, was sure that he would be forgiven. But if the South won the war, he worried about the outcome, telling Secretary of War Edwin M. Stanton, who helped him work outside the legally established system, "If the cause fails we shall both be covered with prosecutions." Stanton replied, "If the cause fails, I do not wish to live." The governor agreed and continued to use his executive power to secure freedom and the Union, helped along by the loyal members of his party. He knew that the stakes were high, but believed that there was no alternative. If he gave up one-man rule, the Democrats would

Fig. 15. Secretary of War Edwin M. Stanton, Republican, Ohio. (Library of Congress)

ruin everything for which he had worked and help destroy the Union. With renewed energy and zealous confidence, Morton became the virtual dictator of Indiana.[2]

THE RETURN TO PARTISANSHIP

The tenuous Union Party movement in Indiana continued throughout the war years, but its spirit of cooperation came to an end after only a few months of collaboration. In part this was due to the ongoing factionalizing of the Democratic Party. The Hoosier Democracy, so long divided between personal and sectional factions, now split over the war and the conduct of it. Peace Democrats emerged to oppose the conflict as a violation of the rights and liberties they had cherished as Jacksonians committed to state's rights and limited government. Some in this group still held proslavery doctrines, but most of them genuinely believed that secession was a legal right and that the South should be allowed to leave the Union in peace. Other members of the peace faction saw the war as an excuse for the Republicans to centralize power and diminish the freedom of all Americans. They worried about the size and scope of government, feared the concentration and abuse of power, suspected the motives of Republican leaders, and saw themselves as the defenders of liberty. Meanwhile, the War Democrats supported the Union, but they subdivided as the conflict escalated. Some of the War Democrats, like Wright, wholeheartedly joined the Union Party effort, cooperating with the Republicans in order to win the war. Others within the War Democrat faction criticized the Union Party as a cover for the Republican Party's own agenda and hoped to take control of the war effort through the winning of elections and political struggle. These men held no great love for the South and wanted to defeat the Confederacy, but they thought the Republicans were going too far in the name of the Union. They believed that the aim of the war was simply to put down the rebellion and restore the Union. This had to be accomplished within the confines of constitutional and legal authority, which meant restricting the ways in which the government and the military operated.

But the political struggle was not limited to the Democrats. While the Republicans were more unified, they, too had their factions. In Indiana this intraparty division largely revolved around Governor Morton. Some antislavery Republicans, like George Julian, thought him too conservative and slow to act. They wanted to expand the scope of the war to including the abolition of slavery and thought that both Lincoln and Morton were too cautious in pursuing the matter. Others worried that Morton was using the war to build his own power and further his own interests. They saw him as an opportunist and a manipulator, a man driven by his personal ambition. Of course, many others—usually the majority of Republicans—supported both the governor and the president. The factions within the Indiana party did not always follow ideological lines, nor did they always mesh with differing views on the issues. They were often personal. If Morton disliked a Republican, that man usually found himself on the outside of the party establishment. Such men often joined with others in one disaffected group or another.

There was much for the critics to address in their complaints. And the fortunes of war lent themselves to mounting criticism, as events outside of Indiana drove the context of politics. Decisions made in Washington and results on the battlefield changed the ways in which Hoosiers argued about the war and their war governor. Morton's expansion and concentration of power brought complaints—and, in the cases of Mansur and Vajen, charges of corruption. The governor's holding of grudges and use of patronage to reward and punish fellow politicians only added to the problem. Beyond the state's borders, the mounting cost of the war in terms of blood and treasure combined with the expansion of the national government to raise concerns about the price of the conflict. Lost battles and failed campaigns hurt the Union Party and Republicans, while victories bolstered their support. Talk about emancipation divided Hoosiers, as the issues of race and slavery always had before. Conservatives in both parties feared that the Lincoln administration would try to make the war of the rebellion a war to free the slaves and argued against the constitutionality of such a policy. When the need for more soldiers resulted in the use of conscription, the draft became an issue. Many who supported the war effort did not agree with the policy, arguing that compulsory military service was a violation of individual liberty. Others noted that a war that needed conscription was by definition not a popular one and believed that the lack of recruits should cause the government to reconsider its approach to the conflict. Thus, libertarian fears about government expansion combined with military affairs and the politics of emancipation to set a context for the struggle for control in Indiana.

By the fall of 1861, the surface spirit of unity that had marked state politics at the outset of the war disappeared. Earlier disagreements that had been couched in the language of collaboration now emerged as full-blown struggles over significant issues. The removal of Jesse Bright proved to be a turning point, as even many of the senator's old friends turned against him and nearly everyone agreed that he had to go. But that unified action against the former powerbroker also signaled the return to partisanship in Indiana. Even as they cooperated in removing Bright, Hoosier Democrats planned their attack on the Republicans. Despite their internal divisions, the opposition party organized protests across the state against the war, but the Republicans countered with Union meetings that often intimidated the advocates of peace. As early as the summer of 1861, there had been complaints about the war tax, but as the months rolled by, the Democrats began to criticize the centralization of power and the ineffective military efforts against the rebellion.

Economics always mattered, and rising prices on the home front combined with the burden of the war tax brought Democratic criticism. Continuing the economic theme, some opposition voices were raised against the Republican plan for the transcontinental railroad. The land grants for the railway favored big business, and the whole scheme seemed designed to create monopolies rather than help farmers and settlers. And mobilization to put down the rebellion brought war contracts, many of which went to Republicans. This opened the door for charges of crony capitalism and corruption. Protectionist tariff policies set the Jacksonian free traders to gnashing their teeth in angry protests against the Republicans helping the eastern manufacturers at the expense of the western states. The Democracy also railed against the suspension of habeas corpus and blasted the government policy of arresting and imprisoning citizens without warrant. The loss of civil liberties had come quickly, and the Jacksonians feared how far Lincoln and the Republicans would go in the name of saving the Union. The Democrats did not yet attack Governor Morton directly but focused on the national scene and the Lincoln administration's conduct of the war.[3]

When they held their state convention in January 1862, Indiana Democrats stoked racial fears by talking about the prospect of emancipation. One speaker, Thomas A. Hendricks, used language that hinted at the creation of a confederacy, the Northwestern Confederacy, that might ally with the South. The future vice president of the United States said that "we are now being so crushed that if we and our children are not to become the hewers of wood and drawers of water for the capitalists of New England and Pennsylvania, we must look to the interest of our section."[4]

Taking an economic view of the war, Hendricks reminded his audience that many in the midwestern states of Ohio, Indiana, and Illinois depended on trade with the rebellious states, saying that their ties to the South would last as long as "grass grows and water runs" and warned that any "political party that would destroy that market is our greatest foe." He called on Hoosiers to think about what Lincoln and the Republicans wanted to do, pointing to pending legislation that contemplated "the freedom of the negroes in the rebel states, in a word the destruction of Southern labor and the ruin forever of our rich trade and the value of our products."[5]

Foreshadowing later Populists and raising ideas about the midwestern states seceding, Hendricks said that the highest priority of the region had to be the preservation of the Union "upon the basis of the constitution." But the Democrat worried that the Republicans would make reunion with the South impossible and would run roughshod over the Constitution. When it came to that point, "then the mighty Northwest must take care of herself and her own interests. She must not allow the arts and finesse of New England to despoil her of her richest commerce and trade by a sectional and selfish policy—Eastern lust of power, commerce and gain."[6]

Other members of the Hoosier Democracy agreed. Defeated for reelection to Congress in 1860, John G. Davis now joined Hendricks at the state convention to lead the Democratic return to partisanship. Davis had protested the war tax the previous summer and was rumored to have visited Richmond,

Virginia, where he had called on his old friend, Jefferson Davis. In his speech to the state party convention, John Davis blasted away at the war tax, arguing that government's attempt to put down the rebellion was costing the taxpayers millions of dollars in interest alone. The former congressman also said that he did not believe that the war could be won and asserted that the Union could not be preserved by force. Davis went on to lament the seizure of Confederate diplomats when a Union naval vessel intercepted the British mail ship, the *Trent,* in November of 1861.

Conveniently forgetting that Old Hickory had opposed secession, John Davis wished that Andrew Jackson could be president again and set things right. The Hoosier Democrat cried out against the abolitionists and Republican corruption. He denounced the Union Party as a farce and declared, "If this government is to be saved from irretrievable wreck, the Democratic Party must do it. From the moment of the defeat of the Democratic Party, you could date the downfall of our country, its institution, the Constitution, and the Union." Davis closed by saying that "the policy of this administration, its ultimate object, is to liberate the slaves" and contending that emancipation was the end goal of the Republican Party. Denouncing the Lincoln administration for higher taxes, trampling on civil rights and liberties, and for thinking about freeing the slaves, Indiana Democrats passed a series of resolutions that included blaming the war on abolitionist fanaticism and the sectionalism of the Republican Party.[7]

But the Democrats praised Indiana soldiers for their brave service and did not directly criticize Oliver Morton. Although they grumbled about his arrogance and usurpation of power and complained about corruption and charged him with nepotism, the Democrats were not yet ready to take on the governor in open political battle. In part this was due to the nature of federalism, as many of the policies and violations of liberty that they hated so much came from the national government. Morton was only indirectly at fault, if at all, since he was not responsible for implementing every national plan. Their reluctance to attack the governor also stemmed from his popularity. It was one thing to protest the faraway government in Washington, DC, but criticizing the state's own leadership in the midst of the rebellion seemed too much at the moment. And, of course, at that point, just about a year into his administration, Morton could be excused for making mistakes because he had done so with good intentions, and the problems had come from his zeal to save the Union rather than outright malevolence.[8]

The Confederate Invasion of 1862

As the year 1862 unfolded, however, the governor began to come under fire from his political enemies. Constantly badgering the national authorities with his demands for supplies, Morton also confidently offered plans to win the war and, incredulously, asked for a military command to achieve the victory on his own. The president and his cabinet officer calmed Morton down, and solemnly thanking him for his ideas, they gently refused his request for a commission as a field commander. His excited enthusiasm mixed with paranoia about enemies real and imagined, Morton always worried about a Confederate invasion, even when there were no Southern troops nearby. He conjured up images of rebel soldiers marching through the defenseless heartland and taking cities like Indianapolis. In April, when he received reports about the operations of Kentucky guerrillas led by a man named John Scott, the governor immediately forwarded the information to the secretary of war and recommended that Scott be arrested. Guerrilla bands crossing the river foreshadowed larger forces coming into the Hoosier State, and Morton kept a vigilant watch as he urged the War Department to send more troops to guard Indiana.[9]

When the Confederate offensive of 1862 actually brought the army of Braxton Bragg into Kentucky, Morton saw his predictions coming true and moved quickly to action. He had been pressuring the Lincoln administration to raise 300,000 more men rather than the 150,000 for which it had planned. He recruited and sent troops to the front, worked the state arsenal overtime to produce hundreds of thousands of rounds of ammunition every day, and borrowed the money from banks on his own credit to pay the bounty for new soldiers. The war governor's initiative brought praise from the *Indianapolis Journal,* the Republican Party organ edited by Berry Sulgrove, who crowed, "Fourteen thousand men have been organized, equipped and sent to the field in four days. We do not believe this promptness has been equaled in any emergency by any state in the Union. The news of the invasion of Kentucky reached Governor Morton on Sunday." Although Ohio would take a week to get ready, Morton moved quickly to stop the invasion south of the river. He thus took action upon his own authority and sent the Indiana men forward.[10]

Such raw troops, rushed to the battlefield with inadequate training, often met with disaster. At the Battle of Richmond in Kentucky, fought on August 30, the inexperienced Indiana regiments were shattered by Confederate veterans. The defeat coincided with the second disaster at Bull Run in Virginia, and that lessened the political impact of the loss for the governor, although it added to the overall decline of morale and worry about the Confederate advance. Battlefield reverses did not stop Morton, however, as he continued raising troops and rushing them forward. When the Confederates moved to Lexington and forced the Kentucky legislature to meet in Louisville, Morton went there to see for himself that the city was defended. The Kentucky lawmakers greeted him with a standing ovation and applauded his leadership as he continued the work he had begun the previous year during Kentucky neutrality. He provided guns and ammunition and sent Indiana units to help secure Louisville. Bracing for a Confederate invasion, on September 5, 1862, Morton declared martial law in the Indiana counties along the Ohio River and began organizing the citizenry to repel the expected foe.

Frustrated with his own state government's lack of speed, the mayor of Cincinnati turned to Morton for help. Like Louisville, the Queen City offered a likely target for the advancing Southerners, and the residents were scurrying about to make preparations for defense. The mayor asked the Ohio governor for cannon but was told to fill out all of the proper paperwork and then send the requisition through the proper channels. The wheels of bureaucracy might eventually turn, but the city leader realized it would be far too late. So he telegraphed Morton and asked him to help. Without hesitating, the Indiana governor replied that he had an artillery battery ready and was sending it immediately by train, along with two railroad cars full of ammunition for the cannon. Morton soon followed his artillery and helped see to it that Lew Wallace was given command in the Cincinnati area. The governor worked closely with the general, who ordered the citizens to help build defensive works south of the river. Morton rushed troops to Cincinnati, and Wallace soon had an army of forty thousand men entrenched and ready to fight. When the Confederates saw what the Union men had done, they decided not to move in that direction. The people of Cincinnati credited Morton and Wallace with saving their city and later commissioned a portrait to be painted of the governor to be hung in the city council chambers.[11]

The Murder of General Nelson

Cooperating so closely with the military soon embroiled Morton in army politics. His good friend Lew Wallace joined many other officers in criticizing General Don Carlos Buell for not stopping Braxton Bragg's invasion of Kentucky. Wallace also hated Buell's friend, General William "Bull" Nelson. A native of Kentucky, Nelson came to Louisville to defend the city during the campaign. Morton's friend and appointee, Jefferson C. Davis, had volunteered to help him secure Louisville and defeat the enemy forces. Nelson, over six feet tall and weighing about 300 pounds, towered over the five-foot seven-inch, 125-pound Davis, whom he put to work recruiting militia to bolster their defenses. Already extremely unpopular in Indiana, Nelson now added Davis and his friends (including Morton) to his list of Hoosier enemies. Unhappy with Davis, he charged the Indiana general with failure to do his duty.[12]

When the Kentuckian asked him how many men he had raised, Davis told Nelson that he had recruited "about 2,500," to which his commander snapped, "About! Damn your 'abouts'! Don't you know how many men you have in your command, sir?" Davis had said he could not give an exact number, but that he needed to equip the men he had and wondered where he could get guns for them. Nelson swore and replied, "You are a pretty general to tell me 'about' how many men—you are not fit to command. Get out of my sight. I will relieve you and send you to Cincinnati under guard, you puppy!" Such language dishonored Davis, especially the use of the insult "puppy," which cast implications upon his mother and had long been a taunt used to goad an opponent into a duel. Davis faced dishonor if he obeyed the order to get out of Louisville and risked military discipline if he disobeyed it and stayed.[13]

Morton heard about the incident, and thinking it insulted the honor of the state of Indiana as well as his friend, promised to resolve the matter upon his upcoming visit to Louisville. On the morning of Sunday, September 28, 1862, Morton met with Nelson over breakfast at the Galt House hotel, which the army used as its headquarters in the city. There the general railed against the *Indianapolis Journal* for its criticisms of him, especially editor Berry Sulgrove's comments about his overbearing manner. After their meal, the two men went out into the hotel lobby. Morton headed across to talk to acquaintances, and the giant Kentuckian went to the main desk, where he stood smoking a cigar while leaning against the counter. Davis approached and asked to speak to Nelson with Morton as a witness, saying that he wanted a clear explanation of the reasons why he was being relieved of his command. His commander taunted him by cupping his hand to his ear and telling Davis to "speak louder, I don't hear very well." When the offended officer replied in a loud voice, demanding an apology, Bull Nelson cut him off and shouted, "Do you know who you're talking to, sir?"[14]

This brought Morton rushing across the room, and he watched as Davis pressed his commander harder for an apology. Nelson roared, "Go away, you God-damned puppy, I don't want anything to do with you!" The Hoosier general was holding a hotel calling card in his hand, and as the confrontation escalated, he began to fidget nervously and twisted the card into a ball. Whether this happened intentionally or not, the card flipped out of Davis's fingers and hit the Kentuckian in the face. Nelson retaliated immediately and slapped Davis across the cheek with the back of his hand before turning on Morton

Fig. 16. Union general William "Bull" Nelson. (Library of Congress)

and snarling, "Did you come here, sir, to see me insulted?" The governor calmly replied, "General Nelson, you astonish me. I was standing here and he asked me to hear what he had to say to you." Nelson turned to a fellow officer, saying, "Did you hear that God-damned insolent scoundrel insult me, sir? I suppose he don't know me, sir. I'll teach him a lesson, sir." The big general then stalked off to his office, but a short time later he came back into the hallway. As he walked toward Morton and Davis, the two men saw that Nelson had his hand in his pocket—and this meant to them that the general was carrying a gun. Davis had previously asked a friend he met in the lobby for a pistol, and the man had given him one. When he saw Nelson now, Davis called out for

Fig. 17. Union general Jefferson C. Davis. (Library of Congress)

him to stop, and when the giant man kept coming, he repeated his warning, shouting, "Stop and defend yourself!" But the Kentuckian continued striding toward the two Hoosiers—and Davis shot him. Amid the chaos that followed, Nelson was carried to his room, where he soon died.[15]

Davis was arrested, and many of Nelson's men talked loudly of revenge. Meanwhile, Davis's men came to the city and began calling for his release, leading to a fear that the two Union forces would fight each other in the streets of Louisville. But the Confederates united them again by moving toward Perryville, and the Northern troops rushed off to fight them there. The common external enemy that had reunited the bickering soldiers soon stopped any talk of action on behalf of the honor of their commanders. The killing had been a matter of honor, if not quite a duel. Although many expected a court-martial, no charges were ever filed, and Davis was released.

This added fuel to the smoldering fires of the conspiracy theorists, who now accused Morton of orchestrating the entire affair. He had not only been a witness, they contended, but had actually planned for the killing to take place. The governor did not deign to answer such ridiculous charges, but the murder of Bull Nelson only added to his growing reputation as a ruthless powerbroker.[16]

The Removal of General Buell

Meanwhile, Morton continued to complain about and work against General Buell (and also criticized General George B. McClellan) during a visit to Washington in early October. Morton thought that the two commanders were incompetent or worse, and in a letter addressed to Lincoln on October 7, 1862, called for their removal. He told the president, "You have generals in your armies who have displayed ability, energy and willingness to fight and conquer the enemy. Place them in command, and reject the wicked incapables whom you have patiently tried and found utterly wanting." The governor thought that he needed capable commanders with whom he could work because of the rising threat to his state. Increasingly, violent events were taking place in Indiana.[17]

In July of 1862, when a band of Kentucky guerrillas crossed the Ohio River and attacked the town of Newburgh, Morton swiftly ordered his state militia to chase them down. He sent available troops, called for volunteers, and rushed to nearby Evansville himself. There he organized a large force of Indiana men to chase the raiders out of the area. His efforts won him praise from the Lincoln administration and helped spur Hoosier Unionists to take matters into their own hands. The small-scale raid led to a mob attacking local Southern sympathizers, whom they accused of helping the guerrillas. Across the state, various groups of Democrats were leading public protests against the war and the government's policies. In the face of this opposition, Morton responded by helping to organize Union Clubs and Union Leagues and other loyal groups to counteract the opposition. The competing groups often clashed, and riots and incidents of vigilante justice carried out by mobs became more frequent as the war continued.[18]

Convinced of Buell's incompetence, Morton kept up the pressure on the general. Beyond the fact that some of Morton's friends, like Wallace, despised Buell, the governor's dislike of the general had developed over time. The trouble stemmed from Morton's tireless efforts on behalf of Hoosier soldiers. When, in late 1861, he learned about poor conditions for Indiana troops from an officer who wrote to him, he complained about it to Buell. The general, a stickler for the chain of command, responded by chastising the officer for going to the governor. Buell had earned a reputation for refusing to consult with his officers and not allowing them to bring problems directly to him. Upset by the outside interference, he wrote to the governor and asked him to respect the chain of command, and Morton agreed to do as the general asked.[19]

But the trouble between the two men continued. Immediately after asking the Indiana executive to respect the process, Buell complained to General McClellan about Morton and other governors interfering with his command. Worried that such meddling was a threat to discipline, he was concerned as well about the political influence state leaders wielded. Buell thought he could correct the situation, but he could not stop Morton from trying to help Hoosier soldiers, and in the summer of 1862 the governor stepped into the chain of command again. He had received reports of poor conditions, confirmed by his own trips to the front. Indiana men were not receiving their supplies, were forced to camp in miserable locations, and were suffering from camp diseases. Morton telegraphed Buell and asked that the general send hundreds of Hoosier men to Lexington, Kentucky, for proper care. The general refused, although he did express sympathy for the soldiers.[20]

Throughout the summer, criticism of Buell mounted in newspapers across the country, especially in the party organs closely affiliated with the governors who disliked him. This included the *Indianapolis Journal,* which was widely known to be Morton's mouthpiece. The Indiana governor turned to getting Buell relieved of command. He enlisted Governor Richard Yates of Illinois and Governor Andrew Johnson of Tennessee to join him in the effort. Yates agreed, and the governors ramped up their efforts to rid themselves of the troublesome general. In addition to being a Democrat, Buell's failures on the battlefield made him especially vulnerable. Like his friend, George McClellan, the general proved too cautious for governors pushing for bold action and an aggressive campaign that would end the war. Morton and Yates criticized the general's conduct at the Battle of Perryville. Not satisfied that the Confederates had been repelled, Morton was convinced that, instead of destroying it, Buell had just let Bragg's army go. He soon had the support of many other governors, who joined him in complaining that Buell had moved too many troops away from Louisville in his efforts to stop Bragg's invasion of Kentucky. In the opinion of the governors, led by Morton, the Union general left Louisville too lightly defended. Buell's disgruntled officers and men joined in the criticism.[21]

When Confederates under General Kirby Smith approached Louisville, Buell sent General Bull Nelson to defend the city and stop the enemy advance. Morton went immediately to observe the situation himself. That summer and

Fig. 18. Union general Don Carlos Buell, 1862. (Library of Congress)

fall the governor traveled back and forth repeatedly between Indianapolis and Louisville, visiting the soldiers, watching the generals, witnessing the shooting of Nelson. He also found time to go to Washington, DC, where he demanded Buell's removal, arguing that the general was "utterly unfit for command." According to Morton, Buell moved too slowly, and was cautious when he should have been aggressive. And politics entered the governor's thinking. That fall, the president issued the preliminary Emancipation Proclamation, and it became a controversial issue. Morton knew that Buell was "opposed to the Emancipation Proclamation," and that was just one more reason the general needed to go. The Indiana governor led the chorus calling for Buell to be sacked, and Governor Yates chimed in nearly as loudly.[22]

When the president finally relieved the general of his command, the two governors telegraphed Lincoln, saying that "the removal of General Buell could not have been delayed an hour with safety to the army or the cause." They assured the president that replacing the hated Buell with General William S. Rosecrans would restore the morale of the Northwest, and the governors called off another visit to Washington to again talk to the authorities about removing the hated officer. Buell languished in Indianapolis, hoping that an investigation would clear him of blame and that he would return to command, but instead he left the army altogether in 1864.[23]

Morton had proved to be a loyal friend and an unforgiving enemy who would not rest until he had achieved his victory. No wonder, then, that some people thought that the governor had planned Nelson's murder at the Galt House. His political enemies despised Morton's interference in military affairs and agreed with Buell that his actions hurt the army. In September 1862 General Henry W. Halleck complained to a fellow officer about Morton and other politicians interfering with the army as they tried to carve up the various departments into commands for their friends and political allies. On October 7, as the governor led the movement to remove General Buell, the *Indiana Sentinel* criticized his meddling and thought this another example of his imperious nature and personal ambition. Democratic editor J. J. Bingham argued that Morton's hatred of Buell stemmed from the general refusing to let him have his way: the general had dared to stand up to the arrogant governor and now suffered the consequences. Still, Morton enjoyed tremendous popularity in Indiana and regionally, as well. His political enemies in the army soon found themselves out of power, while Morton's Republican friends won promotions and achieved victories. To be sure, most of their success came from their own abilities and ambitions and from the support of many Republicans, including the president. But Morton's friendship helped, and as his allies moved up the chain of command, he could count on them to return the favors that he had bestowed upon them during their rise to power. They knew they could count on him to get things done and to be a loyal friend.[24]

Getting things done was practical and necessary, but Morton's actions took place in the context of the war and national politics. The fortunes of war seemed to turn against the Union in the summer of 1862. Thomas J. "Stonewall" Jackson turned back much larger Union forces in his campaign in the Shenandoah Valley, and General McClellan's Peninsular Campaign failed at the gates of Richmond, Virginia. Braxton Bragg's invasion of Kentucky raised fears across the Midwest, and General Robert E. Lee won the second battle at Bull Run before invading Union territory when he marched into Maryland. Even the victory at Antietam came after the bloodiest single day of the war, and General McClellan failed to follow it up, letting Lee's army escape back into Virginia. Other Confederate advances were stopped, but they still added to the sense that things were going badly for the Union. Operations in Missouri continued to keep the status of that border state unclear. September and October 1862 also saw a rebel offensive led by General Sterling Price that was stopped by Union forces commanded by William S. Rosecrans at the Battles of Iuka and Corinth in Mississippi.[25]

The military setbacks came at considerable cost, both in human casualties and in material resources. The government needed more men and called on the states for help. Morton continually sent out his agents to recruit men and organize more regiments. Appeals to patriotism remained the focus of recruitment efforts, but the payment of bounties also helped, especially when local authorities raised funds to offer additional bonuses to the new recruits. But recruiting became much more difficult even as the demand for soldiers continued. The expected short war had become a sustained conflict with no end in sight. So many thousands of volunteers meant labor shortages at home, driving up wages as well as prices, making it harder for men to leave behind employment and their families. And the cause for which a man would fight seemed less clear as the messy mix of politics and self-interest increased as the war went on. In such a context, charges of cronyism added fuel to criticism of government policies. All of it contributed to the growing unpopularity of the war.

THE DRAFT

Desperate for men, the national government turned to conscription, a decision that made the conflict even less popular. In July 1862 Congress passed a bill authorizing the president to call out the state militias and to use a draft to enlist them in national service. Lincoln called for 300,000 men under this law, and the state draft began. Democrats hated the draft on several different levels.

First, conscription violated the liberty of the individual, a basic human right. Second, the draft of the militia violated the principles of state's rights, as the organization was designed for service to the sovereign state, not the national government. Third, the draft indicated that the war was not going well and that the Republicans were failing to save the Union.

Morton had his own reasons to dislike conscription. He had worked tirelessly to recruit men and usually exceeded the quotas set for the Hoosier State, while other states did not always meet the numbers they were supposed to provide. Enforcing the draft in states that had patriotically given more than their share of men to the war effort seemed unfair and unnecessary. Still, the governor implemented the draft in Indiana, setting up a system for enrollment of the militia for conscription; such efforts even came to include enlisting black soldiers to serve in racially segregated units. He tried to have all of the officials in charge of the draft be Republicans loyal to him personally, and to this end he intervened with the War Department to ensure that the draft commissioners were paid on time. His continuing success as a recruiter helped offset the impact of conscription in Indiana. Recruitment often brought frustration with other states as well as with the federal government; even late in the war, Morton bitterly complained to the War Department that other states were not sending their fair share of men to fight while Indiana continued to send more of her sons than required by the quotas set in Washington. But he did not hesitate to institute the policy of forcing men to fight for freedom. His willingness to surrender individual freedom and state's rights, combined with his attempt to extend his own power through the draft system, made the governor an obvious target for those who protested against the new policy.[26]

EMANCIPATION

While the draft made the war more unpopular and elicited mounting criticism, that fall brought an end to all semblance of Union Party cooperation when President Lincoln issued the preliminary Emancipation Proclamation. In making the war about slavery as well as saving the Union, Lincoln deepened the divisions within the Republican Party and forced almost all of the War Democrats out of the Union Party movement in Indiana. At that point, the appointment and commissioning of Democrats came to a halt. The issues of race and slavery marked a decided return to partisanship. Within the Republican ranks, the various factions coalesced into two main groups: the conservatives and the radicals. The president operated between them, using them to his advantage when he could, often playing them off against one another. The conservatives thought the war was about putting down the rebellion and restoring the Union. They hoped to keep within constitutional bounds and saw the abolition of slavery as a dangerous social experiment that would destroy the Union for which they were fighting. The radicals wanted to use the war as a means of ending slavery and moving the country to finally fulfill the ideals of liberty and equality. Lincoln's tentative call for emancipation angered the radicals, who thought him too cautious, but it upset the conservatives even more.[27]

Many Republicans joined the Democrats in criticizing the new policy. Among them was Henry S. Lane, Morton's 1860 running mate, who now served in the US Senate and represented the conservative Republicans of Indiana. Meanwhile, George Julian remained the most prominent of the radicals in the Hoosier State. Morton, the former Democrat, who had switched parties over the issue of slavery, mostly held to a conservative position. In doing so, he remained consistent in his ideological leanings while also serving political expediency. The governor had strongly opposed the expansion of slavery but had not supported abolition of the institution where it already existed. Although not as conservative as Lane, Morton could not yet be called a Radical Republican. He detested Julian and thought that the abolitionists were too extreme. When Lincoln refused to listen to the radicals and insisted that the war was about the Union, Morton had supported him. Still, when the president issued his preliminary policy in September, the governor quickly defended the move and backed emancipation.[28]

While such shifting positions might have indicated opportunistic maneuvering, Morton actually demonstrated ideological consistency once again. In fact, one might have argued that political opportunism would have required him to oppose emancipation on the grounds that the majority of Hoosiers opposed it. But his thinking had changed over time. The antislavery, free-trade, free-soil, free-labor Democrat had become a Republican who developed a nationalist ideology of freedom, Union, and power wielded by party. The rebellion itself changed the context, and Morton's ideas closely matched Lincoln's own thinking, as both of these evolved during the course of the war. For Morton, a clear ideology emerged. The governor had supported freedom and railed against the Slave Power for years before the war, and he continued to see liberty under the law as an ideal for which he fought. Preserving the Union marked the nationalist ideology, and Morton stood ready to defend it at all costs. Power, given to and used by his own party, was the means of achieving those two goals.

In Morton's mind, then, Lincoln chose to issue the preliminary proclamation in order to save the Union and secure freedom, which made it legitimate. Emancipation was a strategy of war, and because he was a fellow Republican,

Morton loyally stood by Lincoln. Thus, his support derived from partisanship, but it was also a matter of ideological principle and not merely an opportunistic move. Supporting emancipation put the governor at odds with the majority of Hoosiers and meant that he and other Republicans in the state were now the targets of criticism for national policies.[29]

THE ELECTION OF 1862 AND THE NORTHWESTERN CONFEDERACY

The election of 1862 occurred in a context, then, that favored the opposition party. The biggest issue was emancipation, which divided the electorate and was wildly unpopular among many in Indiana. Politically that was bad enough, but when it was combined with the draft, higher taxes, the national debt, and failures on the battlefield, the context was simply too much for the Republicans to overcome in the Hoosier State. The Democrats swept to victory, as they won control of the state legislature and took seven of the eleven congressional seats. The Democracy also won significant victories in Illinois and Ohio that fall, as the off-year elections went badly for Morton and his party. Throughout the campaign in Indiana, the candidates focused on the issues of the moment, including economics, emancipation, and the conduct of the war.

The Republicans generally tried to avoid the economic issues because so many Hoosiers were struggling. This was largely due to the interruption of the river trade with New Orleans and other points in the South. The loss of trade with the South meant that large numbers of people in the southern part of the state suffered directly because of the rebellion. Morton himself believed that the economic conditions, not emancipation, were what cost his party the election. This seemed unlikely for much of the state, but the governor was sure that the voters cared more about money than race. With that dubious theory in mind, he began to push more earnestly and frequently for the Union to recapture the Mississippi River and reopen the river trade. Of course, even if economics really did matter more, emancipation had to be defended or denounced in the campaign. The Democrats railed against it, and most Republicans tried to appear moderate while siding with their president. But some conservatives in the party joined the Democrats in criticizing the policy. Mostly trying to avoid the issues, Hoosier Republicans instead raised the specter of internal rebellion by talking about the disloyal factions of the North. For Republican candidates and speakers, anyone who disagreed with them should be called a rebel or a traitor. Gathering information about subversive secret organizations from military investigators, Morton urged Indiana Republicans to be vigilant in their observance of their Democratic neighbors. He shared what he thought were keys to reading secret codes in treasonous conversation and correspondence. While such fears stemmed from his conviction that a fifth column was rising in the Midwest to threaten the Union rear, they also played into his political calculations. That summer the governor hoped that some of the traitors might be arrested and worked to find witnesses who would testify against them.[30]

But talk of treason and the subversive actions of secret societies of Copperheads did not resonate in 1862. While there were some traitors at work in various underground organizations, the voters did not accept the charges the Republicans threw at Democrats. Too many War Democrats and staunch Union men belonged to the Democracy for it to be completely traitorous. Furthermore, the Republicans made claims and leveled charges but had found little actual evidence of treasonous behavior on the part of the Copperheads. The real issues of the day were not disloyalty but Republican policies, especially emancipation. To put it simply, most Hoosier voters in 1862 agreed with the Democrats, who opposed emancipation, higher taxes, the draft, the infringement of civil liberties, and the centralization and expansion of power. Calling someone a rebel or a traitor was a dangerous thing in the midst of the war, and to apply such terms to Democrats who supported the Union seemed to be going too far. Indiana voters rejected such campaign tactics in 1862. Instead, they cast their ballots with an eye toward the issues of the day and they elected the Democrats, setting the stage for a political struggle between the governor and the legislature.

Morton believed that the Democratic victory spelled disaster for the Union. His brother-in-law and private secretary, William R. Holloway, detailed the governor's thinking when he wrote to Lincoln's secretary, John G. Nicolay, on October 24, 1862. The Democrats called for creating a new confederacy, "'*a great Central Government*,' cut off from New England and the Cotton States." This plan for an interior confederacy had first come to light in a speech by Thomas A. Hendricks on January 8, 1862, when he envisioned both a northwestern and a southwestern confederacy free from the meddling easterners.[31]

To make sure that the president got the message, Morton wrote to Lincoln on October 27, 1862, reporting that the Democrats of the Midwest assumed that the rebellion would be successful and that the Confederacy would win independence. Starting from that point, the Democrats moved to asking about the future of their own states and doubted whether they should remain in the Union. Morton thought that the Democrats were finished with their old government and wanted to "secede and form a new one—a Northwestern Confederacy—as a preparatory step to annexation with the South."[32]

Ignoring the fact that many War Democrats had joined him in the Union Party, the governor argued that the Northwestern Confederacy was at the heart of the Democrats' thinking and had been so for the past year. Morton remarked that the Democratic campaign had continually linked the Midwest with the South and tried to separate their states from New England. The opposition party made speech after speech in which they insisted that the Midwest had nothing "in common with the people of the Northern and Eastern states; that New England is fattening at our expense; that the people of New England are cold, selfish, money-making, and, through the medium of tariffs and railroads, are pressing us to the dust." Instead, geography connected the Midwest to the Mississippi Valley, and that meant that the Democrats believed that the social and commercial interests of the heartland were with the South. After all, the Mississippi River was the economic lifeblood of much of the interior of the United States.[33]

Tied geographically, economically, and socially to the Mississippi Valley and the South, the people of the Midwest could "never consent to be separated politically from the people who control the mouth of that river." Morton said that the Democrats, beyond emphasizing the region's connections to the Mississippi Valley, also thought that the war was one of Northern aggression, carried out to force the abolition of slavery upon the Southern states. The Democracy claimed that the South had tried to avoid war and had offered "reasonable and proper compromises" that the Republicans had refused to accept. Although he blamed the South for the rebellion and did not think Southern compromise plans had been at all reasonable, the governor admitted that there was some truth in all of these Democratic arguments. After all, he conceded, "our geographical and social relations are not to be denied," and he advocated for "the free navigation and control of the Mississippi River."[34]

If the South won, then he feared that "Ohio, Indiana, and Illinois can only be prevented from a new act of secession by a bloody and desolating civil war." Bleakly contemplating the future of the country after Southern independence, Morton said that, in that event, the Republicans in government would have to work to save the remnant of the Union in some shape or form. The key to preventing the gloomy future the governor imagined was to win military victories and regain control of the Mississippi River. To achieve this, he offered a plan for retaking the great river and the vital areas along its banks. This meant taking Arkansas and Louisiana, both of which had fairly small populations that had sent many fighting men into the Southern armies in eastern areas. Morton called for a quick strike by a superior Union force, taking the river with a large army and holding it with gunboats. The Emancipation Proclamation played an essential part in his plan, as it would be used to make the "conquest thorough and complete" by freeing the slaves in every conquered area.[35]

The governor confidently assured Lincoln that "All this can be done in less than ninety days with an army of less than one hundred thousand men." He predicted that implementing his plan would isolate Texas and drive that state back into the Union. And the "complete emancipation which could and should be made of all the slaves in Arkansas, Louisiana, and Texas" would bring those states under Union control in a very different way. Freeing the slaves opened the door to new possibilities for readmitting the states to the Union and would also deny their labor and economic production to the rebels. Indeed, Morton's plan would not only secure the midwestern states in their loyalty to the Union, it would also win the war. The Lincoln administration agreed that recapturing the Mississippi was an essential component of achieving victory. But it was easier said than done. Morton's plan did not provide detailed strategies for the campaign, but the military already had such operations in the works. It would take General Ulysses S. Grant longer than ninety days, but he eventually reopened the Mississippi River and achieved much of what Morton had hoped such success would accomplish. But Grant's victory at Vicksburg, which finally completed the retaking of the vital river, did not come until the summer of 1863, and Morton had to deal with the Democrats sooner than that.[36]

Governor versus Legislature, 1863

The governor's military suggestions stemmed from his fears about what the Democrats would do after winning the 1862 elections. He believed that the new majority in the legislature would do their best to rein in his power and take away his control over the state's military effort. His fears were confirmed when the legislative session opened in January 1863, as the Democrats moved to do just what Morton feared they would do. Many of the new members unabashedly called for peace and letting the South go. Others pushed for secession and the creation of the Northwestern Confederacy. Some of the Democrats openly expressed violent threats against Morton, predicting that he would be murdered by members of the Knights of the Golden Circle, a secret society opposed to the war. The Democratic majority confidently said that they would take the state's military efforts, including the arsenal, away from Morton and give Democratic officials control of them.

The Democrats also hoped to elect Thomas Hendricks to the US Senate seat formerly held by Jesse Bright. Morton had appointed Joseph Wright to fill the vacancy created by Bright's expulsion until the legislature could elect a replacement. That was expected to occur early in the session, but the term would expire and a full-term senator be elected as well. The Democrats soon chose David Turpie to serve for about a month before they went ahead and elected Hendricks over the objections of the Republicans. The minority in the legislature argued that they could not elect a man who was not fully supportive of the war effort, and they pointed to Hendricks's speeches about the Northwestern Confederacy as evidence that he could not be trusted. But elections had consequences, and the Democrats used their majority to put their man in the US Senate.

Morton prepared his message to the legislature and sent it to the Indiana house of representatives. In it he summarized the activities of the government over the past two years and also defended the Republicans' conduct of the war. In strong nationalist terms, he denounced those who wanted to gain peace by simply letting the South go: "Peace, temporary and hollow, might be had upon such terms, but not a restoration of the Union. It would be a dishonorable and shameful surrender, forever tarnishing the character of the nation." He also dismissed the idea that Indiana should separate itself from New England and said that if high tariffs were the problem, then the other states should repeal them. After all, the New England states were outnumbered in the Union and in Congress. He argued that Democrats criticized New England because of that region's political principles, which were dominated by the radical Republicans. The governor rejected the idea that those who held offensive or extreme views should be turned out and declared that the real reason that the Democrats wanted to be rid of New England was a "desire to construct a republic in which they can hold the power. Such a project would be criminal to the last degree, if it were not insane."[37]

The partisan politician then attacked partisanship: "The fortunes of party are variable. The party in power today is cast down tomorrow." Morton thought that the business of building a republic and "taking in such states as are favorable and turning out such as are not, presents the last stage of partisan insanity. It would be forming the republic for the party, and not the party for the republic." He was sure that "a government founded upon such ignoble purposes could not stand, and would not deserve to." Once again turning to the rhetoric of unity and the idea of the Union Party, Morton believed most Northern men were loyal and called upon all sides to unite in "the great cause of preserving our national honor and existence." Hoping for the best, he expressed confidence that the new legislature would protect and preserve the Union.[38]

Despite Morton's rhetoric, the legislature refused to receive his message and instead substituted the message of New York governor Horatio Seymour, a newly elected Democrat and critic of the Republican war effort who had especially railed against the Emancipation Proclamation in his address. Amid the wrangling and technical complications involved in rejecting their own governor's message and adopting one given by the executive of another state, the Democrats also elected Turpie and Hendricks to the Senate, even though the Republicans bolted the session to deny the majority a quorum. Because most Hoosiers did not agree with those Republicans who thought Hendricks a traitor, the bolt was widely criticized. It also marked a clear return to partisanship, as it renewed the old tactic of running away to deny the majority party the power to elect the man that they wanted even though they obviously had the right to do so. Instead of living up to the rhetoric of the Union Party movement, the Republicans bolted and returned Indiana politics to the bitter partisanship of the 1850s. The Democrats held strong, the Republicans eventually returned, and the majority sent their own men to Washington. Having flexed their muscles in rejecting the governor's message and the Senate election, the Democrats now turned to attacking Morton directly. Desperate to stop him, they looked for whatever means they could to curb his power.

During the campaign of 1862, there had been talk about Morton misusing public funds. The Democrats held that the governor was corrupt and would use his power to avoid an investigation. Eager to head them off, Morton had one of his close friends in the state senate, Thomas M. Browne, introduce a resolution calling for an investigation and accounting of all public expenditures. Surprised but sure that this was just a bluff, the Democrats responded by requesting that the governor give them a financial statement accounting for the military contingency funds that had been voted for in the special session in 1861. Morton responded the next day and gave them a full account, proving that there was no fraud in his use of those funds.

The Democrats kept up the pressure by asking to examine the books for the quartermaster's department, the state arsenal, and other funds. Rather than resist, the governor and his Republican allies insisted on a full investigation. After several weeks of study, the Democrats found about $800 that could not be accounted for, and they cried out against corruption, asking, "In whose pocket was this money, by what authority and for what purpose?" The governor's private secretary, Will Holloway, responded to the charges, showing that the money had been deposited in a bank account and was being sent to the state treasury. Not satisfied, the Democrats on the senate finance committee charged that the governor had paid for some items out of the military account that should have been paid for out of the contingency fund. They argued that $25,000 supposedly used for equipping the troops had been taken from the wrong fund and that this was evidence that Morton had pocketed the money. In fact, the mistake had been made by the state auditor, and Morton had nothing to do with it. When the finance committee investigators brought the charges forward, not even the Democrats in the legislature were convinced, and the mistake was noted as such. The investigation of the arsenal fund revealed that Morton's creation had earned a good profit.[39]

Fears of corruption, always a potent political issue, became even more pronounced in the war years. Charges of wrongdoing and profiteering took on new meaning as the expansion of government stirred worries about power being abused. Republicans offered easy targets as they worked closely with business in order to fight the war. Fraud and criminal behavior served as symbols for the expression of other fears, ranging from the centralization of power to capitalism to conspiracy theories about secret cabals trying to destroy liberty or the country as a whole. In Indiana the Democrats rushed to attack Morton, sure that they would find corruption on the part of the governor. Confident that they would implicate him, the Democrats insisted on being allowed to go to New York to investigate his expenditures in buying arms. Morton agreed and funded the trip for the committee. They found nothing wrong and ended up proving that Morton was honest in his use of public money.[40]

Disappointed that their political enemy had not been guilty of financial crimes, the Democrats now took up attacks on other fronts. Acting under the order of the president, who authorized such policies, the military had arrested many Hoosier citizens suspected of providing aid and comfort to the rebels or of discouraging enlistments or resisting the draft. Because of the suspension of habeas corpus, those arrested were held indefinitely without trial. The Democrats had railed against the Republican attacks on civil rights and liberties during the campaign in 1862. Now they formed a legislative committee to investigate the arbitrary arrests and pin them on the governor. Morton had said nothing publicly about the arrests, and this enraged the Jacksonian defenders of liberty, who claimed that he should have helped the citizens and secured their rights in the face of encroaching national power. They criticized Morton because "he has seen fit to pursue a very arbitrary and self-opinionated course in regard to the arrests made in Indiana. He has kept his lips sealed!" The Democrats also blamed Morton for throwing Hoosiers in jail, saying, "Not one intelligent man, woman or child in the state doubts that he has been the sole cause of every arrest that has been made—at all events, that he could have prevented every one of them."[41]

The Republicans responded that those who opposed the arrests and complained about the suspension of habeas corpus should be more patriotic. Morton maintained his silence, knowing that there was no evidence that he had been behind the arrests. To be sure, he probably thought that many of them were necessary, as he despised those who obstructed the draft and thought that those who protested against the war were rebel sympathizers. And he worked closely with the military authorities in the region and had plenty of opportunity to be involved in the investigations and arrests of those citizens suspected of undermining the Union cause.

General Horatio Wright, commander of the Department of the Ohio, which included all of the troops in Illinois, Indiana, and Ohio, readily gave the governor whatever information he wanted. Another commander, Henry B. Carrington, arrived in 1862 to work with Morton in getting draftees ready to fight. Carrington, a native of Connecticut, had taught school before moving to Ohio to practice law with that state's future Civil War governor, William Dennison. Carrington, an abolitionist who had served as the Buckeye State's adjutant general in the early months of the war, took charge of Indiana's intelligence operation in 1862, and he worked closely with Morton to investigate the Knights of the Golden Circle and other secret Copperhead organizations. Both men did their duty, although sometimes that meant violating rights and liberties if it seemed necessary to do so to preserve the Union. But their enemies cried out against them. The fact that Carrington often insisted on civil trials and hoped to preserve the rights and liberties of citizens was conveniently overlooked and later forgotten. Morton also worried about the bounds of the law and tried to preserve civil liberties in some cases. But he was often more willing to trample on constitutional rights than the army officers were. Early in 1863, however, most of that was yet to come, and the Democrats claimed that Morton's cooperation with Carrington served as further evidence of his abuse of power.[42]

At the outset of the 1863 legislative session, the Democratic majority moved to take control of the state's military operations. This would curb the governor's power and give them more options for resistance as the war continued. Rumors about the creation of a state military board to take away the governor's authority had been circulating since the election, and finally, on February 17, the Democrats introduced their military bill. Sure enough, the legislation called for a four-man military board to administer Indiana's military efforts. The board was to consist of four state officers—the treasurer, secretary of state, auditor, and attorney general. As Morton remembered it in an 1870 speech, these men would do what the governor had been doing, including "the appointment of all officers in the militia," and "that they should have command of the militia." The board would also "have the custody of the arms and munitions of war, thus placing the whole military power of the state in the hands of those four state officers." Of course Morton disagreed, arguing that "the command of the militia belonged to the Governor, as it does in every state, necessarily and properly, as part of the executive power." The Democrats also called for the dissolution of the Indiana Legion, the military force that Morton had raised for the defense of the state and which was then guarding the southern counties along the Ohio River against "the incursion of the guerrillas from Kentucky." In Morton's view, "the bill was unconstitutional in every particular, it was simply revolution in the form of a legislative act."[43]

The Democrats actually tried to make the bill constitutional through a technicality. They held that the governor would still formally commission the officers appointed by the board and argued that the constitution indicated that the militia was to be organized in the manner provided by law. The existing law placed too much power in the hands of one man, they said, and their new law would still provide for the militia while dividing and sharing the power among four elected officers instead of one. Morton thought that the bill was designed "to take the state bodily into the rebellion, or, if that could not be done, to make her neutral, so as to furnish no aid to the government." Determined to stop the bill, the governor encouraged his fellow Republicans in the legislature to bolt the session to deny the majority the quorum they needed to pass the new law. The Republicans quietly left Indianapolis by train and went to Madison, making it more difficult for the Democratic leadership to force them back into session. The bolters succeeded in defeating the military bill and the legislative session came to an end on March 8, 1863. But the Democrats remained confident of their ultimate victory because they had not passed an appropriations bill. Without money, Morton could not hope to govern the state, and he would be forced to call the legislature back for a special session to pass a funding bill. When they convened, the Democrats planned to push through their military bill. Morton and his party had won for the moment, but they would soon fall to the Democracy. Or so the Democrats thought.[44]

The Dictator of Indiana

Instead, Morton refused to call the legislature back. Not only did he not convene a special session, he did not call the legislature back until 1865. For nearly twenty-two months he ran the state himself. The Democrats frothed and fumed, criticized and complained, taunted and threatened, hoping to force the governor to call the legislature back into session. Republicans mostly supported his actions and rallied to help him accomplish his plans whenever possible. To fund his one-man rule, Morton demonstrated his great influence and personal reputation as well as his ingenuity as an executive leader. He broke the law by taking directly the large payment due to the state arsenal from the national government. Instead of being disbursed to the Indiana state treasury as prescribed by law, the money was paid to him personally on one of his visits to Washington. The state embezzlement act said that any state officer who took public money for his own use or loaned, deposited, or exchanged it contrary to law was guilty of a felony. But the legislature had never officially authorized the state arsenal because the Democrats did not want to give the governor control of it. Now they regretted their decision, as Morton argued that the arsenal was not actually state property and this allowed the federal authorities to pay the money to him. The arsenal funds helped, but they were not nearly enough to cover the budget for the entire state government, so Morton also borrowed money from county governments. Many Republicans at the local level agreed to this scheme and sent amounts varying between $2,000 and $20,000. Private businesses and citizens also contributed, including a group of one hundred Wayne County residents who borrowed $20,000 and sent it to Morton, while the Terre Haute and Richmond Railroad loaned him $15,000 to help run the government.[45]

The governor also borrowed money from various banks, and when he needed funds to pay the interest on the state debt and to provide for the soldiers and their families, he made a secret trip to Washington to ask the Lincoln administration for assistance. He met with the president, who wanted to help but said that, "I know of no law under which I can give you the money." Lincoln sent Morton to Secretary of War Stanton, a man much like the governor himself. Abrupt, touchy, and quick-tempered, Stanton also returned loyalty to those who gave it and respected those who demonstrated competence. Although Morton had peppered him with so many messages as to be an annoyance and Stanton had first refused to see him during a visit to the capital early in the war, the governor had won his trust. When the secretary refused to listen to him during that initial visit, Morton had refused to leave until he did. Stanton in the interim learned that he could count on Morton, and now the Hoosier politician was counting on him. Morton told the secretary what he needed and repeated what Lincoln had told him about knowing of no law that would allow the national government to help him. Stanton listened and replied, "By God, I will find a law!" And he did, using an appropriation given to the president for organizing and supplying arms to loyal citizens in states threatened by the rebellion. Deciding that the rebellion now threatened Indiana, Stanton saw to it that Morton received $250,000 from the War Department for the military operations of the state. Although he might have used the money to pay the interest on the debt, Morton instead went to New York and met with J. F. D. Lanier, an Indiana native and head of the Winslow, Lanier & Co. bank. The firm already administered Indiana's finances in New York, and Lanier had loaned Morton $400,000 to arm and equip new recruits. The governor had repaid that loan, proving himself creditworthy. Now he asked Lanier to loan him the money to pay the interest on the debt, and Lanier agreed.[46]

The Democrats fought back, but they ended up hurting their own cause. They said that not calling a special session would result in default and that this was illegal under state law. They hoped to use repudiation of the debt to force Morton to call the legislature back. Although previous administrations of Democratic governors had borrowed money to pay the interest on the debt, the Democrats now argued that such methods were illegal. Suit was filed and cases were heard by the Democrat-controlled Indiana Supreme Court, which held that nonpayment of the interest would dishonor the state. The court ruled that state officers must not assume doubtful powers. The decisions issued by the court urged a special legislative session.

But Morton ignored them, arguing that the Democrats were playing politics with the law and trying to force him into surrendering his authority. When he successfully borrowed the money to make the interest payment, John C. Walker, the state's New York agent, joined the Democratic repudiators. A Southern sympathizer who only reluctantly supported the Union cause, Walker hated Morton, who had gotten him kicked out of the army for insubordination. Seeing an opportunity for revenge, the agent now refused J. F. D. Lanier's request for a list of genuine holders of state bonds. The banker asked for the list because there had been some fraudulent bonds sold, and he wanted to be sure about the particulars when he paid the interest due by July 1, 1863. When Walker refused to provide the list, Lanier offered to allow the agent to pay the interest, using the bank's checks. Again, Walker refused, and the state defaulted on its debt.

While the Democrats had praised and defended Walker, hoping that his actions would help destroy Morton, the incident ultimately damaged them instead. There was widespread disgust at Walker's refusal to cooperate. Although the state bonds did suffer a loss in value, the public notification for the reason for default offset the financial setback, and Indiana's credit remained strong. It took some time, but Morton found another copy of the list of bondholders, and the New York bank paid the interest that had been due on July 1. The bank also paid the amount due on January 1, 1864. In explaining the situation to Stanton and requesting that he be allowed to use the War Department funds for other expenditures, Morton reported that "the credit of the state and of my administration has been saved by providing the money in New York with which to pay the interest, and the disgrace must rest upon a weak copperhead officer and his wicked advisers."[47]

The governor took great care to account for the money that he obtained and spent during his period of one-man rule. He knew that eventually there would be calls for a full investigation of his handling of those funds. His caution paid off, and by December of 1864 he could tell Stanton that he was ready to return more than $100,000 of the money that the War Department had provided. When the secretary of war said that the money should be charged to the state and assumed as part of Indiana's debt, the governor and the Republicans in the legislature refused. Morton insisted that the money had not been given to him to be put into the state treasury and that he legally could not allow it to be assumed as debt. So he repaid the balance of the money he still had on hand. Democratic charges of corruption came up empty in the light of investigations, and seizing the opportunity, Morton turned the tables by accusing his opponents of financial misdeeds. In February 1864 he accused the state auditor and state treasurer, both Democrats, of misconduct. The governor pointed out that while the two men had supported Walker in his refusal to pay the interest on the debt, when the default lowered the price they used state money to buy bonds for themselves.[48]

Having secured the money for governing alone, Morton continued to run the state from his office. He virtually became a state dictator during this period, and while the Democrats gnashed their teeth and raged against him, they were powerless to stop him. They cried out against his abuse of power, accused him of corruption, and charged him with trampling on the rights and liberties of the people. But he responded by redefining patriotism to mean loyalty to himself and his party. He exercised his power as he saw fit, and when there were complaints, he declared that those who criticized him were traitorous Copperheads who supported the rebellion. Supported by the Lincoln administration and the majority of Indiana Republicans, the governor outwitted and outmaneuvered the Democrats who had thought that 1863 would bring about the end of Oliver Morton's power. Instead of curbing his authority, the Democratic efforts failed and ended up leaving him in complete control of the state government.

BATTLING WITH BURNSIDE OVER FREE SPEECH

Ironically, civil liberties combined with personal loyalty and caused Morton to break with the US Army authorities and defend state's rights later that spring of 1863. In late March the War Department replaced General Wright as the commander of the Department of the Ohio with an Indiana native, General Ambrose Burnside. The new commander had performed poorly at the Battle of Antietam, and then, having reluctantly agreed to take command of the Army of the Potomac, he led his army to disaster at the Battle of Fredericksburg in December of 1862. Now widely reviled, he came back to the Midwest, where resistance to the draft had escalated when Congress authorized national conscription in March of 1863. The new law angered Democrats even more than the state draft had because it provided for substitution, allowing a draftee

Fig. 19. Union general Ambrose Burnside, 1863. (Library of Congress)

to provide an actual substitute to take his place or to pay $300 to commute his conscription. This led to cries of "rich man's war, poor man's fight," and antidraft violence became common across the state. Eager to put down such opposition and to help redeem himself by helping defeat the South, Burnside immediately butted heads with Governor Morton.[49]

Ordered to raise troops to repel any Confederate invasion of Kentucky, Burnside began figuring out how many men he had in the department, including in Indiana. Morton's secretary, Will Holloway, dutifully informed the general of the troop strength and informed the governor of the request. Morton, busy on a trip to the East, quickly sent word back to General Carrington telling him to not allow any troops to be taken from Indiana because all of them were needed to defend the state. But this was only the beginning of friction between the governor and the general. Burnside soon issued his infamous General Order No. 38, which called for military punishment of anyone who expressed opposition to the national government and sympathy for the rebels. The order included the statement that military force would be used to regulate both speech and publication, a clear violation of the First Amendment.

Morton did not speak out against the order but tried unsuccessfully to arrange a meeting with Burnside to discuss the situation. In late April General Carrington reported to Burnside on a series of violent altercations in Brown and Hendricks Counties that expressed alarm over the growing protests against the war and the draft in particular. Burnside dismissed the report as panic and showed that he did not recognize the relationship that Carrington had with Morton when he advised his subordinate to consult the governor. Convinced that Carrington had won his place only through political connections, Burnside relieved him of command and replaced him with General Milo S. Hascall. This left Morton terribly upset, and he exchanged telegrams with Burnside, telling the general that he had just learned about Carrington's removal and that "it is a blow to the Union cause in Indiana in my judgement. Will occasion great dissatisfaction among Union men and rejoicing among the rebels. Look well to your advisers in this matter, my dear General. They are misleading you." The governor organized a campaign to keep Carrington in the Hoosier State, but the officer was sent to Cleveland, Ohio, and Hascall set to work causing trouble in Indiana.[50]

The new military commander in the state was a native of New York who had lived in Indiana since the late 1840s. An attorney, businessman, and staunch Republican before the war, Hascall had the West Point credentials to win a commission as a colonel of an Indiana regiment. Promoted to general in the spring of 1862, he served at the Battle of Shiloh and helped block the Confederate invasion of Kentucky. General Rosecrans sent him to capture deserters

Fig. 20. Governor Oliver P. Morton. (Library of Congress)

in the winter of 1863, and he was headquartered in Indianapolis that spring. On the surface, then, he seemed a likely candidate to win Morton's trust and become a close ally.[51]

But the governor resented the fact that Hascall had been appointed to replace Carrington and that Burnside had failed to consult him on the matter before doing it. Morton had trusted Carrington, who had organized a spy network across the state, but Hascall knew nothing about that operation. In fact, he ignored the governor's staff's suggestions that he investigate the secret groups of Copperheads. Then the new commander quickly obeyed Burnside's orders and sent troops from Indiana to the front, ignoring Morton's objections that it would leave the state vulnerable.[52]

The governor gave the general the cold shoulder, and the cooperation between the army and the state government was temporarily interrupted. When Hascall decided to enforce General Order No. 38 and prepared to send troops to crush opposition in Brown County, Morton intervened. He persuaded Hascall and Burnside not to send soldiers, getting them to agree instead to sending a bipartisan committee to investigate the situation. Meanwhile, the governor continued to push for Carrington's return to Indiana. He delayed a planned trip to Washington because he did not trust Hascall and did not want to leave the state under his command even for a brief time.[53]

Then, Hascall issued his own General Order No. 9, which supplemented Burnside's General Order No. 38 and made it specific to Indiana. He proclaimed that he had evidence of violations of the order being carried out across the state and that he would hold newspapers and stump speakers "to the most rigid accountability." Anyone who spoke out against the draft or criticized the government's policies "will be considered as having violated the order," and he spoke of such speech as being "implied treason." The general said, "The country will have to be saved or lost during the time this Administration remains in power, and therefore he who is factiously and actively opposed to the war policy of the Administration, is as much opposed to his Government."[54]

Thus, General Hascall implemented in Indiana the Republican definition of patriotism: one was either for or against the United States; one either supported the Lincoln administration or one was a rebel. Burnside enthusiastically supported Hascall's order and encouraged him to enforce it. The state commander did just that, arresting Democratic newspaper editors, including those who spoke out against the General Order No. 9. In some instances, armed crowds gathered and prevented the soldiers from arresting editors, while other newspapermen were carried off to jail or forced to suspend publication. Meanwhile, Burnside's General Order No. 38 brought similar arrests across the entire department. In response, Democrats protested and the Union League came out to fight them. The most famous seizure was the arrest of Clement L. Vallandigham, an Ohio Copperhead who had served in Congress the previous year. The Buckeye Democrat had criticized the president and the Republicans repeatedly while serving in the House of Representatives, and his rhetoric encouraged those who resisted the government across the North. After Ambrose Burnside led the Army of the Potomac to its disastrous defeat at Fredericksburg in December 1862, Vallandigham blasted the administration and its war effort in a blistering speech in Congress. Having lost his seat in the previous election, the Ohio Copperhead continued his opposition to the war and to the Republicans as a private citizen. He defied Burnside's order with another speech early in May 1863 and was promptly arrested, setting off a storm of protest across Ohio.[55]

Within a few days the army also arrested Indiana state senator Alexander J. Douglas in Ohio. Douglas had given a speech in the Buckeye State on May 7, 1863, in which he criticized the Lincoln administration and its policies. He returned to Indiana, but when he went back to Ohio for a family wedding, he was apprehended. The arrests of leading Copperheads set off widespread protests across the Midwest, and it seemed like a full-scale insurrection might well ensue.[56]

The Battle of Pogue's Run

Alarmed by such incidents, Democrats across the region, including Indiana, voiced their opposition to the new policies and promised to take whatever action was needed to defend their rights. When the Hoosier Democracy held a meeting in Indianapolis on May 20, 1863, they featured many prominent speakers and drew a large audience of Jacksonians, who expected fiery rhetoric and criticism of the government's policies. Many came prepared to take violent action by bringing along their pistols. Governor Morton conveniently left town for one of his frequent trips to consult with the federal authorities in Washington. but General Hascall remained in the city. He posted soldiers and artillery at strategic points around the Democratic meeting, and the troops kept a close eye on the proceedings. While a few speakers railed against the administration, most were intimidated and moderated their speech accordingly. Even newly elected US senator Thomas A. Hendricks was threatened by Hascall and his men. When the Democrats boarded trains to leave Indianapolis, many of them were carrying pistols, and some chose to fire shots out the windows in protest of the military intimidation. General Hascall responded by stopping the trains. On the Indiana Central route, he had a cannon placed on the tracks and ordered his soldiers to accompany a policeman in searching the passenger cars and demanding the surrender of all weapons. The train heading to Cincinnati was also searched, and many Democrats threw their revolvers out the windows into the creek that ran alongside the tracks just where they had been stopped. This altercation became known as the Battle of Pogue's Run, which ended with Hascall's men confiscating about five hundred pistols from the several trains that were stopped. The so-called peace and pistol democracy had been intimidated and forced to back down from their promises to defend liberty.[57]

In this context, Indiana congressman Joseph K. Edgerton, a Democrat from Fort Wayne, decided to confront General Hascall. The two exchanged letters in the partisan papers, with Edgerton asking the general to clarify what he meant in his General Order No. 9. Hascall replied that he defined the government's war policy to include the Emancipation Proclamation, the war tax, conscription, and the confiscation of rebel property. He contended that those laws had been deliberated and debated and passed by the Congress and signed by the president. He admitted that they possibly were "not the wisest and best that could have been enacted," but he refused to allow criticism of them. They had been passed and were the law. Anyone who spoke against them was aiding and abetting the rebellion. Edgerton responded by denouncing Hascall's policy and said that it did not deserve respect or obedience. He also asked the general, "Where is Governor Morton, the constitutional civil Governor of Indiana, that he does not at once speak and rebuke your claim to exercise authority and do acts, that you cannot exercise or do, without a clear violation of the Constitution and laws of the State of Indiana, and of the United States, and without degrading him to a mere cipher and pageant in the State?" Once again, the Democrats accused Morton of complicity by silence.[58]

Although he remained silent publicly, the governor thought that Burnside and Hascall were reinvigorating the antiwar movement. Far from crushing dissent, they and their harsh policies were actually helping it to spread. Morton responded to Douglas's arrest by intervening on behalf of the state senator with the Lincoln administration. The governor then contacted General Burnside and told him that the president disagreed with the arrest, and the commander saw to it that Douglas was found not guilty and released. In this case, Morton defended civil liberties against the army and defused a volatile situation that threatened to spark the kind of uprising for which the Copperheads had been hoping and planning.[59]

But he also outmaneuvered Burnside politically. When the governor met with Hascall on May 15, the general reported to Burnside on the conversation. Morton had insisted that General Order No. 38 was not practical and he did not think that it could be enforced. Saying that the orders had accomplished nothing but political trouble, the governor had denounced the arrest of Vallandigham and argued that citizens could not be tried by military tribunals. Hascall admitted to Burnside that he was embarrassed by the situation and told the general that "the trouble seems to be that you issued order 38 without consulting him and removed Genl Carrington in a similar manner. He [doesn't] seem to find so much fault with either act as he does the fact that *he* was not *consulted*." The state commander remembered Morton's campaign against Buell and warned Burnside to be careful: "General Buell, incurred his displeasure in a similar manner when he first took command of the Dept and the Govr never ceased in his exertions against him till he was removed. . . . I have considered it important to you to know. Forewarned is forearmed."[60]

But it was too late. Morton told Indianapolis banker Calvin Fletcher that he planned to have both Hascall and Burnside removed, and he began to bring pressure against them, organizing a full-scale campaign for their removal. He gathered support from across the state and also among friends of the president like US Supreme Court justice David Davis, who had served on the federal court in Indianapolis. Morton made several trips to Washington that spring, urging the administration to remove Burnside and Hascall. And he leaked his opposition to them to the Democratic paper, the *Indiana Sentinel*, ending his silence on the violation of civil liberties. Soon the Lincoln administration was admonishing Burnside to take caution in exercising his military power so as "not to excite the apprehensions of the State Executives who are loyal and diligent in maintaining the authority of the Government." Secretary of War Stanton related that the president wanted to keep a "good understanding" with governors like Morton and hoped to leave the governance of the states to those elected officials who knew the people and the situation on the ground.[61]

Meanwhile, Burnside had sent troops to shut down the *Chicago Times,* the leading Democratic organ in that city and the voice of antiwar and antigovernment sentiment. This led to unrest, as crowds gathered to protest the general's action and petitions were sent to Lincoln calling for the paper to be reopened. The president relented, embarrassing Burnside. When Republicans in Illinois howled that the *Times* should remain closed, Lincoln changed his mind and further embarrassed the department commander, who had allowed publication to resume but now had to close the newspaper again. Stanton also urged Burnside to replace Hascall, and on June 5 the general telegraphed the state commander telling him that he had reorganized the department to include Michigan and that General Orlando B. Willcox would take over in Indiana. When Willcox arrived on June 8, Hascall revoked General Order No. 9 and left Indiana. Under his brief command, at least ten Indiana newspapers had been sanctioned by the military. Other Democratic editors had been intimidated, and for a brief time they moderated their criticism of the government. But they soon resumed their attacks on the Republicans, and the suppression of the papers seemed to energize them, giving them another motivation in the struggle.[62]

Hascall's removal, then, could be seen as a victory not only for the freedom of speech but also for the Union cause. His actions had actually made the situation worse instead of better. If he had stayed, things likely would have gotten worse still, since he promised that he would make more arbitrary arrests. Morton's opposition proved to be the key factor in the decision to relieve Hascall of his command. But Morton did not really mind the violation of rights so much as he disliked the way that they had been violated. In reality, the governor never actually opposed the suppression of the press. In 1862 he had complained to Secretary of War Stanton about "the insidious and vituperative attacks" from

Democratic newspapers like the *Chicago Times* and the *Indiana Sentinel.* The governor thought that "their continued apologies for Confederate crimes" and continual attacks on both his and Lincoln's administrations deserved punishment. So he did not necessarily mind suppressing the freedom of speech by closing down opposition publishers. And his administration had suggested that Copperhead speakers should be arrested, including Lambdin P. Milligan, a Democratic attorney and congressional candidate who had criticized the Lincoln administration in the summer of 1862.[63]

But Hascall's removal was not about free speech, it was about Morton's power struggle with Burnside. When he argued that General Order No. 38 and No. 9 were illegal, Morton said that they were infringements upon state authority. He supported other violations of civil liberty, including suppression of free speech and arbitrary arrests. But he wanted to be involved in such actions, and Burnside's style made the governor jealous, and he asserted state's rights to defend his own power. Thus, on June 11, 1863, he issued a proclamation restating the national laws authorizing the arrest and punishment of those who resisted the draft and conspired against the government. Morton was no great defender of free speech; instead he was involved in a fight with the army commander of the Department of the Ohio for control of the state.[64]

While he managed to get rid of Hascall, Morton failed to achieve complete victory in his power struggle with the military authorities in 1863. Burnside remained at his post and refused to return Carrington to Indiana. And he took troops out of Indiana and sent them where he thought they were needed, leaving Morton to complain about the inadequate defense of the state. The governor tried to remove Willcox and replace him with another commander more to his liking, but he failed in that attempt as well. The 1863 conflict over free speech and state's rights versus federal authority should not be seen as mere opportunism or ambition on Morton's part. Nor should it be seen as a contradiction of his nationalist ideology. Rather, the events fit the pattern of his thinking about freedom, Union, and power exercised by his party. For Morton, freedom under the law did not give citizens license to incite rebellion with their public speech and publications. Saving the Union required extreme measures, and that might include the suppression of free speech.[65]

At the same time, the Union was a federal system, and Morton hoped that cooperation between state and national authorities might be the standard mode of operations. When Generals Wright and Carrington were in charge, the governor worked closely with them, and he found the situation to his liking. But when Burnside and Hascall took over, they failed to recognize the governor's role in the fight against treason on the home front. Surely, personality and style played a part in the conflict between Morton and Burnside. It was personal as well as political. Morton's defense of state's rights was not meant to champion individual liberty, nor was it an inconsistent break with his nationalist thinking. In fact, he thought that if the military were to be given orders to arrest civilians, the command had to come from "the highest authority," the president. Here again was his nationalist view of power wielded by his own party. The problem was not that Burnside arrested civilians. It was that he did so on his own initiative without consulting Morton and without being ordered to do so by Lincoln.[66]

Morgan's Raid

Meanwhile, the governor continued to argue that Indiana was vulnerable to attack and that the state needed more troops to prevent an invasion. With casualties mounting, the army needed more men on the front. This meant that the War Department and the Lincoln administration did not think such personnel could be spared to fend off the attacks about which Morton worried. But his argument that the state needed more men for its own defense gained credence in July of 1863, when Confederate general John Hunt Morgan led a cavalry force across the Ohio River and brought the war to Indiana soil. While Morgan's Raid became a footnote in the Civil War thanks to the Union victory at Gettysburg on July 1–3 and the fall of Vicksburg on July 4, the invasion of Indiana and Ohio by Confederate forces demonstrated Morton's skills as an executive and mattered a great deal in the Hoosier State.[67]

When General Burnside gathered troops in Kentucky, the Confederates believed that he would join other Union forces in an invasion of Tennessee. General Braxton Bragg feared that the Union armies would attack him and prevent his move to Chattanooga, where he hoped to defend that important rail junction. To cover his march, Bragg ordered Morgan to take his cavalry on a raid through Kentucky that would divert Burnside and keep him in the Bluegrass State. Morgan went beyond the scope of his orders to confine his attacks to Kentucky, when he decided to cross the Ohio and raid Indiana and Ohio. He hoped that his raid would divert Union troops and demoralize the citizenry of the Lower Midwest. Copperheads in the region had promised an uprising, and if Morgan achieved success, the fifth column might appear in the Union rear. With these plans and hopes in mind, Morgan crossed the river on the second of July with between 2,000 and 2,500 cavalrymen under his command.[68]

Burnside had taken most of the troops raised in Indiana and forwarded them to Kentucky, and the state militia had been depleted by the draft. There were few cavalry units in the state to counter Morgan's fast-moving raiders.

When reports of the raiders moving through Kentucky reached Indianapolis, Morton urged his commanders to intercept Morgan and arrest him and his men. Without the military forces needed to fight the Confederates, such ideas proved impossible to carry out, but the governor thought that the army officers in Kentucky should have done a better job of catching Morgan before he reached the Ohio. When the Southern raiders crossed into Indiana, Morton responded to the crisis with his trademark energy and determination. He called for the citizens of the state to rally to her defense, and within forty-eight hours some 65,000 men gathered to chase the Confederate cavalry.[69]

About 20,000 of these men came to Indianapolis. Untrained, many unarmed, without mounts, the volunteers were organized into infantry companies for the defense of the capital. Rumors abounded, and many feared that Morgan planned to ride to Indianapolis to raise a Copperhead army, free the prisoners at Camp Morton, and take Indiana out of the Union. Reports exaggerated the size of the Confederate force, with estimations of 4,000 to 6,000, often more than doubling the actual size of Morgan's command. Indiana's adjutant general, W. H. H. Terrell, reported that the citizenry responded to the governor's call with "such a display of patriotic energy and devotion as may safely challenge a comparison with any similar exhibition in history." And the overwhelming response was bipartisan, as Democrats and Republicans set aside their differences to rush to the defense of the state. The Copperhead uprising did not materialize, but a Union militia did.[70]

Morgan and his men seemed more interested in stealing horses and robbing businesses than they did in military objectives. They stole cash and food and burned bridges and barns, tore up railroad lines, and drove off the militia who did manage to find and confront them. Small battles, skirmishes really, smacked more of robbery than of true military engagements. Along the way, Morgan tapped the telegraph wires to learn about his pursuit. Just south of Seymour, he turned eastward and eventually crossed into Ohio on July 13, having spent about four days in the Hoosier State. There, in Ohio, he continued his raid as larger Union forces gathered. Unable to get back across the river, Morgan and most of his men were captured and sent to prison. In Indiana, the raid briefly renewed the spirit of the Union Party movement, and Morton tried to capitalize on the situation by calling for the patriotic volunteers to be organized into a permanent part of the state militia. But partisanship quickly returned, as the Democrats and Republicans argued over who should be praised and credited for the patriotic reaction to the invasion of Indiana. The Republicans made Morton the hero, arguing that his timely leadership and appeals to the citizenry led to such an effective response that Morgan had to change his plans and go east instead of continuing on to Indianapolis. Democrats disagreed, arguing that Morton actually instigated the raid by constantly reporting that there were so many Copperheads in Indiana. The governor's critics said that such false charges led the Confederates to believe that they could inspire a disloyal uprising with the raid. The raid resulted in extensive property damage and thousands of stolen horses, as well as tons of food and supplies being taken. This led to years of legal wrangling, as the law governing the Morgan's Raid claims allowed citizens to apply for compensation for what they had lost in those four days in the summer of 1863.[71]

By that fall, the state seemed safe enough from a Confederate invasion to allow the governor to consider going to Ohio and Pennsylvania to campaign for Republicans in those states. He worried that the Democrats of Indiana were sending large numbers of Irishmen to the Buckeye State to swing the election there by fraud. Military successes at the front reopened the Mississippi River and pushed the Southern forces farther away from Indiana. Guerrilla operations along the Ohio River continued but did not pose a serious threat. The governor was now entrenched in his control of the state, which was militarily secure for the moment, at least. But Morton did not rest easy. How could he? He knew that thousands of traitors lived in Indiana and were plotting against the Union. Although the Confederates had been pushed back, they might well advance again, a concern that seemed especially valid given the way the war had gone thus far. If the Copperheads continued to organize and timed their attacks in coordination with the Confederate military, disaster might well occur. Morton remained vigilant for good reason. How could Indiana be safe and the Union secure if traitors lurked on the home front, plotting to destroy the state and the nation from within?[72]

CHAPTER SIX

Copperheads, Treason, and the Election of 1864

THE QUIET WARMTH of the summer night in 1863 was shattered by the sound of the shot that flew past the governor's head as he left his office at the Indiana State Capitol. Oliver Morton had been working late, as usual, and was ready to head home for a few hours of rest before returning to work early in the morning. But the assassin's shot from the darkness that narrowly missed him sent Morton hurrying to the Bates House hotel, where he awakened General Carrington, who had returned to Indiana in July, to tell him about the at-tempted murder. He urged his trusted friend to investigate and see what was going on under the cover of night. The general agreed to accompany Morton and see him safely home. Carrington, now serving on the governor's personal staff, quickly dressed, and the two men made their way to Morton's house. As they approached the door, the would-be assassin fired a second shot but again missed the mark. Carrington searched the area but could not find the shooter. Morton calmly told the army officer that the Copperheads were trying to kill him: "They want to kill me because I am governor. They can't do it. Indiana will support me, but you must watch those fellows. There must be no risk just now." The next day the governor told Berry Sulgrove, the editor of the *Indianapolis Journal*, about the attempt on his life, but he urged the newspaperman to help him keep the story quiet, as he did not want to worry his wife, Lucinda. Within a few months, however, the public came to know about the plot to kill Morton and much more about the Copperheads and their plans in Indiana.[1]

Governor Morton supported the military's move against the secret societies of Copperheads across the state and arrested the ringleaders in the late summer of 1864. The resulting treason trials in Indianapolis coincided with the election campaign and helped the Republicans win a great victory at the polls, as both Morton and Lincoln were reelected and Republican majorities returned in Congress and in the state legislature. The attempt on the governor's life demonstrated the high stakes of Civil War politics and showed how Morton

Fig. 21. Governor O. P. Morton, carte de visite distributed during the Civil War.

dealt with the Copperheads in opportunistic ways, even as he saw them as a very real threat to the Union and himself.

By 1864 the war seemed endless. The Confederate offensive in the summer of 1863 had resulted in the Northern victory at Gettysburg, coinciding with the surrender of Vicksburg and the reopening of the Mississippi River. While Hoosiers had rushed to defend their state against Morgan's Raid, Union armies continued to advance. By the end of 1863 Confederate general Braxton Bragg had failed to follow up on his victory at Chickamauga, and the federal forces led by Ulysses S. Grant held Chattanooga. Grant's success in the western theater led to Lincoln making him the commander of all Union armies, and the general made his headquarters in the field with General George Meade's Army of the Potomac.

Morton worried about what was to come and feared that the Confederates would surprise the Union with larger numbers of men than expected. He hoped that another call for troops would not be needed because he was afraid it would demoralize the Northern populace. In the spring of 1864 Grant began his offensive against Robert E. Lee's Army of Northern Virginia, and the bloody Overland Campaign that included the Battles of the Wilderness, Spotsylvania, and Cold Harbor ended in the siege of Petersburg. Meanwhile, Union general William Tecumseh Sherman led the campaign to take Atlanta, which was finally achieved in September. That fall, General John Bell Hood took the initiative and led his Confederate army to disaster in Tennessee, while Union general Philip Sheridan undertook his Shenandoah Valley campaign. The long list of Union victories made heroes of military leaders and bolstered support for the government as the election of 1864 approached.[2]

In that context, then, occurred both the reelection of the president and that of Governor Morton. In hindsight, these elections seemed a foregone conclusion, an inevitable result of battlefield victories that secured the Union and won the election for the Republicans. But that result did not seem so clear at the time. In the heat of the summer, as the war raged on and casualties mounted ever higher, it seemed likely that the voters might turn against the Republicans who had led them throughout the long conflict. A military setback at the wrong time might very well turn the election, as many in the North grew weary of the war and feared that the growing numbers of dead and wounded men would never end.

Governor Morton's period of one-man rule continued throughout 1864 and criticism of his executive style and use of power grew as the months rolled by. Talk of curbing his dictatorial authority via the coming election often mingled with threats of violence, as Democrats opposed to the Republican conduct of the war mixed with those who resisted the conflict itself. The lines between legitimate dissent and treason continued to blur, even as Morton himself continued to define patriotism as loyalty to his leadership as well as the Union cause. Loyal Democrats who supported the Union but criticized the Republicans or the governor's conduct needed the support of those Peace Democrats who wanted to let the South go.[3]

COPPERHEADS

In such a context, the Copperheads took advantage of legitimate outrage over abuse of power or the expansion of government at the expense of liberty to promote their own plans to foment rebellion in the North. Even the term *Copperhead* was controversial, as it conjured the image of a poisonous snake in the grass, and some applied it too often and indiscriminately. What the term referred to was Northerners who took their Southern sympathy to the extreme point of carrying out treasonous acts against the United States. In many parts of the Midwest, especially in places like southern Indiana, large portions of the population hailed from the South or claimed Southern ancestry. These so-called Butternuts (a term that originated with the use of butternuts to dye the homespun clothing worn by residents in the Lower Midwest—a technique also used in many Southern states) had often left the South to avoid living in a slave society. But they usually maintained strong ties to and sympathies for the South. Now, with old friends and relatives living in the Confederacy, some of them no doubt felt antagonistic to the government because of the war. But not all Butternuts were Copperheads, and not all Copperheads were Butternuts. Antigovernment activities occurred in the northern part of Indiana as well as the southern regions of the state. Some Copperheads became active because of legitimate concerns about the encroaching power of government and the violation of constitutional rights and civil liberties.

Often dismissed as a myth concocted by Morton and other Union leaders or seen as a few misguided crackpots who really had no support, the Copperheads were hard to identify and difficult to assess. They certainly existed and may well have constituted a real threat to the Union, but judging the Copperheads in the context of the war years required understanding what the governor and other leaders in the government and military understood at the time. To Morton, the Copperheads were a real threat and a dangerous enemy who had to be eradicated. Some men might change their stripes, as Morton informed General Sherman in regard to extending the leave of a soldier who had escaped Copperhead influence to become a "a very active and loyal man." But that was an exception to the Republican executive's general rule that Copperheads, like rebels, had to be crushed. Accused of paranoia, the governor had the memory of a bullet flying close by his head to remind him that he was not paranoid if someone was really out to get him.[4]

To be sure, Morton often worried about the Copperheads and anyone else who disagreed with the Republicans. In August of 1861 the *Indianapolis Journal* printed reports that its crosstown rival, the *Indiana Sentinel,* sympathized with the rebels in its criticism of the Lincoln and Morton administrations. The *Sentinel* denounced the charges against it and also printed Morton's denial of the rumors swirling about that the governor had set up a secret police force to investigate those suspected of being disloyal to the Union cause. He snorted that the story was "a damned lie." Of course, the Democratic paper also indicated that they expected no less, since Morton's "espionage" required secrecy, and it reminded readers that Morton had warned critics of the government "to be cautious" in what they said. Indeed, the *Sentinel* accused the governor of redefining loyalty to the Union to mean fealty to the Republican administrations.[5]

RAILROAD ACCIDENT OR ASSASSINATION ATTEMPT?

In the spring of 1862, Morton traveled to visit Hoosier soldiers in the aftermath of the bloody Battle of Shiloh. He had worked hard to bring men wounded in the conflict home to Indiana and worried about the conditions of those still in the field, so he went to investigate the situation. Adjutant General Lazarus Noble and a physician accompanied him to inspect the troops. Morton had invited Calvin Fletcher to go along, but the banker was overwhelmed with work and suggested that the governor take along his son, Miles, instead. Miles J. Fletcher, an Indiana Asbury University (later DePauw University) professor, had won election to a two-year term as the state superintendent of public instruction in 1860. The school superintendent agreed to take the trip with Morton, a fellow Republican who was friendly with his family and who could help him win reelection that fall.[6]

The governor's party went by train, first going west to Terre Haute. They left there about midnight and headed south toward Vincennes. The governor, adjutant general, doctor, and professor ate some food that Fletcher had in his carpetbag and enjoyed "much merry conversation." After eating, the men lay down to sleep, stretching out on the seats. As the train pulled into Sullivan, Indiana, it hit a freight car parked incorrectly on a switch track so that part of it still remained on the main line. Morton wrote to Calvin Fletcher at two o'clock in the morning on Sunday, May 11, 1862, relating what happened next: "I had but fallen asleep when a heavy jar as if the train had struck some heavy obstruction roused me and I sprang to my feet." Nearby, the professor rose and raised the window. He stuck his head out the window to see what was going on just as the passenger car passed the now-derailed freight car. The derailed car struck Miles Fletcher, and he collapsed. Morton related that "I immediately caught him and drew him out of the window, when his head dropped to one side and I perceived the blood and his fatal wound." As Morton held him in his arms, the professor died. The governor immediately wrote to his friend, Calvin Fletcher, telling him the awful news of the tragic accident and the loss of his son.[7]

But he also expressed suspicions about the incident. After relating the details of the accident and his personal investigation of how it happened, the governor said that the incident left little doubt, "at least in my mind, that this is the result of an obstruction deliberately placed upon the track by persons whose wickedness of heart cannot be conceived." Morton thought that some group of enemies had moved the freight car and suspected that they had placed it there in order to derail the train carrying him and his party. Rather than an accident, the tragedy had been an assassination attempt.[8]

Or so the governor thought. He told Calvin Fletcher that although he would like to return to Indianapolis with Miles's body, he could not. Regardless of whether it was an accident or an assassination attempt, Morton would not allow the incident to thwart his plans. After closing his middle-of-the-night missive by urging Fletcher to find solace in his Christian faith and in the accomplishments of his fallen son, the governor realized that his thoughts about the event being an assassination attempt on him might seem inappropriate in such a letter. He drew a squiggly line through the paranoid section and added a postscript: "On reflection I have marked out that part of my letter attributing this design, fearing injustice might be done" and admitting that his suspicions were simply conjectures.[9]

Or perhaps not. Within a few weeks, a man arrested for putting the car on the tracks confessed to the crime and turned state's witness against several accomplices. In exchange for a lenient sentence for himself, he agreed to testify against his fellow conspirators. Whether they really targeted the governor remained unclear to some, especially some Democrats, who scoffed at the reports and thought that the Republicans had made wild accusations and then found someone to arrest and blame in order to cover their story. As word of the supposed attempt on the governor's life spread, the Democrats claimed that Berry Sulgrove had lied about it and made up the story he printed in the *Indianapolis Journal*. They alleged that Sulgrove admitted this when called before a grand jury. But grand jury proceedings were sealed, and the Republicans insisted that Sulgrove had never renounced his story. Whatever the reality was, Morton and his allies no longer doubted that it was true.[10]

In the context of his ongoing battle with the Democrat-controlled legislature and mounting criticism of the government's war effort, Morton feared that he had been the target of assassins on that awful spring night. But those fears also sprang from his growing concern about the enemy within the Northern home front. In the early days of the war, the governor had received numerous reports from informants across the state who told him about Southern sympathizers and even secessionists at work in Indiana. An anonymous informer reported to the governor in November 1861 about rebel sympathizers in southern and western Indiana. The report indicated that the Sullivan County area was a nest of Copperheads who were plotting violence against the government, especially making plans to sabotage trains to kill army officers. No wonder, then, that the governor suspected an assassination attempt when the train incident occurred. As the conflict escalated and the war dragged on, Morton continued to receive reports from across the state about Copperhead activity, and he moved to thwart the traitors' efforts even as he investigated them further. This included his support for the Unionists in Kentucky and sending troops to guard the railroads.[11]

FIRE IN THE REAR

Especially worrisome were rumors that the Copperheads planned to burn the railroad bridges between Indiana and Louisville, cutting that vital connection. Morton telegraphed the War Department in the late summer of 1861 to report the suspected attack on the railroads and tell the national government that he had sent troops to protect the bridges. By 1862 the governor's investigations had led him to believe that there was a widespread network of Copperheads. These traitors represented a real threat, a fire in the rear that might well cause the Union to lose the war. On June 25, 1862, Morton wrote to Secretary of War Edwin Stanton and told him, "The fact is well established that there is a secret political organization in Indiana, estimated and claimed to be 10,000 strong." He said that the Copperheads aimed to disrupt recruiting efforts and to sway public opinion against the war. Wanting to make sure that the administration fully understood the danger, he followed up his letter to Stanton with a note to the president saying that he had sent his warning to the secretary of war.[12]

The governor worried about disloyal newspapers, especially the *Indiana Sentinel*, the *Cincinnati Enquirer*, and the *Chicago Times*, publications that he thought were "doing incalculable injury to the Union cause" with their attacks on Union leaders and "their continued apologies for the crimes committed by the leaders of the rebellion." Morton thought that Copperheads spread dissent and encouraged resistance to the laws and that they gave aid and comfort to the enemy. He especially criticized the *Indiana Sentinel*, which he accused of always opposing the government in order "to show that . . . we cannot carry the war to a successful termination without violating and breaking down the

Constitution which we profess to be fighting to preserve." Morton maintained that Indiana's leading Democratic newspaper asserted "that the responsibility for the war rests wholly upon the North, without a single word in condemnation of the traitors of the South, charging repeatedly and boldly that the sole aim and object is to interfere with their rights by securing the abolition of slavery." Convinced that the Copperheads were organized and operating in every part of the state, the governor believed that they threatened both the conduct of the war and the Union itself. He called for the War Department to furnish him with "at least ten thousand stand of good arms" to be used by the state militia, the "Indiana Legion," which he planned to use against the Copperheads.[13]

Worried about a treasonous conspiracy to create the Northwestern Confederacy, the governor filled his stream of correspondence to Washington with warnings about the dangers of a fifth column rising in the rear, fears of a possible Confederate invasion, and admonitions to carry the war to a quick and successful conclusion. On October 7, 1862, Morton had written to Lincoln with the dire warning that "if our arms do not make great progress in the next sixty days, our cause will be almost lost." His concerns included economics: "Our financial system must speedily end. The Government may subsist for a time upon issues of an irredeemable paper currency . . . but the time will come when the people will refuse to sell their commodities and receive this currency in payment," which would then lead to ruin. Morton worried that "the system may collapse in a single day" and feared that "national and individual bankruptcy would be followed by public despair, and the war would be abandoned by common consent." Economic peril was made all the worse by the possibility of foreign intervention by England and France.[14]

Worried that the rebels stood on the brink of independence, Morton told Lincoln that the Union armies needed only the right general to win the war. The governor urged the president to find a "man of strong intellect, whose head is inspired by his heart, who believes that our cause is sacred, that he is fighting for all that is dear to him and his country." Such a man, even if he lacked military training, would do better than the "cold professional" leaders who continued to fail. Morton gloomily feared that "another three months like the last six and we are lost—lost." He knew that Lincoln had generals with ability and the aggressive nature needed to conquer the South and recommended that the president "place them in command, and reject the wicked incapables whom you have patiently tried and found utterly wanting."[15]

Morton's entreaties to the administration continued as the war dragged on and his dire predictions for defeat did not come true. When the Democratic majority in the legislature tried to seize control of the war effort from him and he responded by running the state from his own office, Morton relied heavily on the support of the national government, especially Lincoln and Secretary of War Stanton. The governor's expansion of his power enraged the opposition and fed the fears of government overreach that strengthened the Copperheads. This led to the so-called Battle of Pogue's Run, on May 20, 1863, when the Copperheads tried to use a Democrat mass meeting in Indianapolis as a launching pad for overthrowing the government but were foiled by Morton and General Milo Hascall. That summer brought Morgan's Raid, which stoked Morton's fears about a fifth column rising in Indiana.[16]

THE 1864 ELECTORAL CAMPAIGN

By 1864 the governor had grown accustomed to cooperating with military authorities like Carrington, who took the lead in the investigations of the disloyal organizations in the state. Now, Morton would take the lead to make treason a political issue. On February 23 he delivered a speech at the Union Party State Convention in Indianapolis in which he officially began to campaign for the election of 1864. There was some question as to whether Morton was eligible to run for the gubernatorial chair, as state law limited the governor to one term. But Morton and the Republicans argued that, since he had been elected lieutenant governor in 1860, he was therefore eligible to seek reelection in 1864. Remarkably, after an initial period of complaint about this legality, the Democrats let the matter drop and did not make it an issue for the remainder of the campaign.[17]

In his Union Party speech, Morton laid out the problem quite clearly: "If we fail in this great struggle, then all is lost." If the Democrats won the election and tried to compromise with the rebels, it would lead to Southern independence and that "then all for which so much blood had been shed, and so much treasure expended, the unity of the nation and her institutions, would be lost forever." He then reviewed the situation in Indiana and placed the blame for his having to adopt one-man rule on the "Copperhead Action in the Legislature." Morton remembered that the Democratic majority had refused to accept his message, choosing instead to adopt New York Governor Seymour's address to his legislature. That had set the tone: "From the beginning it was not hard to predict the end." The Democrats had tried to seize control of the war effort and limit Morton's power. The Republicans had bolted to deny them a quorum and prevent disaster. In the midst of their partisan political struggle with the governor, the Democrat majority had failed to adopt an appropriations bill to fund the state.[18]

When the legislative session ended, Morton had refused to call a special session, knowing that the Democrats would use the opportunity to continue their attempt to curb his power. He had funded the state's benevolent institutions out of the treasury despite there being no budget, arguing that it was lawful to do so because they were "provided for in the Constitution of the State, and are regularly organized by statute—the people of the State have been taxed for their support, and have paid their money into the treasury." Thus, he paid for the operation of the state prisons and the institutions for "the deaf and dumb, the blind and the insane." To pay for the rest of state government, Morton reported that he had taken money from the arsenal, borrowed from county governments, and from banks and railroads. Those funds, as well as appropriations from the War Department, were sufficient to support the state government until February 1, 1865.[19]

After outlining the financial and political struggles in Indiana, Morton turned to national issues. He defended the government's conduct of the war and argued that the Emancipation Proclamation was well within the president's right if he freed the slaves as a means of putting down the rebellion. Morton conceded that "in time of peace there is no power vested in the President or in Congress to interfere with slavery in the States where it exists." But the rebellion gave the government the right to free the slaves of rebellious slave owners. Of course, freeing the slaves was also a moral issue, and Morton argued that the president's action was "not only sanctioned by the laws of war and upheld by the Constitution, but is in especial harmony with the principles of Eternal Justice and the revealed word of God." The governor went on to denounce the so-called Peace Men and argued that they were "men of one idea, and that idea is the preservation of the institution of slavery." He defended the government's arrest of those "who, by speeches and writings, were striving to destroy the Government, and giving aid and comfort to the rebellion." Morton did not dwell on that divisive issue, on which even he had reason to oppose the military on occasion, but instead reminded his audience of the sacrifices of the North. He defended the violation of civil rights and liberties by pointing out the terrible treatment of Union soldiers in Confederate prison camps. He pointed to the way that Unionists were attacked in the rebel states and used Southern atrocities to justify government action. Morton charged that the Peace Democrats were actually Copperheads and that they were collaborating with the rebels.[20]

Later in the year, during the campaign, the Democrats responded to Morton and published a long rebuttal. They countered his arguments point by point, accused him of tyranny, and criticized Lincoln as well. When the Republicans were not deliberately abusing their power, they proved incompetent, as they interfered with the military commanders and thwarted their efforts to win the war. After disagreeing with Morton on every point, the Democrats said, "The truth is, Morton is a tyrant by nature, and, like all other tyrants, he is afraid to oppose superior power. If the people of Indiana desire to have their money squandered on favorites, their personal safety endangered, their liberties stolen from them, they can effect that object by voting for Mr. Morton for Governor."[21]

The Democratic response concluded by listing "the grand result of three years" of "Republican Rule." They argued that the war had cost the lives of a million men. Although that number was too high, the point was relevant, as the casualties of war continued to mount. The Democrats also reminded Hoosiers that the United States now had accumulated a huge national debt and that the war had destroyed much of the nation's wealth. Morton's opponents argued that emancipation had "blotted out" all vestiges of pro-Union sentiment in the South. Meanwhile, the critics asserted that the "the whole country is one vast pest-house of sickness and disease," and the whole country was in mourning for lost loved ones. Overwhelmed by the disastrous conflict, the country was demoralized, and this meant that there "is no longer much regard for human life" and that included a vast increase in the number of "lewd women" and more "rascality and public plunder." Indeed, the opposition even blamed Morton and Lincoln for the decline of Christianity: "atheism and infidelity are seizing on the public mind, and corrupting all the purer and better feelings of the human heart." Then, the Democrats turned to race: "God created the white man and the black man. The one he created superior, the other inferior. Our rulers are guilty of the folly of trying to make that equal which the Creator made unequal." This brought "the anger of the Lord" and God had "afflicted us with war." The Republicans were to blame for the war, for vast numbers of dead men, for debt and disease and destruction. The Republicans had brought mourning, immorality, and atheism. And they had done it all in the name of trying to make blacks equal to whites. The Democrats closed their diatribe: "We, therefore, appeal to you, men of Indiana, to cast from before your eyes the heavy mist that blinds you; rise out of the darkness of the slough of Abolitionism into the light of liberty—the liberty of the WHITE MAN." In a few months, the president would respond to this Democratic argument that the war was caused by attempts to make the races equal: in his second inaugural address, Lincoln would declare that slavery caused the bloody conflict.[22]

Such rhetoric mattered and often fed into actions that brought danger to the state. On June 13, 1864, Morton received a warning that racism and rage against the recruiting of black soldiers were leading some draftees in the southern part of Indiana to not only flee conscription but actually join up with guerrillas operating out of Kentucky. The draft resisters swore to take revenge on Union men in the name of individual freedom from conscription and to defend white supremacy. Of course, the fact that recruiting African American troops would lessen the need for the draft escaped the logic of men expressing their racism as well as their opposition to the government's conduct of the war.[23]

As the campaign heated up, some Democrats spoke openly of the North-western Confederacy, and most criticized the Republicans while blaming the North for the war, railing against the Emancipation Proclamation—often in vile racist terms—and attacking Lincoln and Morton as tyrants who abused their powers. Even some War Democrats separated themselves from the Republicans. One former Union man, Judge Samuel E. Perkins, a chief justice of the state supreme court, delivered a speech in Centerville attacking Morton as a tyrant in the governor's hometown. The judge also claimed that the state treasury now rested in the governor's own pockets, leveling the charge that Morton was using state funds to enrich himself. Incensed, Morton fired back in the pages of the *Indianapolis Journal,* arguing that the state had had no funds, thanks to the legislature not passing a budget and asking the judge to show where the money was if he had stolen it. The governor argued that the charge was "so utterly destitute of truth" that it was scandalous that it "should be uttered by a Supreme Court judge." Questioning Morton's honesty became standard fare for the Democrats, but Morton and his allies countered the charges, and the governor's records eventually convinced even his enemies that he had been scrupulously honest with funds during his one-man rule, even if he did skirt the rules to raise the money.[24]

The Morton-McDonald Debates

In July the Democrats nominated Joseph E. McDonald, former state attorney general and a friend of Morton's, to run against the governor. A War Democrat, McDonald had refused to join the "Peace and Pistol Democracy" and had mostly supported both Morton and Lincoln throughout the war. Reluctant to stand for the nomination when it seemed like the Democrats would win the election, McDonald agreed to run when Union victories on the battlefield made it more difficult for the opposition. His main opponent for the Democratic nomination was an attorney named Lambdin P. Milligan, an outspoken critic of the Republicans and the war who was a known member of the Copperhead secret societies.

McDonald carried the nomination by a wide margin, and the campaign began in earnest. An Ohio native who had moved to Montgomery County, Indiana, as a boy, McDonald had been a saddler's apprentice before attending Wabash College. He transferred to Indiana Asbury University, graduated, and became an attorney in Crawfordsville. He worked as a prosecuting attorney, was elected to Congress in 1849, and in the 1850s he won election as state attorney general. Along the way he and Morton became good friends, despite their political differences, and it was no great surprise that McDonald supported the Union and the war. In fact, he may have given information about

Fig. 22. Congressman and senator Joseph McDonald, Morton's Democratic opponent in the 1864 election. (Library of Congress)

the Copperheads to the army, especially regarding their strength in the state Democratic Party. In 1864, however, McDonald took up his party's cause and began to attack Morton and his one-man rule, making the usual accusations about tyranny and the misuse of funds. The governor followed his opponent's early speeches with lengthy replies of his own, denying all charges and accusing the opposition of aiding and abetting the rebels and of using empty rhetoric to whip up votes. He said that they claimed to care for the sick and wounded, but only at election time. They professed to stand for liberty but actually defended slavery. They blamed the Republicans for not winning the war but really did not want to achieve victory.[25]

The two gubernatorial candidates agreed to a series of debates during the campaign, and the first of these was held on August 10, in LaPorte. The two men had agreed to an equal number of debates, one in each congressional district, with alternating choice of location. Morton had the first choice, and he selected LaPorte because it was a staunch Republican town. The format called for Morton to open with an hour-long speech, and then McDonald would follow with an hour and a half of his own. Morton would conclude with a half-hour rebuttal. The governor complained of a sore throat that he said would have caused him to cancel an ordinary speech, but that he felt he had to continue despite the pain because this was such an important debate.[26]

He then proceeded to the defense of his own actions and those of the Republican Party, of President Lincoln, and the Union military effort. He blamed the state legislature for having to carry the government forward on his own and argued that Democrats had set precedents for each of his policies. Morton believed that he "was sustained by every Union man in the State of Indiana, and I know that very many men who claimed to belong to the Democratic party justified me in refusing to call your Legislature back—pronouncing it to be the most extraordinary and worthless body known to Legislative history." He pointed repeatedly to actions taken by Democratic governors that justified his own executive decisions. And even if such precedents did not allow him to do what he had done, Morton said that "the plea of necessity is as good in 1864" as it had been previously.[27]

After a long defense of his actions to fund the government and run the state without the legislature, Morton argued his case with an emotional appeal to the wartime ideology that served as the foundation of his thinking. Although McDonald tried to evade "the great national questions which . . . overshadow all others at this time," Morton said that "my position is easily defined: I am in favor of sustaining the National Government, restoring and maintaining the Union of these States, and suppressing the rebellion by force of arms." Despite McDonald's career as a War Democrat, he now insisted that he was opposed to the war being "prosecuted under the ideas and policy of the Administration," and he believed that it was "entailing upon the country unmixed evil, and I would be false to my country if I did not say so." Thus, Morton could attack him for flip-flopping on the issues as well as charging him with sympathy for the rebellion.[28]

Furthermore, the governor reminded his audience that McDonald agreed with the state Democratic Party's platform. The Democracy claimed that they supported a war to maintain the Constitution and the Union, but they declared that "we are opposed to a war for the emancipation of the negroes or the subjugation of the Southern States." Morton attacked his opponent by arguing that the rebellion itself was unconstitutional. McDonald had to tell the voters exactly what he and his party meant when they argued for a Constitutional war and said that they opposed freeing the slaves. The Democrat was trying to equivocate and take a middle ground, but Morton declared that "there can be no neutrals in this war. There is no half-way house. There is no place in the Constitution where a man can stand midway between the rebellion and the Government."[29]

The governor then appealed again to the emotions of his audience, and they responded with rounds of applause as he tried to back McDonald into a political corner where he could not escape. Morton cried, "If you are for unconditional peace, if you are in favor of abandoning this war and giving up the rebellious States, giving up the Mississippi river, dividing the Union, you want a man who will carry out your views . . . you want to know who and where he is. If you want such a man, don't vote for me." He raised the specter of defeat if the Union abandoned the conflict and withdrew its armies and predicted that it would result in the war coming to the North. The governor did not want to abandon the cause, especially now when the war was nearly won. The Union had met with many disasters, but "we have now our hold upon the throat of the Confederacy. . . . General Grant and General Sherman have their hands upon its throat, and they will never let go until the monster is dead, unless they are pulled off by the peace men of the North." He predicted that "we will conquer this rebellion; we will crush it out, unless we shall be defeated by men in the North who seek to divide our people." Making the election about saving the Union and downplaying emancipation as only a means to win the war allowed Morton to paint McDonald as the radical. The Democrat, not the Republican, was the one who trampled on the Constitution because he supported secession. For Morton, all of the expansion of power and supposed tyranny of the Republicans stemmed from the root cause of rebellion. He had sworn an oath and had committed himself to saving the nation, and he said, "I have tried to do my duty." Morton and the Republicans defended the Union while McDonald and the Democrats wanted to snatch defeat from the jaws of victory and allow the South, rebellion, and slavery to win.[30]

McDonald responded, saying that his differences with the governor were not personal, but political. He remembered well that he and Morton were old friends who had "stood shoulder to shoulder in the Democratic ranks of old, and we have still remained friends, although he has separated from me and my political household." He then launched into a rebuttal of Morton's defense of his gubernatorial career. He blamed one-man rule on the Republicans, reminding the voters that the legislative minority had bolted the session and prevented the Democratic majority from passing an appropriations bills. McDonald drew laughs when he remembered that the Republican bolters (McDonald called them "seceders") fled by train to Madison: "Now they started South. They were certainly going in the right direction."[31]

The challenger denied that his party's military bill violated the state constitution and argued that the Republicans were using the controversy over the proposed law to carry out a revolutionary plan to prevent democracy from working. After all, McDonald said, to pass the military bill would have required a two-thirds majority vote and the Republicans could have prevented it. And even if it had passed, the Republicans would have been able to challenge it in the courts. The real reason that they bolted and denied a quorum was to prevent the Democrats from curbing the governor's executive power. McDonald did not deny that there had been precedents for some of Morton's actions, but he argued that those Democratic governors had been wrong, just as Morton was wrong. McDonald had been attorney general when some of the precedents had been set, and he now declared that the governor at the time "did wrong" and that he had told him so at the time. The Democratic candidate went into detail in refuting Morton's arguments in defense of his means of funding the state government without the legislature. He declared that he was "a candidate for but one branch" of government, not all three, and drew applause when he exclaimed that if the voters "want your State carried on by the one-man power, don't elect me."[32]

When he at last came to the national issues that Morton had made the central issue, McDonald argued that his position was the conservative, constitutional one. He quoted from the Democratic Party platform of 1840 and that of the Whig Party in 1852 to show that the current Democratic platform was not a radical attack on the Constitution. He claimed that his own views had been consistent throughout his career. Furthermore, McDonald said that "when this war came upon this country there was no man who more than myself took pride in that prompt and patriotic effort that was made by the volunteer soldiers of this country to save it, when its statesmen refused to reach forth their hands to save it by the arts of peace." The Republicans had refused to compromise and they were to blame for the war. They had faced the question of "whether they would lose their party and save their country, or save their party and lose their country, and they chose the latter alternative. They preferred their party to their country." The North had responded with patriotism and fought to save the Union. But, after three and a half years, the war still raged on.[33]

McDonald admitted that he wanted peace but denied that he wanted to allow the South to have its independence. However, he opposed fighting the war "under the idea of the Abolition minority that rules this Administration." He argued that the "Federal Government has no right to infringe upon the rights and institutions of any State. Therefore, I say, I am opposed to a war for the subjugation of States." To put down a rebellion by individuals, by rebels, was one thing, but to trample on the sovereign rights of a state was another. For McDonald and the Democrats, the issues had not changed. They stood for state's rights and wanted to limit the power of the national government. Morton had quoted his opponents correctly but incompletely, and McDonald now finished what he maintained was his motto: "No war for the subjugation of States or the emancipation of negroes, and no peace that looks to a dismemberment of the Union." The challenger riled the audience when he said that after three and a half years it was "time to try some other remedy." The crowd became angry, and men shouted for him to explain what he meant by "other remedy." Finally, Morton rose and quieted the Republicans who made up the bulk of the audience, telling them to listen patiently to McDonald. When he was able to continue, the Democrat asserted that his alternative was to enforce the Constitution. That meant putting down the rebellion, but it did not mean emancipating the slaves. Lincoln and Morton had violated the Constitution and state's rights and threatened the rights of all Americans with their expansion of executive power.[34]

When his opponent finished, Morton spoke again, claiming that McDonald had failed to state where he stood on the question of the Union. The governor denied that the Democrats, including his opponent, had been consistent over the years. Instead, they had changed their minds about the extension of slavery, which had caused Morton to leave the party in 1854. The Republican again denied any wrongdoing in his actions as governor and said, again, that if his actions were wrong, he had done them for the right reasons. He blamed Democrats for agitating the slavery question and accused McDonald of flipping back and forth on the issue. He denied that Lincoln and the Republicans had started the war, reminding the audience that Southerners had seceded and taken up arms before Lincoln even took office. He quoted Confederate leaders who claimed that secession had been "the work of years" as evidence that the South had wanted a war. Morton closed by again defending his executive power, saying that, "if my acts are unconstitutional it could not do any harm." But the Democratic majority in the legislature had tried to do irreparable harm to the state and to the Union. Indeed, Morton said, the militia bill that the Democrats had tried to pass was "insurrection in itself." He called on the voters to try to figure out exactly where McDonald stood "on the war question. If you are for peace, and think he is a peace man, vote for him." But if they wanted "to vote for a man who has tried to stand by the army and the soldiers; who believes that this Union must and shall be preserved, then vote for me."[35]

That first debate set the tone for all thirteen meetings between the two candidates. Sometimes emancipation became the focus of their discourses. In Brownstown, on August 16, McDonald asked Morton what was to become of the more than 150,000 black soldiers then wearing Union uniforms. Were they to become citizens with full equality? The governor replied that "it is not for me to decide what their fate will be, but I trust that they will be forever free; that the men who have gone forth to fight for the Union will never be enslaved again." When faced with such questions, Morton found that his ideology of freedom, Union, and power served as a firm foundation from which to argue his case. Seizing the opportunity to trap his opponent, he asked if McDonald preferred that "we shall fill up the ranks with white men instead of using the negroes? I have heard a good deal from Democrats against negro soldiers, and the provost marshal says that Democrats were the very first to put in negro substitutes." Here the governor attacked his racist opponent for hypocrisy. McDonald opposed the draft and did not want white soldiers to die, but he did not want black troops to serve. Yet, at the same time, members of his own party who decried African American soldiers were the first to employ them to avoid serving themselves.[36]

Embracing racism, McDonald responded by saying that "I have been opposed to making soldiers out of negroes, not because I am not willing that they should stand in place of white men in battle and camp, but because I do not believe any people ever made use of a servile race in war that did not suffer from it." The opposition candidate readily expressed his racism, saying that "the negroes are an inferior race. I have always looked upon this government as made for the white man. I am not in favor of slavery or equality." Thus, the Democrat parried Morton's forensic thrust by playing the race card. The two men remained friendly on a personal level and traveled to the debate sites on the same train, often sitting and smoking together. Once, on the way to Lawrenceburg, the train derailed and their car rolled off the tracks and came to a rest on its side. Shaken but unhurt, the two candidates had to climb out the windows. Their private friendship often gave way to emotional criticism on the debate platform, especially when Morton attacked McDonald on the issue of the Copperheads, eventually forcing his opponent to denounce the secret societies.[37]

Throughout the campaign, Morton made the election about saving the Union, as he defended his record, blamed the Democrats for the war, called them peace men who wanted to destroy the country and maintain slavery, and predicted that anything short of a complete victory would result in another war fought on Northern soil. McDonald remained on the defensive even as he kept trying to paint Morton and the Republicans as tyrants, blaming Lincoln for the war, arguing that emancipation was not simply a war measure but was part of a broader agenda designed to destroy state's rights and the Constitution. In the summer of 1864 Union morale reached a low point, as the mounting casualties on the battlefield brought war weariness. The conflict seemed endless and lent credence to Democratic calls for pursuing an alternative course. While military victories might swing the election to the Republicans, one ill-timed setback could mean that the Democrats would win. Continuing opposition to emancipation, to the draft, and to Republican violations of civil rights and liberties combined to bolster those who challenged the incumbents.[38]

Meanwhile, the Republicans divided. Many in the party thought that Lincoln should be replaced because he was unfit to lead the country. They joined Democrats in blaming the president for the lack of success in the war. For a time, there was a movement to nominate Salmon P. Chase, the secretary of the treasury. Although he did not openly seek the nomination, Chase quietly pursued it. When his beautiful daughter, Kate, married wealthy Rhode Island senator William Sprague, it seemed likely that Chase would have the money to fund a well-organized campaign. He enjoyed the support of a number of Washington politicians, including Kansas senator Samuel C. Pomeroy, who led the push to put Chase in the White House in 1864. But the Chase movement fell apart after the publication of documents criticizing Lincoln went too far. Especially damaging was a pamphlet written by Pomeroy that not only said that Lincoln was incompetent but also called for Chase to replace him. The Pomeroy Circular claimed that there was a national organization in place for Chase and called on its readers to join the movement for him. Pomeroy disliked Lincoln in part because he thought he should have more control over patronage in Kansas, and he hoped that Chase would let him have free rein over appointments. Despite his hopes that the circular would officially set in motion the movement to nominate Chase, Pomeroy overplayed his hand. The circular backfired. Instead of helping the secretary, it hurt him and helped the president. Chase was embarrassed by the public linking of him, a cabinet member, to criticism of the president. He immediately wrote to Lincoln, denying any connection to the circular, and the movement to nominate him collapsed.[39]

Although he usually supported Lincoln, Morton also had his disagreements with the president. In addition to the always-frustrating issue of who controlled patronage, the governor thought that Lincoln had made mistakes in choosing commanders and that his administration had neglected Indiana and the Midwest. As a matter of fact, in April of 1863 he had made speeches in New York City that expressed a clear-eyed assessment of the president's efforts even as he blamed the rebels for the war and defended a nationalist position. Furthermore, General Carrington, to whom Chase had been a political mentor, advocated replacing Lincoln with the secretary of the treasury. The general tried to convince Morton to throw his weight behind the Ohioan's candidacy until the Pomeroy Circular brought such ideas to an end. But other possibilities existed.[40]

Radical Republicans also temporarily mounted a campaign to defeat Lincoln, supporting John C. Frémont under the banner of the Radical Democracy. Radicals thought Lincoln was too cautious or too incompetent to carry forward their agenda of freedom and equality, and their public criticism marked sharp differences within the party. Even some moderate Republicans doubted whether Lincoln could win and urged that the party choose another candidate. It certainly seemed possible that the Democratic candidate, George B. McClellan, could win the presidency and that McDonald could become governor of Indiana.[41]

Morton genuinely feared that a Democratic victory would bring dire consequences. He knew his old friend McDonald well, but he believed that the Democratic Party contained too many Copperheads and rebel sympathizers. When even McDonald toed a party line that attacked Morton in ways that the governor saw as unfair, it was a sign that the opposition party was out to derail not only the Republicans but also the Union as a whole. He knew that large numbers of Democrats were part of the Copperhead conspiracies. On the campaign trail he accused all Democrats of being part of the traitorous secret societies, knowing that McDonald could not afford to alienate portions of his political base by taking too strong a stand either for or against the Copperheads.

McDonald found himself caught in a political trap. As a War Democrat, he supported the Union and knew that the majority of voters agreed with him on that. But a significant portion of his own party opposed the war. If he attacked the Copperheads, he would lose a large number of the voters in his political base. If he did not attack them, his opponent could accuse him of being too soft on treason or even say that McDonald himself was a traitor because of his sympathies with the antiwar Democrats. Morton had him over a barrel. Other War Democrats also found themselves in the same precarious position politically. William H. English supported the war and broke with most of his party by throwing his lot in with Republicans on economic issues, including their banking policies. He so despised the Copperheads that he actually wrote to General Carrington recommending that the leaders of the movement be arrested. But he could not let anyone know that he had done so if he hoped to keep his congressional seat. English, like McDonald, had to appease the Peace Democrats and not attack the Copperheads too vigorously if he hoped to remain in power.[42]

Even with his opponents in the Democratic establishment trapped by the internal dynamics of having to appease the Copperheads, the governor worried that his efforts to paint the opposition as traitors might not work. He needed something more to guarantee victory, so Morton tried desperately to persuade the War Department to allow Indiana soldiers to vote. The governor had received many letters of support from Hoosier officers and men, and he was sure that they would help turn the election in favor of the Republicans. He feared a repeat of the disaster of 1862, with Democrats sweeping to power.

On September 12, 1864, he petitioned Secretary of War Stanton to suspend the draft and to return fifteen thousand soldiers to Indiana in time to vote. In the local elections in the spring of 1863, soldiers home on furlough had helped carry the Republicans to victory in some parts of the state, and the governor hoped to use their support again. Although the plan for returning thousands of troops in time to vote did not happen in 1864, some friendly commanders who could spare them furloughed Hoosier soldiers, who rushed home to cast their ballots in support of the Union. Other states allowed their troops to cast absentee ballots, a measure that won widespread Republican approval, even as many Democrats saw it as evidence of the Republicans trying to rig the election. Looking for whatever edge he could, Morton wanted to use treason as a wedge issue to swing voters to support him and his party. Convinced that most of his opponents were traitors ready to surrender to the South, Morton cooperated with the military authorities to make Democratic treason a central issue in the election. He pushed the War Department—and, therefore, the Lincoln administration—to coordinate the timing of the arrests of half a dozen Indiana Copperheads to coincide with the political campaign. The resulting treason trials in the fall of 1864 helped decide the election.[43]

THE INDIANAPOLIS TREASON TRIALS

The story of the Indianapolis treason trials began when Indiana's Copperheads organized themselves into secret societies. They turned first to the Knights of the Golden Circle (KGC), a group founded in the 1850s to support the expansion of the United States, especially in the Southwest, where they hoped to carve off more of Mexico to create new slave territory. When the Civil War began, the KGC rallied Southern sympathizers. Although its exact origins remain unclear, Dr. William A. Bowles, an eccentric resident of French Lick with a checkered past, helped lead the Indiana chapter of the organization. A physician who built the first resort at the French Lick mineral spring, Bowles had served in the Mexican-American War and brought infamy to Indiana when his apparent drunken behavior at the Battle of Buena Vista prompted his regiment's retreat. The hero of Buena Vista, Jefferson Davis of Mississippi, defended Bowles at the subsequent court-martial trial, but the near disaster disgraced Indiana troops who were now labeled as cowards. A Southern sympathizer, the doctor held proslavery views and reportedly brought slaves to French Lick to work at his hotel. When the war began, Bowles openly proclaimed his sympathy for the Confederate cause and readily told anyone who would listen about his plans to take Indiana out of the Union and make it a slave state. When new societies with new names organized, he readily joined them to continue his resistance to the government.[44]

Another Copperhead ringleader, Harrison H. Dodd, was a native of upstate New York who first moved to Ohio and then to Indianapolis, where he worked as a printer and became active in the Democratic Party. Long concerned with the encroachment of government power on the freedom of individuals, he grew especially worried about what he considered the unchecked abuses of the military authorities in Indiana during the war. He joined the Order of American Knights, another offshoot of or front for the KGC, formed in 1863. Still later, in 1864, Dodd became the leader of the Sons of Liberty, still another clandestine group that sprouted from or fronted for the KGC. Through his secret network, Dodd began resisting the policies of Lincoln and Morton, the Republicans he most blamed for exploiting the war to trample on individual rights and liberties. Soon his printing business in Indianapolis became the headquarters of the secret organizations opposed to the war.[45]

A third leader of the Indiana Copperheads, Lambdin P. Milligan, was a Huntington, Indiana, lawyer and political candidate. Milligan held to the old Jeffersonian-Jacksonian principles of agrarianism and limited government. In his view, the Republican Party, in promoting industrial capitalism and the centralization of power in the national government, threatened the fabric of the American experiment. Republican policies directly contravened the agrarian capitalism and state's rights outlook that Milligan held dear. He strongly criticized the Lincoln administration from the outset of the war and feared that with each passing day the country drew closer to tyranny and the end of liberty. Milligan believed his bitter outcries and secret activities represented nothing less than a last stand for freedom. In his mind, the Sons of Liberty carried on the tradition of the American Revolution, and when his bid for the Democratic nomination for governor failed in 1864, he concluded the time for violent action had arrived.[46]

Opposition to the war ebbed and flowed over time in Indiana. It grew strongest when the war went badly for the North or when specific government policies seemed to confirm Copperhead charges of tyranny. In 1862 battlefield defeats, combined with the beginning of conscription and the preliminary Emancipation Proclamation, pushed many Hoosiers to the Democratic Party to express their disappointment in the unsuccessful war effort, their outrage at the draft, and Lincoln's decision to make the war about slavery. In 1863 the same issues continued to plague Republicans politically. Resistance to the draft prompted military action at home, with patrols of soldiers seeking deserters and confronting those who refused conscription.

The Emancipation Proclamation upset many whites in Indiana who supported a war to save the Union but not one to free the slaves. Whether they opposed emancipation because of racism or because they thought it unconstitutional (or both), these citizens hoped to curb the growing power of the government. When Northern officials arrested newspaper editors, they raised the issue of freedom of speech. In addition, some of those arrested languished in jail for long periods, thanks to Lincoln's suspension of habeas corpus. Governor Morton's one-man rule added fuel to the fires of opposition, as Democrats called him a tyrant and accused him of malfeasance.

To many Hoosiers, Republicans appeared to trample on civil rights and liberties at every turn, all in the name of defeating the rebellion. As a result, resistance to the war stretched across a broad spectrum of Indiana politics. Some, like many Quakers, embraced nonviolent religious views and opposed the draft because it forced men to fight. Others, mostly Democrats, held to libertarian principles of individualism and feared the growing power of government that Republicans centralized in Indianapolis and Washington, DC. Still others supported the Confederacy and the Southern cause, espousing state's rights and proslavery views. Indiana Democrats divided into factions, with the War Democrats joining the Republicans in support of the Union, while Peace Democrats consisted of a coalition of opponents of the war.[47]

Many, probably most, of the Democratic opponents of the war remained loyal to the Union. They opposed Republican policies on legitimate, constitutional grounds and hoped to win elections in order to stop the abuses of power they feared would destroy the country. But some, like Dodd and Bowles, considered taking action against the government, led the Sons of Liberty, and openly recruited new members. In their zeal to enlist others, their organizations became not-so-secret societies. They concocted various plans, including gathering weapons, assassinating politicians, and even overthrowing the state government. The conspirators dreamed of seizing control of Indiana and taking the state out of the Union either to join the Southern Confederacy or to create what would be the independent Northwestern Confederacy. These men simultaneously pursued legitimate politics, vying for nomination to office within the Democratic Party. But in the context of the war, the line between treason and loyalty blurred as men of principle struggled to find the means to oppose the government. Even loyal Democrats who won office knew men who belonged to the Sons of Liberty, and some elected officials belonged to the organization themselves. The blurring of lines and loyalties enabled Republicans like Morton to paint the Democrats with a broad brush and declare that only War Democrats—now part of the Union Party—were loyal. All other Democrats, the Republicans argued, were traitors.[48]

The Indiana Sons of Liberty began to plan an uprising in Indianapolis in the late summer of 1864. They made contact with Confederate agents operating out of Canada and received money for the purchase of weapons to carry out their attack. The plan called for the Sons of Liberty to seize the state arsenal and free the Confederates held prisoner at Camp Morton in Indianapolis. Although later historians believed that only a few hundred Copperheads, at best, were willing to take up arms against the government, the leaders of the movement asserted that they had tens of thousands of men. With chapters of the Sons of Liberty in forty counties across the state, even a few men in each locale could wreak havoc and require the Union military to divert troops to put down the uprising. When Harrison Dodd received a shipment of four hundred revolvers, it seemed that the specter of a fifth column rising up in the Union rear could become a real threat.[49]

But Morton did not stand idly by. Instead, he vigorously hounded his political opponents, including the conspirators. The not-so-secret societies of Copperheads attracted the attention of the press as well as the governor, who discussed them in his annual messages to the legislature and missives to the national government. He badgered the War Department with constant telegrams and revelations of traitorous activities in the state. He continually urged the army to investigate the Copperheads. When the national authorities finally responded, he tried to cooperate with them as best he could. Morton worked closely with the chief of military intelligence in the Midwest, General Carrington, who employed detectives and spies to infiltrate the secret societies. The army gathered information on the Copperheads, which was forwarded to the War Department in Washington. Carrington also shared such reports with Morton, who used it as evidence in his own continuous correspondence with the national government. Although the Lincoln administration largely ignored their initial communications, the governor and the general continued to send along intelligence about a treasonous conspiracy in Indiana. By June of 1864 Morton was urging Carrington to publicize their intelligence about the secret societies, but the general was reluctant to do so. The governor wanted to appeal directly to the loyal citizens of the state and expose the Copperheads. Eventually, however, the national government paid attention.[50]

Carrington's investigation depended on spies who infiltrated the Sons of Liberty. He employed a number of detectives who served as covert operatives, and several of them, including Felix G. Stidger, gained access to the secret Copperhead organization to gather information. It did not prove difficult to infiltrate the Sons of Liberty, as the eccentric, talkative, and always hospitable William Bowles openly shared incriminating information with anyone who would listen, and Copperheads eagerly accepted new members because they

Fig. 23. Union general Henry B. Carrington, ca. 1865. (Library of Congress).

wanted to build their movement and increase their political and military strength. Going undercover required little effort for Union detectives like Stidger, whose information enabled Carrington to submit a full-scale exposé to Governor Morton that detailed the activities of the Sons of Liberty. Carrington's report estimated that some thirty thousand Sons of Liberty across the state were actively arming for an insurrection that would bring an internal civil war to Indiana and the entire Midwest. With this information in hand, the governor and the national authorities waited.[51]

The Copperhead plan, as reported by Stidger, called for an armed uprising in early August of 1864. Attacks on Chicago, Indianapolis, and Springfield, Illinois, would be coordinated with assaults on prison camps to free captured Confederates. Copperheads and freed Confederates would join with guerrillas from Kentucky in carrying out the plan that demanded cooperation across state lines and with the Confederacy. William Bowles would lead an armed force in taking Louisville as part of actions in five states: Indiana, Illinois, Ohio, Kentucky, and Missouri. If successful, the insurrection would overthrow the state governments of Ohio, Indiana, and Illinois and take them out of the Union, along with the two border states.[52]

Soon, however, the conspiracy began to fall apart. As more members of the Sons of Liberty learned of the plan, some concluded it was a bad idea that smacked of treason and would not work. Others argued against the timing of the uprising, believing it would rally support for Morton and Lincoln just before the fall elections. Instead of stopping abuses, such men believed the uprising would enable Republicans to win the election. Divided by internal bickering, the Copperheads failed to strike as planned, as their leaders kept changing the date for the attack to begin. Meanwhile, Carrington continued gathering information on the conspiracy, discovering incriminating records and reports of men trying to buy guns.

Among the revelations, the army found correspondence of Democratic congressman Daniel Voorhees that indicated he planned to buy some twenty thousand rifles to help arm the Copperhead insurgents. The *Indianapolis Journal* exposed the report about Voorhees almost immediately, which raised the alarm among the people of the state. Voorhees denied that he had anything to do with the plan to buy guns and said that the evidence had been planted by the government to discredit him. In an attempt to rally sentiment against the army, the crosstown *Indiana Sentinel* accused Carrington of drunkenness. Morton quickly defended his ally in a telegram to Secretary of War Stanton.

Fig. 24. Congressman Daniel W. Voorhees, Democrat, Indiana. (Library of Congress)

From across Indiana came other reports of disloyal activity, including armed bodies of men searching for Union veterans or soldiers home on furlough. Rumors circulated about armed attacks on towns like Terre Haute as the Copperheads prepared for the coming insurrection.

Then, on August 17, 1864, Morton received an anonymous letter from Buffalo, New York, saying that the "Copperheads of Indiana have ordered and paid for 30,000 revolvers" along with more than forty boxes of ammunition that were to be distributed for the planned uprising. The letter explained that some of the arms had been shipped to Indianapolis in boxes marked "Stationary" and "Hardware," while the rest remained stored in New York City. The shipment to Indianapolis had been addressed to a business partner of Harrison Dodd. The governor immediately informed the army, and soldiers confiscated boxes of guns from Dodd's office and a warehouse located in the Old Sentinel Building—where the Democratic newspaper had once been headquartered.[53]

With reports of Copperhead activity mounting, the situation looked dire for the government as the blistering heat of August continued. There were few troops left in the state to defend against an armed uprising. If the Copperheads took action, they might very well manage to seize control of Indianapolis and other cities. Carrington asked for more soldiers, and Morton supported the general by asking that the commander be given more money to use for surveillance of the Copperheads. The traitors delayed their attack, and in mid-August relief came. The army sent reinforcements to guard the prisons, and soon hundreds of veterans and new recruits alike arrived in Indianapolis. This allowed Morton and Carrington to prepare for the Copperhead attack, should it ever begin.[54]

The Copperheads continued to delay, even when a guerrilla commander crossed from Kentucky into Illinois, where his men captured steamboats and stole cattle. Ultimately the uprising never happened, as public knowledge of at least parts of their plans combined with the arrival of Union reinforcements and internal squabbling to stop the traitors. Nonetheless, at Morton's urging, the army moved in and military officials seized Harrison Dodd's papers and the pistols he had stockpiled in his office. With evidence in hand, the authorities arrested a handful of Copperheads, including Dodd, Milligan, Bowles, Horace Heffren, Stephen Horsey, and Andrew Humphreys, in late August and early September.[55]

The government charged the men with treason and brought them before a military court. Dodd escaped and fled to Canada, which many saw as evidence of his guilt. Tried in absentia and found guilty, he received the death sentence. A military court convicted three others—Milligan, Bowles, and Horsey—and gave them the death penalty, while Humphreys received a sentence of hard labor for the duration of the war. The government dropped the charges against

Heffren, the former legislator to whom Morton had given a military commission, when he agreed to testify against the others and released him after the trial. After the war, in *Ex parte Milligan,* the US Supreme Court decided that the conspirators had a constitutional right to a trial in civilian court. The decision resulted in commuted sentences and the government released the remaining prisoners. With Union victory, the charges of treason had become superfluous, and the Copperheads had collapsed and faded from memory. During the war, however, the trials captured the public's fearful imagination at a moment advantageous to the Republicans, and leaders like Carrington and Morton emerged triumphant.[56]

In the fall of 1864, the treason trials influenced the election the way some Sons of Liberty worried it might. The press splashed the story across newspaper headlines, and fears of a Copperhead rebellion behind the lines swept across the Midwest. The partisan press helped Morton and the government by reporting on the arrests and trials in sensationalized fashion. Some opposition editors were probably cowed into silence when J. J. Bingham, editor of the *Indiana Sentinel,* was arrested for participating in the conspiracy. He turned state's evidence and testified against the other conspirators, revealing inside knowledge that belied his public protestations of innocence. In this climate, few Democrats summoned the courage to speak out against the government's actions.[57]

Despite the cloud of treason hanging over them thanks to the trials, some Democrats continued to criticize Morton and argued that a vote for the Republicans was a vote for the draft. Undaunted by Bingham's arrest, the *Sentinel* appealed to racism when it claimed that a vote for the "Black Republicans" meant that there would be "Negro Equality." The opposition party called Morton and Lincoln tyrants and cried out against the Emancipation Proclamation. But it did not work. Instead, the trials rallied support to the Union cause and the Republicans carried the election. Governor Morton and President Lincoln both won reelection by wide margins over their Democratic opponents. Indiana's October elections resulted in the voters returning Morton to office by a majority of more than 20,000 votes. The Republicans also won a majority in the state legislature, won seats on the state supreme court, and carried the state's congressional delegation. In November Lincoln won Indiana by about the same margin as the governor had in October. Secure in his office, Morton saw his victory as vindication, with the voters expressing their approval of his period of one-man rule with their ballots.[58]

The governor and the president were helped by the vote of Union soldiers who rallied to support the government by overwhelming margins. The men furloughed home to vote remembered that the governor had been the "Soldiers' Friend" in his tireless efforts to keep them supplied and equipped, and they

Fig. 25. "Copperhead Leaders Arraigned for the Indianapolis Treason Trials" (Benn Pittman, ed., *The Trials for Treason at Indianapolis* [Cincinnati: Moore, Wilstach, and Baldwin, 1865]). Starting at the top and moving clockwise, the Copperheads are William A. Bowles, Andrew Humphreys, Stephen Horsey, Horace Heffren, and Lambdin P. Milligan.

returned the favor at the ballot box. The charges of treason left soldiers feeling betrayed by traitors at home and intensified their support of the government. By 1864 Union veterans and troops at home on leave were often helping the state militia battle Copperheads who dared to hold public meetings in Indiana communities. Voting that fall allowed them to strike another blow against the hated traitors. Civilian voters joined the soldiers in supporting Morton and the Republicans, and large majorities flocked to express their disdain for the Copperheads by supporting the government.[59]

By the time of Morton's inaugural on January 6, 1865, the tide of war had turned dramatically toward Union victory. Desperate peace overtures by the Confederates and Southern prayers for a miraculous deliverance paled next to the crushing victories won by Union armies. In just a few months, worries about the Union surviving turned to confidence in victory. Now Morton began to help prepare for achieving the hard-won peace. He worked diligently to take care of the soldiers and sent out more agents to see to their care and to help prepare for their anticipated return home. He also labored to reestablish constitutional government with the help of the now-friendly legislature. The Republican majority set out to cooperate with the governor and to affirm what he had done in the previous months. The governor could count on accomplishing much in his second term, supported by the legislature, with a clear mandate from the voters. How he would apply his ideology of freedom, Union, power, and party after the war remained uncertain for the moment. Meanwhile, the practical matters of governing kept Morton busy, and he continued with a heavy workload, pushing himself to get things done. Until the Confederacy surrendered and the government conquered the rebels, the cause demanded the governor's due diligence. So Morton continued on and did his duty.[60]

CHAPTER SEVEN

Peace and Paralysis

THE CIVIL WAR brought economic expansion, and Governor Morton proclaimed in his 1865 inaugural address that "Indiana shows signs of prosperity and power she never knew before." Delivered on January 6, 1865, Morton's speech began to lay out his second-term agenda in preparation for what now seemed to be an inevitable Union victory. Morton wanted to be sure to win the peace as well as the war, and he looked ahead with that in mind. But he also recognized that the war had brought revolutionary changes to Indiana as well as the rest of the country. The Civil War did more than save the Union and end slavery, the two main objectives of the Northern effort that brought dramatic changes in their own right. Morton realized that the war had also transformed Indiana economically and socially because it accelerated the transformation of Northern society by industrial capitalism. The dynamics of capitalism that began in the antebellum period increased in scope and speed during the war, as the Republicans and their capitalist allies centralized economics and politics in the name of saving the Union. While Indiana largely remained agricultural, the Civil War had brought industrialization to the Hoosier state, and society had changed dramatically. As Morton noted, "Manufactures have increased and prospered, and commerce has brought to us its richest returns." Even as he tried to plan for peace, Morton realized that there was still much to do. With his characteristic energy, he threw himself into the task of leading Indiana through the turmoil and disruption of a changed but victorious society.[1]

But not everyone saw those "signs of prosperity and power" as a positive development. Three years earlier, on January 8, 1862, Hoosier Democrat Thomas A. Hendricks—a former state legislator and congressman and future governor, senator, and vice president of the United States—decried the changes wrought by the Republicans in the name of the war. Pointing to the policies of the Lincoln and Morton administrations, he asked, "Does not the sobbing voice of civil liberty, coming out of the ruins of a violated constitution, call us to the rescue?" He blamed the Republicans for such violations: "Can we as patriots, without an effort to save it, surrender our country to a party whose history thus far is written in failure, corruption and public ruin?" Hendricks criticized the proposed emancipation of the slaves, railed against the centralization of power, and lamented the trampling of individual liberty by the government. He also feared the growing power of industrial capitalism in Indiana and worried that the rest of the country would become subservient to the Northeast, which was home to the economic barons. Hinting at some sort of plan for the Northwest to defend its liberties against the government, Hendricks struck at the very heart of the changes underway in Indiana and the North as a whole.[2]

The broader context of industrialization helped to explain the transformation of the North during the war, but the political forces of nationalism that expanded the power of government also aided the development of capitalism. The story of the growth of capitalism and government in Indiana demonstrated how Republicans like Lincoln and Morton worked to bring prosperity and power like no one had never seen before. Yet the same nationalism that promoted industrialization laid the foundation for postwar economics and politics. The centralization and expansion of power set in motion the dynamics of future capitalism while eradicating the more laissez-faire and agrarian concepts of earlier decades. The economic side of the war meant that Indiana, like the United States, would never be the same. Some of those changes were clearly positive, but others might be negative. What Morton declared triumphantly to be a success, Hendricks feared was the end of American liberty.

BIG BUSINESS, BIG GOVERNMENT

The governor and his Democratic foes also disagreed about economics. Morton and his party favored policies that spurred the growth of industry. The Republicans used the rebellion as an opportunity to centralize power politically and also tried to implement their long-held economic plans. Just as the war did not give birth to the centralization and expansion of political power but instead provided an opportunity for government to grow more quickly, it did not suddenly create industrial capitalism but simply accelerated it. Overall, the war did not spur an economic boom for the entire country. In fact, as classical economists had noted earlier in the nineteenth century, war could not generate economic prosperity. At best it seemed that military conflict was Frédéric Bastiat's parable of the broken window writ large. In the French economist's story, people mistakenly saw the repair of a broken pane of glass as economic production and, therefore, thought destruction created wealth. But Bastiat pointed to what was not seen, which was that the money spent to repair the

Fig. 26. Governor Oliver P. Morton, ca. 1865. (Library of Congress)

window would have been put toward some other commercial activity that would not now be funded. Destruction did not produce wealth but instead hurt the economy by making people spend money on rebuilding things that they had already bought. The parable could readily be applied to an economic analysis of the rebellion. War destroyed and killed, neither of which created true financial growth. Full employment brought about by military service was not true employment: soldiers killed people and wrought destruction but did not produce. Still, war economies involved wealth redistribution and the shifting of economic activity. Such changes could fabricate the illusion of growth even if the war did not bring true prosperity.[3]

In reality, the Civil War brought a decline in economic growth. But this is not to say that it caused an economic crisis for everyone in the country. Rather, prosperity came to some, in some places. Overall, the nation saw a reduction in prewar rates of economic growth. But some sectors of the economy expanded dramatically. Railroads and other industries prospered. Of course, the Democrats of the day, Hendricks included, would have not been surprised. After all, the Republican economics that the Jacksonians opposed were those of Alexander Hamilton and Henry Clay—the old Federalist/Whig agenda brought forward by leaders like Lincoln. That agenda included many of the familiar ideas long promoted by those who favored an active government that worked to support capitalist economic development: a national bank, protective tariffs, and government spending for internal improvements.

With secession, Republican control of Congress was complete, and the party moved to implement the planks of their platform, including those economic strategies so many of them had long hoped to see become reality. The Republicans set aside the old laissez-faire economics of the Jacksonian Democrats in favor of a more active government that intervened in the economy. In a sense, the Republican policies during the war created a kind of neomercantilism, a form of capitalism in which the government sponsored, promoted, and helped control economic activity through legislation and regulation. This system included the notion that economics should benefit the state as well as individuals. In this case, the primary good would be winning the war and saving the nation. This was no accident. Nor was it a hidden agenda. Instead, it was simply what the Republicans had stood for since their formation as a coalition of former Whigs, antislavery Democrats, evangelical reformers, and anti-immigrant Nativists. Although the new antislavery party did not agree on many other issues, they largely came together on their economic platform. They combined free labor ideology with the economic ideas that Hamilton had passed to Clay, who had updated them for the Jacksonian era. Now Lincoln and the Republicans in the Civil War simply reworked those same ideas to fit their own time and the crisis of the war.[4]

Once in control of the national government, the Republicans quickly moved to achieve their economic goals. They began talking about a national banking system in 1861, although they did not establish it until 1863. In the process of creating this system, they destroyed or coopted the remaining state banks and free banks. Like the rest of the country, Indiana soon had national banks that replaced the older institutions. To be sure, this process came easier in the Hoosier State, where the bank failures in the mid-1850s preceded the Panic of 1857 and the resulting depression that wiped out most of the free banks in the years before the war. The Republicans also eventually turned to fiat currency, with the adoption of greenbacks. This, like the national bank, overturned Jacksonian dogma, and Democrats deplored such measures, railing against the banks and paper money.[5]

But the self-styled defenders of liberty (and too often of racism and slavery) also became apoplectic over Republican tax policy. The Lincoln administration eventually adopted the income tax—ruled unconstitutional after the war, but an idea that returned to favor in the early twentieth century—and also passed the Morrill Tariff in 1861. Even more odious to the Democrats were new excise taxes through which Congress taxed just about every single item produced in the United States. The Democrats were appalled, and the *Indiana Sentinel* daily gave over a full page or more to printing a list of items and rates affected, as it announced in its headline, "The National Tax," to remind its readers of how they were paying for the war. By 1864 Americans were carrying the largest tax burden in the history of the country. Meanwhile, crony capitalism seemed to reign supreme, as financiers and railroad magnates worked hand in glove with the government during the war. Bankers and businessmen joined the cause of the Union and reaped the benefits of doing so. Railroads especially won favor, as the government needed their trains for the war effort, and Washington passed out loans and money from bonds and provided land bounties to encourage the construction of the transcontinental railroad, and lesser railway enterprises benefited as well. To be sure, giving money and land to corporations led to more criticism from the Democrats, but the relationship between the Republicans, industrialization, and the Union allowed leaders to hail such crony capitalism as something needed for the cause. Thus, nationalism hid the sins of an expanding government working closely with an expanding industrial class. The Republicans wrapped their economic policies in the garb of patriotism, attaching economic change to the cause of Union, covering the tying of business to politics with the sacred banner of the nation.[6]

This played out in Indiana as well. Although Morton, the former Democrat, did not yet adhere to all of Republican economic policies, his ideology of freedom, Union, power, and party included the practicality of governing. With so much to accomplish for the war effort, Morton's administration worked closely with business in the name of the cause. Although the state lagged behind some of its neighbors in railroad mileage, various companies built new lines in the 1850s. Indianapolis was the center of the railroad boom, and eight different railroads had come together at the city's Union Depot by 1855. While railroad companies continued to lay new tracks before the war, the depression following the Panic of 1857 hurt the expansion of the industry. The war consumed manpower and resources, and railroad building virtually came to a halt. But the conflict also brought government contracts, and this provided an opportunity for most of the railroad companies to pay the debts that they had accrued over the previous decade. Even though the war meant inflated prices and increased operating costs, the exponential growth in business allowed the railroads to pay dividends while still reinvesting some of their profits by upgrading equipment. This laid the foundation for renewed construction in the postwar period. Indianapolis itself would see four new railroad lines in the immediate postwar years, as businessmen capitalized on the industrial prosperity that the war had brought to the state capital. During the rebellion itself, the railroads worked closely with Morton and his officers to arrange transportation for the troops. The governor enjoyed the power of dispensing railroad passes for those individuals who needed them, and he often took trains himself during his wartime travels.[7]

Railroads were not the only businesses booming in Indianapolis during the war. Industrialization, which had been limited and confined to a very small district in what was a sleepy town before the war, now accelerated, as many new factories and foundries appeared. In addition to factories that built railroad equipment, other manufacturers came to the city. Some of the new foundries started small during the war and expanded rapidly. One such was the Union Novelty Works, an iron foundry that produced a wide range of products, from iron bedsteads to gate latches. While many of these factories produced equipment or parts for railroads or made products that supplied the growing population and resulting building boom in Indianapolis, others related more directly to the war itself. Prewar industries like lumber, coal, and pork processing boomed during the conflict. Kingan and Company, the world's largest pork processors, opened a plant in Indianapolis in 1864 and introduced a new cooling process that allowed them to slaughter hogs in the heat of summer. The building trades all enjoyed expansion, as the city grew rapidly. New

Fig. 27. Senator (and future vice president) Thomas A. Hendricks, Democrat, Indiana. (Library of Congress)

industries also appeared, as the Van Camp family started canning pork and beans in their grocery in 1861 and obtained a contract to supply the army. No wonder, then, that city historians point to the war years as the period when Indianapolis truly industrialized. Clearly, the state capital boomed and enjoyed prosperity, as did some other areas of the state.[8]

But what about the criticisms that Hendricks had leveled against the Republicans in 1862? Did the economic boom in some of the cities also cause the rest of the state to flourish? Many southern Indiana communities found that the conflict brought hard times. Secession and war closed the river trade upon which so many southern Indiana farmers had depended. Kentucky staying in the Union helped somewhat, but even when Union forces reopened the Mississippi River trade, relief was slow in coming. Higher prices for farm products did not necessarily translate into an economic boom. The coincident increase in the cost of labor caused by so many men going into the military offset higher prices for farm products, while higher taxes added to the cost of living. While some towns enjoyed newfound prosperity, others lost ground economically and never fully returned to their prewar leadership in the state's economy.

While Democratic jeremiads about future economic collapse due to the national banks, paper money, increased debt, and higher taxes might have been overblown, they were not completely wrong. Those shrill-sounding Democrats who met in conventions to rail against the coming doom wrought by Republicans spoke to their chief constituents, Indiana farmers who prized local autonomy. True Jacksonian libertarians, those farmers and the politicians who represented them rightly saw the transformations accelerated by the war as leading to the eventual end of their way of life. To be sure, those Democrats mixed their economics and politics with racism, and their fear of blacks served as a motivating force right alongside their suspicion of the money power. But they, too, had a valid point to make. The end of slavery would mean that African Americans could move wherever they wanted and would be allowed to compete economically with whites. The war shifted the economy, benefiting some at the expense of others, changing their world forever, for good as well as bad.[9]

Whether Morton or Hendricks was right about Indiana's economy during the war depended on where and when one was. It depended on how one defined prosperity and power. It depended on whether one saw the growth of nationalism, government, and industrialization as positive or negative. It depended on whether one valued localism and individual liberty or whether one cherished the Union, equality, and a broader definition of freedom. It depended on whether one lived in Indianapolis or in the southern part of the state; on whether one used the railroads or the rivers. Both men had valid points to make. Hendricks was at least partially right when he decried the loss of liberty and the trampling of the Constitution in his speech. Truly, the war and Republican policies changed America forever. Although freedom certainly remained, the changes wrought by the war included the loss of some individual liberty as prewar Hoosiers knew it.

Additionally, the economic forces accelerated by the war would all but eradicate the agrarian way of life over the course of the next century. Jefferson's dream of an agrarian Empire for Liberty was doomed. But Morton was right, too, when he pointed to the unprecedented power and prosperity that the state experienced. The growth of government would often extend freedom and equality—as in the case of emancipation and civil rights, for example—even as it also benefited some over others in the growth of industrialization and the crony capitalism that foreshadowed the corporate world of the twentieth and twenty-first centuries. In the end, because they won the war, Lincoln, Morton, and their fellow Republicans won the argument, and even Hendricks eventually accepted the victory of nationalism. As he made his inaugural speech that January day in 1865, Morton pointed to the future, talking about coalfields and recommending the creation of a school for the study of agriculture, noting population growth and mentioning the many new businesses in the state. He thought that it was "indeed a strange anomaly, beyond human foresight, that in the midst of a desolating civil war our state should have unusual prospects of prosperity and power." Morton did well to remark on that irony, for the prosperity and power brought by the Civil War accelerated the vast changes that transformed Indiana and the entire North.[10]

DEFENDING REPUBLICAN ECONOMIC POLICIES

The governor's analysis of the economic transformation of Indiana during the war included another irony, population growth, and Morton was proud to note this at the outset of his second term. Even with tens of thousands of Hoosier men away at the front, Indiana's "towns are filling up. New lands are being brought into cultivation, and new enterprises in manufactures and commerce set on foot." But the reality was that the state's population growth had slowed dramatically. Immigration to Indiana had been an issue for the governor, as he worried about the shortage of labor and the demand for more military recruits that never seemed to end. State leaders often engaged in boosterism, hoping to attract new residents and businesses. Immigration had become more important for population growth in the decades before the Civil War but had come nearly to a standstill during the war. Most of those who had come to America hailed from European countries, especially famine-stricken Ireland and the politically divided German states.

But the waves of immigrants stopped with the war. Few would-be immigrants wanted to land in the United States only to face conscription and military service on the battlefield. Some unfortunate men experienced just that, but most simply chose not to migrate during the conflict. In 1864 Morton sought to sell Indiana to foreign immigrants by publishing *Emigration to the United States of North America: Indiana as a Home for Emigrants.* The forty-two-page pamphlet was an advertisement pitched to Europeans. The governor began by listing the advantages that the United States as a whole offered, including naturalized citizenship, high-wage jobs, cheap land, "light taxes," and readily available education. Morton maintained that the United States offered immigrants "the highest wages with the cheapest lands, living, and education, and the highest political privileges, that laboring men ever received in any country."[11]

Of course, he soon went on to push Indiana in particular. He extolled the rich and well-watered land, proudly told would-be immigrants that most farmers in Indiana "own their lands and work for themselves" rather than toiling for others. The Hoosier State was healthy and the land so rich that even minimal effort in agriculture produced tremendous results, to the point that the "great fertility of the soil has really perpetuated a sluggish and careless mode of farming," as farmers usually "let the soil, sun, and rains work for them." He listed the crops and provided tables containing the 1860 figures for agriculture production, including livestock as well as crops. Morton declared that settling in an older state like Indiana was preferable to moving to Western territories. Transportation and the cost of living were cheaper in the Hoosier State, and the availability of "improved lands" allowed an immigrant to buy an existing farm or start a new homestead without the difficulties of having to go it alone in the West.[12]

If farming did not sound attractive, Morton urged the immigrant to consider manufacturing and gushed about Indiana's "abundant facilities for manufactures," including "immense quantities of timber, and cheap transportation both for raw material and manufactured goods." He again used 1860 census numbers for Indiana as evidence of the potential for industry. While businessmen would find much to their liking, workers would find high wages, and the governor dutifully listed the typical rates of pay for various skilled and unskilled occupations. Morton devoted several pages to the railroads, proudly writing about the expansion of the existing lines and the ways in which they facilitated economic life. Public and private schools, newspapers, and libraries all made Indiana communities attractive.

The governor asserted that Indiana had low taxes, although he admitted that "since the commencement of the civil war the General Government of the United States . . . has established a system of taxation." He contradicted his earlier arguments by saying that the immigrant would not have to pay national taxes, including the new income tax, because only those who spent a lot of money as consumers or made a lot of money as income had to pay such taxes. He also admitted that the state carried a debt, but he asserted that it was actually very low and concluded that an immigrant "need have no fears of his crops or wages being eaten up by taxes." Morton boosted his state by extolling the banking system, including the new national bank. He thought that Indiana was an excellent site for vineyards and wineries, and he devoted a long section of his pamphlet to selling the idea. For those who wanted mineral wealth, the governor noted that the Hoosier State had mining opportunities, especially for rich coalfields that needed to be developed. Salt and iron production, stonecutting, and mining for lead, zinc, and other metals all existed in Indiana. And mineral springs offered opportunities for establishing resorts as well as medicinal uses.[13]

To be sure, the 1864 pamphlet was simply a marketing tool that Morton hoped would help boost immigration as the war ended. But it also presented a defense of Republican economic policy and pointed to the ways in which the war had brought prosperity. In early 1865 the governor worked with the new legislature to deal directly with the state's finances during his period of one-man rule. The Republican majority passed bills that paid the debts accrued by Morton and formed a bipartisan committee to investigate the charges of corruption that Democrats leveled against him. The committee carefully examined the books and found that Morton had been very careful with the state's money and that he and his secretaries had accounted for all funds. Even the Democrats who wanted to find that Morton had absconded with the money had to admit that he had been scrupulously honest. The committee's report allowed the legislature to pass bills paying back the counties, towns, and individuals who had helped the governor keep the state afloat. The legislature also agreed to pay back the money that the War Department had given to Morton. The 1865 legislative session proved to be the sweeping vindication that the governor had wanted.[14]

The End of the War

That legislative session also saw the majority ratify the Thirteenth Amendment abolishing slavery. The Democratic minority tried to organize a bolt to deny a quorum in order to stop the ratification, but they failed. They eventually settled for making racist speeches about the coming doom of the Republic and the white race. Soon, however, triumph and thanksgiving reigned as the country realized that the victory was nearly won. Division about what would happen next seethed under the surface as President Lincoln made his second inaugural address and spoke of moving forward "with malice toward none, with charity for all." On March 18, when Morton was in Washington on one of his many trips to the capital during the war, the president came to the governor's rooms at the National Hotel and presented him with a rebel flag captured by an Indiana regiment fighting in North Carolina. The two Republican leaders made remarks and congratulated each other and the Union soldiers. In his brief speech, Lincoln humorously jabbed at the Confederacy's desperate plan to enlist slaves in their army, saying that, while he did not know if the slaves would actually fight to keep themselves enslaved, he heartily endorsed the idea, as it would deprive the South of workers needed to keep their army fed. Black soldiers enlisting, in either army, helped the Union cause. Morton received the flag on Indiana's behalf and soon headed home to lead the state during the push to final victory. Soon the North turned jubilant with Lee's surrender at Appomattox, as it became obvious that the war was ending and that the cause had been won.

But the victory celebration turned to shock with Lincoln's assassination. When the news reached Indiana, Morton asked the citizens of Indianapolis to close their shops and meet at the statehouse for a solemn remembrance and time of prayer. He invited a number of Democrats as well as Republicans, and the governor spoke about the calamity. When Hendricks stepped up to speak, however, many in the crowd turned angry and began shouting, "Kill him! Don't let the traitor speak!" Some Union men pulled weapons and moved forward to eliminate the Democrat they saw as one who had aided and abetted the Confederacy and contributed to Lincoln's death. Morton stepped in front of Hendricks and restored order "with his terrible eye and ringing voice." At noon on April 19, 1865, communities in Indiana joined others across the country and held funeral services simultaneously with the official funeral in Washington, DC.[15]

Morton planned to meet Lincoln's funeral train when it came to Indiana, but in the meantime, he led a delegation of Hoosier leaders to meet the new president. The governor had corresponded with Andrew Johnson before and, early in the war, had invited the Tennessee Unionist to come stay in Indiana if it was too dangerous for him in his home state. Now Morton called on the president in the Treasury Building in Washington, where he delivered a formal address to Lincoln's successor. He denounced the rebellion and reaffirmed that the states had had no right to secede. He argued that each individual rebel "is politically and criminally responsible for his action" and reasoned that because treason was an individual crime, "so must be its punishment." Morton wanted the Southern states readmitted quickly, under the leadership of Unionists protected by federal troops. Johnson replied in agreement and said that he "might well have adopted Governor Morton's speech as his own."[16]

Confident that Johnson shared his views about the rebellion—punishing rebels and readmitting the Southern states—Morton returned to Indiana. He met the late president's funeral train at Richmond just after midnight on April 30 and rode it back to Indianapolis. Plans for a funeral in the state capital included the governor delivering an address, but driving rain forced the cancellation of the ceremonies. Despite the weather, over 100,000 people filed past the casket as Lincoln lay in state in the rotunda of the capitol building. The following month, Morton's office began collecting funds, often from soldiers, to pay for the building of a monument to Lincoln in Indianapolis.[17]

Morton continued his role as the Soldiers' Friend, even as the troops began returning home in the spring and summer of 1865. He pushed a tax bill through the legislature that funded support for the soldiers' families and continued to lend aid to the hospitals that cared for the wounded. He knew that those still recovering from wounds, and the maimed veterans especially, needed care. The governor created the state Soldiers' Home, which first opened in a hospital in Indianapolis but soon relocated to a site near Knightstown. Additionally, Morton worried about the many orphans of those who had died fighting for the Union cause, so he established the Indiana Soldiers' and Sailors' Children's Home, which was also located in Knightstown when it opened in 1867. To remember those who had made the ultimate sacrifice and died fighting, he wanted to build battlefield cemeteries, including a national burial ground at Gettysburg. No wonder, then, that in 1865, when a military officer and member of Morton's staff was publishing a song he had written about the soldiers and their yearning for home while they were off at war, he dedicated it to Governor Morton.[18]

For those veterans marching back home in triumph, the governor did his best to give them a hero's welcome. Morton gave each returning regiment a public reception that began with a cannon firing early in the morning to mark the beginning of a celebratory breakfast at the Soldiers' Home. The regiment then marched through the streets in a parade to the statehouse. There, amid musical performances and prayers, the governor or one of his representatives welcomed them home with a speech extolling their brave service and sacrifices to the cause. Morton excelled at such greetings, as he extended his personal gratitude as well as that of the state and the nation to the soldiers who had fought for freedom and Union. His sincerity rang true to the men, and they appreciated that Morton and his administration had long supported them and that the governor now treated them as conquering heroes.

While he clearly cared about the soldiers he had helped send off to war, Morton's motives stemmed from his ideology and from his considerations of political power. Like other Republicans during the Civil War era, Morton held to the ideology of freedom, Union, and power. For him, freedom meant freedom under the law, and it meant that slavery had to be contained—and, like Lincoln, during the war he came to believe that it had to be abolished. He saw secession as a treasonous act that would destroy the Union that guaranteed freedom and created the fabric of the American nation. To protect and extend freedom and to preserve the Union, Morton thought it necessary to centralize and use the power of government.

His actions in supporting the soldiers often reflected his ideological principles, but they also demonstrated that Morton knew how to play politics. Yes, his duty demanded helping the soldiers, but such work also helped him politically. The celebrations he held for the returning troops sealed his friendship with most of Indiana's veterans, and they remember him at the ballot box. Being the Soldiers' Friend made the governor even more powerful. For Morton, of course, power meant party, whether he called it the Union Party or the Republican Party. His dedication to party extended beyond using patronage in appointments to laying the foundation for a political organization that would dominate Indiana. He realized the potential for building a power base among the soldiers, and he would help create the Grand Army of the Republic, the veterans' organization that became a potent political force in the postwar era. Having seen the impact of the military vote in 1862 and 1864, Morton now welcomed home the soldiers, not only as heroes but also as potential voters who would help him and his party secure the peace they had achieved through victory.[19]

RACIAL QUESTIONS RAISED BY PEACE

The question of how to secure the peace often absorbed the governor's thoughts. One of the most pressing and obvious issues was the matter of the freedmen and -women. The passage of the Thirteenth Amendment guaranteed the legal freedom of the former slaves, but that was only the beginning of the problem. Whether or not they were equal citizens or whether they would have the right to vote raised further constitutional considerations. Added to this were economic and social questions about the condition of the freed people. Hearing about some schemes to revive the old plan of colonization that would send blacks to Africa, Morton responded with an 1865 speech entitled "What Shall be Done with the Negro?" Denouncing colonization, he took the view of many Republicans at the time, arguing from the principles of free labor ideology to make the libertarian case for freedom and individualism.[20]

The Hoosier leader seized on the old economic arguments that had long been made by racists who feared that blacks would take jobs away from whites. "Some timid souls fear competition with [the freedman], and seem to think that unless he is deprived of his liberty, and kept down by law, and all the means of rising in the world withheld from him, he will outstrip them in the race for fame and fortune." Ironically, some white supremacists wanted the government to give white people advantages over African Americans that "God did not give them." Other racists openly feared that white Americans would be "overrun and subjugated" by the former slaves. Morton dismissed this notion by pointing out that white people in the United States numbered 28 million and that the white population was rapidly growing, while blacks numbered about 4 million. Thus, there was "no great danger" to prevent whites from "treating them with justice and humanity." In keeping with the prewar Republican ideology of free labor, the governor contended that "what the negro requires at our hands is that he shall be made secure in his person and family, that his liberties shall be guaranteed; that he shall be paid for his labor, and secured in all the rights of property, that his education shall be provided for, and then we shall . . . require him to take care of himself."[21]

On September 29, 1865, Morton delivered a speech in Richmond, later published as *Reconstruction and Negro Suffrage.* Ostensibly given in honor of the contributions to the war effort by the citizens of Wayne County, the discourse came in the context of the chaotic months following the war, the oration later haunted Morton, as it became a leading example of the political opportunism with which his opponents charged him. Still feeling the exuberance of the recent Union triumph, he took a positive view of Reconstruction, favorably comparing Andrew Johnson's plans for the postwar settlement to those of the martyred Lincoln. Although he recognized that Northerners could not "expect that the people of the rebel States have come to love us," nor would they any time soon, he proudly argued that the idea of secession and the institution of slavery both had been defeated and "banished once and forever." Adhering to the ideas behind Presidential Reconstruction, the Indiana governor especially supported the legal argument that the war had been a rebellion perpetrated by individuals and that the Southern states had never left the Union. At this point, he backed the administration's plan for amnesty and the restoration of state governments and readmitting the rebel states to the Union.[22]

Most of his discourse in Richmond, however, dealt with the question of whether or not African Americans should have the right to vote. He was quick to again reject the idea of colonization as impracticable and said that the former slaves were Americans who would eventually enjoy the full rights of citizenship. But that was the future, not now. When it came to giving black Southerners the right to vote, Morton admitted that he believed in "the equal rights of all men," and he thought that "in time all men will have the right to vote without distinction of color or race." But the governor also believed that, "in the case of four millions of slaves just freed from bondage, there should be a period of probation and preparation before they are brought to the exercise of political power."[23]

Despite his assertion of egalitarianism, Morton considered the material and social conditions of the freed people in the South and decided against granting them suffrage. After all, the right to vote also carried the right to seek, win, and hold office. He did not think the former slaves were ready for such power. "Perhaps not one in five hundred—I may say one in a thousand—can read, and perhaps, not one in five hundred is worth five dollars in property of any kind. They have no property, personal or real. They have just come from bondage, and all they have is their own bodies." And many of the former slaves lived on their former masters' plantations and worked for them. Such a situation meant that the freedmen would be influenced by their former masters, quite probably with threats and violence as well as the possibility of losing their homes and jobs.[24]

Morton recognized that the freed people were in a precarious position economically and worried about the consequences of that situation. Surely, he thought, until they achieved some measure of social and economic independence, the United States should not give them political rights. He did not think that any group of men in a similar situation, whatever their race, would be ready for citizenship and the franchise. As Morton argued, "To say that such men—and it is no fault of theirs, it is simply their misfortune, and the crime of the nation—to say that such men, just emerging from this slavery, are qualified for the exercise of political powers, is to make the strongest pro-slavery argument I ever heard. It is to pay the highest compliment to the institution of slavery." After all, if slavery made men ready for full citizenship, then it must not have been such a great evil, and the governor refused to accept such an argument.[25]

Next Morton turned to the hypocrisy of Indiana telling the Southern states what to do about black voting rights. He did not make a case for rights but rather pointed out that although Indiana had some twenty-five thousand black people—and most of them were literate property owners—the state not only denied them voting rights but also did not allow them to testify in court. Hoosiers excluded African Americans from public schools and had made it "unlawful and a crime for them to come into the State of Indiana at any time subsequent to 1850." The exclusion article of the 1851 state constitution meant that any black person who had come into Indiana since then could not "make a valid contract; he cannot acquire a piece of land, because the law makes the deed void, and every man who gives him employment is liable to prosecution and fine."[26]

During the war, Morton had helped to recruit and organize the 28th Indiana, a regiment of black soldiers. The black troops, many of them from Delaware and Maryland rather than the Hoosier State, had "fought well on many occasions, and won the high opinion of officers who had seen" them in action. Still, the state denied at least half of the men in the regiment the right to live in Indiana. Given that context, how could Hoosiers "go to Congress and insist upon giving the right of suffrage to the negroes in the southern States?" Morton said that if the state's congressmen did that, they would be asked, "What have you done with these people in your own State?" Morton answered the question clearly: "You have done nothing." Yes, Indiana had fewer African Americans than the Southern states, but to deny even a small minority civil rights gave the lie to the theories of liberty and equality upon which the nation was founded. If Northern states like Indiana refused to grant the vote to their own black residents, then they were hypocrites to expect such in the South. The governor told his home county audience that "these Northern States can never command any moral force on that subject until they shall first be just to their negroes at home."[27]

Charles Sumner had recently proposed that the government should deny the vote to most rebels and give the franchise to the freedmen as a counterbalance to white votes. Morton worried that if the United States pursued this policy, African American voters in the South would outnumber whites by at least twenty to one and this would "erect colored state governments." While he agreed that there were some black politicians qualified and ready to serve in such governments, he feared that the result would be a massive outmigration by whites who would refuse to live under black rule. Morton admitted that there were some Northerners who would accept sharing power with or being governed by African Americans, but he thought racism was still too strong even among those who opposed slavery. "You can't find the most ardent anti-slavery man in Wayne County who will go and locate in a state that has a colored State government." European immigrants would refuse to move to such states even as the native whites fled, meaning that "they will remain permanently colored States in the South." Ultimately, this would lead to a situation where "the colored states will be a balance of power in this country." The former slaves "would constantly vote and act together, and their united vote would constitute a balance of power that

Fig. 28. President Andrew Johnson. (Library of Congress)

might control the government of the nation," just as Southern slaveholders had once been "able to govern this nation a long time" under the Slave Power. This would eventually lead to "a war of races." Thus, in 1865 the man who eventually helped lead the fight for the Fifteenth Amendment argued that blacks were not yet ready for voting rights.[28]

The governor understood all too well that many Hoosiers held racist views. Just two months earlier, he had received word that a group of Union veterans in Evansville had taken it upon themselves to plan an attack on blacks living in the area. The former soldiers may have fought to help free the slaves, but they did not want African Americans living in their own state. They proudly proclaimed that they would act in order to enforce state laws excluding blacks from living in Indiana. Morton directed his military aide to write to one of the leaders of the soldier vigilantes and admonish him not to carry out the plan. The letter shamed the soldiers for such racist thinking and encouraged them to avoid violating the laws of the country they had served so well throughout the long war. Such racial views were widespread across Indiana, and the governor publicly expressing his reluctance about black suffrage fit well with many of his constituents.[29]

Morton's views on black voting changed over time, just as Lincoln's thinking about the issue had changed before his assassination. But when the Hoosier leader came to support black voting rights, his enemies blasted him as an opportunist. And there was truth in that charge. However, considering the context, Morton stood in the mainstream of the Republican Party at the time. The complete break between Johnson and the Radical Republicans had not yet occurred, and it was not immediately clear how former rebels in the South would behave. Some Radicals complained about Johnson, and some ex-Confederates soon controlled state governments and began passing so-called black codes, which were designed to support white supremacy by restricting the activities of African Americans and limiting the impact of freedom. But the wholesale resistance to Reconstruction in the South had not yet emerged when Morton spoke in Richmond.

The governor was on firm ground when he pointed to the hypocrisy of Northerners pushing for black suffrage in the South when they still denied rights to African Americans in their own states. In 1865 Morton supported an apportionment of congressional seats in the South based on the number of voters rather than on population as a temporary measure. Meanwhile, blacks would have a period in which to be educated and to gain independence from their former masters. Later, some would argue that the governor pandered to racism in this speech, rallying support from voters who did not want to extend rights to African Americans. Such arguments ignored the context and the audience. Most of those gathered before him in Richmond that September night were Republicans and opposed to slavery. They applauded Morton's statements about equality and were silently ashamed when he spoke of their hypocrisy. They, like most Republicans, agreed with Morton's ideas about a period of probation before giving former slaves political rights.

About the only Indiana Republican who disagreed was Morton's longtime foe, George W. Julian. When the abolitionist attacked Morton's views and called for black suffrage, other Hoosier Republicans quickly defended the governor and denounced Julian and Sumner as "ultras" whose radical ideas would disrupt the party and the nation. That fall Morton's friend, Solomon Meredith, attacked Julian in the railroad station at Richmond. Having run unsuccessfully against the congressman in the 1864 election, Meredith still held a grudge against Julian for having criticized his appointment at the outset of the war. He also blamed him for publishing newspaper accounts that criticized him as an incompetent military commander. He approached the congressman, knocked him down, and then beat him with a whip. Julian was not seriously injured, and although Meredith was arrested and charged with assault and battery, the case was dismissed. Not even a physical attack by a friend of Morton could dissuade the old abolitionist, however, and Julian continued to criticize the governor. His Centerville foe's radicalism may have contributed to Morton's conservatism: he wanted to set himself apart from the man he hated. Eventually, however, as the context changed, Morton's thinking would evolve, and he later took on many ideas that seemed too radical in 1865.[30]

Morton's First Stroke

By the time of his Richmond speech, the governor had exhausted himself. Long years of labor in leading the state had worn him out. When he met the returning troops in Indianapolis, his haggard appearance betrayed his weariness, and he sometimes barely managed to deliver his speech to the returning veterans. Back pain and other aches plagued him almost constantly. He was forced to cancel planned trips and speaking engagements. By July his health had forced him to be confined to bed to recover some of his strength. In August of 1865 he took a vacation to Niagara Falls, hoping that the trip would distract him, allow him to rest, and recover some of his vitality. It seemed to work. He wrote to Lucinda, saying that he had arrived and was feeling better than he had in a long time and that even his back pain had subsided. The location helped, too, as "the soft moist breeze from the Falls is delightful," and the beauty of Niagara invigorated him. Alone at last, he found relief and was able to relax and escape the pressures of office. Upon his return to Indiana, however, his health again began to decline.[31]

By October he was having trouble thinking clearly, and he "felt an indisposition to read or study. I did not care to read so much as a newspaper." This was unusual for the voracious reader who had long devoured books and daily went through the newspapers. Furthermore, he found himself forgetting things and becoming easily confused. The indefatigable governor lost interest in what was going on, until even "the duties of the state no longer engaged my close attention." The decline continued until October 10, 1865, a day that Morton said that he would never forget. "It was a beautiful one, the air was crisp, and I walked a long distance." He went to bed that night somewhat tired, but otherwise in good health. When he woke early the next morning, he read the morning newspapers while still in bed, as he often did. But when he tried to get out of bed, he "discovered that I was unable to lift my limbs. Again and again I made the effort, when it flashed through my mind that I was paralyzed. I felt no pain, but from my hips downward I was unable to move. My head seemed clear as a bell, and I recalled to mind incidents I had forgotten." Morton had suffered a stroke, and the paralysis that it brought meant that he would never walk again without some sort of support.[32]

At first the governor feared that he might not survive, and he sent for his lawyer as well as his physician, hoping to make a will and put his affairs in order. When he did not die, Morton looked toward recovery, but he could not follow the doctor's orders to rest. Instead, he threw himself back into his work, convening a special session of the legislature. Over the objections of his doctors, on November 14, 1865, the governor addressed the legislature and delivered a message in which he gave them a charge for the session. He apologized for having to sit down while delivering it, but his paralysis demanded it. Drawing attention to the state of his health underscored the importance of the special session, which Morton called because a number of bills had failed to pass in the previous legislative meeting. Financial matters topped the list, including his request for a plan to pay the state's debt. The governor also asked for the reapportionment of legislative seats based on population shifts and asked for the creation of a juvenile detention center.

The soldiers still occupied his mind, as he recommended a revised bill for the relief of military families and wanted the legislature to create a new soldiers' home. He wanted Indiana to promote itself to immigrants and asked for a new agency to take up that task. Morton also pushed for the state to take part in the Paris World's Fair. Education and funds to pay for damages incurred during Morgan's Raid also made his list. Finally, the governor called for changing the law to fund education for African Americans and to allow them to testify in court. He reiterated the views on black suffrage that he had given in his Richmond speech and still recommended support for President Johnson's plan for Reconstruction. Within a matter of weeks, the full break between the president and the Radical Republicans was to bring deep divisions and disagreements that eventually led Morton to change camps on the matter of how to secure the peace in the conquered South. But for the moment he remained hopeful and moderate in his views.[33]

Seeking Treatment and Treaties in Europe

After delivering his message to the legislature, Morton turned the executive branch over to Lieutenant Governor Conrad Baker and prepared to travel to Europe to seek treatment for his paralysis. His physicians worried that he might die during the trip, and a number of friends came to wish him well and to say good-bye, including his electoral opponent in 1864, Joseph McDonald. The governor went first to Washington, where he met with Andrew Johnson and expressed his support for the president. Johnson asked Morton to take on a secret mission to Emperor Louis Napoleon of France. Working outside the normal diplomatic channels, the president hoped through Morton to achieve the French withdrawal from Mexico. This was necessary because the French had recently asked the United States to recognize the government of Emperor Maximilian in Mexico in exchange for pulling their troops out of the country. Johnson wanted Morton to inform Napoleon of the impossibility of such recognition and explain the political situation in the United States, where the people overwhelming supported sending troops to expel the French by force. Officially, Morton would meet with Napoleon to discuss matters like sanitation, transportation, and the supplying of the French armies. But he carried letters from Secretary of War Stanton authorizing his secret mission when he, Lucinda, his son John, and the former editor of the *Indianapolis Journal,* Berry Sulgrove, took ship for Europe.[34]

A short visit in England over the Christmas holiday preceded the trip to Paris. Once in the French capital, Morton met with Louis Napoleon and fulfilled both his official and secret missions. He managed to do a little sightseeing, including visiting the Louvre, before he received treatment from French doctors. They used the Asian moxa procedure, which required the burning of parts of the mugwort plant on or near the skin. The famous actress Clara

Morris received the moxa a few years later, and, supposedly, it cured her so-called "nervous affliction." Because of this, in the 1870s, newspapers linked her name with Morton's in advertisements for and articles about the treatment that they promoted, alongside acupuncture and other alternative procedures. Although some experts thought the moxa was effective for spinal injuries, it proved unsuccessful for Morton. But the recovery period meant that he remained in Paris until February 1, 1866. Now realizing that his paralysis was permanent, he took his little party to Switzerland and Italy. He had hoped that a successful operation would allow him to walk again and had planned to spend more time in Europe. In fact, Andrew Johnson had offered to appoint him minister to Austria if he wanted the job, but Morton declined. Reports about the political battles over Reconstruction stirred him, and he returned home in March to rejoin the fight.[35]

In December of 1865 President Johnson had declared that his plan for Reconstruction was complete and that the state governments in the South were again in operation. The states had ratified the Thirteenth Amendment, and Presidential Reconstruction had followed a magnanimous course of amnesty rather than punishment for the former leaders of the rebellion. But the Radical Republicans would have none of it. The new state governments in the South passed black codes that all but returned the freed people to slavery. It became clear that the former Confederates had not been reconstructed after all, and when Congress convened, the national legislature began to fight with the president for control of the situation. Led by Radicals like Thaddeus Stevens, Charles Sumner, and Benjamin F. Wade, the congressional Republicans began passing bills that expanded the power of the Freedman's Bureau by extending the military occupation in states that denied civil rights to the former slaves. Johnson vetoed the bill. Meanwhile, the battle turned to the Fourteenth Amendment, granting citizenship regardless of race, and the president railed against it in such a way as to erode his support among moderates. The Radicals passed a civil rights bill and Johnson vetoed it. Congress overrode the veto and the fight intensified.

In the midst of these dramatic political events, Morton arrived back in the United States. He landed in New York and then spent a month in the East, meeting with various Republicans, who explained the situation to him. He went to Washington, met with the president, and urged him to sign the civil rights bill. When Johnson said that he would not, Morton informed him that his refusal would bring the final break with the Republicans and the political fight between the administration and Congress would only grow worse. He did his best to persuade Johnson to change his mind but left the president convinced that his efforts were to no avail and that it was time for the Republicans to take control of Reconstruction.

He headed back to Indiana, where he found a political mess. Hoosier Republicans had continued to support Johnson until the president embarrassed them and they found themselves demoralized and adrift. When supporters of Congressional Reconstruction began to assert themselves, the state party tried to please everyone and adopted a contradictory platform that expressed the party's indecision and weakness. Meanwhile, Republican confusion invigorated the Democrats, who began to attack their opponents with charges of corruption. They took up support for Johnson against the Republicans, an easy move when one considered that the president had been a Jacksonian Democrat chosen as Lincoln's second vice president because he was a Southern Unionist. As the 1866 elections approached, the Democrats confidently prepared to take full advantage of the situation and once more win control of Indiana. Many Republicans feared that they would lose the elections, and that would mean losing the peace that had been won with such sacrifice during the war.

But then Morton came home.[36]

CHAPTER EIGHT

Waving the Bloody Shirt

RETURNING ENERGETICALLY TO POLITICS in 1866, Morton soon emerged as a national leader in the Republican Party during Reconstruction. Despite his paralysis, he led his party in developing a new political style and method, which the Democratic opponents of Reconstruction called "waving the bloody shirt." Using the symbolism of blood-soaked garments worn by martyrs to the cause of freedom and Union, Morton rallied his party in order to win and keep power by reminding voters that Democrats had led the rebellion and the treasonous secret societies. He saw Reconstruction as a continuation of the Civil War, and motivated by his core ideology of freedom, Union, power, and party, he worked hard to achieve a final victory over rebellion and treason. Morton may well have been the very first Republican to wave the bloody shirt during Reconstruction when he used the imagery in the election of 1866. Upon his arrival in Indiana, the governor found his party weakened and adrift. Quickly taking command of the election campaign, he denounced the defeatism of his party, arguing that he would not allow Indiana to fall into the hands of rebels and traitorous Copperheads. For him, the issues of Reconstruction continued the issues of the war. The off-year elections would determine control of Congress, a significant matter as the battle with Johnson would determine the future of the country. Furthermore, the election would decide which party controlled the state legislature. Here Morton's own ambitions came into play, as the new legislature would elect a United States senator early in 1867. The governor wanted the seat for himself and enjoyed overwhelming support among Indiana Republicans.[1]

But he also saw the election in personal terms because the Democrats had once again been charging him with corruption. They also said that he had placed the state arsenal in the middle of the city, where it posed a threat to public safety, and he had also located military facilities and hospitals in such a way as to spread disease among the population. During his period of one-man rule, his enemies said, Morton had siphoned off money for himself and for his

198

friends. According to the Democrats, with these stolen funds he bought carriages, land, and an opulent house in Indianapolis. They claimed that he had lined the pockets of his businessman friends and had used cloth designated for wrapping cartridges to cover the billiards tables in the pool halls where he and his cronies spent their many leisure hours.

Within a few years his enemies had added tales to these scandalous charges. Supposedly his paralysis stemmed from his dissipation, especially his sexual habits, and his political opponents claimed that he was such a womanizer that the respectable ladies and gentlemen of Indianapolis refused to receive him. The Democrats cast aspersions on his moral character, hinting that the moxa procedure that he had received in Paris was really a treatment for syphilis or some other venereal disease. They told stories about how he had supposedly given men commissions and offices only if their pretty wives visited the governor's office and had sex with Morton in exchange for their appointments. His political enemies spread rumors that he had kept a mistress throughout the war years. The woman supposedly lived in Knightstown, conveniently located between Indianapolis and Morton's home in Centerville, and he could stop off to visit her when taking the train back and forth. Despite the fact that a bipartisan committee had already cleared him of the charges of stealing money, the Democrats again called for an investigation of Morton's financial records and his alleged misuse of funds.[2]

Frankly, most of the charges were ridiculous. Morton lived comfortably but not extravagantly. Taking up residence in the Governor's Mansion on the corner of Market and Illinois Streets in Indianapolis made it convenient when the pressures of the war made it difficult to travel even the short train ride home to Centerville. Built without proper consideration to drainage, the official residence of the state executive was notoriously damp and unhealthy. As a matter of fact, Governor James Whitcomb had blamed the mansion for his wife's illness and death. Morton had soon realized the derelict condition of the house and had given up on the Governor's Mansion. He had moved into the Bates House hotel and ordered the executive residence torn down. Later he purchased a house in Indianapolis at 149 North Pennsylvania Street that was located on the corner of that avenue and New York Street.[3]

Morton's Indianapolis house, like his Centerville residence, was a large, comfortable home that befitted the lifestyle of a prominent man. But his residence in the state capital was not the luxurious mansion that the Democrats described. A newspaper report about the house at 149 North Pennsylvania Street said that it was large but plain, especially in comparison to several nearby mansions. Tasteful verandas graced the front of the two-and-a-half-story-high residence, a former duplex that had been renovated into a single-family dwelling. Inside,

A House with a history in the down town district which should be owned and preserved by the State.

the hall led to double parlors and a small library on the left. The back parlor was connected to the dining room beyond by large folding doors that allowed for more space for entertaining. The reporter said that Morton's "furniture is rich but plain." The walls were painted a rose color and were adorned with "handsome paintings and fine engravings of Lincoln, Sherman, and Grant." The pictures of the Union heroes were probably added after the war, but at least some of the family photographs in the living room could be found there from the time they moved in. It was a large, comfortable house. But it was not an opulent display of the governor's power and wealth.[4]

Besides, he paid for the house with his own money. His rather large income as an attorney had laid the foundation for a solid financial situation. He and his wife kept careful records, and Lucinda's pecuniary habits helped keep things in order. Actually, he lived somewhat modestly for one who had reached such heights of political power. The newspaper article describing his house also noted that he kept a carriage and horse, but that the vehicle was "much-worn" and the "old black horse much the worse for spavin." The reporter said that Morton was not a rich man, although "he is ambitious, but not avaricious, and cares nothing for display." This virtue and Lucinda's management allowed him to live within his means. Morton invested wisely, both before and after the war, taking tips from his businessman friends and using his knowledge

Fig. 29. (*opposite*) Morton House, Indianapolis (1890s postcard). Published by the Sentinel Printing Co. in Indianapolis, this color postcard served as an advertisement for the Polar Ice and Fuel Company, but it also promoted historic preservation. The Polar Ice Company was founded by Henry Louis Dithmer in 1892 and operated regionally with headquarters in Indianapolis until 2000, when it was bought and became a subsidiary of Home City Ice Company, Inc. Postcards like this were a popular form of advertising in the 1890s but fell out of fashion in the early twentieth century.

The Morton House address changed over the years, as the city grew. Across the top it read, "A House with history in the down town district that should be owned and preserved by the State." The sign on the front of the house at the time was for the YWCA then occupying it. The sign read, "Young Women's Christian Academy and Home for Girls. Dining Room, Gymnasium, and Offices are at Rear of 329 N. Pennsylvania St." On the reverse side the postcard read, "A house with a history, is located at the southeast corner of Pennsylvania and New York streets and was at one time owned and occupied by the Hon. Oliver P. Morton, the famous war Governor of Indiana. Governor Morton died in this house November 1, 1877." Unfortunately, the house was not preserved. Another black and white photograph postcard from 1909 showed the house shortly before it was torn down to build a larger facility for the YWCA. The address of the corner lot is now 241 N. Pennsylvania Street and is occupied today by an office building. Across the street is University Park.

of current events to make money. But he did not make off with state funds. Charges that he did so were simply untrue, and when they opened the books, even his enemies had to admit that Morton was honest. The ludicrous accusations that he covered his pool tables with flannels intended to wrap cartridges hardly required a response.[5]

But the governor took the slanderous attacks personally and set out to defend his record and his honor. As usual, this meant attacking his opponents, and he began to turn the campaign in favor of the Republicans with a speech at the Masonic Hall in Indianapolis on June 20, 1866. According to the current editor of the *Indianapolis Journal* and state printer, who also happened to be his brother-in-law and secretary, W. R. Holloway, a committee of prominent party leaders had prepared an address for the governor to deliver. Morton handed the draft of the committee's speech to Holloway and had him read it aloud. It was a long essay warning voters of the dangers the country faced and discussing the Republican platform. Within minutes Morton had interrupted Holloway: "Stop, the committee have made a failure of it. They do not seem to know what is needed. . . . We must remind the people of the Democratic record, and arraign that party for the crimes and infamies it has perpetrated against society and the government during and since the war." The governor then dictated to Holloway a speech of his own that did just what he wanted. Rather than playing defense, Morton would destroy his opponents in what was nothing less than a continuation of the war.[6]

DECLARING WAR BY ANOTHER NAME

Greeted with tremendous applause at the Masonic Hall, the governor gave his famous Masonic Hall speech sitting down. But his superb performance proved that, despite his paralysis, he was still a formidable orator. Somehow, being unable to walk or stand seemed to sharpen his mind and give more power to his voice. His broad shoulders and powerful torso made him seem huge as he sat in his chair. He still gestured to emphasize his points, and the restless energy that once made him pace to and fro on the stage now made him sway in his seat as he delivered his oration. He declared that "the war is over—the rebellion has been suppressed—the victory has been won, and now the question presented to us at the coming election, is whether the fruits of victory shall be preserved or not." Morton immediately went to work attacking his political foes, arguing that "the temper of the Democratic party is not changed or improved since the termination of the war." Instead he thought that his opponents had grown bitter after suffering defeat both on the battlefield and at the ballot box. He criticized members of the Hoosier Democracy for having gone to a convention in Louisville, where they "mingled their tears with those who wept over Southern heroes," and having "uttered glowing eulogies upon the memory of Stonewall Jackson and John Morgan, and endorsed their most ultra and treasonable doctrines."[7]

For Morton, the leaders of the Indiana Democrats in 1866 were the same men who in 1861 had proclaimed that any Union army passing through Indiana on its way to fight the rebellion "must first pass over their dead bodies." The current Democrats were the same men who had declared during the war that "Southern defeats gave them no joy, and Northern disasters no sorrow." They were the same men who had tried to hamper recruitment efforts and who had resisted the draft, the men who had "corresponded with the rebel leaders in the South," who had tried to take over the state government in 1863. Morton charged the Democrats with treason, arguing that many of them had been Copperheads who belonged to secret societies like the Sons of Liberty. It was the Democrats who had organized and led the conspiracy that had tried to overthrow the government. He admitted that it was not all of them, but even those who did not join the Copperhead secret societies had known what was going on and had stood ready to accept the results if the conspiracy worked. Morton reminded the audience of the events of the summer of 1864, when the Copperheads had planned to seize the arsenal and free the prisoners at Camp Morton. Such charges hit their mark, since Lambdin P. Milligan, the Copperhead leader convicted in the treason trials in 1864, had been released from prison in April and, the next month, delivered a political speech in Bluffton, Indiana. For Morton, such events provided clear evidence of the true nature of his political opponents. Beyond opposing the war, the Democrats had opposed helping the soldiers and their families. Morton remembered that they had not contributed to the Sanitary Commission, and that they had made "foul imputations on the chastity of soldiers' wives."[8]

On and on the Republican orator went, the pace of his words quickening as he railed against the traitorous Democrats. Every rebel and every Copperhead had been a Democrat, every one of those who murdered Union prisoners, every man who promoted rebellion, "every dishonest contractor who has been convicted of defrauding the government . . . every officer in the army who was dismissed for cowardice or disloyalty, calls himself a Democrat." Morton accused his foes in the other party of defending slavery and said that "everyone who shoots down negroes in the streets, burns negro school-houses and meeting-houses, and murders women and children by the light of their own flaming dwellings, calls himself a Democrat."[9]

Although many Northerners associated racial violence with the South, there had been a race riot and lynching of two black men in Evansville in August of 1865. And Daviess County, Indiana, saw another lynching just the month before Morton's June 1866 Masonic Hall speech, as a black man accused of assaulting a white woman was hanged while he was being taken to jail following his arrest. Reports that prominent Democratic citizens had supported or even led the mobs that lynched black citizens outraged Morton and other Republicans. The governor cried, "The Democratic party may be described as a common sewer and loathsome receptacle, into which is emptied every element of treason North and South, and every element of inhumanity and barbarism which has dishonored the age."[10]

According to Morton, the Democrats, having lost the war that they started, would not accept defeat. Instead, they sought a return to office and hoped to regain political power. Thus, the governor revealed their real goal: "Having failed to destroy the constitution by force, they seek to do it by construction." He called on the voters to support the Fourteenth Amendment and to reject the Democrats, who had "committed treason against liberty in behalf of slavery; against civilization in behalf of barbarism" and whose deeds would be remembered as those of one "of the most dangerous and malignant factions that have ever afflicted government and retarded the progress of mankind."[11]

On July 18, 1866, he addressed a Union meeting in New Albany, Indiana, and continued his attacks on the Democrats. This time he criticized a Democratic convention held the previous month in New Albany, where his political foes had declared that the war had been "just and necessary" to preserve the Union and thanked the soldiers for their service. Morton denounced those resolutions and speeches made by Daniel Voorhees and Joseph McDonald as being too little, too late. To say that the war was "just and necessary" sixteen months after it ended was disingenuous on the part of the Democrats. Morton refused to let them say that they had supported the war and again called his enemies traitors who had worked to undermine the government and who had failed to support the troops. Far from being patriots, the Democrats were criminals, and Morton would not let them "blot out the story of their misdeeds, nor erase from the pages of history the record of their crimes against the country." Speaking to a gathering of Union veterans on August 13, 1866, Morton again condemned the Democrats as traitors and used imagery that would become one of the most significant political symbols of Reconstruction. He asked the assembled men if the soldiers wanted the Democrats "whose garments are yet red with the blood of their comrades to legislate for them, to say how much bounty they should have and what pensions they and the widows and families of their slaughtered brethren should have, if any." Invoking the image of traitors wearing garments dripping with the sacrificial blood of martyrs to the cause foreshadowed the way that Morton waved the bloody shirt throughout Reconstruction.[12]

He hit the Democrats hard on the issue of how they treated the soldiers during the war and their stand on veterans' affairs after it ended. Upon his

return from Europe, the governor had begun promoting the Grand Army
of the Republic, seeing that the Union veterans' organization could serve as
a valuable source of political support. Rallying the men of the GAR would
become stock in trade for Morton, and other Republicans would continue the
practice for the rest of the century. His audiences across Indiana responded
enthusiastically to his speeches. Republican newspapers praised his continued
leadership and reminded readers of his superb record throughout the war.
Who better for them to follow into the next round of battle against the traitors
threatening to overturn the Union victory?[13]

In his 1866 speeches, then, Morton first began to wave the bloody shirt—in
this case, the garment was worn by traitors drenched in the blood of the brave
soldiers the Democrats had betrayed. Over time, the bloody shirt came to represent the blouse of a Union soldier's uniform drenched in sacrificial blood shed
while fighting the rebels and traitors. Both uses of the image blamed his political
opponents for the war and reminded supporters of the Union that they should
continue fighting the enemy, albeit with ballots instead of bullets. Morton's first
use of the tactic was aimed at the Hoosier Democracy and largely confined to
denouncing them as Copperheads. But he would soon add attacks on the Southern
rebels as a means to whip up audiences against his political foes. Reminding voters that the Democrats had started the war, and might have engaged in treason
in opposing it while his own party had struggled to preserve the Union and win
freedom, proved a powerful method of achieving electoral success.

In time the symbolism of the bloody shirt would wear thin. But it spoke
volumes during Reconstruction and remained effective among Union veterans
for decades. The term *waving the bloody shirt* became popular for Reconstruction a few years later, when Radical Republican Benjamin F. Wade, senator from
Ohio, reportedly held aloft the shirt of a martyred victim of the Ku Klux Klan
during a speech. That apocryphal tale of Wade waving an actual bloodstained
shirt popularized the symbol, but Morton may have been the first politician
of the era to evoke such imagery. According to the mythologists, the term had
been used before the Civil War in regard to the 1856 caning of Charles Sumner
by Preston Brooks, and some claimed that his blood-soaked shirt was often
held aloft to fan the flames of Northern hatred toward the South. Whoever
was first responsible for the idea of the bloody shirt, Morton used it early and
waved it often throughout the Reconstruction period.[14]

The governor's attacks worked in 1866. He maneuvered within his own
party's ranks to unite them against the Democrats. His own support for
Johnson became an issue when some Republican moderates insisted that the
state party convention should adopt the president's plan for Reconstruction.
Having shifted his views on Johnson and his plans, the governor now had to

move his party in a more radical direction in order to rally Hoosier Republicans to sustain Congressional Reconstruction. Consequently, Morton fought hard in support of the Fourteenth Amendment, throwing his weight behind it in order to garner support for black citizenship among Republicans both in Indiana and elsewhere. His efforts paid off in the fall, when his party carried Indiana's October state elections by a wide margin and won wide-ranging victories in the national November elections as well. The South proved to be an exception, and this caused the Radical Republicans to redouble their efforts to reconstruct the rebellious states.[15]

Feeling triumphant, Morton delivered his annual message to the state legislature on January 11, 1867. In addition to the usual reports on finances and government agencies, he again called on the legislature to make changes to the state constitution and to the state law code in order to accommodate the rights of African Americans in light of the end of slavery. He also urged the lawmakers to provide for the veterans and their families. Early in his speech the governor spoke glowingly about the service of Lieutenant Governor Conrad Baker during Morton's illness and absence in Europe. This was significant, as Morton was eyeing the Senate and hoped to leave the state government in Baker's hands on a more permanent basis.[16]

But much of his message on the state of the state focused on national issues. He now fully embraced the Radical Republican position while blaming the necessity for it on the rebels. Morton said that the Northern people had not sought revenge but had hoped that the South would accept their defeat. If they had done so and "adjusted their Constitutions and laws to the new order of things, rendered justice and given equal protection to all of her citizens," then it would not have been necessary for the congressional Republicans to push for "confiscation, disfranchisement, and punishment." Initially the South had surrendered without making any conditions, and their defeat "inspired in the North feelings amounting almost to compassion and forgiveness." But then the former rebels had "undergone a radical change. They have passed from submission to defiance, and the mercy which was extended to them has been requited in bloody persecutions upon the Union men and negro population in their midst." In light of Southern belligerence, Northerners turned "from mercy and forgiveness to the stern demands of justice, and the exaction of the penalties for treason." Morton argued that the changing context meant that men had to change their positions. "The logic of events" outweighed the arguments of politicians, molding public sentiment and sweeping aside previously held ideas. "The impossible of yesterday is the possible of today, and the radicalism of today becomes the conservatism of tomorrow." Therefore, the governor of Indiana had moved from moderate support for Johnson and Presidential

Reconstruction to the promotion of the Congressional Reconstruction of the Radical Republicans. He had to shift his political position to meet the new threats raised by the rebels and Copperheads. Changing his position was not political opportunism on the part of an ambitious man. It was historical necessity.[17]

Morton made it clear who had changed the context and made his shifting views necessary: the rebels. Even the Radical Republicans had taken on new policy ideas in light of the recalcitrant South. What had been acceptable to the Radicals at the end of the war they now saw as not going far enough. And the rebels were at fault because they refused to accept moderate Reconstruction. The North could not stand for such defiance. Morton declared that it had been obvious from the beginning that the Northern people could not allow the rebels, those who had fought against the Union, to "return to their places in the Government, and retain, in perpetuity, the right to represent four millions of colored people, whom they deprive of all political rights."[18]

He discussed the Fourteenth Amendment and detailed each section of it, showing how the amendment rectified the wrongs of the past and guaranteed the future of freedom and Union. It would prevent the rebels from returning to power and help secure Northern victory over the vanquished South. With the Republicans holding the majority, the governor knew that Indiana would ratify the Fourteenth Amendment. Still, he warned the Southern states that they must ratify it too. "But what if the Southern people reject the amendment? But what if they continue this reign of terror, this flagrant disregard of liberty and life?" He said it was impossible for the North to let the rebels take back control and use their bloody terrorism to force blacks and Unionists into submission. "A quarter of a million lives have been lost, billions of money wasted, the tears of the widow and orphan are flowing, the shrieks of the murdered freedmen are heard, Union men are flying for their lives, and now the blood of the nation is up, and the cry for vengeance is abroad in the land." Morton cried out his warning, "Let the people of the South flee from the wrath to come. Let them put away the perjured traitors who hurried them into rebellion, now darken their counsels, and make haste to abandon their sins." True redemption for the South, Morton argued, could be found not in restoring former rebels to office, but in accepting the consequences of the Civil War by ratifying the Fourteenth Amendment and agreeing to Congressional Reconstruction.[19]

And Morton now indicated that he supported black suffrage. Although he realized that giving the former slaves, "the great mass of whom are profoundly ignorant," and most of whom were not fully prepared for political participation "is repugnant to the feelings of a large part of our people," the governor now argued that it was necessary. Only by giving African American men the right to vote could the North "maintain loyal republican State governments." And that mattered more than the problems of having unprepared voters and officeholders. Morton thought that the situation meant that Republican governments were needed to protect the life and liberty of the freed people and Unionists in the South. That necessity for Republican power in the conquered states "must override every other consideration of prejudice or policy." In the space of two sentences, he conflated a republican form of government with Republican control of the states. This was deliberate because he thought that the Democrats would bring back rebellion and treason. That was unacceptable.[20]

In the face of rebel defiance, only government power could defend freedom and Union and only the Republican Party would use that power to win the peace. Morton warned that if the federal government had "to exercise the great power which has hitherto lain dormant in the Constitution, the people of the South will have the consolation of knowing it is their own act and deed." He blamed the terrorism of the rebels in their slaughter of African Americans in cities like Memphis and New Orleans, in their "murder of loyal men" for making the threat of continued force necessary. Unreconstructed white Southerners were "fast proving" that the government would have to use its "extraordinary powers . . . to cure the evils under which the land is laboring." If the South did not repent, the North would establish new governments and force them to accept their defeat. Indiana's governor promised that "come what will, the Nation will live, and its unity and power be established."[21]

ELECTED TO THE US SENATE

His attention to national issues was appropriate because Morton was the Republican candidate for the US Senate to replace the outgoing Henry Lane. The Democrats nominated Daniel Voorhees, whose opposition to the war and support for Johnson and a soft peace made him a clear alternative to Morton. Republicans rallied behind the governor, and he enjoyed widespread support from Union veterans. He confidently expected to be elected and assured a friend that he could not lose "unless by some very desperate and reckless measure."[22]

Morton's confidence proved to be well placed. The legislature held the election on January 22, 1867, and the governor won 28 to 19 on a party-line vote, although two Republicans cast their ballots for Lane to honor his service. The next day Morton resigned as governor, allowing Conrad Baker to take the gubernatorial chair. The war governor had become a Reconstruction Senator.[23]

Indiana Republicans hailed Morton as a hero, but Democrats gnashed their teeth and used the occasion to praise incoming Governor Baker as a means to attack Morton. Some Democrats despaired the fate of their party and blamed

Fig. 30. Senator Oliver P. Morton, ca. 1870. (Library of Congress)

themselves for choosing bad candidates, with one lamenting that he "never expected to see the Democracy so helpless" in Indiana. Even before he served a day in the Senate, some thought Morton might become a presidential candidate in 1868, a possibility that thrilled Hoosier Republicans and caused the Democrats to froth in anger. As the pro-Morton *Indianapolis Journal* put it, the new senator's "very name vexes" the Democrats and any praises heaped upon him "drive them frantic." For his political enemies, Morton was "the embodiment of their defeat, despair and shame, and they ought to hate him." Loved by his supporters, hated by his foes, Senator Morton set out for Washington, DC, ready to join the national fight over Reconstruction.[24]

He took his seat in the US Senate on March 4, 1867, and quickly established himself as a leader of the Republican Party. Eschewing the tradition for freshmen senators, he vigorously took part in debates and sometimes disagreed with party leaders and committee chairmen. Before long the Reconstruction battles between Johnson and the Radical Republicans in Congress took center stage in the national political arena. Morton hurled himself headlong into the fray, waving the bloody shirt and becoming one of the strongest supporters of African American rights in the Senate.

The battle had already begun by the time he arrived. When the Southern states (except for Tennessee) rejected the Fourteenth Amendment, the Radical Republicans set out to force the defeated Confederates to accept Northern terms for peace. Just two days before Morton took his Senate seat, Congress passed the Reconstruction Acts, a series of laws that established five military districts for an extended occupation and required that each rebel state write a new constitution for congressional approval, ratify the Fourteenth Amendment, and grant black men the right to vote. The laws made the military commander of each of the military districts the supreme authority. This meant that the provisional state governments organized during Presidential Reconstruction were now subject to the army. Soon the new senator from Indiana joined his fellow Radical Republicans in offering other legislation to expand on and enforce the initial Reconstruction Acts.[25]

When Charles Sumner proposed several additional measures in the wake of the initial Reconstruction Act that established the military districts, the Senate initially tabled them. On March 12, however, Morton insisted that the Senate take them up for discussion and a vote, and some of them won approval. Knowing that the president would veto the acts, the Republicans fought hard to win public support for them, and the Indiana senator made several speeches on their behalf that spring. On April 16 he addressed a mostly African American audience gathered to celebrate the anniversary of abolition in Washington, DC. He told them that he was glad that they were "proving to the world that you intend to qualify yourselves to become useful, patriotic and intelligent citizens of this great republic." He urged them to accept immigrants from the North and from Europe and to "encourage all men to come among you—to take up their residence with you. They must have absolute and perfect protection for life, liberty and property."[26]

In the spring of 1867 Morton envisioned an integrated society that would benefit everyone, but he did not pander to the crowd, filled with black citizens who would come to count him a friend and ally. Instead, he urged them to focus on education, which would be the means through which they would achieve full equality. Promoting the hope of a liberal education, Morton told Washington's African Americans that "if this generation is able to do nothing but to educate the children and prepare them for their duties in life, it will have done well. The intelligence, the education of your children must stand to them in the place of position, in the place of worldly advantages." He discussed the Fourteenth Amendment and called for extending the franchise to black men. The senator assured his audience that Northern states like Indiana would reform their own constitutions to eliminate the hypocrisy that plagued their arguments against the rebel states.[27]

Finishing his first session in the Senate, Morton returned to Indianapolis, where he set up a new law firm with partners E. B. Martindale and John S. Tarkington. The senior partner in Morton, Martindale, & Tarkington would be mostly a figurehead, but the senator needed additional income, and he was also planning for a time in which he might not hold political office. He voted in the elections that spring and apparently tried to cast his ballot in the wrong precinct, which brought Democratic charges of voter fraud. His health had not improved and he went to Hot Springs, Arkansas, to take the waters in hopes that such treatment might help him overcome his paralysis. The difficult trip by railroad, steamboat, and the last leg of the journey taken in a horse-drawn ambulance probably made things worse, but mineral waters and hot springs continued to hold the public's imagination with promises of miracle cures. On his way back to Indiana in July, he stopped in Little Rock and gave a speech there, again warning Southerners that they must accept defeat and Reconstruction. He declared that "the colored man today is free and no power can again reduce him to bondage." The Hoosier senator cautioned white Southerners that if they did not submit, the measures taken against them "will grow more and more severe." That summer and fall, Morton went to Ohio to campaign for Rutherford B. Hayes, the Republican candidate for governor of the Buckeye State, where the senator again waved the bloody shirt and called for extending the franchise to black men.[28]

He made his way back to Washington and the Senate in the fall of 1867 and continued to take part in the debates over Reconstruction. In December he battled with his fellow senator from Indiana when Democrat Thomas

Hendricks, opposing Reconstruction legislature, argued that Hoosiers did not want black equality and had not fought for it in the war, a fact that he claimed was shown in the election results in 1864 and 1866. Morton vigorously refuted Hendricks's contentions, saying that the people of Indiana had strongly supported both the prosecution of the war and the congressional policies for Reconstruction.

In late December Morton spoke to the Soldiers' and Sailors' Union of Washington and waved the bloody shirt before an audience of Northern veterans. He argued that there were "two ideas paramount in the American mind[,] antagonistic and irreconcilable, each struggling for the supremacy." One of those ideas was "the justice and propriety of the war to put down the rebellion and preserve the integrity of the Union. The other is the rightfulness of the rebellion and the wickedness and injustice of the Government of the United States in putting it down by force of arms." As always, he blamed the rebels and the Democrats for the nation's problems. He claimed that the "financial embarrassment in the country, depression of labor, and stagnation of trade" all stemmed from the disturbing situation in the South. Morton argued that that situation was caused by the "persistent and determined efforts of the Southern rebels and Northern Democrats to defeat Reconstruction." The turmoil, he thought, was nothing short of a continuation of the rebellion. He accused the Democrats of trying to give political power in the Southern states to the former rebels and that they tried to distract and "deceive the people" with outright lies and by trying to cause chaos by complaining about the "alleged oppression" of white Southerners. Morton argued that the real oppressed people of the South were not the rebels but the Unionists who had fought them and the former slaves whom they were trying to again subject to their power.[29]

The senator detailed the issues of the moment, discussing Johnson's plans and those of Congress, countering the arguments made by Democrats. He appealed to his audience that January day by denouncing proposals to have the national government assume Confederate debts, and he spoke directly to the Union military men when he criticized the idea of paying pensions to rebel veterans, their widows, and orphans. Morton cried out against putting the rebels on "a level with the soldiers of Union," warning that if the Democratic Party won elections and took power, "the elevation of the rebel soldier will follow." Indiana Democrats worried that "Morton proposes to fight the next political battle on the 'war issues of 1863–4'" and hoped that their party would nominate a candidate who would let them avoid facing the argument that Reconstruction was the war continued. But the Hoosier senator took the fight to his enemies and left them reeling under his relentless assaults.[30]

Morton's Great "Reconstruction" Speech

In January of 1868 Morton won his place as a leader of the national Republican Party when he delivered the most significant speech of his career. Once again basing his views on the firm foundation of his ideology of freedom, Union, power, and party, the senator defended the constitutionality of the Reconstruction Acts. He spoke in response to Senator James Rood Doolittle of Wisconsin, who like Morton was a former Democrat who had turned Republican. Unlike his Indiana colleague, however, Doolittle remained a moderate Republican and thought that some of the Radical policies for Reconstruction went too far. He argued that the right to vote had to remain within the bounds of the Constitution, which meant that each state had to decide for itself, although he called for Congress to establish criteria that allowed some blacks to vote but also would let the former rebels cast ballots. He thought that the Radical plan for giving African Americans the franchise but denying it to former Confederates made race war inevitable, and he hoped to prevent that by offering amendments to current legislation working its way through the Senate.

In making a case for his amendments on January 23, 1868, the Wisconsin senator referred to Morton's 1865 Richmond speech in which the Hoosier governor had argued against black suffrage. Doolittle claimed that the Radicals had used their power within the party to force men like Morton and Ulysses S. Grant to change their positions on the issue of voting rights. He said that he had been grateful for Morton's Richmond speech, which helped him in his "struggle against the radicals in my own state, to prevent them from reversing the policy upon which the Union party had fought and mastered the rebellion." Then Morton had changed his views and Doolittle lamented it, saying, "Of all the surrenders to the radical, negro suffrage policy of Reconstruction, none gave me so much pain as that of the honorable senator from Indiana, except one. I refer to that of General Grant." Most observers agreed that Grant would be the Republican candidate for president in the 1868 election, and moderates like Doolittle feared that, like the Hoosier politician, the Union war hero had come under the sway of the Radicals. Morton heard his name mentioned, and because the hour was late, announced that he would reply the next day.[31]

On Friday, January 24, 1868, the Indiana senator sat in a chair in the Senate chamber and spoke for an hour and twenty minutes, his sentences falling "like sledge-hammer blows" upon the attentive audience. At times he paused to allow the secretary to read portions of court decisions and pieces of legislation, but he spoke mostly without notes throughout the discourse. Morton's speech argued that Congress had the right to control Reconstruction and defended the policies of Radical Reconstruction. He began with the proposition that when the war ended in 1865, "the rebel states were without state governments of any kind." The rebels overthrew the original governments after secession, and then Union armies overturned the rebel administrations. President Johnson's proclamations that began Reconstruction in Southern states like North Carolina clearly recognized this reality, and Morton quoted the fourth article of the Constitution that said that "the United States shall guarantee to every state in this Union a republican form of government." This clause gave the national government a "vast, undefined power that has never yet been ascertained" that allowed it to prevent "anarchy, revolution, and rebellion." That authority, then, gave the federal government whatever other power "may be necessary to maintain in each state a republican form of government." Johnson had used this power to appoint governors and establish provisional governments in the former Confederate states under his plan for Presidential Reconstruction. He had provided also that "the military commander of the department . . . shall aid and assist the said provisional Governor" in governing the states.[32]

Having established that there were no governments in the defeated rebel states and that the national government had the right and power to create new administrations to govern them, Morton then turned to the question of who should control that process. The Constitution gave the power to the national authorities, which the senator argued meant all three branches of government, not just one. The proper way to establish new governments in the rebel states, then, was for there to be "a legislative act, a law passed by Congress, submitted to the President for his approval, and perhaps, in a proper case, subject to review by the judiciary." Of course, if the president did not approve such legislation, Congress could override him with a two-thirds majority. Morton cited *Luther v. Borden,* an 1849 Supreme Court decision regarding the Dorr Rebellion, an attempt to overthrow the government of Rhode Island. In that case, the Court held that the national government had the authority "to interfere in the domestic concerns of a state," during times of emergency, and that the power to do so rested with Congress except when it could not be convened or when the emergency was a military matter, like invasion. Hence the president had the power to administer provisional governments during the rebellion, but after the Confederacy was defeated, the Court said that "it rests with Congress to decide what government is the established one in a state." Morton referred also to an 1864 law dealing with insurrection and rebellion that said that rebel states could not cast votes in national elections and could not send representatives to Congress until the rebellion was suppressed. Doolittle himself had voted for the law, which allowed Morton to strike back at the man who had used the Hoosier's own words against him.[33]

While the national government clearly had the power to establish new governments for the rebel states, Morton argued that Johnson had overstepped his authority and had tried to do so "without the cooperation of Congress." The president's provisional governments had quickly moved to adopt new constitutions, but these state charters were produced by conventions "elected by a small minority even of the white voters" and had not been ratified by the people of the states. Therefore, Morton said that they were arbitrary constitutions, established "simply by force of executive power." In his Reconstruction proclamations, Johnson had declared that only loyal men would be allowed to form the new governments. Instead they had been "organized by the disloyal; every office passed into the hands of a rebel." That meant that those new governments provided no protection for Unionists, white or black, and the "loyal men were murdered with impunity."[34]

Morton challenged "any senator upon this floor to point to a single case in any of the rebel states where a rebel has been tried and brought to punishment by the civil authority for the murder of a Union man." He assured them that they would not be able to find even one example. Instead, the provisional governments formed under Presidential Reconstruction had "utterly failed to answer the purpose of civil governments." The rebels controlled the South through the new governments, and they used that power to return "the colored people to a condition of *quasi* slavery; they made them the slaves of society instead of being, as they were before, the slaves of individuals." Using vagrancy laws, the new Southern governments deprived the former slaves "of the rights of freemen, and placed them under the power and control of their rebel masters, who were filled with hatred and revenge."[35]

Then, in 1866, when Congress brought forward the Fourteenth Amendment, the Southern states rejected it. Morton charged that those who opposed the amendment did so because they were rebels or rebel sympathizers. The senator carefully summarized what the Fourteenth Amendment did, starting with it granting citizenship to all men born in the United States. It said that any group of people denied the franchise did not count as population for representation purposes. It made ex-Confederates ineligible to hold office and said that the United States would "never assume and pay any part of the rebel debt" and "should never pay the rebels for their slaves." Morton blamed white Southerners for the harsher terms of Reconstruction. They had "contemptuously rejected" the Fourteenth Amendment, and Congress had to face the reality that "every proposition of compromise had been rejected, every half-measure had been spurned by the rebels" themselves.[36]

Therefore, the Republicans had no choice but to take control of Reconstruction. So they passed the Reconstruction Acts. Congress had the authority to do it, and if the president did not approve, Morton's party had the votes to override his veto. Congress gave white Southerners their chance to have power over much of Reconstruction, including "leaving the suffrage with the white men" and "leaving with the white people of the South the question as to when the colored people should exercise the right of suffrage, if ever." Given the opportunity, white Southerners showed that they would not be reconstructed. Instead, "it was found that those white men were as rebellious as ever; that they hated this government more bitterly than ever." Across the South the rebels had returned to power and "persecuted the loyal men, both white and black, in their midst."[37]

Morton cried, "What was there left to do? Either we must hold these people continually by military power, or we must use such machinery" of power as the law allowed to build loyal republican (and Republican) governments. That meant giving black men the right to vote, despite the many "dangers we apprehended" in doing so. Morton frankly admitted that he "approached universal colored suffrage in the South reluctantly. Not because I adhered to the miserable doctrine that this was a white man's government, but because I entertained fears" about whether the freedmen were ready for political power. He argued that practical matters, not racism, gave him pause. He quoted from his Richmond speech to remind his colleagues that he stood for equality, saying once more that he believed in "the equal rights of all men." In 1865 he had worried that a period of probation and preparation was needed for former slaves just liberated from bondage, who were mostly illiterate and uneducated, susceptible to being swayed by their former masters. But then came "the bloody experience of the last two years," and Morton realized that "we could not reconstruct upon the basis of the white population." The unreconstructed rebels refused to accept their defeat and were now trying to win the peace. They threatened to win through politics what they had lost on the battlefield. Reconstruction simply continued the rebellion by other means, through terrorism and politics rather than military efforts. Freedom and Union were still at stake, and Morton maintained that only power wielded by his party could secure those precious national ideals.[38]

Insisting that the Republicans remained within their constitutional bounds as they designed Congressional Reconstruction, Morton jabbed back at those who continually protested against what they perceived as violations of the Constitution. He lamented, "How many crimes against liberty, humanity, and progress are committed in the name of the constitution by these men who, while they love it not and seek its destruction, yet now, for party purposes, claim to be its special friends." Although the senator continued the legendary partisanship that he had brought with him from Indiana, he still blamed the Democrats for being the ones putting their party before the good of the country. Raising the issue of partisan politics brought him to his favorite enemies, at last. Once again, Morton waved the bloody shirt. Agreeing with his debate opponent, Senator Doolittle, he declared that the radicals of the South were the secessionists. And he asserted that "the secessionists of the South are Democrats today, acting in harmony and concert with the Democratic party. They were Democrats during the war who prayed for the success" of their peace candidates over Republicans like Morton and the martyred Lincoln. He argued that the Northern Democrats had "sympathized with the rebellion" and had helped cause it. To those who claimed that the Reconstruction Acts were "intended to establish negro supremacy," Morton retorted that such charges were untrue, that he and his fellow Radicals wanted only "to divide the political power between the loyal and the disloyal."[39]

Dismissing Doolittle's proposed changes to the legislation in question, Morton also disingenuously denied that he had ever endorsed Johnson's Reconstruction policy. He dubiously claimed that he had only been trying to save the president by keeping him united with the Republicans. His apparent support for Johnson's policies had been a party measure, designed to help promote cooperation between the Republicans and the Tennessean, not true adherence to the president's schemes. The Hoosier politician argued that his own ideas and actions stemmed from his being "in harmony with the great body of the Republican party of the North."[40]

Once more he admitted that his views had changed, but he said that they had changed because the context had changed, because the rebels had given him and his party no other choice. He was not alone in his shifting position on issues like black suffrage. "The American people have been educated rapidly, and the man who says he has learned nothing, that he stands now where he stood six years ago, is like an ancient mile-post by the side of a deserted highway." Morton compared his evolution on the issues to the course taken by Abraham Lincoln, whose Emancipation Proclamation "was dictated by the stern and bloody experiences of the times. Mr. Lincoln had no choice left him." As always, he faulted the rebels, the Democrats, and their treason for changing the context. They forced the Republicans to embrace emancipation, forced them to use black troops during the war, forced them to pass the Thirteenth Amendment, forced them to pass the Fourteenth Amendment. All of those were radical ideas that came to be necessary policy because of the traitorous Democrats. Now their treason required the passage of the Reconstruction Acts and, probably, an amendment to allow black suffrage, too.[41]

Morton said that the Republicans had "done nothing arbitrarily." They had not sought revenge, had not set out to punish the rebels. They had been magnanimous and forgiving. Indeed, they had been too soft, perhaps, because "Justice has not had her demand. Not a man has yet been executed for this great treason." As for Jefferson Davis, the "arch fiend himself is now at liberty upon bail." Rather than vengeance, the Republicans insisted upon a secure future. All they wanted was to make sure that the "evil spirits" who caused the war could not "again come into power during this generation, again to bring upon us rebellion and calamity."[42]

That was the great difference between the Republicans and the Democrats, he argued. For him and his party, "our principles are those of humanity, they are those of justice, they are those of equal rights; they are principles that appeal to the hearts and consciences of men." But the Democrats appealed to racial prejudice and tried to stir up hatred. Despite the fact that whites vastly outnumbered blacks in the country as a whole and in all but two Southern states, the Democrats continued to use racism as a political weapon. They hoped to make white supremacy the main issue, to stir white racial fears and bigotry to prevent African Americans "from rising to supremacy and power." Morton found "nothing noble, nothing generous . . . nothing lovely, in that policy." The Republicans stood on the foundation of the Declaration of Independence and human rights, which "are the gift of God to every man born into the world."[43]

Here, like Lincoln, Morton interpreted the Constitution in the light of the Declaration of Independence and made his party the defender of both. He cried out, "How glorious is this great principle compared with the inhuman—I might say the heathenish—appeal to the prejudice of race against race." Democrats hoped to stir up "the strong against the weak . . . to deprive the weak of their right of protection against the strong." The differences were stark, the stakes were high, and Morton argued that his side fought for the right against the wrong.[44]

When he finished, Morton's Republican colleagues rushed over to congratulate him, and excited senators wanting to shake his hand and express their agreement with him surrounded the seated paralytic who had spoken with such power. The scene was so moving that *Frank Leslie's Illustrated Newspaper* published a sketch of Morton surrounded by his colleagues after his great speech. He sat tall in his chair, his crutch leaning beside him, in the heart of the Senate, part of the Radical leadership with men like Charles Sumner of

Fig. 31. (*opposite*) "Senator Morton, of Indiana, Receiving the Congratulations of Senators, After His Speech, in the Senate Chamber, Washington, on the 24th of January Last" (*Frank Leslie's Illustrated Newspaper,* February 15, 1868).

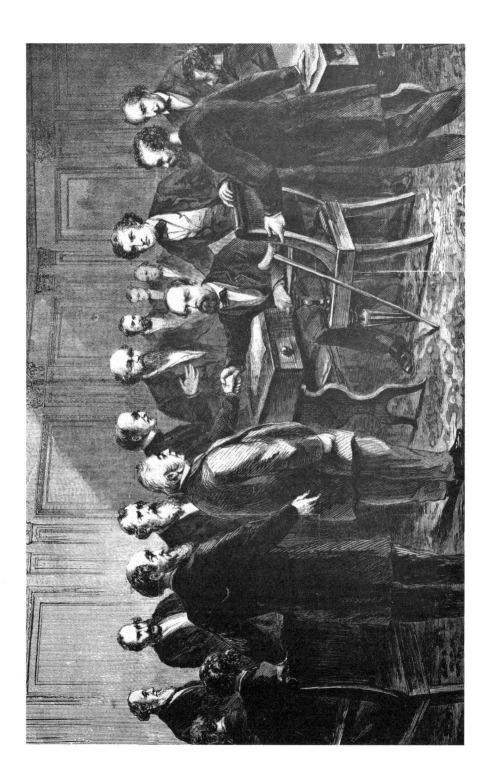

Massachusetts and Roscoe Conkling of New York. Horace Greeley's *New-York Tribune* declared that he had "delivered one of the most powerful arguments in vindication of the Congressional policy of Reconstruction that has yet been made."[45]

Almost immediately, Republican newspapers printed the speech and several different publishers produced it in pamphlet form, eventually distributing over two million copies of the oration across the country. Some Democratic papers criticized it as another example of the Republicans trying to justify their violations of the Constitution and their tyrannical plans to usurp power and establish a military dictatorship, first in the South, then over the entire country. His Democratic colleague from Indiana, Senator Thomas Hendricks, responded to Morton, and the New York City organs of the Democratic Party offered serious attempts at rebutting his arguments, but the positive responses overwhelmed the criticism. Morton received over six hundred letters of congratulation and saw his speech translated into several different languages and reprinted in Europe. When an aide read it to him, General Grant said, "That settles it . . . That one speech, if not another word is said, insures a Republican victory in the fall." Some Democrats feared the same, especially as more Republican candidates began to follow Morton's example in waving the bloody shirt and attacking their opponents so strongly that they were put on the defensive.[46]

Overnight, it seemed, Oliver P. Morton had emerged as a national leader of the Republican Party. His speech had clearly drawn the lines of battle and cast the Republicans as the constitutional defenders of freedom, equality, and the nation. He had waved the bloody shirt more subtly than was his usual practice, but he had skillfully connected the Democrats with rebellion and blamed them not only for the war and the terrorism that followed but also for making the Republicans and the nation have to change policies. He had couched Reconstruction as a continuation of the rebellion and grounded his arguments in the same ideology that had served the Republican Party so well throughout the years of the Civil War. Morton had showed that the Union and freedom were still in danger at the hands of traitorous rebels now using political means and terror to achieve their ends.

He had effectively argued that the Constitution authorized the expansion and use of power at the national level to eliminate those threats. He had also made it clear that only his party could be trusted with such power. His speech had come in debate with a moderate Republican, but he had also assailed the rebels and Northern Democrats, shrewdly taking on all of the enemies of the Radical Republicans. He had aligned himself with the Radicals while still admitting that he had been reluctant to embrace black suffrage, explaining how his views had evolved. At the same time he established himself as a friend and ally of the freed people and as a defender of equality and of all loyal Unionists, black and white. No wonder, then, that some Republicans renewed their hopes that he might become president in 1868. To those who knew him as Indiana's war governor, his emergence on the national stage was surprising only in the sense that some had wondered whether his disability would diminish his abilities. Clearly, his paralysis had not stopped him from taking on a leadership role.[47]

RADICAL REPUBLICAN LEADER

Reconstruction consumed much of Morton's career in the Senate, as it often dominated the political scene throughout the 1870s and constantly remained on the agenda, even when other matters demanded public attention. He became chair of the Committee on Privileges and Elections and served as a member of the Committee on Foreign Relations chaired by Sumner. Morton's chairmanship proved to be a significant post during Reconstruction, as the political battles over election laws and the seating of elected officials often came through his committee. His characteristic energy and enthusiasm for the fight continued to win him a reputation as a great orator and debater, even though he spoke sitting down. Perhaps his paralysis helped him channel his energy, as he had long been known for his dramatic gesturing and pacing back and forth on the platform when he spoke standing up. Sitting in a chair limited his movements, but that served to make his hand gestures more powerful. He always prepared for his speeches but rarely read them, pausing only occasionally to consult his notes.

In addition to his speaking ability, his skills as an organizer also helped make him a national leader, as he became an effective floor manager who could be counted on to shepherd legislation through the Senate. Other Radical Republicans took their place in American history and memory as the leaders of Congressional Reconstruction, writing laws to which their names forever would be attached. Thaddeus Stevens and Benjamin Butler in the House, Benjamin Wade and Charles Sumner in the Senate famously led the way, stirring the imaginations and, often, the hatred of their fellow Americans. Oliver Morton ranked among the first tier of Republican leaders, although not as the author of bills or as the most eloquent of orators. Instead, he was the blunt force of nature who spoke directly and plainly, who attacked his enemies in frontal assaults. And he was the man who got things done, a vital part of the process of lawmaking.[48]

Unlike many former governors who found it difficult to work as legislators when later elected to the Senate, Morton flourished. He adapted quickly to his new role, effectively fulfilling the prophetic prediction made by his Quaker friend in 1861 that he could serve well as either a governor or a senator while Lane would not have done well in an executive capacity. To be sure, the pressure of Senate business sometimes seemed overwhelming, even for a man as indefatigable as Morton. But he learned to enjoy the legislative process, and the recovery of his health, if not his ability to walk, put him in good spirits as he began his work in Washington. He kept a vigilant eye out for Indiana's interests, and early in his first term in the Senate he stopped an attempt to sell federal land in the state that he thought would have disadvantaged his constituents. Throughout his career as a senator he remained loyal to his party, a matter of consequence when the Republicans decided to impeach the president.[49]

During the impeachment and trial of Andrew Johnson in 1868, Morton sided with the Radicals trying to remove the president from office. At one point rumors flew around Washington that Morton's vote on the removal of the president was controlled by the Republican senator from Kansas, Samuel C. Pomeroy, but those who knew the Hoosier dismissed such stories. Although he voted to convict, the Indiana senator made no speeches and remained mostly above the fray. This was not a political consideration on his part but was rooted in the simple fact that Morton liked Johnson and considered him a friend. Despite their political differences, they remained cordial, and even after Morton voted to convict the president they maintained their personal liking for one another. The attempt to remove Johnson failed when the articles to convict him fell one vote short in the Senate trial, but his power over Reconstruction was effectively curbed by his impeachment. When the ex-president returned to Washington as a senator, he and Morton greeted one another warmly. When Johnson died not long after taking his seat in the Senate, Morton delivered a moving tribute to him. Although he refused to apologize for his vote for impeachment because he believed that Johnson "had violated the law," he chose to forget the other man's faults and "to remember only his virtues and his services to his country."[50]

Later that year he joined his Republican colleagues in debating the counting of votes. With the presidential election looming in the fall, the Democrats nominated New York's Horatio Seymour for president and adopted a platform that directly challenged the Radical Republicans. Former Republican Frank P. Blair Jr. of Missouri was the Democracy's candidate for vice president, and he argued that a Democratic president would have to use the military to demolish the new governments formed under congressional policies and overthrow the unconstitutional Reconstruction Acts. In accepting the Republican nomination, Ulysses S. Grant had said, "Let us have peace." But now the Democrats spoke openly of armed violence. The Radicals moved to strengthen the Reconstruction Acts and secure what they had accomplished by tightening the election laws and thereby preventing the Democrats from overturning the results in Southern states. Once again, the Democrats pushed for state's rights, arguing that the states had the right to make the election rules. The Republicans insisted that the Congress had the right to regulate voting.

On July 10, 1868, Morton spoke on the question of peace or war, arguing that the Democrats encouraged the Southern rebels to commit violence, that the party's platform "invited them again to insurrection and rebellion." The Democrats drew the lines, dividing the country again, calling for the renewal of the war. Morton had the clerk read Blair's remarks and used them as evidence that the Democrats wanted war, calling for "resistance by force of arms to Congressional legislation; the overthrow by force of arms of the governments that have been erected in the rebel States." The struggle in Reconstruction was nothing less than "the continuance of this rebellion . . . in a somewhat different form, but still the same struggle, contending for the same principles." Morton noted that this time the announcement of rebellion came not from the South but from the Democratic convention in New York. He thought it made the issues in the election clear and the job of the Republicans easier. Rather than having to argue about currency questions or taxation or other issues, Blair had "unmasked the enemy with whom we have to deal, and has placed before the country the very issue, peace or war."[51]

The Republican Party published Morton's speech and distributed it for use throughout the campaign. With congressional rules excluding several unreconstructed Southern states from voting, Grant and the Republicans carried the fall elections, and many observers thought that Blair's comments helped swing the voters against the Democrats. This meant that Congressional Reconstruction continued, although the Radicals turned mostly to defending what they had accomplished already rather than enacting new policies. Throughout the summer and fall of 1868, Morton campaigned for Grant and the other candidates of the Republican Party. He gave speech after speech, waving the bloody shirt, denouncing Democrats as rebels and traitors, and working to preserve the power his party needed to maintain freedom and Union.[52]

Building a Political Machine

Meanwhile, Morton worked hard to solidify and expand his own political base back home in Indiana. This included the usual business of constituent service, which involved handling correspondence from Hoosiers and forwarding their requests and petitions to the appropriate government office. He often worked from his rooms in the boardinghouse or hotel where he lived in Washington. Because of his paralysis, he usually spent a large part of his morning in bed and often conducted business from there. He took breakfast in bed, reading as many newspapers as he could as he ate and reclined on his pillows. His secretaries came in, bringing paperwork and correspondence, and the senator often received visitors in his bedroom or in the adjoining parlor. When possible, he tried to walk, making his way about with the aid of crutches. Unflagging in his dedication, he rarely missed a day when the Senate was in session, taking a carriage between his hotel and the Capitol building. Even with his crutches, he could not negotiate the flights of stairs, so he had to be carried in a chair. African Americans on the Senate staff often carried Morton to his place in the Senate chamber, and there were times he stayed in his seat only with great difficulty. But his indomitable willpower overcame his poor physical condition. As he had throughout his career, he proved tireless and relentlessly conducted the work of his office. And, as always, he devoted himself to his party. He made trips to other states to campaign for Republican candidates. And he traveled to the West, spending time in Colorado, Idaho, Washington, Oregon, and California, rallying the party faithful while also laying the foundation for his own future ambitions. Morton thought that the West presented an opportunity to build the nation anew, on the basis of equality, and helping to build the Republican Party in the states he visited, he envisioned a bright future for the region.[53]

Of course he usually returned home after each congressional session. His trips to Indiana involved maintaining his friendships in the state and allowed him to continue building his political organization. Morton always stood ready to help Republicans who were loyal to the party and to him, especially if they happened to be former soldiers. Like all politicians of the time, he attached his endorsement to the requests of men he considered allies and friends. But he also wanted to destroy his enemies. Morton was a great hater, and he refused to forget the Copperheads and others who had resisted the war. Early in his first term as senator, he intervened when a Copperhead convicted of murder asked President Johnson for a pardon. A jury convicted the man, William Whitesides, of conspiring to kill an army officer trying to carry out the draft in Daviess County, Indiana. Sentenced to death, Whitesides had not pulled the trigger but had helped murder the soldier, and Morton wrote to the president offering his "solemn protest against executive clemency in this case."[54]

Other enemies were fellow Republicans. He continued his machinations against his old political rival, Congressman George W. Julian. At Morton's behest, the Republicans in the state legislature had redrawn Julian's congressional district in 1867, taking away three solidly Republican counties and adding four Democratic ones. Despite this effort, Julian narrowly won reelection in 1868. The election also brought controversy within the Republican Party of Indiana. When the Republicans again won a majority in the state legislature, they had to elect another US senator to replace Democrat Thomas A. Hendricks, whose term had expired.[55]

Hoping to build a political machine in his home state, Morton backed certain Republicans over others, and he wanted to influence the choice of his new colleague in Washington. His handpicked candidate for the Senate, Lieutenant Governor William Cumback, became the favorite. Morton had recommended his longtime friend and political ally for a postmaster position at the outset of the war, and the two had remained close ever since. With Morton's help and his own high position, Cumback seemed sure to go to the Senate, but scandal prevented him from winning the office. The scandal broke early in 1869, when Governor Conrad Baker made public a series of letters written to him by Cumback. In these letters, written the year before, the senatorial favorite promised not to challenge Baker's reelection in exchange for an appointment to the US Senate if the sitting senator, Democrat Thomas Hendricks, chose to resign before his term ended in order to run for governor. This would give Cumback the power of incumbency and enhance his position for winning election to a full term. Governor Baker saw this as an attempt to bribe him, and despite Cumback's desperate pleas to the contrary, that was the way that others also perceived the letters. Instead the Republicans turned to a compromise candidate, Logansport attorney and longtime Republican operative Daniel D. Pratt, who eventually joined Morton in the Senate. With Cumback eliminated, Morton stayed out of the election for the most part, preferring to support Baker and to bide his time waiting to defeat his nemesis, George W. Julian.[56]

MORTON'S GETTYSBURG ADDRESS

The next summer Morton delivered the keynote address at the dedication of the National Soldiers' Monument at Gettysburg. There he once again waved the bloody shirt in the ongoing struggles of Reconstruction. Located in the national cemetery at the battlefield, the monument honored the fallen soldiers with sculptures that depicted an allegory, as its inscription read, of "peace and plenty under freedom . . . following a heroic struggle." Because Morton had proposed the monument and fought for its construction, he was a logical choice for speaker. That he had sat on the platform beside Lincoln when the cemetery was dedicated in November 1863, had promoted the GAR, and was now a leader of the Radical Republicans all made the choice even easier.

General George Meade also spoke, and Bayard Taylor wrote and delivered an ode to the soldiers at the ceremony on July 1, 1869. Morton extolled the courage and prowess of the Union soldiers and praised Meade for leading them as he recounted the three days of battle at Gettysburg.

The senator remembered Pickett's Charge as a defeat "inflicted upon the Confederacy from which it could scarcely recover." He spoke of the terrible loss suffered by families who wept for their loved ones who now lay in graves marked "Perished at Gettysburg, in defense of their country." Morton nodded to the Southern soldiers who also fell at the battle and lamented that "they were our countrymen—of our blood, language, and history." He used the vocabulary of reconciliation when he said that the Confederates had "displayed a courage worthy of their country" and noted that the news of their defeat and casualties "carried agony to thousands of southern homes." But he called them "rebels" and said that their bravery was worthy of "a better cause," crying out, "Would to God that these men had died for their country and not in fratricidal strife, for its destruction. Oh, who can describe the wickedness of rebellion, or paint the horrors of civil war!"[57]

Morton might be willing to shed tears for dead Southerners, but he made it clear who bore the responsibility for their deaths: "The rebellion was madness. It was the insanity of States, the delirium of millions, brought on by the pernicious influence of human slavery. The people of the South were drunk with the spoils of the labor of four millions of slaves." The rebels had deluded themselves, believing that honor belonged only to slaveholders and that free labor meant that Northerners were cowards. They thought that Northerners were interested only in profits and "would not fight for their Government or principles." So the South tried to break up the Union and establish a new government built on human slavery. "The lust of power, the unholy greed of slavery, the mad ambition of disappointed statesmen impelled the people of the South to a fearful crime, which drenched the land with fraternal blood."[58]

He blamed the rebels for the war caused by slavery. But out of the bloody war God brought "Liberty universal, soon to be guaranteed and preserved by suffrage universal." Like Christ's blood atoning for the sins of the world, the blood of the soldiers washed out the sin of slavery. With the rebellion crushed, the United States could live up to its founding. "The principles of liberty, so gloriously stated in the Declaration of Independence, had hitherto existed in theory." But the reality had been hypocrisy, a contradiction of those very principles upon which the American republic had been founded. A country born in freedom had brutalized millions of slaves under its flag. But now "slavery lies buried in the tomb of the rebellion. The rebellion, the offspring of slavery, hath murdered its unnatural parent, and the perfect reign of liberty is at hand." Morton then turned to the "ratification of the fifteenth . . . amendment to the Constitution of the United States," which he believed would soon be accomplished. With "impartial suffrage," he argued, the nation would achieve "the equal rights of man" and would begin a millennium during which the hopes of the Founding Fathers would finally become reality. He recounted a history of freedom since 1776, taking his audience on a survey of various European and South American countries and their struggles for liberty, arguing that it was the Declaration of Independence and American Revolution that inspired the world.[59]

The senator remembered how difficult it had been to put down the rebellion and argued that Northern victory resulted from several different causes. The brave Union soldiers drew strength from "the conviction that they [were] fighting in a just and patriotic cause." The North fought to preserve freedom and "the best government in the world" and to destroy the evil of slavery. This gave them a great moral advantage over Southerners fighting in the name of "bitter prejudices." Furthermore, the Union took advantage of the fact that their men were shaped "by habitual labor, and by that self-reliance and confidence which free labor only can inspire." Intelligent and independent, hardworking and devoted to duty, the Union soldiers fought better and showed more courage than did their rebel counterparts. Morton celebrated at length "the patriotic and gallant men who fell upon this field" and testified of "our love to the great cause in which they perished." He remembered their sacrifices and thanked them and God for having escaped the terrible dangers that would surely have followed a successful secession and rebellion. He recalled Lincoln's words in the Gettysburg Address and cited Edward Everett as well, comparing the darkness of that November dedication in 1863, when the war remained undecided, with the current joyful moment of celebration. "How powerful the contrast between now and then! The dark cloud which overspread the horizon is gone and all is brightness." Despite his earlier references to the rebels and their crimes, he did not want to celebrate a triumph over them. Instead, he said, it was time to celebrate the Union cause. He hoped that Southerners would come to recognize that "our triumph is theirs, and their children's children." Morton rejoiced that peace and prosperity reigned supreme and "HENCEFORTH DISUNION IS IMPOSSIBLE [emphasis in the original]."[60]

Passing the Fifteenth Amendment

Soon Morton took up the task of making future disunion impossible by helping pass the Fifteenth Amendment to the Constitution. Although he and some other Radicals had pushed for the amendment for the past couple of years, it was not until the election of 1868 that the majority of the party came to share their view. The Seymour-Blair campaign convinced Republicans that if the Democrats came to power they would sweep away all that Congressional Reconstruction had accomplished. Now the party as a whole realized that black voting rights needed stronger protection than that provided by mere legislation. An amendment providing that voting and the holding of office should not be denied to an individual because of race, color, or condition of previous servitude once seemed too radical even for some Radical Republicans. Now it stood as the logical measure needed to preserve freedom and the Union.

Support grew for the Fifteenth Amendment, and it came to the Senate floor for debate on January 23, 1869. Morton objected to the version of the amendment that came forward. Written in the House of Representatives, it addressed only race, color, and condition of previous servitude. The Hoosier senator feared that this left too much power in the hands of the states. He worried that white Southerners would use other criteria—like education, property ownership, and residency—to prevent blacks from voting. He also advocated giving women the right to vote, pointing out the paradox of enfranchising uneducated black men while denying the vote to educated women. Morton also thought that the amendment conceded the power to regulate voting rights to the states, and he insisted that such power actually resided in Congress. Despite his objections, however, he realized that the stronger Senate version that he personally favored had little chance of passing, so he supported the wording from the House.[61]

Throughout the debates in February 1869, Morton faced off against his colleague from Indiana, outgoing senator Thomas Hendricks. Long an opponent of Reconstruction, Hendricks fought a rearguard action, hoping to defeat the Fifteenth Amendment before he left office and Pratt arrived to vote for it. The Democrat argued first that the Republicans planned to force through the amendment and have it ratified by legislatures not elected to office on the issue. Because the Republicans had not included an amendment in their platform, Hendricks said, the Senate should delay the amendment so that the people could vote for legislators based on whether or not they supported the change to the Constitution. Morton dismissed such arguments, arguing that President Grant won the election, in part, on the issue of black suffrage and that the people had given him a mandate. Further, many other Republicans had campaigned on the issue. He argued that Hendricks wanted a delay only to distract the nation from other matters and to keep the public mind agitated in hopes of defeating the Republicans in the next election.

Undaunted, Hendricks next resorted to racism, arguing that blacks were inferior to whites and that the moral, physical, and intellectual differences between the two races were enough to reject the idea of black suffrage. The

Democrat asked for evidence of African American abilities, wondering what, if anything, a member of the black race had ever invented. Rather than stooping to such a level, Morton replied by saying that such capabilities had nothing to do with civil rights. In fact, a lack of power made the argument for the expansion of suffrage. "The strong can protect themselves. The weak require to be furnished with the means of protection." All men had natural rights, and civil rights were the extension of those rights, the means by which society protected those rights that people enjoyed. When one of Hendricks's Democratic colleagues argued against the amendment by saying that the United States was not a nation and thus voting regulations came under state sovereignty, Morton retorted that "the heresy of secession is not dead; it lives."[62]

Working closely with his fellow Republicans, Morton skillfully managed the debate in the Senate, and when that body voted on February 26, 1869, it passed 39–13. The House had passed the amendment the day before, so it went to the states for ratification. With three-fourths of the states needed for it to become part of the Constitution, the amendment faced an uphill battle. No matter how one counted the numbers, some Southern states had to vote for it to ratify the amendment. This meant that the Republicans had to keep Northern states together as well—and, because of the divisive nature of its politics, Indiana sat in the balance. Morton immediately turned his attention to ensuring that the Hoosier State ratified the amendment. The problem was that the state constitution clearly stated that such a vote required two-thirds of each of the two legislative bodies and the Democrats held more than one-third of the seats in both the state house and senate. This set the stage for another battle between Morton (through his friend and successor Conrad Baker) and Democrats in the Indiana state legislature.[63]

Worried that it might pass because some moderates might switch sides, Hoosier Democrats chose to stop the amendment cold by resigning their seats. With seventeen senators and forty-one representatives resigning (the total numbers were fifty state senators and one hundred representatives), the legislature lacked a quorum, and the Democrats thought that this settled the matter for the moment. Governor Baker called for special elections to fill the vacant seats, and, sure enough, almost every single Democrat won reelection. When Baker called for a special session to consider the Fifteenth Amendment, the Democrats showed up at the outset of the meeting but soon resigned their seats again. In previous battles with the executive, partisan groups had bolted the session but had not resigned. To prevent the bolting from happening again, the Republicans, who had used the method so skillfully in 1863, passed a law making it a misdemeanor to bolt, and doing so brought punishment in the form of a thousand-dollar fine. To get around this, the Democrats chose to resign.

Morton was in Indianapolis when the opposition party resigned the second time, and he seized the opportunity. He sent word to the Republican leadership not to adjourn the session and asked them to meet with him. When they came, he explained his plan. He examined the language of the constitution and argued that the legislature made a quorum when the session opened. The resignation of the Democrats meant that the legal passage of legislation, including ratification of the amendment, required only two-thirds of the remaining members, not two-thirds of the total number of seats in each body. Following Morton's advice, the Republicans dutifully passed the Fifteenth Amendment. The outraged Democrats gnashed their teeth and published long tirades against the maneuver, arguing that the ratification was illegal. Morton defended the action, although even some Republicans were skeptical about it. Still, Indiana ratified the amendment, and Morton once again outwitted and defeated the Democrats. When they won control of the legislature in the next election, Indiana Democrats passed a resolution declaring the ratification null and void, but it was too late. By that time three-fourths of the states had ratified it, and the Fifteenth Amendment became part of the Constitution of the United States. Still, when the Indiana Democrats brought their complaints to Congress, Morton took the time to respond to their resolutions in a Senate speech refuting their arguments, which Republicans then published and distributed to reassure voters of the legality of the amendment.[64]

While still planning to secure its passage in Indiana, Morton had turned to ratifying the amendment in other states, especially in the South. While other Radicals feared that the amendment was doomed, Morton had fought to make ratification happen and saw his opportunity in the readmission of the unreconstructed states of Virginia, Texas, and Mississippi. On April 9, 1869, even as the battle over ratification in Indiana remained a stalemate, he offered an amendment to the readmittance legislation. Morton called for requiring the states to pass the Fifteenth Amendment as a condition of their return to the Union. This set off a debate over whether such a requirement was right, given that the states had already held conventions and passed constitutions. Senator Lyman Trumbull of Illinois led those who opposed Morton's plan. Trumbull, like Morton, had switched parties over the slavery issue and became a staunch Republican supporter of the Union. A powerful opponent of slavery, he had coauthored the Thirteenth Amendment. As Reconstruction progressed, however, Trumbull began to doubt the legality and motives behind the Radical agenda. He broke with other Republicans and voted against the conviction of President Johnson. After that he continued to resist what he considered overreach by the Radicals. By the time Morton offered his plan that spring, Trumbull knew that he faced a difficult path to reelection when his term ended in 1872, but he again decided to stand on his principles. The Illinois senator objected to Morton's amendment, saying that it broke faith with the states in question, and he asked that his Indiana colleague withdraw his proposal.[65]

Morton refused, arguing that his plan was necessary to guarantee the passage of the Fifteenth Amendment and that the Democrats hoped to stall it until after the elections that fall. They hoped to use it as a political weapon because they knew that racial prejudice made black voting rights a volatile issue in the Midwest. He pointed to the situation in Indiana, where the Democratic legislators had resigned to prevent the ratification vote. They did so because they had calculated that without three of the unreconstructed states in the South, "Virginia, Texas, and Mississippi, the amendment cannot be ratified, unless it receives the vote of Indiana." Realizing that Indiana was the pivotal state for the amendment's ratification, the Democrats had sought to block the vote. But if the three unreconstructed states were required to ratify the amendment as part of their return to the Union, then the Hoosier Democracy's plan was for naught, as the state's vote would prove unnecessary. Throughout his debate with Trumbull, Morton called the Indiana Democratic resignations "a revolutionary movement" and refused to agree that the opposition party represented the will of the people. Here again he accused the Democrats of rebellion.[66]

Morton's amendment passed and so did the bill, another important step in ratifying the amendment. Soon, Georgia presented a problem and an opportunity. Previously reconstructed, Georgia seemed settled. But the state legislature expelled its African American members and put white Democrats in their seats. They ignored the Reconstruction Acts by putting in white legislators who were not eligible because of their participation in the rebellion, rejected the Fifteenth Amendment, and elected two Democrats to the US Senate. When those men presented their credentials to take their seats, Morton moved against them. He opened the December 1869 session by introducing a bill rejecting the two senators and directing the governor to reconvene the legislature, complete with its black members and excluding white members prohibited from serving by the Reconstruction Acts.

His bill also required Georgia to ratify the Fifteenth Amendment before Washington accepted any of its representatives or senators. Once more Morton argued his case in debates with his colleagues, sometimes taking on fellow Radicals on the details of his plan. He continually blamed the rebels and Democrats for the situation. After all, "it is not our fault that Georgia has not been reconstructed. It is the result of her treachery, the treachery of her legislature." And he refused to accept defeat, arguing that his plan was critical for the future of black people and the nation as a whole. "Without the fifteenth amendment there is not security for colored suffrage in any of the Southern states. When the late rebels shall get the power . . . they will disfranchise the colored man in every Southern state." And without the ballot, the freed people would be subject to oppression. The "whole work of Reconstruction" had to be protected "by putting universal suffrage in the constitution and under the protection of the laws of the United States." With such arguments, Morton carried the debate in 1869, and his bill passed. As the states ratified the Fifteenth Amendment, Democrats tried various strategies to delay or defeat the measure with new legislation. Every step of the way, Morton was there to block them. His heated response during one such debate in the spring of 1870 nearly led to a duel between two men in the correspondent's gallery of the Senate who began arguing over the senator's speech. The Indiana Republican's oratorical skills and masterful logic helped him frustrate the Democrats. Time after time he outmaneuvered and out-argued his opponents. At the same time Morton proved that he was a practical politician. He got things done. He also embraced the idea of government control. If freedom and the fate of the nation required it, then it was necessary to exercise power. In so doing he not only secured the ratification of the Fifteenth Amendment, he also expanded the authority of Congress over Reconstruction. Ironically, however, his party chose not to continue to use that power to the extent that Morton and some other Radicals hoped they would.[67]

Sure enough, the Fifteenth Amendment became the law of the land and a political issue in the election of 1870. Railing against the measure, the Democrats returned to power in Indiana, as the mood of the voters turned against the Radical Republicans. Although the Republicans held on to their majority in Congress (and lost only one congressional seat in Indiana), accomplishing the ratification of the Fifteenth Amendment cost Morton's party the state legislature. Despite his efforts during the campaign, the senator's party played defense. And they lost.

Morton worked hard for a legislative majority partly out of personal ambition. Eyeing the White House, he entertained conversations with President Grant and other party leaders about the possibility of a prominent diplomatic post or a cabinet seat. In the fall of 1870 it looked like he might well be appointed minister to England. When the Democrats won control of the legislature, such talk ended, as Morton could not afford to resign his Senate seat and give it up to the other party. Eventually the Fifteenth Amendment proved to be the last major piece of Radical policy passed during Reconstruction. But the political battles over the issues of race and equality were far from over, and Morton remained in the fray. Throughout the rest of his career, he continued to fight for freedom, Union, power, and party, always waving the bloody shirt, always unrelenting in his attacks on the Democrats he called rebels and traitors. But after 1870 his efforts, like those of other Radicals, turned to implementing and enforcing the legislation that they had passed earlier. Perhaps no issue concerned them more than the Ku Klux Klan. Throughout the ensuing years, Morton sought to defeat the Klan and worked to secure the positions of black officeholders across the South.[68]

CHAPTER NINE

A Radical Champion for African Americans

His work in helping to pass the Fifteenth Amendment made Morton a champion for the rights of African Americans. Throughout the 1870s he continued to support legislation that protected blacks and extended their civil rights and liberties. He did much of this work in the name of defending the Reconstruction policies already enacted, but he also labored for African Americans on behalf of his party. He knew that maintaining a Republican majority required the support of black voters. Without them, the Republicans could not possibly hold the South. Certainly, keeping power mattered to the senator. But he also believed sincerely that African Americans deserved freedom, equality, and protection under the law. In championing the rights of black Americans, he was continuing to fight the rebellion and defending the cause derived from his ideology of freedom, Union, power, and party. It was no contradiction for him to want to maintain both black rights and the power of the Republican Party. Instead, when seen through the lens of Reconstruction being the continuation of the Civil War, the two were interconnected parts of his consistent ideological thinking. Being a champion for African Americans also meant championing the Republican Party and his own power.

Fighting the Ku Klux Klan

In the spring of 1870, Morton again turned to fighting against secret societies of traitors. This time his enemies belonged to the Ku Klux Klan, the secret organization created by some former Confederates to resist Reconstruction. During the ongoing debates over reconstructing the Southern states, Morton worried about the terrorism used by the Klan and other such organizations to intimidate African American voters. He introduced legislation to make it a crime to intimidate black voters and then threw himself into the debates surrounding the issue. In Senate debates he cited reports from the Freedman's Bureau and from the military officers commanding the districts in the South

234

as well as voting statistics to show that the escalation of violence lowered black voter turnout. After comparing the new threat to the Copperhead conspiracies that he had fought during the war, Morton cried out that the "Union men of the south are everywhere falling, silently in most cases, their fall noted only by their Father in heaven." He urged the administration and congressional leaders to do something about it: "The time for action has come. There is the smell of blood in the air. . . . When men go to bed at night apprehensive that before morning they will be aroused by the smoke of fire or be summoned to the door by the hoarse voices of the Ku-Klux, all resistance, all endurance gives way; the father trembles for his family; he will abandon his principles, he will surrender his property." The Hoosier senator lamented that the government had not punished any of the criminals responsible: "No, not one . . . not for treason, not for murder, nor for all the nameless crimes committed by the rebellion." He supported continued military occupation, hoping that the army would root out the secret societies and protect white Unionists and black Southerners.[1]

But the Klan continued to operate even as Congress began passing a series of Enforcement Acts to give teeth to Reconstruction. In December of 1870 Morton introduced a resolution asking President Grant to provide the Senate with all information that the administration had about the secret society. When the president sent reports of widespread violence, Morton decided to move against the Klan, and on January 18, 1871, he called for the creation of a Senate committee to investigate the organization. Senate Democrats accused him of waving the bloody shirt and trying to whip up fear and hatred in order to rally the voters to the waning Republican standard. They denounced his plan for an investigation as an official excuse to establish martial law and claimed that reports of violence were overblown and that the real cause of any actual incidents was Republican corruption. Despite these protests, however, the Republican majority in the Senate supported Morton and created the committee. Subsequently the committee did find evidence of terror and violence, which they reported to the full Senate in March. This coincided with Grant's request for a law to suppress the night riders, and Morton joined other Republicans in working to pass the Ku Klux Klan Act of 1871.[2]

The law, called by various titles—including the Third Enforcement Act, the Force Act, and the Civil Rights Act—required a great deal of maneuvering in Congress. In the Senate Morton joined other Radicals in leading the fight for the new law, although some of his former allies now lined up with others to oppose him. On April 4, 1871, he gave a long speech entitled "Protection of Life at the South," in which he made the case for African American rights and, once again, waved the bloody shirt against the Democrats. He scoffed at Democrats who claimed that they did not want to abolish black voting rights

Fig. 32. "Too Thin Massa Grant" (*Frank Leslie's Illustrated Newspaper,* September 14, 1872). In this racist cartoon, the Ku Klux Klan is portrayed as a scheme by the Republicans to scare voters to win the election. Oliver P. Morton is shown as the puppet master behind President Grant, who is the puppet master over the Ku Klux figures. Although mostly hidden in the picture, Morton is seen as the power behind the president. The cartoon caption reads: "U. S. G. (as manipulator of Ku-Klux figures)—'Look here, Sambo; if you don't vote for Grant, these Ku-Klux fellows will put you back into slavery.' [Black Sambo character]—'Massa, it am no use to get up dem horrid figgers. Sambo knows dat he's free, and dat neider you nor any oder man can make him a slave again. I vote for Greeley, dat good man who helped make me free.'"

but merely wanted to experiment with different forms of elections to see if they would better promote racial equality. Dismissing such calls for using the states as experimental laboratories, Morton snorted that the Democrats would always decide that equality did not work and would abolish black voting rights. He disagreed with their contentions, charging that the whole Democratic Party was "opposed to granting negroes the right of suffrage. They opposed all constitutional amendments; they opposed the abolition of slavery; they opposed the enfranchisement of negroes at every step."[3]

What rights African Americans had obtained came from Republicans. In truth, "every right they have got, civil and political, has been given to them in spite of the stern resistance of the Democratic party." Morton predicted that if the Democrats took power, "the very first step they would take would be to deprive the colored people of the right of suffrage." He made the case again for the right of blacks to vote before turning to the subject of the Klan. He argued that the organization's oath "excludes every Federal soldier, every Republican, every negro, every member of the Grand Army of the Republic, every member of the Union League, so that no Republican, nobody but a straight-out Democrat, and I may say a secession democrat at that, can belong to that order." For Morton the Klan was another example of how the rebels and traitors in the Democratic Party continued to fight the rebellion.[4]

He refuted the arguments that the violence in the South was the result of Republican policy and corruption. Although his opponents said that the night riders attacked only to stop corruption, Morton could not find a single case where that was true. Instead, "the victims have been innocent men, so far as I know, in no case connected with this maladministration." To those who maintained that the Klan was simply another example of vigilante justice being carried out against thieves and criminals, the Indiana senator responded by pointing out that "these outrages are committed upon men of certain politics, men of certain political views" rather than on horse thieves or other outlaws. He also denied that the Republicans were running corrupt governments in the South. Democrats said that the Reconstruction governments were running up public debt to line the pockets of their cronies as well as their own, but Morton insisted that the debt accrued in the Southern states was the result of having to rebuild the infrastructure destroyed in the war, especially to build railroads. Far from being evidence of corruption, the state debts showed that the Republicans were rebuilding the South and laying the foundation for economic prosperity. He compared this favorably to the financial obligations in Northern states—including Indiana—that accumulated debts in the name of internal improvements. No, the Klan did not ride against corruption: it rode to spread terror to intimidate blacks and white Unionists. For emphasis, Morton asked the clerk to read a message from the governor of Mississippi requesting more Federal cavalry to help against the Klan because the state militia lacked the strength to defeat the night riders.[5]

In the course of his argument, Morton reminded his listeners that Tammany Hall controlled the New York Democratic Party as a means of rebutting the charges of Republican corruption. A Democratic senator objected, denying that Tammany Hall had any undue influence, but Morton ridiculed him in response: "The Senator . . . of course I do not question his sincerity, I never do that with any senator—has given me a bit of news. I thought it was a notorious fact that the influence of the Tammany Society was the controlling power in the Democratic party in New York, and in fact throughout this nation." The Hoosier senator insisted that Tammany was in control of the Democrats—although not absolutely—and that the corruption in politics could be found in Democratic ranks, not in the Republican fold. The Klan did not ride to stop corruption. If it did, it would organize against Boss Tweed in New York. Morton argued that corruption always traced back to the Democrats and that all Klansmen were Democrats. Therefore, the Klan did not oppose corruption.[6]

However sound or unsound his logic was on that particular matter, Morton denounced Democratic calls for reform and the restoration of self-government in the South because he believed it meant a return of the rebels and traitors who had caused the war. He contended that such arguments meant that the Democrats wanted "to restore the government to the white people, to take it from all the people and give it to part of the people." But Morton said that the Democrats had created the very situation that they wanted to reform: "Southern Democracy resisted Reconstruction, as did the Democracy of the North. They resisted it; they refused to take any part in it. It was thereby thrown into the hands of those whom they call carpet-baggers and scalawags and the colored people." Had they accepted their defeat and joined in Reconstruction, he added, they would have had the self-government that they claimed to want. Instead, they refused to cooperate and "they resisted the action of Congress by every means in their power, and the work of Reconstruction was thus thrown into the hands of the men who they denounced." Morton criticized the language that Democratic politicians used, saying that their vitriolic verbal attacks on Reconstruction encouraged the Ku Klux Klan to take violent action. When Democratic senators said that the Reconstruction Laws were unconstitutional and, therefore, null and void, it created a state of anarchy within which the secret terrorist society could operate. Once again he blamed the Democrats for creating a problem and encouraging treason and rebellion.[7]

The government had a duty to enforce the new amendments and Reconstruction Laws. As a matter of fact, Morton argued, "the protection of the people in their lives, liberty, and property is the highest duty of a government." Facing the widespread terror wrought by the Klan, loyal whites and blacks were in danger. The senator stated that the facts showed that Unionists were threatened and "that the colored people, because of the prejudices against their race, because they were formerly slaves and have been released against the will of their masters, and because they, too, are Republicans, have no protection for life and property." Morton raised his voice to "plead for the security and protection of these people, not because they are Republicans, but because they are human beings" entitled to their rights and to "the equal protection of the laws."[8]

To Democratic charges that blacks and Unionists also committed violence, Morton admitted that such claims were probably true. After all, "it is not to be supposed that the colored people of the South, hunted, oppressed, and outraged as they are, would submit to everything tamely; that they would not in some cases retaliate." This was not sufficient evidence to justify the Klan's actions, however, even if it did go beyond the bounds of self-defense. Morton said that it was "clear beyond all question that the aggressions, as an organized thing, as a systematic thing, is justly chargeable to those who have been the friends of and engaged in the rebellion." To him, the night riders continued the rebellion and the government needed to crush it. The Ku Klux Klan was "a confederacy, existing in a number of States, and binding them together by its secret and murderous ties." The Hoosier politician defended the Union Leagues that sometimes fought the Klan, listed at length the evidence against the secret society, and repeatedly accused the Democrats of creating, fostering, and belonging to it. This was not a heroic fight for freedom against military occupation and corrupt government. Instead, he said, "the Ku Klux is the result of a general purpose, of a matured plan for the subjugation of the south by a party that is in hostility to the Government of the United States, by the party which organized and conducted the rebellion." Instead of trying to win elections, the Klan "electioneers by murder, and persuades men by the lash and destruction of their property." Morton thought that such tactics would fail in the long run and said that the Democrats could absolve themselves of their crimes by admitting the existence of such methods and uniting with the Republicans to suppress the Klan.[9]

He defended the so-called carpetbaggers and scalawags, arguing that the South needed *more* such migrants from the North. The Union soldiers and businessmen who moved to the South joined with those Southerners who had given up the rebellion to lay the foundation for a stable society and a flourishing economy. The Democrats stirred the same old fears, played to the same old racism, and continued to lead white Southerners down the wrong path. Morton cried out, "Will the people of the South never learn that for thirty years the Democratic party has been their most deadly enemy?" The Democrats had led the South to rebellion and ruin. Now they were leading white Southerners in futile resistance to Reconstruction, all so that the Democracy could win political power. If they did win power, Southern Democrats would then take control of the party, and that meant that they would overturn the hard-won Union victory. For Morton, then, the "southern question will be the great issue in 1872 that will dwarf into insignificance every other." Economics and reform would matter, but Reconstruction remained the paramount concern of the nation. He promised that his Republican Party would "struggle for life, for the privilege of living in peace and security, while the Democratic party will struggle to regain their former power," using terrorism as the means to do so. The senator called on good Union men to see that because "everything is at stake for which we struggled and suffered through ten years of war and storm," they needed to "unite again as a band of brothers, and . . . move forward resolved to conquer for the right."[10]

In a letter to his wife the next day, Morton remarked that by the time he had finished his speech, he was "so weak I could scarce sit in my chair." Beyond his ongoing and ever-fluctuating health issues, he faced strong opposition. Looking toward 1872, a number of Republicans, including some Radicals, were seeking to replace Grant on the ticket, and this led them to oppose Morton, the president's strongest ally in the Senate. Despite the fact that many of them agreed with him on the issues and hoped to pass the Ku Klux Klan Act, these men worked to undermine the Hoosier senator before the election. He told Lucinda that "the combination against me here is very strong and are pulling every string." He reported that when he began to speak, a group of senators, including longtime allies like Roscoe Conkling, William Stewart, Lyman Trumbull, Justin Smith Morrill, and John Sherman, "went into a cloak room and remained there until I was through. It was generally noticed." Despite that public snubbing by his fellow Republicans, Morton continued to lead the fight for Reconstruction and gained even more influence across the country.[11]

A NATIONALIST AND NATIONAL FIGURE

Fighting for Reconstruction confirmed Morton's nationalism. Although he had defended aspects of state's rights doctrine as governor and had helped maintain federalism in the course of the war that greatly expanded the national government's power, the senator now shared the nationalism of so many others in his party. He still held to his foundational ideology of freedom, Union, power, and party, but he began to apply it in ways that took a broader, nationalist perspective. After campaigning throughout the summer of 1871, he and Lucinda joined a group of fellow Republicans and their wives on a trip to California. Morton returned in November to give the Franklin Lyceum Lectures in Boston, Massachusetts, and Providence, Rhode Island.

The invitation to speak was an honor that reflected the senator's growing reputation, and he did not disappoint his audience with his lecture, "The National Idea." He traced the history of "the doctrine of state sovereignty" back to the Virginia and Kentucky Resolutions of 1798. He argued that it was a mistake to think that the state's rights doctrine of state sovereignty "was devised for the benefit of slavery" and that it had existed only for slavery and died with slavery. He insisted that "slavery was the immediate cause of the war," but he also said that the South could not have started the rebellion without "this idea of the sovereignty of the states." Holding to the same arguments he had made in his 1861 Rockville speech, Morton thought that "this doctrine is a perpetual threat against the life of any nation. The nation is not safe so long as there is any considerable number of people who entertain this doctrine." He declaimed that the idea of a sovereign state "is a poisoned dagger always at hand to be clutched by some desperate factions." The political weapon of state sovereignty lay at a hand, a "ready-made instrument of destruction." He recalled how state sovereignty had put such a "great strain upon the government in 1798 and 1812 and 1832," as the idea of nullification threatened to destroy the Union.[12]

The senator proclaimed that Republicans and all true Unionists opposed this dangerous doctrine with "what we call 'The National Idea.' We assume that this government was formed by the people of the United States in their aggregate and primary capacity. We assume that instead of thirty-seven nations, there is but one sovereignty." While he insisted that there were some rights retained by the states because the "preservation of local self-government is essential to the liberties of this nation," he claimed that such rights were "consistent with national sovereignty." Morton could allow state's rights, but state sovereignty with its powers of nullification and secession was dangerous and treasonous. He said, somewhat dubiously, that Jefferson and Madison had been forgiven for their writing the resolutions of 1798 because of their subsequent service and dedication to the "the national character of our government." Of course, the notion of state sovereignty had returned in 1861. Nationalism was the answer to the evil that had caused the rebellion, and Morton urged all Americans to embrace it. "The idea that we are a nation, that we are one people, undivided and indivisible, should be a plank in the platform of every party. It should be taught in every school, academy, and college. . . . It should be the central idea of American politics." The senator believed that "we must have a nation. It is a necessity of our political existence." The nation protected the citizens "in the enjoyment of life, liberty and property," and the national government needed the power to fulfill the duty of securing individual rights and liberties.[13]

In the South, then, this meant that the federal government had to protect the rights of black citizens, and Morton continued his fight for the rights of African Americans in a speech to the Senate on January 23, 1872. The issue at hand was a bill that would remove the political disabilities against former rebels under the Fourteenth Amendment. Morton vigorously opposed the legislation, arguing that in effect it granted universal amnesty to the rebels and "is a violation of the spirit of the amendment, if not its letter." He claimed that the rebellion was a top-down movement. It did not arise from the mass of white Southern people but was the work of nefarious politicians. The leaders of the defeated Confederacy deserved to "go down into history as they have lived, rebels. They must die as they have lived." To grant the rebels amnesty would not win over white Southerners but "will only conciliate them by being a concession that they were in the right and that we were in the wrong." Morton reminded the Senate of the "consequences of this rebellion," which he said were greater than the impact "of all the crimes that have been committed in the United States from the time this Government was formed until the present day." He added up the costs—at least half a million lives lost, countless widows and orphans, the load of debt—and concluded that the rebels had "brought these untold, incalculable calamities and woes upon this nation." Such men deserved punishment. To let them return to citizenship and office "would be to educate the children of this country and all future generations in the belief that treason is no crime, that there is nothing wrong in rebellion."[14]

As always, he waved the bloody shirt, blaming the Democrats for the rebellion and hoping that they would not win control of the government in the coming election. He denounced those who would overturn the Fourteenth and Fifteenth Amendments and the Reconstruction Acts. He pointed to the "intelligence and fidelity displayed by the colored people of the South" and argued that blacks had more than proven that they were worthy of their rights and of protection against terrorism. African Americans worked "under the greatest difficulties, from the want of education, want of political experience, and want of property, their very homesteads owned by their former oppressors." Their former masters hated them and resented their emancipation and enfranchisement, but the former slaves showed "independence, firmness, and courage." Morton vowed that his "Republican party will stand by them to the last, to protect them in the enjoyment of their civil and political rights." He concluded by arguing that "there can be but two parties in this country until the issues of the war are settled. Whoever is not for us is against us. . . . Every man must take his choice upon which side he will be in this conflict." He predicted that passing the legislation under consideration and electing Democrats would be a pledge "not to interfere, not to execute the Ku Klux law." It would mean that there "would be no security for the life, liberty, or property of the Union people. . . . The civil and political rights of at least four million people are dependent upon the continued supremacy of the Republican party."[15]

THE SOUTHERN QUESTION AND THE ELECTION OF 1872

In the election of 1872, Morton tried to make the Southern question the focus of the campaign while also supporting President Grant's reelection bid against both the breakaway Liberal Republicans and the Democrats. The Liberal Republican Party opposed the Grant administration, arguing that the president and his cabinet members were corrupt. In addition to running reform-minded candidates, the Liberal Republicans supported civil service reform and local (or state) government and control to offset the centralization of national power. They also thought that the goals of Reconstruction had been achieved—namely, guaranteeing the end of slavery and permanently destroying the Confederacy by bringing the rebellious states back into the Union. With the Thirteenth Amendment and the readmittance of the Southern states having accomplished those goals, the Liberal Republicans called for withdrawing the occupying troops and ending Reconstruction. Despite their continued support for civil rights for blacks, the Liberal Republicans attracted Democratic support because of their plan to end Reconstruction and their calls for returning to a more decentralized government that featured state's rights.[16] In fact, the Democrats chose not to field a presidential candidate of their own, instead rallying behind Horace Greeley, the Republican candidate.

Facing off against this new threat, Morton waved the bloody shirt, which again proved effective. He focused his efforts in Indiana, where the October elections would decide the governor's race as well as the state legislature. With Morton's own term ending early in 1873, he worked hard to secure a Republican majority that would reelect him. He feared that the Democracy might carry the election after they won a majority in 1870 and prevented him from resigning to take another post. His own party trusted in the Hoosier senator's abilities, however, as they elected him to the Republican National Executive Committee at the Republican National Convention in June. There he worked unsuccessfully to help Schuyler Colfax keep the vice presidency, seeing Henry Wilson replace the Indiana politician on the ticket with Grant. Still, Morton enthusiastically worked for the president's reelection, helping ensure that his friend secured the nomination and then making a speech on his behalf at the convention. A few weeks after the convention, Morton fired the "First Guns" of the Indiana campaign of 1872 on June 24, in his speech with that title at a

Republican rally at the Masonic Hall in Indianapolis. He defended the Grant administration and Republican policy, covering the financial issues, denying charges of corruption, and discussing civil service reform. Although his loyalty to Grant probably caused him to too quickly dismiss charges of corruption in the administration, Morton believed the president was honest and knew that Grant shared his ideological commitments. He then turned to Reconstruction and accused the Democrats of being the party of rebellion and slavery. He asked the voters to guarantee the victories won thus far by voting for Republicans. The Democrats threatened the Reconstruction Amendments and Acts, he said, and if elected they would enable the rebels to win the peace where they had lost the war.[17]

He continued to hurl his accusations at the Democrats when the campaign began in earnest in late summer. At Rushville, Indiana, on August 7, 1872, he again cited Frank Blair Jr. and made him the voice of the Democratic Party. Morton aimed his venomous darts at Horace Greeley, accusing him of being a secessionist and too soft on the Ku Klux Klan. Greeley, who had long opposed slavery, now betrayed African Americans in his quest to win office. It seemed that Morton waved the bloody shirt against all opponents, whatever their party, whatever their actual stand on the issues. Many thought Morton was the power behind the throne of the Grant administration and that he manipulated the president's campaign. A political cartoon published on September 21, 1872, in *Frank Leslie's Illustrated Newspaper* expressed such sentiment. It showed Morton behind Grant, controlling the president as he fired ineffective issues at a towering Greeley[18] (see Fig. 32).

Back in Indianapolis in September, Morton ramped up his bloody shirt rhetoric, spending less time on economic issues and more accusing Democrats of denying the existence of the Klan while actually supporting the terrorist organization. He cited evidence and quoted various sources to show that the Ku Klux Klan did exist and that their actions were rebellion by another means. Throughout the campaign, Morton repeatedly attacked the Democratic candidate for governor, Thomas Hendricks. He accused the former senator of corruption and treason, painting him as a power-seeking Copperhead. Indiana's state elections on October 8, 1872, resulted in the Republicans recapturing the state legislature, most statewide offices, and a majority of the congressional seats. The Democrat Hendricks took the governor's chair, however, returning him to office and setting up future battles with Morton.[19]

But the national elections, including the presidential contest, came in November, and Morton believed that the Republicans had to maintain control of the federal government in order to have the power to protect freedom and Union from the forces of rebellion and treason. Having canvassed heavily in

Fig. 33. "Grant's Strategy" (*Frank Leslie's Illustrated Newspaper,* September 21, 1872). Once again Oliver P. Morton is depicted as the power behind the throne, the one who is manipulating the president. Grant is sending bubble after bubble at Liberal Republican Horace Greeley, hoping that issues blown up by the *New York Times,* including bolts from state party conventions and issues like free trade, will defeat his rival. In the caption Grant says, "Confound those bubbles!—they all burst. I really thought that last one would knock him over; but that's gone, too." It also contains a confession by a delegate to the Pennsylvania convention, admitting that the Grant campaign paid his way, implying that the president was buying his reelection.

Indiana, he now headed to Illinois, where he kicked off a series of speeches with an address in Chicago. There he focused on financial matters rather than Reconstruction, pointing to the city's rapid growth and economic prosperity as reasons to stay the course politically by reelecting Grant and the Republicans. After stumping at three more stops in Illinois, he traveled to St. Louis, where he repeated his arguments in defense of his party's candidates and policies while waving the bloody shirt against their opponents. Morton then returned to Indiana to speak in Aurora, where he closed the campaign.

In this speech, he denounced the various candidates talking about reconciliation between the North and South. Both Greeley and the Democrats claimed that "they want to be reconciled." But "to whom?," he asked. "To the loyal men of the South?" Then, he answered his own question: "No, they propose to be reconciled to those who were engaged in the rebellion; to the violent elements of the South; the part of the Southern people who have refused to accept" the outcome of the war and the policies of Reconstruction. Morton agreed that it was "a beautiful thing to talk about reconciliation. I am in favor of it. . . . But I have always said there could be no reconciliation, except upon sound principles." The Democrats and Liberal Republicans would pursue a plan for reconciliation that would result in war. No, Morton said, "we shall have reconciliation if the Republican party is continued in power, and it will be upon correct principles." True reunion would come between the Union men of the North and Southern Unionists, white and black. Yes, Americans could achieve reconciliation, but only on Northern terms, on the principles of the victorious, not on the desires of the conquered. The Hoosier senator declared that he did not "propose to be reconciled by placing the loyal colored men of the South, and the loyal white men of the South, under the control and government of their ancient enemies." As always, his foundational ideology animated his arguments: "If there is to be a division of parties down there—if those who were engaged in the rebellion are to be upon one side, and the loyal men upon the other side, and if the power is to go into the hands of one side or the other, for my part, I would indefinitely prefer to keep it in the loyal hands of those who have been loyal men."[20]

The Republicans swept to victory in the November contest, with President Grant reelected and the party extending their congressional majority by picking up sixty-two more seats. Despite rumors that there was support for Schuyler Colfax or Richard W. Thompson among the Republicans and fears that the Democrats might elect James D. Williams because the majority would not show up, the state legislature reelected Morton to the Senate. In fact, Hoosier Republicans overwhelmingly supported him and showed their enthusiasm by taking the vote in late November instead of waiting for his term to expire in

January. Although the elections in the legislature usually occurred at the end of a senator's term, the Indiana lawmakers voted early as a show of support for the man who led their party in the state. The Democrats despaired over the Republican victories, and the *Louisville Courier,* lamenting Morton's re-election, called him "an unscrupulous and desperate conspirator" who joined other Republicans in rallying around "the drunken and half-witted voluptuary Grant." But the Hoosier senator could afford to ignore such criticisms in the wake of his party's triumphs as well as his own.[21]

Morton's stump speaking proved so effective that Ohio Republicans invited him to help them in their state campaign in 1873. He traveled to the Buckeye State and spoke on the campus of Ohio University in Athens. Urging his audience to support the reelection of Governor Edward F. Noyes, Morton decried the Democrats as traitors who supported nullification, secession, slavery, and the Ku Klux Klan. He repeated his message in Dayton the following month, speaking to a large crowd in front of the courthouse. Waving the bloody shirt was not enough this time, however. In the midst of the financial crisis following the Panic of 1873, Ohio voters cast their ballots, and William Allen, the Democratic candidate, won the gubernatorial race.[22]

A PLAN TO ELIMINATE THE ELECTORAL COLLEGE

Elections dominated much of any politician's career, but Morton went beyond his own office-seeking and spent a great deal of time in his second term in the Senate thinking about elections and the electoral process. Early in 1873 he argued successfully that the Senate should authorize his Committee on Privileges and Elections to investigate changing the Electoral College that elected the president of the United States. He had long thought that the system did not work as intended, but when the Senate threw out the electoral votes of Arkansas in 1872, effectively disenfranchising the voters of the state, Morton decided it was time for action. The Senate approved his resolution, and as chair of the committee he set to work on investigating the problem. He went to the Library of Congress and conducted research, then called his committee to New York in September 1873. There they met, and he persuaded them to support a proposed constitutional amendment providing for the direct election of the president by the people. By the fall of 1873 he was urging President Grant to support his plan to eliminate the Electoral College by amending the Constitution. But when his report and the proposed amendment finally reached the floor in May of 1874, the Senate took no action. By that time his Democratic enemies were convinced that his plan to change the voting system was a scheme to steal the presidency for the Republicans, perhaps with a third term for Grant or with a new Morton administration. Despite his failure to bring his amendment up for a vote and the attacks of his enemies, the senator continued to push for abolishing the Electoral College, but he failed to persuade his colleagues to support his plan.[23]

LOUISIANA

It was fitting that the denying of votes in Arkansas spurred Morton to action on the Electoral College. He dedicated himself to the problem of elections in the reconstructed South, particularly regarding African Americans elected to office. While Morton worried about Arkansas and other Southern elections, perhaps no Southern state required the attention of the powerful chair of the Committee on Privileges and Elections as much as Louisiana. In 1868 the Republicans had elected Henry Clay Warmoth as governor, but he hewed to a more conservative line than they had expected. Using his patronage, he appointed many Democrats to office across the state, and the fact that he was a native of Illinois lent credence to charges about Yankee carpetbaggers, in addition to cries against corruption. Accused of cronyism and bribes, Warmoth denied only general charges of corruption, avoiding comment about any specific details. But the evidence was overwhelming that the dashing young Union veteran from the North was using his office to get rich. The Radicals took heart when Warmoth sided with the Liberal Republicans in the party divisions of 1872, and they nominated US senator William Pitt Kellogg to oppose him. Having lost his own party's nomination, Warmoth threw his support to the Democrats, officially creating a Fusionist campaign that united the Liberals and the Democracy.[24]

The African American lieutenant governor, P. B. S. Pinchback, reported the intimidation of black voters but thought that the Republicans should have a majority of thirty thousand votes. Louisiana, already infamous for its political corruption, now demonstrated how to steal and steal back an election. Knowing that most African American voters were illiterate, Fusionists printed and distributed fake ballots that looked like the official Republican ticket on one side but actually listed Warmoth and the Democrats on the other. Intimidating and defrauding voters at the polls helped, but the Fusionists also packed the electoral boards with Democrats, who ensured the results when it came time to count the ballots. They declared victory for their candidate, John McEnery, and a majority of Democratic candidates for the legislature.[25]

Republicans fought back with an electoral board of their own that declared Kellogg and a Republican legislative majority the winners. The state legislature began impeachment proceedings against Warmoth. State law required him to step aside during impeachment, so Pinchback became the acting governor. But

Fig. 34. Governor William Pitt Kellogg, Republican, Louisiana. (Library of Congress)

the Republicans knew that time was short, so they asked the federal government for help. The attorney general ordered the US marshal for the area to
back up the federal courts and promised that the administration would send
as many troops as were needed to enforce the laws. The Republicans then had
a federal judge order the marshal to seize the Louisiana statehouse and admit
only those legislators certified by the pro-Kellogg board. Soon the state had
two legislatures meeting, one dominated by Fusionist/Democrats, the other
led by Republicans. Each claimed legitimacy and issued resolutions denouncing the other. With competing governors and legislatures, violence followed
the political chaos, as whites lynched African Americans and butchered black
soldiers in the spring of 1873.

Louisiana demonstrated the chaos of Reconstruction, complete with corruption and racial violence. There was enough blame to go around, as the Democrats had stolen the election and the Republicans had stolen it back using force. News of the turmoil created political tensions, and President Grant thought about calling for new elections, but his cabinet pressured him not to do it. The federal intervention in the election outraged the Democrats, of course, but it also upset many Republicans. Meddling in elections and setting up puppet governments with armed troops were hardly the ways to achieve a successful Reconstruction.[26]

During the chaotic events of early 1873, Morton maintained that the federal government should not interfere in Louisiana. He opposed congressional efforts to overturn the existing Kellogg government and create a new one—despite the fact that the supporters of such legislation used the same argument that he had made previously regarding the authority to guarantee a republican form of government. Morton now argued against congressional action, saying that had the Democrats not stolen the election, Kellogg would have won anyway. The Indiana senator called for "masterly inactivity" rather than intervention in Louisiana. Despite the violence that followed, the senator remained steadfast in his position. Because the issue split the Republican leadership, Morton soon became the undisputed leader of those Radicals who supported the Grant administration. Rumors swirled about him taking a cabinet seat or a diplomatic post, while some talked about Morton running for president or accepting an appointment to the Supreme Court. His consistent ideological commitment to freedom, Union, power, and party had combined with his skills as a speaker and political operator to make him a formidable force in the Republican Party. In shaping Reconstruction policy, he repeatedly used his power as an advocate for the rights of African Americans, and Louisiana soon presented another opportunity for him to do so.[27]

P. B. S. PINCHBACK

The Kellogg government elected P. B. S. Pinchback to the US Senate. The man who had been the first African American elected as a lieutenant governor sat in the governor's chair for a few weeks after Warmoth was forced out, making him the first black governor of a state. Elected to Congress in the disputed 1872 contest, Pinchback also became the first African American member of the House of Representatives elected in Louisiana history. But he wanted the Senate seat that was left vacant when Kellogg resigned to become governor. However, charges of corruption followed Pinchback. and he eventually admitted to using his office for personal gain. While serving on the New Orleans

Park Commission, he had arranged for the city not only to buy property that he owned but to pay far more than it was worth. Despite this scandal, the pro-Kellogg Republican legislature elected him to the Senate early in 1873. But the pro-McEnery Fusionist/Democrat legislature elected Republican and Union veteran William L. McMillen, and the seating of the next senator became a political issue.[28]

Unsurprisingly, Morton supported Pinchback. When others called for a new election, he held against it, saying that African Americans needed one of their own to represent them and to protect them. New Orleans businessmen needed stability and order. Only the murderous members of the White League (as commentators now called the Klan-like organization in Louisiana) wanted the continuing turmoil. The seating of a new senator was delayed throughout 1873 but came back to the floor early in 1874. Morton had again taken the waters at Hot Springs, Arkansas, and while there had prepared to give a speech denouncing the Colfax massacre. He hoped his vivid description of the events would remind his colleagues that this was a continuation of the war and underscore his argument that a new election would mean giving in to the rebels. He included the violent episode when he delivered his speech, entitled "Louisiana Affairs," over the course of two days, on January 30 and February 2, 1874. Given in response to a fellow senator who was calling for a new senatorial election in Louisiana, Morton's discourse defended the rights of African Americans in general and Pinchback in particular. But he also repeated his oft-made argument that Reconstruction was a continuation of the war. He blamed the Democrats for the problem but claimed that "the best part of that party are opposed" to a new election. Only the rebels wanted more blood. He recounted the history of the election of 1872 in Louisiana, calling the movement to put McEnery in office a fraud.[29]

Morton told the story of how the Bayou State was now "covered with blood" because of the Louisiana Democrats he called "the assassins of 1866, 1868, and of 1873." He reminded his listeners of how more than three hundred blacks had been killed or wounded in a New Orleans riot in 1866. In 1868 members of the White League—which Morton continued to call the Ku Klux Klan—caused more than two thousand African American casualties in the two months leading up to the presidential election. And the terrorists often murdered under the authority of local government. Morton remembered that "Louisiana was a vast slaughter-house; blood was shed in every parish and almost upon every plantation." But not a single person came to trial or received punishment for the crimes.

The worst event came on Easter Sunday, 1873, when a force of black militia faced off against a white posse in Colfax Township in Grant Parish. The African American troops, finding themselves outnumbered and outgunned, took up a

Fig. 35. P. B. S. Pinchback, Republican, Louisiana. (Library of Congress)

defensive position in the courthouse. The white attackers set the building on fire and shot the defenders as they tried to escape. In the end, the Colfax massacre resulted in sixty-nine dead black men buried in a mass grave. Morton told how the white attackers burned out their victims, detailing how "when the flames had spread throughout the building the colored men in the court-house held out white handkerchiefs" to surrender. But when they came out, some of them on fire, "they were met at the door and murdered, and stabbed, and mutilated." Hoping to shock his fellow Republicans and spur them to action, the senator described the gory scene. He read from the grand jury report that told how "three or four men would seize a colored man and another man put his pistol in his mouth and blow his brains out; and that they were mutilated and their abdomens ripped open after they were dead." The posse captured some of the black soldiers and took them down to the river. There they experimented in killing the African Americans, as they "put them breast to back, three or four or five each, and then a man would stand at the end of the line to see through how many bodies he could send a bullet with his rifle."[30]

In the context of Louisiana during Reconstruction, murder had become commonplace. Morton lamented that "the life of a colored man in Louisiana is considered of no more account than that of a mad dog; and . . . not one of the murderers has been punished." Faced with ongoing violence, what could the national government do? Morton worried that a new election would result in additional massacres. He believed that the best course was for the current Reconstruction government to continue, but he did not speak in defense of Kellogg and promised that he would prosecute Pinchback or any other Republican if his duty required it. The senator carefully went through the various arguments for a new election, logically dissecting each point, refuting them all. He argued strongly for seating Pinchback, appealing to questions of legality and process as well as right and wrong.

He did not want Congress to step into Louisiana affairs, and he warned President Grant not to intervene as well. The senator said that the Constitution authorized presidential intervention only in the case of an insurrection that the state government could not suppress. The Grant administration had certified the Kellogg government, and that meant that the Republicans controlled the state. There had not been an insurrection, so the national government could not interfere with Louisiana. Although he was a Radical Republican, Morton did not want Washington to call for a new election because the state government established by Congressional Reconstruction remained in place. To step in now would question the legitimacy of the Kellogg government. Violating state's rights was dependent on which party controlled a state. Therefore, he did not want to undermine the Republicans in Louisiana. He waved the bloody shirt again, blaming the Democrats for the violent situation. Those who had caused the war still refused to accept defeat and resisted Reconstruction. Louisiana had a government that had elected Pinchback to the Senate. That body needed to seat him and move on, even if the way that the Kellogg government had come into power was wrong. After all, Morton said that he had presented "the history of politics in Louisiana for the last seven years as furnishing a substantial vindication for the mass of the Republican party in that State." The Democrats had slandered Louisiana Republicans long enough. It was time to defeat the rebels and murderers, the Democrats and the Klan, by seating Pinchback. If the Senate did not do that, they would be giving ground to the enemy.[31]

Despite the weight of Morton's influence, Pinchback never served in the Senate. The Hoosier senator counted on the weight of the Republican Party to put the African American into office, but he could not get it done. A political cartoon published in *Frank Leslie's Illustrated Newspaper* in February 1874 showed Morton as the ringmaster encouraging Pinchback to ride the camel of the Republican Party, but the animal was simply too loaded down with all of the politicians trying to stay aboard. Other Republicans caricatured in the illustration advise President Grant not to follow Morton's advice, warning him that such an attempt will break it down. It seemed that Morton's attempt to seat Pinchback was the final straw that broke the camel's back. Still, the Indiana leader fought to accomplish the task. As chair of the Committee on Privileges and Elections, Morton kept pushing to seat the African American from Louisiana. Morton's speeches on Pinchback's behalf became a familiar refrain, to the point that in the spring of 1875 Democratic senator Allen Thurman of Ohio complained that the Hoosier's speech was the same one given again and again, offering nothing new, but simply repeating the same arguments. Still, Morton fought on. Constant delays dragged the issue out for years, and eventually the Democrats took control of Congress. They voted to pay Pinchback thousands of dollars in salary and travel expenses, but they would not let him join the Senate. Instead, the seat remained vacant until the term expired and a white Democrat won the seat following the end of Reconstruction. Increasingly, Morton's power fell short of the mark. Although he fought hard for African Americans' rights, by the middle of the 1870s the American people had grown tired of Reconstruction and the Southern question. Even as chairman of the

Fig. 36. (*opposite*) "The Last Straw on the Camel's Back" (*Frank Leslie's Illustrated Newspaper*, February 21, 1874). In this cartoon, Morton is caricatured as the ringmaster of the Republican Party that is overloaded with corrupt politicians. Hoping to seat another African American Republican in the Senate, Morton urges P. B. S. Pinchback to climb aboard, assuring him that they can throw Grant off if they need to do so to secure the African American his seat in the Senate. The caption reads: "The Dying Scene in the Farce of 'The Republican Party,' to Slow Music by [Wisconsin Republican Senator] Matt Carpenter's Unrivaled Brass Band. U. S. G. [Ulysses S. Grant]—'This poor old beast has so long been staggering under its burden, that we must throw off a few of the monstrosities if we would make it rise with me. I must unload.' Ring-Master Morton—'Climb on, Pinchback. The old thing can stand another straw; and if it can't rise, we'll throw off Grant, and so unload.' [Pennsylvania Republican Senator Simon] Cameron—'Mr. President, if you persist in driving this performing animal for your own benefit, you will ruin it as a beast of burden. It was not raised for your benefit.' [New York Republican businessman] Tom Murphy—'These fellows are only making the old man mad. He'll have his own way, and throw them all off before he gets through.'"

Committee on Privileges and Elections, Morton found it difficult to bring more African Americans into office. Undaunted, he continued his fight and even took on new issues related to freedom and equality.[32]

A VOICE FOR WOMEN'S RIGHTS

In an 1874 bill that proposed to divide the Dakota Territory, a fellow Radical Republican included an amendment granting women the right to vote. Morton then took up the cause of women's suffrage. Following what was now his formula in defending African American rights, he began by turning to the Declaration of Independence. He said that the nation's founding document expressed the natural rights of all human beings, including women. The Hoosier senator countered opposing arguments that said that it would upset the marriage relationship by again asserting that women were equal and saying as well that making them legally equal would actually improve marriage. He found it shameful that women were paid only about half of what men earned for the same kind of work and said that the gender pay gap could not be fixed until women had political rights.[33]

Arguing the cause of women's rights, he reminded his colleagues that American democracy rested on the foundation of a government formed with

Fig. 37. (*opposite*) "The Late Terrible Democratic Storm" (*Frank Leslie's Illustrated Newspaper,* October 9, 1875). Many saw the widespread Democratic victories in the elections of 1875 as a repudiation of Grant and the Republican Party. Even before the election, it was clear that the Democrats would win in New York and many Southern states as well. But Morton managed to avoid being hurt politically by the attacks on the president and his party. The illustration published at the time shows Morton crawling out of the floodwaters, having escaped the storm that swept over his party. The caption under the soon-to-be victorious Democrats of New York, depicted standing on the right, lists what they claimed to stand for: "The public credit must be sacredly maintained, and we denounce repudiation in every form and guise. Steady steps towards specie payments. No step backward. Home rule, revenue reform, no centralization. No private use of public funds by public officers. The party in power responsible for all legislation while in power. The Presidency a public trust, not a private perquisite; no third term. Economy in the public expense, that labor may be lightly burdened." The caption under the cartoon reads: "U. S. G. [Ulysses S. Grant]—'What a sorry plight we are in! See what bad holes the storm has made in the umbrella! Blaine, can't you stop that one?' [Maine senator] James B[laine]—'I am trying my best, but this Bloody Shirt won't do it; I am afraid we are all lost.' [Pennsylvania Republican congressman William D.] Kelley—'Oh, my poor baby! It is getting very wet. It won't take much more to kill it.' [New York Democratic governor Samuel] Tilden—'Ah, my men, "Honesty is the best policy." If your umbrella ever was of good firm stuff, it has become too rotten in your hands to protect you against this storm.'"

the consent of the governed. Morton asked "whether the women of this country have ever given their consent to this Government." He rhetorically inquired whether women had ever possessed the means to express such consent. Taking up an oft-used comparison, he noted that African American men had also been denied the right to give their consent to the government because they had not been enfranchised. Morton insisted that there was only one way that the consent of the governed could be given, and that was by "the right to vote."[34]

Knowing that some opponents of women's suffrage claimed that women's consent was given through their husbands, the Indiana Radical again compared the issue to slavery. In the past it had been argued that masters voiced the consent of their slaves and had their good at heart when he cast his ballots. Morton snorted at such a ridiculous idea: "We denied that. We know it was not true." Under the old system of common law, the father represented his daughter and the husband represented his wife. But under that system, patriarchy reigned supreme and females had no rights, no property, and no voice. They were under the control and authority of their male guardians. And those men could be tyrants, if they chose, because the law protected them, not those supposedly represented by them.[35]

Morton was glad that the United States had made progress since the days of common law, noting that American women had the right to own property, at least. Now, he thought that it was time to take the next step toward an egalitarian society. It was time for the United States to live up to its ideals and founding principles. He opined that "the theory of our Government is expressly violated in regard to woman." Only by granting women their natural rights could the country fulfill its own promise and live up to its own principles. Morton contended that making "woman the equal of man in regard to civil rights, rights of property, rights of person, political rights, you elevate her, you make her happier." Extending rights to women would also elevate men.[36]

The senator dismissed arguments that letting women have the right to vote would degrade them. Those who claimed the validity of such ideas failed to recognize the true nature of civilization. Other countries did, indeed, prohibit women from voting. But other countries also did things like requiring women to go barefoot or wear a veil. In the end, Morton rejected all arguments against the assertion that women would be degraded by having the franchise. Instead, he said that women having political rights would bring virtue to politics. The idea of women attending campaign events during election season had once been unthinkable, but Morton applauded the fact that, now, women were an expected part of the audience and they often spoke their minds on the issues. Although the Senate voted down the amendment and the bill to create a new territory failed as well, Morton had voiced a case for women's rights.

The Indiana senator had already supported women's suffrage earlier that year, and he became a consistent advocate for giving women the right to vote in the District of Columbia. Working in the wake of Victoria Woodhull running as the first female candidate for the presidency in 1872, and in a period when the momentum seemed to be on the side of granting equality to women, Morton fought hard on their behalf. In a February 1875, debate about a civil rights bill that focused on African Americans in the South, Morton stated that he also favored women's equality and always had. At a convention supporting women's rights the following year, he said that the Declaration of Independence included both sexes. When one considered that he had also worked to protect the rights of Native Americans over the years, it was quite clear that Morton followed a consistent course when it came to standing on the side of equality.[37]

Presidential Possibilities

By 1875 speculation about the presidential election of 1876 had begun in earnest. Many observers thought Morton a leading candidate, but so too was Indiana's former senator and current governor, Democrat Thomas A. Hendricks. Longtime rivals and political foes, the two Hoosier politicians now seemed likely to face off for the highest office in the land. In the summer of 1875, the *Indianapolis Journal* and the *Indiana Sentinel* engaged in a battle for their respective candidates, attacking the man from the other party, often making it personal with vilification of his character. Hoping to build his support for a presidential run and to keep his party in power, Morton headed to Ohio to stump once again for Buckeye Republicans in their gubernatorial race.

He made a series of speeches, including an address at Urbana on August 7, 1875, in which he attacked the Democrats like always and continued to argue for African American rights. After nine years of waving the bloody shirt, Morton had perfected the method. He equated Ohio Democrats like Governor William Allen with Confederate leaders. The Democrats were responsible for the rebellion, he insisted, and outlined the now familiar list of costs and consequences of their treason. He made Reconstruction a continuation of the war and blamed Democrats for resisting congressional policies and causing the Republican plans to fall short of expectations. He claimed that the Democrats committed all corruption in politics and blamed them for economic crisis and currency problems. Morton celebrated his own party as the champion of freedom, Union, and equality—making the Republicans the true heirs of the American Revolution. He closed his speech by pointing to the upcoming Centennial celebration, which he said would be a time for Americans to be thankful not only for the birth of their country but also for the Republican Party that had saved it.[38]

This time his efforts in Ohio paid off, as he helped Rutherford B. Hayes win the governor's office. The 1875 elections did not go well for Republicans in many parts of the country, especially in Southern states where Democratic Redeemers swept to victory and in New York, where the Democracy elected their whole state ticket. White Southerners celebrated the return of Democrats to power and called them "Redeemers" because they brought "Redemption" by ending Reconstruction wherever they were elected. In both the Southern contests and the New York elections, charges of corruption had boosted the candidates who promised to bring reform in the wake of so many high-profile scandals. But Morton escaped any negative consequences from the Democratic gains and actually increased his political clout. During the campaign, national observers saw how he was able to avoid being hurt by the storm of issues that the Democrats hurled at the Republicans. A political cartoon, "The Late Terrible Democratic Storm," published before the election in *Frank Leslie's Illustrated Newspaper,* showed Morton crawling out of the floodwaters to safety even as many other Republicans drowned or continued to be buffeted by the Democratic tempest[39] (see Fig. 37).

Morton's effective campaigning that fall incensed his Democratic enemies back in Indiana. They saw his work in Ohio for what it was: the senator laying the foundations for an 1876 presidential run. He followed up his stump speaking in Ohio with a trip to Maine. There, much to the chagrin of Maine politicians and newspapers editors who hoped to nominate their native son, James G. Blaine, for president, Morton worked for Republican candidates seeking election that fall. In late October the *Sentinel* raged against him, calling him a glory-seeking "revolutionist" and saying that the paper hoped to wave a bloody shirt itself, in hopes that it would warn voters in time to prevent a Morton presidency.[40]

But the Hoosier Republican continued the political fight undeterred. In addition to saving the Union, Republicans also stood for the freedom and equality of black Americans and had worked hard to secure their rights, a fact that Morton trumpeted with pride in his Urbana speech as he recalled the fight for the Reconstruction Amendments. And he refused to give up the struggle for African Americans even as many of his colleagues turned away when the political winds began to shift. Like a true champion, Morton would not give up. Throughout his Senate career, he fought alongside colleagues like Charles Sumner of Massachusetts and Zachariah Chandler of Michigan to enact legislation protecting the civil rights of African Americans. To be sure, his motives included maintaining the power of the Republican Party, and he wanted to punish the rebels for their treason. He constantly complained that the government had punished no traitors after the war (except for Jefferson Davis, who the Hoosier thought got off lightly), but if he could not try them in court and send them to prison or the gallows, at least Morton could force the rebels to accept black equality. He fought amnesty for former Confederates and applied the Fourteenth Amendment to bar them from seeking office. And he used his position as committee chairman to try to secure the offices of elected African American politicians. Afraid that the return of the Democrats to power would mean sacrificing the safety and freedom of black Southerners and the authority of the Republican Party, he vigilantly monitored elections in the South.[41]

MISSISSIPPI

In addition to Louisiana's disputed contests and the seating of Pinchback, Morton also got involved in Mississippi. In January 1870, for example, he had introduced a bill readmitting Mississippi to the Union and called for investigations by his committee to ensure that the state really had been reconstructed. He then pushed through the Magnolia State's readmission in February and guided the seating of "carpetbagger" senator Adelbert Ames. A few months later, he supported and applauded the election of Hiram Revels to the Senate by Mississippi.

When Revels made his first speech in the Senate chamber, Morton praised the African American Republican, saying "that the Senator from Mississippi has so well vindicated the ability and the intelligence of his race, that he has so well vindicated the cause of liberty and showed to the country that in receiving him in exchange for Jefferson Davis the Senate has lost nothing in intelligence while it has gained much in patriotism and loyalty." Fittingly, Revels's speech had been in support of Morton's plans for Reconstruction in the state of Georgia, and *Harper's Weekly* published a Thomas Nast cartoon depicting Revels surrounded by Radicals, including Morton, while a Shakespearean caricature of Jefferson Davis lamented the loss of his power outside of the Senate chamber (see Fig. 39). Although Revels served for only about a year, Morton later helped Blanche Bruce win the actual seat once held by Davis. Both African American Republicans from Mississippi proved to be valuable allies in the struggle for equality. Despite sending Bruce to the Senate and having a population with a black majority that would overwhelmingly vote Republican, Mississippi continued to demand Morton's careful attention throughout the 1870s.[42]

In the 1875 election the Democrats won large majorities in the Magnolia State, taking power away from the Republicans, who had controlled the government since the implementation of Congressional Reconstruction. Adelbert Ames,

Fig. 38. Senator Hiram R. Revels, Republican, Mississippi. (Library of Congress)

the Republican Morton had helped to seat in the Senate in 1870, had previously served as governor in Mississippi and had returned to that post after four years in Washington. A native of Maine, Ames was a Radical whose rigid adherence to principle made him so inflexible politically that even fellow Republicans grew frustrated with him. Few white Mississippians supported the Reconstruction government, and this resulted in a state Republican organization made up mostly of African Americans and white carpetbaggers from the North. One exception was James L. Alcorn, a former Confederate general who joined the Republican Party and served as governor before replacing Revels in the Senate. Despite his new party affiliation, however, Alcorn resisted most Reconstruction policies and became a thorn in the side of both Ames and Morton. Meanwhile, the majority of white Mississippians who chose to act politically tended to join terrorist organizations like the Klan, the White League, and an informal white militia called the Red Shirts, using violence to suppress the black vote. Unlike the night riders of the Klan, the Red Shirts and the White Leaguers took openly to the streets in large armed gangs. They forced white Republican officeholders to resign and massacred large numbers of African Americans in 1874, setting the stage for the election the following year.[43]

Helpless in the face of mounting violence, Ames refused to muster the militia because he feared a race war between black soldiers and white vigilantes. Even though race riots eventually forced him to call out some African American troops, he first looked to the national government for help. But the Democrats took the election that fall and celebrated what they called Redemption. They began impeachment proceedings against Ames and set out to restore Democratic power and white supremacy. When the reports of widespread violence, intimidation, and election fraud reached Senator Morton in December of 1875, he called for the creation of a committee to investigate. This set off a debate in the Senate, as Delaware Democrat Thomas Bayard argued against Morton's resolution for a committee, intimating that the Indiana senator was making up stories and facts about violence in the South.[44]

On January 19, 1876, Morton renewed his call for an investigation and gave a long speech in which he waved the bloody shirt and defended the rights of black citizens. He opened by asserting that "the late pretended election in Mississippi was an armed revolution, characterized by fraud, murder and violence in almost every form." He then made some general observations, saying that Southern Democrats had deprived Republicans of basic rights and freedoms even before the war. Prohibiting the Republican Party from organizing and suppressing freedom of speech and assembly, the Mississippi Democracy demonized their political opponents in order to protect the evil institution of

"TIME WORKS WONDERS."

IAGO. (JEFF DAVIS.) "FOR THAT I DO SUSPECT THE LUSTY MOOR
HATH LEAP'D INTO MY SEAT: THE THOUGHT WHEREOF
DOTH LIKE A POISONOUS MINERAL GNAW MY INWARDS." — OTHELLO.

slavery. The persecution of Republicans continued during and after the war and was so pervasive that few white citizens dared to join the party because they feared the Democrats would ostracize or murder them. And their fears were well-founded ones, because the Mississippi Democrats wanted "not only to defeat the Republican party of the South, but to extinguish it." Morton thought that fear kept the Southern middle class, a natural constituency for the GOP among whites, from joining the Republicans. This meant that the Republican Party consisted mostly of African Americans and that "power has thus been thrown into the hands of the colored people to a much larger extent that it otherwise would have been."[45]

And the Democrats set out to intimidate black Mississippians. The White Leagues refused to lease land to African Americans who voted Republican. Nor would they employ them. Consequently, Morton said, the Democrats starved black voters unless they gave up their political efforts on behalf of Republicans. Even though some former Confederate officers and men had accepted defeat and tried to collaborate with Republicans during the early stages of Reconstruction, the Democrats had turned on them as well. Morton reminded his audience of General James Longstreet as the most famous example of a former Confederate who turned Republican only to face "social punishment" for what Southern Democrats considered a crime. His once-promising insurance business ruined by political persecution, Longstreet had to take a government job to make a living. Treating Republicans as social outcasts and resorting to violence to intimidate any potential opposition, Southern Democrats like those in Mississippi set out to bring their states back under their control. They cried out against carpetbaggers and scalawags, but Morton maintained that the Southern Democrats were themselves the ones guilty of corruption and criminal activity.[46]

Fig. 39. (*opposite*) "Time Works Wonders" (*Harper's Weekly*, April 9, 1870). In this Thomas Nast cartoon Jefferson Davis is reacting to the election of Hiram Revels to the Senate as Morton and other Radical Republicans stand beside Revels, the first African American to serve in the United States Senate. Davis is depicted as Iago, the antagonist in Shakespeare's Othello, and says, "For that I do suspect, the lusty Moor hath leap'd into my seat: the thought of whereof doth like a poisonous mineral gnaw my inwards." The robe Davis wears in the cartoon reminded readers of how he had been captured with a shawl wrapped about him, a fact that brought Northern accusations that he had dressed as a woman. Such a depiction mattered in the face of Southern conceptions of manhood and honor, as the former leader of the defeated Confederacy was humiliated, emasculated, and shamed by the African American being elected to the Senate.

The senator admitted that most Southern blacks were not well prepared for citizenship. After all, "slavery was a bad training school, not only intellectually, but morally. The cruel and inhuman laws which made it a penitentiary offense to teach a colored child to read and write" had kept generations of African Americans illiterate. Morton begged his colleagues to remember the context when they heard Democrats denouncing black ignorance. He also urged them to ignore denials of "atrocities committed upon the colored people." He thought that the evidence showed clearly that blacks had "been hunted down like wild beasts, and the white sportsmen went gunning for them." The murder of an African American became familiar and expected among whites, and no murderers went to prison, faced execution, or even went to trial, for that matter. Morton refuted the stories about "negro plots to murder the white people," saying that such tales had "become exceedingly stale and disgusting." White Southerners often told such stories as a prelude to a violent riot, with massacres sure to follow the rumors of a black uprising. Especially popular, and therefore especially stale, were stories about how the freed people of Georgia were going to kill all of the white men and ugly white women of that state, implying that the plan made it possible for African American men to rape the attractive white females. Morton declared that "this infamous lie was intended as pretext for a slaughter." The wholesale murder of African Americans based on doubtful threats reminded the Indiana senator of how, nearly "every year before the war there were stories of plots among the slaves to 'rise' and murder their masters and families," and that supposed slave rebellions had been used to justify "the greatest cruelties."[47]

Morton praised Southern blacks for their general refusal to seek vengeance. Even when opportunities presented the possibility for violence, they rarely took advantage of such moments. Their "peaceable conduct . . . during the war in remaining upon the plantations and working with their usual industry, while their masters were in the field fighting for the professed purpose of perpetuating slavery, has been the subject of . . . surprise." Throughout Reconstruction African Americans had continued to be peaceful. Such nonviolent behavior stood as stark evidence against the charges of murder and atrocities that Southern whites claimed were the reason for their own violence. The senator thought that blacks "possess far greater intelligence than their enemies give them credit for. They know full well that their enemies are trained in the art of war, possess the best quality of arms, are skilled in the use of them, and are daring and aggressive." Realizing that they would suffer the most from a violent confrontation, most blacks thought that "their interests lie in peace and the observance of the laws."[48]

While duty required all men "to maintain the rights of the colored people," Morton said that his Republican Party especially carried the burden of responsibility for African Americans. The Republicans had abolished slavery, had "elevated the colored people to equal civil and political rights," and had given them a share of power. In doing so, they had placed blacks in a precarious position. Republicans needed to continue to fight for civil rights, but Morton worried that they would not fulfill their obligation. And he feared the result if his party "should become tired and so act that their enemies can say that they admit that the brief experiment of negro freedom and suffrage is a failure." To do so "would deserve the execration of men, and I doubt not receive the punishment of Heaven."[49]

But, Morton said further, too many Republicans were wavering and talking about giving up on Reconstruction. They were tired of the Southern question, tired of the issues of race and equality and the Ku Klux Klan. Already, many Northerners thought that "it is the genteel thing to abandon the colored people and to join in the crusade against them by professing a high regard for a good government in the South." Increasingly, Republicans were choosing to avoid the issue and focus instead on "questions of currency, tariff, civil-service reform, and other economic subjects." Some hoped to achieve reconciliation by ending Reconstruction and avoiding divisive issues. The Hoosier politician now warned his party not to "become indifferent to the fate of the colored people and ignore the atrocities committed upon them." Doing so would doom African Americans, as nothing else could "prevent them from sinking rapidly into a state of vassalage." If the Republicans abandoned blacks, as soon as the Democrats were elected they would "hurl them from the platform of equality and reduce them to a vassalage but one remove from slavery."[50]

Democrats pursued what Morton called a "white-line policy" in the South, meaning that they thought that "the Government should be exclusively in the hands of the white people, and that colored people should be excluded from all participation therein." The Democracy in Mississippi and other Southern states charged that black Republicans had used a "color-line policy" to take power during Reconstruction, but the senator denied that this was true. Although there were few white Southerners in the Republican Party, he claimed that this was because of the rebel Democrats intimidating those who might join African Americans in the party from the North. He described the ongoing violence that the Ku Klux Klan and White League had used throughout Reconstruction. He cited reports about the Klan operating across the South, noting that in Louisiana alone the Ku Klux inflicted more casualties "than fell at the battle of Bull Run." This "bloody record shows that the white-line

Democracy of Mississippi" was another part of the broader effort by rebels to continue their rebellion by violent resistance to Reconstruction. He denied that Republicans were corrupt, and responding to Democratic charges of misgovernment and abuse of power, said that he had "no faith in that virtue which assails with fury fraud and corruption, but connives at murder, outrage, and oppression." In the end, it came down to the "national question," which was "the political, civil, and industrial condition of the South, the violation of the political, civil, and social rights of millions of people, and the subversion of the majority by violence and intimidation." Once again, Morton drew the lines starkly between the two parties. The Republicans stood on one side as the defenders of freedom and the nation. On the other side were the Democrats, who promoted rebellion and murder.[51]

There were many people who "deplore any reference to the outrages committed in the south as inimical to reconciliation and harmony between the sections." Such individuals were "exceedingly anxious that in this Centennial year all past differences shall be forgotten," and they hoped that "the North and South, forgetting and forgiving, and mindful only of our great national future, shall meet and embrace as a nation of brothers." Morton claimed that he, too, wanted peace and harmony, but he reminded those who pushed for forgetting the past that any reconciliation accomplished "while the dearest rights of millions are systematically violated" would be "the rankest hypocrisy." No, he would not yield. The senator contended that true healing had to come from below and "be thorough to be permanent and healthy." He insisted that "the only highway to peace," the "one highway to reconciliation," remained open to the Democrats and rebels of the South. It required them to embrace the ideas contained in the phrase, "EQUAL RIGHTS TO ALL; TO ALL THE EQUAL PROTECTION OF THE LAWS [emphasis in the original]."[52]

These general remarks set up his discussion of the events in Mississippi. He first examined the financial situation over the past few decades, arguing that the Republican government during Reconstruction had inherited an impoverished state. Outlining money spent and taxes raised, Morton praised the Republicans and criticized the Democrats. He asserted that the Democracy was responsible for all of the incidents of corruption across Mississippi. Democrats simply stole taxpayer funds and made off with money from the state treasury, even robbing the people of the land and revenue earmarked for education. The 1875 election, Morton insisted, was a contest decided by violence and fraud. He read into the official Senate record excerpt after excerpt of newspapers reporting on incidents of violence or editors encouraging whites to intimidate blacks. Closing at last, Morton quoted an editor who said that when white Southerners managed to "escape from what they style 'negro rule,' no matter how, nothing but the active power of the Federal Government can restore it again." Page after page of evidence lent weight to his argument that the election deserved an investigation and made it clear that he intended to use such an inquiry to overturn the Redeemer government in Mississippi. After all, freedom and Union were at stake, and the Republicans had lost power. This put African Americans in jeopardy, but it also threatened the very fabric of the nation, the authority of the federal government, and the continued success of both the Indiana senator and his party.[53]

Despite Morton's eloquence, Mississippi senator Blanche K. Bruce charged Grant and the party with deserting black Southerners. An African American Republican whom Morton had supported in his successful bid to win the seat formerly held by Jefferson Davis, Bruce embodied all the principles of Radical Reconstruction. But fighting for equality included accepting the possibility that those for whom you fought might disagree with you. Speaking on the Senate floor on February 10, Bruce said that his race could no longer trust the Republican Party, and unless his colleagues returned to their former policies, African Americans would have to make a deal with Southern Democrats to guarantee their safety. He had heard Morton's speech on January 19, but rhetoric no longer satisfied him. Now, when the Indiana senator made some movement that indicated he might try to interrupt his colleague, Bruce turned to him and cried out, "Shake not your bloody shirt at me!" He accused the Radicals of selling out the cause and called them hypocrites and liars.[54]

Although he was dismayed that Bruce had criticized the party, Morton knew that his colleague was right. Too many Republicans were giving up on the Southern question. Too many had grown tired of fighting the long battle for equality. Besides his own principles, the Hoosier senator also continued his valiant efforts on behalf of African Americans for political reasons. Morton was relying on black delegates to deliver the South to him at the party's national convention, so he had to keep beating the drum for Reconstruction or he would have no chance to secure the nomination. But many Southern African Americans presciently worried that Northern Republicans were all talk and would sell them out in some deal with white Southerners.

Waving the bloody shirt and defending the rights of black citizens remained potent in early 1876, and Morton's speech paid off in the short term. The Senate passed his resolution and a committee investigated the Mississippi election. Sure enough, when the members of the committee reported in August 1876, they said they had found exactly what the Indiana senator had predicted that they would: Democrats had used violence and fraud to steal the election. By then, however, it was late summer, and the congressional session was nearly finished. There was not enough time left for Morton to do anything with the

Fig. 40. Senator Blanche K. Bruce, Republican, Mississippi. (Library of Congress)

investigating committee's report. Furthermore, the 1876 election campaign had begun and everyone was now focused on the presidential race. Most Republicans agreed with the Indiana senator that white Southerners were using armed force and corruption to carry out Redemption. But many of Morton's colleagues had grown weary of Reconstruction and did not think that the Southern question had a clear solution. For them it was time to move on. Even among the Radicals, only a diehard few held the line in favor of continuing and even expanding Congressional Reconstruction. By 1876 Morton had become one of the most vocal and visible of those who kept up the fight and, especially, unwaveringly supported African Americans.[55]

His struggle to seat Pinchback continued into 1876, as well, and it led to another bitter debate. In a speech supporting Pinchback, Morton quoted at length from an address by Georgia's Robert A. Toombs, who had resigned his seat in the US Senate in 1861 to become the secretary of state of the Confederacy. In his 1876 address, made as a private citizen, Toombs had blasted away at Republicans and African Americans, and he had called for a constitutional convention to redeem Georgia, promising his audience that "if you have a convention, I can make you a convention by which the people will rule and the nigger will never be heard from again." The former Confederate eventually made good on his word when he led the movement for a state constitutional convention in 1877. But in 1876 Morton used Toombs's speech as evidence of the rebel Democrats plotting to overthrow the Republican Reconstruction governments.[56]

This led Georgia senator John B. Gordon to denounce Morton for his anti-Southern rhetoric. Gordon, a former Confederate general who had helped create the Ku Klux Klan, denied the charges that Morton had made against the Democracy and accused him of having a poisoned mind. He made these charges in a speech in his home state of Georgia, but upon his return to the Senate, Gordon called for an investigation of Republican corruption, pointing to famous scandals like the Whiskey Ring and Crédit Mobilier as examples of how the Grant administration operated. As a Stalwart Republican, Morton had long battled against such accusations. In the elections of 1875, in which the Democrats won significant victories, corruption had been a powerful issue. Now, a year later, the Indiana senator was once again defending his president and his party and accusing Georgia Democrats of stealing elections.[57]

In March 1876 the two senators fired away at one another, until Morton finally quoted Gordon, who had said that the enemies of Georgia included "the world, the flesh, and the senator from Indiana." The Hoosier politician thought it significant that the Georgian had not included the devil in his list, saying that the Democrats were allies with Satan. Then he took aim at Gordon himself: "The devil is understood and believed to be the progenitor of the great and noble order of the Ku-Klux which did so much in revolutionizing the politics of Georgia. It would not do to speak of him disrespectfully." Gordon snapped back that Morton had taken the devil's place. The Northerner replied that of course Gordon replaced Satan with the Indiana senator because the Georgia Democrats considered the devil a close friend.[58]

African Americans in Washington expressed their gratitude a few days after the debate, as they serenaded Morton and Pinchback, who greeted them from the balcony of the Ebbitt House Hotel. The Indiana leader made a few remarks to the crowd and Frederick Douglass delivered a speech that praised the senator's efforts. Clearly, African Americans recognized Morton as one of their champions and appreciated that he had so long supported Pinchback and continued to fight against Southern Democrats like Gordon. Although he did manage to inflict some verbal damage on the Confederate-turned-Klansman-turned-Senator, Morton failed to seat Pinchback. And his plan to overturn the Mississippi elections fell short. In March 1877 Morton fought the seating of newly elected Mississippi senator Lucius Q. C. Lamar, a Democrat Redeemer. The Hoosier Radical said that Lamar had been elected by fraud and violence and once again began reading reports about the situation in Mississippi to the Senate. A great many of his Senate colleagues, including some Republicans, refused to listen, and groups of Southern senators openly chatted and ignored Morton's speech. Gordon finally stood and asked that the remainder of the Indiana senator's report not be read aloud. And when Alabama senator George Spencer, a white Republican, said that he was anxious for the report to be heard, Gordon looked around and replied, snidely, "It must be very apparent to the senator that nobody is listening to it." Morton forged on, saying that if it was "right to seat Lamar, it was a great wrong *not* to seat Mr. Pinchback." The Radicals were appalled at the boldness with which the Redeemers openly rejected the policies of the past decade. But as old Radical Republicans lost elections, died, or gave up on Reconstruction, Morton increasingly found himself standing nearly alone.[59]

Reconstruction became more unpopular as the American people tired of it and even Republicans began to turn away from it. Still, Morton refused to give up and continued to fight the rebels. State's rights might have worked earlier in the decade, when Republicans controlled Southern statehouses, but he now thought Washington needed to intervene. The Democrats had taken power and were winning the war by another name. To achieve victory and to secure the rights and freedoms all citizens deserved, the federal government had to act, which meant giving it the power to do so. And for the government to act in a way that would achieve the cause of freedom and Union, he thought the Republican Party had to keep power. Even as he boldly championed the rights of African Americans, Morton supported his party, earning a reputation as one of the most loyal members of the Republican organization that he had helped to create and continued to lead. For him, championing the cause of African Americans through Reconstruction required party loyalty.

Chapter Ten

Stalwart Republican

IN THE COURSE OF HIS SENATORIAL CAREER, Oliver Morton became a Stalwart Republican and proved to be one of the most reliable supporters of the Grant administration in the Senate. But the Hoosier's loyalty was not just to the president. He was, instead, faithful to the Republican Party, which remained an essential part of his foundational ideology of freedom, Union, power, and party. Throughout his career, Morton consistently held to that ideology, although it sometimes required him to contradict his own prior thinking on particular matters. On the Reconstruction policies that dominated his time in the Senate, he usually managed to reconcile the different principles upon which he had stood since the beginning of the Civil War. He fought against the same enemies and hoped to defeat the same rebellion. He defended freedom and the Union, both of which needed sustaining by the power of a strong national government. His party stood for the cherished doctrines of the Declaration of Independence and could, therefore, be trusted to employ the power of government in the right way. Should Democrats take that power or if freedom and Union somehow began to conflict, it would raise serious problems for the line of thinking that Morton had followed since 1861.

But his party engaged other issues besides Reconstruction and often divided over them. A staunch Radical on Reconstruction, Morton's stand on matters ranging from the economy to civil service reform made him a reliable vote for the administration, and he defended the president against those who decried the corruption of "Grantism." He joined with Roscoe Conkling of New York and Zachariah Chandler of Michigan in leading the administration's supporters in the Senate. Although his party loyalty meant that he often based his decisions on practical considerations and political concerns, as a leading Stalwart the Indiana senator helped lead the way on issues involving foreign policy, currency, economic policy, and internal improvements.[1]

Foreign Affairs

Morton broke with his fellow Radicals and sided with President Grant on the question of American expansion in foreign policy. The Hoosier politician had long been an expansionist, and as a senator he pushed for policies that would encourage the annexation of new territories. In February 1870 Morton contended for the passage of a bill making it a misdemeanor for anyone in the United States to sell or give arms to a foreign power for the suppression of an insurrection. Ironically, the Radical Republican who had spent his career fighting rebels supported colonial rebellions against imperial powers, especially the prospect of Cuba winning its independence from Spain. He noted that the United States had deplored and denounced French intervention in Mexico during the attempt to enthrone the Emperor Maximilian, and he thought Cubans deserved to have the Monroe Doctrine applied on their behalf as well. Keeping the European powers out of the Western Hemisphere followed traditional American policy, and Cuba, he felt, should be encouraged to follow the course of other Latin American countries that had successfully fought to free themselves from colonialism. American filibusterers had tried on several occasions to break the island colony free from Spain, usually with an eye toward eventual annexation as a slave state. Northerners had usually opposed such schemes in the antebellum period, but Morton had been an expansionist before the Civil War, and he still thought that annexing new territory was a good idea. Although he couched his arguments in the libertarian language of the struggle for freedom, he also made remarks that hinted that he believed that Cuba would become part of the United States. After all, he argued, "Cuba belongs to this continent; she is an adjacent isle, and is a part of the American system."[2]

Expansion in foreign policy again became an issue later that same year when the Grant administration began pushing for the annexation of Santo Domingo. Nationalists like Secretary of State William Seward had made annexation part of the Republican mainstream since the party's inception in the 1850s. At that time such expansionist ideas had fit well with the widespread popularity of the "Young America" movement. In keeping with such ideas, in 1860–1861 Seward had urged Lincoln to start a war with Spain to unite the country and prevent civil war while also bringing in new territories or at least new markets for American agricultural and industrial products. The secretary of state also directed the purchase of Alaska from Russia in 1867. Although "Seward's folly" remained the subject of ridicule by many wags until the gold rush of 1896, expansionism had long been supported by many Republicans, and adding new territory remained popular in the party's ranks after the Civil War.

This impulse was quite evident as the expansionist Republicans continued to look for new territory when Hamilton Fish succeeded Seward as head of the State Department in 1869. The island of Santo Domingo (or Hispaniola), ruled by Spain (and, at times, by France) for several centuries, consisted of two countries, Haiti and the Dominican Republic. Haiti, which had won its independence and saw the only successful slave rebellion in the history of the Western Hemisphere, controlled the western part of the island and had roughly a third of the land and nearly four-fifths of the population. It struggled economically even as the country was required to pay France for official recognition and seemed unable to resolve deep social divisions. The Haitians ruled the rest of the island for about twenty years after the Dominican Republic declared independence from Spain and united with its eastern neighbor. The Dominicans won independence from Haiti, but long decades of corruption followed, along with intermittent invasion attempts as the Haitians tried to reunite the island. In the 1860s Buenaventura Baez emerged as president, and he attempted to sell his country to European nations. When that failed, he turned to the United States, which he hoped would annex the Dominican Republic.[3]

President Grant and Secretary of State Fish tried to oblige Baez. With visions of plantations producing sugar and coffee and strategic ports facilitating America's naval power, the president negotiated a treaty annexing the Caribbean nation in exchange for the United State paying off the Dominican Republic's debt. The administration sent the treaty to the Senate, which referred it to the Committee on Foreign Relations for consideration. The committee's membership included Morton, and he supported the administration's plan. However, the committee chair, Charles Sumner, and a majority of the members did not agree with it. In 1869 Morton had supported Sumner's plan for Reconstruction, and the two senators had become allies on matters related to the South. Now they disagreed on foreign policy.

In a long speech over the course of two days in March of 1870, Sumner explained why the majority on the committee opposed the annexation of Santo Domingo. He thought the expense was too large and that it involved too many uncertainties. Furthermore, he feared that it would lead to a long, expensive war. After discussing finances, Sumner held forth against the treaty on moral grounds. He worried that the annexation might lead to the United States taking all of the Caribbean islands. Defending the right of the people of the West Indies to be independent and free, Sumner made claims that carried the racial views of the time. He said that the United States was "an Anglo-Saxon Republic" and would remain so, but that the Dominican Republic—like the other Caribbean islands—contained "colored communities" and the "black race was predominant." Sumner insisted that the black race was better suited

Fig. 41. President Ulysses S. Grant. (Library of Congress)

for the tropics and that white Americans needed to help them, but let them remain separate and self-governing.[4]

Morton responded to Sumner with a strong defense of the treaty agreement. He claimed that the people of the Dominican Republic wanted to join the United States and appealed to questions of national security by pointing out the island's strategic advantages. The Indiana senator predicted that the United States was destined to become a power in the Caribbean and that annexation began the fulfilment of what must inevitably come in the future. He also extolled the richness of the island nation, listing the various things it produced that the American people wanted and needed. For dramatic effect, he brought out samples of some of the goods. This led to two senators playing tug-of-war with a rope made of Dominican hemp and two others—one black, the other a race-baiting hater of blacks—licking a big block of Dominican rock salt—on opposite sides, of course. Despite the flair and force of his arguments, Morton was unable to sway many of his colleagues, and the treaty failed when the Senate voted on the question of ratification in 1870. Charles Sumner had broken with the administration, and the rift between the president and the senator from Massachusetts derailed the treaty.[5]

But Grant would not let the annexation issue go and made Santo Domingo a major part of his annual message to Congress. He asked Congress to appoint commissioners to go to the island to negotiate a new treaty, one that the Senate would ratify. Morton and other Stalwarts maintained that trying to appoint commissioners went too far, too fast. They realized that Sumner's influence could stop the process because the Massachusetts Radical and his friends made up a bloc of votes that could prevent the two-thirds approval needed to ratify a treaty.

Eventually Grant and Sumner took to openly fighting one another. The senator blocked appointments and tried to stop the administration's agenda, while the president fired Sumner's friends and attempted to drive him out of the leadership. Entangled in this personal battle within the Republican ranks, the question of annexation also coincided with the *Alabama* claims, an issue upon which Morton had given his views in the spring of 1869. The United States was trying to make Great Britain pay for the destruction wrought by the British-built Confederate raider, the CSS *Alabama*. Since his good friend John Lothrop Motley, who had helped prevent the Europeans from supporting the Confederacy during the war, was serving as minister to England at the time, Sumner was able to dictate terms in the negotiations, much to the chagrin of Secretary of State Hamilton Fish. Eventually, Fish accused Motley of hampering the claims, and Grant fired the ambassador. By then everyone realized that the firing was actually an attack on Sumner. Unsatisfied, Grant and his secretary of state worked until they successfully removed the Massachusetts Radical from his position as chair of the Committee on Foreign Relations.[6]

In December 1870, with this bitter struggle going on, Morton introduced a resolution to create an investigatory committee to gather information and report to the Senate about the possibility of annexing Santo Domingo. He hoped that this fact-finding commission would remove annexation from the personal feud and political wrangling between Sumner and Grant. But Sumner opposed the resolution and delivered a speech saying that he had read in the newspapers that President Grant had said that if he were not in office, he would call the Massachusetts senator out for slighting his honor. While the president clearly held a personal grudge against Sumner, it was also obvious that the senator hated Grant, too. In fact, much of his opposition to annexation stemmed from his personal dislike of the president. In the course of his speech, Morton tried several times to interrupt him to ask questions or make remarks that defended Grant, but that only caused Sumner to accuse him of being a friend and crony of the president. At some points, he even refused to let Morton interrupt him, and at least once he said he already knew what the Hoosier was going to say.[7]

Sumner finally finished speaking on the afternoon of December 21, 1870, and that evening Morton got his chance to reply. He immediately took up the issue of his relationship with Grant: "If the Senator means to impute to me that fact that I am a friend of the President, personally and politically, he is quite right." Morton proudly said that he had been Grant's friend and admirer since the early days of the war. He added that he sometimes disagreed with the president, but he slapped Sumner when he said that "I always try to differ with him in such a way as not to assail his personal character or to demoralize the party of which he is the head." Morton denounced the assaults on Grant by fellow Republicans and gladly reported that every attack had failed. Despite Sumner's treachery, the Indiana senator announced that "this Administration is thus far a great success." Taking the Stalwart position, he said that the senator from Massachusetts had made an indefensible personal attack on the president. Rather than disagreeing about "mere political principles," Sumner had "charged the President with usurpation, with crimes." Against these charges, Morton offered a careful defense of Grant's policies and his agenda as outlined in his State of the Union speech.[8]

He then argued for the Senate's approval of his resolution, saying that this was not the same agreement that they had rejected in the spring. This was a new start to the process, and the resolution authorized only the gathering of information about annexation so that senators could make up their minds when the time to consider a new treaty finally came. In the course of his arguments,

Fig. 42. Senator Charles Sumner, Republican, Massachusetts. (Library of Congress)

Morton predicted that "the annexation will come. I prophesy here to-night that it will come." He did not know if it would happen in his lifetime, but he believed that "it is destined to come." He argued that Sumner could not stand in the way of American manifest destiny, could not stop the inevitable. Morton also thought that the United States would annex Cuba and Puerto Rico. The islands in the Caribbean were friendly and wanted to join the American experiment in liberty and self-government. Sumner had spoken about the annexation of

Canada, but Morton insisted that the West Indies would join the United States far sooner than her northern neighbor. Santo Domingo was thus the first step toward fulfilling a national destiny, and Morton urged his colleagues to pass his resolution. Forensic fireworks followed as senators jumped into the debate, firing acrimonious charges at one another and at the president. The Radicals divided, as some supported Sumner and others rallied to Morton and the Stalwart defense of the administration. The exchange lasted long into the night, and when the Senate voted, Morton's resolution passed, 32–9. But defeat followed short-term victory. When the commissioners reported to the president in the spring of 1871, they recommended annexing the Dominican Republic. But the public mood had shifted and support had diminished, so Grant decided not to push the issue.[9]

The Radicals disagreed on other foreign policy issues as well. Hoping to strike a blow against Grant, Sumner called for an investigation of all arms sales by the government during the Franco-Prussian War. Because of French support for Maximilian in Mexico and the public seeing Louis Napoleon as the aggressor in the conflict with Prussia, Sumner thought that he might catch the administration selling guns and ammunition to the villains. The "French Arms" debate in February 1871, once again featured the Hoosier senator battling against his colleague from Massachusetts. Taking the Stalwart perspective, Morton denounced Sumner's resolution as an example of political chess and accused the Bay State leader of trying to influence the 1872 election. The Indiana senator not only tried to defend Grant on the details of the issue, he also held that Republicans needed to unite in the face of the coming election. Already the Liberal Republicans had emerged as a third-party threat, and the Democrats hungrily eyed the possibility of a victory over their divided foes. Party mattered to Morton, and he hoped that his colleagues would remember how important it was that they present a united front in the face of the opposition. If they did not, they would enable the Democrats to win the election and the Ku Klux Klan to ride to victory in the South. Appealing to Reconstruction and the vital issues of freedom and Union, Morton hoped to strengthen the ties that bound his party together and allowed them to exercise the power of government.[10]

When the administration deposed Sumner from his committee chairmanship in the spring of 1871, Grant relied on Morton to help the new chair, Simon Cameron, shepherd the Treaty of Washington through the Senate. That treaty resolved the *Alabama* claims, and the Hoosier senator served as floor manager to keep the Republicans united. This proved a delicate maneuver, as he had to tread carefully to avoid offending Cameron, who worried that Morton was the one that Grant wanted to chair the Committee on Foreign Relations. Cameron worried with good reason, as he had been replaced by Edwin Stanton after serving incompetently as Lincoln's first secretary of war. With Morton's reputation eclipsing his own, the Pennsylvanian jealously guarded his role as chairman. Fortunately, Morton handled the situation adeptly by putting party unity ahead of any personal ambition for the seat. Concerns for the party continually marked his relationship with Charles Sumner. Despite the bitterness of their debates over Santo Domingo and the French arms question, Morton and Sumner remained friends and allies as they led the Radicals in Reconstruction. In August 1871 they corresponded frequently, expressing their cordiality toward one another. Sumner again raised the old debate, trying to defend himself and arguing about the details of what he had and had not said to and about the president. Morton did not take the bait and simply ignored that part of Sumner's letter and wrote a warm and friendly response. Stalwart that he was, Morton valued party unity and recognized that it would be impractical to argue about now-dead issues.[11]

Economic Issues

Money also mattered. The Republicans divided on financial issues, including monetary policy, and Morton soon found himself at the heart of the debate about currency. During the war, the Republicans, led by the Lincoln administration, had directed the transformation of the American economic system. Much of the change came in the name of fighting the rebellion, but the individual policies reflected long-standing portions of the Federalist/ Whig economic agenda. Even before the Republicans took office in 1861, James Buchanan had signed off on the Morrill Tariff. Named for its sponsor, Congressman Justin Smith Morrill of Vermont, the tariff had passed because Southern politicians who had previously blocked the raising of taxes on imported goods had resigned their seats in the wake of secession. Pennsylvania publisher and economist Henry Charles Carey had helped Morrill write the law, which raised rates to protect certain American industrial interests and promised to increase wages for certain industrial workers. Carey, the author of a number of economic treatises, had worried about the impact of the Panic of 1857 on the iron and steel industries of his home state. Originally a proponent of free trade, he had become a protectionist, and he had guided Morrill's efforts to pass a higher tariff. Many Republicans had supported the law favored by many of the businessmen in their constituencies. The new tariff had overturned the long-standing free-trade policies that the Jacksonians had pursued in the prewar decades.[12]

But that was only the beginning. The Republicans created a new national banking system, permanently ending the separation of the national government from financial institutions. To raise revenue, they passed excise taxes and the income tax. And they took the United States into the world of paper money. Many Whigs had loved the idea of soft money and carried their dream with them into the Republican Party. They wanted a monetary system in which the government could regulate inflation and economic growth or contraction through control of the money supply. In 1861 the Republicans suspended specie payments in order to raise revenue for the war and to prevent the Treasury from draining its supply of gold and silver. The staggering costs of the conflict made it difficult for the government to pay the bills and paying for arms, equipment, salaries, and supplies with banknotes redeemable for specie would have quickly exhausted its reserves of precious metals. To pay for the war, the Union leadership turned to debt and to soft money.

Borrowing against the future and printing fiat currency enabled the Republicans to pursue a monetarist policy, using the money supply to regulate the economy in ways that expanded the power of the national government, favored the interests of their business cronies, and tied the country's financial future to inflationary money and centralized banking. This resulted in the printing of billions of dollars of government banknotes that the people called "greenbacks" and smaller denominational notes popularly known as "shin plasters." Printed under the authority given to the Treasury in the Legal Tender Act of 1862, the Union used United States notes to pay for the expenses of the war. The government continued to pay the interest on its debt in specie but used paper money for everything else. The law made the national notes legal tender, and greenbacks were not convertible to other kinds of money. An initial printing of $150 million in notes proved insufficient, and additional printings followed. The greenbacks experienced inflation almost immediately. They depreciated rapidly against specie, and despite the efforts of secretary of the treasury Salmon P. Chase to halt inflation, their value continued to decline. The Republican monetarists refused to accept responsibility for inflation. Instead they blamed "gold speculators," and Chase spent the remainder of the war years trying to stop inflation, eventually eliminating the gold market in an unsuccessful attempt to do so.[13]

In the name of the war, the Lincoln administration pushed through their revolutionary economic agenda. Chase was a Radical Republican and used the threat of resignation to pressure President Lincoln when the chief executive seemed too cautious. The Ohioan used his position as treasury secretary to influence the entire course of the administration. Since he had been a rival for the presidential nomination in 1860, Lincoln suspected that Chase wanted to run things himself. Like Morton, the Ohioan was a former Democrat and a free trader. Chase thus presented a stark alternative to Lincoln, the former Whig who supported tariffs. Although he often clashed with the Radicals, Lincoln generally agreed with them on most economic issues, and so he allowed Chase to implement a monetarist policy.[14]

Soft money related to the national debt, which expanded rapidly to keep up with the massive expenditures required to fund the Union military effort. It was possible to borrow without fiat currency, but it would have meant that bond prices would have gone higher and interest rates on them would have increased as well. The Republicans chose inflationary money over alternative methods of accruing public debt. Jay Cooke became the official promoter of government bonds and made a fortune for himself and his friends along the way. He joined Chase and Senator John Sherman of Ohio in pushing through the National Banking Acts of 1863 and 1864. These laws destroyed the old decentralized banking system of the Jacksonians and replaced it with a national, centralized, inflationary banking system controlled by the government in Washington and New York banks. The law required that the new national banks purchase government securities. These national banks sprang up across the country, often owned or indirectly controlled by Jay Cooke and his New York friends. After the Banking Act of 1863 passed, 66 new national banks appeared. By 1866 there were over 1,600 national banks across the United States. Meanwhile, the number of state-chartered banks dwindled from over 1,400 to 297, as a 10 percent tax on state banknotes prevented them from competing with the new national banks. Clearly the national banking system, based on the debt and greenbacks of inflationary monetary policy, had replaced the old financial apparatus.[15]

THE CURRENCY QUESTION

When the war ended, the nation found itself using depreciated paper money and carrying a heavy load of debt. The question of what to do next divided Republicans. Salmon P. Chase no longer directed the administration's economic policy. Maine senator William Fessenden had succeeded Chase in the cabinet post when the Ohioan resigned in 1864 and was later appointed chief justice of the Supreme Court. With Chase gone, Lincoln now relied on the moderate Fessenden to help him keep the Radicals at bay. When Fessenden returned to the Senate in March 1865, President Lincoln appointed Fort Wayne, Indiana, banker Hugh McCulloch as his third secretary of the treasury. Within days the new secretary had begun the long Republican fight over monetary policy when he set out to stop inflation through a currency contraction. He proposed returning to the gold standard and paying off the national debt as quickly as possible. The soft money interests—an alliance of the followers of Carey that included politicians like Morrill, businessmen like railroad tycoon Thomas A.

Scott, and Wall Street speculators like Richard Schell—responded by passing a law that called for Congress to cooperate with the Treasury in resuming specie payments "as soon as the business interests of the country will permit."[16]

The debates and controversies over financial policy continued after Oliver Morton arrived to take his seat in the Senate. Bills to limit contraction or to limit the amount of money printed all brought renewed arguments about whether or not the government should return to the gold standard. On June 15, 1868, the Indiana senator jumped into the fight when he opposed an increase in the money supply. He said that he had "hoped that the Senate had got past the time when it was necessary to argue the evils of an inflation of the currency—the increase of speculation, and the diminution of productive industry." He argued that the government should try to provide stability and avoid inflation. Saying that he believed "the best way to return to specie payment is to fix some time when this government will redeem its legal-tender notes," he called on his colleagues to work toward that end. A month later, on July 13, 1868, he joined the debate on legal grounds. While he still called for the resumption of gold payments, he reasoned that the law as written did not mean that the government had to pay principal on the national debt in specie. Instead, he argued, the Treasury had to pay the interest on the debt with gold, but could use greenbacks to pay the principal on government bonds. This led to charges that he was inconsistent or had flip-flopped on the issue. In fact, Morton remained a goldbug supporter of hard money, a position he had held since his days as a Jacksonian Democrat. With his party divided on the question, his support of McCulloch made him a Stalwart in the sense of supporting the current administration. By that time, however, he had already broken with President Johnson on Reconstruction, so the term "Stalwart" had limited application.[17]

During the 1868 presidential race, the candidates responded to questions that focused on the currency question. Some thought that the reason that Andrew Johnson had escaped conviction by the Senate was because of the money issue. This idea also held that the lead prosecutor for the House of Representatives, Benjamin F. Wade, would probably win the presidency if he managed to remove Johnson from office. His support of paper currency made him a "Greenbacker" as well as a prominent Radical Republican. Fearing that Butler would oppose a return to hard money, some thought that Republicans who supported specie resumption had changed their votes to defeat his presidential bid. Capital gossip about the currency issue continued to spread throughout the campaign in 1868 and often included Morton. Rumors spread that if Grant won the election, he would appoint Morton to his cabinet, possibly as treasury secretary. Although the rumors were untrue, Grant shared the Hoosier's affection for the gold standard, and when the Civil War hero won the presidency, Morton introduced a bill on December 14, 1868, that called for the resumption of specie payments. He would welcome Grant to office by returning the United States to a hard-money policy. His bill prohibited the government from selling gold and required that all surplus specie go toward redemption of United States notes. He set July 1, 1871, as the date for resumption of payment by the Treasury, with all national banks required to redeem notes with gold a year later. Of course, the soft-money men in the Senate opposed his plan, and word that the debate was about to begin spread rapidly.[18]

Two days after introducing his legislation, Morton carefully read a prepared speech in support of his bill, setting off the discussion. He rarely read his discourses, preferring to speak extemporaneously from memory, consulting prepared notes that he usually had on his desk as he delivered his speech. On this occasion, however, he decided to write out his oration and read it into the record. A large audience packed the Senate chamber that day, December 16, 1868, as interested parties gathered to watch and hear the debate about money. Bankers and other businessmen from various cities came to listen to Morton's speech, and the House of Representatives adjourned early so that congressmen could go to the Senate to hear it. In January his great speech on Reconstruction had made him a national leader who helped direct government policy in the South. Now, in December, the nation looked and listened as he tried to shape the economy.[19]

Ever ready to charge right in, Morton began boldly: "Among the mighty changes wrought by the war is the revolution in the character of our currency." In the name of fighting the war, the nation had abandoned the gold standard and adopted paper money. Now the problem was how to return gold and silver to the currency. Inflation meant that the fiat money had greatly depreciated and the value of the notes continued to fluctuate. Anticipating some of the arguments against his plan, Morton tried to address some of the problems that might hinder a return to the gold standard. He refuted assertions that resumption could not happen until after contraction because the currency was redundant. He dismissed claims that the country must first halt the outflow of gold to Europe by arguing that specie followed the laws of supply and demand. Since the only demand for gold in the United States was to pay for imported goods, of course it went to Europe. If an internal demand returned, the supply would follow. He claimed that wherever "paper money has been made legal tender, it has invariably driven gold and silver" out of circulation and out of the country. Holding to orthodox economics, he denied that the debt had anything to do with the depreciation of the currency. Instead, the government caused inflation by daily breaking its promise to pay the amount indicated on the notes. Paper money was a promissory note, and because the government kept printing more of it and did not redeem the money in specie, the result was an inevitable depreciation in value.[20]

Refuting the arguments of those who supported various other schemes, Morton carefully made the case for his own plan. Resuming the payment of specie was sound financially, he argued; it was also morally right. To continue with soft money was to continue to break promise with the American people. He thought that the "currency of a country bears an intimate . . . relation to every form of credit and security, both public and private, and, if it be depreciated, inevitably drags them down." Inflationary policy stood in the way of economic growth. Morton dissected McCulloch's plan for contraction and claimed that it would not work. Too many of the proposed currency policies tried to get around the reality of the situation. "You cannot pay a debt without paying it, and every trick or device to bring the currency up to par, without making preparations to redeem it according to the promise on its face, will be abortive and disastrous." No, Morton did not buy into plans like contraction. He refused to accept the arguments that tried to blame inflation on other circumstances. "The currency is depreciated because it is overdue and dishonored."[21]

But the senator did not agree with those who wanted to resume specie payment immediately. To do so would create chaos. Fixing a time for resumption would give the greenbacks a fixed value in gold and it would give the country time to prepare for the return to the gold standard. This included allowing the government to pay down its debt and accumulate enough gold to redeem its currency. Morton insisted that the Treasury must stop selling gold and start setting aside surplus specie as a reserve toward eventual resumption. He expected the country's mines to produce more than enough gold and silver to provide the necessary amounts for resumption to occur, and he predicted that prosperity would follow the end of soft money. Like the calm after a storm, "so with our country when peace, Reconstruction, and resumption have come." After the tempest of the Civil War, "peace has come, and with it Reconstruction. The bright sun of prosperity shines forth in a cloudless sky." With flowery oratory, Morton pointed to the gleaming future under the gold standard, as industry flourished, immigrants poured into the West, and the United States "moves on gloriously to its great and final destiny."[22]

The debate that ensued played out in the pages of the *New-York Tribune* as well as on the floor of the Senate. Morton found himself embroiled in a long argument with Horace Greeley, the famous editor of the newspaper, who favored immediate resumption. And his speech brought a variety of responses from colleagues and commentators. Even those who supported him thought Morton might have the timing of resumption wrong. The *New York Times* said that his speech did a better job of refuting the plans of others than it did in supporting his own. The *Washington Chronicle* led the capital newspapers in saying that the speech stood as an important event in the nation's economic history. The senator received over five hundred letters of congratulations, but those at the extreme ends of the debate disagreed with him. The soft-money men did not want resumption at all, while many goldbugs thought that the Hoosier's plan was too slow. The Senate finally referred Morton's bill to the Committee on Finance, but it did not go beyond that point. The goldbug Republican had failed to achieve resumption. But he had emerged as an acknowledged leader on economic issues and rumors circulated that he would be appointed secretary of the treasury in the new Grant administration. His 1868 plan contained many of the practical considerations and political compromises that would eventually mark a successful return to specie payments, including his call for a staged resumption with fixed dates for redemption of notes to begin. Disappointed, he turned to other matters, although the currency question did not go away.[23]

With the Panic of 1873, overinflated banks and railroad companies with empires built on inflationary money went bankrupt. Jay Cooke, who had moved from fearing inflation and favoring resumption in 1866 to embracing soft money just a few years later, saw his mighty banking and railroad kingdom come crashing down. The fall of Cooke sparked the panic, and of course the followers of Carey called for more greenbacks, hoping that government monetary policy would save them. Despite the financial crisis, the national economy as a whole continued to expand. Even the money supply increased and, overall, national production grew at extraordinary rates. Prices fell, but they had been falling since the end of the war, and they continued to decrease after the crisis passed. Still, there was a financial crisis, as some companies and financial institutions collapsed. With farmers and workers worrying about their livelihoods and businessmen desperately trying to avoid losing everything, the panic spurred the Republicans to return to the money question. And once again Morton found himself in the center of the debate.[24]

By 1874, however, he had changed his mind about resumption. Although his transformation on the issue had caused a break with the administration, he remained steadfast in his faithfulness to the Republican Party. The panic had created a demand for currency, especially in the West, and Morton began to rethink his position about specie payments. Perhaps it was the wrong time to return to the gold standard. The extent to which he had changed his mind about inflationary policy appeared in the immediate aftermath of the panic, when he advised Grant to use the government's full reserve of greenbacks in an attempt to stabilize the banks. The president did not heed his advice, so Morton led the fight to increase the limit of greenbacks, and the legislation passed. But the president vetoed it, and Morton's reliable mouthpiece back home, the *Indianapolis Journal,* wrote that the president was "controlled by Eastern capitalists in this matter." Taking up the language of populism, the editorial voice of Indiana Republicans worried that "the voice of the West and South in favor of a moderate increase of the currency, has been unable to make itself heard over the loud and imperious protests of the rich men and money kings of the East."[25]

In Washington's heated debates over resumption, Morton often took on fellow Republicans in the Senate, especially Carl Schurz of Missouri. The German-born Radical had broken party ranks to create the Liberal Republican movement that had supported Horace Greeley for president in 1872, and like Greeley, he held to the hard-money position. Ironically, Morton ended up arguing against the very ideas he had promoted in 1868. Next to his evolution on the question of black suffrage, his flip-flop on the currency question was his most famous political reversal. And as with African American voting rights, at least part of the reason he switched positions was his loyalty to party. In this instance, he recognized that greenbacks mattered a great deal to the people in the West and South, particularly to farmers and workers. The issue threatened the power base he had worked so long to build, so, hoping to avoid a dangerous party split, Morton tried to walk the fine line between the different currency camps. He wanted to advocate a moderate expansion of paper money while keeping the peace with the goldbugs by still blasting away at those who promoted soft money. Democrat Thomas Hendricks tried to take the same moderate position, but Morton accused his rival of extreme inflationary policies. Most Democrats toed the hard-money line, but already some Hoosiers were at work to take political advantage of the economic crisis and the currency question. Eventually, this led to the creation of the Greenback Party, a third-party movement that supported populists like James D. "Blue Jeans Bill" Williams, who split the Democrats and rode the issue to power in the Indiana gubernatorial election in 1876.[26]

THE PANIC OF 1873

Back in 1873, however, the course to take on money matters had remained unclear for many Republicans. That September Morton made a speech at the Agricultural Exposition held at the State Fairgrounds in Indianapolis. He avoided the currency question and instead devoted his time to extolling the virtues of education, railroads, and Bessemer steel. He barely mentioned agriculture, except to praise the richness of Indiana's soil, and spent more time talking about the future celebration of the Centennial in Philadelphia in 1876 than he did about farming. The senator did manage to mention farmers when talking about the virtue of having a diversity of labor, but he merely put them alongside mechanics and factory workers. While snubbing farmers at an agricultural event, Morton gave a rather workmanlike speech that promoted the state's economic progress and potential. His lackluster performance no doubt derived from the fact that the Exposition was organized under the leadership of Democrats, including Governor Thomas Hendricks, who spoke immediately after Morton. Despite the bitterness between them, Morton and Hendricks would sometimes work together on the issues. In 1868, while both of men were serving in the Senate, they had come together in support of an unsuccessful attempt at a law establishing an eight-hour workday. But such cooperation between the partisan enemies was rare, and in 1873 Morton did the duty required of him by his office; but he knew that the audience of farmers attending the event was mostly a supporter of his political foes. Rather than praise them or attack them outright, he chose moderation while still boosting Indiana's economy. Within days, however, the United States found itself in the midst of a financial meltdown, as Jay Cooke & Company, one of the country's largest banking concerns, declared bankruptcy. The Panic of 1873 began that September, and a depression followed. Suddenly, economics became the most important political issue to most voters and politicians.[27]

As the panic spread, Morton set out to prevent his party from dividing over money. He found himself embroiled in controversy just a month after the financial crisis began, when debate ensued over his support for a congressional pay raise. Morton tried to argue that he had spoken in favor of removing the pay raise from a bill that he otherwise supported. But Ohio Democrat Allen Thurman took him to task on this and quoted extensively from the Senate record to show that the Hoosier had supported the pay hike. As the economic depression began, austerity measures seemed in order, and the voters were watching to see if their members of Congress would deny themselves first. Of course, the fact that many blamed monetary policies like the Coinage Act of 1873 for the crisis served to keep currency in the forefront as a political issue. Despite his own claims to hold a moderate position on money, Morton found plenty of Republicans ready to fight against him on the subject.[28]

The Indiana senator renewed the fight about currency on March 23, 1874, when he delivered a Senate speech on the money question. The oration was given in response to Schurz, who had attacked Morton during a spirited exchange on February 25. At that time the Indiana senator had made remarks implying that because Schurz was foreign born, he could not fully understand the United States. The German immigrant passionately fought back and accused Morton of switching his position. The Hoosier said that he had changed his mind but not his party, slamming Schurz for having created the Liberal Republicans in 1872. The Missouri senator fired back that while Morton had never left his party, Schurz had never left his principles, and that was the difference between them. Ohio Republican John Sherman pitched into the fray on the German's side, snorting that Morton was the leader of a "new school" that "throws [economic] theory to the dogs."[29]

Having gotten the worst of the personal altercation, Morton now turned to trying to win the political debate over money. He began by dividing the different opinions on currency into three camps. First, there were those goldbugs who favored returning to the gold standard as quickly as possible and were arguing for an immediate resumption of specie payments. Second, the soft-money interests wanted to do nothing, as they hoped to keep the inflationary banking and currency system. Lastly, there came those like Morton, who believed that the financial crisis prevented a return to specie payments for the time being but wanted to expand the number of greenbacks in circulation and extend the benefits of the money system to all sections of the country. Morton contended that the goldbugs needed to show where the gold and silver to redeem banknotes would come from, as the forced resumption of specie payments without adequate reserves to pay them would cause further problems. Increasing the amount of paper money available, he asserted, would help the southern and western states where currency was scarce. He made much of the right of those states to share in the benefits of the system and called for the creation of new national banks in those areas. Printing more paper currency would help offset the damage wrought by the depression and bring equity across the country. At the same time, Morton asserted that the laws of supply and demand would keep down inflation even as the increased circulation of United States notes helped spur an economic recovery.[30]

Schurz replied by quoting Morton's own words from 1868, reminding the Senate of their Indiana colleague's arguments against inflation and opposing the establishment of new national banks in states in the South and West. The Missourian went on at great length, reading from the *Congressional Globe* the relevant passages of Morton's previous speeches on the Senate floor. Faced with the stark reality of his own contradictions caused by his political flip-flop on the issue, Morton had to reply. He admitted that his opponent quoted him accurately, but said that he had gone over his old speech and found it remarkable that Schurz followed his 1868 arguments so closely. He hinted at plagiarism and pointed to details that Schurz had not attributed to him. The

Hoosier drew laughs by saying that he had recognized the resemblance at once and that Schurz had now shown the Senate where he got his ideas. Listening to the German's speech, Morton "did not say a word about its origin for I was a little ashamed of it myself." He said that he had changed his mind over the course of the past five years and that what he had once thought "a tolerably good thing" he had reconsidered, and he was now "satisfied that there was no sense in it." He pointed out that some of his information in his 1868 discourse had not been original to him, but he thought that Schurz still should have given him credit.[31]

Using humor and evasion, Morton deflected the damage inflicted by having his own words thrown back at him in debate. He did not answer Schurz's charge about his partisanship because it was true. Morton was a Stalwart Republican whose steadfast loyalty to the party often helped dictate his positions on policy. Some argued that such political switching was mere opportunism or the result of always following the latest trends. For the Indiana politician, however, party played a central role in his ideology. Without it, power could not be trusted, and without power he could not win the ongoing struggle on behalf of the cause of Union and freedom. This meant that he sometimes had to flip his position on some issues. Furthermore, his thinking on important matters did evolve over the years, so his changing views sometimes did reflect a genuine changing of his mind that resulted from further thought, additional information, and the practical lessons learned from experience. Whatever his real reasons were for changing his position on the currency question, it was not a simple matter of political opportunity. In Oliver Morton's case, party *was* principle.[32]

His vindication seemed to come in April 1874, when Congress passed a bill raising the greenback limit and authorizing national banks in states with a shortage of currency. Having led the fight for the measure, Morton had mustered the votes of most Republicans in support of the bill and thought he had the president's approval as well. But then Grant vetoed it, saying that an expansion of paper money would violate sound principles of economics and national interests as well as break the government's promise to return to the gold standard. Surprised by the veto, Morton was absent when Congress tried to override the presidential nullification of the law. The attempt to override failed, and many criticized the Hoosier for not being there to cast his much-needed vote. Although it was doubtful that he could have made a difference, Morton faced mounting displeasure on the issue. National newspaper cartoons in pro-administration organs portrayed him as the chief proponent of inflationary soft money. One published in *Frank Leslie's Illustrated Newspaper* put the argument between Morton and Schurz in terms many readers could understand. "The Currency Question in a Tumbler" featured the inflationist Morton watering down a glass of whiskey and insisting that he had more in his glass while Schurz pointed out that the Indiana senator had only diluted the drink (see Fig. 43). Back home in Indiana, the cry for currency expansion meant that many voters were unhappy that their senator had failed to get the job done. The pressure was so great that Morton deemed it necessary to publish a letter in the *Indianapolis Journal* defending himself.[33]

The currency issue remained a potent and dangerous issue for the Stalwart dedicated to his party. In the end, after nearly another year of debate in which the Indiana senator often participated, Congress passed a compromise currency bill. The Specie Payment Resumption Act of January 14, 1875, which contained elements of Morton's 1868 plan, set 1879 as the date for resumption and set agreed-upon limits on the amount of legal tender to be in circulation. Morton worked closely with goldbug senators John Sherman of Ohio and George F. Edmunds of Vermont in drafting the compromise bill. Because the date for resumption was more than three years away, however, the money issue continued to raise its divisive head throughout the remainder of Morton's career. Populists gained strength and pushed for the coinage of silver as well as gold. The soft-money interests continued to hope for avoiding specie payments altogether. But despite his changing positions and willingness to take a moderate stand for compromise, Morton found satisfaction in the Resumption Act because it passed in the Senate by a large margin, with almost every single Republican supporting it. But although his shifting views made sense within the broader framework of his ideological commitment to party as a principle, his taking different positions on currency made him the butt of the joke in many political cartoons. One of them, "Comedy of Errors," published in *Harper's Weekly* on August 28, 1875, showed Morton arguing with himself, with one caricature arguing for hard money and the other for inflationary paper currency[34] (see Fig. 44).

TRADE POLICY AND REGULATION OF THE RAILROADS

The senator from Indiana also took a Stalwart position on other economic issues. Formerly a Democratic free trader, he came to support the mainstream Republican policy of moderate protectionism. In the summer of 1870 he campaigned for Republican candidates across the Hoosier State, and on July 18, in Terre Haute, he expounded on the issue of the tariff. He thought that a tax on imports was necessary to help domestic manufacturers. If a free-trade policy set the duties too low or eliminated them altogether, American industry would suffer, wealth would decrease, and jobs would be lost. If a protectionist tariff

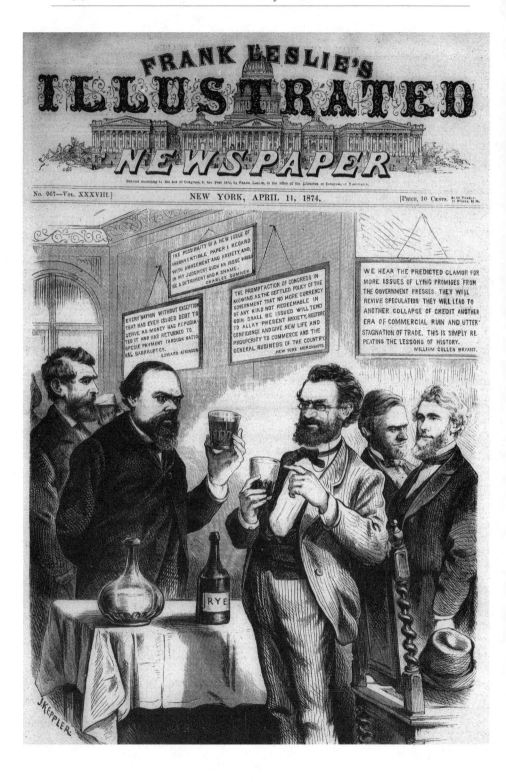

set the rates too high, it would eliminate foreign competition and domestic monopolies would dominate the market. Morton believed that the role of government was to pursue a wise tariff policy, setting the rates in such a way as to create fair competition between domestic and foreign manufacturers while also keeping prices at a level that favored consumers. The Hoosier senator held to the party tradition and also tried to help his Indiana constituents by consistently supporting internal improvement legislation and pushing for funding to build railroad bridges across the Ohio River.[35]

But he did not take the traditional party line on all economic matters. Throughout his career as an attorney and politician, Morton had supported railroads. He had worked as a railroad lawyer, and, as governor, he had seen their importance during the war; as a senator, too, he had encouraged their expansion during Reconstruction. But in the months following the Panic of 1873, he introduced a resolution asking the Senate Committee on Transportation to draft a bill to promote interstate commerce that included government controls on the very industry that he had so long supported.

In his Senate speech on January 27, 1874, he called for congressional legislation to regulate the railroads. In lawyerly fashion, Morton outlined the legal and constitutional history of the subject, concluding that it was clear that the "power given to Congress is to regulate commerce among the several States, and whatever is necessary to execute the power must be included in it." He anticipated arguments that the state governments chartered and regulated the railroads and rebutted them by saying that a state "can make no contract with a corporation which would limit or restrict Congress in the exercise of its power to regulate commerce." Here, again, nationalism trumped state's rights. Morton asserted that "the power of a railroad company to fix the rates for freight and passengers is but the power of the State granted in the charter of its creation." He noted that state regulations might be used to harm the railroads as well as

Fig. 43. (*opposite*) "The Currency Question in a Tumbler" (*Frank Leslie's Illustrated Newspaper,* April 11, 1874). This cartoon pokes fun at Morton's support of inflationary paper money in his debates with goldbug senators like Carl Schurz. The caption reads: "Senator Morton—'Put plenty of water in your whisky, and see how the volume increases. I've got a tumblerful, and you've got only two fingers. Make more of it, Senator.' Senator Schurz—'But, Mr. Morton, you've got no more whisky than I have, and your full glass is of no more value than the unadulterated quantity that I have. You have weakened your whisky and spoiled your water.'" On the wall behind the senators are quotations from New York merchants, prominent businessman Edward Atkinson, Charles Sumner, and William Cullen Bryant warning of the evils of paper money and predicting that a return to specie payments will be required following the financial collapse of the government.

Fig. 44. "Comedy of Errors" (*Harper's Weekly,* August 28, 1875). In this cartoon depicting Morton's changing and contradictory views on the currency question, he is shown arguing with himself. "Hard Money" Morton argues to "Inflation" Morton that paper money is no longer needed to offset the crisis of the depression. The caption reads: "Dromio Morton (of today) to Dromio Morton (of yesterday): 'The period has gone by when any increase of the currency would do good in checking the panic, I am free to say, and believe that it must run its course until the times are relieved by the economy, industry, and the operation of general causes.'"

protect them, so it was to their advantage that the national government should exercise its sovereign powers over transportation. But he played to the growing number of populists when he noted that "in the absence of restraining clauses in the charter . . . or legislation by the State or by Congress," the power to fix rates "may be exercised by the company at its discretion." He thought that the law as it stood now "would be ineffectual to restrain legislation by a State in fixing rates and creating burdensome regulations" and said that the answer was "the action of Congress" in passing laws to regulate interstate commerce.

But instead of passing his resolution, the Senate created an investigatory committee. When the committee submitted its report in April 1874, Morton discovered that it was focused almost exclusively on improving river, lake, and canal routes for commerce, and it wasn't until 1887, years later, that some of what the senator suggested in his speech found its way into the Interstate Commerce Act.[36]

In this case, it seemed that Morton had broken with the Republican Party line by attacking the railroads. In reality, however, he had proposed regulating the railroads for the express purpose of strengthening his party. Across the South, the Republicans held tenuously to power. In addition to the ever-present threat posed by the Democrats who hated Reconstruction, Southern Republicans now faced the growing populist movement. Even in the North, populism made significant gains in the wake of the Panic of 1873. Farmers and workers had real complaints about real abuses when it came to railroad companies charging exorbitant rates and banks committing usury or foreclosing on the indebted, and Democrats used charges of corruption and cronyism to counter the Republican practice of waving the bloody shirt. They also found that linking Republican corruption to the banks and railroads appealed to many Americans, especially in rural areas. The fact that many instances of actual bribery and cronyism existed lent credence to the political argument. Furthermore, the Democrats were beginning to win elections. If they followed through on their promises to the voters who elected them, they might very well undertake the regulation of the railroads themselves and would do so in ways far more injurious to business interests than what the Republicans would do. Therefore, it was in this context, to help his party, that Morton introduced his call for railroad regulation. What seemed like a divisive issue could have become a practical and moderate piece of legislation that actually strengthened and united the Republicans. It did not work in 1874, but the speech was far more than just the senator playing politics or switching his position. The following year, he opposed the regulation of so-called "horse railways," because he said that the streetcars used in the cities across the country were "the people's carriages," and that where they were wanted, they should be allowed. Furthermore, such companies were usually local enterprises that operated in an urban area rather than larger national industries that ran across state lines. Consequently, federalism applied and the streetcars were not subject to congressional regulation. So the Hoosier leader thought that freedom should reign over the horse railways. Again, despite those who might see his actions as opportunistic, Morton's stand on the regulation of business proved consistent with his ideology.[37]

CORRUPTION AND CIVIL SERVICE REFORM

Corruption, long an issue in American politics, became vital in the 1870s. It continued to gain momentum in the wake of widespread religious revivals led by preachers like Dwight L. Moody. As it often did, morality mingled with politics. Actual crimes that broke as political scandals splashed across the newspaper headlines and gave people a reason to suspect that there was more going on. Throughout the Grant administration, Morton defended his president and his party against charges of corruption amid the troubles brought by real scandals. In the election of 1875, for example, he tried desperately to save the Republicans from defeat at the hands of Democrats promising reform, but over time scandals continued to rock the administration, and many now associated "Grantism" with corruption. But the brave Stalwart senator labored on, even when others in his party turned away from the president. On April 3, 1875, *Frank Leslie's Illustrated Newspaper* printed a cartoon that captured Morton's loyalty to Grant. In the illustration, entitled "A Hopeless Case," the Indiana senator was bent over a river, trying to rescue a drowning Ulysses S. Grant, who was flailing and calling for help. On the shore, his former friends and allies were pictured turning away, abandoning him to his fate. Only Morton's fellow Stalwart Roscoe Conkling stood by, holding on to the Hoosier as he reached out to help the president. Although Morton managed to help some of his fellow Republicans win in the election that fall, the 1875 contest was seen as a repudiation of Grantism and an electoral swing toward those who called for reform.[38]

Fig. 45. (*opposite*) "A Hopeless Case" (*Frank Leslie's Illustrated Newspaper*, April 3, 1875). Here Morton calls out to fellow Radical Republican senator Roscoe Conkling of New York as they try to save their party from the scandals of the Grant administration, the unpopular Civil Rights Act of 1875 that gave teeth to Reconstruction, and talk of the president seeking a third term. Hoping that the elections in Connecticut (where candidates took strong stands for or against the administration) will shift the political winds that have been blowing against him, Grant desperately struggles to stay afloat. The president cries for help as most of his former friends and allies turn away. The cartoon caption says: "Morton—'Hold on to me, Conkling, or I shall lose my life trying to save this fellow. Why is it we cannot rescue him?' Conkling—'Confound him, he's a dead weight. I'm afraid we shall all perish with him—everything, I feel, is giving way.' U. S. G. [Ulysses S. Grant]—'I am stuck fast in the mud and quicksand. Will nobody help me? Where are all my friends? Keep my head afloat and I'll pay you well. If I could only get hold of that Connecticut plank I might save myself.'" Vice President Henry Wilson, Maine senator James G. Blaine, and "other Old Friends" are looking on with indifference or walking away, saying, "Connecticut plank or not; that obstinate chap is beyond our help. If he drown with those dead men, 'twill be his own fault. Self-preservation is the first law of Nature—let's leave him to his fate."

No. 1,018—Vol. XL.]   NEW YORK, APRIL 3, 1875.   [Price 10 Cents.

Always seen as a partisan, Morton was accused of helping set up "carpetbag" senators (like George Spencer in Alabama, a Republican Morton helped seat by blocking a Democratic rival following a disputed election) in the Southern states during Reconstruction. His enemies said that he used his position as chair of the Committee on Privileges and Elections to help put corrupt Republicans into power, packing the Senate with party allies loyal to himself. Furthermore, he was charged with lending aid to Yankee carpetbagger governors (like William Pitt Kellogg in Louisiana) and this, when combined with his loyalty to Grant, opened Morton to criticism on the issue of political corruption.

He managed to at least dilute the power of such accusations when his committee investigated the two Republican senators from Kansas in 1872–73 on charges of electoral misconduct and bribery. Samuel C. Pomeroy, a native of Massachusetts, had moved to Kansas in the 1850s during the disputes over the extension of slavery. Alexander Caldwell, a Pennsylvanian, had moved there at the outset of the Civil War. Both men were seen as carpetbaggers by Southern Democrats, who thought that the Republican senators used fraud and bribery to win the offices they used for their own enrichment as well as that of their friends. When formal charges were laid against Pomeroy and Caldwell, Morton's committee held hearings, called witnesses, and investigated the cases against the senators. Although Pomeroy was found not guilty and proven to be a victim of an elaborate scheme to smear his reputation, he was tainted by the corruption case and defeated in his reelection bid in early 1873. Caldwell, however, was shown to have bribed rivals in order to prevent them from running against him and of having paid at least $60,000 to win his seat. When Caldwell offered a strong defense in the committee hearings, Morton destroyed his fellow Republican's case in his brutal, lawyerly fashion, pointing out the flaws in the senator's testimony and showing him to be guilty. Rather than be expelled from the Senate, Caldwell resigned. Morton's role in the corruption investigation of Caldwell, especially, cleared his own name and served as a bulwark against charges that he was a mere partisan who always supported the carpetbaggers and unscrupulous Republicans.

Corruption was a powerful issue that could swing elections, and Morton knew this well, as his Democratic enemies had accused of him of stealing the state's treasury when he was governor. He also understood that one of the causes of such accusations was the patronage system. When one party took power away from the other, civil servants and bureaucrats lost their jobs and political loyalists took their place. Cronyism and party fealty usually took precedence over the question of whether someone was qualified for a position. Always an intense partisan, Morton used his patronage to build the foundation of a political machine. This had started when he was governor, and he continued the practice as senator. The traditional custom of the "courtesy of the Senate" meant that whenever the president sent over a nomination for the approval of the Senate, that body deferred to the senators from the nominee's state. If the two senators from a state were from the same party, they conferred about such decisions. If they were from opposing parties, the man in the majority nearly always got what he wanted. This meant that very few nominations ever actually received close consideration or debate.[39]

One office that senators used to reward loyalty was that of postmaster. Much-sought-after positions such as these switched hands whenever a new president won election to the White House, and there were always local disputes over which man should have the job. Whenever there was a vacancy, friends of the candidates for the position sent letters recommending them to their congressman, the state's senators, and the president. Morton often endorsed men for postmaster, always with an eye toward party and personal loyalty. On July 18, 1873, however, he wrote Will Holloway telling him that he was tired of a particular controversy over replacing a sitting postmaster in an Indiana town and agreed to go along with the man selected by other party leaders. Although he expressed his frustration over the difficulty that arose in choosing a replacement, he did think that the current postmaster's appointment had been a mistake and remarked that the man "is as unpopular as he is ugly."[40]

The system meant that senators like Morton had a lot of patronage power. Unsurprisingly, in January 1871, when Senator Trumbull of Illinois introduced legislation that would end congressional patronage, Morton opposed it. He declared that the proposed law was unconstitutional and that the decision actually rested with the president. Senators only advised the executive which men to choose for appointments. The Indiana politician insisted, doubtfully, that he preferred to be relieved of such duties himself but that it was a responsibility of the office. After all, the people should elect men of good character, and they should help make such decisions. He also argued that, generally, good men filled the civil service and they did good work for the government. Although he claimed that he wanted some kind of civil service reform, he actually thought that because the system was not broken, there was no need to fix it. He rallied the majority of his party to help him in defeating the measure, and civil service reform stalled. A political cartoon published on August 3, 1872, in *Frank Leslie's Illustrated Newspaper* showed Morton asking for more money from Grant, who was campaigning for reelection himself. The senator needed the funds to help him secure more power in Indiana, warning that without the cash, the election would not go well for the Republicans that fall. The president's running mate, Henry Wilson of Massachusetts, drawn on the other side of the president, told Grant that he has already given Morton all of the patronage in his state and more besides. The cartoon poked fun at the president for not being his own man as well as jabbing at the power of Republican insiders like the Indiana senator. Caricatures aside, Morton did have access to the president and used his patronage power to his advantage[41] (see Fig. 46).

On patronage and civil service reform, too, power and party motivated Morton. He believed that the Democratic Party threatened the Union and would destroy liberty. He was convinced that Democrats were corrupt and traitorous and that securing individual freedom and saving the Union required the use of government power. That power needed to rest in the hands of his party to prevent the destruction of the Democrats, and it was only through patronage that good Republicans could guarantee that the civil servants in the bureaucracy remained loyal to the cause. When the issue came back up later, Morton continued to insist that he favored the proper kind of civil service reform even as he worked to undermine any legislative attempts to carry forward any changes.[42]

Fig. 46. (*opposite*)"Behind the Scenes at Long Branch, July 12th, 1872" (*Frank Leslie's Illustrated Newspaper,* August 3, 1872). In this cartoon depicting the charges that Republicans tried to buy elections during the Reconstruction Era, Oliver P. Morton is shown asking the president for money. He says, "Mr. President, you must give me money to spend in Indiana. We are both in the same boat, and if the State is lost, you and I are both gone." Meanwhile, Grant's vice presidential running mate, Massachusetts senator Henry Wilson, complains, "Mr. President, you have given Morton all of the patronage in his State, and a good slice of the New York Custom House. Now, it is much more important to spend money in North Carolina because the election there is the first in the campaign, and if we don't carry that State, it's up with all of us." Grant replies, "Well, I don't get much now from Leet's Custom House business, and I shall have to get [Secretary of the Treasury George S.] Boutwell to let us have some cash and charge it to Court Expenses." The text boxes above the men read (left), from Secretary Boutwell's speech at Greensboro, NC: "General Grant shrinks from the exercise of power. He never seeks to enlarge his authority as a magistrate," and "If, during this Administration, the power of the National Government has been felt in this and in some other States, all candid men must admit that occasion existed for its use"; (right) from ex-Senator [James] Doolittle [Republican, Wisconsin], "I say, and all the world knows, in New Orleans Grant's agent controlled the Convention by the bayonet. In Wisconsin and New York his agents and appointees controlled the Conventions by his patronage. I arraign before the bar of public opinion the officers, agents and tools of Grantism in North Carolina, upon the authority of Governor Vance and many others, honorable men, and charge that the power of the Federal Government is used to control them. I charge that numbers of men, three thousand and upward, having been charged with offenses and arrested, and upon their giving their political support to the Grant party, have been released and discharged from imprisonment without trial and without costs. That to others the promise of pardon or of suspending prosecution has been and is held out upon the condition of changing their political action; that among them all, and in all parts of the State, it is held out that immunity will come if they give support to the political party."

No. 870—Vol. XXXIV.]   NEW YORK, AUGUST 3, 1872.   [Price, 10 Cents. $4 00 YEARLY. 13 WEEKS, $1 00.

"General Grant shrinks from the exercise of power. He never seeks to enlarge his authority as a magistrate." "If, during this Administration, the power of the National Government has been felt in this and in some other States, all candid men must admit that occasion existed for its use."

[Secretary Boutwell's Speech at Greensboro', N. C.

"I say, and all the world knows, in New Orleans Grant's agent controlled the Convention by the bayonet. In Wisconsin and New York his agents and appointees controlled the Conventions by his patronage. I arraign before the bar of public opinion the officers, agents and tools of Grantism in North Carolina, upon the authority of Governor Vance and many others, honorable men, and charge that the power of the Federal Government is used to control them. I charge that numbers of men, three thousand and upward, having been charged with offenses and arrested, and upon their giving their political support to the Grant party, have been released and discharged from imprisonment without trial and without costs. That to others the promise of pardon or of suspending prosecution has been and is held out upon the condition of changing their political action; that among them all, and in all parts of the State, it is held out that immunity will come if they give support to the political party."

EX-SENATOR DOOLITTLE.

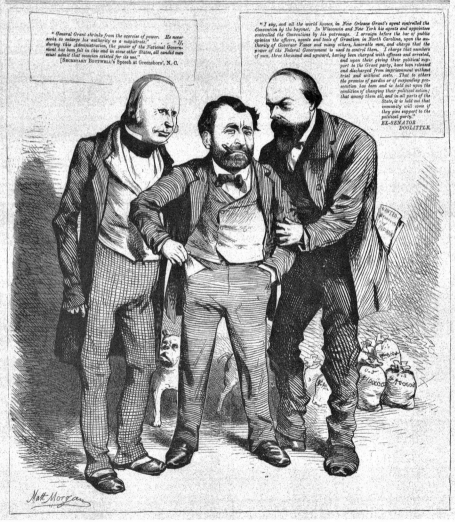

The Mortons in Washington Society

Corruption and cronyism plagued the Grant administration, as scandal after scandal rocked the president's cabinet. Morton's instincts and honesty allowed him to remain free from most of the charges of corruption that were raised continuously throughout the 1870s. Still, as a Stalwart Republican, he had become a trusted friend and adviser to the president and other important political and social figures. Senator Morton and his wife became fixtures in Washington society, and Lucinda a close friend of First Lady Julia Dent Grant as well. Attending the many parties, balls, banquets, dinners, and charitable functions was an expected part of a senator's duties, but it also afforded Morton the opportunity to influence President Grant and many other leaders with whom he talked in the course of such an event.[43]

The society columns in the Washington newspapers kept tabs on the comings and goings of prominent figures in the city and contained gossipy reports about parties and receptions, complete with guest lists and descriptions of what the fashionable ladies attending wore that evening. Senator and Mrs. Morton made many appearances over the years, often in the company of the Grants. But Morton had also continued his friendship with Andrew Johnson, even after the bitter impeachment and trial of the president. Despite having voted for Johnson's conviction and supporting Grant in the election of 1868, Morton still attended the outgoing president's last White House reception on January 1, 1869. Upon his arrival, Morton shook hands with the president and "conversed with him for some minutes." The following month, in February, Morton was among the guests at a private party held by the incoming vice president, Indiana's own Schuyler Colfax. In November of 1869 the Hoosier senator attended Thanksgiving services at the Metropolitan Methodist Church and, a few days later, joined other dignitaries in a visit to the Naval Yard, then went to a party hosted by Secretary of State Hamilton Fish. Washington tradition required the president to hold a New Year's Day reception each year, and Morton, who happily began each year by attending the event at the White House, was always on the list of guests during the Grant administration. In February 1870 Lucinda Morton helped the first lady greet her guests at a White House party, and she did so again in April 1872. In 1874 the two women worked together as the organizers of a charity benefit.[44]

Sometimes, when the senator's health or schedule prevented him from being present at an event, Lucinda went alone, such as when she attended a wedding in July 1870, when she turned up at a society party in January 1874, and when she went with the Grants to the conservatory on January 21, 1876. When Lucinda was at home in Indianapolis, Morton attended society functions without her, including making the trip to be at President Grant's banquet at his private home in Long Branch, New Jersey, in July 1871 and going to a party with the president in December 1873. He attended parties hosted by fellow senators and showed up at the Washington galas held by the Indiana Republicans. Morton was also a guest at state dinners at the White House and at parties hosted by foreign diplomats, such as when he and Lucinda attended a grand ball held by the British minister to honor the visiting Prince Arthur in January 1870.[45]

Of course, the Mortons also hosted parties themselves. Over the years, he lived at the Metropolitan, the National, and the Ebbitt House Hotels, and these establishments were the venues where he and Lucinda hosted their social events. The couple kept their house in Indianapolis, and Lucinda often remained there while Oliver went to Washington for congressional sessions. But his rented rooms at capital hotels were always large enough to accommodate her as well as himself and were also chosen with an eye both toward entertaining guests and his comfort in conducting business at home.

Living in Washington hotels sometimes caused confusion that led to funny family stories. In January 1874 young Walter Morton made the papers when he came to visit his parents in Washington. Senator and Mrs. Morton had lodged at the Ebbitt House for several years, and when his train arrived in the city, Walter rushed to the hotel to greet his mother and father. He reached the door to their rooms and began knocking excitedly. Unbeknownst to him, the senator and his wife had changed their lodgings and had forgotten to tell Walter. A young couple now lived in their old quarters. The boy's knocking awakened the new lodgers, and the sleepy husband asked his wife to open the door for "the man who lights the fires." The lady left her bed to unlatch the door, then hurried back to bed before the employee could see her in her nightgown. When he heard the door bolt slide, Walter eagerly threw open the door and ran into the room. He followed the woman to the bed, embraced her, and as she cried out at the sight of the stranger and covered her head with the blankets, attempted to kiss her. Her husband awoke and began stammering, "Wh—wh—at's the matter? Wh—wh—at's up? Wh—who are you, sir?" Realizing his error, young Walter, embarrassed, blushingly began to explain that he had mistakenly thought it was his parents' room. The woman realized what had happened, and uncovering her head to show her "beautiful young face," broke into "a hearty and forgiving laugh." Shamefaced, Walter retreated from the room, sputtering, "I–I–I thought you were my mother!" The couple appreciated the humor of the situation and laughingly told the story about Washington, with the husband vowing to always keep an eye out for "the man who builds the fires."[46]

Their sons often visited the Mortons in Washington, but the senator and his wife also entertained many other guests at their parties. On January 1, 1872, Mrs. Morton held a reception at the Metropolitan Hotel that was well attended, even though her husband managed to sneak away to go to the White House for President Grant's reception being held at the same time. On January 22, 1874, the Mortons held a reception at the Ebbitt House Hotel and Rosalind "Rose" English, the daughter of former Democratic congressman and Indianapolis banker William H. English, helped Lucinda receive their guests. The evening before, the Mortons were the center of a "jolly little impromptu party" at the hotel. Lucinda and other ladies, including young Rose English, were gathered in the parlor while the senator joined other gentlemen for after-dinner conversation. Someone among the ladies suggested that they should dance, and "a gallant army officer" staying at the hotel found instruments and musicians to play them. The men joined the ladies and the fun began, with society columns reporting that the unplanned party "presented as gay an appearance as those at many of the formal parties of the city." Not all social functions were so happy, as on December 18, 1873, when Senator Morton attended President Grant's father-in-law's funeral. But he shared joy with the president, too. When the Mortons' son John got married in February 1874, the Mortons hosted many prominent guests, including President Grant. A couple of years later, when John and his wife came to Washington for a visit from their home in San Francisco, the senator and his wife held a large party in their honor. In January 1876 Lucinda Morton's reception at the Ebbitt House was "the center of gayety," as she hosted "a very large reception." By that time the Mortons were familiar with "the season" in the capital city and knew well how to throw a society party. Thus, it was not a surprise that their reception topped the long list of social events reported in the papers that day.[47]

Naturally, Senator Morton's relationship with President Grant extended beyond social events to more official meetings. The senator had the privilege of greeting and officially notifying Grant and Colfax of their election on February 13, 1869, and he fulfilled his duty by offering a welcoming speech. Thereafter, Morton was a regular and frequent visitor to the White House and often met with the president even on days when the doors of the executive mansion were closed to most callers. The Washington newspapers reported many of his meetings with the president, often noting that Morton had "a lengthy interview" with Grant. During such visits, the Stalwart Republican consulted with Grant on various political matters, offering his advice, receiving the president's instructions, and planning their strategy for governing the country and getting bills passed. Sometimes other leaders joined them, but Morton often met with Grant alone, a fact that indicated the significance of his close friendship and influence with the president. At least some of his long meetings at the White House focused on his own position, such as in the fall of 1870, when Morton was considering accepting the post of minister to Great Britain.[48]

In addition to meetings in Washington, the senator and the president sometimes traveled together. In the spring of 1871 they took the same train westward, with Grant heading to his family farm in St. Louis and Morton going to Indianapolis; when they reached the Indiana capital, they each delivered speeches to an enthusiastic crowd. That trip went so well that Grant asked Morton to accompany him on a trip to the Pacific Coast that summer. Although the president eventually changed his plans, Morton did travel to the West Coast, where he survived a train wreck in California while riding on the Central Pacific Railroad in October 1871. Back in Washington, Morton's visits to the White House became routine, with meetings taking place nearly every week, and when the issues demanded it, sometimes he called on Grant daily to work out their plans. Although neither man left a record of their meetings, the newspapers often knew the subjects of the meetings (as with the possible appointment to England), and the timing of Morton's visits provided clues about many others, as he visited more frequently when managing important legislation or helping figure out campaign strategy. During his discussions with the president, the Indiana senator learned what Grant wanted the Stalwart Republicans to do while also exercising his own influence in matters ranging from foreign affairs to economic policy to Reconstruction to patronage appointments.[49]

Morton and Pratt

Another man with whom Morton often conferred about patronage decisions and other political matters was Daniel D. Pratt, the Logansport lawyer elected to the Senate in 1869 amid the controversy about Will Cumback's letters. Although he had favored Cumback for the Senate initially, Morton had bowed to his friend and successor in the governor's chair, Conrad Baker. The Indiana governor had pushed Pratt as an alternative while vehemently opposing Cumback, and Morton, busy with his work in the Senate and not wanting to offend Baker, went along with the plan. He did not actively support Pratt, but neither did he try to prevent him from taking office. Although he knew Pratt, who like himself had been a member of the Republican Party from its inception in Indiana and who had been a candidate for various high offices, he was not close to the Logansport attorney, who had been relatively inactive politically throughout the war years. Pratt's wife had died in 1861, and although he still campaigned for the party and was the unsuccessful Republican candidate for the Senate in 1863, he had scaled back his efforts to focus on his family and local community. With his own choice eliminated from consideration and the state party situation in turmoil, it was not surprising that Morton had remained quiet about the decision. After all, the good of his party demanded that he support Baker's choice.[50]

There might have been bad blood between the senior senator and Pratt, however. During the war, when Pratt traveled to Washington to check on the condition of soldiers from his home county, Morton thought he was questioning the governor's implementation of draft quotas. Suspicious, the state executive had his secretary, Charles Jacobs, write and send a letter that brusquely inquired about what Pratt was doing. Morton was prickly about his honor and was always quick to defend himself and his authority. Ever suspicious of anyone who might threaten or undermine his efforts, he certainly did not want Pratt making accusations that the governor had been unfair in his treatment of the soldiers. Pratt had in no way intended anything of the sort, and nothing came of the incident at the time. But when Pratt won the election, Morton did not join the parade of writers sending letters to congratulate him, and when the new junior senator from Indiana arrived in Washington, his senior colleague corresponded with him only through his secretary.

This was not a personal slight, even if Pratt had imagined it a breach of etiquette. Morton had developed the habit of having his secretary (or secretaries during the depth of the war) write his correspondence for him. Not only did they send out letters to subordinates and constituents, they often wrote on Morton's behalf to national political leaders. Morton often delegated his authority and trusted his secretary with his correspondence. Sometimes he dictated letters; at other times he gave the actual writer more general instructions. Furthermore, with the decline of his health, Morton relied more heavily on his assistants to help him carry the heavy load of correspondence.[51]

Morton could be arrogant, haughty, and tyrannical. Pratt knew his colleague's reputation, and Morton may very well have been cold toward him at first. Regardless of how it began, their relationship soon became more cordial. Shortly after Pratt assumed his seat, Morton sent him a hasty but friendly note, saying, "You may have the use of my Committee's Room for your documents and for any purpose at any time, and I will furnish you a key so that you can go out and in as you see proper." However arrogant he might otherwise have been, Morton clearly reached out to his junior colleague in an accommodating and friendly way. The relationship between Morton and Pratt changed over time and they eventually became friends who forged a working arrangement that suited both men. Their committee assignments and roles reflected this. Morton had taken a leadership role among Republicans in the Senate, serving as chair of the Committee of Privileges and Elections and as a vocal member

Fig. 47. Senator Daniel D. Pratt, Republican, Indiana. (Library of Congress)

of the Foreign Affairs Committee. When Pratt arrived two years later, he became chair of the Committee on Pensions. He also served on the Committee on Public Lands and the Committee on the District of Columbia. Pratt's personality was not suited to the high-profile politics that Morton preferred. Instead, the junior senator's work on pensions required many thankless hours of dealing with petitions and appeals and making decisions that reflected more of constituent services than national leadership. Indeed, Morton forwarded to Pratt the pension requests that came to him, happy to have the other man deal with such matters.[52]

The two senators agreed on most issues, and their votes reflected that. Pratt joined a select committee that looked at the revision of the law and another that investigated racial violence in the South. Both of these assignments touched on matters critical to Morton, and the two senators cooperated on them, especially as they related to Reconstruction, which the two Republicans realized was the most important issue that they faced. The senators both advocated for black rights and for a hard peace in the South, although Morton waved the bloody shirt, making a stronger and more public stand than his colleague. The two men shared notes and information about the Ku Klux Klan and the activities of Democrats across the country. Beyond Reconstruction, they also received many requests for patronage. Both dealt with office-seeking letters and other such requests in the expected way, making recommendations and writing to appropriate cabinet secretaries on behalf of those they wanted to help. Taking advantage of the "courtesy of the Senate," Morton often used patronage to reward those loyal to him and to help maintain his personal political power. But he was careful not to overstep his bounds when he thought a request was more properly within Pratt's authority. When he received a letter from two Lafayette, Indiana, Republicans recommending an appointment, Morton had his secretary forward it to Pratt, and his assistant scrawled an explanation on the outer fold: "Senator Morton prefers that you should control this patronage as it is in your own dist[rict] and you will better understand it." Far from being a sign of arrogance and a slight, such a communication from Morton's secretary marked the senior senator's deference to his colleague's authority and knowledge on a particular matter, as well as keeping with the custom of the era before civil service reform.[53]

Beyond their cooperation on the issues and patronage, Pratt sought and Morton provided political advice. While still in Logansport preparing to move to Washington, Pratt wrote to Morton about a patronage request that he had received. He wanted to help the man, who was seeking a position, but was unsure of how the applicant should proceed. He asked Morton for his opinion, saying that "I myself am too fresh in political life to know much about the etiquette of such matters." Upon assuming office, Pratt soon began to regret his election. He worried that he was not suited to the Senate and contemplated resigning from office. He wrote to Governor Conrad Baker on December 22, 1869, giving him forewarning of his intention to step down and saying, "Whatever capabilities I possessed as a mere lawyer, I have none as a statesman—and it is too late in life to qualify for this place." Two days later, on Christmas Eve, he sent his formal letter of resignation, citing personal reasons for resigning, including his declining legal practice. He also said that his son was "embarking on the profession of law" and he thought the young man needed his help. Pratt told Baker that "I have no taste for public life or ambitions for its honors." Furthermore, he feared that his diffident personality, "which I cannot overcome, disables me from participating in the debates of Congress."[54]

When Morton learned of Pratt's intended resignation, he fired off a letter to his colleague, saying, "I hope you have reconsidered your determination to resign. It would in my opinion be a very great mistake." He urged Pratt to stay in office and confidently assured him that he could overcome his reluctance to speak on the floor, telling him that "I have no doubt of your entire reception in the Senate if you but make an effort." He was sure that "one who is so able and successful at the bar cannot fail in the Senate. You greatly underrate your ability and if you will but make a speech upon some question you have examined, you will make a fine impression and be released effectually from the timidity which oppresses you." Morton said that "I sincerely hope you will remain in the discharge of the duties to which you have been so honorably elected." Still, if Pratt refused to change his mind, Morton hoped that he would let him know, as there would be "an immense scramble for the place and I shall feel a deep interest in the character of your successor." Morton signed the letter, "Truly Your Friend." Pratt's resignation soon became public, as the newspapers published his intention and rumors swirled about who might replace him. Meanwhile, Governor Baker and other friends begged Pratt to reconsider, and in the face of mounting pressure and flattering arguments about his abilities, Pratt changed his mind and did not resign. When Morton heard about his fellow senator's change of heart, he wrote to him on December 30, 1869, saying, "I am sincerely rejoiced at this and believe you have decided wisely for yourself and friends. I am sure of your success in the Senate, and know that you have but to try." Pratt soon followed Morton's advice, taking to the Senate floor to make his first speech on January 15, 1870, and sure enough, although he never matched Morton's oratorical fame, Pratt overcame his timid personality and served effectively throughout the rest of his term.[55]

Over the years, Morton and Pratt continued to cooperate and became friendly allies. While working together on economic policy in January 1874, they conferred frequently, and both expressed their views to President Grant as well as to other senators. In the midst of the crisis following the Panic of 1873, Indiana's senators considered remedies and advised the administration. Amid their work, Morton wrote a quick note to Pratt, who was about to go to the White House, saying, "Please do not go to the President until I see you again. I have heard an additional item." In the fall of 1874, while on a trip to California, Morton wrote to Pratt telling him that he was about to head east.

Afraid that he might arrive too late for the organization of the Senate committees, he told Pratt that, "I shall be glad to retain my present state—that is
as chairman of Priv. & Elections and the second place on Foreign Relations."
He asked his colleague to convey his wishes to the party leadership and signed
the message, "Your Friend."[56]

That summer of 1874, Pratt was a candidate for reelection, but he was ill and
worn out, and his dislike for the Senate had returned. He ran a brief, lackluster
campaign. His friends, including his fellow senator, urged him to work harder
and held out hope that the Republicans would retain their legislative majority
and return Pratt to the Senate. With the campaign heating up, Morton wrote
a personal note to Pratt, advising him to speak in "close or doubtful districts,"
where the Senator's appearance could "help the state ticket just as much and
at the same time look after the legislature." Pratt's illness prevented him from
doing much, and his party worked desperately to help him. They brought in
speakers from outside the state, and Morton himself cut short his vacation to
take the waters in Arkansas to stump for his colleague. During the campaign,
the new civil rights bill being debated in Congress raised controversy because
of its call for equal education for African Americans. Indiana Republicans tried
to downplay the issue, even avoiding any mention of the civil rights bill in
their state party platform. But the Democrats played the race card, opposing
integrated schools and railing against the proposed bill. Campaigning for Pratt
and other Republicans, Morton tried to take a moderate stand, arguing that
the proposed bill did not require integrated schools, only equal educational
opportunities. This would allow for segregated schools in Indiana. This was
a naked political ploy, because an amendment to the proposed bill allowing
segregation in schools had been rejected by the US Senate that spring. Furthermore, Morton strongly supported the legislation and voted for what eventually
became the Civil Rights Act of 1875. But on the campaign trail he tried to ride
the fence and strike a moderate position that would appeal to Indiana voters.
It seemed that Morton would say or do anything to keep his party and his fellow senator in power. Even telling an outright lie was not enough, however,
and the Democrats swept to victory and elected Morton's old friend and foe
Joseph E. McDonald as Pratt's successor in 1875. Although the 1875 elections
were devastating to his party, Morton was widely seen as having escaped the
carnage, a fact that lent further credence to his presidential hopes.[57]

Pratt hoped to return home to Logansport to rejuvenate and revive his struggling law practice. But President Grant appointed him commissioner of internal
revenue, an important position in the wake of Republican scandals that had rocked
the tax office. Pratt decided to do his duty and accepted the post. Upon hearing
the news, Senator Morton wrote to "My Dear Friend" and said that he was "very

Fig. 48. Senator Oliver P. Morton, ca. 1875, carte de visite.

glad you have accepted the position of Com. of Int. Revenue." He noted that the job was "a very important one" and thought that Pratt could "make it equal to a cabinet position" while also giving "to it a character it never had." After congratulating his friend, Morton conveyed a personal sorrow, saying that his "only brother was buried last Sunday after a long and painful illness." He also reported that his son Walter had been ill, "but is up again." Meanwhile, he was happy to say that his "own health is still improving." He sent his "regard to Mrs. Pratt" and signed off as "Your Friend." Clearly, whatever coldness or animosity he might have once held, Morton no longer harbored any ill feelings toward Pratt, whom he now considered a friend.[58]

While his relationship with Pratt fit well with his Stalwart Republican views of party, Morton did not feel the same way about his longtime nemesis, George W. Julian. The animosity between the two men stretched across decades of time, and its root causes were lost even to Julian. After failing to oust his old enemy in the 1868 election by gerrymandering, Morton quietly supported a conservative candidate to oppose the congressman in the 1870 Republican primary. Connersville judge Jeremiah M. Wilson won the party's nomination and took the seat in the fall contest. By 1872 Julian was so disgusted with Morton and Ulysses S. Grant that he turned to the Liberal Republicans. Considered seriously as the vice presidential candidate, Julian was disappointed when the Liberals nominated Greeley. But he ran for Congress as a Liberal, and Morton orchestrated a series of political attacks on him. Morton's friends spun the story of Meredith beating the congressman into a story about how Julian abused veterans. They accused him of nepotism because some of his relatives received appointments as postmasters in Wayne County. Sure enough, Julian and the Liberals went down to defeat and Wilson held on to his seat for a second term. The loss was so devastating that Morton's rival left Centerville and moved to the Indianapolis suburb of Irvington. There he worked as a writer and later enjoyed appointments to government jobs, but he never again sought elected office. Morton's vengeance was complete.[59]

Finally satisfied that he had settled the old score, Morton could now forget about Julian, but other Republican rivals continued to worry him. Congressman Godlove S. Orth, the former Know Nothing, remained a possible threat within Indiana's party ranks. Morton feared that the Lafayette nativist might challenge the senator's control of the state organization to further his own ambitions. An affable, good-natured man with a sense of humor, Orth was a skillful political operator who was often named as a possible candidate for Morton's Senate seat. Although he kept it somewhat quiet, it was widely known that Morton disliked Orth and had worked behind the scenes to defeat him in several of his congressional reelection bids. When Orth tried to secure the nomination for governor in 1872, hoping to follow Conrad Baker in the office, Morton threw his support behind one of his own loyal supporters, Congressman Thomas M. Browne. Many state Republicans thought this cost them the governor's chair, as Browne proved no match for Thomas A. Hendricks in the general election that fall. Later, in 1876, Morton threw his support behind Orth's candidacy in the gubernatorial race, possibly to deflect the criticism he had faced four years earlier. Or perhaps he wanted to use Orth to block the ambitions of another possible candidate for governor who also might threaten Morton's power in the Indiana Republican Party.[60]

MORTON AND HARRISON

Benjamin Harrison, the grandson of President William Henry Harrison, had volunteered to help Governor Morton during the war, and the state executive had asked him to raise a regiment of troops and eventually gave him a colonel's commission. Later Morton recommended Harrison's promotion to brigadier general to President Lincoln. After the war, the general stood in for the governor on several occasions when Morton's health prevented him from speaking to the returning veterans. The two men agreed on most political issues, and Harrison's law partner, William P. Fishback, was one of Morton's trusted friends and allies in Indiana. As senator, Morton watched Harrison win his reputation as a prosecuting attorney and approved of the lawyer's skillful arguments against Lambdin P. Milligan when the Copperhead tried to sue for damages upon his release from prison.

However, when Harrison defended Fishback and Morton's brother-in-law, W. R. Holloway, in a much-discussed newspaper case, a rift formed between the rising attorney and the senator. Holloway had owned and edited the *Indianapolis Journal* during and just after the war, effectively making the paper Morton's personal mouthpiece. Fishback took over from Holloway, maintaining the newspaper's loyalty to the Republican cause and kept up its tradition of fighting with its crosstown Democratic competitor, the *Indiana Sentinel*. The two newspapers followed the nineteenth-century practice in serving as party organs and in securing the contract as the state printer whenever their party was in power. The friction between the two papers led to a lawsuit when the Democrats charged the *Journal* with defrauding the state treasury. Harrison defended the *Journal* well, and then, when Fishback accused the editor of the *Sentinel,* used his office as prosecuting attorney to bring the Democratic paper's editor to trial for perjury.[61]

The editor was acquitted, much to the disappointment of the Republicans. In the course of pursuing the case, however, Harrison carefully went through the account books of the newspapers and discovered that W. R. Holloway and a group of his Republican friends had been involved in some shady dealings with treasury bonds. The prosecutor admitted this in court, embarrassing Morton, who did not forgive him for what he considered a political betrayal. This resulted in the senator working behind the scenes to deny Harrison the nomination for governor in 1872 and driving his potential rival into a period of political exile. In 1876 he again blocked Harrison's path to the governorship. The rift between the two men caused some anti-Morton Republicans to hope that Harrison could be used to break the senator's stranglehold on the state party. Partly to distract from Morton's own ambitions, they began pushing the young lawyer as a possible presidential candidate. But Harrison refused to go back into politics, saying that he preferred to remain in the legal profession. Not seeking office helped restore some faith in him among Morton's close friends. Orth won the nomination for governor, but a scandal involving fraudulent claims against the government of Venezuela forced him to withdraw from the race. The senator stuck with Orth as long as he could, and when asked what he thought the gubernatorial nominee should do about the scandal, replied that it was up to the candidate to decide for himself. When Orth stepped aside, Morton agreed to support Harrison, and the general was allowed back into politics, although he lost the governor's race to James D. Williams.[62]

Even as he continued to control the Indiana party with an iron fist and followed through on his grudges to punish those who crossed him, Morton also remained loyal to his own ambitions. By the mid-1870s he was a serious candidate for the presidency of the United States. One of the foremost politicians who waved the bloody shirt in debates over Reconstruction, Morton also helped create and define the term "Stalwart Republican." His stand on the issues and years of service to his party had won him many friends across the nation, while his championing African American rights made him a favorite among Southern Republicans. With the election of 1876 approaching, Morton eyed the White House and prepared to take his fight for freedom, Union, power, and party to the highest office in the country.

CHAPTER ELEVEN

The Election of 1876 and the End of an Era

ON MAY 10, 1876, the Centennial Exhibition in Philadelphia officially opened, and a huge crowd of at least 100,000 people gathered around the platform filled with dignitaries there to help begin the nation's one hundredth birthday celebration. President Grant led the political lineup, and a number of Republicans hoping to succeed him in the White House gathered around the chief executive. The candidates for the party's nomination at the Centennial included Secretary of State Hamilton Fish and Treasury Secretary Benjamin Bristow. But Grant's cabinet members were not the favorites to take the nomination that year, thanks to the many scandals that had rocked the administration, so most observers expected the party's standard-bearer to hail from the US Senate. As one might have expected, the senators who would be president made their way to the Philadelphia Exhibition for opening day. Near the president sat James Blaine of Maine, a clear favorite who had waved the bloody shirt against the Democrats but had also criticized Grant on a number of issues, making him an independent and distinctive choice. New York's Roscoe Conkling, a leading Stalwart and Radical who had used his patronage power to build a formidable political base, enjoyed being Grant's handpicked candidate to succeed him and he, too, joined the president on the platform. Among the contenders for the nomination on the platform that day was another Stalwart Radical who had used patronage to build his political power and who had often battled with Conkling in the Senate: Oliver P. Morton of Indiana. As the Centennial celebration opened that spring day, the race for the White House was already underway, and Morton was one of the leading candidates.[1]

Some Republicans hoped that Grant would seek a third term, and the president seemed open to the idea. A June 12, 1875, political cartoon published in *Frank Leslie's Illustrated Newspaper* included Morton among the other candidates joining Grant at "The Great American Rifle Match." The setting played to the popularity of sport shooting at a time when many Americans closely followed the performance of their national rifle team, which often traveled abroad to compete with foreign marksmen. In the cartoon Grant proclaimed that he had hit the mark twice and was ready to try a third shot. But the other candidates argued that he should not do it. In the drawing Grant's gun seemed to be aimed right at Morton's face, although it was supposed to be behind the Indiana senator. Grant did listen to the advice of his party leaders, and once it became clear that he would not seek a third term, a scramble for the nomination began[2] (see Fig. 49).

Morton enjoyed clear advantages going into the campaign. His many years as a party loyalist meant that he had worked for candidates in many states and could now count on their support. Being a Stalwart also meant that members of the outgoing administration, including Grant, would lend him whatever support they could. But his independence on some issues gave him an argument against the charges of "Grantism" that could link him too closely to the scandal-ridden administration. His own political organization in Indiana guaranteed him a powerful base on which to build his national efforts. And his staunch efforts throughout Reconstruction meant that he ranked as the first choice for most Southern Republicans. He was also very strong in the other Midwestern states, and his supporters were working to locate the national convention in Cincinnati, where Morton could be nominated on what would seem like his home field. Among the many endorsements for president that he received was the support of William T. Sherman. The Union war hero had been mentioned as a possible candidate himself, but he quickly dismissed such notions before praising Blaine, then saying, "Morton is a remarkable man and fitted for any political position . . . I love Morton for his war record. He was the best war governor we had. He never complained that Indiana had furnished more than its just quota. The demand for more troops had only to be made to be complied with. Thousands of war democrats would vote for him." Whether General Sherman correctly judged the old War Democrats after a decade of Reconstruction was arguable, but Morton did enjoy a lot of support.[3]

But he also faced certain disadvantages. Foremost among them were his health and paralysis. There were concerns that his disability might detract from his appeal, and his poor health raised questions about what would happen if he should die in office. When he became a serious candidate for the presidency, more political cartoons began to depict him with his crutches and canes, a not-so-subtle reminder of his health problems. Newspapers in Washington had monitored Morton's health over the years, reporting on his illnesses, telling readers when he fell, and printing rumors about him dying. This included his having to leave the Senate chamber in April of 1869, when he was overcome with weakness that he blamed on the "close air" in the room. Later that same year newspapers reported on Morton falling on the platform

No. 1,028—Vol. XL.]   NEW YORK, JUNE 12, 1875.   [PRICE 10 CENTS.

at the railroad depot in Philadelphia. In 1871 the senator was "robbed of his wallet while entering the cars" in Jersey City during a train trip to Washington. While many healthy people fell victim to crime, the story reinforced the image of Morton being crippled and helpless. The papers also reported his physical improvement, including his growing strong enough to plan a trip to the Pacific Coast with President Grant in the summer of 1871 and being able to deliver speeches while standing on his feet during the election campaign in the fall of 1872. When the congressional session opened in December of 1875, Morton seemed strong and was "walking easily on canes." In March 1876, however, he fell while getting off the elevator at the Ebbitt House. Although he returned to the Senate the next day, such reports reminded readers of his paralysis. So, too, did the false rumors that he was dying in March 1874 and May 1876.[4]

Second, Morton's unrelenting attacks on Democrats, repeated calls to complete the destruction of the South, and unwavering support of African Americans made him too much of a radical for conservatives and moderates in the party, who hoped to nominate a candidate who had taken less extreme positions. Third, his ruthless nature and often arrogant personality combined with his forceful and confrontational style to make him rather unlikable. While that did not necessarily hurt him with the mass of voters in the 1870s, it did damage him among Republican leaders who had crossed him in the past. Finally, there were the charges of corruption and immorality that Democrats had been hurling at him since his time as governor.[5]

As always, the charges of misconduct came from the *Sentinel*, as the Indianapolis Democratic organ raised again the accusations that Morton had stolen

Fig. 49. (*opposite*) "The Great American Rifle Match" (*Frank Leslie's Illustrated Newspaper*, June 12, 1875). This illustration's setting fit well with the national newspapers, which were covering the American team of marksmen who went abroad that summer to engage in rifle matches against international competition (for examples, see *Harper's Weekly*, July 10 and July 17, 1875). In this depiction focused on Ulysses S. Grant thinking about a third term, Morton (with his crutch beside him—a not-so-subtle message about his health that began to appear when he became a serious candidate for the presidency) joins other Republican presidential aspirants in advising the president not to do it. The caption reads: "Grant—'I hit the first target, easy. I managed to get in on the second. Now, gentlemen, shall I try for the third, or be satisfied with two out of three!' [Pennsylvania governor and possible presidential candidate] John F. Hartranft (speaking for the Lancaster Convention)—'The unwritten law of the Republic wisely, and under the sanction of the most venerable examples, limits the Presidential service of any citizen to two terms. We are unalterably opposed to a third term.' Morton, Cameron, Conkling, Wilson (in chorus)—'Don't try again! Even if you hit you'll miss, and the shot would be fatal.'"

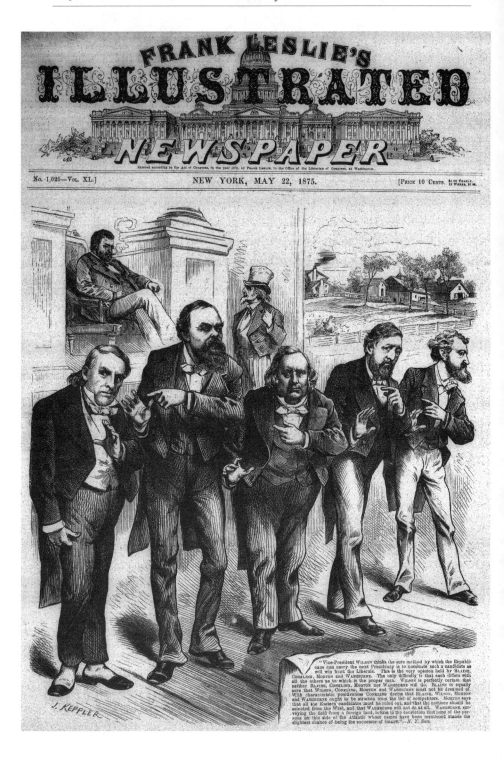

state money and abused his power. They also claimed that he had been part of the Whiskey Ring scandal that had been exposed in 1875. Morton quickly denied that he had been part of that scheme, which had allowed politicians connected to the Grant administration to siphon off millions of dollars of taxes paid on liquor. He continued his teetotaling ways in his personal life and remained a staunch supporter of temperance throughout the 1870s, so charges that he made money off of alcohol raised the charge of hypocrisy as well as criminality. Moral issues mattered, and a candidate's personal character was often raised during political campaigns. Democrats had spread rumors about Morton's sexual habits for years, never quite publishing the actual stories, but making insinuations about his character. They had called him "Moxa Morton," alluding to the Asian treatments for his paralysis and suggested that it was actually used to treat venereal disease. They used the moxa to link him to actress Clara Morris, implying that the two had been together.[6]

Such accusations about a sex scandal may have led to earlier attempts to blackmail the senator. In 1870 a drunken woman had repeatedly called on Morton in Washington, demanding money from him and insinuating that she and her family would spread a "vile article" that had been published in

Fig. 50. (*opposite*) "Counting Each Other Out" (*Frank Leslie's Illustrated Newspaper,* May 22, 1875). In this early look at the Republican field for the presidency in 1876, Morton is shown as one of the top candidates as he argues with the others as each explains why all the rest are not good choices. The caption reads: "Uncle Sam to [Ulysses S. Grant]—'You're tired of sitting in the Presidential Chair—so Sargent says you told him. Each one of those fellows expects to take it when you leave for yonder farm.' U. S. G. [Ulysses S. Grant]—'But I needn't be in a hurry to leave on their account, for, while each is counting himself in as my successor, they're all counting each other out.' Above: 'Vice-President [Henry] Wilson thinks the sure method by which the Republicans can carry the next Presidency is to nominate such a candidate as will win back the Liberals. This is the very opinion held by [Maine senator James G.] BLAINE, [New York senator Roscoe] Conkling, Morton and [Illinois Republican, former secretary of state, and currently minister to France Elihu] Washburne. The only difficulty is that each differs with all the others as to which is the proper man. Wilson is perfectly certain that neither Blaine, Conkling, Morton nor Washburne will do. Blaine is equally sure that Wilson, Conkling, Morton and Washburne must not be dreamed of. With characteristic positiveness Conkling deems that Blaine, Wilson, Morton and Washburne ought to be stricken from the list of competitors. Morton says that all the Eastern candidates must be ruled out, and that the nominee should be selected from the West, and that Washburne will not do at all. Washburne, surveying the field from a foreign land, is firm in the conviction that none of the persons on this side of the Atlantic whose names have been mentioned stands the slightest chance of being the successor of Grant.'"—N. Y. Sun.

a Philadelphia paper. The senator wrote to his wife explaining the situation, informing her that the woman had shown up at the Senate chamber, where she sent word to Morton demanding fifteen dollars that she needed at once. At first he refused her, but "afraid of a scene," he gave her ten dollars so that she would go away for the time being. He told Lucinda that he did not "know how to get clear of her," saying that the woman was desperate. Later, the woman returned to Washington and forced her way into Morton's rooms at the Ebbitt House. She was drunk again and demanded money from him, saying she needed it to go home. Morton thought about calling for a policeman but wanted to keep it quiet, so he paid her and asked his landlord to prevent her from coming to his room again. Clearly, he had denied any wrongdoing to his wife and now told her about the incident so that rumors of it would not bring shock and trouble in his marriage.[7]

In whatever manner, Morton finally managed to silence the drunken woman, and whether or not she was actually trying to blackmail him, the stories about his sexual debauchery did not go away. He seemed to have written a heartfelt defense against such charges to Lucinda. At first pleading his case in a legal fashion, he argued that scandalous charges were made for political reasons and that he could make such assaults on others as well, if he stooped so low. He gave examples of how one might level false charges against an opponent, even when there was no basis for it. And he blasted his enemies for repeating such vile stories about him. "They have accused me, but they dare

Fig. 51. (*opposite*) "Republican Candidates in Training for the Presidential Race" (*Frank Leslie's Illustrated Newspaper*, July 24, 1875). By the summer of 1875 Morton was one of many possible Republican nominees in the 1876 election. Here he is shown with his crutch and cane, running with the other contenders as they train for the upcoming campaign. The cartoon makes reference to his support for paper money ("rag-money"). The caption says: U. S. G. [Ulysses S. Grant]—'It really looks as if those fellows think I have no chance for the Third Term. They leave me sitting here while they all run themselves.' [Elihu Washburne]—'As President, you made me Secretary of State and then Minister to France. Why not also back me as Presidential Candidate, as you seem to count yourself out?'[Pennsylvania governor John F.] Hartranft to Washburne— 'You have had your full share already. You, too, should be counted out. As for the rest, Wilson and Blaine have only strength enough to defeat each other; Morgan may beat Conkling in New York, thanks to Fenton and Federal Office-holders, but he cannot carry the country; Morton and Ben Butler both bid high for the support of rag-money speculators and the carpet-bag fraternity, but such support would be fatal to candidates of any party; the last shall be first, they say, but Bristow may yet find that the promise doesn't always hold good. So I might as well strip for the race myself. If Old Winnebago don't sell me out, my chances will be as good as those of any other—Republican.'"

not face me with their accusation. They can utter their dirty insinuations," but they did so undercover and were nothing more than "cowardly skulk[ers] when called to account."[8]

But he soon began to appeal to her Christian faith, as he turned to the bonds of marriage, which he said was a union made by God himself. He spoke of those who would rather commit suicide than cut or break the sacred cord of marriage. Morton became emotional, telling Lucinda that she had "awakened within me a new life. You have made me conscious of possessing a higher and purer nature. You have inspired me with sentiments of love so pure and lofty, that I know them to be the true expressions of my nature." He closed his defense by crying out, "May that God who searches the heart judge me in this; and may he have you in his protection from every ill, is the prayer of him who is devoted to you in life to death." Such an emotional plea surely indicated that Lucinda must have at least worried that the charges against him were true.[9]

His wife accepted his heartfelt arguments, but the rumors persisted. Even Republicans recognized Morton's reputation as a ladies' man. An 1871 Republican newspaper story about the senator praised him for his personal habits, saying that he was a voracious reader, that he was ambitious but not greedy, that he was "tender and just, inspiring the warmest devotion and respect." The fawning account related that the senator loved being at home but was seldom there because of his duties. The female newspaper reporter wrote that Morton had a good marriage and said that Lucinda had "uncommon ability, is a shrewd observer . . . there is nothing in politics she does not know." The Republican scribe declared that the senator's wife was modest, slightly shorter than average height for a woman at the time, and she was "slightly built [with] a graceful bearing." The writer thought that Lucinda had "a well-shaped head and comely features. Her smile is lovely, and her eyes and voice bewitching." Overcome by Mrs. Morton's charms, the lady reporter wrote that Lucinda was "the most womanly of women" and was the reason that the senator was in favor of women's rights. Morton had spoken in support of equality for women just a few months before, and the article included a brief interview with him about that issue. He held to a strong egalitarian position, arguing that women should have political and economic equality.[10]

Yet even such a positive story hinted at scandal when the female writer included the subheading "Senator Morton and the Ladies." When discussing Morton's habits at home, the article mentioned how he received visitors to his Indianapolis house in the parlor or living room, usually sitting on a lounge situated near the fire. Certainly he received many callers, but he preferred them to be female: "If the visitor be a lady, and she can sing, the happiness of the Senator is complete." To be sure, the piece focused on Morton's love of music, which he had apparently inherited from his mother. He could sup-posedly remember every opera he had ever heard, and he knew the various musical passages by heart. His Republican admirer exclaimed, "Imagine then his delight when listening to a sweet voice, even in conversation." Certainly, the story was not a direct reference to infidelity. And the flowery language of mid-nineteenth-century Romanticism lent itself to such sentiments. The article was perfectly innocent and clearly favorable to its subject. In fact, the writer claimed that Morton was "the worst abused man in America" and admired him for not allowing "any personal abuse, prejudice, or hatred to stand in the way" of his duty. Still, printing such a story played into the ongoing rumors about Morton's dalliances with women.[11]

Throughout the 1870s, the Democrats played dirty politics, publishing more stories about Morton's supposed sexual misconduct. In April 1873 the *Milwaukee Daily News* again referred to him as "Moxa Morton of Indiana" and claimed that "there is not, probably, in this country, a more conscienceless, corrupt, and utterly profligate man in public life than Morton. He is rotten physically, morally and politically." When he spoke in favor of women's rights in 1874, the Democratic *St. Paul Daily Pioneer* snorted, "Why shouldn't Morton espouse the woman's cause? It is woman that has made him what he is—so the gossips say." Supposedly, Morton's paralysis resulted from his immorality, caused either by a sexually transmitted disease or by having too much sex. In February 1876 the *Raleigh Sentinel* expressed North Carolina Democrats' views of the Indiana politician when it proclaimed that Morton "is a vice-reeking Hoosier bundle of moral and physical rottenness, leprous ulcers and caustic bandages, who loads down with plagues and pollutions the wings of every breeze that sweeps across his loathsome putrefying carcass." Obviously, the Democrats wanted to prevent him from winning the presidency.[12]

"A Bloody Shirt and a Pair of Ripe Ruby Lips"

When a national convention of African Americans met in Nashville and voted to back the Hoosier senator for president, it indicated that he enjoyed the support of the South as well as widespread popularity in the Midwest. Their hatred for their old enemy rising with his growing political aspirations, the Democrats decided that he might well win the nomination, and so they set out to destroy him. On April 15, 1876, the *Chicago Times* published the most scandalous tale about Morton that they could find. Splashed across the two pages of the daily edition in lurid detail, the stories charged the Republican with using the power of his office to procure sexual liaisons with the pretty wives of office seekers. The long article purported to be a comparison between the two Indiana senators,

Morton and Hendricks, both of whom were considered possible presidential candidates for their respective parties. While it mostly praised Hendricks, the essay was actually a scurrilous personal attack on Morton's character. What set it apart from other newspaper assaults was the level of shocking particulars it included. The headlines on page one announced that Morton's name "Reeks with Filth and Slime," and promised to relate just "A Few of the Hellish Liaisons of and Attempted Seductions by Indiana's Favorite Stud Horse."[13]

Sure enough, after leveling the now-stale accusations about Morton stealing funds and running Indiana like a petty tyrant and blasting him on the current issues, the newspaper stooped to new levels of mudslinging. His enemies declared that he was not the teetotaler that he claimed to be but rather was often found drunk. Of course, his loyal minions on his staff and in the military kept this all a secret. The Democratic writer declared that "the reign of Morton as governor was reckless, swaggering, full of vim, noisy, personal, with an atmosphere of demoralization, impurity, and unchaste womanhood about it." According to the rumors, Morton had surrounded himself with men and women of low character and sated his lust with every pretty woman he could seduce. He used the power of his office to procure sexual favors from them. The *Times* cited General Robert Milroy, whom Morton had commissioned as colonel of an Indiana regiment when the war began, as the source of one story. The general said that "Morton is a lecherous scoundrel . . . He is a damned stud-horse" and related a story that he had heard from a certain Judge Frazer about how the governor had tried to seduce a pretty girl seeking a pardon for her imprisoned brother. When the "comely, attractive, and pleasing" young woman entered his office, Morton "took her dimensions," and "asked her to call" on him late in the evening. He met with her alone, although she brought along a male friend who remained outside, unbeknownst to the governor. When the girl did not respond to his advances, Morton told her directly that she would have to spend the night with him if she wanted her brother to go free. Shocked at "the infamous proposal of the 'great war governor,'" the young lady ran from the room "in shame and tears." Her escort confronted him, and he agreed to pardon her brother if they agreed to keep quiet about the incident. Within days of the story appearing in the *Times,* Judge Frazer denied having ever told such a story, but the newspaper made it part of a pattern.[14]

Democrats claimed that Morton's sexual habits had begun when he was a young attorney in Centerville, and the same newspaper quoted an old man from Richmond as the source of stories stretching back to that time: "Why, he had a reputation over at Centreville before he was 25 as bad as he has now—or had before he became disabled." Supposedly, the young lawyer's affair with a married woman was common knowledge in his hometown, where stories abounded about how he often had to make his escape out of the bedroom window when his lover's husband came home early. The governor's lechery was supposedly so well known that even children were aware of his predilections. The wags joked that, when two boys got into an argument, one threatened to lick the other in a fight. His opponent replied, "I know one thing. I can't lick you, but Gov. Morton sleeps with your ma!" The punchline came in the response: "Shucks! That's nothing. Gov. Morton sleeps with *everybody's* ma!"[15]

The rumors held that during the war, Morton had made it his practice to give commissions to men seeking a place in the military if they allowed their wives to sleep with the governor. Knowing this, one unmarried captain hired an attractive blonde woman who lived in Louisville to pose as his wife to help him secure a promotion to lieutenant colonel and win a bet with a fellow officer. The Kentucky beauty traveled to Indianapolis and sent the governor a perfumed letter inviting him to meet her at her hotel and when he arrived explained how she wanted to help her "husband" get a promotion. The attractive young woman "looked her prettiest, was careful not to conceal her dainty foot and No. 1½ boot, and it was arranged that the 'great war governor' was to call again that evening 'after office hours.'" That night, Morton came to her room, where the blonde pled her case for the officer's promotion. She employed her "winsome smiles and sparkling eyes," while Morton "dallied listlessly with her lily white hand and golden hair." He claimed to be overworked and too tired to go home and asked to sleep on her sofa. She agreed and he spent the night. The blonde left Indianapolis with the promotion for her "husband" in hand.[16]

Insinuating the sale of offices and favors and including the blonde's shoe size was significant. The lovely Louisville lady's boot was the same size as that worn by Amanda Tomlinson Bowers Belknap, the beautiful wife of Secretary of War William W. Belknap. Mrs. Belknap had been the secretary's widowed sister-in-law, but when his wife (her sister) died shortly after giving birth to a child, she agreed to marry him. A fashionable beauty who enjoyed life in the center of high society, she supposedly delayed her marriage so that she could go shopping in Paris. She returned with a load of expensive furniture, dresses, and forty pairs of size 1½ shoes. All of Washington talked about Mrs. Belknap and her dainty feet, and people across the nation learned about her shoe size and her fashionable tastes. Early in 1876, the Belknap scandal broke when a congressional investigation revealed that Mrs. Belknap had persuaded her husband to sell a government contract and post-trader position at a fort in the West. The sutler at Fort Sill, Oklahoma, made quarterly payments that went directly to Mrs. Belknap. Even though the secretary might not have actually known the full extent of what was going on, the scandal forced him to resign—and he claimed he did so only to protect his wife. With other recent scandals still fresh in the minds of the voters, Belknap's resignation hurt the Republicans as they entered the presidential campaign. Connecting Morton to Belknap mattered, then, in the context of the swirl of corruption charges surrounding the Grant administration that he had so long supported.[17]

The titillating article in the Chicago newspaper related that Theodore Scribner, a newspaper reporter who had once worked for the *New-York Herald* before moving to work for the *Indianapolis Journal,* had seen Morton's infidelities firsthand. While Scribner lived in the Indiana capital, he got to know his neighbor across the street and also made the acquaintance of the man's "beautiful, voluptuous young wife." Apparently Morton knew the couple as well. The neighbor told the *Journal* reporter that the governor had called him to the statehouse, where he offered him a commission as a lieutenant colonel of a regiment then serving in Georgia. The man accepted the commission and within the week reported to duty in the South. Scribner remembered that, "As my journalistic duties kept me up till from midnight to 2 o'clock a.m., I was an unwilling discoverer of what was very painful to me." The late-writing reporter looked out his window and saw that "night after night Morton's carriage would drive up there and the festive governor would alight, and go into Mr.—-'s house, remain three or four hours, and before day-light re-enter his carriage and drive away." The woman cheating on her soldier husband soon became a widow, as the colonel died and was buried in the South. The Democratic rumormongers reminded readers that in the Old Testament King David had sent Uriah the Hittite off to war so that he could be with the beautiful Bathsheba. In Indianapolis in the 1860s, the gossips said, Governor Morton sent a colonel to fight in the Civil War so that he could be with the man's lovely wife. According to his enemies, Morton's depravity reached biblical proportions.[18]

The *Chicago Times* suggested that Morton had continued his lustful predations after he won election to the US Senate. Edited by the Copperhead sympathizer Wilbur F. Storey, the *Times* repeatedly fired scurrilous attacks at the senator. The DC grapevine related that "he had a salacious intrigue with a little woman in Washington" and used his patronage power to give her husband a position as postmaster of the Senate to cover up the affair. Apparently, the affair began when Morton moved into the National Hotel, which the *Times* called a "sinkhole of immorality, lobbying, corruption, and nastiness." If anyone should know that the hotel was a den of iniquity, it was Storey. The editor of the *Times* was legendary for his own sexual appetites and infamous orgies. Whether or not he ever spent time at the National Hotel, Storey eventually contracted syphilis and died from complications of the disease—ironically suffering a paralytic stroke that stemmed from his venereal disease, the very thing that Democrats said caused Morton's paralysis. Despite the hypocrisy of such an editor publishing scandalous charges against Morton, the paper went on to say that the senator met the wife of an obscure resident of the capital while living at the nasty hotel.[19]

This "scrawny little brunette was also a boarder there and occupied much of her time in Morton's apartments." With Lucinda Morton back home in Indianapolis, the crippled senator was lonely and "the black-eyed little woman was kind." What started out with her compassionate desire to help the paralyzed man soon became an affair filled with mutual passion between them. The gossip spread rapidly through the hotel, and her husband became upset. When he confronted his wife, the "little brunette was infatuate and reckless" and refused to break off the affair. Her husband demanded a separation, and soon all of Washington was whispering about the illicit relationship. Morton bought off the cuckold with the job as Senate postmaster, a position he held until the scandal became so public that he had to resign in order to protect the senator.[20]

The paper reported that the senator's sexual appetites continued to consume him, however, and he supposedly paid "hush money" to prevent a writer from publishing tales about the concupiscent escapades at the National Hotel. Capital gossips whispered that Morton played a central role in the stories about the morally bankrupt hotel. The *Times* found the senator deficient in every aspect of his character. The author of the article claimed that "he is not a scholar—not even a well-read man. He has the breadth and grasp of intellect to have become one of our most cultured and accomplished men of letters," but he had squandered it all away in his dissipation. Morton was deficient in conversation and lacked "that personal charm that arises from sweetness, purity, and a tone of manhood." Instead, the senator changed his personality depending on his own needs and the type of person with whom he was interacting. "His manners with pretty women melt into sunshine. With men, ordinarily, he is austere and vulgar." The paper allowed for the possibility that "perhaps Morton has deteriorated socially, in consequence of his physical calamity." The writer hinted that Morton had hurt Lucinda deeply with his philandering ways: "His wife is a quiet, solemn lady, and to a stranger seems to wear the shadow of a secret melancholy."[21]

The piece concluded by comparing what the hypothetical administrations of Hendricks or Morton might look like. Arguing that "Hendricks would not startle the country as pig-headed Grant did when his first cabinet was announced," the *Chicago Times* admitted that, under the Hoosier Democrat, "of course the moss-back democracy of ante-bellum days would stalk forth like Mummies stepping out of their cerements" to enter the cabinet. Yes, the writer admitted, if Hendricks were president, "there would be a flavor of the confederacy about the capital," but he argued that it would be no different than under Grant, when he claimed that former rebels had held prominent positions. The article promised that a Hendricks presidency would have a higher moral tone than either that of Grant or a possible one under Morton, despite the fact that the Indiana Democrat would be tempted to give in to Southern Democrats and let them have their way on matters concerning the "everlasting nigger." But the writer thought that the Democratic candidate was too wise to go too far in appeasing the South, which would antagonize the voters of the North. Hendricks had the examples of "Jimmy Buchanan and poor Andy Johnson" to warn him against being too pro-Southern.[22]

But if Morton were elected, the paper predicted that he would appoint African Americans and Radicals to his cabinet. There would be scandals and fraud, as all of the corruption under Grant would be repeated under Morton. Because the Hoosier Republican was so bold and so depraved, he would not even try to conceal his dishonesty, inaugurating a new period of "personal government" in which bribes and payoffs would be expected even as Morton waged "relentless war on all enemies." Under the Republican, lobbyists would flourish, while the "scalawag and 'soldier' fraud elements" would enjoy new levels of prosperity under his government. Under President Morton, the *Chicago Times* writer prophesied, "Nepotism would find a new and more fruitful lease of power." Of course the ruthless and degenerate tyrant would unleash his lustful appetites when he took up residence in the White House. "Buxom Beauty would be rampant and ruling at Washington. A man there without a mistress would be spurned from respectable administration circles." The *Times* thought that such decadence would at least be committed openly and boldly. According to his Democratic enemies, the emblem of Morton's presidency would be "a bloody shirt and a pair of ripe ruby lips."[23]

As usual in the nineteenth century, other newspapers picked up the story and printed it or excerpts of it in their own editions. Republican papers like the *Indianapolis Journal* denied the charges of corruption, although they chose to ignore the sexual accusations as unworthy of reply. Realizing that sex scandals might not be enough to stop Morton, the Democrats turned back to charges of official misconduct. In March 1876 the senator faced accusations that he had been part of the Emma Mine scandal, a silver mine swindle in which Morton had supposedly been bribed as part of a plan to remove a Utah judge from the bench in an attempt to save the culprits, including Nevada Republican senator William M. Stewart. Vigorously denying the story, Morton defended himself and the government accepted his explanation, but the charges added to the perception of wrongdoing.[24]

Hoping to bring down a leading Radical Republican candidate, the *New York World,* the Democratic-leaning newspaper that Joseph Pulitzer had transformed into a successful and sensationalist publication, accused Morton of stealing money from the federal government during the war and claimed that there were documents to prove it. Soon an Illinois Democratic congressman, William M. Springer, began calling for an official investigation and audit of the accounts in the federal departments in Washington to see if Morton had indeed misappropriated funds while serving as governor. He especially questioned $250,000 that he thought the governor had taken without cause. The senator called on the congressman and told him that he welcomed yet another full investigation but insisted that his longtime aide and former adjutant general, W. H. H. Terrell, be present for the accounting because he had kept many of the books and could offer explanations and clarifications. He then telegraphed Terrell and another aide and had the two men come to Washington to help with the investigation, confident that they would be able to clear him on all counts with their knowledge of the facts. The two former aides met with Springer, who then backed off and wrote to Morton that he had no charges to bring against him. Unsatisfied with that result, Morton decided to explain himself in a long vindication that he wrote and had published in the *New York World*. On May 3, 1876, he read the explanation on the floor of the Senate, once again defending his conduct during his period of one-man rule and blaming the traitorous Democrats for creating the situation in the first place. His personal defense turned into another opportunity to wave the bloody shirt, as he painted his opponents as friends of the rebellion and portrayed himself as the heroic warrior for freedom and Union.[25]

The *World* apologized and withdrew the charges. In the wake of these accusations and a number of scandals involving other candidates like James Blaine that seemed to be based on information obtained through the theft of confidential correspondence, Morton called for an investigation of American privacy laws. The Indiana senator questioned whether the existing rules were obsolete in an era of new technology that made surveillance and the theft and exposure of information much easier. He worried that the law had fallen behind the telegraph and other magnetic dispatch technologies. At the same time, Morton defended free speech by opposing a proposal for a new, stronger obscenity law. Of course, in light of his own scandals raised by the Democratic attacks, the Hoosier Republican's interest in these laws certainly seemed self-serving to some, as he hoped to protect himself and cover his behavior.

Despite the fact that he was now seen as unscrupulous by many voters because of the unfounded charges, Republican papers triumphantly announced Morton's vindication and declared him a great hero. His old friend Murat Halstead, the *Cincinnati Commercial* editor, was not surprised at the nasty charges made against the Hoosier senator. "It is a lovely exhibition of Democratic policy to have this matter raked up just now. There are red hot coals still on the old ash heap." Morton himself had been working for the presidential nomination for a long time, but he had really begun to sound like a candidate when he disputed the Redeemer victory in the 1875 Mississippi election. Waving the bloody shirt against the Bourbons (as the white Democrats often called the Redeemers in many areas of the South) reminded voters about the dangers of ending Reconstruction. But many Republicans were giving up on the Southern question, and Morton's calls to continue occupying and punishing the rebels had grown stale.[26]

Morton for President

Still, his friends set out to make Morton president. They published the customary campaign biography, made arrangements to hold the national convention in Cincinnati, and began rounding up delegates to cast their votes for him. That spring P. B. S. Pinchback came to Indiana and stumped for Morton, repaying the Hoosier senator for his steadfast support for the African American's election to the Senate. While Morton enjoyed widespread popularity among Southern blacks and could probably carry most of the South, Indiana seemed to be the only Northern state firmly committed to him. Still, he remained in the top tier of the long list of candidates for the Republican nomination in 1876. Although Vice President Henry Wilson, one of the top candidates, had died in the fall of 1875, the field was still crowded. Others included Morton's fellow senators Matthew Carpenter of Wisconsin, Pennsylvania's Simon Cameron, James G. Blaine of Maine, and New York's Roscoe Conkling, as well as Secretary of State Hamilton Fish of New York, Secretary of the Treasury Benjamin Bristow of Kentucky, Postmaster General Marshall Jewell of Connecticut, Minister to France Elihu Washburne of Illinois, and governors like Pennsylvania's John Hartranft and Ohio's Rutherford B. Hayes. The top tier seemed to be Morton, Conkling, and Blaine, with most of the others losing support except in their home states. Some, like Hayes, were dark-horse candidates who might be nominated as a compromise if the favorites failed to win.

Going into the convention in June, the presumptive favorite for the nomination was Blaine of Maine. In mid-May a group of reform-minded Republicans had gathered in New York to discuss how to deny the nomination to Blaine, Morton, and Conkling. The reformers had linked the three leading Radical candidates to Grantism, and even though both Blaine and Morton had remained apart from the administration's scandals, all three men had supported the president enough to be tainted and abhorrent to those who wanted civil service reform. The reformers liked Benjamin Bristow, who had cleaned up after the Whiskey Ring scandal, but the Kentuckian had not gained any traction. Soon the reformers had begun talking about finding "anyone but the top three" to push through the process.[27]

In the days leading up to the convention, Blaine had gained strength and Morton's supporters began to worry. The Hoosier could count on most of the Southern delegates, as African Americans overwhelmingly supported him, but Indiana still seemed to be the only Northern state he had in his pocket. For a while his supporters had hoped that he might emerge as a compromise candidate, because while Blaine had enjoyed a groundswell of support, there were many who were beginning to say that they wanted anyone else but him. Because Blaine and Morton shared views on most major issues, perhaps the Indiana senator would be the fallback candidate should Maine's favorite son prove unable to secure the nomination. Meanwhile, Southern blacks represented a crucial constituency, and they made it clear that they wanted a candidate dedicated to Reconstruction. Morton remained their first choice. Conkling of New York was the ultimate Stalwart and was legendary for his use of the spoils system of patronage. Although he supposedly had Grant's support, he lacked widespread popularity and too many factions opposed him.[28]

In Cincinnati things did not turn out well for Morton. The convention opened on June 14, and the party platform that started by declaring that the United States was a nation was adopted the next day. Then the nominations began. Hoosier Republicans had nominated Morton back in March, and the Indiana delegation at the national gathering put forward the senator's name, as expected. Immediately, things went badly. The nominating speech was made by Terre Haute Republican powerbroker Richard W. Thompson, a renowned orator. But on this occasion his effort fell flat. His speech sounded more like a boilerplate eulogy or obituary than a rousing campaign endorsement. A former Whig who had joined the Know Nothings and then turned to the Constitutional Union Party in 1860, Thompson was nowhere near as radical as Morton. Perhaps that contributed to his less-than-impressive speech. He called Morton "the old war governor," and much to the dismay of the senator's chief operatives (led by his brother-in-law, Will Holloway, and longtime friend and ally Will Cumback), made reference to his paralysis. Thompson concluded his workmanlike recommendation of this old, paralyzed man by saying that "his head is clear, his heart is sound, his will is uncontrollable, his devotion to the Union is unabated, and he is ready now, tomorrow, or the next day to give his life for the honor of the old flag." This was hardly the ringing endorsement one hoped for on such an occasion. Things looked up when P. B. S. Pinchback of Louisiana seconded Indiana's choice, and Morton's nomination brought many cheers from the audience.[29]

That evening, Simon Cameron of Pennsylvania called Holloway to his room and told him that he was working at all costs to prevent Blaine from getting the nomination. He asked the Morton camp to throw a few votes to the Keystone State's governor, John Hartranft, on the second ballot to help Cameron keep the Pennsylvania delegates united. Holloway agreed, hoping that this would help stall Blaine and also build support for Morton on subsequent ballots. On June 16 the first ballot was taken, with Blaine getting 285 votes and Morton coming in second with 124. Secretary of the Treasury Bristow got 113, and Roscoe Conkling came in fourth with 99, with the rest scattered among various candidates. According to custom, after the first ballot states that had voted for their favorite sons now turned to the leading contenders. In the second round of voting, Morton's total fell to 111, as Holloway kept his bargain and gave some votes to Hartranft. Blaine increased his amount to 298. As the balloting continued, little movement occurred, and no one seemed able to get the required 379 votes. On the sixth ballot, Morton's votes fell to 85 and Blaine's went up to 308. At that point, it became clear that neither Morton nor Conkling could beat Blaine. If they wanted another nominee, now was the time to move. Morton's Southern support began to defect, and Will Cumback withdrew Morton's name and gave most of Indiana's votes to Ohio's Rutherford B. Hayes, who was elected on the seventh ballot with 384 votes to Blaine's 351.[30]

Hayes had become the compromise candidate that Morton's supporters thought that the Indiana senator might be. Acceptable to all, the Ohio governor had offended almost no one. Knowing his home state well, he had embraced the nativist push for a law against Catholic schools. While Morton and Conkling had avoided the issue for fear of offending Catholic immigrants and because they genuinely did not agree with such nativism, Blaine had pushed for changing the laws to prevent "sectarian" involvement in publicly funded education. The term *sectarian* was code for "Catholic," and the nativists knew it. They soon attached Blaine's name to proposed state constitutional amendments against sectarianism. Over the ensuing years, Protestant voters and politicians responded to the pressure brought by the nativists, and eventually thirty-eight states passed Blaine Amendments forbidding public funds to be paid to religious schools. Hayes had used anti-Catholicism to his advantage before, and he knew that, although Cincinnati had a large number of German immigrants and many of them were Catholics, there was a strong anticlerical sentiment among the Queen City's ethnic population. One could attack the Catholic Church or Catholic schools without coming across as a rabid hater of all immigrants. Doing so would rally liberal and radical Germans, as well as many members of the Protestant majority. Hayes's political savvy combined with his winning the gubernatorial race in Ohio in 1875 to make him a dark horse in the race. Thus, following the blueprint used by the Lincoln campaign in 1860, Senator John Sherman worked hard to make his fellow Buckeye the compromise candidate, and when the front-runners faltered, their supporters turned to Hayes.[31]

THE ELECTION OF 1876

Disappointed, Morton still remained loyal to his party, and he sent the first telegram of congratulations to Hayes, pledging to "labor earnestly for your success." And he kept his word, throwing himself into the campaign for president on behalf of the Republicans, especially Hayes and his vice presidential running mate, William A. Wheeler of New York. The Democrats nominated New York governor Samuel J. Tilden and Morton's old enemy from Indiana, Senator Thomas A. Hendricks. As if his party loyalty was not enough, Morton was now motivated by the fact that the hated Hendricks was running for vice president. Soon every issue seemed to be caught up in the politics of the election. In July the Indiana Republican joined other members of his party in delivering speeches in the Senate on the seemingly bland topic of internal improvements. The House of Representatives, now controlled by the Democrats, had reduced the appropriations for infrastructure, but when a bill to fund work on rivers and harbors—with most of the projects located in Democratic districts—they passed a large increase. The Senate added even more money to the bill, and Ohio's Democratic senator Allen Thurman, a longtime critic of the railroads who opposed such increases on principle, called for sending it to the Committee on Appropriations with instructions to cut it back.[32]

Morton spoke in response to Thurman's motion, making it an opportunity to campaign for the Republican Party. He asked his colleagues in the other party, "What good thing has been done of any character by the democratic party in the last twenty-five years?" When a Democratic senator told him that the Democracy had exposed the corruption of the Grant administration, Morton replied that they all knew that his opponents had "assumed the role of the detective." He doubted they would find any real misconduct but charged that his enemies were "dodging the question." He then explained that the Democrats had done nothing good in the past several decades. Instead, the party had been the source of much evil, including the Fugitive Slave Act, the Kansas-Nebraska Act, Bleeding Kansas, the Dred Scott decision, secession, disloyalty during the war, and opposition to Reconstruction. Once again, Indiana's senator waved the bloody shirt against the Democrats and made them responsible for the rebellion. He remembered "the outrages of the Ku Klux and white leagues who received protection and encouragement in the tents of the democratic party."[33]

The Democrats, Morton declared, were "continually evil" and had "the blackest and most damnable record in the history of parties in this or any other country." As always, he blamed his opponents for all of the problems the nation faced. The Democrats were responsible for the increased cost of government and for higher taxes. When a Democratic colleague interrupted him to ask whether or not they ought to reform the many abuses in government, Morton thought that whatever problems there were stemmed from the war. He argued that "if these things are the natural and legitimate consequence of the rebellion," then it was not wise for those who started the rebellion to try to blame others for what they had caused. But that was what the Democrats did. They had started the Civil War, but they tried to say that it was the Republicans who were at fault. Whatever the Republicans did, the Democrats resisted it and then blamed their enemies for the problems caused by their resistance. He pointed to Reconstruction, where his party had tried "to protect the colored people of the South and the white republicans from the numerous slaughters that have fallen upon them," but the Democrats screamed in protest, arguing that such measures were the use of force and a violation of rights, liberties, and the spirit of democracy.[34]

Morton then brought the point home, pointing to the Hamburg Massacre in South Carolina. Just days earlier, on July 8, a mob of more than a hundred white men had attacked about thirty black militiamen as part of a plan to disrupt Republican campaign activities. At least six black soldiers and one white man were killed and many others wounded. With white Southerners still using violence and terror to intimidate voters, it was easy to wave the bloody shirt at the Democrats. Morton made the most of it, saying that the Democrats had only two arguments to make in the political campaign. "The argument has been in the South, violence, intimidation; and the argument in the North is the cry of reform and corruption. The first argument is the shotgun, the revolver, the bowie knife, and it is sharp and murderous; and the second argument is false and hypocritical."[35]

He continued to attack the Democrats when he began to deliver stump speeches late that summer. In Indianapolis on August 11, he spoke at the Academy of Music and blasted the Democratic presidential ticket as "slanderers of our good name." His bitter discourse focused on the nasty charges the Tilden-Hendricks campaign had made against the Republicans and Morton personally. He answered their accusations of wrongdoing by calling them hypocrites and pointing to their own misdeeds. Who supported these slandering hypocrites? In the Democratic Party of 1876, Morton saw "assembled the mourners for slavery, the organizers of rebellion, the Ku-Klux and White Liners, the Northern sympathizers and dough-faces, the advocates of state sovereignty, and the representatives of every element that had torn the country with civil war, drenched it with blood, and watered it with the tears of widows and orphans." He attacked Hendricks with relish, using humor while still spitting venom at his old rival. Morton thought that the Hoosier Democrat's career surpassed all others in being "barren of good or important results." His longtime competitor had backed Buchanan, blamed the rebellion on the Republicans, led the Peace Democrats in foolish criticism of the Union, and helped create the Copperhead Sons of Liberty with his rhetoric. Hendricks hated blacks and had opposed emancipation. Even after the end of slavery, Morton recalled that the Democrat "had been against the repeal of the Fugitive Slave law, and had opposed propositions to allow negroes to ride in the street cars or sit on juries or hold office." The aspirant for the vice presidency had resisted Reconstruction, voting and speaking against all three of the constitutional amendments. He had opposed enlisting black soldiers, had voted to allow slavery to go into Kansas, and had promoted the exclusion clause in the Indiana state constitution. With such an "unbroken record of blunders, unredeemed by any good measure," Morton wondered how Hendricks could be considered "promising material for a great reformer."[36]

The *Sentinel* thought the August 11 speech was "one of the poorest of Morton's efforts" and said that his "low and scurrilous attack upon Mr. Hendricks' political record" was "the most indecent and ungenteel" assault "that even Morton ever uttered against a political opponent." The Democratic paper lamented that Morton had then assaulted Tilden with "vituperations and venom," arguing that the Republican's criticism was worse than if the New York governor "had spent twenty years of his life at Sing Sing" prison. In Shelbyville, a few days later, Hendricks defended his own record and agreed with a member of his audience who called Morton a liar.[37]

The Republican campaigner responded in a speech at Laporte, once again waving the bloody shirt as he described the history of the Democrats and their efforts to "subvert the government." He insisted that he had not lied, that Hendricks had a long record of riding the fence or taking the wrong side of an issue. He quoted at length from past platforms of the Indiana Democratic Party and from Hendricks's speeches. Morton defended his own record, once again blaming the traitorous Democrats for forcing him to run the state on his own when he was governor. He praised Hayes, reminding his audience that the Republican candidate had fought for freedom and Union. He called Tilden and Hendricks the "Confederate Democracy," saying that "I use that name purposely and understandingly," arguing that the Democrats still stood for rebellion. He concluded that the 1876 election was "a struggle between the blue and the gray: between the loyal and the disloyal. . . . They say we wave the bloody shirt; that we keep talking about the war. They would have us forget about the war, but they do not forget about it. Everything, in the South, turns on the war." Only rebels could get elected by the Democrats of the South, which the senator insisted was evidence that the war remained the central issue. He warned the voters of Indiana that "if the Democratic party shall carry the election this year, depend upon it, it will not be a triumph of Northern Democracy, but the triumph of Southern Democracy." Even though some Northerners and some in his party wanted to end Reconstruction, Morton stressed that the rebellion was still going on.[38]

For the rest of the campaign Morton dogged Hendricks, taking on the job of attacking the opposition's vice presidential candidate on his home turf. Clearly, the Republicans hoped that Morton's machine could deliver Indiana, even though Hoosiers might be tempted to vote for one of their own Democrats. Although he focused on the national election, the senator also supported Benjamin Harrison for governor in the Indiana race. While the Republican eventually lost his bid to take the governor's chair that fall, astute observers saw what Morton had feared years before: that Harrison had the character, charisma, and ability to replace the senator as the leader of the Grand Old Party in the Hoosier State. As one Republican paper put it, Harrison was "exceedingly popular as a speaker, adding to party logic fine strokes of humor and wit. His personal magnetism is only equaled in this state by that of Morton."[39]

Physically, Morton was feeling better than he had in a long time. Perhaps the campaign invigorated him, like it had back in 1873, because the papers reported that he was able to walk without help except for his crutches or canes and that he now moved faster across the stage to the platform than he had since his stroke. The rigors of the campaign trail took their toll, however, and by October he had returned to delivering his speeches while seated. The Democrats cruelly sneered and called him "Sitting Bull," using the hint of racism to smear Morton for remaining in his chair. The *Boston Post* jabbed that he stayed in his seat because "his views were too narrow to stand on." They also claimed that the only reason he accepted the outcome of the convention and campaigned for the Republican ticket was because he knew that "Hayes would be a piece of potter's clay in Morton's hands."[40]

Although losing the nomination had stung, the senator remained, as ever, the Stalwart Republican. He liked Hayes and thought that the Buckeye governor would make a good president who would stand by the Republican agenda. Morton had helped Hayes campaign for governor the year before, and he thought the presidential candidate would continue Reconstruction while leading the nation forward into economic prosperity. Furthermore, he truly believed that the situation was dangerous. If the Democrats won, it would be the end of Reconstruction and the rebels would return to power. This would destroy most, if not all, that the Radicals had accomplished. African Americans were in jeopardy; their rights and liberties were at risk. The Democrats would encourage the rebels, and the South would try to rise again. It might very well lead to another rebellion, another civil war. Freedom and Union were again in peril. And, once again, Morton believed that only the power of the national government, wielded by his Republican Party, could save the country. Waving the bloody shirt was by now familiar, but Morton thought it absolutely necessary as he continued the fight, confident that the various pieces of his ideology remained compatible and cohesive. He hoped that his ideas and methods would again prove effective in bringing out the voters to save the republic from the looming threat of rebellion.

Hayes lost the popular vote, but Tilden came up one vote short in the Electoral College. This precipitated the very kind of crisis that Morton had warned the country about three years earlier when he tried to get the Senate to support his committee investigating the Electoral College. The election attracted the highest turnout in the history of the country, with 81 percent of eligible voters casting ballots. Despite Morton's efforts, the Democrats carried Indiana in both the state elections in October and the presidential contest in November by more than five thousand votes. Benjamin Harrison, whom Morton had finally allowed back into politics, lost the governor's race to "Blue Jean Bill" Williams. Nationally, Tilden won by more than a quarter million votes, and Democrats celebrated their victory.

When the Electoral College totals came in, however, Tilden had 184 votes, while Hayes had 165, and 20 votes were disputed. Because 185 electoral votes were needed to win, Tilden was one vote short. Although one Oregon vote was in question, the rest of the disputed votes came in three Southern states: Florida, which had 4 electoral votes; Louisiana, which had 8; and South Carolina, which had 7. While the other Southern states had been redeemed by the election of Bourbon governments, these three remained under military occupation and Republican control, making them all the more significant. In all three states it appeared that Tilden and Hendricks had won the popular vote. But the Republicans cried fraud and pointed to deceptive ballots used by the Democrats to trick illiterate voters. As they had done in Mississippi and other Southern states in previous years, the Democrats listed their candidates on a ballot printed with Republican symbols—and this time they used a picture of Abraham Lincoln. Voters unable to read the names of the candidates dutifully cast their ballots for the Democrats while thinking that they had voted for the party of Lincoln. Violence influenced the results as well, and the Republicans gathered reports about Red Shirts and White Leaguers intimidating voters in various precincts in the disputed states. In the end, both parties claimed to have won all three states, and each declared their candidate the winner. If

Hayes received all twenty of the outstanding electoral votes, he would win the election by one vote. With the presidency in the balance, congressional leaders began to argue about how to resolve the dispute.[41]

With the contested election, the possibility of Morton becoming president again began to take shape. It was a long shot, but if Washington powerbrokers did not resolve the election by Inauguration Day on March 5, 1877, there would be no president or vice president. In fact, there had not been a vice president since the death of Henry Wilson in November of 1875. The line of succession made the president pro tempore of the Senate the next to be commander in chief. Michigan's Thomas W. Ferry still held the position, which he had assumed in 1875. But there were rumors that Morton might replace him, and if so, the Indiana senator's presidential ambitions might be fulfilled after all. His Democratic enemies would not want it to happen, as they saw Morton as the worst possible Republican to take the presidency.

In the end, the rumors turned out to be false and Ferry kept the job. To be sure, Morton had not pursued the office of president pro tempore. Nor did he believe that whoever held the position in the Senate should become the commander in chief. Although he still wanted the White House, Morton was looking ahead toward 1880. He would be only fifty-seven years old in 1880, and he knew from experience that the changing context of politics might well make him the Republican nominee in the next campaign or in 1884. He liked Hayes and was friends with the Ohioan, so he did not want to betray that relationship by trying to take the office for himself. And Morton also sincerely believed that Hayes had won the election. The Democrats had stolen it by using violence and voter intimidation. White thugs had bulldozed black voters, and in some states they had committed murder to prevent Hayes from winning. One infamous example came from Louisiana, where an African American woman testified that her husband had been murdered by white Democrats while on his way to vote for Hayes and that the same men had killed the baby she carried in her arms before raping her. For Morton, this was still another battle in the ongoing struggle: the rebels refused to accept their defeat and were continuing the Civil War by others means. Already restored to power in most of the South, they had stolen the presidential election to ensure that Reconstruction ended in the last three states where Republicans still held the upper hand.[42]

Of course, if Morton had gotten his way, there would have been no dispute. He had proposed a constitutional amendment to eliminate the Electoral College. He had argued against the rules that established the technical details that the Democrats now used to contest the Republican attempts to accept the election results forwarded by the boards in the three states. Foremost among his concerns was the Twenty-Second Joint Rule that the Republicans had pushed through in 1865. This was not a legal statute but said that when the president of the Senate opened the electoral votes during the joint session of Congress, any senator or representative could object to any state's electoral vote for any reason. The two bodies would then vote separately on whether to sustain the objection or not. By this method a state's electoral votes could be excluded by the vote of either the Senate or the House, even if the other body approved them. A few years earlier, Morton had feared that the Democrats would someday control one house of Congress and use the rule to deny the election to a Republican candidate. He supported his argument with the results of the 1872 election, when Congress had thrown out the electoral votes of Louisiana and almost rejected those of Arkansas, Texas, and Mississippi. That time, the exclusion did not matter, as Grant had won anyway. But the Indiana senator had warned that it might someday cost a winning candidate the election. His party had listened to him and the Senate passed his amendment, but the House did not, and it had been referred back to Morton's own committee, where he allowed it to sit because he knew he could not get it passed. Early in 1876 he had tried again to repeal the Twenty-Second Rule but was unable to accomplish it. Now his warnings came true, and the rule was being used to reject votes that he believed belonged to Hayes.[43]

Obviously the Democrats thought that Tilden had won, and they wanted to ensure that he did. The turmoil continued, with dual legislatures submitting their returns while Republican-appointed electoral boards presented different results. The Republicans in the Senate voted to repeal the Twenty-Second Rule, but the Democratic-controlled House insisted that it still stood. Radical Republicans asserted that, with the rule gone, the president of the Senate had the power to resolve any disputed votes. Democrats warned that they might refuse to attend a joint session, denying a quorum and preventing the electoral votes from counting. They began considering impeachment proceedings against Grant because he had used the military to overturn the popular vote in the three Southern states.

THE COMPROMISE OF 1877

When Morton arrived in Washington in December 1876 for the tense congressional session that would decide how to settle the disputed election, he had shaved off his signature goatee and now wore only a mustache and a small tuft of hair below his mouth in what would be called a "soul patch" in the twentieth century. His bushy goatee had symbolized his ferocity and the newspapers thought that his new look made him look younger and less intimidating. Perhaps some of his colleagues hoped that shaving off his beard had produced a gentler Morton, one who might be willing to compromise. They soon found out that, beard or no beard, the senator remained fierce in the defense of his principles.[44]

Some congressional leaders began trying to forge a compromise through the traditional use of committees. The House voted to create a committee of seven representatives to join a similar number of senators to forge some kind of agreement on a process to resolve the election. The Senate agreed to the proposal, and Morton was one of the senators appointed to the committee. At first the men from the two sides of Congress met separately, and although they agreed to meet to discuss proposals, they would vote on their own. One idea was to have a committee of judges from the federal courts or the United States Supreme Court decide the matter. This led to arguing about the composition of such a committee and how it might work. Eventually, however, they settled on appointing a fifteen-man commission made up of five senators, five representatives, and five associate justices of the Supreme Court. Only one of the fourteen members of this committee voted against the plan: Oliver P. Morton. He insisted that Hayes had won the election and that all of this talk about process and compromise was just another step toward allowing the rebel Democrats to steal the presidency and end Reconstruction.[45]

The plan then went to the House and Senate on January 18, 1877, for debate and a final vote. The wrangling centered on how to choose the judges, with both parties hoping to gain the upper hand. Although the plan contained some of the same language that he had drafted in his earlier attempts to overturn the Twenty-Second Rule, Morton opposed the bill. He sneered that this was another compromise that history would judge harshly, remembering it alongside the Missouri Compromise of 1820 and the Compromise of 1850 as another example of the North yielding to the South. He argued that, with the compromise bill, "the shadow of intimidation has entered this chamber" and thought that senators were "acting under the apprehension of violence, of some great revolutionary act that will threaten the safety and continuance of our institutions." Morton disagreed. He believed "that Rutherford B. Hayes has been elected President of the United States; that he has been elected under the forms of law and according to law, and . . . that if he shall be counted in . . . he will be inaugurated, and there will be no violence and no revolution." The debate pitted Morton against some members of his own party, even his fellow Stalwart Radical, Roscoe Conkling, whom the Hoosier handled "without gloves" in a rough exchange on the Senate floor. Other Republicans joined Morton in opposition to the plan, but when the vote came on January 29, the bill passed the Senate, with forty-seven in favor and only seventeen opposed. Morton and fifteen other Republicans were in the minority, joined by one

Fig. 52. Senator Oliver P. Morton, ca. 1876. (Library of Congress)

Democrat. The House passed the bill as well and the commission was created, and Morton was one of the five senators to serve on it.[46]

His arguments against the plan set the tone for the commission's work: the members advocated for their party rather than trying to achieve some principled compromise. This meant the debates were partisan (with the judges joining the party of whichever president had appointed them), with Republicans supporting Hayes and Democrats fighting for Tilden. Working on behalf of his party to give Hayes the White House *was* principled for Morton, however. As he had done for so many years, he fought for his ideology of freedom, Union, power, and party. The issues were the same. The stakes were the same. His ideas were the same. Despite what his critics contended then and later, if his actions were understood in the context of events and the principles of his ideology, Morton was remarkably consistent. Opportunistic as he was, Morton did not maneuver to make himself president. Instead, he fought for his party to hold the office. In his official opinions as commissioner, he argued vigorously for accepting the returns submitted by the Republican-controlled election boards and giving the contest to Hayes. He held that to do otherwise was to violate the Constitution and help the Democrats steal the election. The partisan debates brought about a partisan result: the Commission voted to award all twenty disputed electoral votes to Hayes, with the eight Republican members carrying the decision over the seven Democrats.[47]

The Republican-controlled Senate voted immediately to adopt the Commission's decision, but the Democrats used their majority in the House to stall the decision. They challenged the eligibility of electors in other states beyond the three in the South, slowing down the vote count in an attempt to filibuster the final resolution. There was talk of impeaching Grant, or of turning to armed confrontation. Although Southern Democrats had spoken with the most bitter and militant voices throughout the process, they now became more conciliatory. They calmed their rash colleagues calling for such bold moves and began to negotiate. Talks had been underway since at least December, and Southern Democrats joined Northern men in calling for a compromise that would end Reconstruction and promote internal improvements in the South in exchange for Hayes taking the presidency.

Rumors had it that railroad tycoons like Jay Gould and Tom Scott wanted to resolve the issue in a way that would let them build more tracks across the South, adding to their empires. The negotiations took place between a group of Southern Democrats and Northern Republicans that included a number of newspapermen as well as congressmen and senators. This would mean that Hayes would have to agree to Redemption, removing the last occupying troops from the South and allowing white Southern Democrats to take power over the black (and the few white) Southern Republicans. The negotiators for the Southern Democracy also wanted one of their own in the Cabinet. Supposedly, the deal would also include the president endorsing economic development in the South, including not only the building of new railroads but also the river and harbor construction projects that Morton had opposed the previous year. Although Hayes tried to avoid making specific promises and there may not have been an actual deal involving business interests, the agreement was made, and the Compromise of 1877 was accomplished.[48]

But the Republicans who carried out the plan worried about the reaction of Morton and other Radicals. Although many in the party were now abandoning their black friends and the policy of Reconstruction, Morton continued the fight alongside other diehard Radicals like Zachariah Chandler and Benjamin Butler. Hayes liked the Indiana senator who had done so much to further his political career, and this meant that he remained politically powerful. Morton could not simply be ignored if the party hoped for any kind of unity moving forward. Especially important was Louisiana, where the senator had devoted so much of his energy to helping African Americans and the Republican Party. He had already declared that any kind of agreement would rank with the compromises that had given the South more power in the past. If he or another prominent Radical chose to fight the deal, the whole process might be derailed, and so Hayes needed to keep Morton on his side to keep the party united at least through the inauguration. To do that, he needed to give them political cover.

So, on February 26, a group of Ohio Republicans, including future president James Garfield, met with white Southern Democrats at the Wormley House hotel in Washington. The hotel provided an ironic setting for the meeting, as it was owned and operated by James Wormley, a wealthy free African American and self-made man. The Southerners promised that the Democratic governments of Louisiana and South Carolina would protect the civil rights of African Americans if the federal troops were withdrawn from the state. Garfield protested that the Ohio delegation had no right to speak for Hayes and insisted that he wanted no part of such a bargain. But the other Republicans present at the meeting followed through on the deal suggested. Democrats pledged to uphold black rights in exchange for the end of Reconstruction. How many Southerners were swayed by the negotiations remained unclear, but a few of them joined Northern Democrats in supporting the Compromise of 1877.[49]

One man who attended the Wormley Conference kept notes and later testified before Congress that the meeting was designed to placate Morton, Garfield, and John Sherman with assurances from the Southerners that they would protect black rights in Louisiana, especially. Morton demanded such an agreement in order to support the election compromise, and his coming over to do so gave Hayes political cover with the Radical Republicans. A few days later, when Morton was at the Ebbitt House in Washington, he was serenaded by a group of Ohio friends who had gathered outside the hotel. He responded to them with a short speech in which he declared that any conciliatory policy with the South had to guarantee the safety of African Americans by granting "protection to life and liberty and to the political rights of all classes, without regard to color or politics." He stated that "there can be no compromise, no peace which is not based on the political and civil rights of all classes of men. When there shall be such protection to life and liberty then there will be peace and tranquility, but not before." His unyielding rhetoric indicated that he still stood by his earlier insistence on protecting black rights, even as he accepted the deal made at the Wormley Conference, hoping that it would guarantee equality. The Hoosier senator said that there could be no compromise at the same time that he adhered to his party's bargain with the Southern Democrats.[50]

In the end, Hayes became president of the United States on March 5, 1877. Many Democrats gnashed their teeth and cried that the Republicans had stolen the election. A political poster entitled "The Political Farce of 1877" put Morton at the top of the list of "the Two Negroes and Ten Whites Who Defeated the Will of the American People." Others were shocked that Morton seemed to have sold out his principles and abandoned the Radical cause for which he had fought so long. Some thought that he had made the deal to further his own presidential ambitions, having bargained to get the nomination in 1880. A political cartoon published in February in *Frank Leslie's Illustrated Newspaper* portrayed Morton as the supposed expert on elections as he wrote on a

Fig. 53. (*opposite*) "The Political Farce of 1876" (Library of Congress). In this Democratic lithograph decrying the contest as a stolen election, which was published in 1877 by Joseph A. Stoll, Morton is listed along with other congressional members of the committee that finally decided the 1876 presidential race. He and the legislators are joined by two white and two black members of the Louisiana Election Board and are called here the "Two Negroes and Ten Whites Who Defeated the Will of the American People, as expressed through the Ballot Box, on the 7th day of November, 1876."

The Library of Congress description of the lithograph reads: "Print showing bust portraits of eight men, identified as, clockwise from top, Oliver P. Morton, James A. Garfield, George F. Hoar, William Strong, Joseph P. Bradley, Samuel F. Miller, George F. Edmunds, and Frederick T. Frelinghuysen; also a group of four men identified as the 'Louisiana Returning Board,' from left, Kenner, Casenave, Anderson, and Wells. Includes text of four quotes regarding election fraud, such as this by Messrs. Clifford, Field, Bayard, Abbott, Hunton, Thurman & Payne, 'We can prove beyond a shadow of doubt that Louisiana and Florida voted for Tilden by decisive majorities, and we are prepared to show up the villainous frauds of the Returning Boards. All we ask is investigation by this commission,' and this by U. S. Grant, 'No man worthy of the office of President should be willing to hold it if counted in, or placed there, by any fraud. Either party can afford to be disappointed in the result, but the country cannot afford to have the result tainted by the suspicion of illegal, or false returns.' In the 1876 presidential election, the election returns in four states were disputed; the final tally of votes showed Democratic candidate Samuel Tilden with approximately 250,000 more popular votes than Republican candidate Rutherford B. Hayes, though Hayes ended up with one more electoral vote than Tilden. On March 2, 1877, Congress met in a joint session and declared Hayes and Wheeler president and vice-president."

THE POLITICAL FARCE
OF 1876.

LOUISIANA RETURNING BOARD.

No man worthy of the office of President should be willing to hold it if counted in, or placed there, by any fraud. Either party can afford to be disappointed in the result, but the country cannot afford to have the result tainted by the suspicion of illegal, or false returns.

U. S. Grant.

I could never have been reconciled to the elevation by the smallest aid of mine of a person, however respectable in private life, who must forever carry upon his brow the stamp of fraud first triumphant in American history. No subsequent action, however meritorious, can wash away the letters of that record.

Charles Francis Adams.

We can prove beyond a shadow of doubt that Louisiana and Florida voted for Tilden by decisive majorities, and we are prepared to show up the villainous frauds of the Returning Boards. All we ask is investigation by this commission.

Clifford, Field, Bayard, Abbott, Hunton, Thurman & Payne.

We would be perfectly willing to examine into the merits of the case, but the evidence is all against us. We therefore declare it "Aliunde," 7 into 8 once, and "Joe Bradley" over.

Miller, Strong, Morton, Garfield, Frelinghuysen, Edmunds, Hoar & Bradley.

THE TWO NEGROES AND TEN WHITES

Who defeated the will of the American people, as expressed through the Ballot box, on the 7th day of November 1876.

Entered, according to act of Congress, in the year 1877, by JOSEPH A. STULL, in the office of the Librarian of Congress at Washington.

Copies of this sheet may be had by addressing Publisher.

97 South Orange Ave., Newark, N. J.

chalkboard that the Constitution said that Hayes should be president in 1877 and that he, Morton, should be president in 1881[51] (see Fig. 54).

To be sure, the Indiana senator celebrated the election of Hayes along with the rest of his party, assured that the Wormley meeting had fulfilled his demands. Clearly, then, the Radical warrior did not think that he had compromised any of his principles. And there were no indications that he had been bought off with a new job. The senator's efforts on behalf of the new president brought an offer of a cabinet post, but he refused one, saying that he would never take a position from which he could be fired by any man. He stayed in the Senate, where there was a strong push to make him chair of the Committee on Foreign Relations, but he refused that job as well, preferring to keep his familiar post on Privileges and Elections.

Party versus Principle

One reason for that was that Louisiana and South Carolina were still problems. In both states the Republican election board had certified the victories of a Republican governor and legislature, but the Democrats formed rival governments, insisting that they had won the election. Even after the inauguration of Hayes, the tense situation continued. Among the Republicans elected from Louisiana was a new US senator, none other than the former carpetbag governor, William Pitt Kellogg. When he arrived in Washington, Democratic senators objected to him being seated, setting off a debate. Morton, unsurprisingly, supported Kellogg and argued the case for him against fellow Republicans as well as Democrats. When the Senate referred the case to Privileges and Elections, Morton used his influence to push through a report favoring Kellogg, but the Senate adjourned without considering the committee's report. By the

Fig. 54. (*opposite*) "The Double-Faced Head of Republican Radicalism" (*Frank Leslie's Illustrated Newspaper,* February 10, 1877). This cartoon depicts Morton as a manipulator who swung the 1876 election to Rutherford B. Hayes while planning to put himself in the White House four years later. With his canes leaning beside him, the Indiana Senator has written on a chalkboard: "The Constitution as I understand it makes Hayes president in 1877 and me president in 1881. O. P. Morton." To the left, a politician reads a list entitled "Morton vs. Morton" that lists quotations from Morton that seem to show his inconsistencies on how to resolve the disputed election. In the upper right, leaders line up to sign a petition titled "Honest Men of Both Parties are United in Demanding a Fair Count." In the center a bewildered judge stews over a volume entitled "Constitutional Law on the Counting of Electoral Votes."

FRANK LESLIE'S ILLUSTRATED NEWSPAPER

No. 1,115—Vol. XLIII.]　　　NEW YORK, FEBRUARY 10, 1877.　　　[PRICE, 10 CENTS.

THE DOUBLE-FACED HEAD OF REPUBLICAN RADICALISM.

time the Senate was ready to reconvene, Hayes had withdrawn the last federal troops from the South, and when the president did not support the Republican governments, the Redeemer Democrats took control of both Louisiana and South Carolina.[52]

As the new congressional session approached, there was a lot of talk about what Morton might do next. A group of more than one hundred Southern Republicans published an open letter to him in the *New York Times,* asking him to express his opinion. The senator responded in a letter dated May 24, 1877, saying that despite the change of governments in the two states, "unless Kellogg voluntarily withdraws, the Senate will have to decide the question of his election as it stood at the time of adjournment." As always, Morton proceeded directly and bluntly: "The Republican governments of Louisiana and South Carolina have yielded to force. They have gone down before an armed minority whose threats of future violence were guaranteed by a long train of bloody deeds in the past." He regretted having to say so, but "stripped of all disguises and pretenses, the simple fact is" that the Republican Reconstruction governments "were not able to maintain themselves in authority, and the Government of the United States . . . refused them its support." Indefatigable to the end, Morton waved the bloody shirt in the spring of 1877: "The Democratic Party in Louisiana, an undoubted minority . . . were determined to govern, whatever it might cost in the way of life. Their pretended majority at the late election had cost many lives, and was the product of the most infamous and damning of crimes. The murder and crimes have been proved, and the blood-stained majority set aside by lawful process." The Hayes administration had decided that "such a case of insurrection and violence" did not require federal intervention. Instead, the situation was left to the warring parties. The Indiana senator managed to win at least one battle when Kellogg took his Senate seat, a position he held until 1883. But Reconstruction came to an end. Morton pointed to the Wormley Conference and the Compromise of 1877 when he remarked that the policy "was apparently worked out through the presence of the commission and seemed to take the form of negotiations. Assurances were given that the rights of all classes should be protected." But he allowed that "general promises of this kind amount to little, especially when left to the voluntary execution of a party that thought the colored man ought not to have political rights—even personal freedom, and who have never considered him a part of the people."[53]

Ever the realist, the Indiana senator admitted defeat: "President Hayes was urged to give up Louisiana and South Carolina at once, and was told that it was only a question of time; that at the next election they would" be redeemed by the Democrats just like the rest of the South. "However repulsive this argument," Morton said, "it was unfortunately too true." Terrorism had worked. The use of violence had allowed the Democrats to recapture state after state.

Fig. 55. Rutherford B. Hayes. (Library of Congress)

Faced with the reality that "Republican governments in Louisiana and South Carolina could only be kept in place by the army," the president had yielded to "an argument of expediency—not of right and justice." The senator doubted whether the administration could have continued Reconstruction, given that the Democrats in the House had withheld military appropriations until it was agreed that such money would not be used to support troops occupying the South. Even in the Senate, Morton thought, the Republican majority who supported Reconstruction was "but nominal, if it exists at all." Without the support of even his own party, Hayes faced an inevitable result. The Hoosier insisted that the president had the authority to uphold the Reconstruction governments, but "the undertaking would have been futile and the failure disastrous."[54]

As usual, Morton contended that the blame lay with the Democrats. They used their power to destroy the army to threaten the administration and force the president to keep the bargain made in the compromise. All of the talk about reconciliation and peace meant nothing to Morton. After all, the foremost proponents of peace were "the very men who planned the massacres" of African Americans across the South. But Northerners had grown tired of the Southern Question. "The painful truth is that political murders in the South have ceased to be shocking." The Democrats always tried to justify the racial violence "by energetic talk about carpet-baggers, scalawags, and Radical thieves." And not a single person had been "punished for the butcheries" committed at a long list of places, including Hamburg and Colfax.[55]

At long last, the various pieces of Morton's ideology had become incompatible. His party had refused to employ government power to ensure freedom. The true Union cause was lost, as reconciliation had been achieved on Southern terms. The rebels had won. Faced with this stark reality, Morton swallowed the bitter pill of defeat and took the practical choice. Choosing party as his principle, he remained a Stalwart Republican and supported Hayes. He did not believe "that President Hayes intends to desert or destroy the Republican party . . . I believe in his patriotism and high integrity, and in his undivided purpose to make his administration" accomplish good for the country. The senator had admired the new president's inaugural address, which he thought "was strong and beautiful," and he especially liked its "declaration of his devotion to the great doctrines of human rights." He thought that Hayes would be a good Republican president, "not in a mere partisan way," but in his principles and in his maintenance of the party's organization. Morton knew well that "political principles do not execute themselves, they need a party to do that. Organization in politics is as necessary as in war." It was not enough to have a huge number of people committed to a shared principle. If they lacked organization, they would be helpless before a smaller, disciplined force.[56]

He still presented the Republican Party "as a grand and indispensable instrumentality for carrying into operation the true principles of government and human rights." He reminded his readers that it was "the Republican organization, consolidated and disciplined with great labor, that carried the country through the war, preserved the Union, abolished slavery, placed the amendments in the constitution, and that now stands as the guardian of the Nation's liberty and honor." Although his fellow Republicans were abandoning the fight to which he had given so much, Morton remained loyal. Party was a principle, for without party a cause could not be won.[57]

Despite the troops being withdrawn and Redeemer governments in control across the South, he did not agree with those who said "that the Republican system of Reconstruction is a failure." He insisted that it was a good policy based on just and unchanging doctrines. The "only sense in which it has failed is that it has been resisted by armed and murderous organizations, by terrorism and proscriptions the most wicked and cruel of the age." And if the Southern Democrats followed through on their promises to Hayes by protecting citizens and civil rights, Reconstruction "will not be a failure, but a grand success." He declared that the defining elements of Reconstruction "are the Fourteenth and Fifteenth amendments to the constitution, establishing the equal civil and political rights of all men" as well as the laws enacted to enforce the amendments. The ultimate success or failure of Reconstruction depended entirely on them: "So far as these have failed Reconstruction is a failure; so far as they succeed Reconstruction is a success."[58]

And, in some ways, he judged Reconstruction a success. White Southerners no longer pushed for secession. They were focused on rebuilding after their failed rebellion, hoping to recover their economic losses. But Morton had no illusions about the situation. Reconstruction had failed, too. Yes, there would be peace and quiet in the South now that the Democrats "have gained complete power and the Republican party has ceased to struggle . . . There will be peace when there is abject submission." Wiping out the Republican Party across the South "was not the harbinger of prosperity or happiness." He worried about the direction of the country, noting that there were calls to treat Confederate veterans the same as Union soldiers and to accept claims for repayment of property losses suffered by Southerners. If the distinctions were blurred in the legal system, the Union cause would truly be lost. It would not happen immediately, "but step by step, already becoming more rapid, until the public mind has become demoralized, the rebellion has ceased to be a crime—scarcely a mistake." He predicted that reconciliation and reunion would demand that there be no difference "between loyalty and treason." Prophesying the future of Civil War memory, Morton thought that the American people would forget that the war was fought to crush the rebellion. They would forget the principles of freedom and Union. They would forget about the crimes of slavery and treason. They would remember the fallen soldiers of both sides on equal terms and praise them all alike. In the name of reunion, they would forget the reasons the Union had fought. That would mark the failure of Reconstruction.[59]

But he hoped for success and, as always, looked to party for the answer. The Republican Party, he declared, "was never more necessary to the nation than it is today." He dismissed talk about abandoning or disbanding the Republican organization to create a new political party because Southerners hated it so much. Morton found it absurd that there were those who thought that "the party which saved the nation" and that embodied its most cherished principles should "commit suicide as an act of conciliation to the late enemies of the republic." The Republicans in the South had been overthrown by force. Since 1868 the rebels had been using terrorism and murder as weapons, and their insurgency against the United States had "culminated in the bloody field of last year." They had lost, but Republicans could not allow their party to be destroyed. That would "make the Democratic party supreme and fasten upon the country its odious policy and principles." Morton knew better than to believe that Southern Democrats had converted on the race question. No, he was sure that they "have not changed in regard to the civil and political rights of the negro," and if they had won the presidency, they would have repealed the Fourteenth and Fifteenth Amendments.[60]

Realistic and practical as he was, Morton still held fast to his argument that true reunion and reconciliation, "to be honest and durable, must be based upon the concession of equal civil and political rights, peace and protection to men of all races and creeds." If the former slaveholders who had resisted Reconstruction over the last decade had suddenly converted and would enforce the amendments by implementing civil rights, it would be the consummation of the senator's most devout wishes. But he demurred, admitting that "I do not believe in this sudden conversion." He did not think that his disbelief should bring charges of prejudice on his part. After all, he had a lot of recent evidence to go with a long past record of crime to make him doubt what the rebels had to say. Morton reasoned that although it had made mistakes, the Republican Party in the South had "waged a noble contest for the right, and the courage and self-sacrifice displayed by its members" would long be remembered. In response to the rise of the Redeemer governments and their creation of "a solid South by force," Morton called on his fellow Republican to build "a solid North by vigilance and the eternal justice of their cause." If Northern Republicans did not unite and win in their home states, they would "fall prey to a solid Confederate South." This would mean that "the rebellion will have been suppressed in vain" and "the fruits of the war will be lost."[61]

Despite the fact that the Republicans had sold out the principles of freedom and Union by giving up on the use of power, Morton clung to his party. He could see no alternative. The only hope was to keep the Republicans united in hopes of resisting the rebels, who had already retaken so much. He distrusted white Southerners, but his loyalty required him to trust Hayes. What else could he do? If he broke with the administration, he would be isolated or would break up the party. His own words summed it up well: "Political principles do not execute themselves, they need a party to do that." The Stalwart Republican did not turn away from the other pieces of his ideology. He still believed in freedom and Union and power. He still promoted equality, still hoped to achieve protection and civil rights for African Americans. But without his party, he could not hope to achieve the power necessary to fight for the universal doctrines that he traced to the Declaration of the Independence. A hundred years had passed since the nation's birth, but the very ideas upon which it had been founded were threatened by violent terrorism being practiced by an organized enemy. Only through a well-managed and disciplined party could Morton hope to win back the power necessary to continue the fight to which he had been so long dedicated.[62]

THE IMMIGRATION ISSUE

That spring and summer, Morton turned to the nation's founding when he once again took up the issue of the Electoral College. He wrote a two-part article for the *North American Review* that was published in the May-June and July-August editions of the journal. Expounding on the Constitution and the writings of the Founding Fathers, he repeated his call for abolishing the current system, arguing that "the electoral college is not only useless, but dangerous." Immigration also occupied his mind that summer, as he wrote a minority report for the Committee of Investigation on the issue of excluding Chinese immigrants. The 1876 Democratic national convention had called for an exclusion act to prohibit the Chinese from coming to America. Nativists in the Republican ranks had pushed for a similar resolution, but the party platform made a more moderate call for an investigation of the subject. A joint committee of the House and Senate, with Morton as chair, conducted the work. They traveled to San Francisco, where they questioned sixty witnesses and gathered data and information. They returned to the campaign and the disputed election, which pushed back their report. Morton disagreed with the majority of the so-called Morton Committee, who favored exclusion.[63]

   Thus, in the spring of 1877, when time finally allowed, he began to write his dissent. He proved unable to complete the task, although the portions that he had finished were published by the Senate in January 1878. In the dissent, Morton argued that a nation founded on the principles of liberty and equality could not exclude the Chinese. He defended them on every front, arguing on behalf of their culture, work ethic, and social relations. He doubted that open immigration would result in "an inundation" of Chinese migrants but said that if such occurred the government could take action then to stop it. Morton challenged Americans to live up to their ideals. "We profess to believe that God has given to all men the same rights, without regard to race or color," he wrote, but that doctrine had taken a century to be established in American law. Slavery was the most obvious violation of the sacred principle of equality, but immigration presented another area where the country fell short. Morton asserted that "our country is open to immigrants from all parts of the world." He dismissed arguments about the Chinese being too isolated to assimilate and that their refusal to receive immigrants in their home country meant that they should be unwelcome in the United States. He praised their intelligence and accomplishments and urged his colleagues to reject exclusion in favor of inclusion. The Indiana senator thought that someday China might be freed from foreign intervention and, if so, would "outstrip the western nations" culturally and economically. He found no reason to exclude them and called for open immigration because of the great value that they would add to the nation.[64]

Morton did not complete his dissenting opinion on immigration because no sooner had he started it than he had to travel to Oregon with other members of a Senate subcommittee to investigate charges of election fraud and the disputed Electoral College vote. Before leaving, he gave a Decoration Day speech at Crown Hill Cemetery in Indianapolis, honoring the fallen soldiers in a way that reminded his audience why he had been called the Soldiers' Friend when he served as governor. It was a nationalist discourse, filled with praise for the dead heroes. But he again took the opportunity to blast away at the Democrats and Southern rebels, saying that the North must never forget the cost and sacrifices of the rebellion. Reunion and reconciliation with the South must be accomplished on Unionist terms, not the Lost Cause values of the rebels. Reconciliation did not mean erasing the memory of the rebellion and who was responsible. "But while we cannot forget, yet we can forgive, and we will forgive all who accept the great doctrines of equal liberty and of equal rights for all and equal protection for all." Reconstruction had ended, but Morton did not forget: "We must remember that there is an eternal difference between right and wrong, and that we were on the right side, and that they were on the wrong side. . . . We were grandly in the right, and that they were terribly in the wrong."[65]

THE DEATH OF MORTON

Lucinda and his son, Oliver, traveled with Morton as he left on June 7, 1877, for his trip to the West Coast. He was very sick and could barely get out of the bed in the sleeper car, but wherever he went, crowds of people gathered to serenade him and beg him to speak. From San Francisco, the Morton family took a ship to Portland, Oregon, and the sea voyage improved the senator's health. He worked hard on the eighteen-day investigation of possible election fraud, leading the examination of more than 150 witnesses. Afterward he made his way to the state of Washington, visiting several towns there. Upon his return to Oregon, he delivered an extemporaneous hour-and-a-half-long speech at Salem in which he waved the bloody shirt and urged the president to sustain Reconstruction before heading back to the coast and to a resort to take the waters. By early August he was in San Francisco, and his health seemed better than it had been since his stroke in 1865. He was able to walk several blocks with minimal reliance on his crutches. Then, on August 6, he noticed a numbness on his left side and woke Lucinda, telling her that he felt very weak. Within hours, he began to experience paralysis on his left side, and by morning he had lost the use of his arm as well as his leg. After consulting a doctor, the family decided to head east for Indianapolis. When they arrived, they decided that he should try to recover at his mother-in-law's home in Richmond because their house in the state capital was not arranged for his care.[66]

Back home in Indiana, Morton received visits from many friends and letters from many more well-wishers. Word that he had suffered another stroke spread quickly, and so did the news that he was not recovering the use of his limbs. On September 13 President Hayes came to visit him in Mrs. Burbank's Richmond home. When Morton told the president that he hoped he would soon return to the Senate where he could support the administration, the doctor stopped the conversation. Hayes kissed Morton good-bye and began sobbing as soon as he left the room. He considered the senator a friend and knew that he was losing a powerful ally in the party. Republicans worried about what would happen to their party if Morton died and speculated about how they would replace him as a leader. Political bitterness came through when the *Indiana Sentinel* coldly printed a bold headline that asked, "Will He Die Soon?" and suggested that Democrat Daniel Voorhees should replace Morton in the Senate.[67]

The senator finally improved enough to move back to his own home in Indianapolis. He managed to help his old law partner, E. B. Martindale, who now served as editor of the *Journal,* write an article about the relationship between Hayes and congressional Republicans. Morton contributed much to the piece, and he expressed his continuing opposition to the civil service reforms that Hayes promoted. He also made it clear that he did not like the administration's Southern policy. But disagreement on the issues did not prevent him from praising Hayes as a party leader and a good man. Still, he argued that if the South did not keep up its end of the compromise agreement, the president should be prepared to use force to make them respect and enforce the laws that protected citizens and guaranteed civil rights.[68]

The *Journal* opinion piece was his last expression of his political views. His health deteriorated throughout the month of October, as newspapers across

Fig. 56. Morton funeral, Indianapolis, November 5, 1877 (*Frank Leslie's Illustrated Newspaper,* November 21, 1877).

the country continued to print regular updates about his condition. Then, on a gloomy fall afternoon, he suffered yet another stroke. His family gathered around him as he uttered his last words: "I am dying, I am worn out." At 5:28 P.M. on Thursday, November 1, 1877, Oliver P. Morton died.[69]

The mourning began immediately, with resolutions passed by various organizations, legislatures, and agencies. In Washington and elsewhere across the country, flags were flown at half-staff. President Hayes ordered government offices to close, and the Treasury Building was draped for mourning. The postal service delivered hundreds of letters of condolence to his widow over the next few weeks. Morton's body lay in state at the courthouse, and thousands of Hoosiers walked past his coffin to pay their respects. That Sunday, eulogies were delivered in churches around the city, state, and country. Morton had not been a churchgoer since childhood and had never professed to be a Christian, but his wife attended services regularly at the Robert's Park Methodist Church. The funeral service was held there on Monday, November 5, and special trains brought attendees from all over the state. The Reverend Joseph Bradford Cleaver of the Christian Church delivered the funeral sermon, "Saul Is Dead," drawing his text from the Old Testament story of Israel losing its first king. The minister concluded his oration by telling the audience to "bury your illustrious dead—bury him to the dirge of a nation's lament. . . . Bury him gratefully, with the flag for a winding-sheet—no star obscured, no stripe erased. Lay him to rest upon the heart of the nation which he, 'worn out,' died to preserve undivided and indivisible."[70]

Lucinda Morton's pastor at the Robert's Park Church followed with a eulogy that emphasized the senator's love for his family and their devotion to him, saying that "I want men to know that this man had something else in him besides ambition and cold power." Morton's old teacher from Centerville, Samuel Hoshour, closed the service with a prayer, and then the long funeral procession made its way through the city's streets, lined with thousands of Hoosier mourners. They buried him at Crown Hill Cemetery, next to the Union soldiers for whom he had done so much, not far from where he had honored those martyrs to the Northern cause just a few months before with his speech on Decoration Day. Hoosiers had laid Morton to rest, but the nation continued to mourn and began to create a cultural memory of Indiana's Civil War governor and Reconstruction Senator.[71]

CHAPTER TWELVE

Morton and the Politics of Memory

OLIVER P. MORTON DIED IN 1877, but his memory lived on. Newspapers across the country printed obituaries, and both *Frank Leslie's Illustrated Newspaper* and *Harper's Weekly* carried pictures of his funeral to a national audience. In the months after his death, state and national political leaders offered eulogies, as Americans mourned Indiana's Civil War governor and Reconstruction Senator in ways that allowed them to express their different views of the recent past. While the eulogists reached consensus on Morton as a defender of the Union and the Soldiers' Friend, they disagreed on important matters, including the late leader's use of power, the issues of race and slavery, and the meaning of the Civil War. Unsurprisingly, then, Morton's legacy became a political matter, as orators invoked him at Grand Army of the Republic gatherings and at ceremonies dedicating statues of the Hoosier politician. The act of recalling the man who helped lead his state and country through the Civil War and its aftermath often led to contested memories, as speakers and writers selected what to remember and what to forget about the Civil War era. Consequently, reminiscences about Morton became a platform for the politics of the present as well as a means of promoting different historical interpretations. Despite, or perhaps because of, this fact, Morton's legacy remained strong after his death. By the early twenty-first century, many knew him only as the Great War Governor, forgetting his significance during Reconstruction. But Morton still retained potent political power as a symbol for Americans who continued to use the past to construct meaning in their own time.[1]

EULOGIES

The first historical accounts of Morton came in the eulogies after his death in 1877 and included memorial speeches given in the US Capitol on January 17–18, 1878. Delivered in the aftermath of the contested presidential election and the end of Reconstruction, these tributes came at a time when many Americans were ready to forget the bitterness of sectionalism and the Civil War. Instead they looked forward to a brighter future in a unified nation poised to enjoy the wealth and power of the new industrial age and more westward expansion. Forgetting the past, however, meant setting aside or glossing over differences, often a difficult task. For many, it meant abandoning the fight for racial equality and redefining nationalism in ways that embraced both North and South instead of Union triumph. In a sense, then, Morton's death represented the passing of an era.

Many dozens of obituaries and eulogies appeared in newspapers across the country. Two examples served to demonstrate the ways that Northerners looked back at their fallen leader. Just days after the senator's death, the *Christian Recorder,* an African American newspaper published in Philadelphia, lamented Morton's passing, remarking on his role in the crusade against slavery and his indefatigable fight for equality. The black editor mourned the passing of one of the great champions of his race, mentioning especially Morton's work in passing the Fifteenth Amendment and standing strong against the Ku Klux Klan. In their obituaries and eulogies, white Republicans wept over the loss of a great defender of freedom and the Union, a man who had helped to crush the rebellion and save the nation. The *Rockland County Journal,* published in Nyack, New York, remembered Morton's energetic leadership as governor, including his creation of the state arsenal and his vigilance in rooting out the Copperheads. In his story of Morton's senate career, the editor nodded to his staunch support of African Americans and noted that the Hoosier Republican had been "a champion of the oppressed."[2]

When the congressional memorials began in January 1878, they reflected the memories of those who had known Morton, but they also expressed the speakers' own political views. Indiana's junior senator, Joseph E. McDonald, rose first to commemorate his late colleague. The Democrat had unsuccessfully challenged Morton for the governor's chair in 1864; he defeated Daniel D. Pratt in the 1874 Senate race and took office in 1875. This former political foe set the tone for generations of remembrance as he praised his Republican colleague's energy and ability. Although McDonald, a War Democrat who had supported the Union, had been critical of Morton's leadership as governor, especially his centralization of power, he quickly passed over such differences in his portrayal. Rather, he focused on Morton's relentless support for the Union as he argued that "the energy with which he supported and upheld the power of the Federal Government in its efforts to suppress the rebellion won for him the name and title of the 'war governor,' and gave him a permanent place in the front rank of the public men of the country." This was not simply a matter of being kind to the dead, for McDonald still remembered the governor as "naturally combative and aggressive, intensely in earnest in his undertakings, and intolerant in regard to those who differed with him" and remarked that Morton had too often made sound patriots his enemies because of perceived disloyalty. An opponent of Radical Reconstruction, he gently chided Morton for being a "champion of Reconstruction policy" rather than "restoration" and criticized the late leader for his role in helping to elect a Republican to the presidency in 1876. The Democrat concluded that "Oliver P. Morton was a great man" but believed that Americans would always differ in their views of his actions as a political leader. The senator sidestepped controversial issues while also referring to Morton's faults and vaguely criticizing his political positions. Couching his eulogy in such vague language allowed him to share his late rival's positive attributes and staunch Unionism while distancing himself from anything that might stir opposition to his own political future.[3]

Vermont senator George F. Edmunds continued the theme of praising Morton as an energetic Unionist, but he also recalled the Hoosier Republican's support for emancipation and equality. A fellow Republican who had supported Radical Reconstruction, Edmunds argued that Morton's partisanship had served sacred principles. As governor, the Hoosier leader had "brought a fervent love of real liberty and equality of rights among men that can exist only under the security of provisions of fundamental law, and can only be practically defended and promoted by the enactment of statutes, and their fearless and vigilant enforcement by judiciary and executive power." The governor had believed in freedom and Union, both defended by the power of the state and national governments and by the Republican Party. Edmunds declared that Senator Morton had held to his fundamental nationalist ideology by fighting for the Fourteenth and Fifteenth Amendments, as well as for the laws that Republicans passed to enforce those constitutional changes. He maintained that Morton "firmly believed that there had been a great and beneficent change, a lawful revolution in the form of the Government in the direction of equal rights, as the fair fruit of a revolution that had been attempted in the interest of slavery and secession." For Edmunds and the majority of politicians who spoke over the course of the two days set aside for the tributes, Morton stood for freedom, equality, and the Union and his career had been a triumph over rebellion and slavery.[4]

Following several other speakers, former Union general Ambrose Burnside of Rhode Island expanded on the story of Morton, recalling that the governor's "great care and love for the soldiers of his State, not only while they were in the field but after their return to their homes, won for him their great respect and affection." Indeed, the idea of the "Soldiers' Friend" served as a standard foundational piece of Morton's legacy. Burnside also complicated historical memory by discussing how Morton had opposed the general's arrest of a number of Northern civilians for treason when they made speeches criticizing Morton, Abraham Lincoln, and other Republicans for their wartime conduct. While others would remember Morton for attacking those who opposed the war, Burnside recalled that the governor had fought for the dissenters and had demanded the release of a state senator who "was one of his most bitter political opponents." Burnside had experienced Morton's wrath firsthand when the governor resisted his departmental command, but he now memorialized his old political foe in a measured way. Such an account fit well in the days following the end of Reconstruction, as politicians rushed to set aside past bitterness in the name of reconciling differences and healing old wounds.[5]

But some of Morton's Senate colleagues were not ready to let go of the past. When Reconstruction ended in Alabama, the Democrats returned to power in the state legislature and elected John Tyler Morgan to the US Senate in 1877. Morgan was a spokesman for the Lost Cause who had championed the end of Reconstruction in the South. A lifelong Democrat, he had fought for the Confederacy, rising to the rank of general. At the end of the war, Morgan remained a staunch defender of slavery and state's rights, and he was probably a leader of the Ku Klux Klan during Reconstruction. Indeed, he supported legal lynching and promoted racial segregation and white supremacy for the remainder of his long senatorial career. When Reconstruction ended in Alabama, the Democrats returned to power in the state legislature and elected Morgan to the senate. The Southern Democrat noted that Indiana had "suffered a bereavement in the death of an honored son" and claimed that Alabama extended her condolences, complete with "emblems of peace" and feelings of sympathy and friendship. But Morgan quickly moved on to his main point, arguing that Morton "did not live to see the states all reassembled in this Chamber," discrediting with a sentence the Republican governments that had controlled the Southern states during Reconstruction and for which the Indiana senator had fought long and hard. Morgan grumbled that Morton had resisted the return of the Democrats in the South "under his views of the Constitution" and recalled that "States stood arrayed against him."[6]

The Senate's new voice of the Lost Cause couched his remarks in the language of reconciliation: Morton had "believed that he was compelled to lay his hand on the sword of military power. He grasped it firmly. He wielded it without pause or questioning, but with perfect loyalty to his country. In this he only did his duty; for the country of his soul's allegiance required it of him." Speaking of the politician as a soldier reflected the style of reconciliation and the Lost Cause, both of which extolled the courage and virtue of those who had fought for that in which they believed. But while the Alabama leader could forgive Morton for his actions in the war, he could not forget that the Indiana statesman had been a Radical Republican during Reconstruction: "When others thought that the sword had served its full purpose and should be sheathed . . . he held to it with a firmer grasp." Remembering how Morton had waved the bloody shirt throughout the postwar period, the unreconstructed Southerner noted that "in this the South was opposed to him, and its wail of anguish was bitter against him. While he held the sword suspended the South had no shield for its uncovered bosom."[7]

Even as Morgan complained about Morton as the enemy of the South, he made excuses for his criticisms of the late statesman, saying that he was sure that Morton would have asked for no less, would have made "no plea for lenient consideration. His opinions are too bold and too broadly and confidently stated to be diverted off into neutral ground." The Alabamian predicted that Morton's views, though flawed, would "always be respected." Morgan argued, implausibly, that the differences between Morton and the South were those of opinion: "The hostility was not in the intent or the purpose." Rather, the differences between the North and South were "based on misconceptions of fact, the correction of which other evil influences rendered for the time impossible." Morton's war to save the Union and support of Radical Reconstruction became a misunderstanding that, in a different context, the combatants might have avoided. Thus, one defiant supporter of the Lost Cause couched his eulogy in the language of reconciliation. Rather than honoring Morton, the Southern Democrat seemed to taunt the fallen champion as he celebrated Redemption and the defeat of the principles for which the Hoosier Republican had fought.[8]

Several other Republicans continued the earlier arguments made by Edmunds and added remarks about Morton's fight against slavery and racial inequality. Then the senator from Mississippi, Blanche Bruce, stood and delivered a eulogy that focused on Morton's fight for emancipation and equality. An African American Republican elected in 1875, Bruce represented well those aspects of the Civil War that the Lost Cause preferred to forget. Born a slave in Virginia, Bruce gained his freedom when his master—also his father—manumitted him and sent him off as an apprentice to learn a trade. He worked as a printer, and when the Union Army rejected him as a volunteer because of his race, he attended Oberlin College. After a stint as a steamboat pilot, he opened a school for blacks in Missouri. When the war ended, Bruce moved to Mississippi, where he bought land and entered politics during Reconstruction. The second black man elected to the US Senate, he held Jefferson Davis's old seat until 1880, when he lost to a white Southern Democrat. In his memorial address in 1878, Bruce predicted that in the future Morton's views would be as "revered as are now those of the fathers of the Republic." Speaking as an African American leader and a friend of the

Indiana senator, Bruce argued that "no public man of his day, with the possible exception of Abraham Lincoln and Charles Sumner, was better known to the colored people of the South than Oliver P. Morton, and none more respected and revered."[9]

Bruce recalled that Morton had initially been reluctant to give the vote to the freedmen but had changed his mind. The senator insisted that Morton should be judged on his later actions—especially his leadership in the fight for the Fifteenth Amendment—rather than his momentary hesitation. Morton's work in the Senate, he claimed, rested on two fundamental issues: first, that the "emancipation of more than four millions of former bondsmen was an accomplished fact"; and, second, that the "political relations of eleven great communities were ruptured and imperatively demanded restoration." These two issues of emancipation and Reconstruction of the Southern states, according to Bruce, were related and revolutionary. Emancipation "involved reorganization of both the social and industrial elements of the South," and Morton had believed that a "just, harmonious, peaceful" process "demanded the enfranchisement of the negro." The freedman needed the right to vote because true freedom "could only be sufficiently attained when he was clothed with the power of self-protection by becoming a personal and actual participant in the creation and administration of government." The progress of black Southerners during the 1870s attested to the potential power of egalitarianism, but policies promoting equality were already beginning to fade as Southern Redeemers took political control. For Morton, Reconstruction of the South could be achieved fully only when black Americans were "equally protected by the law and enjoyed citizenship and the right to vote. The Indiana senator, Bruce stated, "looked not only to the elevation of a race but the Reconstruction of a great country." That his vision for the future was now fading did not diminish the importance of what Morton had helped to accomplish.[10]

Senator Bruce concluded that all Americans owed Morton a debt of gratitude, but African Americans especially loved and respected him and his faithful loyalty to their cause. Coming after the end of Reconstruction, as more Americans were turning their backs on racial equality, Bruce's speech stood as a bold contrast to Morgan's Lost Cause narrative and he offered a far more radical recollection of Morton than the one that focused on the Unionist war governor and friend of the soldiers.[11]

In the House of Representatives, none of the majority Democrats chose to participate in the event and the speakers were all Northern Republicans. Such partisanship marked the lower chamber of Congress and reflected the ways in which many Democrats refused to forget the past. Congressman John Hanna, a Republican from Greencastle, Indiana, remembered that "the preservation of the Union in the interest of liberty and humanity was with [Morton] a conviction of duty so intense that no earthly power ever presented obstacles which he deemed insurmountable." Hanna argued that Morton had helped extinguish "a heresy which has cost so much blood and treasure—that we are simply a confederation of States, bound only by a rope of sand." The Greencastle politician also evoked the issue of emancipation, remarking that Morton "was equally devoted to securing beyond all question for the weak and humble the inalienable rights of man." Congressman Thomas M. Browne from Winchester, Indiana, recalled that "to the cause of the Union" Morton "consecrated every energy and impulse" and said that "to him the war was a contest in which slavery was measuring swords with free representative government, and he believed the victory of the insurgents would be the doom of the Republic." Other speakers sidestepped the issues of Union and slavery by focusing on Morton's personal qualities. August A. Hardenburgh of New Jersey waxed on in flowery language about Morton's public spirit and future US President James A. Garfield of Ohio spent time talking about the late leader's organizational skills and force of will. All of them agreed that Morton had been a significant leader blessed with great abilities.[12]

However, even in these early accounts, Americans expressed different views of Morton. Everyone commended his energy, his organizational skills, his great leadership abilities, and his commitment to the Union. Almost everyone recalled his dedication to his party, his tireless support of the soldiers, and his love of freedom. Some eulogists talked about his legal career and the power of his intellect. Almost all of them extolled the force of his oratory, his habit of stating clearly, even bluntly, what he meant. They lamented the decline of his health and praised him for continuing to work after strokes left him paralyzed. Even his enemies recognized that he could be a warm and loyal friend, although many also noted that he could be ruthless to those who crossed him. But beyond the consistent themes that united the memorials, different eulogists presented different views of Morton that reflected their memories of the Civil War. Therefore, African Americans remembered him differently than did unreconstructed ex-Confederates; Northern Democrats focused on personal matters rather than sharing the Unionist recollections of Republicans.[13]

A Phrenological Memory

The same month as the congressional eulogies, the *Phrenological Journal and Life Illustrated* published a study of Morton. Written by Professor Alexander Wilder, one of the country's leading phrenologists, the January 1878 article combined the widely popular interest in science and pseudoscience with a Unionist memory of the Civil War. Based on the scientific idea that local areas of the brain controlled certain parts of the mind, phrenology moved into pseudoscience with arguments about the shape and size of the skull and how that determined one's thoughts, actions, and personal traits. The phrenologist wrote that Morton's head and body indicated his character and personality, remarking that the senator was solid and stocky, which meant that he was strong and vital. Wilder also contended that Morton possessed "a massive forehead, the upper part of which is large, indicating intellectual force, breadth of thought and purpose, and ability to comprehend matters of extended and weighty character." He went on to argue that the Hoosier leader's skull indicated an acquisitive nature as well as a tendency toward destruction and combat. Wilder argued that Morton was courageous and thorough and had the qualities to be a strong executive officer. Despite his fighting characteristics, the professor thought that the senator was also a generous "man of liberal spirit" who wanted to do good and help others. His analysis found that Morton should have avoided "coffee, tobacco, and all excesses in food" as well as alcohol. This was because "excess at table kills its hundreds."[14]

After providing his expert phrenological perspective with the benefit of hindsight, the phrenologist outlined the facts of Morton's life and career in Unionist terms. He hailed the Hoosier politician's patriotism and outlined his work to raise and supply the troops in defense of the Union. He noted that while some had thought that Southerners were really patriots devoted to the Union and would not secede, Morton had not doubted that they were rebels and traitors. Wilder quoted his subject at length, mustering the late politician's words as evidence of his hatred of rebellion and love of the Union. He recalled the governor's efforts on behalf of the soldiers and in rooting out the Copperheads. He also touched on Morton's "investigations of the Ku-Klux organizations of the South," declaring that he "was as earnest as ever in favor of vigorous measures to enforce the laws" of Reconstruction. However accurate his claim to science might or might not have been, the phrenologist clearly expressed a pro-Northern interpretation of Morton and the war that did not forget about rebellion, race, and Reconstruction.[15]

THE GRAND ARMY OF THE REPUBLIC

Across the ensuing years, as anniversaries and memorial dedications returned the nation's attention to the Civil War and Reconstruction, they also provided opportunities for remembering Morton's career and historical legacy. Of course, the family's private grief also continued. Writing home to his mother from Oxford University in England in 1881, Oliver T. Morton, the widow's youngest son, noted the fourth anniversary of his father's death. He said that the thought of "that terrible day fills me with great grief" and cried out, "Oh,

Mother, if you only knew how my heart goes out to you tonight, how much I love you." He encouraged her to "bear up, my darling, Mother." He knew that nothing could make up for the loss of her husband but assured her that the love of her children could bring her comfort.[16]

Public memories continued as well. On November 1, 1891, the fourteenth anniversary of Morton's death, Republican lawyer and politician William P. Fishback delivered an address to the Grand Army of the Republic (GAR) encampment in Indianapolis. He argued that Morton was the greatest states-man that Indiana had ever produced, and he recalled that long before other leaders, including Lincoln, recognized the reality of secession, "Morton pro-claimed that there should be no compromise with rebels." Fishback picked up on a theme that often reappeared over the decades following the Civil War, as speakers hinted at sinister conspiracies designed to undermine the Union victory when rallying the GAR members for political purposes. He asserted that there were dark forces at work in politics—a matter of consequence in his own career as a civil service reformer and advocate for education. Then, looking back at the scene of Morton's career during the war, he noted "in the background other forms, dark, ambiguous, and sinister, the shadows of those who were deaf to the calls of patriotism, who sulked in the hour of battle or caballed and conspired to cripple and defeat the Union army."[17]

Recalling Morton's struggles against the Copperheads, Fishback also re-minded the gathered veterans that Morton—in contrast to his enemies—had been the Soldiers' Friend, purchasing overcoats for Hoosier troops, creating the Indiana Sanitary Commission to keep the men supplied, and making efforts to treat the wounded at the front and bring them home to Indiana hospitals for care. In return, he recalled, the soldiers supported Morton politically, both as governor and as senator, making it a reciprocal relationship between the politician and his constituency. Of Morton's Senate service, Fishback called to mind his role in "the Reconstruction legislation and the constitutional amendments" and in leading the Radical Republican effort to help African Americans in the South. The Republican speaker also recounted Morton's powerful 1868 speech on Reconstruction that "was an assault upon the policy of President Johnson, who was organizing governments in the seceded States upon the basis of white population alone." Morton had defended "the congres-sional plan which was to go upon the basis of loyalty to the Nation, regardless of color." Such remarks were significant in light of the fact that Republicans had recently pushed for a bill to enforce the Fifteenth Amendment but had failed to pass it in the face of a Senate filibuster. With the egalitarian vision of Reconstruction fading in the South, where Mississippi had disenfranchised African Americans, the inclusion of Morton's staunch support for it signaled an attempt to rally Republican voters to renew the fight. Fishback closed his address with the senator's "dying words, that he was 'worn out'—worn out in the service of his State and Nation."[18]

In his 1891 speech, Fishback remembered the aspects of Morton's career—his efforts to clean up politics and his work in starting the Indiana law school—that spoke to the attorney's own interests in reforming society. But Fishback also used Morton to remind the Union veterans of the cause which they had fought, recalling the past in ways that rallied his listeners to continue their support for reform and for the Republican Party. Morton had worked to earn the soldiers' support during his lifetime, and for many years after his death, his memory remained a potent means of mustering veterans to vote for Republicans.[19]

PUTTING MORTON IN STATUARY HALL

Different views of Morton that hinged on shifting historical explanations came into play again in 1900. The federal government had allowed each state to put two statues in the Capitol's Statuary Hall, and Indiana chose the state's first to memorialize Morton, passing a law commissioning the monument in 1897. Although the Democrats had quickly returned to power in Indiana following the Civil War, the Republicans generally dominated national politics, and this helped to set the stage for the 1900 portrayals of Morton. As the century closed, the United States had finished its western expansion even as the population rose, fueled by immigration and internal growth. The growth of industrial capitalism created immense national wealth and power, but battles between labor and management brought violence and upheaval. In 1896 the US Supreme Court had established racial segregation in *Plessy v. Ferguson*. The case legally confirmed the power of white supremacy and marked the abandonment of African Americans freed by the Civil War. A new generation of Americans who had not known slavery in their lifetimes embraced the doctrine of "separate but equal," and a majority of white Americans advocated segregation in the North as well as the South. The populist movement that had animated politics waned in the late 1890s, especially after the Spanish-American War in 1898, and nationalism reigned supreme in the wake of military victory. The United Sates seemed poised for greatness, and on April 14, 1900, as Indiana's senators joined colleagues in celebrating the acceptance of the Morton statue, their speeches expressed the nationalism inherent in their own time and connected that to the Civil War era and Morton's own career.[20]

Senator Charles W. Fairbanks of Indianapolis began his address with emancipation, noting that Morton came from Wayne County, Indiana, where the people "have been intensely patriotic and liberty loving. The institution of

Fig. 57. Morton statue, Statuary Hall, US Capitol, Washington, DC. (National Statuary Hall Collection, Architect of the Capitol)

human slavery was repugnant to them, and they were strongly antislavery prior to the civil war. The 'underground railroad' had many stations in that part of the State, where countless colored refugees found succor and asylum in their search for liberty." After recounting Morton's early career, Fairbanks quoted at length from the governor's words in defense of the Union. Morton had recognized the dangerous nature of secession long before others did, realizing that it threatened to destroy the nation. The Civil War governor had remained firm, and "when others doubted he was certain. Compromise was impossible, for right and wrong opposed each other. Freedom and slavery were engaged for the mastery; there could be no compromise." Fairbanks, an important adviser to President William McKinley during the Spanish-American War, had crafted a historical analysis that fit well with his own nationalist views of war and American power.[21]

The soon-to-be vice president told how Morton had supported Lincoln and that he "was, indeed, the soldiers' friend" both during and after the war and did not forget that "provision was to be made for the widow and the orphan by a grateful Republic." After outlining Morton's work as war governor, Fairbanks turned to his career in the Senate, explaining that the nation had to be rebuilt without abandoning the cause of African American freedom, as "a race must be secured in the rights of citizenship." Fairbanks himself had interceded on behalf of black soldiers during the war with Spain, and despite his conservative philosophy (or perhaps because of it), he held fast to ideas of racial equality.[22]

Now he argued that Senator Morton "possessed convictions, and convictions possessed him" and that he had proved himself "an aggressive and zealous advocate of the policy of Reconstruction." The speaker recounted Morton's 1868 Reconstruction speech and quoted its nationalist sentiments: "The States are but subordinate parts of one great nation. The Nation is over all, even as God is over the universe." Fairbanks also said that "it was largely due to his championship that the fourteenth and fifteenth amendments to the Constitution were adopted." He again quoted Morton, recalling how the senator had rejected "the appeal of prejudice of race against race; the endeavor to excite the strong against the weak; the effort to deprive the weak of their right of protection against the strong."[23]

Remembering Morton's fight for racial equality mattered in the years following the 1896 landmark Supreme Court decision in *Plessy v. Ferguson*. Fairbanks's analysis challenged prevailing attitudes about white supremacy but were couched in terms easily understood to an audience living in the early stages of the Progressive Era, when reformers hoped to curb the excesses of capitalism and battle sin in the name of extending the American Dream. Helping the weak, the poor, the downtrodden meant much to voters at the turn of the century—and Fairbanks knew that his own party often led the way in calling for reform and government action. Lionizing Morton as both the Civil War governor and Reconstruction Senator, Fairbanks portrayed him in heroic terms that included his support for the Union, the soldiers, the veterans, war widows and orphans, and African Americans.[24]

Indiana's junior senator, Albert J. Beveridge, rose to remember Morton in even more overtly nationalist terms. Elected the previous year, Beveridge—a longtime rival of Fairbanks—was a progressive reformer and spokesman for imperialism, who held to a nationalist ideology that combined religious zeal with intellectual rigor. He would later express his own nationalism in his writing of history, including works on Lincoln and Chief Justice John Marshall. Still in the early days of the first of his two Senate terms, he began his speech by invoking the Almighty, arguing that "great men are the instruments of God." Morton, he declared, had been divinely inspired to save the Union and to provide for the soldiers and their families. Beveridge thought that the governor had done it all "in a holy cause. A single passionate belief inspired his life—a single irresistible resolution. A Nation in reality the American people ought to be, and a Nation in reality he would give his powers to make us."[25]

In this view, Morton was a national statesman, one of "God's incarnations of national life." Like Lincoln, the Hoosier statesman had understood that only in the nation could "the sovereignty of the people, the prosperity of the people, the happiness and safety of the people" be secured. Beveridge discussed the governor's wartime career at length before returning to his main theme: "Morton's whole career was based upon profound belief in the common people," in "the living vital, human faith of one who in himself is of the people. That is why he was a Nationalist." Speaking to a Progressive Era audience just after the Spanish-American War, the Republican reformer merged Morton's nationalism with his own.[26]

Beveridge celebrated the fact that Morton had been a partisan politician, arguing that "America needs to-day more partisanship like that." Morton's dedication to party showed that he "understood that principles were greater than personalities, and that a party standing for a principle is greater than any man standing for a personality." Because he believed "in the sovereignty of an idea," Morton led his party to save the Union and used his power as a party leader to destroy slavery. Beveridge argued that, thanks to Morton, "slavery is gone forever, and on the seat of independence, dignity, and power, free labor sits enthroned. . . . Thought is free, speech is free; liberty at last is dwelling among the sons of men." The future historian placed Morton among "the heroes of the people" who "led the people's cause to victory, and enshrined the people's rights in the people's imperishable Nation." Champion of the people, defender of the Union, supporter of freedom, partisan of principle, hero of the nation, Morton stood tall in a story that clearly displayed the continuing vitality of a nationalist memory of the Civil War era amid calls for expanding an American empire in the new age of Progressive reform.[27]

Speakers in the House of Representatives also presented their historical interpretations of Morton, and, once again, the subject of Morton proved a complicated matter. Indiana's George W. Steele recounted how Morton had attacked "the hateful doctrine" of state's rights. Fellow Hoosier Abraham L. Brick said that for Morton, the "Union was more sacred than even human blood, than his own life." Another Indiana Republican, Jesse Overstreet, contended that the War of the Rebellion had brought Morton his opportunity for greatness and emphasized "his courageous stand for the Union" and dedication to the soldiers. Many of the speakers discussed how Morton had rooted out traitors in Indiana, thwarting the efforts of the Copperheads, and nearly all praised his efforts as the Soldiers' Friend.[28]

Emancipation remained an important part of the story, as Ohio's Charles H. Grosvenor talked about how Morton "entered upon a war against the proslavery tendencies of the Democratic party" and New York's De Alva S. Alexander analyzed Morton's close association with Charles Sumner and their collaborative "efforts to secure the passage and ratification of the fifteenth amendment." Edgar D. Crumpacker of Indiana continued the focus on emancipation when he recalled that slavery had been the cause of the Civil War: "Slavery became aggressive and demanded new territory," but Morton, "a man of powerful convictions . . . dedicated to the cause of human liberty," resisted that aggression. Hoosier James E. Watson used the occasion to argue that slavery "ruled this entire nation with absolute sway." He described how Southern slavery "sought to tear the Stars and Stripes into shreds and from the tattered fragments to construct the Stars and Bars. She sought to crush the Union, and from its ruins to erect a new nation, whose foundation should be the stooping and lacerated backs of 4,000,000 human beings."[29]

While the Republicans harkened back to Morton's fight against slavery, the Democrats in the spring of 1900 remembered him from a very different perspective. Indiana's Robert W. Miers admitted that Morton worked tirelessly despite his health problems and remained strong in his convictions. But Miers also reminisced that "his life was one constant criticism and censure; he made strong friends and bitter enemies." Continuing, Miers said, "We regret that the conditions of his time made him violent in some of his methods." The Hoosier Democrat then made the argument that Morton had still been a great man whose "services to his State and his nation will live forever, while the enmities which he engendered have already been buried." Another Indiana Democrat,

Francis M. Griffith, pointed out that Morton was the subject of much criticism and that he was greatly feared by many, especially his political enemies. But "old prejudices are forgotten," Griffith said, offering reconciliation: "The sound of hasty words has died away. We can view Oliver P. Morton as he really was, and Democrats can unite with Republicans to-day in doing homage to that iron will and great intellect which assisted to restore order out of chaos in Indiana and assisted in guiding the ship of state safely through the most stormy waters it ever encountered."[30]

A Memorial to the Great War Governor

Seven years later, Hoosiers officially bestowed on Morton the title of Great War Governor. The GAR had proposed that the state erect a monument to Morton in front of the east entrance of the Indiana State Capitol. Indiana lawmakers dutifully responded to the veterans with a bill that provided for the statue, stating, in Unionist terms, that "No man in civil life, save Abraham Lincoln, did more for the Union during the Civil War than Oliver P. Morton, the great War Governor of Indiana," and appropriating $35,000 dollars to fund it. On July 23, 1907, the statue was dedicated, complete with a parade, a full band, and a crowd of thousands singing "America." Morton's widow and son-in-law, Lucinda Morton and William R. Holloway, evaluated and approved the planning for the statue, ensuring that it would memorialize Morton as a hero of the Union. Although it left out his contributions to Reconstruction, the bronze tablet on the monument boldly stated the sentiments of nationalism and continued the now-familiar Progressive Era themes regarding Morton and the Civil War: "Oliver Perry Morton . . . In all ways and at all times the friend of the Union soldier, the friend of the country, the upholder of Abraham Lincoln, the defender of the flag and the Union of the States. Patriot, statesman, lover of liberty, heroic in heart, inflexible in purpose, and ever to be known as THE GREAT WAR GOVERNOR [emphasis in the original]."[31]

The dedication speeches began with Warren R. King, a GAR leader and president of the monument commission, who remembered fallen comrades and living brothers in arms who carried the scars of battle. King suggested that the monument to Morton was also a symbol of something much larger: it would not only commemorate the war governor but would "also perpetuate the fact that the citizens of Indiana who lived at the time of its building did not lack in three of the greatest virtues, love, memory, and gratitude."[32]

Governor J. Frank Hanly followed with flowery oratory, accepting the statue on behalf of the state. He, too, argued that Morton's monument was a symbol of something greater. The statue would "tell the story of a people's crucial trial," a matter of importance at a time when Hanly was pushing for

Fig. 58. Morton monument, Indiana State Capitol. (W. H. Bass Photo Company Collection, Indiana Historical Society)

progressive reforms in Indiana. The Republican governor listed Morton's many accomplishments, especially in preparing Hoosier soldiers for war. Speaking to his Progressive Era audience, Hanly argued that the Morton story was one "of love and pity and tender care for the sick and wounded, the widowed and the fatherless; of a state betrayed and yet preserved; of days of toil and nights of waking; of high resolve, of solemn consecration; of carnage and of sacrifice; of wounds and death and prison walls." Yet the monument would also remind those who saw it "of a land redeemed . . . of a government saved from dishonor and dismemberment; of the establishment of national solidarity, of peace achieved, of a union reconstructed; of slavery abolished by constitutional enactment." Thus, Hanly brought together Union and emancipation in a nationalist vision of the Civil War. Morton had become a symbol of the nation "in its unity, and in its indivisibility." His statue stood to remind future generations that the nationalist Civil War leader had "freely admitted that it would cost much to save the Union (how much none knew better than he), but insisted that it would cost everything to lose it."[33]

Detailing the many contributions that the war governor had made during the Civil War, Governor Hanly held forth for a long time more, praising Morton for his efforts, excusing him for those times when he acted "outside the constitution and beyond the law," because he did so "always for the public good." In an era of progressive reform, one's good intentions mattered, even if it involved redefining the law. Hanly's own progressive agenda achieved little, as the conservative Democrats in the state legislature thwarted most of his efforts. A supporter of Prohibition before, during, and after his term as governor, he did not live to see the unintended consequences of that policy. But as he spoke that day in 1907, the governor, eager to reform Indiana in light of his own moral principles, told his audience that, before Morton, "the state had not known his equal, nor shall we know his like again, till in the unfolding purpose of the Infinite another crisis great as that in which he lived bursts upon the land, and his great soul reincarnated returns to earth to lead again his countrymen through its gloom and sacrifice."[34]

When the governor finally completed his flowery speech, Vice President Fairbanks responded to calls from the audience and spoke extemporaneously. Although scheduled to make a speech to the GAR gathering that night, Fairbanks took the opportunity to affirm that Morton was a symbol for Indiana and the nation: "We have met, it is said, to do honor to the memory of Oliver P. Morton. That is in a sense true, but in a larger sense, we have met to do honor to the people of our state. For we honor ourselves when we honor those who have done arduous service in the cause of liberty." He also argued that Morton stood as a symbol of "republican institutions" and extolled the virtues of liberty and republican government.[35]

The afternoon ceremonies closed with a group of ladies from the Daughters of the American Revolution laying a wreath on the pedestal of the monument and the president of the Woman's Relief Corps putting a folded silk flag beside it. That evening, Vice President Fairbanks continued the celebration in his brief remarks to the Union veterans, remembering that Morton had worked to save the Union and adding that, as senator, "he did much to secure the adoption of the fourteenth and fifteenth amendments to the Constitution of the United States." Speaking before an audience dominated by Union veterans and their families, Fairbanks again brought together emancipation and the Union in a nationalist ideology that made Oliver P. Morton a symbol of the state and the nation, of freedom and equality, of American power and American victory.[36]

THE CALL OF OLIVER P. MORTON

But his memory mattered at the local level, too. Sixteen years after the dedication of the statue at the statehouse, on Friday evening, August 3, 1923, residents of Centerville, Indiana, gathered to observe the centennial of Morton's birth. A full weekend of activities renewed interest in the life of the town's most important native, while also reviving a sense of pride in Wayne County residents. The festivities included speeches by Morton biographer William Dudley Foulke and the current governor of Indiana, Warren T. McCray, but history was accompanied by music, invocations, the reading of poems dedicated to the governor, and a triple parachute jump. The central event came in the form of a play, "The Call of Oliver P. Morton," written by Bessie M. Buhl, and performed in the high school auditorium to an audience of more than five hundred people. Miss Buhl's drama illustrated how Hoosiers constructed historical memory in ways that interwove the life of the governor with the history of the community. The play invoked the Civil War while also extolling the virtues of Morton's ideology in a nationalist portrayal that reflected much about the celebrants' own time. In commemorating their native son, Centerville's residents also told a story about themselves.[37]

The pageant included characters looking back at the founding of Centerville, and it related the story of the town's first hanging—of an African American man convicted of murdering another black man. Including such a fact meant much in Indiana in the 1920s, as it was the era of the Ku Klux Klan's popularity in the state, and the lynching of black men in the Hoosier State became an all-too-frequent occurrence. Buhl did not have to include the story, but doing so spoke loudly to many white citizens in her own time.[38]

Her selection of music for the drama included several hymns, another example of the playwright's context shaping her historical account, as Christianity had not only remained strong but had expanded its influence in the Hoosier State. Regardless of her subject's religious views, Buhl made sure that songs like "The Sweet Bye and Bye," and "Nearer, My God, To Thee," were part of the centennial. Christian faith also played a prominent role in the play itself, as Buhl had characters invoking divine blessings on three-year-old Oliver Morton, whose later love of reading centered on the Bible. While he did read the scriptures thoroughly, Buhl made no mention of other books the young man might have read. Instead, she wrote long conversations in which Morton discussed the Ten Commandments and promised to read the Bible through every year. Doing so made the past relevant to Indiana's present, a time when Evangelical Christianity and fundamentalism were gaining new strength. Although Morton was not a devout Christian, Buhl made him seem like one in order to make him fit more comfortably in her own time.[39]

Other parts of the play further indicated the context of the 1920s. Buhl's emphasis on education certainly mirrored Morton's own passion for learning, but she also spoke to a Progressive Era audience. They understood the "call of education" to be the public education system of the twentieth century, instead of what Morton had experienced decades earlier. So, too, the playwright's nationalism spoke of her own time, as the drama dripped patriotism. Morton's own nationalist ideology certainly included his devotion to the United States, but Buhl expressed a full-throated nationalism that took such love of country to new levels. As a song entitled "The Weaving of the Flag" played, "six fairies, in white," danced across the stage. The fairies recited lines about courage, purity, and hope during an imagined dream of young Morton that spoke volumes to a post–World War I audience. From her opening with the founding of Centerville to the closing patriotic lines spoken to the Civil War veterans seated front and center, Buhl revived Morton in the terms of the 1920s. In doing so she defined the meaning of the Civil War in ways that her audience could understand and embrace. Yet, even as she constructed a memory for her own time, the playwright did capture some of the essence of her subject and continued the tradition of Hoosiers and Americans remembering Morton in ways vital to their present.[40]

Morton at Vicksburg

About three years later, on Wednesday, June 16, 1926, a large party of visitors made their way to the Indiana Circle at the Vicksburg Battlefield National Military Park in Mississippi to dedicate the Hoosier State's battlefield monument. Although most state monuments on such battlefields depicted a famous general or combat hero or tried to memorialize the common soldier who had fought there, Indiana had chosen to erect a statue of Oliver P. Morton. In the late afternoon sun, the quiet ceremony began with the unveiling of "Morton in Bronze." The dedication poem and the speeches that followed oozed nationalism, but this was not the same memory that previous generations had admired. Instead, participants in the ceremony now explained the Civil War in the vocabulary of reconciliation. Slavery and emancipation received scant attention; the fight for the Union was no longer triumphant but was seen as equal to the Southern cause. For the sake of reconciliation, the language of friendship encompassed treating both sides as noble and patriotic Americans, recognizing the bravery of the individual soldiers, and not remembering the causes of the conflict.[41]

Clearly, things had changed. Morton still stood as a symbol of nationalism and the Civil War, and those who had opposed him during his lifetime still managed to reconstitute their memories of him in ways that conveniently forgot past battles over issues like race, slavery, and the power of the national government. Morton had not changed, but the historical context of his memorialization had. By the mid-1920s the expansion of industrial capitalism, urbanization, and world war had transformed Indiana. With modernity came tensions, as people looked for answers to many bewildering new questions about economic change, immigration, the migration of African Americans from the South to northern states, the role of government in Progressive reforms, and social and cultural shifts. By the 1920s segregation was taking hold in many northern areas as well as the South. White supremacy, long an accepted view, remained the law under Jim Crow. It was not surprising that in such a context historical memory of the Civil War also began to change, as many chose to forget race, slavery, and emancipation. Emancipationist memories—still held by African Americans and some whites—began to diminish as more Union veterans passed away and new generations constructed different interpretations of the past.[42]

Like other Americans, Hoosiers responded to this transformative period in a variety of ways. Defense of tradition and community came in many forms. Many returned to religion, as some Christians embraced progressive reform while others chose a nonpolitical path or pursued a more fundamentalist faith. Another response was the growth in popularity of various "patriotic" organizations. The American Legion and various fraternal orders attracted individuals worried about the loss of community and wanting some way to band together in order to deal with change. In that era of "joining," many white Hoosiers turned to the Ku Klux Klan. The Klan in Indiana wrapped itself in the American flag and held high the Christian cross. This state branch of the second Klan that rose in the early twentieth century often emphasized anti-immigrant sentiments, a popular stance in Indiana, where many feared losing their jobs to ethnic minorities. To be sure, the hatred of blacks that dominated in the South also animated the Indiana Klan, as racism fueled lynching and the creation of "sundown towns"—towns in which African Americans were likely to be killed if they remained there after the sun went down—in the Hoosier State. The arrival in the state of many African Americans from the South during the early twentieth century's great migration exacerbated racial tensions.

By 1925 at least a quarter of white male Hoosiers belonged to the Ku Klux Klan, and the organization held political influence. Many Hoosier politicians joined the hooded order, mostly at the local level, but their ranks included some state legislators as well. In the 1924 gubernatorial election, Edward L. Jackson, the Republican, openly accepted Klan support. Jackson won the election by almost one hundred thousand votes and carried ninety of the state's ninety-two counties. It looked as though the Ku Klux Klan now had a governor with whom the organization could work to bring about the reforms they hoped would mitigate the strain of rapid change.[43]

It was in this context that the 1926 dedication of the Morton statue at the Vicksburg Battlefield took place. This monument came at the behest of the Vicksburg National Military Park Commission, headed up by William T. Rigby, a Union veteran from Iowa who had fought in the Vicksburg campaign as well as other major battles. The federal government established the Vicksburg National Military Park in 1899, and Rigby then received his appointment as the resident commissioner. The commission designed the park for the convenience of tourists, including a plan for each state to have a circle with various monuments, including a large statue dedicated to that state. When the commission invited Indiana to erect its statue on the Indiana Circle, the state legislature appropriated $15,000 for the project and appointed a commission to take up "where the Commission of 1908 left off." Harkening back to the Morton statue at the State Capitol spoke volumes, both in the content and sentiments behind the state memorial at Vicksburg. First, Indiana chose to replicate its earlier shrine by building a statue of Oliver P. Morton, still their symbol of the Civil War. Second, the 1926 statue would be similar to the 1907 sculpture in that Morton would symbolize nationalism. But those similarities belied real differences between 1907 and 1926.[44]

The 1926 commission report, published as *Morton in Bronze,* revealed both the similarities and the differences between the efforts behind the two statues and showed the different ways in which Hoosiers constructed their account of the Civil War. The biggest difference involved race. While the 1907 dedication mentioned slavery, emancipation, and the Reconstruction amendments, the 1926 ceremonies did not. Slavery came into the later report only in extracts taken from an article by Foulke. Contained in an early section of the booklet-length report, the Foulke extracts provided "A Sketch of the 'Great War Governor.'" The few lines about slavery stated that Morton had broken with the Democratic Party over slavery and had joined the Republicans in opposing it. Foulke's two-volume biography had detailed the ways in which Morton's views on slavery changed and how he became staunchly opposed to the institution; the 1926 extracts were few and carefully chosen. The booklet quoted Foulke on the late 1850s: "During the next four years the pro-slavery element won the supremacy but the Dred Scott decision and the Lecompton

Constitution aroused the anti-slavery sentiment of the North and added to the strength of the Republican party." That was it. Not another word about slavery appeared in the speeches at the dedication or in the sixty-four-page report, except for a passing anecdotal reference to slave quarters located near a mansion in a veteran's account of a battle. And those few lines dedicated to slavery made the abolitionists as much a cause of the war as the defenders of the peculiar institution. Clearly, Hoosiers excised slavery and emancipation from their history when they dedicated their Vicksburg monument.[45]

Americans still held a vibrant nationalist vision, but it, too, had changed. The 1907 dedication had emphasized the cause of the Union, celebrating the North's victory, with only passing nods to later reconciliation. In 1926 the celebrants inverted the two, as the nationalist perspective now rested on a foundation of reconciliation, with the Union victory pushed to the background. While no speaker at Vicksburg managed to rival the flowery oration of Governor Hanly in 1907, the nationalist poem read by Captain Francis M. Van Pelt, a member of the commission and a Union veteran, almost reached such levels. "To the Statue of Morton," the poem, ran on for more than three pages in the published report. In his opening stanzas the poet evoked the Union cause, drawing attention to how the image of Morton brought memories of the great conflict. The poem remembered that time: "When waves of secession caused well nigh to dip / Our old union vessel; he stood by the ship, with red, white and blue at the mast." Then, a few lines later, he trumpeted: "We'll now nail this motto high up overhead, / *One country, one Morton, one flag* [emphasis in the original]."[46]

This nationalism conjured up images of reconciliation with the South, not a record of Union victory: "Flag that takes us way back yonder / 'Neath historic apple tree, / Where one chieftain makes surrender, / And while shaking hands with Lee. / Grant said, 'Thank God comes the ending / Of this bitter, cruel war, / Now let's put our time in mending, / Healing up the bloody scar.'" Appomattox now became a hastening toward reunion and a nation reconciled.[47]

In 1907 Governor Hanly had charged the South with "despotism," "error," and "dishonor," while hailing Morton as a tower of "magnificent manhood," who "crushed and overwhelmed" his foes in defense of moral right. In contrast, in 1926 the poet said very little about Morton himself, rushing on from Appomattox to reconcile the North and South in the Spanish-American War of 1898: "When the cry from Cuba came, / Blue and gray interwoven / Under one flag just the same. / O'er each school house, north and southland, / One flag flutters in the breeze, / Not alone at home but elsewhere / Far away o'er foreign seas." Then came the Boxer Rebellion in China: "Later on when Major Conger, / Standing for the Christian world / In command at siege of Peking /

Fig. 59. Morton at Vicksburg. (National Park Service Photo, United States Department of the Interior)

The first flag he saw unfurled / That was coming to his rescue / There in China, could it be? / Twas the same one he marched under / From Atlanta to the sea." From there, the poem went on to the Great War when a reconciled America answer the divine call: "Christians held their breath and wondered / What the great U.S. would do, / While the Kaiser's cannon thundered / With all barriers broken through. / God then seemed to touch the button. / If not, how else could it be? / Moulding into one great army, / Champions of both Grant and Lee." The poet paid homage to the mythological view that Americans fought only for freedom: "Yes, they knew the starry banner / Says tis right that makes the might, / We ne'er fight for land or lucre, / But humanity and right." Closing his song of nationalist reconciliation, the writer cried, "Then let us all rejoice to say / All our efforts were not vain, / While some wore blue, and others gray, / *Thank God*, we now are friends again [emphasis in the original]. / Then let each stand, with hat in hand, / From valley up to mountain crag, / Rejoicing that in all this land, / We've just *one country and one flag* [emphasis in the original]."[48]

A short speech by Governor Ed Jackson followed the long poem, and the Indiana executive quoted Morton's speech of November 22, 1860. As secession loomed, Morton had said, "I would rather come out of a struggle defeated in arms and conceding independence to successful revolution than to purchase present peace by the concession of principles that must inevitably explode this nation into small and dishonored fragments." Jackson nodded to the Unionist cause but used a few lines from Morton that poorly reflected his usual sharp attacks on the South. Then the Klan-backed politician offered a ridiculously inaccurate reconciliationist view of the war, asserting that both the North and South fought for the Union: "This Union was preserved by heroes, both from the north and south, who fought on this battlefield. Each made a great sacrifice for what he believed to be right and by their joint sacrifices they cemented the Union forever."[49]

The remaining speeches at the dedication and the letters from various veterans reprinted in the published report continued in the spirit of reconciliation, redefining nationalism to mean reunion instead of victory. The Union cause remained but was diminished and constructed in new ways, now made subservient to reconciliation. The celebrants excised emancipation from the narrative. One might argue that such language stemmed from the fact that Indiana was putting up a monument in Mississippi, where it would be impolite to push Northern victory and emancipation in a Southern state. Perhaps Hoosiers shaped their memories to meet the time and place where they were remembering the past. But the context indicates that this was not just a display of Northern manners. Appropriating the same nationalist symbol of their state and the Civil War, Hoosiers had constructed a new understanding of Oliver Morton, quite different from those they had held two decades earlier.

THE CENTENNIAL OF THE CIVIL WAR

By the time Americans reached the centennial of the Civil War in the early 1960s, their analysis of Morton had changed again. In 1961 the Indiana Civil War Centennial Commission published *Indiana and the Civil War,* a collection of essays written by scholars for a popular audience. In his brief introduction, commission chair Carl A. Zenor couched the state's official memories of the Civil War in the terms of reconciliation, making much of "the bonds of unity." The collected essays reflected the context of the period, including the Cold War with its constant worries about Communism and the threat of nuclear war, as well as the rising civil rights movement. Many pages were dedicated to Abraham Lincoln, the Great Emancipator, and emphasized Hoosier support for the martyred president. One essay delved into Indiana's divided reactions to the Emancipation Proclamation, analyzing the complexity of the issue in ways that reflected current racial politics. But little was said about Morton's opposition to slavery and his senatorial support for racial equality, despite the fact that many saw the civil rights movement as a second Reconstruction that aimed to achieve the goals not reached in the post–Civil War era. Instead, Hoosiers' official recollections of Morton in the mid-twentieth century focused on his gubernatorial record.

Butler University historian Emma Lou Thornbrough contributed a piece on "Morton's One-Man Government" that asked if he was a dictator or a patriot. Reflecting the critical scholarship of the preceding decades, Thornbrough took Morton to task for his political opportunism, his centralization of power, and his skirting the bounds of the state constitution and the law. Despite her groundbreaking work on African American history, in this essay she accepted the prevailing historical analysis that Morton had used the Copperhead threat for political advantage. In the aftermath of the McCarthy hearings and the Red Scare of the 1950s, the theory that Morton and the Republicans had exaggerated the Copperheads and used the treason trials of 1864 to win the election seemed obvious and appropriate. Far from preventing a fifth column from rising in the rear, Morton had used his power to promote his own and his party's interests and created a constitutional crisis in doing so. Thus, Thornbrough—more balanced in her analysis of Morton in her book on the Civil War era in Indiana—accepted the consensus of historians who saw the governor as a dictator. She concluded by contrasting him with Lincoln, saying that while the President's "reputation has grown with the years, the luster of Morton's reputation has dimmed." Thornbrough thought that Morton lacked the qualities that made Lincoln great, "magnanimity and forbearance and political genius without narrow partisanship."[50]

A few years later, Centerville celebrated its sesquicentennial with a pageant and other events that venerated Morton in the 150th anniversary of the founding of his hometown. Like the centennial of the war, this celebration included obvious signs of the contemporary context shaping a view of the past. Even the title of the program reflected it—"From the Flintlock to the Missile"—made a Cold War reference to the nuclear age. Scenes in the performance of *The Builders of History* included the Morton wedding and the governor speaking about his role in the Civil War. As always, Abraham Lincoln helped shape the view of Morton, as the Gettysburg Address earned as much attention as the governor's speech. Bare mention was made of his Senate career, and the festivities conflated him with George Julian, a fact that would have dismayed the two men who had hated one another for so long. By the mid-twentieth century Morton's memory had faded into a shadow of his life, even in his own hometown.[51]

Americans remembered Oliver Morton in different ways at different times, and their accounts of him usually reflected their own context and their own concerns. Because his complex and complicated career spanned the defining events of the Civil War and Reconstruction, one could choose to emphasize different aspects of his life that allowed his legacy to be appropriated for current political purposes. But that same complexity also allowed others to contest recollections of Morton and offer their own views, often in political opposition to a previously constructed meaning.

The eulogists who memorialized their late colleague in 1878 set the stage, as they agreed on aspects of his character, praised his abilities and tremendous energy, applauded his efforts on behalf of the soldiers, and hailed him as a hero of the Union. But they differed as they recalled his legacy, disagreeing about his use or abuse of power and arguing over whether he should be seen as a patriot or a tyrant. They created a pattern for the memories of future generations, as they criticized or extolled his partisanship, expressed horror or approval of his attacks on the Copperheads, and either included or forgot his fight against slavery and for racial equality. Morton became a positive symbol of the Union and of emancipation but stood as a negative emblem for the Lost Cause and for those who promoted reconciliation. All of the memorialists agreed that he was a nationalist, but they also claimed that ideology and worked to redefine his thought to fit their own as they conjured up Morton in ways that fit their own political needs.

Over time, Morton's memory shifted and dimmed, as those who remembered him in life passed away and succeeding generations looked for consensus in their historical accounts of him. By the 1890s Morton was representing the Union cause for Republican voters and was hailed at gatherings of the Grand Army of the Republic. In 1900 some Hoosiers speaking at the US Capitol chose to make Morton a symbol of Northern victory and emancipation, while others tried to couch their recollections in terms of reconciliation. Audience mattered, as speakers pitched their stories to fit the venue. Consensus was more likely in Indiana and reigned at Republican gatherings, while conflict came in national settings as Democrats appropriated history for purposes different from their GOP rivals.

In 1907 Union and emancipation again dominated remembrances of Morton at the dedication of his statue in front of the Indiana State Capitol. But by 1926 reconciliation had swept away recollections of emancipation, and speakers downplayed Unionism as they dedicated the Morton statue at Vicksburg. When the United States reached the centennial of the Civil War, memories of Morton had shifted again, as his senatorial career was forgotten and historians reached a consensus that he had been a dictator during his time as Civil War governor. On each occasion, Americans evoked Morton to speak to contemporary audiences about current issues, employing the past for political purposes. History was for the living.

Memories of Morton in the Twenty-First Century

And historical memory lived on. During the sesquicentennial anniversary of the Civil War, a group of about one hundred people gathered in Centerville, Indiana, on August 4, 2013, to celebrate the 190th anniversary of Oliver P. Morton's birthday and to dedicate two markers along the town's main street. One of the signs commemorated the National Road and the other marked the site of the home of George Julian, a longtime opponent of slavery and Republican political rival of Morton. Speakers talked about Julian's fight against the peculiar institution and remembered the importance of the National Road as a thoroughfare uniting the nation before moving down the road to the Morton House, then in the early stages of restoration. That Centerville no longer flourished, and the historical markers were erected in hopes of promoting cultural tourism in a small town where the effects of globalization and a postindustrial economy helped to set the context of the event. Organized by the owner of the Morton House—Ball State University professor and town historian Ronald Morris—the day came to a close with speeches, a tour of the house, and a display of paintings of the home by a local artist.

Throughout the day, Morton was resurrected as a staunch nationalist, an opponent of slavery, and the Soldiers' Friend. Although one speaker did mention his differences with Julian, the event again conflated the two rival Republicans, remembering them as fighters for freedom, equality, and justice. Focused on his early life, the ceremonies did not delve deeply into Morton's political career. But much was made of the roots of his nationalist ideology and his opposition to slavery. The appearance of a Lincoln impersonator—who declared that the president had to appear at a celebration of one his strongest supporters—completed the image of Morton as an antislavery Unionist. Once again, historical interpretations had changed, as emancipation and Union returned to the center of the story. Brief mention was made of Morton's actions against the Copperheads, but they were now interpreted as legitimate and a sincere response to a real conspiracy, no matter how significant or insignificant a threat it might have been. One speaker admitted that Morton might have gone too far and made reference to the government spying on civilians under the administrations of George W. Bush and Barack Obama. The same speaker also mentioned Morton's work as a senator, especially his efforts on behalf of the Reconstruction amendments to the Constitution, and praised his work on behalf of African Americans.[52]

On April 19, 2015, as the sesquicentennial of the Civil War drew to a close, Centerville residents gathered at the Methodist Church to commemorate the Lincoln funeral services held there 150 years earlier. In 1865 communities across the country had held memorials for the fallen president at the exact same time that the official funeral took place in Washington. One such community was Centerville, which held its service at noon in the Methodist Church. Now, on the sesquicentennial, a crowd of people filled the same room in the same building at the same exact hour, and, of course, they included Oliver Morton.

"Remembering Lincoln Exactly 150 Years Later" was a solemn occasion, and attendees wore dark colors of mourning and pinned on black paper ribbons. Presentations included a prayer given at Lincoln's actual funeral, readings of the accounts of the 1865 Centerville event written by those who were there, a discussion of the national ceremonies, hymns sung by the church choir, and reflections on the men of Wayne County who fought and died in the Civil War. Also on the program was a lecture about Lincoln and Morton, "Partners for the Union." The speaker outlined the ways that Indiana's Civil War governor supported the president and the Union cause. He also spoke at length about how Morton carried on the project of Reconstruction after Lincoln's death. As always, the story of Morton meant that the North fought to preserve the Union and to end slavery, complete with a brief account of his helping to stop the Copperheads. But Civil War memories made on a rainy day in the spring of 2015 also included the Reconstruction amendments and the fight against the Ku Klux Klan in the postwar period.[53]

In the context of the early twenty-first century, Morton's legacy had shifted once more, reflecting the time's broader acceptance of racial equality and the now widely held view that the Civil War was primarily about slavery. In the era of the War on Terror, conspiracies against the government did not seem so far-fetched, and an audience familiar with increased government action in the name of security accepted, with some concern, that a leader might use surveillance and spying to root out enemies hidden within the society itself. As Americans marked the 150th anniversary of the Civil War, they had an African American as president, were fighting a continuing war against terrorism, and were holding on to the still-cherished ideals of freedom and equality existing within a surveillance state that diminished personal liberty. By the end of sesquicentennial celebrations in 2015, race riots and questions about inequality at home, as well as the ongoing struggle to rebuild societies torn by conflicts in Middle Eastern countries like Iraq, Afghanistan, and Syria, were making Reconstruction seem relevant once again. In such a context, then, some Americans looked back to the Civil War and Reconstruction and Oliver P. Morton again became a symbol in the politics of historical memory.

Notes

ABBREVIATIONS

JDPIHS   John Dowling Papers, William Henry Smith Memorial Library, Indiana Historical Society, Indianapolis

OPMIHS   Oliver P. Morton Papers, William Henry Smith Memorial Library, Indiana Historical Society, Indianapolis

OPMISL   Oliver P. Morton Papers, Indiana State Library, Indianapolis

OPMLB   Oliver P. Morton Letter Books, Indiana State Archives, Indianapolis

OPMPSA   Governor Oliver P. Morton Papers, Indiana State Archives, Indianapolis

OPMTBS   Oliver P. Morton Telegraph Books and Slips, Indiana State Archives, Indianapolis

PPISL   Daniel P. Pratt Papers, Indiana State Library, Indianapolis

INTRODUCTION

1. For an account of the statue at the State Capitol, see chapter 12. The statue on what was then called Governor's Circle was erected in the 1880s; see *Harper's Weekly*, Jan. 19, 1884. Mention of the statue remaining on Monument Circle at the time of the construction of the Soldiers' and Sailors' Monument in the center of Indianapolis, is found in *Harper's Weekly*, Sept. 7, 1889.

2. For examples of Drew Cayton's work, see Cayton, *Frontier Indiana*, and Cayton and Onuf, *Midwest and the Nation*. Towne, "Scorched Earth or Fertile Ground?"; the quotations here are taken from p. 406.

3. French, *Life, Speeches*; N.A., *Oliver P. Morton of Indiana: Sketch of His Life*.

4. Walker, *Sketch of the Life*.

5. Foulke, *Life of Oliver P. Morton*.

6. Gray, *Hidden Civil War*; Milton, *Abraham Lincoln and the Fifth Column*.

7. Hesseltine, *Lincoln and the War Governors*.

8. Stampp, *Indiana Politics*.

9. Barnhart and Carmony, *Indiana from Frontier to Industrial Commonwealth*; Nevins, *Ordeal of the Union*; Klement, *Copperheads in the Middle West* (see as well his later works, *Limits of Dissent* and *Dark Lanterns*).

10. Thornbrough, *Indiana in the Civil War Era*; Sylvester, "Oliver P. Morton and Hoosier Politics."

11. For Madison's positive treatment from a New Left perspective, see Madison, *Indiana Way* and *Hoosiers,* and for an example of a New Left scholar giving Morton meager and negative treatment, see Bensel, *Yankee Leviathan.* For the neglect of his postwar career, see Foner, *Reconstruction.* For a New Left scholar whose earlier view saw him negatively but who later began to question Morton's supposed opportunism, see Neely, *Fate of Liberty,* and his *Union Divided,* esp. 56–60. A recent study that misinterprets Morton in making him fit a broader analytical framework is found in Stanley, *The Loyal West.*

12. Etcheson, *A Generation at War;* Harris, *Lincoln and the Union Governors;* Engle, *Gathering to Save a Nation.*

13. Towne, *Surveillance and Spies.*

14. I searched for Morton's personal papers but could find nothing beyond the few pieces that others had identified in the standard archive collections. I heard the story about him burning his papers from Lloyd Hunter of Franklin College, who did preliminary work when considering a biography of Morton. Lloyd Hunter, conversation with author, Society of Civil War Historians Biennial Meeting, Lexington, Kentucky, June 15, 2012; Green, *Freedom, Union, and Power;* Green, "Reconstructing the Nation, Reconstructing the Party." The aspect of party was suggested (albeit in a negative light) in Schultz, "Oliver P. Morton and Reconstruction."

15. For a study that sees the conflict as a war for the Union, see Gallagher, *Union War.* An insightful study on motives that invites further exploration and argues that Northern ideology did not change during the war is Hess, *Liberty, Virtue, and Progress.* Another important book, Christopher Phillips, *The Rivers Ran Backward,* appeared too late for me to incorporate its provocative borderlands approach into my own thinking about Morton. While it would not change my overall interpretation of Morton, it would certainly require me to rethink certain issues and argue about them differently.

16. The postmodern concept of interpretive biography is best known in sociology, and a theoretical study of it can be found in Denzin, *Interpretive Biography,* and Denzin, *Interpretive Autoethnography.* For one example of my mentor's views on writing biography, see Michael O'Brien, "Biography and the Old South: A Review Essay," which originally appeared in the *Virginia Magazine of History and Biography* in October 1985 but has been conveniently reprinted in his *Placing the South.*

1. A NATIVE SON

1. Foulke, *Life of Oliver P. Morton,* vol. 1, 9.

2. Ibid.

3. Scholars have neglected the importance of the National Road and we need more studies of its role in places like Indiana. Until a full history of it is written, see Raitz, *National Road;* Sky, *National Road and the Difficult Path;* Rose, "Upland Southerners"; and Rose, "National Road Border."

4. Sky, *National Road and the Difficult Path* repeats the oft-told story of immigrants using the road, while Gregory S. Rose argues its role has been exaggerated in Rose, "Extending the Road West," 178–79. Rose's chapter also includes his argument that immigrants along the road came from the South.

5. Nation, *At Home in the Hoosier Hills;* Etcheson, *Emerging Midwest.*

6. For this analysis of the architecture, see Wilhelm, "Road as a Corridor for Ideas."

7. For the clash between the ethics of individualism and honor, see Wyatt-Brown, *Yankee Saints and Southern Sinners.* For the changes and tensions wrought by the new transportation revolution, see Taylor, *Transportation Revolution,* and Larson, *Internal Improvement.* Interpretations of Jacksonian America abound, but a few titles of importance will suffice here. A broader synthesis that demonstrates the dynamic nature of capitalism, without falling into the Marxist interpretation of the early nineteenth century experiencing a "market revolution," is found in McDougall, *Freedom Just Around the Corner.* The standard New Left/neo-Marxist view of the Jacksonian period that sees capitalism in a negative light is Sellers, *Market Revolution.* A fine synthesis that refutes Sellers with an interpretation of the communications revolution that emphasizes the more positive developments of the period without ignoring its flaws and shortcomings is Howe, *What Hath God Wrought.*

8. For a brief history of the National Road, see Sky, *National Road and the Difficult Path.* The differing interpretations of the libertarian policies of the Jacksonian era are found in Larson, *Internal Improvement,* and in McDougall, *Freedom Just Around the Corner,* esp. 429. The politics of the Jacksonian era are discussed in the notes in chapter 2.

9. For more on the National Road culture in Centerville, see Whallon, *Centerville, Indiana,* 8–9. See also newspapers from the era, esp. *Centerville Western Times, Wayne County Record, Indiana True Democrat,* and *Richmond Palladium.*

10. Foulke, *Life of Oliver P. Morton,* vol. 1, 3–4. Foulke had access to Morton's son and widow as well as some papers now missing, which makes his account the most reliable source for Morton's early life. Apocryphal stories appear in the script of a play performed in Centerville, Bessie M. Buhl's "Call of Oliver P. Morton." (Note that the Buhl play script can be found in Indiana Pamphlets, Indiana State Library, Indianapolis, Indiana.)

11. Foulke, *Life of Oliver P. Morton,* vol. 1, 6–8; Walker, *Sketch of the Life,* 10–11. Without personal papers or public statements that touch on such matters, it is impossible to prove what Morton truly thought about religion and the role that it played in his thinking. This speculation draws connections from the context to the various bits of information that are available and to later documented facts.

12. Foulke, *Life of Oliver P. Morton,* vol. 1, 8–9. In the nineteenth century, the town's name was spelled "Centreville," but I have chosen to employ the later and still-used modern spelling of "Centerville" in this narrative. French, *Life, Speeches of Morton,* 11–12.

13. Foulke, *Life of Oliver P. Morton,* vol. 1, 9.

14. Ibid., 9–10.

15. For some important examples of the vast literature on the Second Great Awakening, each offering unique interpretations, see Cross, *Burned-Over District;* Smith, *Revivalism and Social Reform;* Johnson, *A Shopkeeper's Millennium;* McLoughlin, *Revivals, Awakenings, and Reform;* Ryan, *Cradle of the Middle Class;* Johnson, *Islands of Holiness;* Hatch, *Democratization of American Christianity;* Butler, *Awash in a Sea of Faith;* Carwardine, *Evangelicals and Politics.*

16. William H. McGuffey became a legendary figure at Miami when he began to publish what became his *McGuffey's Reader* in the 1830s. Albert T. Bledsoe, who often interrupted his mathematics lectures with rants in support of state's rights and slavery, went on to serve as an assistant secretary of war for the Confederacy during the Civil War. For the history of Miami University in the 1830s–1840s, see Havighurst, *Miami Years, 1809–1984,* esp. 39–89.

17. Ibid.

18. Foulke, *Life of Oliver P. Morton,* vol. 1, 10–12; Walker, *Sketch of the Life,* 12.

19. Foulke, *Life of Oliver P. Morton,* vol. 1, 13; Walker, *Sketch of the Life,* 12.

20. Foulke, *Life of Oliver P. Morton,* vol. 1, 14–15.

21. For assertions that he left college to marry Lucinda, see *Indianapolis Sun,* clipping of June 25, 1871, story in edition dated July 1871, in Oliver P. Morton Scrapbook, Oliver P. Morton Papers, William Henry Smith Memorial Library, Indiana Historical Society, Indianapolis, Indiana (hereafter OPMIHS).

22. French, *Life, Speeches, State Papers,* 13–14; Foulke, *Life of Oliver P. Morton,* vol. 1, 13–14. The house Morton rented is located at 115 South Morton Avenue (Centerville Road) in Centerville. A sign on the outside of the home marks it as a historic site and provides what seem to be inaccurate dates of the family's residence there.

23. Foulke, *Life of Oliver P. Morton,* vol. 1, 15–17.

24. *Indiana Sentinel,* Feb. 26, 1852; Foulke, *Life of Oliver P. Morton,* vol. 1, 17–18.

25. Foulke, *Life of Oliver P. Morton,* vol. 1, 18–19.

26. Ibid., 18–20.

27. Walker, *Sketch of the Life,* 14–21; Foulke, *Life of Oliver P. Morton,* vol. 1, 19–28.

28. Foulke, *Life of Oliver P. Morton,* vol. 1, 21–28. Foulke described cases and examined papers no longer available. Rumors that there are papers stored in the Wayne County Courthouse persist, and if they prove true, perhaps Morton's cases are among them, but I was unable to gain access to any such archives. Otherwise, few of his legal documents survive, and beyond those we must rely on Foulke and the other nineteenth-century biographers for accounts of his legal career.

29. On the Morton House in Centerville, see Hoagland, *Historic American Buildings Survey.*

30. For Morton sitting on his porch and gazing out at the view, see Foulke, *Life of Oliver P. Morton,* vol. 1, 28. Ronald Morris, who recently purchased the Morton House, is restoring it to its 1850s splendor. Ron, a professor at Ball State University, previously restored the Raridan House just up the street, and he works hard to keep the history of the town alive. In 2013 he extended the author his kind hospitality as well as a walking tour of Centerville on a rainy afternoon. The Morton House is located at 319 West Main Street. For George Julian's claim to have encouraged Morton's legal career, and his account of their feud, see Julian, *Political Recollections, 1840 to 1872,* 270–71.

2. A RISING REPUBLICAN STAR

1. Foulke, *Life of Oliver P. Morton,* vol. 1, 38–39. Morton's opposition to party discipline over the Kansas-Nebraska bill is ironic in light of his later views on the importance of party and loyalty. This account of the expelling of delegates at the state convention was given by Othniel Beeson, the Wayne County delegate who claimed to respond to the crowd when the expelled men reached the door. It is possible that Beeson conflated events, as the press did not mention the state convention expelling the anti-Nebraska men. Morton himself was not mentioned in the newspapers at the time. See Thornbrough, *Indiana in the Civil War Era,* 57n33. For another account of the split in the Democratic Party, see Stoler, "Insurgent Democrats of Indiana," esp. 11–13.

2. Foulke, *Life of Oliver P. Morton,* vol. 1, 29–35. The Compromise of 1850 is treated in all of the major studies of the politics of the 1850s. Potter, *Impending Crisis, 1848–1861,*

remains an important interpretation that laid the foundation for many future studies that see slavery as the central issue of the decade. Holt, *Political Crisis of the 1850s,* and Silbey, *Partisan Imperative,* as well as Silbey's *American Political Nation,* are splendid examples of how the "new political history" that emerged after the 1960s focused on ethnocultural issues rather than ideology, while putting local politics and other issues at the center of the 1850s instead of privileging national policies and slavery above everything else. For the politics of slavery returning to the center of things in a short, engaging synthesis designed for general readers as well as scholars, see Green, *Politics and America in Crisis.*

3. For the 1851 congressional election and Julian's bitterness, see Riddleberger, *George Washington Julian,* 81–83. The vote totals are found in Riker and Thornbrough, *Indiana Election Returns,* 123. The exact nature of the personal differences between Julian and Morton remain unknown, if they ever were clear to even the two men themselves. See chapter 1, note 30, for reference to Julian's account of their disagreements.

4. For newspaper stories mentioning Morton leaving the Democrats during the controversy over the Kansas-Nebraska Act, see *Indiana Free Democrat,* Apr. 27, Aug. 24, Sept. 14, Nov. 2, 1854. On the Missouri Compromise, see Forbes, *Missouri Compromise and Its Aftermath.* Older, but still useful, is Moore, *Missouri Controversy.* The 1820 agreement is treated in the major works of synthesis of early nineteenth-century America, including Sellers, *Market Revolution;* Wilentz, *Rise of American Democracy;* McDougall, *Freedom Just Around the Corner;* and Howe, *What Hath God Wrought.*

5. For the politics of the Kansas-Nebraska Act, see Potter, *Impending Crisis,* 145–76; Green, *Politics and America in Crisis,* 67–71. The definitive biography of Douglas is Johannsen, *Stephen A. Douglas.* For another insightful interpretation of Douglas, see Huston, *Stephen A. Douglas.*

6. Foulke, *Life of Oliver P. Morton,* vol. 1, 35–38.

7. Foulke, *Life of Oliver P. Morton,* vol. 1, 38. For more on Jesse Bright, see Wickre, "Indiana's Southern Senator." A still useful study of Bright's political career is Murphy, *Political Career of Jesse D. Bright.* Classic nineteenth-century "public man" accounts of both Bright and Wright, and one of Morton as well, are found in brief in Woollen, *Biographical and Historical Sketches,* 223–32, 94–103, 130–46.

8. Foulke, *Life of Oliver P. Morton,* vol. 1, 38. Emma Lou Thornbrough has pointed out that there is a discrepancy between Foulke's account and what appeared in the Indianapolis newspapers at the time. Foulke said that McDonald refused to follow Morton's call for opposition to the bill, but the newspapers said that McDonald did try to introduce substitute resolutions. See Thornbrough, *Indiana in the Civil War Era,* 57n33.

9. Foulke, *Life of Oliver P. Morton,* vol. 1, 39–40.

10. For the Free Soil movement, see Earle, *Jacksonian Antislavery.* On the Whigs, see Michael F. Holt's massive study, *Rise and Fall of the American Whig Party,* and Howe, *Political Culture.* The best examination of the American Party is Anbinder, *Nativism and Slavery.* The nativist party in Indiana is covered in Brand, "History of the Know Nothing Party," pts. 1 and 2. For more on the prohibition movement of the 1850s in Indiana, see Thornbrough, *Indiana in the Civil War Era,* 57–59.

11. Foulke, *Life of Oliver P. Morton,* vol. 1, 41–43.

12. For mention of Morton as a possible state senate candidate, see *Evansville Daily Journal,* Jan. 11, 1855.

13. Foulker, *Life of Oliver P. Morton,* vol. 1, 43–44. For more on the complexities and confusion surrounding the fusion of the People's Party in Indiana, see Gienapp, *Origins of the Republican Party.*

14. For more on the Pittsburgh convention, see Gienapp, *Origins of the Republican Party,* 254–59.

15. Despite Morton's stand against nativism, Democratic newspapers in Indiana and elsewhere still thought that he enjoyed the support of the Know Nothings; see *Nashville Union and American,* Jan. 2, 1857. An insightful study of the American Party that examines the political organization as more than just a precursor to the Republicans and refuses to dismiss it as right-wing extremism is Anbinder, *Nativism and Slavery.* An older treatment that sees nativism as an extension of Evangelical Christian reform is Billington, *Protestant Crusade.* Mid-twentieth-century historians largely dismissed the Know Nothings as irrational, accepting the interpretation of Hofstadter, *Paranoid Style in American Politics.* An example of the ethnocultural view that renewed interest in the American Party was a significant part of the Republican coalition is found in Holt, *Political Crisis of the 1850s.* Gienapp, *Origins of the Republican Party,* follows in this later tradition and includes the positions of Orth and Colfax; see esp. 180–84, 281–85.

16. Randolph's coining of the term *doughface* is recounted in Moore, *Missouri Controversy,* 104, and explored fully in Richards, *Slave Power,* 83–106. Democrats in the North often combined racism—usually in the form of blackface minstrelsy—with political ideology in ways that appealed to their constituents; see Jean H. Baker, *Affairs of Party.*

17. Twentieth-century historians tended to dismiss the Slave Power conspiracy as outlandish or as one of many conspiracy theories that reflected the "paranoid style" that Richard Hofstadter identified in American politics, but more recent scholars have revived at least part of its validity. For the Progressive Era "death blow" to the Slave Power thesis that argued it was simply antislavery rhetoric, see Boucher, "In Re That Aggressive Slaveocracy." For the mid-century view influenced by Hofstadter, see Davis, *Slave Power Conspiracy.* For examples of later examinations that gave at least some credence to the conspiracy theory as part of a broader interpretation, see Holt, *Political Crisis of the 1850s;* Sewell, *Ballots for Freedom;* and Gienapp, "Republican Party and the Slave Power." More recent studies show how the very real power of Southern slaveholders made the conspiracy theory credible for Northern voters. For an example, see Earle, *Jacksonian Antislavery.* For a full-scale return to the Slave Power thesis as an interpretation, see Richards, *Slave Power.*

18. *Indianapolis Journal,* Jan. 30, 1856 (note that the *Indianapolis Journal* went through several different names, including *Indianapolis Weekly Journal* and *Indianapolis Daily Journal.* For clarity, I call it and cite it as the *Indianapolis Journal*); Foulke, *Life of Oliver P. Morton,* vol. 1, 47. For the free labor ideology that animated the Republicans and the role of former Democrats like Morton in its development, see Foner, *Free Soil, Free Labor, Free Men,* esp. 149–85.

19. For a brief biography of Henry Lane, see Woodburn, "Henry Smith Lane." I take this view of Lane and Republican conservatism in the politics of the 1850s in Indiana from Peek, "Upland Southerners."

20. In addition to his role as a powerbroker, Bright became something of a fixture in the Washington, DC, scene; see Shelden, *Washington Brotherhood,* 55, 82, 130, 137, 152–56, 87–88, 92–94, 117.

21. For the 1856 state convention and the battle between Bright and Wright, see Thornbrough, *Indiana in the Civil War Era,* 71. Also useful for the details of the election of 1856 in Indiana are Zimmerman, "Origin and Rise of the Republican Party," pts. 1 and 2; Van Bolt, "Rise of the Republican Party in Indiana." For a brief biography of Joseph A. Wright, see Sample, "Joseph A. Wright." For a splendid account of Jesse Bright's role in the 1856 presidential election, see Nichols, *Disruption of American Democracy,* 2–51. Wickre, "Indiana's Southern Senator," 163–87, provides a more recent update on Bright's managing of the presidential election.

22. St. Clair, "Ashbel P. Willard." See also Haffner, *Hoosier Governor,* and Woollen, *Biographical and Historical Sketches,* 104–12.

23. *Evansville Daily Journal,* May 3, 1856. For praise of Morton as a candidate, see *Evansville Daily Journal,* June 17, 1856. For Know Nothing praise of Morton, see *Indiana American,* May 16, 1856. For Democratic criticism of him, see *Indiana Sentinel,* July 3, 1856. For a Democratic politician's views of the campaign of 1856, see Thomas Dowling to John Dowling, Oct. 20, 1856, John Dowling Papers, William Henry Smith Memorial Library, Indiana Historical Society, Indianapolis, Indiana (hereafter JDPIHS).

24. Foulke, *Life of Oliver P. Morton,* vol. 1, 49–57. No full record of the debates in the gubernatorial campaign in 1856 exists. Bits and pieces can be drawn from various firsthand accounts and from scattered newspaper references. Foulke provides the most detailed summary of them. See also *Marshall County Republican,* Oct. 9, 1856; *Indiana Sentinel,* Aug. 13, 14, 18, 1856; *Plymouth Republican,* Oct. 9, Aug. 9, 1856. More on the campaign can be found in the *Indiana Sentinel,* June 5, July 23, 31, Aug. 4, 7, Sept. 13, 1856.

25. The most important recent interpretation of Kansas, and its place in American politics, is Etcheson, *Bleeding Kansas,* a book that focuses on the ways in which whites on both sides of the conflict understood themselves to be fighting for freedom and returns popular sovereignty to the center of the story. Etcheson's work challenges the emphasis on race rather than slavery that is found in Rawley, *Race and Politics.* An economic interpretation is Gates, *Fifty Million Acres.* A still useful and balanced narrative that argued the violence was a battle over the morality of slavery is Nichols, *Bleeding Kansas.* David Donald's *Charles Sumner and the Coming of the Civil War* is the first volume of the splendid definitive biography, and the account of "Bleeding Sumner" is on pp. 278–311. Frémont, a Catholic, received the nomination of the northern Know Nothings as well as the Republicans. For more on the presidential campaign, see Potter, *Impending Crisis,* 249–56.

26. *Indiana Sentinel,* Aug. 14, 1856. The *Indiana Sentinel* went through several name changes, including *Indiana State Sentinel, Indiana Weekly Sentinel, Indiana Daily State Sentinel, Indianapolis Weekly Sentinel,* and *Indianapolis Daily Sentinel.* For the sake of clarity, I have chosen to simply call it the *Indiana Sentinel* and I cite it as such, except when citing it as a publisher of other documents besides the newspaper. Note that there were times when there were separate editions—a weekly and a daily. This can cause confusion for researchers, but both editions are available.

27. Foulke, *Life of Oliver P. Morton,* vol. 1, 49–57.

28. Holmes County *Republican,* Sept. 25, 1856; *Indiana Sentinel,* July 3, 1856.

29. Thornbrough, *Indiana in the Civil War Era,* 74–75; Van Bolt, "Rise of the Republican Party," 213.

30. Ibid.; for Wright's influence on the old Whigs, see Peek, "Upland Southerners," esp. 209–25. Peek also argued that Morton's failure in 1856 hinged on his inability to rally Whigs to the Republican cause. See Peek, "'True and Ever Living Principle,'" 414.

31. For Morton's reaction to his defeat in 1856, see Foulke, *Life of Oliver P. Morton,* vol. 1, 57–58; for the gubernatorial election returns, see *Evansville Daily Journal,* Oct. 16, 1856.

3. The Election of 1860

1. Portions of this chapter were previously published as a theoretical study in A. James Fuller, "The Election of 1860 and Political Realignment Theory: Indiana as a Case Study," in Fuller, *Election of 1860 Reconsidered,* 193–224. For reports on Morton's friends working for his nomination and general support for him, see *Marshall County Republican,* Dec. 8, 1859; *Evansville Daily Journal,* Feb. 25, 1860; *Wabash Express,* Feb. 1, Mar. 7, 14, 1860.

2. For post-election newspaper comment on the Republican deal to elect Lane to the Senate and make Morton governor, see *Wabash Express,* Nov. 29, 1860.

3. Foulke, *Life of Oliver P. Morton,* vol. 1, 66–67; *Jasper Weekly Courier,* Nov. 7, 1860; *Wabash Express,* Nov. 28, 1860; Turpie, *Sketches of My Own Times,* 183–84. Turpie, Morton's opponent in the race for lieutenant governor, also describes a similar deal being made by the Democrats.

4. Lucinda Morton kept many grocery lists and receipts from certain periods in the 1870s that provide insights into the meals at the Morton home. They are found in OPMISL. Her recipe book also survives, although with a badly stained and burned cover, a fact that makes one question the abilities of the cook while also indicating that it was heavily used. See Mrs. Oliver P. Morton, Recipe Book, OPMIHS. For more on John Miller Morton, see *Harper's Weekly,* Mar. 6, 1880.

5. Walter Morton to Lucinda Morton, Dec. 9, 1874, OPMIHS.

6. For an account of Oliver T. Morton as a teenager and mention of Morton's home life, see *Harper's Weekly,* Aug. 7, 1874. There is one surviving letter from Morton to Ollie. In it, he thanked the boy for a recent letter and told him that he was sure that he is doing well in school. The father described his rooms at the Ebbitt House hotel, mentioning the convenience of the elevator, which was significant for a paralyzed man. He promised to send money for his son to buy ice skates and assured him that he would not forget to bring diamond earrings, probably a gift to be given to Lucinda. See Oliver P. Morton to Son, Dec. 5, 1872, OPMISL; Oliver Morton Jr, to Lucinda Morton, Oct. 31, 1881, OPMIHS. For an example of Ollie's writing, see Oliver T. Morton, *Southern Empire,* which he dedicated to his mother.

7. Foulke, *Life of Oliver P. Morton,* vol. 1, 61.

8. Ibid., 60–61. The *Indianapolis Journal,* which was published under various titles, became the Republican Party organ in Indianapolis and the state. The Journal Company, a group of men led by Ovid Butler, bought the paper, which had been a Whig organ, in 1854 and turned it Republican. They made Sulgrove, who had worked as an assistant editor with the previous owner, the editor, and in 1856 Sulgrove purchased

enough stock in the company to gain control of it, continuing as editor. In 1864 he sold the newspaper to William R. Holloway, Morton's brother-in-law, but in 1866 Sulgrove returned as editor and held the post for several more years. Holloway sold the business in 1865 and it went through several owners in the 1870s, but remained a Republican paper loyal to Morton throughout his political career. For information about the paper, see Miller, *Indiana Newspaper Bibliography,* 273–74. For more on Sulgrove, see newspaper sketches published at the time of his death in 1890, conveniently reprinted as "Berry R. Sulgrove, Journalist."

9. Foulke, *Life of Oliver P. Morton,* vol. 1, 62; Riddleberger, *George Washington Julian,* 116.

10. There is a vast literature on the ideology of republicanism and it seems that a majority of scholars now accept it as the dominant philosophy from the era of the American Revolution to the Civil War. Some scholars still argue for liberalism, which dominated the scholarship of the mid-twentieth century. I see the two as existing simultaneously, often in tension, sometimes not, with the conflict between them mostly arising from differences over capitalism. While liberalism promoted capitalism, republicanism feared the disorder of free markets. Thus, liberalism favored freer markets, while republicanism demanded government regulations. Of course, republicanism changed over time and made peace with capitalism, at least to some degree, as the Whigs promoted government intervention in the economy both to control and extend the market. No doubt many American citizens failed to see much distinction between the two idea systems. I take this definition of republicanism from Rodgers, "Saving the Republic," 177. For some examples of reviews and syntheses of the scholarship on republicanism, see Shallhope, "Toward Republican Synthesis"; Rodgers, "Republicanism"; Silbey, *American Political Nation;* and Watson, *Liberty and Power.* For two examples of the case for liberalism and its triumph over revolutionary republicanism, see Appleby, *Capitalism and the New Social Order,* and Wood, *Empire of Liberty.*

11. Foulke, *Life of Oliver P. Morton,* vol. 1, 62–64; Riddleberger, *George Washington Julian,* 120–22.

12. Foulke, *Life of Oliver P. Morton,* vol. 1, 64; notes in Oliver P. Morton Scrapbook, OPMIHS.

13. For more on the Lecompton constitution, see Etcheson, *Bleeding Kansas,* 139–67. On the Dred Scott case, see Green, *Politics and America in Crisis,* 109–13, and the classic treatment in Fehrenbacher, *Dred Scott Case.*

14. Sample, "Joseph A. Wright," 116–19. For more on William H. English, see Nicholas, "William Hayden English."

15. St. Clair, "Ashbel P. Willard," 127–29.

16. Thornbrough, *Indiana in the Civil War Era,* 78; Foulke, *Life of Oliver P. Morton,* vol. 1, 59–60.

17. Thornbrough, *Indiana in the Civil War Era,* 81. Gregory Peek argued that Indiana politics allied the Douglas Democrats and Republicans between 1857 and 1858; see Peek, "'True and Ever Living Principle,'" 381–421.

18. Huston, *Panic of 1857,* 14–28; Rothbard, *A History of Money,* 90–114. In their zeal to avoid economic determinism, scholars have neglected the Panic of 1857 as a cause of the Civil War, but there are notable exceptions. In addition to Huston, another historian who gives the economic crisis more than a passing reference is Stampp, *America in 1857,*

221–38. Allan Nevins also gave a thorough look at the panic and resulting depression in the third volume of his eight-volume classic study of the Civil War era, *The Ordeal of the Union;* see Nevins, *Emergence of Lincoln,* 176–97. A more typical example is Nevins's fellow Progressive historian Roy F. Nichols, who gives the crisis 3 pages out of more than 500 in *Disruption of American Democracy,* 132–34. Consensus scholar David M. Potter mentions the Panic of 1857 only once in his nearly 600 pages of *The Impending Crisis.* Sean Wilentz manages about 5 pages out of some 150 dedicated to the 1850–1861 period in *Rise of American Democracy,* 719–25. Scholars looking at Indiana vary in their treatment of the depression following the panic. Kenneth M. Stampp, in *Indiana Politics,* 10–11, 43, 54, notes the panic's role in setting the context for the 1860 election and integrates it into his first fifty-odd pages of background leading up to the Civil War. Emma Lou Thornbrough, *Indiana in the Civil War Era,* 84, admits that "economic conditions, although they did not receive much attention in political speeches or in the press, were no doubt an ingredient in the political upheaval," while incorrectly blaming the bank failures throughout the 1850s on lack of proper regulation through the Free Banking Law. All she gives the Panic of 1857 is a phrase: "In 1856 there were widespread crop failures and in 1857 a general depression."

19. Huston, *Panic of 1857,* 130, 131–38.

20. On the Mormon War and Mountain Meadows massacre, see Denton, *American Massacre;* Brooks, *Mountain Meadows Massacre.*

21. For an interpretation of corruption as a political issue in the antebellum period, see Summers, *Plundering Generation.* On the Revival of 1858, see Smith, *Revivalism and Social Reform,* esp. 63–79; Carwardine, *Evangelicals and Politics,* 292–96; Stampp, *America in 1857,* 236–38. A more skeptical view that challenges the argument for the revival's influence is found in Long, *Revival of 1857–58.*

22. Fletcher, *Diary,* vol. 6, *1857–1860,* 208–9, entry dated Mar. 27, 1858; *Indianapolis Locomotive,* Mar. 27, 1858, quoted in ibid., 208.

23. On the corruption of the Buchanan administration, see Nichols, *Disruption of American Democracy,* esp. 331–32. For the ways in which the perception of scandal allowed the Republicans to cast their opposition to the Democrats in terms of republicanism, see Morrison, "President James Buchanan," 152–53. On the swamplands scandal, see St. Clair, "Ashbel P. Willard," 129–30.

24. Stampp, *America in 1857,* 231–32, 246–48.

25. Thornbrough, *Indiana in the Civil War Era,* 83.

26. St. Clair, "Ashbel P. Willard," 130. Willard died in office in October of 1860 and was replaced by Lt. Gov. Abram A. Hammond, who held office until January 1861. For more on John Brown and his raid on Harper's Ferry, see Reynolds, *John Brown, Abolitionist;* Finkelman, *His Soul Goes Marching On.*

27. Stampp, *Indiana Politics during the Civil War,* 15–21.

28. On the Democratic split and the nominations of Douglas and Breckinridge, see Nichols, *Disruption of American Democracy,* esp. 303–20; Potter, *Impending Crisis,* 404–13; Fuller, "A Forlorn Hope." For the situation in Indiana following the national split, see Thornbrough, *Indiana in the Civil War Era,* 89–90, and Stampp, *Indiana Politics,* 31–41.

29. Peek, "Upland Southerners," outlines the Republicans taking this more conservative position and sees this as the result of a political culture rooted in the world

of the upland Southerners who had settled early Indiana. Here I am drawing on his excellent account of the events and am indebted to him for his detailed research on the intricate maneuvering of the Republicans in the 1850s. I do think that he might take his interpretation of the move to conservatism too far, however. While upland Southern culture did matter and certainly informed the thinking and actions of former Whigs with Southern backgrounds—like Henry S. Lane—I think the Republican shift to a more moderate position on slavery reflected the changing context of politics in the years leading up to 1860. Nor would I agree with an interpretation that held that men like Morton were just opportunists suppressing their real views to get elected. Rather they came to the more conservative position because of the same shifting nature of politics that ruined Stephen Douglas's presidential hopes. Morton, for example, held to a consistent position on slavery throughout the period. But his views that were too radical in 1854 to remain a Democrat and too strident in 1856 to win the election appeared more conservative by 1860. I think Peek is correct about Lane, and he is also right to note that Morton toned down his rhetoric in 1860.

Without Morton's personal papers, we may never be able to know why he took the more conservative position. This leaves his actions open to interpretation, and one can argue that he was merely an opportunist, a party loyalist, a true conservative, and so on. For a fine study of upland Southern culture and its influence, see Etcheson, *Emerging Midwest.* A splendid look at upland Southerners in Indiana is Nation, *At Home in the Hoosier Hills.*

It is past time that other parts of Indiana culture receive the kind of attention that scholars have given the upland Southerners. Even in southern Indiana, different groups of people lived just one county away or even within the same county. More studies of Quaker communities, for example, are needed. So, too, are works that look at those who came to Indiana from the Northern states. And immigrants deserve more study, as large groups of Irish and German migrants came to the state well before the Civil War. The diversity of Hoosiers in the antebellum period belies the emphasis so far given to upland Southerners.

30. For the results of the 1856 presidential election in Indiana, see Thornbrough, *Indiana in the Civil War Era,* 76. For more on John Bell, see Fuller, "Last True Whig."

31. Oliver P. Morton, "Speech delivered at Terre Haute, March [10th], 1860," in French, *Life, Speeches, State Papers,* 31–53. Note that French incorrectly cites the date as March 18, but newspapers report it as the 10th and published it before the 18th. For a newspaper account of the speech, see *Wabash Express,* Mar. 14, 1860.

32. Morton, "Speech Delivered at Terre Haute," 54–55.

33. Ibid., 55.

34. Rothbard, *A History of Money,* 115–22; Huston, *Panic of 1857,* 210.

35. Oliver P. Morton, "Campaign of 1860, Speech at Fort Wayne."

36. Ibid. The way that Morton placed economics within the Slave Power conspiracy fits well with the interpretation found in Huston, *Panic of 1857,* esp. 231. On the Panic and Republican free labor ideology, see also Foner, *Free Soil, Free Labor, Free Men,* 24–29.

37. Morton, "Campaign of 1860, Speech at Fort Wayne," 103–15.

38. Ibid., 117–18.

39. *White Cloud Kansas Chief,* Aug. 16, 1860.

40. Fletcher, *Diary,* vol. 6, *1857–1860,* 596, entry dated Sept. 11, 1860, 596.

41. Ibid., 602–603, entry dated Sept. 28, 1860; ibid., 603, entry dated Sept. 29, 1860.

42. For the Revival's role in the election of 1860, see Carwardine, *Evangelicals and Politics,* 296–307. For the true meaning of "Black Republican," see Randall, *Lincoln the President,* 182. Corruption also mattered in the context of republicanism, the ideology that underlay much of antebellum politics; see Knupfer, *Union As It Is.* For a study of Southern republicanism that emphasizes the extolling of virtue and the denunciation of corruption, see Greensberg, *Masters and Statesmen.*

43. William H. English to Nahum Caper, Feb. 1, 1860, William Hayden English Papers, William H. Smith Memorial Library, Indiana Historical Society, Indianapolis, Indiana; *Wabash Express,* Mar. 7, 1860.

44. For historians outlining the Republican claim to conservatism in Indiana, see Peek, "Upland Southerners"; Stampp, *Indiana Politics,* 43; Thornbrough, *Indiana in the Civil War Era,* 90–92.

45. For Lane's racist statements and doubts about Julian, see Peek, "Upland Southerners," 327, 341.

46. Morton, "Speech delivered at Terre Haute," 31–38.

47. Ibid.

48. Ibid.

49. Ibid., 38–47. In the political turmoil of the 1850s, Kansas came to be a symbol for white liberty, making Morton's use of it as a valence issue all the more significant. See Etcheson, *Bleeding Kansas.*

50. Morton, "Speech at Terre Haute," 38–47.

51. Ibid., 47–54.

52. Turpie, *Sketches of My Own Times,* 188. For more of Morton's 1860 campaign speeches, see French, *Life, Speeches, State Papers,* 31–135; Foulke, *Life of Oliver P. Morton,* 67–84.

53. For these vote totals, see *Wabash Express,* Oct. 17, 1860; *Evansville Daily Journal,* Dec. 17, 1860.

4. The War Governor

1. For an example of Morton's recruitment efforts, see his published call for troops, *Evansville Daily Journal,* July 3, 1862.

2. Foulke, *Life of Oliver P. Morton,* vol. 1, 183–88; Morton to Col. Vawter, Aug. 13, 1862, in Oliver P. Morton Telegraph Books and Slips, Indiana State Archives, Indianapolis, Indiana (hereafter OPMTBS); Edwin M. Stanton to Oliver P. Morton, Aug. 19,1862, OPMTBS.

3. French, *Life, Speeches, State Papers,* 123–35. Here Morton linked the preservation of the Union with freedom in a way that demonstrated that Republicans already connected the two, meaning that emancipation was part of the party's ideology from the beginning of the conflict. This fits well with the interpretation found in James Oakes, *Freedom National.*

4. French, *Life, Speeches, State Papers,* 123–35.

5. Foulke, *Life of Oliver P. Morton,* vol. 1, 104–5. Along with the varying, noncommitted replies of other governors, Morton's response that he wanted to postpone any such peace convention until after the inauguration was published in newspapers across the country; for an example, see *Newark Advocate,* Feb. 1, 1861.

6. For Morton's questions and responses to him from the delegates, see Morton to "Compromisers in Washington, D.C.," Feb. 1, 1861, Oliver P. Morton Papers, Indiana State Library, Indianapolis, Indiana (hereafter OPMISL); Caleb B. Smith to Morton, Feb. 1, 1861, OPMISL; Pleasant A. Hackleman to Morton, Feb. 1, 1861, OPMISL; Godlove S. Orth to Morton, Feb. 1, 1861, OPMISL; Erastus W. H. Ellis to Morton, Feb. 2, 1861, OPMISL; Thomas C. Slaughter to Morton, Feb. 3, 1861, OPMISL.

7. *Indianapolis Journal,* Feb. 12, 1861; *Cincinnati Daily Commercial,* Feb. 13, 1861; *Boston Daily Advertiser,* Feb. 12, 1861; *Farmer's Cabinet,* Feb. 15, 1861. Here again, the language that Morton and Lincoln used fits well with the interpretation of James Oakes in *Freedom National.* From the outset of the war, the Republicans connected the Union with freedom—which included emancipation. Of course, different definitions of "liberty" or "freedom" mattered, as did disagreements over how to achieve those ends.

8. The introduction to a volume on the Indiana governors discusses how Morton was the most powerful governor in the nineteenth century and set a precedent for Paul V. McNutt, who centralized power as governor during the Great Depression; see Gugin, St. Clair, and Wolf, "Indiana Governors," esp. 8–9. In the early twenty-first century the governorship of Mitch Daniels was transformative in ways that might make him part of a triumvirate of state leaders who shaped Indiana history. For evidence to support this suggestion, see the later chapters of Madison, *Hoosiers.*

9. For the reports on the state's financial situation, see *Journal of the House . . . January 10, 1861,* esp. 29–32, 181–82, 282–83, 877–82; Foulke, *Life of Oliver P. Morton,* vol. 1, 108–9.

10. *Journal of the House . . . January 10, 1861,* 853–59, 1050–66; On the Swamp Lands frauds, see ibid., 62, 374, 572, 703–5; Foulke, *Life of Oliver P. Morton,* vol. 1, 109; Thornbrough, *Indiana in the Civil War Era,* 366–68. For later discussion of the fraud investigation, see W. R. Holloway to Indiana attorney general Oscar B. Hord, Oct. 22, 1863, Oliver P. Morton Letter Books, Indiana State Archives, Indianapolis, Indiana (hereafter OPMLB).

11. "An Act to Organize the Militia, Providing for the Appointment, and Prescribing the Duties of Certain Officers Thereof, Approved June 14, 1852," Apr. 1861, OPMISL; Foulke, *Life of Oliver P. Morton,* vol. 1, 110–11.

12. Ibid.; for Morton searching for guns, see examples of replies from his correspondents in the Governor Oliver P. Morton Papers, Indiana State Archives, Indianapolis, Indiana (hereafter OPMPSA), esp. A. J. Harrison to Oliver P. Morton, Jan. 30, 1861; James A. Weldman to Oliver P. Morton, Feb. 5, 1861; D. Cumbacher to Oliver P. Morton, Feb. 6, 1861; William Stivers to Oliver P. Morton, Feb. 6, 1861; E. Banks to Oliver P. Morton, Feb. 6, 1861; John Gardner to Oliver P. Morton, Feb. 7, 1861; M. L. Marsh to Oliver P. Morton, Feb. 8, 1861; E. Dulley to Oliver P. Morton, Feb. 9, 1861; B. C. Martin to Oliver P. Morton, Feb. 12, 1861. See also H. K. Craig to Oliver P. Morton, Jan. 9, 12, Feb. 7, 1861.

13. For Owen's appointment, see Oliver P. Morton, Letter Book, Apr. 1861–Sept. 1862, p. 45, OPMLB. For more on Robert Dale Owen, see Owen, *Threading My Way,* and Woollen, *Biographical and Historical Sketches,* 289–308. A full biography of Owen is found in Leopold, *Robert Dale Owen.*

14. For examples of Owen reporting to the governor on his travels and arms purchases, see Robert Dale Owen to Oliver P Morton, Apr. 19, June 3, 25, July 10, Aug. 19, Sept. 6, 7, Oct. 22, 1862, OPMPSA; also, Official Report, Sept. 4, 1862, OPMSA; also, Thornbrough, *Indiana in the Civil War Era,* 164–67. An example of Morton issuing

orders regarding the state arsenal is found in O. P. Morton, Special Order, Nov. 11, 1863, OPMLB. For the military reporting on the arsenal, see L. Thomas to Simon Cameron, Report to Secretary of War, Oct. 21, 1861, *Official Records,* ser. 1, vol. 4, 313–14.

15. *Lowell Daily Citizen and News,* Apr. 6, 1861; *Daily Cleveland Herald,* Apr. 9, 1861; *Wisconsin State Journal,* Mar. 30, Apr. 2, 6, 1861.

16. Morton to Lincoln, Apr. 15, 1861, OPMTBS; Simon Cameron to Morton, Apr. 15, 1861, OPMTBS. For Morton's proclamation calling for volunteers, see *Evansville Daily Journal,* Apr. 18, 1861.

17. Morton's message to the special session in 1861 was printed in the legislative journal but was later extracted and published separately in pamphlet form. Morton, *Message of the Governor to the Legislature,* 577–79.

18. Ibid., 579–82.

19. Ibid, 570–82.

20. For the debates and legislative actions, see *Journal of the House . . . April 24, 1861.* A balanced secondary account is found in Sylvester, "Oliver P. Morton and Hoosier Politics," esp. 95–104.

21. The Johnson County legislator was named John A. Polk, and his lone dissent can be found in *Journal of the House . . . January 10, 1861,* 66, 155–56. Sylvester, "Oliver P. Morton and Hoosier Politics," 95–102, provides one account of the special session, while Thornbrough, *Indiana in the Civil War Era,* 106, offers a concise assessment. The most detailed accounts of the session are found in Draper and Draper, *Brevier Legislative Reports.* The rejection of the Polk motion is covered on pp. 105–8.

22. For the racist measure, see *Journal of the House . . . January 10, 1861,* 58, 77, 123, 162–63, 370.

23. For the move against Bright, see ibid., 210–11, 393; also Draper and Draper, *Brevier Legislative Reports,* 120, 253, 256.

24. "An Act to Organize the Militia, 1852," in Oliver P. Morton Scrapbook, OPMIHS.

25. For more on these commissions and appointments, see Thornbrough, *Indiana in the Civil War Era,* 127–31; Foulke, *Life of Oliver P. Morton,* vol. 1, 149–54. For more on John Love, see John Love Papers, William Henry Smith Memorial Library, Indiana Historical Society, Indianapolis, Indiana.

26. Morton appointed so many Democrats that some disgruntled Republicans claimed that he had forgotten his friends and called for him to move back toward the old system of patronage. Over the course of the war, however, he did appoint more Republicans than Democrats. This occurred largely because after the Emancipation Proclamation it became much more difficult to find Democrats who were politically reliable. After all, Morton did not want to do favors for men who would turn on him and the Lincoln administration at the first opportunity—especially during election season—and try to persuade the soldiers in their commands to vote against the Republicans. See *Indiana Sentinel,* May 2, 1864. For additional criticism of Morton's appointments, see William Dudley Foulke, *Life of Oliver P. Morton,* vol. 1, 151–52.

27. For the Meredith appointment and controversy, see Foulke, *Life of Oliver P. Morton,* vol. 1, 152–53. For complaints about Morton's failure to commission Meredith quickly enough, see M. L. Bundy to C. B. Smith, May 8, 1861, Smith-Spooner Collection, Huntington Research Library, San Marino, California. I thank Gregory Peek for sharing this letter with me. For more on Meredith as a commander, see Nolan, *Iron*

Brigade, passim. Morton's recommendation for Meredith to be promoted to major general is found in O. P. Morton to Abraham Lincoln, Feb. 1, 1865, OPMIHS.

28. Thornbrough, *Indiana in the Civil War Era,* 127–31.

29. For the Heffren appointment and call for censure, see Draper and Draper, *Brevier Legislative Reports,* 179, 243–44.

30. Oliver P. Morton to Abraham Lincoln, June 3, 1861, OPMTBS. In a paper delivered to the Civil War Study Group, Daniel Stowell provided an excellent overview of the way the 1861 appointments worked in Indiana. He shared his paper with me, and I have drawn on it for this story as well as for the others that immediately follow. Stowell, "Mobilizing Hoosiers."

31. Oliver P. Morton to Abraham Lincoln, June 7, 1861, OPMTBS; Oliver P. Morton to Abraham Lincoln, June 9, 1861, Indiana History Manuscripts, Indiana Univ., Bloomington.

32. Oliver P. Morton to Abraham Lincoln, June 19, 1861, OPMLB.

33. Oliver P. Morton to Abraham Lincoln, July 31, 1861, OPMLB.

34. For an example of Morton's travels to DC, see telegrams dated Feb. 8, 1862, OPMTBS. For the governors complaining to the War Committee, see Engle, *Gathering to Save a Nation,* 132–33.

35. The Rockville speech is reprinted in Foulke, *Life of Oliver P. Morton,* vol. 1, 172–74. Stampp, *Indiana Politics,* 73; Foulke, *Life of Oliver P. Morton,* vol. 1, 115; *Indiana Sentinel,* Apr. 15, 1861.

36. Oliver P. Morton to Abraham Lincoln, Aug. 9, 1861, OPMIHS; Abraham Lincoln to Morton, Aug. 15, 1861, OPMTBS.

37. Oliver P. Morton to Abraham Lincoln, Sept. 10, 1861, OPMLB; Oliver P. Morton to Abraham Lincoln, Sept. 20, 1861, OPMTBS; Abraham Lincoln to Morton, Sept. 21, 1861, OPMTBS; Oliver P. Morton to Abraham Lincoln, Sept. 22, 1861, OPMLB; Abraham Lincoln to Morton, Sept. 22, 1861, OPMTBS.

38. For the Kentucky situation, see Foulke, *Life of Oliver P. Morton,* vol. 1, 131–38.

39. Ibid.

40. For a report on the meeting between Morton and Dennison, see Gen. O. M. Mitchell to Edward D. Townsend, Sept. 26, 1861, *Official Records,* ser. 1, vol. 4, 276.

41. Foulke, *Life of Oliver P. Morton,* vol. 1, 131–45. For examples of Morton's worrying about Kentucky, see Oliver P. Morton to Thomas A. Scott, Aug. 29, Sept. 2, 1861; and O. P. Morton to Simon Cameron, Sept. 12, 1861, *Official Records,* ser. 1, vol. 4, 255, 257. For Confederates warning Magoffin not to be like Morton, see Marshall to Governor Magoffin, Mar. 23, 1862, *Official Records,* ser. 1, vol. 10, 468–75. For more on the situation in Kentucky, see the dated Coulter, *Civil War and Readjustment.* A brief overview is found in Harrison, *Civil War in Kentucky.* Rightmyer, *Torn,* is a recent account by a public historian. Important insights are found in Marshall, *Creating a Confederate Kentucky,* and Ramage and Watkins, *Kentucky Rising.* On Beriah Magoffin, see Harrison, "Beriah Magoffin."

42. *Evening Star,* Sept. 25, 1861; Oliver P. Morton to Thomas Scott, Sept. 25, 1861, OPMTBS; Abraham Lincoln to Morton, Sept. 26, 1861, OPMTBS; Oliver P. Morton to Abraham Lincoln, Sept. 26, 1861, OPMLB.

43. Abraham Lincoln to Oliver P. Morton, Sept. 29, 1861, Abraham Lincoln Papers, Library of Congress, Washington, DC.

44. Oliver P. Morton to Abraham Lincoln, Oct. 7, 1861, OPMTBS. I again thank Daniel Stowell for this story and the sources for it.

45. Wilson, *Business of Civil War,* 27–28. For the story of the overcoats, see Morton telegrams, Aug. 20 to Nov. 11, 1861, in OPMTBS. The controversy with Meigs is outlined in Foulke, *Life of Oliver P. Morton,* vol. 1, 160–61.

46. *Indiana Sentinel,* Nov. 27, 1861; Oliver P. Morton to J. J. Bingham, Nov. 28, 1861, OPMISL. The *Sentinel* was a Democratic paper from its inception in 1841 and remained the party's organ in Indianapolis and the state throughout the nineteenth century. Joseph J. Bingham bought the newspaper in 1856 and served as editor until 1865, when he sold it to new owners, who briefly changed the title to the *Indianapolis Herald.* Another change in ownership returned to the old title in 1868. Under Bingham and later editors like James B. Maynard, the *Sentinel* relentlessly criticized Morton and remained the leading voice of his enemies throughout his entire career. For more on the paper, see Miller, *Indiana Newspaper Bibliography,* 275–76. See also the Indiana State Library blog entry: S. Chandler Lighty, "The *Indiana Sentinel:* Indianapolis's Democratic Voice," Oct. 17, 2013, *Hoosier State Chronicles: Indiana's Digital Historic Newspaper Program,* https://blog.newspapers.library.in.gov/indiana-sentinel.

47. For examples of Morton sending military agents to visit the soldiers, see letters dated Aug. 9, 1864, OPMLB. For Mrs. Morton's leadership, the letter to Wallace, and his reply, see Lucinda Morton and Others to General Wallace, Apr. 17, 1861, and Wallace to Ladies, Apr. 17, 1861, both reprinted in *Evansville Daily Journal,* Apr. 20, 1861. Mrs. Morton continued her work with the Sanitary Commission and bought supplies for the soldiers; see Bill from M. H. GM Dry Goods to Mrs. Morton, Nov. 3, 1863, OPMISL. For examples of Morton working to supply Indiana troops, see Oliver P. Morton to Edwin M. Stanton, Mar. 1, 1862, OPMTBS; W. R. Holloway to Edwin M. Stanton, Oct. 28, 1862, and Oliver P. Morton to Edwin M. Stanton, Jan. 24, 1865, OPMLB. The governor also reorganized the state commissary department in July 1862 to better supply the soldiers; see Oliver P. Morton order, July 1, 1862, OPMLB. For examples of Morton referring soldiers' families to the Sanitary Commission, see W. R. Holloway to Mrs. Sarah C. Baker, Mar. 3, 1864, and J. M. Commons to Mrs. Sarah Riley, June 13, 1864, OPMLB. For Morton giving letters of passage to sanitary commissioners, see letters dated July 7, 8, 18, 1864, OPMPLB.

48. Oliver P. Morton, Notes, Feb. 13, 1862, OPMPSA; Stampp, *Indiana Politics,* 123–27; Thornbrough, *Indiana in the Civil War Era,* 170–71; Foulke, *Life of Oliver P. Morton,* vol. 1, 162–65.

49. For an example of the governor trying to find surgeons, see Oliver P. Morton to General C. P. Buckingham, July 17, 1862, Gov. Oliver P. Morton Letters, William Henry Smith Memorial Library, Indiana Historical Society, Indianapolis, Indiana. For Morton's concerns for the wounded after Fort Donelson, see Oliver P. Morton telegrams dated Feb. 17, 1862, OPMTBS; Thornbrough, *Indiana in the Civil War Era,* 171–73; Foulke, *Life of Oliver P. Morton,* vol. 1, 165. Peggy Brase Seigel argued that Morton's actions created opportunities for women nurses to gain independence; see Seigel, "She Went to War." Although he did help female nurses, Morton initially refused their offers to serve; see W. R. Holloway to Miss Mollie A. Conner, Oct. 16, 1862, OPMLB. Thomas E. Rodgers has argued that Hoosiers did not see any significant changes in gender roles during and because of the war; see Rodgers, "Hoosier Women." For the Battle of Shiloh, see McPherson, *Battle Cry of Freedom,* 405–18.

50. Examples of the numerous pieces of correspondence about doctors are found in OPMSL and OPMLB. For examples of Morton worrying about the wounded, see O. P. Morton to Edwin M. Stanton, Oct. 3, 1863; O. P. Morton to W. H. De Motte, June 28, 1864; O. P. Morton to James H. Turner, June 28, 1864, OMPLB. For the case of Frank E. Johnson, see O. P. Morton to Lieutenant Commander Fitch, Aug. 19, 1863, original letter in author's personal collection. For the governor working to help obtain the release of captured Indiana soldiers, see O. P. Morton to Abraham Lincoln, Jan. 12, 1865, OPMIHS. An example of the governor trying to help Hoosiers held prisoner is found in *Evansville Daily Journal,* Nov. 23, 1863. An example of Morton intervening on behalf of a Confederate-held prisoner, see Oliver P. Morton to Edwin M. Stanton, May 31, 1864, OPMLB. For an example of Morton worrying about Union prisoners, including "contraband," see Oliver P. Morton to General Halleck, Feb. 24, 1862, OPMTBS. Another example of the governor seeking advice about the freed slaves brought to Indiana is found in Oliver P. Morton to Gen. George M. Cullum, Mar. 1, 1863, OPMTBS. Cullum responded and told Morton to feed and care for them until the War Department gave further instructions; see Gen. G. M. Cullum to Oliver P. Morton, Mar. 3, 1862, OPMTNS. The issue of African Americans displaced by the war is also found in O. P. Morton to Lucius Eaton, Apr. 11, 1863, OPMLB.

51. Excellent accounts of the complex roles of women in Indiana can be found in the work of Nicole Etcheson. See, esp., Etcheson, *A Generation at War,* 123–47, and Etcheson, "No Fit Wife." For a summary of the literature that suggests that Morton's work afforded women more workplace opportunities, see Anita Ashendel, "'Women as Force,'" 14–15.

52. O. P. Morton to S. D. Bayless, May 23, 1865, OPMLB.

53. Thornbrough, *Indiana in the Civil War Era,* 177.

54. Ibid., 177–79. For Morton's call for increasing the soldiers' pay, see *Evansville Daily Journal,* Dec. 5, 1862. For the Thanksgiving Proclamation, see *Indiana Sentinel,* Nov. 17, 1862. Morton, like other governors, called for a Day of Thanksgiving every year of the war. For his other Thanksgiving proclamations, see *Indiana Sentinel,* Nov. 13, 1861; *Plymouth Democrat,* Nov. 19, 1863; O. P. Morton, "Thanksgiving Proclamation," Nov. 12, 1864, OPMPSA; and copies of the printed proclamations preserved in the Oliver P. Morton Scrapbook, OPMIHS. One might argue that the pride so many leaders took in private charities represented both the influence of Evangelical Christian ideals and the vestiges of Jacksonian principles about individualism and the proper role of government. As Emma Lou Thornbrough noted in *Indiana in the Civil War Era,* 177–79, later criticisms emphasized that the care of the families should not have been a problem for private charity to solve but was something owed to the military families by the government. For an example of the soldiers appreciating Morton as their friend and supporting him, see *Evansville Daily Journal,* Jan. 21, 1863.

55. For this view of the Northern war governors, see Stephen Engle, *All the President's Statesmen,* and Stephen Engle, *Gathering to Save a Nation.* A similar view is found in Harris, *Lincoln and the Union Governors.* An older interpretation that argued that the war governors were outsmarted and wisely used by the superior genius of Abraham Lincoln is found in Hesseltine, *Lincoln and the War Governors.*

56. Thornbrough, *Indiana in the Civil War Era,* 108–10. For more on Caleb B. Smith, see Bailey, "Caleb Blood Smith."

57. Oliver P. Morton to Abraham Lincoln, Dec. 26, 1860, Abraham Lincoln Papers, Library of Congress, Washington, DC. I thank Daniel Stowell for reference to this

letter. For an example of Smith turning out a Democrat in the Indiana office of his own department, see Caleb B. Smith to John Dowling, Apr. 21, 1861, JDPIHS; Thornbough, *Indiana in the Civil War Era*, 108–10. On John P. Usher, see Richardson and Farley, *John Palmer Usher*. For an example of Morton corresponding with Usher on political matters, see O. P. Morton to John P. Usher, Sept. 25, 1863, OPMLB.

58. Stampp, *Indiana Politics*, 111–12; Foulke, *Life of Oliver P. Morton*, vol. 1, 151; *Brevier Legislative Reports, 1861*, V, 36, 156, 199–200.

59. Stampp, *Indiana Politics*, 111–12; Foulke, *Life of Oliver P. Morton*, vol. 1, 153–54.

60. Thornbrough, *Indiana in the Civil War Era*, 116; Stampp, *Indiana Politics*, 84–86. For a full view of Garber's side of the story, see Garber, *Concerning the Quarrel*.

61. For Bright's expulsion from the US Senate and Morton appointing Wright, see Stampp, *Indiana Politics*, 96–98; Thornbrough, *Indiana in the Civil War Era*, 115–16. For an example of Morton receiving advice about replacing Bright, see W. R. Holloway to Oliver P. Morton, Feb. 9, 1862, OPMTBS.

62. *Indiana Sentinel*, Feb. 25, Mar. 5, 7, 1862; Stampp, *Indiana Politics*, 98–99. For Democratic charges of Morton becoming a tyrant, see *Plymouth Weekly Democrat*, Sept. 18, 1862.

5. One-Man Rule

1. For the installation of the safe, see receipts dated July 29 and Sept. 7, 1863, in Adjutant General's Records, Indiana State Archives, Indianapolis, Indiana. The purchase of the safe is found in letters dated May and June 1863 in OPMLB.

2. Foulke, *Life of Oliver P. Morton*, vol. 1, 260–61. Lincoln authorized the money from the War Department on June 18, 1863.

3. For Democratic criticism of the Republicans and the Union Party in this period, see Stampp, *Indiana Politics*, 139–42. For a private correspondence discussing Democratic views of the situation in early 1862, see Thomas Palmer to John Dowling, Jan. 26, 1862, JDPIHS. A good overview of the shifting economic situation in Indiana during the war is found in Sylvester, "Oliver P. Morton and Hoosier Politics," passim.

4. Hendricks, "Speech of Mr. Hendricks."

5. Ibid.

6. Ibid.

7. *Richmond (Va.) Times Dispatch*, Jan. 23, 25, 1862.

8. Some Democrats kept their criticisms general and vague because pro-Union postmasters and military officers opened and read their mail. For an example of such vague critiques, see Thomas Dowling to John Dowling, May 19, 1862, and Patrick Donahoe to John Dowling, July 14, 1862, JDPIHS.

9. Anonymous, "Lt. Coffin's Statement," to Oliver P. Morton, Apr. 28, 1862, OPMPSA. Morton's recommendation for Scott's arrest is found on the back of the letter.

10. *Indianapolis Journal*, Aug. 21, 1862. I do not attempt to cite all relevant titles from the vast literature on the Civil War. There are, of course, studies of individual commanders, battles, and campaigns available. But this volume is focused primarily on the political side of the conflict, so I do not include such secondary sources except when they are directly related to Morton and the political situation. Instead, I have chosen

to refer the reader to a classic and widely respected one-volume history of the conflict. On the 1862 Confederate invasion, see McPherson, *Battle Cry of Freedom,* 511–45.

11. For the commissioning of the portrait of Morton, see *Evansville Daily Journal,* Jan. 9, 1866. In 1872, Cincinnati again honored Morton, this time with a banquet; see *Evening Star,* Nov. 26, 1872.

12. On General Buell, see Engle, *Don Carlos Buell.*

13. For newspaper accounts of the incident with Bull Nelson, see *New York Herald,* Sept. 30, Oct. 2, 1862; *Abingdon Virginian,* Oct. 17, 1862; *Harper's Weekly,* Oct. 18, 1862. An excellent historical study of the affair is found in Clark, *Notorious "Bull" Nelson,* esp., 119–52. A slightly different version of the event is found in Foulke, *Life of Oliver P. Morton,* vol. 1, 193–95. The account as told here is drawn mostly from Clark, but it includes some of the dialogue as found in Foulke.

14. Clark, *Notorious "Bull" Nelson,* 140–52; *New York Herald,* Oct. 2, 1862.

15. Clark, *Notorious "Bull" Nelson,* 140–52.

16. Ibid., 153–66. For criticism of Morton's role in the killing of Nelson, see *Indiana Sentinel,* Oct. 7, 1862.

17. Foulke, *Life of Oliver P. Morton,* vol. 1, 196–98.

18. For the Newburgh raid, see Stampp, *Indiana Politics,* 150–51. On the Union Clubs and Union Leagues, see ibid., 192–93. For coverage of the political tension and violence in one Indiana community, see Etcheson, *A Generation at War,* esp. 99–122.

19. For an excellent account of the dispute between Morton and Buell, see Engle, *Don Carlos Buell,* passim; William C. Moreau to Oliver P. Morton, Nov. 25, 1861, OPMTBS; Don Carlos Buell to Oliver P. Morton, Nov. 25, 1861, OPMTBS; Oliver P. Morton to Don Carlos Buell, Dec. 3, 1861, OPMTBS; Don Carlos Buell to John Love, Dec. 7, 1861; Engle, *Don Carlos Buell,* 94–95.

20. Ibid., 115–16; Oliver P. Morton to Don Carlos Buell, June 4, 1862, OPMTBS; Morton to Buell, June 5, 1862, OPMLB; Buell to Morton, June 6, 1862, cited in Engle, *Don Carlos Buell,* 253.

21. Ibid., 273, 280, 289.

22. Ibid., 296–97, 300, 314.

23. Yates and Morton to Lincoln, Oct. 25, 1862, *Official Records,* ser. 2, vol. 16, II, 642; Engle, *Don Carlos Buell,* 319–20.

24. H. W. Halleck to John Schofield, Sept. 20, 1862, *Official Records,* ser. 1, vol. 13, 654; *Indiana Sentinel,* Oct. 7, 1862. Morton maintained a friendly relationship with the owner of the Galt House and later wrote the man an introduction to President Lincoln; see O. P. Morton to Abraham Lincoln, Dec. 16, 1864, OPMLB.

25. While visiting Indiana troops in the field, Morton worried about the Confederate forces at Corinth in the spring of 1862 and wrote to the secretary of war warning him to reinforce Union armies to defend against them; see O. P. Morton to Edwin M. Stanton, May 22, 1862, *Official Records,* ser. 1, vol. 10, 209–10.

26. On the state draft in Indiana, see Thornbrough, *Indiana in the Civil War Era,* 131–132; Stampp, *Indiana Politics,* 144. At times, Morton's recruiting efforts were so successful that the government temporarily suspended the draft in the Hoosier State; see *Marshall County Republican,* Mar. 24, 1864. For a summary of the governor's 1862 appointments of draft commissioners, see O. P. Morton to W. Scott Ketchum, Jan. 14,

1864, OPMLB. For Morton intervening on behalf of the draft commissioners, see O. P. Morton to W. Scott Ketchum, Jan. 21, 1864, OPMLB. An example of Morton discussing the raising of black troops is found in a letter from one of his military aides, William H. Schlater, to G. W. Brodie, Nov. 12, 1863, OPMLB. Early in 1864 the governor began receiving the applications of white officers wanting to command regiments of African American soldiers; for examples see William H. Schlater to George W. Hines, Jan. 6, 1864; William H. Schlater to L. Conrad, Jan. 7, 1864; William H. Schlater to J. Smith, Jan. 22, 1864, OPMLB. For Morton complaining that other states did not make their quotas, see Oliver P. Morton to James B. Fry, Feb. 1, 1864, OPMLB.

27. For studies on the Emancipation Proclamation, see Franklin, *Emancipation Proclamation;* Guelzo, *Lincoln's Emancipation Proclamation;* Holzer, Medford, and Williams, *Emancipation Proclamation.*

28. Morton and many other Republicans saw the Emancipation Proclamation as a means to win the war, although even many who supported the measure worried that it would punish loyal Unionist slaveholders and would hurt the party politically. See, e.g., *Indianapolis Journal,* Sept. 27, 1862. For more on the Emancipation Proclamation as a war measure, see Gallagher, *The Union War,* 75–118.

29. For praise of Morton's support of emancipation and for the measure as a means of winning the war, see *Marshall County Republican,* Mar. 3, 1864.

30. For Morton sharing secret codes and seeking witnesses to testify against the Copperhead secret societies during the 1862 campaign, see Oliver P. Morton to E. B. Allen, May 10, 1862, July 15, 1862, in Edward B. Allen Papers, William Henry Smith Memorial Library, Indiana Historical Society, Indianapolis, Indiana.

31. William R. Holloway to John G. Nicolay, Oct. 24, 1862, OPMLB; Hendricks, "Issues of the War." At the time, the plan to take the Midwest out of the Union was called both Northwest Conspiracy and Northwestern Conspiracy.

32. Morton to Lincoln, Oct. 27, 1862, repr. in Terrell, *Indiana in the War of the Rebellion,* 25–28.

33. Ibid.

34. Ibid.

35. Ibid.

36. Ibid.

37. Oliver P. Morton, *Governor's Message,* Jan. 10, 1863, printed in *Evansville Daily Journal,* Jan. 12, 13, 1863. Many other Republican papers also published the governor's annual message.

38. Ibid.

39. Foulke, *Life of Oliver P. Morton,* vol. 1, 221–22.

40. On the fear of corruption as an issue during the war, see Smith, *Enemy Within.*

41. *Report and Evidence of the Committee on Arbitrary Arrests,* 23.

42. Towne, *Surveillance and Spies,* 208–9, 268–69, showed that Morton and Carrington disagreed about what should be done with the evidence that the army was gathering about the Copperheads. Morton wanted the army to arrest suspects and try them in military tribunals, but Carrington argued for civilian arrests and trials. Overall, the two men cooperated closely and agreed most of the time, but Carrington

reported that he and the governor also disagreed when Morton wanted to make the evidence public and the army commander did not; see ibid., 268–69.

43. Foulke, *Life of Oliver P. Morton,* vol. 1, 236; Oliver P. Morton, "History of Indiana Democracy Ventilated."

44. Foulke, *Life of Oliver P. Morton,* vol. 1, 236–40; Stampp, *Indiana Politics,* 176–79.

45. Foulke, *Life of Oliver P. Morton,* vol. 1, 254–55. For Democratic criticism of his one-man rule, see reprint of *Cincinnati Enquirer* editorial in *Indiana Sentinel,* Dec. 21, 1863, Apr. 9, 18, 1864. For an example of Republicans expressing support for Morton in his battle with the Democratic legislature, see *Evansville Daily Journal,* Mar. 30, 1863. For an example of Morton borrowing $3,000 from the St. Joseph County government, see Oliver P. Morton to John H. Harper, Feb. 5, 1864, original letter in author's personal collection. This letter, and others like it, served as receipts for the loans and outlined the purposes for which the money was to be used: "in defraying the proper and necessary expenses of the Benevolent Institutions of the State and the Northern Prison, and for the relief of sick and wounded Indiana soldiers." The letter also said that the loan and reasonable interest would be repaid to the county in a manner "as may be provided for by law hereafter."

46. Ibid., 260–62.

47. For examples of how the payment of the interest on the debt quickly became an issue upon which the Democrats attacked Morton, hoping that they might use it as another means to force him to recall the legislature, see *Indianapolis Journal,* May 4, 1863; *Indiana Sentinel,* May 9, 11, 1863.

48. For Democratic charges in 1864 that Morton mishandled state money, see *Indiana Sentinel,* Feb. 17, 1864; Morton, *Speech at the Union State Convention.*

49. For the disaster at Fredericksburg, see McPherson, *Battle Cry of Freedom,* 570–75.

50. I take this story and interpretation of the power struggle between Morton and Burnside, including the telegram quotations cited here, from Towne, "Killing the Serpent Speedily." For Morton expressing concern about the removal of Carrington, see Oliver P. Morton to J. J. Brown, Apr. 29, 1863, OPMTBS.

51. Towne, "Killing the Serpent Speedily," 49–50.

52. Ibid.

53. Towne, *Surveillance and Spies,* 79.

54. Towne, "Killing the Serpent Speedily," 50–53.

55. Ibid, 50–53. In May 1863, friends back home in Wayne Country reported to the governor that "Confederate Sympathizers" were causing trouble, and the Union League asked for Morton's permission to take up arms against them; see A. C. Harris to O. P. Morton, May 6, 1863, OPMPSA. For more on Vallandigham from a different interpretive angle, see Klement, *Limits of Dissent.*

56. For the full story of Douglas's arrest and the response to it, see Towne, "Worse than Vallandigham."

57. Towne, "Killing the Serpent Speedily," 53–54; Foulke, *Life of Oliver P. Morton,* vol. 1, 273–77.

58. Towne, "Killing the Serpent Speedily," 54–55.

59. Towne, "Worse than Vallandigham," 1–39.

60. Towne, "Killing the Serpent Speedily," 56–58.

61. Ibid.

62. Ibid. 60–61. For more on the suppression of the *Chicago Times,* see Tenney, "To Suppress or Not to Suppress."

63. Tenney, "To Surpress or Not to Surpress"; Oliver P. Morton to Edwin M. Stanton, June 25, 1862, OPMLB. The letter books, of course, provide copies. The letter is also found in *Official Records,* ser. 3, vol. 2, 176. The suggestion to arrest Milligan is found in William R. Holloway to John Hanna, Aug. 15, 1862, John Hanna Papers, Lilly Library, Indiana Univ., Bloomington, Indiana.

64. Towne, "Killing the Serpent Speedily," 60–65.

65. Ibid., 62–65.

66. Ibid.

67. For the major campaigns in the summer and fall of 1863, see McPherson, *Battle Cry of Freedom,* 626–88.

68. For more on Morgan and Morgan's Raid, see Ramage, *Rebel Raider;* Wilson, "Thunderbolt of the Confederacy"; Ramage, "Indiana's Response"; Roller, "Business as Usual."

69. *Madison Daily Courier,* July 10, 11, 1863; Terrell, *Indiana in the War of the Rebellion,* 178–79. For Morton's correspondence with Gen. Jeremiah T. Boyle, commander at Louisville, during the raid, see Morton to Boyle, July 4, 6, 1863; Boyle to Morton, July 6, 1863, OPMTBS. For examples of Morton's response to the raid, see Oliver P. Morton, "General Military Orders," July 9, 1863, OPMPSA; O. P. Morton to R. E. Ricker, July 10, 1863, OPMPSA; O. P. Morton, "John Morgan on the Wing," July 13, 1863, OPMPSA.

70. Terrell, *Indiana in the War of the Rebellion,* 178–79.

71. Oliver P. Morton, "To the Officers and Soldiers of the 'Legion' and 'Minute Men' of Indiana," July 15, 1863, OPMIHS. For examples of Morgan's Raid claims coming to Morton, see W. R. Holloway to Messrs. Leonard and Swinson, Mar. 17, 1864, OPMLB; Thomas E. Brambelle to O. P. Morton, June 22, 1864, OPMPSA.

72. For Morton considering campaigning in Ohio, see W. R. Holloway to A. Anderson, Sept. 22, 1863; W. R. Holloway to C. M. Allen, Sept. 22, 1863; W. R. Holloway to William E. Davis, Sept. 22, 1863, OPMLB. For Morton's concerns about the Democrats committing fraud by sending Irish voters to Ohio, see W. R. Holloway to William Dennison, Sept. 26, 1863, OPMLB. The governor's direction of the Republican campaign in the state and local elections that year are found in Holloway's letters to various recipients (including Richard W. Thompson) in late September 1863, OPMLB.

6. Copperheads, Treason, and the Election of 1864

1. Part of this chapter was published as an article: Fuller, "Oliver P. Morton, Political Ideology, and Treason." The account of the assassination attempt on Morton is found in Foulke, *Life of Oliver P. Morton,* vol. 1, 383–84. Horace Heffren, the Democratic state legislator to whom Morton gave a commission, testified at the Indianapolis Treason Trials in 1864 and confirmed that the Copperhead organizations had plotted to assassinate the governor; see *Farmer's Cabinet,* Nov. 11, 1864. For a later example of the Republicans using the assassination attempt as a means to rally Union veterans to vote for Morton's party, see *Indiana American,* Jan. 17, 1868.

2. For Morton worrying about what was to come, see O. P. Morton to Edwin M. Stanton, Jan. 19, 1864, *Official Records,* ser. 3, vol. 4, 39–40. As he had throughout the conflict, Morton continued working diligently to recruit soldiers and get them ready to be sent to the front. For an example of him reassuring General Grant that Indiana soldiers would soon be on the way, see O. P. Morton to Ulysses S. Grant, Feb. 12, 1864, OPMLB. He also continued to advise Lincoln on how to win the war and argued that victory had to be achieved in 1864; see O. P. Morton to Abraham Lincoln, Jan. 18, 1864, OPMLB. For an overview of the Overland Campaign and other operations in 1864, see McPherson, *Battle Cry of Freedom,* 718–50.

3. For examples of criticism of Morton in 1864, see *Indiana Sentinel,* Apr. 30, July 13, 1864. For an example of doubts about the election, see Fletcher, *Diary,* vol. 8, *1863–1864,* 446, entry dated Oct. 8, 1864.

4. O. P. Morton to William Tecumseh Sherman, Nov. 17, 1865, OPMLB. The literature on the Copperheads continues to grow as the debate continues over whether or not they constituted a real threat to the Union. Progressive historian Wood Gray argued that the Copperheads were a very real expression of an internal Civil War on the Northern home front; see Gray, *Hidden Civil War.* A popular history published that same year took the same view: Milton, *Abraham Lincoln and the Fifth Column.* Frank L. Klement disagreed with Gray, arguing that self-serving or paranoid Republican politicians largely created the Copperhead threat and used the actions of a few unstable individuals to engage in a witch hunt designed to label the loyal opposition as traitors in order to win elections. See Klement, *Copperheads in the Middle West.*

Trained as a Progressive historian, Klement saw history in economic and class terms. He thus portrayed Morton and other Republicans as the tools of the capitalist class who attacked the poor Democrats struggling to defend the liberty of farmers and workers. Writing in the immediate context of the McCarthy hearings and the Cold War, Klement's revisionist interpretation saw government overreach, as leaders got swept up in the hysteria and went too far in trying to root out internal enemies. The Klement thesis enjoyed a long period of dominance, accepted by Consensus historians eager to see the North as a unified nation and who saw themselves as revisionist scholars correcting the errors of the past. Despite their love of Lincoln and most Radical Republicans, the New Left historians also embraced the Klement thesis, and it became a standard part of the race-nationalist narrative of the late twentieth century. For those New Left scholars reluctant to criticize politicians of the past with whom they agreed on issues like race, Klement's interpretation stood as a foil against any who might criticize the Republicans and, by extension if not directly, Abraham Lincoln. For an example, see Neely, *Fate of Liberty.* More recently, historians reflecting the context of the age of the War on Terror have begun to challenge this long-standing interpretation. Jennifer Weber argued that the Copperheads were a real threat, and that had they timed some of their actions better, might have damaged Union prospects for victory; see Weber, *Copperheads.* Another work that raised questions about the prevailing view was the section on the Sons of Liberty in Churchill, *To Shake Their Guns in the Tyrant's Face,* 107–44. Stephen Towne attempted to fully dismantle the Klement thesis with a devastating refutation based on the most complete archival research on the subject yet undertaken. Not only were the Copperheads real and a true threat, but only the diligent efforts of Union military officers, politicians like Morton, and a network of spies and detectives thwarted the traitorous plans of an internal Civil War. See Towne, *Surveillance and Spies*. Like William Blair in *With Malice Toward None*, I take more of a middle-ground position on the Copperheads in my analysis of Morton's actions. I think that he both sincerely believed that there was a threat and used that threat to further his own political ends.

5. *Indianapolis Journal*, Aug. 13, 1861; *Indiana Sentinel*, Aug. 14, 1861.

6. For more on Miles Fletcher, see Robert W. Smith, "Biographical Sketches," Calvin Fletcher Jr. Family Collection, 1850–1977, Indiana Historical Society, Indianapolis, Indiana.

7. O. P. Morton to Calvin Fletcher, May 11, 1863, Calvin Fletcher Papers, William Henry Smith Memorial Library, Indiana Historical Society, Indianapolis, Indiana. The background to and an account of this story can be found in Fletcher, *Diary*, vol. 7, 1861–1862, 420–27.

8. O. P. Morton to Calvin Fletcher, May 11, 1863, Calvin Fletcher Papers, William Henry Smith Memorial Library, Indiana Historical Society, Indianapolis, Indiana.

9. Ibid.

10. The *Indianapolis Journal*, May 18, 1862, printed an account of the accident that said it was a plot to kill Morton. The crosstown Democratic organ, the *Indiana Sentinel*, scoffed at that idea the next day, May 19, 1862, and again on May 26, 1862. The arrest of the man who put the car on the tracks and his confession were reported in the *Journal* on June 20, 1862, and republished in the *Pomeroy Weekly Telegraph*, June 27, 1862. The *Sentinel* continued to deride the story and saw it as a romance concocted by Berry Sulgrove, the editor of the *Journal*; see *Indiana Sentinel*, Nov. 24, 1862. For the Democrats saying that Sulgrove admitted making up the story in his grand jury testimony, see Draper and Draper, *Brevier Legislative Reports*, vol. 6, 1863, 70.

11. Morton forwarded the report to Terre Haute native and assistant secretary of the interior, John P. Usher, who endorsed it and sent it on to Senator Henry S. Lane. The original is "Memorandum handed me by J. P. Usher on the 26th Nov 1861 (Opposition to the War and Lincoln's Administration)," in Lane-Elston Papers, William Henry Smith Memorial Library, Indiana Historical Society, Indianapolis, Indiana. The report has been conveniently reprinted in Nation and Towne, *Indiana's War*, 173–77. When Morton gave the report to the *Journal*, it set off a firestorm of newspaper controversy because it implicated leading Democrats like John G. Davis and Daniel Voorhees; see *Indianapolis Journal*, Dec. 30, 1861, Jan. 1, 16, 29, 1862; *Indiana Sentinel*, Dec. 31, 1861, Jan. 3, 15, 17, 1862. Other newspapers joined the fray as well; for an account of the arguments, see Towne, *Surveillance and Spies*, 19–20. For another example of Morton receiving a report about Copperhead activity (in this case, from his hometown of Centerville), see A. Jones and others to Oliver P. Morton, May 2, 1863, OPMTBS.

12. For Morton's early worries and actions against the Copperheads, see Towne, *Surveillance and Spies*, 17–21; Morton to Stanton, June 25, 1862, OPMLB; Morton to Lincoln, June 25, 1862, OPMLB.

13. Ibid.

14. Morton to Lincoln, Oct. 7, 1862, reprinted in Terrell, *Indiana in the War of the Rebellion*, 24–25.

15. Ibid.

16. The Battle of Pogue's Run is recounted in Foulke, *Life of Oliver P. Morton*, vol. 1, 273–78.

17. For questions about his eligibility, see *Evansville Daily Journal,* Jan. 8, 25, 1864; *Marshall Country Republican,* Jan. 28, 1864.

18. Thornbrough, *Indiana in the Civil War Era,* 210; Morton, *Speech at the Union State Convention.*

19. Ibid.

20. Ibid.

21. *Facts for the People.* For an example of Morton's involvement in the campaign that summer, see John Brough to O. P. Morton, Aug. 27, 1864, OPMISL.

22. *Facts for the People.*

23. James H. McNeely to Oliver P. Morton, June 13, 1864, OPMPSA.

24. Foulke, *Life of Oliver P. Morton,* vol. 1, 298, 299n.

25. On a brief summary of McDonald's early career, see Thornbrough, *Indiana in the Civil War Era,* 212n61; Foulke, *Life of Oliver P. Morton,* vol. 1, 300–302.

26. *Gubernatorial Canvass,* 1–5.

27. Ibid.

28. Ibid.

29. Ibid., 6.

30. Ibid., 7–8.

31. Ibid., 8–14.

32. Ibid.

33. Ibid., 14–17.

34. Ibid.

35. Ibid., 17–20.

36. Foulke, *Life of Oliver P. Morton,* vol. 1, 355–63.

37. Ibid.

38. For an example of Morton's campaign rhetoric, see Morton, *National and State Affairs.*

39. For the movement for Chase and the Pomeroy Circular, see Waugh, *Reelecting Lincoln,* 32–45, 115–17.

40. *New York Times,* Apr. 10, 1863; *New York Herald,* Apr. 10, 1863; *New-York Tribune,* Apr. 13, 1863; Towne, *Surveillance and Spies,* 80.

41. On the campaign for Frémont in 1864, see Long, *Jewel of Liberty,* 182–84, 239–43; Waugh, *Reelecting Lincoln,* 137–47, 175–81, 303–5.

42. Towne, *Surveillance and Spies,* 263.

43. Oliver P. Morton to Edwin M. Stanton, Sept. 12, 1864, OPMLB. Democrats complained bitterly about the soldiers tipping the elections, complaining that the Republicans brought them home to "aid the abolitionists"; see John Dowling to Fenelon Dowling, Apr. 15, 1863, JDPIHS.

44. Although secrecy makes it hard to follow Copperheads with great accuracy, it seems that the same group of men made up the leadership of organizations. They changed the name from Knights of the Golden Circle to the Order of American Knights to the Sons of Liberty, probably in hopes of confusing the authorities or to make it appear that they had more followers. Like other secret societies, it is quite likely that the inner circle of leaders kept their plans to themselves, sharing with other members what they thought they needed to know. This meant that many members were not privy to every part of every plot. Towne, *Surveillance and Spies,* outlines the shifting

conspiracies, and useful archival sources include General Hovey's Report, Aug. 1865, in Conrad Baker Papers, box 1, folder 8, William Henry Smith Memorial Library, Indiana Historical Society, Indianapolis, Indiana, and a list of the Sons of Liberty, William R. Holloway Papers, box 2, folder 4, William Henry Smith Memorial Library, Indiana Historical Society, Indianapolis, Indiana. For more on the Knights of the Golden Circle, see Keehn, *Knights of the Golden Circle.* For more on the eccentric Bowles, see Thornbrough, *Indiana in the Civil War Era,* 214; Stampp, *Indiana Politics,* 149–50; and Rehnquist, "Civil Liberty," 932.

45. On Dodd, see Towne, *Surveillance and Spies,* 206; Rehnquist, "Civil Liberty," 932; Blair, *With Malice Toward Some,* 211–15.

46. For more on Milligan, see Towne, "Worse than Vallandigham"; Kelley, *Milligan's Fight Against Lincoln;* and Thornbrough, *Indiana in the Civil War Era,* 216.

47. For opposition to the war in Indiana, see Towne, *Surveillance and Spies,* passim; Stampp, *Indiana Politics,* 186–91; Thornbrough, *Indiana in the Civil War Era,*18–224; and Nation and Towne, *Indiana's War,* 125–27, 155–59. Jacquelyn S. Nelson argues that nearly a quarter of Indiana Quakers joined the Union Army. She contends that Quakers who opposed the war on religious grounds faced little harassment from the authorities. Morton's long acquaintance with members of the Society of Friends in Wayne County no doubt influenced his own approach to such religious objectors. For this and more on Quaker opposition to the war, see Nelson, *Indiana Quakers.*

48. Congressman Daniel Voorhees offers an excellent example of a politician who blurred the line between legitimate opposition and treason. For a study that reveals how loyal Democrats mixed with conspirators in the Sons of Liberty in one Indiana county, see Etcheson, *A Generation at War,* 99–122.

49. Thornbrough, *Indiana in the Civil War Era,* 216–17.

50. Henry B. Carrington to Edwin M. Stanton, June 17, 1864, *Official Records,* ser. 2, vol. 7, 450.

51. Towne, *Surveillance and Spies,* 174–221; Foulke, *Life of Oliver P. Morton,* vol. 1, 373–418.

52. For the details of the planned uprising, see Towne, *Surveillance and Spies,* 256–63.

53. Ibid., 261–64; *Indianapolis Journal,* Aug. 6, 8, 1864; *Indiana Sentinel,* Aug. 3, 1864. Oliver P. Morton to Edwin M. Stanton, Aug. 6, 1864, OPMTBS.

54. Towne, *Surveillance and Spies,* 256–63.

55. Ibid., 264–67.

56. For more on the treason trials and the Supreme Court decision in *Ex parte Milligan,* see Wertheim, "Indianapolis Treason Trials"; Rehnquist, "Civil Liberty," 932–37; and Kelley, *Milligan's Fight Against Lincoln.* For Democratic criticism of Morton's role in the investigation and arrests, see *Indiana Sentinel,* Aug. 25, 1864.

57. Wertheim, "Indianapolis Treason Trials."

58. *Indiana Sentinel,* Oct. 3, 1864; Other Democratic criticisms were reprinted in *Evansville Daily Journal,* Oct. 5, 7, 1864. Election returns are found in Thornbrough, *Indiana in the Civil War Era,* 223, and in *Indiana Sentinel,* Oct. 31, 1864. Comments on Morton's reelection in a national newspaper are found in *Harper's Weekly,* Oct. 22, 1864.

59. Wertheim, "Indianapolis Treason Trials"; Thornbrough, *Indiana in the Civil War Era,* 220, 222. There are differing interpretations of the election of 1864, including several in the last generation of scholarship. David E. Long, in *The Jewel of Liberty,* argues that

the election was the most important in American history and puts Lincoln and the issue of slavery at the center of the story. Long's detailed account includes analysis of the Indianapolis treason trials and rightly portrays the election's outcome as doubtful in the summer of 1864, but he focuses too much on emancipation as a corrective to previous accounts that had ignored slavery. This overcorrection includes too much attention to Lincoln as emancipator—to the point of hagiography—but Long does touch on other issues and is especially good at putting the contest in the context of the war.

John Waugh, *Reelecting Lincoln,* offers a riveting narrative of the presidential election, with useful insights on the candidates. Waugh joins other scholars in arguing that the soldiers' votes made the difference in returning Lincoln to the White House for a second term. In *Decided on the Battlefield,* David Alan Johnson contends that the military delivered the victory to the Republicans by winning battles, an interpretation that fits well with the work of others. But he provides few primary sources, does not engage the current literature, and in his long epilogue he wanders off into a dubious counterfactual musing about what would have happened if George McClellan had won the election.

For his part, Jonathan W. White, in *Emancipation, the Union Army,* challenges the argument that the soldiers supported emancipation and the Republican Party when they voted for Lincoln. Rather than embracing abolitionism and becoming staunch Republicans, many of the 78 percent of the soldiers who cast their ballots for the president did so simply because they believed that the Democrats were traitors and that McClellan's victory would mean losing the war. Adherence to the Union cause remained an important factor, as soldiers and citizens alike chose to vote for the incumbents in hopes of preserving the nation rather than wholeheartedly voting for freedom, equality, and the Republican platform. Finally, Larry E. Nelson, *Bullets, Ballots, and Rhetoric,* looks at the ways in which the Confederacy placed its hopes in the outcome of the Northern election, as Southern leaders counted on war weariness to bolster the Democrats and looked for ways to exploit disunity in the United States to achieve their own independence.

60. Thornbrough, *Indiana in the Civil War Era,* 222, 227. For Morton sending out agents to help the troops and prepare to bring them home, see letters dated Apr. 3 and Apr. 25, 1865, OPMLB. See also O. P. Morton to Edwin M. Stanton, May 22, 1865, OPMLB.

7. Peace and Paralysis

1. Morton, "Inaugural Address, Jan. 6, 1865."
2. Hendricks, "Issues of the War," 451–65.
3. Bastiat, *That Which Is Seen.* Bastiat's parable told the story of a baker who found his window broken by some unknown vandal. A crowd gathered around as the news spread throughout the village. Someone said that the broken window would create work for the glazier and that the baker would pay someone to install it, and soon the argument was made that the broken window brought prosperity because it created jobs. But this was a fallacy, and Bastiat carefully explained that the money that the baker spent on replacing the window was money that he could not spend on other items. The seen—the broken window—seemed to create economic wealth, but it actually hurt the

economy because of the unseen—the products and investments that the baker might have bought and made with money that he now had to spend to replace something that he had purchased previously.

Bastiat used the parable to explain the unintended consequences of government spending. Government took money and spent it on things clearly seen, but this meant the loss of many unseen economic activities that might have occurred otherwise. War served as a prime example of how government spending robbed the economy of wealth creation in the name of destruction. Building armies cost a lot of money, and everyone could see the consequences. But the unseen losses were compounded when one added in the loss of life and the creativity of those individuals now gone from the course of history. In his later debates about currency, Morton would deride the theories of Bastiat that were used to criticize Republican economic policies; see *Harper's Weekly*, Feb. 7, 1874.

For other studies that show that the war did not create economic growth, see Mulderink, *New Bedford's Civil War*; Gallman and Engerman, "Civil War Economy"; Gallman, *Mastering Wartime*; O'Brien, *Economic Effect*.

4. Paludan, *"A People's Contest,"* 143. Paludan admitted that the war brought economic decline despite his interpretation, which was much more sympathetic to the nationalist agenda and the statist policies it brought. For a libertarian alternative that argues for the development of a neomercantilist economy during the war, see Hummel, *Emancipating Slaves*, 231–38. Throughout the war, Morton continued to hold to many Jacksonian economic principles, but practical considerations of governance and his overriding ideological commitments meant that he often violated the free market doctrines that carried over from his days as a Democrat. After the war, he would continue to evolve on economic matters and abandon many free market ideas in favor of statist neomercantilism; see throughout present work, esp. chapter 10.

5. Stampp, *Indiana Politics*, 190; Leary, *Indianapolis*, 84–86.

6. Paludan, *A Peoples' Contest*, 117–20, 136–37; *Indianapolis Daily Sentinel*, 1862–1863, passim. For more on the ways in which Republicans became tied to big business, see Richardson, *Greatest Nation of the Earth*, and her *To Make Men Free*, 25–54.

7. Thornbrough, *Indiana in the Civil War Era*, 337. For an example of Morton working with the railroads during the war, see Oliver P. Morton to M. Prindle, Jan. 9, 1864, OPMLB.

8. Holloway, *Indianapolis*, 344–65; Leary, *Indianapolis*, 97–103, 116–17.

9. Stampp, *Indiana Politics*, 186–90; Thornbrough, *Indiana in the Civil War Era*, 190–96. For the virtue of local autonomy to rural Hoosiers, see Richard F. Nation, *At Home in the Hoosier Hills*, 213–19. For a view of the Jacksonian Democrats as libertarian defenders of the free market and economic liberty (with certain exceptions, such as the obvious example of slavery), see Rothbard, *A History of Money*, 90–122, esp. 91. For a study of the impact of the war on agriculture, see Gates, *Agriculture and the Civil War*.

10. Morton, "Inaugural Address, Jan. 6, 1865."

11. Morton, *Emigration to the United States*, 3.

12. Ibid., 4–17.

13. Ibid., 17–42. Morton continued to encourage emigration, but the war made it difficult to allocate resources for doing much about it; see Charles P. Jacobs to Father John Dauphin, July 10, 1865, in Oliver P. Morton Letter Book, May 10, 1865, to Sept. 1865, OPMIHS.

14. Thornbrough, *Indiana in the Civil War Era,* 227; Foulke, *Life of Oliver P. Morton,* vol. 1, 436–37.

15. Ibid., 436, 438–40. Lincoln presenting the flag to Morton is recounted in *Evening Star,* Mar. 18, 1865. Newspaper coverage of Morton's proclamation calling Hoosiers to pray and grieve is in *Evening Star,* Apr. 17, 1865.

16. Foulke, *Life of Morton,* 441–42; O. P. Morton to Andrew Johnson, Aug. 5, 1861, OPMISL.

17. For Morton's proclamation about the Lincoln funeral train, see Oliver P. Morton Scrapbook, OPMIHS. Please note that in 2014 the Indiana Historical Society obtained another Oliver P. Morton scrapbook that contains newspaper clippings regarding the building of a memorial to him in 1907. I do not cite that scrapbook in this book but am instead citing the scrapbook housed in the Oliver P. Morton Papers that was originally his own and that his widow added to after his death. It is unfortunate that the archivists chose to title the 1907 volume the same thing as the original collection started by Morton himself. For the 1907 collection, which was a gift from the Ohio Historical Society, see Oliver P. Morton Scrapbook, OPMIHS. For more on the Lincoln funeral and train, see Reed, *Lincoln's Funeral Train.* For the governor raising money for a Lincoln monument, see Oliver P. Morton to W. H. Vance, May 29, 1865; George H. West to J. Long, May 30, 1865, OPMLB.

18. There are many letters related to the governor's work to help the soldiers return home in the spring of 1865 in his letter books; see, esp., those dated in May 1865, OPMLB. For Morton thinking about creating the Soldiers' Home, see O. P. Morton to Harvey D. Scott, May 29, 1865, OPMLB. Discussion about appointing a manager of the home can be found in O. P. Morton to Edwin M. Stanton, July 17, 1865, OPMLB. For the song dedicated to Morton, see Lozier, *Cottage of the Dear Ones.*

19. Foulke, *Life of Oliver P. Morton,* vol. 1, 445–47. For Morton's work in support of the cemetery at Gettysburg, see Morton, *Soldiers' National Cemetery.*

20. Morton, "What Shall be Done with the Negro?," Notes, 1865, OPMISL.

21. Ibid.

22. Morton, *Reconstruction and Negro Suffrage,* 1–9.

23. Ibid., 9–14.

24. Ibid. Here Morton made the argument repeated by later historians that such laws meant that the labor conditions in the South were simply slavery by another name; see Blackmon, *Slavery by Another Name.*

25. Morton, *Reconstruction and Negro Suffrage,* 9–14. For an example of the reaction to Morton's Richmond speech, see *Evening Star,* Oct. 9, 1865.

26. Morton referred to the exclusionary clause of the state constitution when asked about how to deal with black refugees during the war, see W. R. Holloway to Dr. Alexander, Mar. 24, 1864, OPMLB.

27. Morton, *Reconstruction and Negro Suffrage,* 14–16.

28. Ibid., 16–19.

29. William H. Schlater to John Thomas, July 18, 1865, OPMLB. Lieutenant Governor Conrad Baker fielded a letter to Morton regarding fears of mob violence against blacks; see Conrad Baker to Mrs. Montgomery, Aug. 23, 1865, OPMLB.

30. Thornbrough, *Indiana in the Civil War Era,* 229–30. A newspaper account of the confrontation between Meredith and Julian is in *Evening Star,* Nov. 30, 1865.

31. Oliver P. Morton to D. L. Goodloe, July 2, 1865, OPMLB; Foulke, *Life of Oliver P. Morton,* vol. 1, 453.

32. Ibid., 453–54.

33. Morton, *Message of Oliver P. Morton, 1865.*

34. For Morton's official and secret missions to France, see Foulke, *Life of Oliver P. Morton,* vol. 1, 457–59. The letters from Stanton are reprinted in the notes on those pages. The mission was not very secret, however, as it was mentioned in the newspapers; see *Evening Star,* Nov. 30, 1865.

35. Ibid., 459–62; for the moxa, see Lu, *Celestial Lancets;* for Clara Morris receiving it, see *Court of Appeals,* 160; a full study of the actress is Grossman, *A Spectacle of Suffering;* Walker, *Sketch of the Life,* 127.

36. Thornbrough, *Indiana in the Civil War Era,* 231–34; Foulke, *Life of Oliver P. Morton,* vol. 1, 464–67.

8. Waving the Bloody Shirt

1. Although the Democrats probably coined the term and used it negatively, I am using it as a more neutral descriptor, and even in a positive sense in analyzing Morton's role in the politics of the postwar era. In Morton's view, the rebels and traitors in the Democratic Party had shed the blood of martyrs, so I employ the term to describe his methods. Although the phrase "waving the bloody shirt" was applied often to Morton throughout the Reconstruction era, it was used infrequently until 1874. There is a vast literature on Reconstruction, and many of the most important books include Morton and his role in the politics of the era. For the purposes of this chapter, I rely on several sources, esp. Summers, *Ordeal of the Reunion;* Foner, *Reconstruction;* Stampp, *Era of Reconstruction;* and despite its racism and unbalanced sympathy for white Southerners and Andrew Johnson, Bowers, *Tragic Era.* I take the general chronology and story of Reconstruction from Summers and Foner, while consulting Bowers and Stampp as well as other scholars on particular matters.

2. Ibid., 468. For a dismissal of the stories about Morton's dissipation, see *Indianapolis Journal,* Oct. 16, 1873. A discussion of the charges of corruption and sexual scandal as they resurfaced in the 1876 election season can be found in Summers, *Era of Good Stealings,* 27–28, 319, 41–42n. In recent months, a woman claiming to be descended from the liaison between Morton and his mistress has approached Indiana State Library staff asking for advice on how to get DNA testing to prove that the story is true. Marcia Caudell, Reference Librarian, Indiana State Library, conversation with author, Feb. 28, 2015, at Indiana Association of Historians Annual Meeting, Indiana Univeristy-Purdue Univ.-Indianapolis, Indianapolis, Indiana.

3. On the governor's residence and Morton's moving out of it, see Holloway, *Indianapolis,* 64; Baker, "James Whitcomb." For Morton possibly selling the house at 149 Pennsylvania Street and buying another, see E. B. Martindale to Oliver P. Morton, Nov. 30, 1872, OPMISL.

4. For the newspaper description of the Pennsylvania Street House, see *Indianapolis Sun,* clipping of June 25, 1871, story in edition dated July 1871, in Oliver P. Morton Scrapbook, OPMIHS. Note that this was a short-lived *Sun* that lasted only about a year. The address of the property changed over the years. It is located on the southeast

corner of the intersection of Pennsylvania Street and New York Street and is today occupied by an office building. University Park is located across the street.

5. Ibid. The Morton family financial records are in several bank account and ledger books in OPMISL. Also insightful are the household receipts that Lucinda kept. Several years of them are in the collection, complete with weekly coal deliveries, detailed grocery lists, and medical expenses. For postwar examples of Morton's personal financial dealings, including his significant holdings in railroad bonds, see Oliver P. Morton to William R. Holloway, letter possibly dated 1870, OPMISL; Oliver P. Morton to William R. Holloway, Dec. 8, 1872.

6. Foulke, *Life of Oliver P. Morton,* vol. 1, 468–69.

7. Morton, *Speech of Gov. Oliver P. Morton . . . Masonic Hall,* 1–3.

8. Ibid. For a report of Milligan's Bluffton speech, see *Evansville Daily Journal,* May 31, 1866.

9. Morton, *Speech of Gov. Oliver P. Morton . . . Masonic Hall,* 3–8.

10. Ibid.

11. For the 1865 Evansville race riot, see Thornbrough, *Negro in Indiana Before 1900,* 209–10. For the Daviess County lynching in May of 1866, see Bigham, *On Jordan's Banks,* 133. Morton, *Speech of Gov. Oliver P. Morton . . . Masonic Hall,* 3–8.

12. Morton, *Speech of Gov.Oliver P. Morton . . . Masonic Hall,* 3–8.

13. Morton, *Speech of Gov. Oliver P. Morton . . . Union Meeting; Indianapolis Journal,* Aug. 13, 1866.

14. Morton, *Speech of Gov. Oliver P. Morton . . . Union Meeting.* For accounts of Morton rallying the veterans, of Republicans honoring him, and of him emerging as a hero for many in his party, see *Evansville Daily Journal,* Sept. 8, 25, 26, 1866. For Morton being the first to try to organize the GAR as a political force, see Wilson, *Grand Army of the Republic,* 16–17. For a more recent study of the GAR, see McConnell, *Glorious Contentment.* A useful correction to McConnell is Gannon, *Won Cause.*

15. For the story of Wade waving the bloody shirt, see Budiansky, *Bloody Shirt,* 1–5. For the myth that the term originated with the caning of Sumner, see Summers, *Ordeal of the Reunion,* 358.

16. Foulke, *Life of Oliver P. Morton,* vol. 1, 482–83; Thornbrough, *Indiana in the Civil War Era,* 235–38.

17. Morton, *Message of Governor Oliver P. Morton,* 1–23, 2.

18. Ibid., 26.

19. Ibid., 25–26.

20. Ibid., 30–31.

21. Ibid., 3

22. Support for Morton's Senate candidacy is found in *Evansville Daily Journal,* Oct. 24 and Dec. 19, 1866. For his confidence in winning, see Oliver P. Morton to Simon T. Powell, Oct. 29, 1866, OPMISL.

23. For the election, see *Indiana Senate Journal, 1867,* 128–29; *Evansville Daily Journal,* Jan. 23, 1867; *Harper's Weekly,* Feb. 9, 1867.

24. For Democratic despair, see Thomas Dowling to John Dowling, Jan. 27, 1867, JDPIHS. For talk of Morton as a presidential candidate in 1868, see *Indianapolis Journal,* Jan. 23, 1867, and *Evansville Daily Journal,* Feb. 1, 1867.

25. For a broader look at the Reconstruction Acts, see Foner, *Reconstruction,* 271–94; Summers, *Ordeal of the Reunion,* esp. 100–106. Charles Sumner and others were impressed by Morton's performance so early in his tenure in the Senate; see *Evansville Daily Journal,* Apr. 1, 1867. Another favorable view of the new senator is found in *Harper's Weekly,* Apr. 20, 1867.

26. Foulke, *Life of Oliver P. Morton,* vol. 2, 1–4; *National Republican,* Mar. 1, 1867; Oliver P. Morton, "Speech to Colored People," Apr. 16, 1867, OPMISL.

27. Morton, "Speech to Colored People." For examples of Morton supporting Reconstruction in the spring of 1867, see *Evening Star,* Mar. 18, 22, 25, 1867.

28. For the charges of voter fraud, see *Plymouth Weekly Democrat,* May 30, 1867. Morton wrote a letter giving an account of his trip to the springs that was reprinted in the newspapers, including the *Chicago Tribune,* which misprinted the location in its headline; see "The Hot Springs of Idaho: An Interesting Letter from Governor Morton," *Chicago Tribune,* July 19, 1867. Taking the waters at resort spas located on mineral and hot springs was a tradition that went back to ancient times. Bath, England, was one famous spot in Europe, but there were many others; see Elliott, *Bath.* In the United States, Saratoga Springs, New York, catered to the wealthy and fashionable people in the era before the Civil War. In the postwar period there were many spas across America offering cures that used the water drawn from natural springs. One such resort was located in Indiana at the French Lick and West Baden Springs, but Morton did not use it, probably because its founder was none other than the Copperhead confidence man William Bowles. For an example of the numerous studies of different resorts located at hot and mineral springs, see Corbett, *Making of American Resorts;* Bullard. On Hot Springs, Arkansas, see Hanley, *Hot Springs;* Brown, *American Spa.* An overview of the spa at French Lick is Bundy, *French Lick Springs.* For Morton's Little Rock speech, see Foulke, *Life of Oliver P. Morton,* vol. 2, 5–6. For Morton campaigning in Ohio in 1867, including making a well-regarded speech in Columbus, see *Evening Star,* Aug. 29, 30, 1867.

29. For the debate with Hendicks, see *Congressional Record, 40th Cong., 2nd Sess., Part I,* Dec. 5, 1867, 37–40; *Evening Star,* Dec. 6, 1867. For his January speech, see Morton, *Issues of 1868,* 1–4. For praise of this speech both in Washington and back home in Indiana, see *Evening Star,* Dec. 30, 1867, and *Indiana American,* Jan. 17, 1868. Note that the speech was actually delivered on Dec. 30, 1867, Jan. 6, 1868.

30. Morton, *Issues of 1868,* 1–4; Thomas Dowling to John Dowling, Jan. 22, 1868, JDPIHS.

31. Foulke, *Life of Oliver P. Morton,* vol. 2, 15–16; for more on James Rood Doolittle, see his lengthy obituary on the front page of *Evening Times,* July 27, 1897. For coverage of the debate between the two senators, see *Evening Star,* Jan. 23, 1868.

32. *Congressional Globe, 40th Cong., 2nd Sess.,* Jan. 24, 1868, 723–27; *New-York Tribune,* Jan. 25, 1868; *Evening Star,* Jan. 24, 1868; Morton, *Reconstruction,* 1–2.

33. Morton, *Reconstruction,* 2–3. On *Luther v. Borden,* see Schuchman, "Political Background."

34. Morton, *Reconstruction,* 4–5.

35. Ibid., 5.

36. Ibid.

37. Ibid.

38. Ibid., 5–6.

39. Ibid., 6.

40. Ibid., 7.

41. Ibid. For more on the implications of interpreting the Constitution in light of the Declaration, see Guelzo, "Apple of Gold in a Picture of Silver."

42. Morton, *Reconstruction*, 8.

43. Ibid.

44. Ibid.

45. *Frank Leslie's Illustrated Newspaper*, Feb. 15, 1868; *New-York Tribune*, Jan. 25, 1868.

46. For examples of Republican newspapers praising or reprinting the speech, see *National Republican*, Jan. 25, 1868; *Wheeling Daily Intelligencer*, Feb. 6, 1868; *Belmont Chronicle*, Feb. 6, 1868; *Gallipolis Journal*, Feb. 13, 1868. For an example of the pamphlet, see *Speech of Senator Morton, of Indiana, on Reconstruction*. For criticism, see *Charleston Daily News*, Jan. 25, 1868; *Staunton Spectator* Jan. 28, 1868; *Alexandria Gazette*, Feb. 1, 1868. For Thomas Hendricks responding to Morton, see *Plymouth Weekly Democrat*, Feb. 13, 1868. For the New York Democratic papers trying to rebut Morton's arguments, see Foulke, *Life of Oliver P. Morton*, vol. 2, 42–43. For a later remembrance of Ulysses S. Grant remarking on the speech, see *Leavenworth Times*, May 16, 1876. For more on Roscoe Conkling, see Jordan, *Roscoe Conkling of New York*. For a Democratic assessment of the 1868 campaign and the influence of Morton on other Republicans (in this case, Richard W. Thompson), see Thomas Dowling to John Dowling, Mar. 8, 1868, JDPIHS. This letter covers a number of matters, including the impeachment of Johnson, the Republicans choosing Grant, the dominance of the Radical Republicans, and Morton's style of speaking influencing others.

47. For renewed talk of Morton running for president in 1868, see *Evansville Daily Journal*, Mar. 6, 1868.

48. The leading authority on the Radical Republicans remains Hans L. Trefousse, whose numerous studies and biographies reinterpreted their contributions as well as their shortcomings. For the leaders listed here, see his following works: *Thaddeus Stevens; Ben Butler; Benjamin Franklin Wade*. See also Trefousse, *Radical Republicans*. On Charles Sumner, see Donald, *Charles Sumner and the Coming of the Civil War*, and Donald, *Charles Sumner and the Rights of Man*.

49. Morton's good spirits, attention to legislative business, and thwarting of the plan to sell government land in Indiana are found in Morton to Dear Friend, Mar. 19, 1867, original letter in author's personal collection.

50. Foulke, *Life of Oliver P. Morton*, vol. 2, 46, 376–80. For the rumors of Morton being controlled by Pomeroy and for his votes on impeachment, see *Evening Star*, May 22, 26, 1868. For a study of the impeachment of Johnson, see Trefousse, *Impeachment of a President*.

51. Morton, *Peace or War*, 1–3.

52. On the 1868 election, Frank P. Blair Jr. and the Democratic platform, see Summers, *Ordeal of the Reunion*, 141–51. For an example of Morton's campaigning for Grant, see *Evening Star*, Sept. 14, 1868.

53. One of many examples of constituent service, this one dealing with the ever-present issue of patronage appointments, is found in Thomas M. Browne to O. P. Morton, Mar. 2, 1877, original letter in author's personal collection.

54. O. P. Morton to Andrew Johnson, Mar. 18, 1868, OPMIHS. For examples of Morton trying to keep control of state political affairs, see Oliver P. Morton to Hiram Iddings, Feb. 4, 1872, OPMISL; Oliver P. Morton to William R. Holloway, Mar. 15,

23, Apr. 22, May 10, Dec. 2, 30, 1872, OPMISL; Oliver P. Morton to Simon T. Powell, Mar. 12, Apr. 22, 26, 1872, June 25, 1876, OPMISL.

55. An example of Morton endorsing a friend is found in O. P. Morton to Ulysses S. Grant, Dec. 21, 1872, original letter in author's personal collection. For Morton's campaigning in 1868, see Foulke, *Life of Oliver P. Morton,* vol. 2, 52–61.

56. For Morton recommending Cumback, see Oliver P. Morton to Abraham Lincoln, Apr. 23, 1861, Abraham Lincoln Papers, William Henry Smith Memorial Library, Indiana Historical Society, Indianapolis, Indiana. For the Cumback controversy, see Thornbrough, *Indiana in the Civil War Era,* 241–42. For the key letter in question, see Will Cumback to Conrad Baker, Jan. 6, 1868, Conrad Baker Papers, Indiana State Library, Indianapolis, Indiana. Hendricks was popular in the state, and for his possible reelection or his possible gubernatorial candidacy giving his party hope for victory, see Thomas Dowling to John Dowling, Aug. 5, 1868, JDPIHS.

57. Morton, *Oration of Hon. O. P. Morton,* 12–19. For newspaper coverage of Morton's speech, see *Harper's Weekly,* July 17, 1869.

58. Morton, *Oration of Hon. O. P. Morton,* 12–19.

59. Ibid., 19–31.

60. Ibid., 31–40.

61. For Morton's objections to the weaker House version of the Fifteenth Amendment, see Schultz, "Morton and Reconstruction," 21–24. For its passage by Congress, see Summers, *Ordeal of the Reunion,* 153–54.

62. *Harper's Weekly,* Feb. 20, 1869. For Morton's floor management and the debates over the amendment in the Senate, see *Congressional Globe, 40th Cong., 3rd Sess.;* Foulke, *Life of Oliver P. Morton,* vol. 2, 103–9.

63. Schultz, "Morton and Reconstruction," 24.

64. Ibid., 24–28; *Indianapolis Journal,* May 25, 1869; Oliver P. Morton, *Fifteenth Amendment.* For Democratic criticism and Republican defense of Morton during the controversy over the amendment and during the election campaign that followed, see *Evansville Daily Journal,* May 5, July 25, 1870.

65. *Congressional Globe, 41st Cong., 1st Sess.,* April 9, 1869, 653–57. For more on Trumbull, see Krug, *Lyman Trumbull.*

66. Krug, *Lyman Trumbull.*

67. *Congressional Globe, 41st Cong., 2nd Sess.,* passim. Newspaper coverage of the Georgia bill is found in *Evening Star,* Apr. 14, 15, 1870. For Morton's speech and the near-duel over it, see *Congressional Globe, 41st Cong., 2nd Sess.,* May 17, 1870, 3512; *Evening Star,* May 25, 1870.

68. For Morton possibly being made minister to England, see clippings of various newspapers in the Oliver P. Morton Scrapbook, OPMIHS; *Harper's Weekly,* Nov. 12, 1870; Thornbrough, *Indiana in the Civil War Era,* 244–46. Additional newspaper coverage in the *Evening Star* includes his possible appointment Sept. 23, 1870; his decision to make it dependent on state legislature, Oct. 8, 1870; Democrats won legislative majority, Oct. 13, 1870; Morton officially declining the post, Oct. 25, 1870.

9. A Radical Champion for African Americans

1. Morton made his remarks on April 17, 1870; see *Congressional Globe, 41st Cong., 2nd Sess.,* Apr. 14, 1870, appendix, 274–80. For the bill to stop voter intimidation, see *Evening Star,* May 21, 1870. For more on the Ku Klux Klan during Reconstruction, see Trelease,

White Terror. Another insightful study of the use of terror to resist Reconstruction is found in Rable, *But There Was No Peace.* A book that puts the Klan violence of the 1870s into the larger context of the politics of black voting rights is Wang, *Trial of Democracy.*

2. Summers, *Ordeal of the Reunion,* 267–71; Foner, *Reconstruction,* 454–59.

3. Morton gathered evidence of the escalating violence across the South and dutifully reported it to the Senate; see *Evening Star,* Mar. 3, 11, 13, 15, 16, 21, 24, 28, 31, 1871. Morton, *Protection of Life,* 3–4.

4. Ibid.

5. Ibid., 5–8.

6. Ibid.

7. Ibid, 8.

8. Ibid., 10–11.

9. Ibid., 11–15.

10. Ibid., 15–16.

11. O. P. Morton to Lucinda Morton, Apr. 5, 1871, OPMISL.

12. Foulke, *Life of Oliver P. Morton,* vol. 2, 202; Oliver P. Morton, "The National Idea," in *Providence Journal,* Nov. 27, 1871. A few years later, Morton gave what appears to be largely the same speech, with the same title, in a Decoration Day speech in Greencastle, Indiana, and "The National Idea," attracted widespread attention with its forceful statement of the nationalist view; see *Harper's Weekly,* June 26, 1875.

13. Ibid.

14. Morton, *Political Disabilities,* 1–2.

15. Ibid., 2–8.

16. For a definitive interpretation of the Liberal Republicans in 1872, see Slap, *Doom of Reconstruction.*

17. For Morton at the Republican National Convention, see *Evening Star,* June 4, 5, 1872; Oliver P. Morton, "First Guns," in *Indianapolis Journal,* June 24, 1872.

18. *Cincinnati Daily Gazette,* Aug. 9, 1872; *Frank Leslie's Illustrated Newspaper,* September 21, 1872.

19. *Indianapolis Journal,* September 19, 1872.

20. *Chicago Inter-Ocean,* Oct. 18, 1872; *Daily Missouri Democrat,* Oct. 23, 1872; *Cincinnati Daily Gazette,* Oct. 26, 1872. For more examples of Morton campaigning for his party in 1872, see *Evening Star,* Sept. 2, 8, Oct 23, 1872.

21. For rumors about Richard Thompson's possible candidacy and his denial that he wanted Morton's seat, see *Evening Star,* Oct. 22, 28, 1872. Morton expressed his fears about a possible 1872 Colfax nomination; see Oliver P. Morton to Hiram Iddings, Feb. 4, 1872. The *Louisville Courier's* lament about his reelection was reprinted in *Evening Star,* Oct. 11, 1872. After the 1872 election, Morton spoke of Colfax's future presidential possibilities; see Oliver P. Morton to William R. Holloway, Dec. 8, 1872, OPMISL.

22. Morton's "Campaign of 1873" speech at Athens, Ohio, followed his proven formula for waving the bloody shirt. The speech was printed in *Cincinnati Daily Commercial,* Aug. 23, 1873. For more newspaper coverage of Morton campaigning in Ohio, including speeches given with his friend Rutherford B. Hayes, see *Evening Star,* Aug 18, Sept. 12, 1873. For more on the election, see Thornbrough, *Indiana in the Civil War Era,* 246–52; *Cincinnati Daily Commercial,* September 12, 1873. After the 1872 election, Morton spoke of Colfax's future presidential possibilities; see Oliver P. Morton to William R. Holloway, Dec. 8, 1872, OPMISL.

23. Morton, *Presidential Elections;* Morton, *Report on Presidential Elections;* Oliver P. Morton to William R. Holloway, Sept. 26, 1873; Foulke, *Life of Oliver P. Morton,* vol. 2, 269–74. O. P. Morton to Ulysses S. Grant, Oct. 22, 1873, OPMIHS. For Democratic charges that Morton's plan was a scheme to steal presidential elections, see *Indiana Sentinel,* May 26, 1874. For Morton continuing to push for his plan, see *Harper's Weekly,* Jan. 23, Feb. 13, 1875.

24. On Warmoth and the disputed 1872 election, see Summers, *Ordeal of the Reunion,* 284–85, 330–32.

25. Ibid.

26. Ibid.

27. Foulke, *Life of Oliver P. Morton,* vol. 2, 275–84. For Morton's own account of one of his efforts to prevent the overturning of the Kellogg government, see Oliver P. Morton to William R. Holloway, 1872, OPMISL. For national newspaper mention of Morton's support for the Kellogg government, see *Harper's Weekly,* Feb. 21, 1874. For a recent study that examines the ways in which violent resistance to Reconstruction occurred on the state and local level, see Egerton, *Wars of Reconstruction.*

28. For Pinchback's corruption, see Foner, *Reconstruction,* 388; for more on Pinchback, see Haskins, *Pinckney Benton Stewart Pinchback.*

29. Foulke, *Life of Oliver P. Morton,* vol. 2, 284–85; Democrats attacked Morton for his support of Pinchback; see *Indiana Sentinel,* Feb. 17, 1874; Morton, *Louisiana Affairs,* 1.

30. Ibid., 2. Newspaper coverage of his *Louisiana Affairs* speech and the debate surrounding it is found in *Evening Star,* Jan. 28, 31, Feb. 3, 1874. In an Indianapolis speech on September 18, 1874, Morton said that the White League was the Klan and also linked it to the Copperheads he had fought in the Civil War: "The White League exists not only in Louisiana, but in other Southern States . . . It is but another name for the Ku Klux organization, and is in the nature of the Sons of Liberty, that once existed in Indiana," Morton, *The South.* For more on the Colfax Massacre, see Keith, *The Colfax Massacre.*

31. Morton, *Louisiana Affairs,* 3–16. Morton continued the fight in the following months and repeated his arguments about Louisiana in the fall of 1874; see Morton, *The South:* For national coverage of his support for Pinchback, see *Harper's Weekly,* Feb. 7, 1874, Jan. 9, 1875.

32. *Frank Leslie's Illustrated Newspaper,* Feb. 21, 1874. For the complaint that Morton kept repeating the same speech, see *Evening Star,* Mar. 13, 1875, and *Congressional Record, 45th Cong., 1st Sess.,* Mar. 13, 1877, 40–41. For examples of newspaper coverage of Morton's support for Pinchback over the years, see *Evening Star,* Dec. 4, 6, 15, 16, 1873, Jan. 26, Dec. 23, 1874, Feb. 2, 16, Mar. 6, 8, 9, 12, 17, Nov. 15, Dec. 14, 1875, Jan. 28, Feb. 2, 4, 5, 7, Mar. 2, 9, 1876. One example of a Southern Democratic perspective of Morton's support for Pinchback is found in the *Alexandria Gazette,* Dec. 23, 1874.

33. In the nineteenth century, the usage was "woman suffrage." *Congressional Record, 43rd Cong., 1st Sess.,* May 28, 1874, 4332–33.

34. Ibid.

35. Ibid.

36. Ibid.

37. Ibid.; *Evening Star,* Jan. 21, 1874; for Morton supporting women's suffrage in DC, see *Evening Star,* Feb. 15, 1875; for his comments during the civil rights bill debate, see

Evening Star, Feb. 26, 1875; for his assertion about the Declaration of Independence including women, see *Evening Star,* Jan. 27, 1876. For a study of the push for suffrage during the Reconstruction years that unfortunately neglects Morton, see Dudden, *Fighting Chance.* For Morton supporting the rights of Native Americans, see *Evening Star,* Apr. 4, 1870.

38. *Indiana Sentinel,* July 15–17, 1875; *Indianapolis Journal,* July 16, 1875; Foulke, *Life of Oliver P. Morton,* vol. 2, 354–55; Morton, *Record and Platforms* . For press coverage of his Urbana speech, see *Evening Star,* Aug. 9, 1875, and *Harper's Weekly,* Aug. 28, 1875.

39. *Frank Leslie's Illustrated Newspaper,* Oct. 9, 1875.

40. For the Maine trip, see Oliver P. Morton to William R. Holloway, Aug. 31, 1875, OPMISL; *Indiana Sentinel,* Oct. 21, 1875.

41. Oliver P. Morton to William R. Holloway, Aug. 31, 1875, OPMISL; Schultz, "Morton and Reconstruction," 47. For more on Zachariah Chandler, see Trefousse, *Radical Republicans,* passim.

42. For Morton readmitting Mississippi and seating Ames in the Senate, see *Evening Star,* Jan. 31, Feb. 15, Mar. 18, 1870. For Revels's speech and Morton's response and remarks about Jefferson Davis, see *Congressional Globe, 41st Cong., 2nd Sess.,* Mar. 16, 1870, 1986–89; The context of politics in Mississippi is outlined in Summers, *Ordeal of the Reunion,* 356–57; and Foner, *Reconstruction,* 558–63.

43. For more on Ames, see Lord, "Adelbert Ames." On Alcorn, see Pereyra, *James Lusk Alcorn.*

44. Morton's call for a committee to investigate Mississippi's election and Bayard's attack on him are found in *Congressional Record, 44th Cong., 1st Sess.,* Dec. 16, 1875. For a remarkably balanced and thorough study of the Mississippi situation, see Harris, *Day of the Carpetbagger.*

45. *Evening Star,* Dec. 15, 17, 19, 1875; Morton, *Democratic Violence,* 3–4. An example of press coverage of the speech is found in *Harper's Weekly,* Feb. 26, 1876.

46. Morton, *Democratic Violence,* 5. There are a number of excellent biographies of James Longstreet, but especially useful for the issues here is Piston, *Lee's Tarnished Lieutenant.*

47. Morton, *Democratic Violence,* 5–6.

48. Ibid., 6.

49. Ibid.

50. Ibid., 7–9. Morton's arguments here fit well with the view of later historians who see the new labor system as restoring slavery by another name, see Blackmon, *Slavery by Another Name.*

51. Morton, *Democratic Violence,* 9; Morton's view of the upcoming Centennial fits well with the interpretation found in Kinslow, "Contesting the Centennial." Kinslow argues that many Northerners held to a pro-Union, pro-Reconstruction, pro-equality perspective during the Centennial, even as others pushed different ideas, including white Southerners already beginning to embrace the concept of the Lost Cause.

52. Morton, *Democratic Violence,* 10–22. A newspaper account of this speech is found in *Evening Star,* Jan. 19, 20, 1876.

53. *Democratic Violence,* 10–22.

54. I take this account of Bruce's speech from Brown, *Year of the Century,* 199–200. For Democratic coverage of Bruce making a speech on March 31 in support of Morton's

Mississippi resolutions, see *Chicago Times,* Apr. 1, 1876. For more on Bruce, see Harris, "Blanche K. Bruce of Mississippi," and Graham, *Senator and the Socialite.*

55. Foulke, *Life of Oliver P. Morton,* vol. 2, 375–76. For newspaper commentary on Morton's waving the bloody shirt, making his Mississippi resolutions, and hopes that he might also lead the fight in South Carolina, see *Evening Star,* Mar. 27, May 18, 1876; *Harper's Weekly,* Jan. 15, Feb. 12, 26, 1876.

56. *Atlanta Constitution,* Feb. 1, 1876.

57. *Congressional Record, 44th Cong., 1st Sess.,* Mar. 7, 1876, 1580–86; *Atlanta Constitution,* Mar. 21, 1876; Foulke, *Life of Oliver P. Morton,* vol. 2, 380–85. For more on the Grant scandals and an interpretation that the era was no more corrupt than other periods, see Summers, *Era of Good Stealings.*

58. *Congressional Record, 44th Cong., 1st Sess.,* Mar. 7, 1876, 1580–86; Foulke, *Life of Oliver P. Morton,* vol. 2, 380–85. For newspaper coverage of this debate between Gordon and Morton, see *Evening Star,* Mar. 9, 10, 1876. Gordon's biographer discussed the debate between the two partisan senators, see Eckert, *John Brown Gordon,* 172–73.

59. For the serenade and Douglass's speech, see *Evening Star,* Mar. 14, 1876. For Morton's effort to block Lamar, see *Congressional Record, 45th Cong., 1st Sess.* (1877), 13–15.

10. Stalwart Republican

1. By 1880, "Stalwart" meant those Republicans opposing the civil service reforms promoted by President Rutherford B. Hayes. At other times, it applied to those who stuck with Radical Reconstruction or to those who supported President Grant. Although he did not use "Stalwart" himself and it really came into usage later, the term described Morton in both his refusal to give up on Reconstruction and his faithfulness to Grant. In this chapter, however, Stalwart Republican primarily means Morton's loyalty to the Republican Party. For more on Chandler, see George, *Zachariah Chandler.*

2. Morton, *Laws of Neutrality;* for more on American filibustering in Cuba, see May, *Manifest Destiny's Underworld.* Morton closely observed events in Latin America, favoring the independence of colonies from Spain. But he also praised Spain on occasion, such as when he congratulated the imperial power for abolishing slavery in Puerto Rico; see *Harper's Weekly,* Apr. 12, 1873. Hispaniola is the proper name of the island, but the colonial term and name of the oldest city, Santo Domingo, remains interchangeable. In the mid-nineteenth century, San Domingo was the accepted name.

3. Summers, *Ordeal of the Reunion,* 209, 220.

4. For Sumner's disagreement with the administration and the quotes included here, see Donald, *Charles Sumner and the Rights of Man,* 434–43.

5. Ibid., 443. Donald explains the bad blood between Grant and Sumner on pp. 433–37.

6. Summers, *Ordeal of the Reunion,* 224–25. A newspaper account of Morton speaking in the debate over the *Alabama* claims is found in *Evening Star,* Apr. 14, 1869.

7. Foulke, *Life of Oliver P. Morton,* vol. 2, 150–55.

8. Morton, *Annexation of Dominica,* 3–4. Morton and Grant became close enough that their wives corresponded and shared personal details about their families; see Lucinda Morton to Mrs. Grant, July 17, 1875, OPMIHS.

9. Morton, *Annexation of Dominica,* 4–8; *Harper's Weekly,* Dec. 31, 1870; Foulke, *Life of Oliver P. Morton,* vol. 2, 185. For some of the extensive newspaper coverage of Morton's role in the politics of annexation, see *Evening Star,* Mar 24, 25, 26, Dec. 20, 21, 1870, Jan. 6, Jan. 9, Mar. 23, 1871.

10. For the French arms debate, see *Congressional Globe, 42nd Cong., 2nd Sess.,* Feb. 14 to March 18, 1872, 1005–782. Foulke, *Life of Oliver P. Morton,* vol. 2, 227–53. Newspaper coverage is in *Evening Star,* Feb. 16, 21, 23, Mar. 1, 1872.

11. For the Treaty of Washington, see ibid., 174–78, and Summers, *Ordeal of the Reunion,* 216; Foulke included the entire letters written between the two senators; see Foulke, *Life of Oliver P. Morton,* vol. 2, 185–87. In 1872 Sumner supported the Liberal Republicans and soon turned away from Radical Reconstruction; see Donald, *Charles Sumner and the Rights of Man,* esp. 529–72; Summers, *Ordeal of the Reunion,* 307–9.

12. Summers, *Ordeal of the Reunion,* 11; for more on Carey, see Richardson, *Greatest Nation of the Earth,* 19–27, 142–43.

13. For this take on the greenbacks, see Rothbard, *A History of Money,* 122–32. Rothbard's libertarian analysis updates and complicates the Progressive interpretation found in the classic work of Charles and Mary Beard, *Rise of American Civilization,* which argued that the Civil War was a "Second American Revolution." The Beardian view saw the Civil War as a struggle between classes that pitted the agrarians of the South against Northern industrialists and business interests. That perspective of Republican financial policies informed Howard K. Beale's interpretation of Reconstruction in *Critical Year.* The revisionists of the Consensus School in the mid-twentieth century challenged the Beard approach and argued that the Civil War was not so revolutionary. This included arguing that the war was less transformative economically than the Progressives thought; see Sharkey, *Money, Class, and Party.* The Consensus revision of the politics of Republican economics is found in Unger, *Greenback Era.* For a brief and engaging nationalist account of the money issue written by a historian, see Brands, *Money Men.*

14. For more on Chase, see Niven, *Salmon P. Chase.*

15. Rothbard, *A History of Money,* 122–47.

16. *Congressional Globe, 39th Cong., 1st Sess.,* 75; Unger, *Greenback Era,* 41–42; Rothbard, *A History of Money,* 148–49. For more on Fessenden, see Cook, *Civil War Senator.* For more on Hugh McCulloch, see his memoir, *Men and Measures.* Morton, of course, supported having another Hoosier in Lincoln's cabinet, but McCulloch was a conservative, and this raised suspicions of him during Reconstruction.

17. *Congressional Globe, 40th Cong., 2nd Sess.,* June 15, 1868, 3157–62; ibid., July 13, 1868, 3992–93. Rather than simply being a matter of shared fiscal views, Morton's support for McCulloch's policies followed careful consideration, and he met with the secretary to discuss the issue; see Foulke, *Life of Oliver P. Morton,* vol. 2, 74. McCulloch spoke highly of Morton in his memoirs; see McCulloch, *Men and Measures,* 72–73.

18. For Wade's inflationist views and presidential ambitions playing a part in failing to convict Johnson, see Trefousse, *Benjamin Franklin Wade,* esp. 299–306. For Morton's bill, see *Evening Star,* Dec. 7, 14, 1868.

19. Foulke, *Life of Oliver P. Morton,* vol. 2, 73–75. For newspaper coverage of Morton's speech, see *Evening Star,* Dec. 16, 17, 1868.

20. Morton, *Resumption of Specie Payments,* 1–4.

21. Ibid., 5–8.

22. Ibid., 8–14.

23. Foulke, *Life of Oliver P. Morton*, vol. 2, 89–102. For the debate with Greeley, see *New-York Tribune*, Dec. 18, 1868, Jan. 1, 1869, and *Evening Star*, Jan. 2, 5, Feb. 13, Mar. 9, 31, 1869. For praise of Morton's speech, see *Evening Star*, Dec. 17, 1868. For mention of Morton as a possible secretary of the treasury, see *Evening Star*, Dec. 28, 1868.

24. For the Panic of 1873 as a period of inflationary bankruptcy and economic expansion, see Rothbard, *A History of Money*, 154–56. For the more traditional view that a deep depression followed the panic, see Unger, *Greenback Era*, 213–48. An example of a historian taking a liberal nationalist approach that tries to strike a balance between Austrian School economists like Rothbard and Marxist interpretations is found in Nelson, *Nation of Deadbeats*, esp. 159–79.

25. *Indianapolis Journal*, Apr. 23, 1874; *Harper's Weekly*, Feb. 2, 1874.

26. Thornbrough, *Indiana in the Civil War Era*, 285–300. For more on the issue in the Hoosier State, see Carleton, "Money Question"; for more on Carl Schurz, see Trefousse, *Carl Schurz*.

27. Morton, "Address to the Agricultural Exposition," 79–83. For Morton and Hendricks working together for the eight-hour workday, see *Evening Star*, June 24, 1868, and *Congressional Globe, 40th Cong., 2nd Sess.*, Pt. 4, June 24, 1868, 3427–29. For the Panic of 1873, see Unger, *The Greenback Era*, 213–48; Barreyre, "Politics of Economic Crises."

28. Oliver P. Morton to William R. Holloway, September 30, 1873. For Thurman attacking Morton's support of the congressional pay raise, see *Jasper Weekly Courier*, Oct. 3, 1873.

29. Oliver P. Morton, *National-Bank Circulation*; Foulke, *Life of Oliver P. Morton*, vol. 2, 323–28. For newspaper coverage of Morton at the center of the currency debates early in 1874, see *Evening Star*, Jan. 9, 17, Feb. 12, 18, 1874. Schurz's attacks on Morton and that of John Sherman are covered in *Evening Star*, Feb. 25, 1874.

30. Morton, *National-Bank Circulation*, passim.

31. Foulke, *Life of Oliver P. Morton*, vol. 2, 329–31.

32. Ibid.

33. Unger, *Greenback Era*, 233–45, 249–63. For "The Currency Question in a Tumbler," see *Frank Leslie's Illustrated Newspaper*, Apr. 11, 1874. Another, earlier, national cartoon on the subject is found in *Harper's Weekly*, July 4, 1874; Foulke, *Life of Oliver P. Morton*, vol. 2, 332–38; Oliver P. Morton, "Currency Question," *Indianapolis Journal*, May 5, 1874.

34. Unger, *Greenback Era*, 249–63. For Democratic criticism of Morton's views on the currency question, see *Indiana Sentinel*, September 16, 1875. For the "Comedy of Errors" cartoon, see *Harper's Weekly*, Aug. 28, 1875.

35. Morton, *Terre Haute Speech*. For examples of Morton's support of bridges across the Ohio River, see *Evening Star*, May 25, June 18, July 18, 22, 1868, Apr. 5, 8, 1869, June 9, 1870, Mar. 24, 1874.

36. Oliver P. Morton, *Railroad Legislation*.

37. Coverage of Morton calling for railroad regulation is in *Evening Star*, Jan. 27, 1874. For background on the railroads in this period and their place in party politics, see Summers, *Railroads, Reconstruction*, esp. 237–49. Morton's stand on streetcar regulation is found in *Evening Star*, Feb. 6, 1875.

38. *Frank Leslie's Illustrated Newspaper,* Apr. 3, 1875. For a study that includes Dwight L. Moody and religion, see Evensen, *God's Man for the Gilded Age,* and Brown, *Year of the Century,* esp. 24–41.

39. Corruption had been a part of Republican politics from the party's inception and had been part of Lincoln's appeal in 1860, when he was cast as "Honest Abe" against Seward's ties to the corrupt politics of New York and his ally, Thurlow Weed. For more on the issue in the prewar period, see Summers, *Plundering Generation.* For Morton being accused of supporting carpetbaggers, see *Evening Star,* Feb. 24, 1872. For the committee's reports on the Pomeroy and Caldwell investigations, see *Congressional Globe, 42nd Cong., 2nd Sess., Report No. 224, Senator S. C. Pomeroy's Election, 1867,* June 3, 1872; ibid., *Report No. 523, Pomeroy Investigation,* Mar. 3, 1873; ibid., *Report No. 451, Senator Caldwell's Election, Kansas, 1871,* Feb. 17, 1873. For newspaper coverage of Morton's role in the Caldwell case, see *Evening Star,* Jan. 10, Feb. 5, 17, 24, 25, Mar. 10, 11, 12, 22, 1873. For an example of the Caldwell investigation clearing Morton's name of corruption charges, see *Evening Star,* Sept. 26, 1874.

40. Oliver P. Morton to William R. Holloway, July 18, 1873, OPMISL.

41. *Frank Leslie's Illustrated Newspaper,* Aug. 3, 1872. Morton's use of patronage sometimes brought complaints from his fellow senators; for an example, see *Evening Star,* Feb. 14, 1870.

42. *Congressional Globe, 41st Cong., 3rd Sess.,* Jan. 4, 10, 12, 1871, 392–473; *Indianapolis Journal,* Feb. 2, 1872; *Harper's Weekly,* Feb. 11, 1871.

43. For an excellent study of Washington, DC, society in the pre-Civil War era that describes how important social events were in the politics of the era and is suggestive of the ways in which social functions in the city were significant during Morton's senatorial career in the postwar years, see Rachel A. Shelden, *Washington Brotherhood.*

44. For these examples of the Mortons in Washington society, see *Evening Star,* Jan. 1, Feb. 27, Nov. 19, 25, 1869. For examples of Morton attending the New Year's Day receptions at the White House during the Grant years, see *Evening Star,* Jan. 1, 1870, Jan. 1, 1872, Jan. 1, 1873, Jan. 1, 1874. For Lucinda Morton helping Julia Grant receive her guests, see *Evening Star,* Feb. 15, 1870, Apr. 20. 1872. For Lucinda and the first lady working together for the charitable benefit, see *Evening Star,* Apr. 15, 1874.

45. For Lucinda Morton going to these events alone, see *Evening Star,* July 1, 1870, Jan. 17, 1874, Jan. 21, 1876. For Morton attending society functions by himself, see *Evening Star,* July 1, 1871, Dec. 4, 1873. For an example of Morton showing up at a party hosted by a fellow senator, this one held by Zachariah Chandler of Michigan, see *Evening Star,* Mar. 7, 1871. Morton turning up at the parties held by the Indiana Republicans can be found in *Evening Star,* Mar. 17, 1871, Feb. 15, 1873. For Morton going to a state dinner and an event hosted by foreign diplomats (this one hosted by the British), see *Evening Star,* Feb. 20, 1873, Mar. 17, 1871. The Mortons' attendance at the grand ball for Prince Arthur was noted in *Evening Star,* Jan. 28, 1870.

46. The story of Walter Morton, the "Man Who Builds the Fires," can be found in *National Republican,* Jan. 6, 1874, and in *Alexandria Gazette and Virginia Advertiser,* Jan. 6, 1874.

47. For Lucinda's New Year's Day reception and Morton also attending the one at the White House, see *Evening Star,* Jan. 1, 1872. For the reception where Rose English helped Lucinda receive her guests and the impromptu party at the Ebbitt House the evening before, see *Evening Star,* Jan. 22, 1874. Morton attending the president's father-

in-law's funeral is found in *Evening Star,* Dec. 18, 1873. For John Morton's wedding and the reception when he and his wife visited from San Francisco, see *Evening Star,* Feb. 12, 1874, Feb. 5, 1876. For Lucinda's "very large reception," see *Evening Star,* Jan. 21, 1876.

48. For Morton officially notifying Grant and Colfax with his speech, see *Evening Star,* Feb. 13, 1869. For some examples of Morton's visits to the White House during the Grant years, see *Evening Star,* Mar. 10, 22, Apr. 5, 20, Dec. 8, 1869, Mar. 26, 1870, Dec. 18, 1871, Jan. 15, 22, 24, Feb. 1, 10, 24, 28, Mar. 12, 18, 20, June 3, Dec. 5, 16, 19, 1872, Jan. 8, 16, 21, Feb. 19, Mar. 10, 14, 27, Aug. 5, 1873, Jan. 19, Apr. 17, 1874, Mar. 12, 1875, Jan. 4, 15, 29, Mar. 6, 15, Apr. 3, 20, May 8, 17, July 20, 28, Aug. 8, Nov. 28, Dec. 4, 1876. For some of his "lengthy interviews," see *Evening Star,* Nov. 8, 16, 1869, Dec. 30, 1870. For examples of Morton being one of the few visitors received on days when the president was not meeting other visitors, see Nov. 22, 1869, Apr. 1, 1872. For meetings that were probably about Morton possibly being appointed minister to Great Britain, see *Evening Star,* Oct. 31, Nov. 2, 1870. Near the end of Grant's term, he offered to make Morton minister to Russia, but the senator declined; see *Evening Star,* Jan. 1, 1875.

49. For Morton and Grant traveling westward together to their respective homes and speaking together in Indianapolis, see *Evening Star,* Apr. 21, 24, 1871. For Grant inviting Morton to accompany him on a trip to the Pacific Coast, see *Evening Star,* June 19, 1871. For Morton surviving the train wreck in California, see *Evening Star,* Oct. 27, 1871

50. For more on Pratt, see Holliday, "Daniel D. Pratt: Lawyer," and Holliday, "Daniel D. Pratt: Senator." Holliday argued that the imperious Morton treated Pratt with disrespect and tried to run roughshod over his long-suffering junior colleague. In "Daniel D. Pratt: Lawyer" he said that "the relationship between the Indiana Senators continued to be a very formal one and never ripened into cordiality during their association in the Senate," 124. I challenge that interpretation and argue that the two men actually became friends who cooperated in the Senate.

51. Holliday, "Daniel D. Pratt: Lawyer," 124.

52. Foulke, *Life of Oliver P. Morton,* vol. 2, 517; Holliday, "Daniel D. Pratt: Lawyer," 124; Morton to Pratt, note dated 1869, Daniel P. Pratt Papers, Indiana State Library, Indianapolis, Indiana (hereafter, PPISL); Holliday, "Lawyer and Legislator," 124. For Morton's Senate career, see Foulke, *Life of Oliver P. Morton,* vol. 2, passim. For Pratt's Senate career, see Holliday, "Daniel D. Pratt: Senator." For Morton referring a pension request to Pratt, see O. P. Morton to Mrs. Martha A. Jones, Feb. 12, 1874, PPISL.

53. For examples of the senators sharing information, see Morton to Pratt, Nov. 12, 1868, and J. D. Vandeventer to Hon. O. P. Morton, Sept. 12, 1876, PPISL; for Morton and Pratt sharing views on the issues, see Holliday, "Daniel D. Pratt: Senator," 19–39; for an overview of the senators working together during Reconstruction, see Thornbrough, *Indiana in the Civil War Era,* 225–96.

54. Pratt to Baker, Dec. 22, 1869, PPISL; Pratt to Baker, Dec. 24, 1869, PPISL.

55. Morton to Pratt, Dec. 23, 1869, PPISL; newspaper clipping dated Jan. 8, 1870, PPISL; Holliday, "Daniel D. Pratt: Lawyer," 125–26; Morton to Pratt, Dec. 30, 1869, PPISL.

56. Morton to Pratt, Jan. 6, 1874, PPISL; Morton to Pratt, Nov. 12, 1874, PPISL.

57. Holliday, "Daniel D. Pratt: Senator," 40–42; Morton to Pratt, Aug. 7, 1875, PPISL; Gillette, *Retreat from Reconstruction,* 239–240.

58. Morton to Pratt, May 6, 1875, PPISL.

59. For Morton's efforts to defeat Julian in 1872, see Oliver P. Morton to William R. Holloway, Mar. 15, 23, 1872, OPMISL; Oliver P. Morton to Simon T. Powell, Mar. 12, May 10, 1872, OPMISL. For Julian's account of the start of the long hatred between the two Centerville Republicans, see Julian, *Political Recollections, 1840–1872*, 270–71; Riddleberger, *George Washington Julian*, 260, 262–75, 277–321.

60. Thornbrough, *Indiana in the Civil War Era*, 247, 298–99. For Morton's relationship with Orth, see John L. Miller to William R. Holloway, Feb. 3, 1872, and Oliver P. Morton to William R. Holloway, Feb. 4, 1872, OPMISL; Sievers, *Benjamin Harrison Vol. 2*, 53–54.

61. Insight into this controversy can be found in William R. Holloway to Governor Conrad Baker, Feb. 27, 1872, William R. Holloway Papers, William Henry Smith Memorial Library, Indiana Historical Society, Indianapolis, Indiana. For documents relating to Holloway's ownership, editing, and sale of the *Journal*, see William R. Holloway Papers, box 2, folders 8–12, OPMIHS.

62. Sievers, *Benjamin Harrison Vol. 1*, 177–79, 278; Sievers, *Benjamin Harrison Vol. 2*, 61–105; Thornbrough, *Indiana in the Civil War Era*, 297–304.

11. The Election of 1876 and the End of an Era

1. For a colorful and engaging account of the ceremonies at the opening of the Centennial, see Brown, *Year of the Century*, 112–37. Most studies of the Centennial fail to mention that Morton was present on Opening Day, but his attendance alongside the other dignitaries was noted in *Philadelphia Inquirer*, May 11, 1876, and in *Godey's Lady's Book*, June, 1876.

2. *Frank Leslie's Illustrated Newspaper*, June 12, 1875.

3. For Sherman's remarks on Morton as a presidential candidate, see *Evening Star*, Mar. 15, 1876.

4. For cartoon depictions of him with his crutches/canes, see *Frank Leslie's Illustrated Newspaper*, June 12, 1875, and July 24, 1875. For other cartoons that did not portray him as a cripple, see *Frank Leslie's Illustrated Newspaper*, Sept.21, 1872, Feb. 21, Apr. 14, 1874, and May 22, 1875. For some of the dozens of reports on Morton's health in the Washington newspapers, see *Evening Star*, July 16, Sept 8, 1868, July 27, Nov. 13, 1874, Dec. 3, 1874, July 12, 1875. For Morton leaving the Senate chamber and falling on the railroad platform, see *Evening Star*, Apr. 23, Dec. 6, 1869. His being robbed in Jersey City was recounted in *Evening Star*, Nov. 29, 1871. A report of his improved health enabling him to plan to travel with the president is found in *Evening Star*, June 12, 1871, while his speaking while standing in the 1872 campaign is recounted in *Evening Star*, Oct. 14, 1872. His walking easily on canes is found in *Evening Star*, Dec. 6, 1875, and his elevator fall is related in *Evening Star*, Mar. 30, 1876. The rumors of the senator dying are in *Evening Star*, Mar. 12, 13, 16, 1874, May 4, 1876.

5. His Democratic foes in Indiana launched unrelenting attacks on Morton, as their fears of him becoming president grew throughout 1875 and 1876. They called him a tyrant, an opportunist, a hateful man, and someone not to be trusted, and they insisted that he would become a dictator because of his record as governor and his support for Radical Reconstruction. For examples, see *Indiana Sentinel*, Sept. 8, Oct. 21, 1875, Jan. 24, Feb. 7,

Mar. 15, June 7, 1876. For examples of how Indiana Republicans supported his presidential bid and defended Morton against such attacks, see *Marshall County Republican,* June 17, Mar. 30, 1875, May 11, 25, June 8, 1876.

6. *Evening Star,* Dec. 16, 1875; *Indiana Sentinel,* Dec. 22, 1875. For an example of Morton's continued support for temperance, see *Harper's Weekly,* Mar. 11, 1876.

7. O. P. Morton to Lucinda Morton, Dec. 12, 1870, OPMISL; O. P. Morton to Lucinda Morton, Nov. 22, 1873, OPMISL. The letters to Lucinda imply that the drunken woman, Mrs. Jim Pritchett, was holding allegations of a sexual scandal over Morton, but it is unclear if that is truly the case. Mrs. Pritchett told others at various times that she was the senator's daughter-in-law and his niece.

8. This unsigned, undated emotional defense in Morton's handwriting is found in Oliver P. Morton Scrapbook, OPMIHS. While it has no addressee, the language used and the fact that it was in his scrapbook that contained so many newspaper clippings and to which his wife had access, I am assuming it was written to Lucinda. The letter is written on the pages of the scrapbook, while surrounding pages have newspaper clippings pasted into them. In other places, Morton also wrote on the scrapbook pages, but these are usually drafts of speeches. I initially thought this letter might be a draft or notes for a speech defending himself against Democratic accusations, but it is too personal and too emotional, and the style is remarkably different from the type that Morton used in public speaking.

9. *Indianapolis Sun,* clipping of June 25, 1871, story in edition dated July 1871, Oliver P. Morton Scrapbook, OPMIHS.

10. Ibid.

11. Ibid.

12. *Milwaukee Daily News,* Apr. 16, 1873; *St. Paul Daily Pioneer,* June 3, 1874; *Raleigh Sentinel,* Feb. 18, 1876.

13. *Chicago Times,* Apr. 15, 1876.

14. Ibid.; *Chicago Times,* Apr. 19, 1876.

15. *Chicago Times,* Apr. 15, 1876.

16. Ibid.

17. For a detailed and entertaining account of the Belknap scandal, see Brown, *Year of the Century,* 97–108. Morton's skills as a constitutional and procedural expert put him at the center of the congressional investigations of the Belknap case. For examples of his role, see *Evening Star,* Apr. 5, 6, 17, May 8, 29, 30, 1876.

18. *Chicago Times,* Apr. 15, 1876.

19. Ibid., 2. Without much evidence, it is difficult to judge the truth about private matters like sexual affairs. The editor of the *Chicago Times,* Wilbur F. Storey, was a rather independent Democratic partisan who often printed scurrilous stories about politicians. Born in Vermont, he had learned the newspaper business as a youth in New York City before moving to Indiana, where his first publishing venture failed. After a time in Michigan, including some years as editor of the *Detroit Free Press,* he purchased the *Times* and moved to Chicago. There he proved to be an innovator by printing local news, and in a time when sensationalism already pervaded much of American journalism, he upped the ante, especially in his attacks on his enemies.

During the Civil War, Storey's Copperhead sympathies and criticism of the Lincoln administration caused General Ambrose Burnside to close down his newspaper in 1863.

Lincoln soon lifted the ban, but Storey made himself out to be a defender of free speech and victim of tyranny. By the late 1870s he was writing little of the paper's content, but he still encouraged sensationalism. For more on Wilbur F. Storey, see Walsh, *To Print the News*. Printing the worst kind of rumors and gossip was typical of Storey and his staff, which makes it quite likely that most of the scandalous material about Morton was simply garbage. But I am one who suspects that where there is smoke, there is fire. While I do not believe that Morton was the kind of sexual predator the *Times* made him out to be, I think that he must have had at least one affair—probably with the Knightstown woman—and that became the basis for the nasty attacks on him. Such an affair would also help to explain the destruction of his personal papers, as they might have contained some sort of evidence about such a liaison outside of his marriage. I think it telling that of the few personal papers that do survive, most of them are letters Morton wrote to Lucinda explaining the situation about a possible female blackmailer and his heartfelt defense in his scrapbook. I think that she kept those as reminders of his denials whenever she saw or heard the sex scandal stories being repeated.

20. *Chicago Times,* Apr. 15, 1876.

21. Ibid.

22. Ibid.

23. Ibid.

24. Foulke, *Life of Oliver P. Morton,* vol. 2, 391–94. For the Emma Mine Scandal and Morton's explanation, see *Evening Star,* Mar. 21, 1876.

25. For the charges that Morton stole money during the war, see *New York World,* Apr. 28, 1876; Oliver P. Morton, *Personal Explanation.* A newspaper account is *Evening Star,* May 3, 1876.

26. *New York World,* May 3, 4, 1876; *Evening Star,* June 21, 22, 30, 1876; *Cincinnati Commercial,* May 4, 1876. For an example of the newspapers covering Morton continuing to wave the bloody shirt in 1876, see *Harper's Weekly,* Feb. 26, 1876.

27. The campaign biography is *Oliver P. Morton of Indiana.* In 1864 William French had written a long life-and-letters style biography for use in Morton's reelection campaign. The Republicans reprinted a revised version in 1866 to support his election to the Senate—see French, *Life, Speeches*—but in 1876 his supporters set the French book aside and published a much shorter, cheaper, pamphlet-style biography designed for wider distribution.

For Pinchback campaigning for Morton that spring, see Dray, *Capitol Men,* 365. For an example of newspapers relating Morton's African American support, see *Chicago Times,* Mar. 20, 1876. Of the numerous accounts of the 1876 election, including several published in the wake of the disputed election of 2000, which had many parallels to the nineteenth-century contest, the most reliable recent study is Holt, *By One Vote.* Holt challenges the traditional interpretation and raises new questions for scholars to consider. Brown, *Year of the Century,* offers more color and intrigue, while Summers, *Ordeal of the Reunion,* 372–93, and Foner, *Reconstruction,* 564–87, provide accurate and insightful syntheses. Studies of the Centennial include the election as well; see, e.g., Bergamini, *Hundredth Year,* passim, and Randel, *Centennial,* esp. 214–39. For an unreliable book that repeats the traditional account of how the Republicans stole the election in order to continue their corrupt and greedy depredations in the South, see Morris, *Fraud of the Century.* In conflating events and seeing the past through the lens of the 2000 election,

Morris largely ignores and dismisses the use of force and fraud by the Democratic Redeemers. *Harper's Weekly,* Mar. 18, 1876; Foulke, *Life of Oliver P. Morton,* vol. 2, 398–99.

28. I draw these calculations of Morton's chances for the nomination from the various studies of the election cited in note 26 as well as newspaper accounts like those found in *Evening Star* in May and June, 1876.

29. Holt, *By One Vote,* 90–93; Foulke, *Life of Morton,* vol. 2, 398–400.

30. For the balloting at the Cincinnati convention, see Holt, *By One Vote,* 91–93; Foulke, *Life of Oliver P. Morton,* vol. 2, 400–401.

31. For Hayes becoming the compromise candidate, see Holt, *By One Vote,* 54–66. Ironically, Blaine Amendments remain the law today in many states, where courts are employing them to overturn educational choice using voucher systems. In response, conservatives who favor school choice, and Protestants who want to use public funds to send their children to private, Christian schools, are calling for repealing the amendment in some states; see, e.g., "Religious Bigotry in Colorado: The Anti-Catholic Blaine Amendment Is Used to Kill Vouchers," *Wall Street Journal,* July 2, 2015.

32. Morton thought he still had strong prospects for future runs at the presidency, and this influenced his loyal pledge to support the nominee; see O. P. Morton to Simon T. Powell, June 25, 1876, OPMIHS. For newspaper coverage of this debate, see *Evening Star,* July 18, 1876. For Morton's speech and these quotations, see Morton, Sherman, and Boutwell, *River and Harbor Bill,* 1–2.

33. Ibid., 1–4.

34. Ibid., 2–3.

35. Ibid., 3–4. Morton used the Hamburg Massacre in the campaign that summer; see *Evening Star,* Aug. 2, 1876.

36. Oliver P. Morton, "Tilden and Hendricks as Slanderers of Our Good Name," *Cincinnati Gazette,* Aug. 11, 1876.

37. *Indiana Sentinel,* Aug. 16, 1876.

38. Foulke, *Life of Oliver P. Morton,* vol. 2, 420; Morton, "The History of Indiana Democracy Ventilated."

39. For the comments on Harrison, see *Evening Star,* Aug. 8, 1876.

40. For examples of Morton campaigning and the Democrats calling him names, see *Evening Star,* Aug. 12, 16, Sept. 4, 7, 29, Oct. 17, 26, 1876.

41. Holt, *By One Vote,* 175–203.

42. For Morton possibly becoming president pro tempore of the Senate and taking the presidency that way, see *Evening Star,* Dec. 20, 1875, Jan. 12, Nov. 21, 1876; Randel, *Centennial,* 235. The term *bulldoze* came from white Southerners calling for one of their own to give a black man a dose of the bullwhip, with "bull dose," becoming "bulldoze." For the accounts of murder and bulldozing, see Holt, *By One Vote,* 182, 200.

43. Even before the election, the Republican mouthpiece in Washington lamented that Morton's plans to change the rules had not been implemented; see *Evening Star,* Oct. 16, 20, 1876. For Morton's attempts to rescind the Twenty-Second Rule, see Holt, *By One Vote,* 26–28, 206–7.

44. For Morton shaving off his beard, see *Evening Star,* Dec. 5, 1876.

45. For the attempts at compromise through committees, see Holt, *By One Vote,* 210–13.

46. For coverage of the Senate debate and Morton's rough handling of Conkling, see *National Republican,* Jan. 25, 1877. Morton's speech can be found in the *Congressional Record* and in *Appleton's Annual Cyclopedia,* 144–47.

47. The report of the Electoral Commission, including Morton's opinions, are found in ibid., 184–218, and in Foulke, *Life of Oliver P. Morton,* vol. 2, 461–77.

48. Holt, *By One Vote,* 236–40.

49. Holt, *By One Vote,* 240–43; Summers, *Ordeal of the Reunion,* 384. Historians continue to debate whether there really was a Compromise of 1877, and if there was, what the details were. C. Vann Woodward famously argued for one in *Reunion and Reaction.* For a challenge to Woodward, see Peskin, "Was There a Compromise of 1877?" For more on the turn away from Reconstruction before 1877, see Gillette, *Retreat from Reconstruction.* For more on James Wormley, see Gelderman, *A Free Man of Color.*

50. I take this interpretation and the following sources from Mark Summers and thank him for sharing them with me. See the testimony of E. A. Burke in *Congressional Record, 45th Cong., 3rd Sess.,* H. R. Misc. Doc. 31, "Presidential Election Investigation," vol. 3: Testimony Relating to Louisiana. The notes of the Wormley Conference were in Burke's handwriting, and he insisted that South Carolina was never part of the deal, only Louisiana. Burke also indicated that Morton demanded protection for African American rights in Louisiana in exchange for agreeing to the compromise and that his support gave Hayes political cover. Gelderman, *A Free Man of Color and His Hotel,* offers a detailed account of the Wormley Conference, see 100–105. For the Morton serenade and speech at the Ebbitt House, see *New York Herald,* Mar. 4, 1877. Many did not accept Morton's arguments that the Compromise of 1877 was not a surrender; see *Harper's Weekly,* Feb. 10, 1877. Charles Calhoun, *Conceiving a New Republic,* includes Morton in his argument that 1877 was not really the end of the Southern Question but was instead the Republicans trying to salvage what they could given the political situation. Although I take a slightly more traditional perspective, Morton's views fit well with Calhoun's interpretation.

51. "Political Farce of 1876"; *Frank Leslie's Illustrated Newspaper,* Feb. 10, 1877.

52. Foulke, *Life of Oliver P. Morton,* vol. 2, 479–86. National newspapers noticed Morton continuing to take a Radical stand on the Southern Question; see *Harper's Weekly,* Apr. 14, 1877.

53. Morton, *President's Southern Policy,* 1–2.

54. Ibid.

55. Ibid., 2.

56. Ibid., 2–3.

57. Ibid.

58. Ibid., 3.

59. Ibid.

60. Ibid., 3–4.

61. Ibid., 4.

62. Morton's calls for party unity underscored the deep fractures in the ranks and the fears that many Republicans had about the long-term consequences of ending Reconstruction; see *Harper's Weekly,* June 23, 1877.

63. Morton, "American Constitution, I"; Oliver P. Morton, "American Constitution, II"; Morton, *Chinese Immigration.*

64. Ibid.

65. For the reasons for going to Oregon, see *Evening Star,* Dec. 12, 1876, July 6, 1877. For Morton's Decoration Day speech in Indianapolis, see *Indianapolis Journal,* May 31,

1877. For a problematic analysis of Morton's Decoration Day speeches over the years, see Rainesalo, "Senator Oliver P. Morton and Historical Memory."

66. For coverage of Morton's Salem, Oregon, speech, see *Evening Star,* Aug. 13, 1877.

67. For Hayes's visit, see *Alexandria Gazette,* Sept. 15, 1877; *Evening Star,* Sept. 13, 15, 1877. For Republicans worrying about the impact of Morton's death on the party, *National Tribune,* Oct. 1, 1877. The brutal hopes of the Democrats are found in *Indiana Sentinel,* Aug. 27, 1877.

68. The *Journal* article was carried by many other newspapers and was the basis of a piece in *Harper's Weekly,* Nov. 10, 1877.

69. For more on Morton's sickness and death, see William R. Holloway Papers, box 1, folder 4, OPMIHS. For examples of newspaper coverage of Morton's declining health throughout the summer and fall and his death in November, see *Evening Star,* Aug. 14, 15, 16, 18, 20, 21, 23, 24, 25, 27, 28, 29 30, 31, Sept. 1, 5, 6, 7, 8, 11, 12, 13, 15, 17, 19, 21, 22, 26, 27, 28, Oct. 3, 4, 8, 9, 11, 12, 15, 22, 23, 25, 30, Nov. 1, 2, 3, 1877; *Christian Recorder,* Nov. 1, 1877; *Alexandria Gazette,* Nov. 1, 1877.

70. For the flags at half-staff and the closing of the government, see *Evening Star,* Nov. 2, 3, 1877. For the letters of condolence, see box 10, folder 4, OPMIHS. For a study that looks more closely at these condolence letters, including many from significant political figures, see Rainesalo, "Senator Oliver P. Morton and Historical Memory," esp. 60–62, 75–76.

71. Foulke, *Life of Oliver P. Morton,* vol. 2, 503–6. An obituary and account of the funeral in a national newspaper is found in *Harper's Weekly,* Nov. 17 and Dec. 1, 1877. For more on Morton's grave and decisions about the monument over it at Crown Hill Cemetery, see Rainesalo, "Senator Oliver P. Morton and Historical Memory," 80–82.

12. Morton and the Politics of Memory

1. A version of this chapter was published as an article; see Fuller, "Oliver P. Morton and the Politics of Civil War Memory." For the funeral pictures, see *Frank Leslie's Illustrated Newspaper,* Nov. 21, 1877, and *Harper's Weekly,* Dec. 1, 1877. Remembering Morton necessarily involved Civil War memory, a subject upon which the literature continues to grow and become more complex as scholars examine the meaning of culture and history as expressed in successive generations. Paul H. Buck began the scholarly literature on the subject with a study that today's historians too often neglect; see Buck, *Road to Reunion.* Gaines M. Foster looked at Southern memories and the development of the Lost Cause, a subject explored extensively by Southern historians, in his *Ghosts of the Confederacy.* An important study that helped spur recent interest in historical memory was Michael Kammen's *Mystic Chords of Memory,* while Stuart McConnell's study of the Grand Army of the Republic outlined the role of Northern veterans in remembering the war; see McConnell, *Glorious Contentment.*

Carol Reardon foreshadowed the complexity of shifting memories in Reardon, *Pickett's Charge.* Kirk Savage looked at the role of race in monuments and statues remembering the Civil War in Savage, *Standing Soldiers, Kneeling Slaves.* A collection of essays edited by W. Fitzhugh Brundage explored the complex nature of Southern historical memory; see Brundage, *Where These Memories Grow.*

The most influential book on Civil War memory in the most recent generation of scholarship is the insightful work of David W. Blight, who extended Buck's interpretation by arguing that the foundation of reunion and twentieth-century American nationalism rested on the reconciliation of the North and the South on terms that preserved racism and white supremacy. He argued that there were three distinct Civil War memories: the Emancipationist, the Lost Cause, and the Reconciliationist, with the last informing reunion on racist grounds; see Blight, *Race and Reunion.* Nina Silber foreshadowed the Blight interpretation in a gendered analysis in Silber, *Romance of Reunion.* A book that shows how women played an essential role in creating Civil War memory is Janney, *Burying The Dead.*

There are a number of insightful studies of Southern historical memory, including W. Fitzhugh Brundage's *Southern Past.* An excellent state study is Marshall, *Creating a Confederate Kentucky,* and useful correctives to and expansions of Blight, especially in challenging his framework of three memories by distinguishing a fourth memory, the Unionist view, are found in Blair, *Cities of the Dead;* Neff, *Honoring the Civil War Dead;* Gallagher, *Causes Won, Lost, Forgotten;* Jeffrey, *Abolitionists Remember;* and Gannon, *The Won Cause.* Caroline E. Janney provides a full correction of the Blight interpretation in her *Remembering the Civil War.*

2. *Christian Recorder,* Nov. 8, 1877; *Rockland County Journal,* Nov. 10, 1877.

3. McDonald, "Address of Mr. McDonald," 8–13.

4. Edmunds, "Address of Mr. Edmunds." For information about Edmunds, see Crockett, *George Franklin Edmunds.*

5. Burnside, "Address of Mr. Burnside."

6. Ibid.

7. Morgan, "Address of Mr. Morgan." For more on Morgan, including his expansion, see Fry, *John Tyler Morgan.*

8. Morgan, "Address of Mr. Morgan."

9. Bruce, "Address of Mr. Bruce." Senator Bruce was not the only African American to mourn Morton; see "Memorial Meeting of the Colored People on Senator Morton's Death," *Indianapolis Journal,* Nov. 8, 1877; the Colored Citizens of Owensboro, Kentucky, to Lucinda Morton, Nov. 5, 1877; and John H. Johnson to Lucinda Morton, Nov. 6, 1877, OPMIHS.

10. Bruce, "Address of Mr. Bruce," 51–57.

11. Ibid.

12. The only non-Northerner to speak in the House of Representatives hailed from West Virginia. For the memorials in the House and the quotations included here, see *Memorial Addresses on the Life and Character of Oliver P. Morton,* 61–125.

13. My interpretation of the memories of Morton and the Civil War differs somewhat from that of James H. Madison, who argued for a view of Indiana's Civil War memory similar to that of David Blight; see Madison, "Civil War Memories."

14. Wilder, "Oliver P. Morton, Late Senator."

15. Ibid.

16. Oliver T. Morton to Lucinda Morton, Oct. 31, 1881, OPMIHS.

17. Fishback, *Address Delivered on the Fourteenth Anniversary.* For more on Fishback, see Phillips, *Indiana in Transition,* 13, 21, 417. For more on the failed 1890 force bill (or the federal elections bill or the Lodge bill [it was introduced by Henry Cabot Lodge]), see *New York Age,* Aug. 9, 1890, and Keyssar, *Right to Vote,* 86–106. A number of states had GAR posts named for Morton, including: Indiana, Iowa, Washington (DC), Nebraska, Minnesota, Texas, Washington, Kansas, and Missouri.

18. Fishback, *Address Delivered on the Fourteenth Anniversary.*

19. Ibid.

20. *Proceedings in Congress upon the Acceptance of the Statue of Oliver P. Morton.* Those responsible for it sought and received approval of the final design from Morton's widow and son, Lucinda Morton and Oliver T. Morton. For the family's approval and more on the decision and planning for the statue, see Rainesalo, "Senator Oliver P. Morton and Historical Memory," 97–101. Rainesalo's thesis research confirms archival evidence indicating that Lucinda Morton played an important role in shaping and maintaining her husband's historical memory.

21. Fairbanks, "Address of Mr. Fairbanks." Here Fairbanks's words about blacks searching for liberty contradict the interpretation of David Blight, who argues that the emphasis of memories of the Underground Railroad was always on the white abolitionists, not on the agency of runaway slaves; see Blight, *Race and Reunion,* 231.

22. Ibid.

23. Ibid.

24. Ibid. For more on Fairbanks, see Phillips, *Indiana in Transition,* 54, 65, 129–30, passim.

25. Beveridge, "Address of Mr. Beveridge," 35–45.

26. Ibid.

27. Ibid. For more on Beveridge, see Phillips, *Indiana in Transition,* 70–72, 95, passim.

28. For the Apr. 14, 1900, speeches in the House of Representatives, see *Proceedings in Congress upon the Acceptance of a Statue of Oliver P. Morton,* 47–141.

29. Ibid.

30. Ibid.

31. Adams, *State of Indiana Dedication Ceremonies,* 3–4, 12–14. For Lucinda Morton and Will Holloway evaluating the work, see Rainesalo, "Senator Oliver P. Morton and Historical Memory," 109–10.

32. Adams, *State of Indiana Dedication Ceremonies,* 15–19.

33. Ibid., 19–23.

34. Ibid. 23–29. For Hanly's career, see Scheele, "J. Frank Hanly."

35. Adams, *State of Indiana Dedication Ceremonies,* 29–31.

36. Ibid., 31–34.

37. Kate Milner Rash, "Morton Centenary Revives Interest in Famous War Governor," in *Centerville Echo,* Aug. 219–23; "Foulke Makes Address at Opening of Morton Centennial Anniversary," in *Richmond Palladium,* Aug. 3, 1923; "Governor McCrary to Unveil Marker," in *Richmond Item,* Aug. 4, 1923; "An Old Indiana Town: Interesting Reminiscences of Centerville," in *Centerville Echo,* Aug. 3, 1923; "Committees Work Hard for Success of Centennial Day," in *Richmond Palladium,* Aug. 3, 1923; R. C. Waters, "Drama-Pageant of Oliver," in *Centerville Echo,* Aug. 3, 1923; "Pageant as Tribute to Indiana's War Governor," in *Richmond Palladium,* Aug. 3, 1923; R. C. Waters, "Historical Fidelity of Incidents in Great War Governor's Life Preserved by Men and Women of Today in Play," in *Richmond Palladium,* Aug. 3, 1923; Buhl, "Call of Oliver P. Morton."

38. Buhl, "Call of Oliver P. Morton," 2; For more on the Indiana Ku Klux Klan and lynching in the period, see Lutholtz, *Grand Dragon;* Madison, *A Lynching in the Heartland.*

39. Buhl, "Call of Oliver P. Morton," 2–6.

40. Ibid., 9–11, 8, passim.

41. Perry, *Morton in Bronze.*

42. For a brief account of Indiana in the 1910s and 1920s, see Madison, *Indiana Way,* esp. 145–232.

43. For more on the Ku Klux Klan in Indiana, see Madison, *Indiana Way,* 289–95; Lutholtz, *Grand Dragon.* For more on Governor Ed Jackson, see Lantzer, "Edward L. Jackson," in Gugin and St. Clair, *Governors of Indiana,* 274–79.

44. Perry, *Morton in Bronze,* 7–17, 31–36. For a study of the creation of battlefield parks and the building of memorials on them that includes Vicksburg and takes the perspective of the Blight interpretation of Civil War memory, see Smith, *Golden Age of Battlefield Preservation.*

45. Perry, *Morton in Bronze,* 18–29.

46. Ibid., 41–44.

47. Adams, *Dedication Ceremonies of Morton Statue,* 19–29.

48. Perry, *Morton in Bronze,* 41–44.

49. Ibid., 46.

50. Zenor, *Indiana and the Civil War.* For Emma Lou Thornbrough's more balanced interpretation of Morton, see Thornbrough, *Indiana in the Civil War Era,* 1850.

51. Centerville, Indiana, 1814–1964.

52. Beth Treaster et al., "Happy Birthday, Oliver P. Morton!"; Louise Ronald, "Looking Back and Forward," *Richmond Palladium-Item,* Aug. 5, 2013. A descendant of Morton attended the ceremonies and the author was one of the invited speakers. I spoke at the event outside the Morton House and emphasized Morton's nationalism, included his actions against the Copperheads, and mentioned his Senate career while joining others in remembering his opposition to slavery and efforts on behalf of the soldiers.

53. The Lincoln funeral event was sponsored by the Centerville-Center Township Public Library and the Centerville United Methodist Church and was organized by Beth Treaster, Kevin Smith, Nancy Merkamp, Carol Detwiler, and Danny Shaver. I delivered the lecture, "Lincoln and Morton, Partners for the Union"; see the printed program, Treaster, "Remembering Lincoln Exactly 150 Years Later" (author's private collection). See also *Richmond Palladium-Item,* Apr. 27, 2015. Twenty-first century memories of Morton continue, of course, and during the campaign for the election of 2016 at the University of Indianapolis, I gave a lecture that involved memories of Morton and his role in the disputed 1876 contest; see "Lecture Connects Corrupt Election of 1876 to Today," *Reflector,* Sept. 28, 2016.

Bibliography

PRIMARY SOURCES

Newspapers

Abingdon (VA) *Virginian*
Alexandria (VA) *Gazette and Virginia Advertiser*
Atlanta Constitution
Belmont Chronicle (St. Clairsville, OH)
Boston Daily Advertiser
Centerville (IN) *Echo*
Centerville (IN) *Western Times*
Charleston (SC) *Daily News*
Chicago Inter-Ocean
Chicago Times
Chicago Tribune
Christian Recorder (Philadelphia)
Cincinnati Commercial
Cincinnati Daily Commercial
Cincinnati Daily Gazette
Cincinnati Gazette
Daily Cleveland Herald
Daily Missouri Democrat (St. Louis)
Evansville (IN) *Daily Journal*
Evening Star (Washington, DC)
Farmer's Cabinet (Amherst, NH)
Frank Leslie's Illustrated Newspaper
Gallipolis (OH) *Journal*
Godey's Lady's Book (Philadelphia)
Harper's Weekly
Holmes County Republican (Millersburg, OH)
Indiana American (Brookville)
Indiana Free Democrat (Indianapolis)
Indiana Sentinel (Indianapolis)
Indiana True Democrat (Centerville, IN)
Indianapolis Journal
Jasper (IN) *Weekly Courier*

Leavenworth (KS) *Times*
Lowell (MA) *Daily Citizen and News*
Madison (IN) *Daily Courier*
Marshall County Republican (Plymouth, IN)
Milwaukee Daily News
Philadelphia Inquirer
Pomeroy (OH) *Weekly Telegraph*
Nashville Union and American
National Republican (Washington, DC)
National Tribune (Washington, DC)
New York Age
New-York Daily Tribune
New York Herald
New York Times
New-York Tribune
New York World
Philadelphia Inquirer
Plymouth (IN) *Democrat*
Plymouth (IN) *Republican*
Plymouth (IN) *Weekly Democrat*
Raleigh Sentinel
Reflector (University of Indianapolis)
Richmond (IN) *Item*
Richmond (IN) *Palladium*
Richmond (IN) *Palladium-Item*
Richmond (IN) *Times Dispatch*
Rockland County Journal (Nyack, NY)
Staunton (VA) *Spectator*
St. Paul Daily Pioneer
Vincennes (IN) *Sun*
Wabash (IN) *Express*
Wall Street Journal
Washington (DC) *Chronicle*
Washington (DC) *Evening Times*
Wayne County Record (Richmond, IN)
Wheeling (WV) *Daily Intelligencer*
White Cloud Kansas Chief
Wisconsin State Journal (Madison)

Manuscript Collections

Huntington Research Library, San Marino, California
    Smith-Spooner Collection
Indiana State Archives, Indianapolis
    Adjutant General's Records
    Oliver P. Morton Letter Books
    Oliver P. Morton Papers

Indiana State Library, Indianapolis
  Conrad Baker Papers
  Daniel P. Pratt Papers
  George W. Julian Papers
  Indiana Pamphlets
  Oliver P. Morton Papers
  Oliver P. Morton Telegraph Books and Slips
Library of Congress, Washington, DC
  Abraham Lincoln Papers
Lilly Library, Indiana University, Bloomington
  Henry Smith Lane Papers
  Indiana History Manuscripts
  John Hanna Papers
  Schuyler Colfax Papers
  William Cumback Papers
William Henry Smith Memorial Library, Indiana Historical Society, Indianapolis
  Abraham Lincoln Papers
  Calvin Fletcher Jr. Family Collection
  Calvin Fletcher Papers
  Conrad Baker Papers
  Edward B. Allen Papers
  Governor Oliver P. Morton Letters
  John Dowling Papers
  John Love Papers
  Lane-Elston Papers
  Oliver P. Morton Letter Book
  Oliver P. Morton Letter Book, May 10, 1865, to September 1865
  Oliver P. Morton Papers
  William Hayden English Papers
  William R. Holloway Papers

Published Primary Sources

Adams, Henry C., comp. *State of Indiana Dedication Ceremonies of Morton Statue and Monument and Report of Commission, 1907.* Indianapolis: W. B. Buford, 1908.

Appleton's Annual Cyclopedia and Registry of Important Events of the Year 1877. New York: Appleton 1878.

Bastiat, Frédéric. *That Which Is Seen, and That Which Is Not Seen* (1850). In Charles Frédéric Bastiat, *The Bastiat Collection*, 1–48. Auburn, AL: Mises Institute, 2011.

"Berry R. Sulgrove, Journalist." Obituary. *Indiana Quarterly Magazine of History* 2, no. 3 (Sept. 1906): 139–47.

Beveridge, Albert J. "Address of Mr. Beveridge." In *Proceedings in Congress upon the Acceptance of a Statue of Oliver P. Morton,* 35–45.

Bruce, Blanche K. "Address of Mr. Bruce, of Mississippi." In *Memorial Addresses,* 51–57.

Burnside, Ambrose. "Address of Mr. Burnside, of Rhode Island." In *Memorial Addresses,* 26–31.

Centerville, Indiana, 1814–1964, Sesquicentennial, Sept. 13–19, 1964, "From the Flintlock to the Missile." Centerville, IN: Sesquicentennial Committee, 1964.

Congressional Globe, 39th Congress, 1st Session.

Congressional Globe, 40th Congress, 2nd Session.

Congressional Globe, 40th Congress, 3rd Session.

Congressional Globe, 41st Congress, 1st Session.

Congressional Globe, 41st Congress, 2nd Session.

Congressional Globe, 41st Congress, 3rd Session.

Congressional Record, 43rd Congress, 1st Session.

Congressional Record, 44th Congress, 1st Session.

Congressional Record, 45th Congress, 3rd Session, vol. 3, House of Representatives Miscellaneous Document 31: Testimony Relating to Louisiana. *Court of Appeals,* vol. 5, 1st div. New York: Benj. Tyrrel, Law Printer, 1892.

Draper, Ariel, and Draper, W. H. *Brevier Legislative Reports: Embracing Short-Hand Sketches of the Journals and Debates of the General Assembly of the State of Indiana, Convened in Extra Session On the 24th Day of April, 1861,* vol. 5. Indianapolis: Daily Indiana Sentinel Printers, 1861.

———. *Brevier Legislative Reports: Embracing Short-hand Sketches of the Journals and Debates of the General Assembly of the State of Indiana, Meeting in the Capitol, in the Town of Indianapolis, in Regular Session Under the Constitutional Provision, January 8th, 1863,* vol. 6. South Bend, IN: South Bend Job Office, 1863.

Edmunds, George F. "Address of Mr. Edmunds, of Vermont." In *Memorial Addresses,* 13–18.

Facts for the People, in Answer to Gov. O. P. Morton's Erroneous Statements to the Republican State Convention, February 23, 1864. Indianapolis: Democratic State Central Committee, 1864.

Fairbanks, Charles W. "Address of Mr. Fairbanks." In *Proceedings in Congress upon the Acceptance of the Statue of Oliver P. Morton, presented by the State of Indiana.* Washington. DC: Government Printing Office, 1900.

Fishback, W. P. *Address Delivered on the Fourteenth Anniversary of the Death of Oliver P. Morton, to the Members of the Grand Army of the Republic, at Indianapolis, November 1st, 1891.* Indianapolis: Frank H. Smith, 1891.

Fletcher, Calvin. *The Diary of Calvin Fletcher,* edited by Gayle Thornbrough, Dorothy L. Riker, and Paula Corpuz. 9 vols.Indianapolis: Indiana Historical Society, 1978.

French, William M., ed. *Life, Speeches, State Papers and Public Services of Gov. Oliver P. Morton.* Cincinnati: Moore, Wilstach, and Baldwin, 1866.

The Gubernatorial Canvass: Debate Between Gov. Oliver P. Morton and Hon. Joseph E. McDonald, at LaPorte, Wednesday, Aug. 10, 1864. Indianapolis: n.p., 1864.

Hendricks, Thomas A. "The Issues of the War. Speech Delivered to the Democratic State Convention, Metropolitan Hall, Indianapolis, Jan. 8, 1862." In *Life and Public Services of Thomas A. Hendricks with Selected Speeches and Writing,* edited by John W. Holcombe and Hubert M. Skinner, 451–65. Indianapolis: Carlton and Hollenbeck, 1886.

———. "Speech of Mr. Hendricks." In *Speeches of Hon. D. W. Voorhees and Hon. T. A. Hendricks, on the Civil War and the Present Condition of the Country.* Indianapolis: State Sentinel Steam Press, 1862.

Holloway, W. R. *Indianapolis: A Historical and Statistical Sketch of the Railroad City, a Chronicle of Its Social, Municipal, Commercial and Manufacturing Progress, with Full Statistical Tables.* Indianapolis: Indianapolis Journal Printing, 1870.

Journal of the House of Representatives of the State of Indiana during the Forty-first Session of the General Assembly Commencing Thursday, January 10, 1861. Indianapolis: Berry Sulgrove, State Printer, 1861

Journal of the House of Representatives of the State of Indiana During the Special Session of the General Assembly, Commencing Wednesday, April 24, 1861. Indianapolis: Barry Sulgrove, State Printer, 1861.

Julian, George W. *Political Recollections, 1840 to 1872.* Chicago: Jansen, McClurg, 1884.

Lozier, John Hogarth. *The Cottage of the Dear Ones Left at Home.* Cincinnati: J. Church Jr., 1865.

McCulloch, Hugh. *Men and Measures of Half a Century: Sketches and Comments.* New York: Scribner's, 1889.

McDonald, Joseph E. "Address of Mr. McDonald, of Indiana." In *Memorial Addresses,* 8–13.

Memorial Addresses on the Life and Character of Oliver P. Morton, A Senator from Indiana, Delivered in the Senate and House of Representatives, January 17 and 18, 1878. Published by Order of Congress. Washington, DC: Government Printing Office, 1878.

Morgan, John Tyler. "Address of Mr. Tyler, of Alabama." In *Memorial Addresses,* 26–31.

Morton, Oliver P. "Address to the Agricultural Exposition, September 10, 1873." In *Twenty-Third Annual Report of the Indiana State Board of Agriculture, 1873.* Indianapolis: Sentinel Company Printers, 1874.

———. "The American Constitution, I." *North American Review* 124, no. 256 (May–June 1877): 341–46.

———. "The American Constitution, II." *North American Review* 125, no. 257 (July–Aug. 1877): 68–78.

———. *Annexation of Dominica: Speech of Hon. Oliver P. Morton, of Indiana, Delivered in the Senate of the United States, December 21, 1870.* Washington, DC: Rives and Bailey, 1870.

———. "Campaign of 1860, Speech at Fort Wayne." in French, *Life, Speeches, State Papers,* 81–102.

——— "The Currency Question." *Indianapolis Journal,* May 5, 1874.

———. *Democratic Violence: Proscription, and Intolerance, Spirit of the White-Line Democracy, Duty of the Republican Party to Maintain the Rights of Colored Men, Startling Democratic Defalcations, Unparalleled Corruption and Maladministration: Speech of Hon. O. P. Morton, Delivered in the United States Senate, January 19, 1876, on the Mississippi Election.* Washington, DC: n.p., 1876.

———. *Emigration to the United States of North America: Indiana as a Home for Emigrants.* Indianapolis: Joseph J. Bingham, State Printer, 1864.

———. *Fifteenth Amendment: Speech of Hon. Oliver P. Morton of Indiana, Delivered in the Senate of the United States, February 15, 1871.* Washington, DC: Rives and Bailey, 1871.

———. "First Guns." *Indianapolis Journal,* June 24, 1872.

———. "The History of Indiana Democracy Ventilated, Speech of Oliver P. Morton at LaPorte, Indiana." *Indianapolis Journal,* Aug. 15, 1876,

———. *Hon. O. P. Morton's Terre Haute Speech, Delivered July 18, 1870, at Terre Haute Indiana.* Washington, DC: Union Republican Congressional Committee, 1870.

———. "Inaugural Address, Jan. 6, 1865." *Indianapolis Journal*, Jan. 7, 1865.

———. *The Issues of 1868: Speech of Hon. O. P. Morton, U.S. Senator from Indiana, Before the Soldiers' and Sailors' Union of Washington, DC, on Monday Evening, January 6, 1868.* Washington, DC: Chronicle Print, 1868.

———. *Laws of Neutrality: Speech of Hon. Oliver P. Morton, of Indiana, Delivered in the Senate of the United States, February 9, 1870.* Washington, DC: Rives and Bailey, 1870.

———. *Louisiana Affairs: Speech of Hon. Oliver P. Morton, of Indiana, in the United States Senate, January 30 and February 2, 1874.* Washington, DC: Chronicle Publishing, 1874.

———. *Message of the Governor to the Legislature, At Its Extra Session, April 24, 1861.* Indianapolis: Barry R. Sulgrove, State Printer, 1862.

———. *Message of Governor Oliver P. Morton, Delivered January 11, 1867.* Indianapolis: W. R. Holloway, State Printer, 1867.

———. *Message of Oliver P. Morton, Governor of the State of Indiana, to the Special Session of the General Assembly, Delivered Tuesday, Nov. 16, 1865.* Indianapolis: W. R. Holloway, State Printer, 1865.

———. *National and State Affairs: Speech of Governor O. P. Morton, at the Union Congressional Convention, Held at Greencastle, Ind., July 27, 1864.* Indianapolis: Indianapolis Journal Printing, 1864.

———. *National-Bank Circulation: Speech of Hon. O. P. Morton, of Indiana, in the United States Senate, March 23, 1874.* Washington, DC: Government Printing Office, 1874.

———. "The National Idea." *Providence Journal*, Nov. 27, 1871.

———. *Oration of Hon. O. P. Morton, Address of Major General George G. Meade, and Dedication Ode, by Bayard Taylor, Together with the Other Exercises at the Dedication of the Monument in the Soldiers' National Cemetery at Gettysburg, July 1, 1869.* Gettysburg: J. E. Wible, 1870.

———. *Peace or War: The Democratic Position Illustrated by Frank P. Blair Jr.* Washington, DC: Union Republican Congressional Committee, 1868.

———. *Personal Explanation, O. P. Morton, Governor of Indiana: Alleged Misapplication of $250,000, Revolutionary Policy of Democratic Legislature, in the Senate of the United States, May 3, 1876.* Washington, DC: Chronicle Printers, 1876.

———. *Political Disabilities—Attitude of the Democratic Party: Speech of Hon. Oliver P. Morton, of Indiana, in the Senate of the United States, January 23,1872.* Washington, DC: Congressional Globe Office, 1872.

———. *Presidential Elections: Speech of Hon. Oliver P. Morton, of Indiana, Delivered to the Senate of the United States, January 17, 1873.* Washington, DC: Rives and Bailey, 1873.

———. *The President's Southern Policy: Letter of Hon. O. P. Morton Upon the Overthrow of the Republican State Governments of South Carolina and Louisiana, May 24, 1877.* Indianapolis: Journal Printers, 1877.

———. *Protection of Life, etc., at the South: Speech of Hon. Oliver P. Morton of Indiana, Delivered in the Senate of the United States, April 4, 1871.* Washington: Rives & Bailey, 1871.

———. *Railroad Legislation: Speech of Hon. O. P. Morton, of Indiana, in the Senate of the United States, January 27, 1874.* Washington, DC: Government Printing Office, 1874.

———. *Reconstruction and Negro Suffrage. Speech of Governor O. P. Morton at Richmond, Indiana, on Thursday Evening, September 29, 1865.* Indianapolis: W. R. Holloway, State Printer, 1865.

———. *Reconstruction. Speech of Hon. O. P. Morton, in the U.S. Senate, January 24, 1868, on the Constitutionality of the Reconstruction Acts.* Washington, DC: Chronicle Printers, 1868.

———. *Record and Platforms of the Democratic Party. Speech of Senator Morton, at Urbana, Ohio, Aug. 7, 1875.* Washington, DC: Union Republican Congressional Committee, 1875.

———. *Report on Presidential Elections.* Washington, DC: Congressional Globe Printers, 1873.

———. *Soldiers' National Cemetery at Gettysburg.* Indianapolis: W. R. Holloway, State Printer, 1865.

———. *The South: The Political Situation, Speech of Senator Morton on Louisiana Affairs.* Washington, DC: n.p., 1874.

———. *Speech at the Union State Convention Held at Indianapolis, IND., February 23, 1864.* Indianapolis: *Indianapolis Journal*, 1864.

———"Speech delivered at Terre Haute, March [10th], 1860," In French, *Life, Speeches, State Papers*, 31–53.

———. *Speech of Gov. Oliver P. Morton, Delivered at Masonic Hall, Tuesday Evening, June 20, 1866.* Indianapolis: W. R. Holloway, State Printer, 1866.

———. *Speech of Gov. Oliver P. Morton, Delivered at the Union Meeting at New Albany, Wednesday, July 18, 1866.* n.p., 1866.

———. *Speech of Hon. O. P. Morton, of Indiana, on the Resumption of Specie Payments, in the Senate of the United States, December 16, 1868.* Washington, DC: Chronicle Printers, 1868.

———. *Speech of Senator Morton, of Indiana, on Reconstruction, in the United States Senate on Friday, January 24, 1868.* San Francisco: Union Republican State Central Committee of California, 1868.

———. *Views of the Late Oliver P. Morton on the Character, Extent, and Effect of Chinese Immigrants to the United States.* Washington, DC: Government Printing Office, 1878.

Morton, Oliver P., John Sherman, and George S. Boutwell. *River and Harbor Bill and the Dead-Lock: Speeches of Senators Morton, Sherman, and Boutwell, July 18, 19, and 22, 1876.* Washington, DC: Government Printing Office, 1876.

Morton, Oliver T. *The Southern Empire.* Boston: Houghton Mifflin, 1892.

Oliver P. Morton of Indiana: Sketch of His Life and Public Services Prepared by Direction of the Indiana Republican State Central Committee. Indianapolis: Journal Company Printers, 1876.

Owen, Robert Dale. *Threading My Way: Twenty-Seven Years of Autobiography.* London: Trubner, 1874.

Perry, Oran, comp. *Morton in Bronze: Indiana Circle, Vicksburg.* Indianapolis: W. B. Buford, 1926.

Pittman, Benn, ed. *The Trials for Treason at Indianapolis.* Cincinnati: Moore, Wilstach, and Baldwin, 1865.

Proceedings in Congress upon the Acceptance of the Statue of Oliver P. Morton, Presented by the State of Indiana. Washington. DC: Government Printing Office, 1900.

Report and Evidence of the Committee on Arbitrary Arrests in the State of Indiana, Authorized by Resolution of the House of Representatives, January 9, 1863. Indianapolis: J. J. Bingham, State Printer, 1863.

Terrell, W. H. H. *Indiana in the War of the Rebellion: Report of the Adjutant General,* vol. 1. 1869. Reprint. Indianapolis: Indiana Historical Bureau, 1960.

Turpie, David. *Sketches of My Own Times.* Indianapolis: Bobbs-Merrill, 1903.

US War Department. *The War of the Rebellion: A Compilation of the Official Records of the Union and Confederate Armies.* 128 vols. Washington, DC: Government Printing Office, 1880–1901.

Walker, Charles M. *Sketch of the Life, Character, and Public Services of Oliver P. Morton. Prepared for the Indianapolis Journal.* Indianapolis: Indianapolis Journal, 1878.

Wilder, A. "Oliver P. Morton, Late Senator of the United States." *Phrenological Journal and Life Illustrated* 66, no. 1 (Jan. 1878): 5–10.

SECONDARY SOURCES

Anbinder, Tyler. *Nativism and Slavery: The Northern Know Nothings and the Politics of the 1850s.* New York: Oxford Univ. Press, 1992.

Appleby, Joyce. *Capitalism and the New Social Order: The Republican Vision of the 1790s.* New York: New York Univ. Press, 1984.

Ashendel, Anita. "'Women as Force' in Indiana History." In *The State of Indiana History 2000: Papers Presented at the Indiana Historical Society's Grand Opening,* edited by Robert M. Taylor, 1–36. Indianapolis: Indiana Historical Society Press, 2001.

Bailey, Louis J. "Caleb Blood Smith." *Indiana Magazine of History* 29 (1953): 213–39.

Baker, David L. "James Whitcomb." In Gugin and St. Clair, *Governors of Indiana,* 84–103.

Baker, Jean H. *Affairs of Party: The Political Culture of Northern Democrats in the Mid-Nineteenth Century.* 1983. Reprint. New York: Fordham Univ. Press, 1998.

Barnhart, John D., and Donald F. Carmony. *Indiana from Frontier to Industrial Commonwealth.* 2 vols. New York: Lewis Historical Publishing Company, 1953 and 1954.

Barreyre, Nicolas. "The Politics of Economic Crises: The Panic of 1873, the End of Reconstruction, and the Realignment of American Politics." *Journal of the Gilded Age and Progressive Era* 10, no. 4 (Oct. 2011): 403–23.

Beale, Howard K. *The Critical Year: A Study of Andrew Johnson and Reconstruction.* New York: Harcourt, Brace, 1930.

Beard, Charles A., and Mary R. Beard. *The Rise of American Civilization.* New York: Macmillan, 1927.

Bensel, Richard Franklin. *Yankee Leviathan: The Origins of Central Authority in America, 1859–1877.* New York: Cambridge Univ. Press, 1990.

Bergamini, John D. *The Hundredth Year: The United States in 1876.* New York: G. P. Putnam's Sons, 1976.

Bigham, Darrel E. *On Jordan's Banks: Emancipation and Its Aftermath in the Ohio River Valley.* Lexington: Univ. Press of Kentucky, 2005.

Billington, Ray Allen. *The Protestant Crusade, 1800–1860: A Study of the Origins of American Nativism.* 1938. Reprint. Chicago: Quadrangle Paperbacks, 1964.

Blackmon, Douglas A. *Slavery by Another Name: The Re-Enslavement of Black Americans from the Civil War to World War II.* New York: Anchor, 2008.

Blair, William. *Cities of the Dead: Contesting the Memory of the Civil War in the South, 1865–1914.* Chapel Hill: Univ. of North Carolina Press, 2004.

———. *With Malice Toward Some: Treason and Loyalty in the Civil War Era.* Chapel Hill: Univ. of North Carolina Press, 2014.

Blight, David W. *Race and Reunion: The Civil War in American Memory.* Cambridge, MA: Harvard Univ. Press, 2001.

Boucher, Chauncey S. "In Re That Aggressive Slaveocracy." *Mississippi Valley Historical Review* 8 (June–Sept. 1921): 13–80.

Bowers, Claude G. *The Tragic Era: The Revolution after Lincoln.* Boston: Houghton Mifflin, 1929.

Brand, Carl Fremont. "The History of the Know Nothing Party in Indiana." Pt. 1. *Indiana Magazine of History* 18 (Mar. 1922): 46–48.

———. "The History of the Know Nothing Party in Indiana." Pt. 2. *Indiana Magazine of History* 18 (Sept. 1922), 266–306.

Brands, H. W. *The Money Men: Capitalism, Democracy, and the Hundred Years' War over the American Dollar.* New York: Norton, 2006.

Brooks, Juanita. *The Mountain Meadows Massacre.* Norman: Univ. of Oklahoma Press, 1970.

Brown, Dee. *The American Spa: Hot Springs, Arkansas.* Torrance, CA: Rose Publishing, 1982.

———. *The Year of the Century: 1876.* New York: Scribner's, 1966.

Brundage, W. Fitzhugh. *The Southern Past: A Clash of Race and Memory.* Cambridge, MA: Belknap Press/Harvard Univ. Press, 2005.

———, ed. *Where These Memories Grow: History, Memory, and Southern Identity.* Chapel Hill: Univ. of North Carolina Press, 2000.

Buck, Paul H. *The Road to Reunion, 1865–1900.* Boston: Little, Brown, 1937.

Budiansky, Stephen. *The Bloody Shirt: Terror After Appomattox.* New York: Viking, 2008.

Bullard, Loring. *Healing Waters: Missouri's Historic Mineral Springs and Spas.* Columbia: Univ. of Missouri Press, 2004.

Bundy, Chris. *French Lick Springs and West Baden Springs: A Brief History of America's Grand Resorts.* Salem, IN: printed by author, c. 2006.

Butler, Jon. *Awash in a Sea of Faith: Christianizing the American People.* Cambridge, MA: Harvard Univ. Press, 1990.

Calhoun, Charles W. *Conceiving a New Republic: The Republican Party and the Southern Question, 1869–1900.* Lawrence: Univ. Press of Kansas, 2006.

Carleton, William G. "The Money Question in Indiana Politics, 1865–1890." *Indiana Magazine of History* 42, no. 2 (June 1946): 107–50.

Carwardine, Richard J. *Evangelicals and Politics in Antebellum America.* New Haven, CT: Yale Univ. Press, 1993.

Cayton, Andrew R. L. *Frontier Indiana.* Bloomington, IN: Indiana Univ. Press, 1996.

Cayton, Andrew R. L., and Peter S. Onuf. *The Midwest and the Nation: Rethinking the History of an American Region.* Bloomington: Indiana Univ. Press, 1990.

Churchill, Robert H. *To Shake Their Guns in the Tyrant's Face: Libertarian Political Violence and the Origins of the Militia Movement.* Ann Arbor: Univ. of Michigan Press, 2009.

Clark, Donald A. *The Notorious "Bull" Nelson, Murdered Civil War General.* Carbondale: Southern Illinois Univ. Press, 2011.

Cook, Robert J. *Civil War Senator: William Pitt Fessenden and the Fight to Save the American Republic.* Baton Rouge: Louisiana State Univ. Press, 2011.

Corbett, Theodore. *The Making of American Resorts: Saratoga Springs, Ballston Spa, and Lake George.* Brunswick, NJ: Rutgers Univ. Press, 2001.

Coulter, E. Merton. *The Civil War and Readjustment in Kentucky.* Chapel Hill: Univ. of North Carolina Press, 1934.

Crockett, Walter Hill. *George Franklin Edmunds.* St. Albans, VT: Vermonter, 1919.

Cross, Whitney R. *The Burned-Over District: The Social and Intellectual History of Enthusiastic Religion in Western New York, 1800–1850.* Ithaca, NY: Cornell Univ. Press, 1950.

Davis, David Brion. *The Slave Power Conspiracy and the Paranoid Style.* Baton Rouge: Louisiana State Univ. Press, 1969.

Denton, Sally. *American Massacre: The Tragedy at Mountain Meadows, September 1857.* New York: Alfred A. Knopf, 2003.

Denzin, Norman K. *Interpretive Autoethnography.* Qualitative Research Methods, vol. 17, 2nd ed. Newbury Park, CA: Sage Publications, 2014.

———. *Interpretive Biography.* Qualitative Research Methods, Series 17. Newbury Park, CA: Sage Publications, 1989.

Donald, David. *Charles Sumner and the Coming of the Civil War.* New York: Alfred A. Knopf, 1960.

———. *Charles Sumner and the Rights of Man.* New York: Alfred A. Knopf, 1970.

Dray, Philip. *Capitol Men: The Epic Story of Reconstruction Through the Lives of the First Black Congressmen.* Boston: Houghton Mifflin, 2008.

———. *Charles Sumner and the Rights of Man.* New York: Alfred A. Knopf, 1970.

Dudden, Faye E. *Fighting Chance: The Struggle over Woman Suffrage and Black Suffrage in Reconstruction America.* New York: Oxford Univ. Press, 2011.

Earle, Jonathan H. *Jacksonian Antislavery and the Politics of Free Soil, 1824–1854.* Chapel Hill: Univ. of North Carolina Press, 2003.

Eckert, Ralph Lowell. *John Brown Gordon: Soldier, Southerner, American.* Southern Biography Series. Baton Rouge: Louisiana State Univ. Press, 1989.

Egerton, Douglas R. *The Wars of Reconstruction: The Brief, Violent History of America's Most Progressive Era.* New York: Bloomsbury, 2014.

Elliott, Kirsten. *Bath.* London: Frances Lincoln, 2004.

Engle, Stephen. *All the President's Statesmen: Northern Governors and the American Civil War.* Frank L. Klement Lectures: Alternative Views of the Sectional Conflict. Milwaukee: Marquette Univ. Press, 2006.

———. *Don Carlos Buell: Most Promising of All.* Chapel Hill: Univ. of North Carolina Press, 1999.

———. *Gathering to Save a Nation: Abraham Lincoln, Union Governors, and the Preservation of the Union.* Chapel Hill: Univ. of North Carolina Press, forthcoming.

Etcheson, Nicole. *Bleeding Kansas: Contested Liberty in the Civil War Era.* Lawrence: Univ. Press of Kansas, 2004.

———. *The Emerging Midwest: Upland Southerners and the Political Culture of the Old Northwest, 1787–1861.* Bloomington: Indiana Univ. Press, 1996.

———. *A Generation at War: The Civil War Era in a Northern Community.* Lawrence: Univ. Press of Kansas, 2011.

———. "No Fit Wife: Soldiers' Wives and Their In-Laws on the Indiana Home Front." In *Union Heartland: The Midwestern Home Front During the Civil War,* edited by Ginette Aley and J. L. Anderson, 97–124. Carbondale: Southern Illinois Univ. Press, 2013.

Evensen, Bruce J. *God's Man for the Gilded Age: Dwight L. Moody and the Rise of Modern Mass Evangelism.* New York: Oxford Univ. Press, 2003.

Fehrenbacher, Don E. *The Dred Scott Case: Its Significance in American Law and Politics.* New York: Oxford Univ. Press, 1978.

Finkelman, Paul, ed. *His Soul Goes Marching On: Responses to John Brown and the Harper's Ferry Raid.* Charlottesville: Univ. of Virginia Press, 1995.

Foner, Eric. *Free Soil, Free Labor, Free Men: The Ideology of the Republican Party before the Civil War.* New York: Oxford Univ. Press, 1970.

———. *Reconstruction: American's Unfinished Revolution, 1863–1877.* New York: Harper-Collins, 1988.

Foulke, William Dudley. *Life of Oliver P. Morton, Including His Important Speeches.* 2 vols. Indianapolis: Bowen-Merrill, 1899.

Franklin, John Hope. *The Emancipation Proclamation.* New York: Doubleday, 1963.

Fry, Joseph A. *John Tyler Morgan and the Search for Southern Autonomy.* Knoxville: Univ. of Tennessee Press, 1992.

Fuller, A. James. "A Forlorn Hope: Interpreting the Breckinridge Campaign as a Matter of Honor." In Fuller, *Election of 1860 Reconsidered,* 69–101.

———. "The Last True Whig: John Bell and the Politics of Compromise in 1860." In Fuller, *Election of 1860 Reconsidered,* 103–39.

———. "Oliver P. Morton, Political Ideology, and Treason in Civil War Indiana." *Ohio Valley History* 13, no. 3 (Fall 2013): 27–45.

———. "Oliver P. Morton and the Politics of Civil War Memory." *Indiana Magazine of History* 110 (Dec. 2014): 324–56.

———, ed. *The Election of 1860 Reconsidered.* The Civil War in the North series. Kent, OH: Kent State Univ. Press, 2013.

Gallagher, Gary W. *Causes Won, Lost, Forgotten: How Hollywood and Popular Art Shape What We Know About the Civil War.* Chapel Hill: Univ. of North Carolina Press, 2008.

———. *The Union War.* Cambridge, MA: Harvard Univ. Press, 2011.

Gallman, J. Matthew. *Mastering Wartime: A Social History of Philadelphia during the Civil War.* New York: Cambridge Univ. Press, 1990.

———. *Northerners at War: Reflections on the Civil War Home Front.* Kent, OH: Kent State Univ. Press, 2010.

Gallman, J. Matthew, and Stanley Engerman. "The Civil War Economy: A Modern View." In *Northerners at War: Reflections on the Civil War Home* Front, edited by J. Matthew Gallman, 87–119. Kent, OH: Kent State Univ. Press, 2010.

Gannon, Barbara A. *The Won Cause: Black and White Comradeship in the Grand Army of the Republic.* Chapel Hill: Univ. of North Carolina Press, 2011.

Gates, Paul Wallace. *Agriculture and the Civil War.* New York: Alfred A. Knopf, 1965.

———. *Fifty Million Acres: Conflicts over Kansas Land Policy, 1854–1900.* Ithaca, NY: Cornell Univ. Press, 1954.

Gelderman, Carol. *A Free Man of Color and His Hotel: Race, Reconstruction, and the Role of the Federal Government.* Washington, DC: Potomac Books, 2012.

George, Mary K. *Zachariah Chandler: A Political Biography.* East Lansing: Michigan State Univ. Press, 1969.

Gienapp, William E. *The Origins of the Republican Party, 1852–1856.* New York: Oxford Univ. Press, 1987.

———. "The Republican Party and the Slave Power." In *New Perspectives on Race and Slavery in America,* edited by Robert H. Abzug and Stephen E. Maizlish, 57–78. Lexington: Univ. of Kentucky Press, 1986.

Gillette, William. *Retreat from Reconstruction, 1869–1879.* Baton Rouge: Louisiana State Univ. Press, 1979.

Graham, Lawrence Otis. *The Senator and the Socialite: The True Story of America's First Black Dynasty.* New York: HarperCollins, 2007.

Gray, Wood. *The Hidden Civil War: The Story of the Copperheads.* New York: Viking Press, 1942.

Green, Michael S. *Freedom, Union, and Power: Lincoln and His Party during the Civil War.* New York: Fordham Univ. Press, 2004.

———. *Politics and America in Crisis: The Coming of the Civil War.* Santa Barbara, CA: Praeger, 2010.

———. "Reconstructing the Nation, Reconstructing the Party: Postwar Republicans and the Evolution of a Party." In *The Great Task Remaining Before Us: Reconstruction as America's Continuing Civil War,* edited by Paul A. Cimbala and Randall M. Miller, 183–204. New York: Simon and Schuster, 2004.

Guelzo, Allen C. "Apple of Gold in a Picture of Silver: The Constitution and Liberty." In *The Lincoln Enigma: The Changing Faces of an American Icon,* edited by Gabor Boritt, 86–107. New York: Oxford Univ. Press, 2001.

Gugin, Linda C., and James E. St. Clair, eds. *The Governors of Indiana.* Indianapolis: Indiana Historical Society Press, 2006.

Gugin, Linda C., James E. St. Clair, and Thomas P. Wolf. "Indiana Governors: Powers and Personal Attributes." In Gugin and St. Clair, *Governors of Indiana,* 1–17.

Haffner, Gerald O. *The Hoosier Governor, Ashbel P. Willard, and His Times.* New Albany: Indiana Univ. Southeast Bookstore, 1980.

Hanley, Ray. *Hot Springs: Past and Present.* Fayetteville: Univ. of Arkansas Press, 2014.

Harris, William C. "Blanche K. Bruce of Mississippi: Conservative Assimilationist." In *Southern Black Leaders of the Reconstruction Era,* edited by Howard N. Rabinowitz, 1–38. Carbondale: Univ. of Illinois, Press, 1982.

———. *The Day of the Carpetbagger: Republican Reconstruction in Mississippi.* Baton Rouge: Louisiana State Univ. Press, 1979.

———. *Lincoln and the Union Governors.* Concise Lincoln Library. Carbondale: Southern Illinois Univ. Press, 2013.

Harrison, Lowell H. "Beriah Magoffin." In *Kentucky's Governors,* edited by Lowell H. Harrison, 603–4. Lexington: Univ. Press of Kentucky, 2004.

———. *The Civil War in Kentucky.* Lexington: Univ. Press of Kentucky, 1987.

Haskins, James. *Pinckney Benton Stewart Pinchback.* New York: MacMillan, 1973.

Hatch, Nathan O. *The Democratization of American Christianity.* New Haven, CT: Yale Univ. Press, 1989.

Havighurst, Walter. *The Miami Years, 1809–1984.* New York: G. P. Putnam's Sons, 1984.

Hess, Earl J. *Liberty, Virtue, and Progress: Northerners and Their War for the Union.* New York: Fordham Univ. Press, 1997.

Hesseltine, William B. *Lincoln and the War Governors.* New York: Alfred A. Knopf, 1948.

Hoagland, Alison K. *Historic American Buildings Survey: Jacob Julian (Oliver P. Morton) House.* Washington, DC: National Park Service, Department of the Interior, 1984.

Hofstadter, Richard. *The Paranoid Style in American Politics and Other Essays.* New York: Alfred A. Knopf, 1965.

Holcombe, John W. and Hubert M. Skinner, *Life and Public Services of Thomas A. Hendricks with Selected Speeches and Writing.* Indianapolis: Carlton and Hollenbeck, 1886.

Holt, Michael F. *By One Vote: The Disputed Presidential Election of 1876.* Lawrence: Univ. Press of Kansas, 2008.

———. *The Political Crisis of the 1850s.* New York: W. W. Norton, 1978.

———. *The Rise and Fall of the American Whig Party: Jacksonian Politics and the Onset of the Civil War.* New York: Oxford Univ. Press, 1999.

Holzer, Harold, Edna Greene Medford, and Frank J. Williams. *The Emancipation Proclamation: Three Views.* Baton Rouge: Louisiana State Univ. Press, 2006.

Howe, Daniel Walker, *The Political Culture of the American Whigs.* Chicago: Univ. of Chicago Press, 1984.

———. *What Hath God Wrought: The Transformation of America, 1815–1848.* New York: Oxford Univ. Press, 2007.

Hummel, Jeffery Rogers. *Emancipating Slaves, Enslaving Free Men: A History of the American Civil War.* 2nd ed. Chicago: Open Court, 2014.

Huston, James L. *The Panic of 1857 and the Coming of the Civil War.* Baton Rouge: Louisiana State Univ. Press, 1987.

———. *Stephen A. Douglas and the Dilemmas of Democratic Equality.* New York: Rowman and Littlefield, 2007.

Janney, Caroline E. *Burying the Dead But Not the Past: Ladies' Memorial Associations and the Lost Cause.* Chapel Hill: Univ. of North Carolina Press, 2008.

———. *Remembering the Civil War: Reunion and the Limits of Reconciliation.* Chapel Hill: Univ. of North Carolina Press, 2013.

Jeffrey, Julie Roy. *Abolitionists Remember: Antislavery Autobiographies and the Unfinished Work of Emancipation.* Chapel Hill: Univ. of North Carolina Press, 2008.

Johannsen, Robert W. *Stephen A. Douglas.* New York: Oxford Univ. Press, 1973.

Johnson, Curtis D. *Islands of Holiness: Rural Religion in Upstate New York, 1790–1860.* Ithaca, NY: Cornell Univ. Press, 1989.

Johnson, David Alan. *Decided on the Battlefield: Grant, Sherman, Lincoln and the Election of 1864.* New York: Prometheus Books, 2012.

Johnson, Paul E. *A Shopkeeper's Millennium: Society and Revivals in Rochester, New York, 1815–1837.* New York: Hill and Wang, 1978.

Jordan, David M. *Roscoe Conkling of New York: Voice in the Senate.* Ithaca, NY: Cornell Univ. Press, 1971.

Kammen, Michael. *Mystic Chords of Memory: The Transformation of Tradition in American Culture.* New York: Alfred A. Knopf, 1991.

Keehn, David C. *Knights of the Golden Circle: Secret Empire, Southern Secession, Civil War.* Baton Rouge: Louisiana State Univ. Press, 2013.

Keith, Lee Anna. *The Colfax Massacre: The Untold Story of Black Power, White Terror, and the Death of Reconstruction.* New York: Oxford Univ. Press, 2009.

Kelley, Darwin N. *Milligan's Fight Against Lincoln.* New York: Exposition Press, 1973.

Keyssar, Alexander. *The Right to Vote: The Contested History of Democracy in the United States.* New York: Basic Books, 2000.

Kinslow, Krista. "Contesting the Centennial: Politics and Culture at the 1876 World's Fair." PhD diss., Boston Univ., forthcoming.

Klement, Frank L. *The Copperheads in the Middle West.* Chicago: Univ. of Chicago Press, 1960.

———. *Dark Lanterns: Secret Political Societies, Conspiracies, and Treason Trials in the Civil War.* Baton Rouge: Louisiana State Univ. Press, 1989.

———. *The Limits of Dissent: Clement L. Vallandigham and the Civil War.* Lexington: Univ. Press of Kentucky, 1970.

Knupfer, Peter B. *The Union as It Is: Constitutional Unionism and Sectional Compromise, 1787–1861.* Chapel Hill: Univ. of North Carolina Press, 1991.

Krug, Mark M. *Lyman Trumbull: Conservative Radical.* New York: A. S. Barnes, 1965.

Lantzer, Jason S. "Edward L. Jackson." In Gugin and St. Clair, *Governors of Indiana,* 274–79.

Larson, John Lauritz. *Internal Improvement: National Public Works and the Promise of Popular Government in the Early United States.* Chapel Hill: Univ. of North Carolina Press, 2001.

Leary, Edward A. *Indianapolis: The Story of a City.* Indianapolis: Bobbs-Merrill, 1971.

Leopold, Richard William. *Robert Dale Owen: A Biography.* Cambridge, MA: Harvard Univ. Press, 1940.

Lighty, S. Chandler. "The *Indiana Sentinel*: Indianapolis's Democratic Voice." Oct. 17, 2013. *Hoosier State Chronicles: Indiana's Digital Historic Newspaper Program,* https://blog.newspapers.library.in.gov/indiana-sentinel.

Long, David E. *The Jewel of Liberty: Abraham Lincoln's Reelection and the End of Slavery.* Mechanicsburg, PA: Stackpole Books.

Long, Kathryn Teresa. *The Revival of 1857–58: Interpreting an American Religious Awakening.* New York: Oxford Univ. Press, 1998.

Lord, Stuart B. "Adelbert Ames, Soldier and Politician: a Reevaluation." *Maine Historical Society Quarterly* 13, no. 2 (1973): 81–97.

Lu, Gwei-Djen. *Celestial Lancets: A History and Rationale of Acupuncture and Moxa.* London: Routledge, 2002.

Lutholtz, M. William. *Grand Dragon: D. C. Stephenson and the Ku Klux Klan in Indiana.* West Lafayette, IN: Purdue Univ. Press, 1991.

Madison, James H. "Civil War Memories and 'Pardnership Forgittin,' 1865–1913." *Indiana Magazine of History* 99 (Sept. 2003): 198–230.

———. *Hoosiers: A New History of Indiana.* Bloomington: Indiana Univ. Press, 2014.

———. *The Indiana Way: A State History.* Bloomington: Indiana Univ. Press, 1986.

———. *A Lynching in the Heartland: Race and Memory in America.* New York: Palgrave Macmillan, 2001.

Marshall, Anne E. *Creating a Confederate Kentucky: The Lost Cause and Civil War Memory in a Border State.* Chapel Hill: Univ. of North Carolina Press, 2010.

May, Robert E. *Manifest Destiny's Underworld: Filibustering in Antebellum America.* Chapel Hill: Univ. of North Carolina Press, 2002.

McConnell, Stuart. *Glorious Contentment: The Grand Army of the Republic, 1865–1900.* Chapel Hill: Univ. of North Carolina Press, 1992.

McDougall, Walter A. *Freedom Just Around the Corner: A New American History, 1585–1828.* New York: HarperCollins, 2004.

McLoughlin, William G. *Revivals, Awakenings, and Reform.* Chicago: Univ. of Chicago Press, 1978.

McPherson, James. *The Battle Cry of Freedom: The Civil War Era.* Oxford History of the United States. New York: Oxford Univ. Press, 1988.

Miller, John W. *Indiana Newspaper Bibliography.* Indianapolis: Indiana Historical Society, 1982.

Milton, George Fort. *Abraham Lincoln and the Fifth Column.* New York: Vanguard Press, 1942.

Moore, Glover. *The Missouri Controversy, 1819–1821.* Lexington: Univ. of Kentucky Press, 1953.

Morris, Roy, Jr. *Fraud of the Century: Rutherford B. Hayes, Samuel Tilden, and the Stolen Election of 1876.* New York: Simon and Schuster, 2003.

Morrison, Michael A. "President James Buchanan: Executive Leadership and the Crisis of the Democracy." In *James Buchanan and the Coming of the Civil War,* edited by John W. Quist and Michael J. Birkner, 134–64. Gainesville: Univ. Press of Florida, 2013.

Mulderink, Earl F. *New Bedford's Civil War.* New York: Fordham Univ. Press, 2012.

Murphy, Charles B. *The Political Career of Jesse D. Bright.* Indiana Historical Society Publications, vol. 10, no. 3. Indianapolis: Indiana Historical Society Publications, 1931.

Nation, Richard F. *At Home in the Hoosier Hills: Agriculture, Politics, and Religion in Southern Indiana, 1810–1870.* Bloomington: Indiana Univ. Press, 2005.

Nation, Richard F., and Stephen E. Towne, eds. *Indiana's War: The Civil War in Documents.* Athens: Ohio Univ. Press, 2009.

Neely, Mark E., Jr. *The Fate of Liberty: Abraham Lincoln and Civil Liberties.* New York: Oxford Univ. Press, 1991.

———. *Union Divided: Party Conflict in the Civil War North.* Cambridge, MA: Harvard Univ. Press, 2002.

Neff, John R. *Honoring the Civil War Dead: Commemoration and the Problem of Reconciliation.* Lawrence: Univ. Press of Kansas, 2005.

Nelson, Jacquelyn S. *Indiana Quakers Confront the Civil War.* Indianapolis: Indiana Historical Society, 1994.

Nelson, Larry E. *Bullets, Ballots, and Rhetoric: Confederate States Policy for the United States Presidential Contest.* Tuscaloosa: Univ. of Alabama Press, 2015.

Nelson, Scott Reynolds, *A Nation of Deadbeats: An Uncommon History of America's Financial Disasters.* New York: Alfred A. Knopf, 2012.

Nevins, Allan. *The Emergence of Lincoln: Douglas, Buchanan, and Party Chaos, 1857–1859.* New York: Scribner's, 1950.

Nicholas, Stacey. "William Hayden English." In *The Encyclopedia of Indianapolis,* edited by David J. Bodenhamer and Robert G. Barrows, 544–45. Bloomington: Indiana Univ. Press, 1994.

Nichols, Alice. *Bleeding Kansas.* New York: Oxford Univ. Press, 1954.

Nichols, Roy Franklin. *The Disruption of American Democracy.* New York: Macmillan, 1948.

Niven, John. *Salmon P. Chase: A Biography.* New York: Oxford Univ. Press, 1995.

Nolan, Alan T. *The Iron Brigade: A Military History.* Bloomington, IN: Indiana Univ. Press, 1961.

Oakes, James. *Freedom National: The Destruction of Slavery in the United States, 1861–1865.* New York: W. W. Norton, 2012.

O'Brien, Michael. "Biography and the Old South." In Michael O'Brien, *Placing the South*, 86–99. Jackson: Univ. Press of Mississippi, 2007.

O'Brien, Patrick K. *The Economic Effect of the American Civil War*. Atlantic Highlands, NJ: Humanities Press International, 1988.

Paludan, Phillip S. *"A People's Contest": The Union and the Civil War, 1861–1865*. New York: Harper and Row, 1988.

Peek, Gregory. "'The True and Ever Living Principle of States Rights and Popular Sovereignty': Douglas Democrats and Indiana Republicans Allied, 1857–1859." *Indiana Magazine of History* 111, no. 4 (Dec. 2015): 381–421.

———. "Upland Southerners, Indiana Political Culture, and the Coming of the Civil War, 1816–1861." PhD diss., Univ. of Houston, 2010.

Pereyra, Lillian A. *James Lusk Alcorn: Persistent Whig*. Baton Rouge: Louisiana State Univ. Press, 1966.

Peskin, Allan. "Was There a Compromise of 1877?" *Journal of American History* 60 (June 1973): 63–75.

Phillips, Christopher. *The Rivers Ran Backward: The Civil War and the Remaking of the American Middle Border*. New York: Oxford Univ. Press, 2016.

Phillips, Clifton J. *Indiana in Transition: The Emergence of an Industrial Commonwealth, 1880–1920*. The History of Indiana, vol. 4. Indianapolis: Indiana Historical Bureau and Indiana Historical Society, 1968.

Piston, William Garrett. *Lee's Tarnished Lieutenant: James Longstreet and His Place in Southern History*. Athens: Univ. of Georgia Press, 1990.

Potter, David M. *The Impending Crisis, 1848–1861*. New York: Harper and Row, 1976.

Rabinowitz, Howard N., ed. *Southern Black Leaders of the Reconstruction Era*. Carbondale: Univ. of Illinois, Press, 1982.

Rable, George C. *But There Was No Peace: The Role of Violence in the Politics of Reconstruction*. Athens: Univ. of Georgia Press, 1984.

Rainesalo, Timothy C. "Senator Oliver P. Morton and Historical Memory of the Civil War and Reconstruction in Indiana." MA thesis, Indiana Univ., 2016.

Raitz, Karl, ed. *The National Road*. Road and American Culture Series. Baltimore: Johns Hopkins Univ. Press, 1996.

Ramage, James A. "Indiana's Response to John Hunt Morgan's Raid." *Journal of the Jackson Purchase Historical Society* 8 (June 1980): 1–9.

———. *Rebel Raider: The Life of General John Hunt Morgan*. Lexington: Univ. Press of Kentucky, 1986.

Ramage, James A., and Andrea S. Watkins. *Kentucky Rising: Democracy, Slavery, and Culture from the Early Republic to the Civil War*. Lexington: Univ. Press of Kentucky, 2011.

Randall, J. G. *Lincoln the President: Springfield to Gettysburg*, vol. I. New York: Dodd, Mead, 1945.

Randel, William Peirce. *Centennial: American Life in 1876*. Philadelphia: Chilton, 1969.

Rawley, James A. *Race and Politics: "Bleeding Kansas" and the Coming of the Civil War*. New York: J. B. Lippincott, 1969.

Reardon, Carol. *Pickett's Charge in History and Memory*. Chapel Hill: Univ. of North Carolina Press, 1997.

Reed, Robert M. *Lincoln's Funeral Train: The Epic Journey from Washington to Springfield*. Atglen, PA: Schiffer, 2014.

Rehnquist, William. "Civil Liberty and the Civil War: The Indianapolis Treason Trials." *Indiana Law Journal* 72 (Fall 1997): 927–37.

Reynolds, David S. *John Brown, Abolitionist: The Man Who Killed Slavery, Sparked the Civil War, and Seeded Civil Rights.* New York: Alfred A. Knopf, 2005.

Richards, Leonard L. *The Slave Power: The Free North and Southern Domination, 1780–1860.* Baton Rouge: Louisiana State Univ. Press, 2000.

Richardson, Elmo R., and Alan W. Farley. *John Palmer Usher: Lincoln's Secretary of the Interior.* Lawrence: Univ. of Kansas Press, 1960.

Richardson, Heather Cox. *The Greatest Nation of the Earth: Republican Economic Policies during the Civil War.* Cambridge, MA: Harvard Univ. Press, 1997.

———. *To Make Men Free: A History of the Republican Party.* New York: Basic Books, 2014.

Riddleberger, Patrick W. *George Washington Julian: Radical Republican.* Indianapolis: Indiana Historical Bureau, 1966.

Rightmyer, Don. *Torn: The Civil War in Kentucky.* El Dorado Hills, CA: Savas Beatie, 2014.

Riker, Dorothy, and Gayle Thornbrough, comp., *Indiana Election Returns, 1816–1851.* Indianapolis: Indiana Historical Bureau, 1960.

Rodgers, Daniel T. "Republicanism: The Career of a Concept." *Journal of American History* 79 (June 1992): 11–38.

Rodgers, Thomas E. "Saving the Republic: Turnout, Ideology, and Republicanism in the Election of 1860." In *The Election of 1860 Reconsidered,* edited by A. James Fuller, 165–92. Kent: OH: Kent State Univ. Press, 2013.

———. "Hoosier Women and the Civil War Homefront." *Indiana Magazine of History* 97 (June 2001): 105–28.

Roller, Scott. "Business as Usual: Indiana's Response to the Confederate Invasions of the Summer of 1863." *Indiana Magazine of History* 88 (March 1992): 1–25.

Rose, Gregory S. "Extending the Road West," In *The National Road,* edited by Karl Raitz, 178–79. Road and American Culture Series. Baltimore: Johns Hopkins Univ. Press, 1996

———. "The National Road Border between the North and the South in the Midwest by 1870," *Geoscience and Man* 25, (1988): 159–67.

———. "Upland Southerners: The County Origins of Southern Migrants to Indiana by 1850." *Indiana Magazine of History* 82 (1986): 242–63.

Rothbard, Murray N. *A History of Money and Banking the United States: The Colonial Era to World War II.* Auburn, AL: Mises Institute, 2002.

Ryan, Mary P. *Cradle of the Middle Class: The Family in Oneida County, New York, 1790–1860.* New York: Cambridge Univ. Press, 1981.

Sample, Bradford W. "Joseph A. Wright." In Gugin and James St. Clair, *Governors of Indiana,* 112–22.

Savage, Kirk. *Standing Soldiers, Kneeling Slaves: Race, War, and Monument in Nineteenth-Century America.* Princeton, NJ: Princeton Univ. Press, 1997.

Scheele, Raymond. "J. Frank Hanly." In Gugin and St. Clair, *Governors of Indiana,* 224–31.

Schuchman, John S. "The Political Background of the Political-Question Doctrine: The Judges and the Dorr War." *American Journal of Legal History* 6, no. 2 (1972): 111–25.

Schultz, Leslie Hamilton. "Oliver P. Morton and Reconstruction, 1867–1877." MA thesis, Univ. of Chicago, 1935.

Seigel, Peggy Brase. "She Went to War: Indiana Women Nurses in the Civil War." *Indiana Magazine of History* 86 (Mar. 1990): 1–27.

Sellers, Charles G. *The Market Revolution: Jacksonian America, 1815–1846*. New York: Oxford Univ. Press, 1992.

Sewell, Richard H. *Ballots for Freedom: Antislavery Politics in the United States, 1837–1860*. New York: Oxford Univ. Press, 1976.

Shallhope, Robert. E. "Toward Republican Synthesis: The Emergence of an Understanding of Republicanism in American Historiography." *William and Mary Quarterly* 29, no. 1 (Jan. 1972): 49–80.

Sharkey, Robert P. *Money, Class, and Party: An Economic Study of Civil War and Reconstruction*. Baltimore: Johns Hopkins Univ. Press, 1959.

Shelden, Rachel A. *Washington Brotherhood: Politics, Social Life, and the Coming of the Civil War*. Chapel Hill: Univ. of North Carolina Press, 2013.

Sievers, Harry J. *Benjamin Harrison Vol. 1: Hoosier Warrior: Through the Civil War Years, 1833–1865*. New York: Univ. Publishers, 1952.

———. *Benjamin Harrison Vol. 2: Hoosier Statesman: From the Civil War to the White House, 1865–1888*. New York: Univ. Publishers, 1959.

Silber, Nina. *The Romance of Reunion: Northerners and the South, 1865–1900*. Chapel Hill: Univ. of North Carolina Press, 1993.

Silbey, Joel H. *The American Political Nation, 1838–1893*. Stanford, CA: Stanford Univ. Press, 1991.

———. *The Partisan Imperative: The Dynamics of American Politics Before the Civil War*. New York: Oxford Univ. Press, 1985.

Sky, Theodore. *The National Road and the Difficult Path to Sustainable National Investment*. Newark: Univ. of Delaware Press, 2011.

Slap, Andrew L. *The Doom of Reconstruction: The Liberal Republicans in the Civil War Era*. New York: Fordham Univ. Press, 2006.

Smith, Michael Thomas. *The Enemy Within: Fears of Corruption in the Civil War North*. Charlottesville: Univ. of Virginia Press, 2011.

Smith, Timothy B. *The Golden Age of Battlefield Preservation: The Decade of the 1890s and the Establishment of America's First Five Military Parks*. Knoxville: Univ. of Tennessee Press, 2008.

Smith, Timothy L. *Revivalism and Social Reform in Mid-19th-Century America*. New York: Abingdon Press, 1957.

Stampp, Kenneth M. *America in 1857: A Nation on the Brink*. New York: Oxford Univ. Press, 1990.

———. *The Era of Reconstruction, 1865–1877*. New York: Alfred A. Knopf, 1965.

———. *Indiana Politics during the Civil War*. 1949. Reprint. Bloomington: Indiana Univ. Press, 1978.

Stanley, Matthew E. *The Loyal West: Civil War and Reunion in Middle America*. Urbana: Univ. of Illinois Press, 2017.

St. Clair, James E. "Ashbel P. Willare." In Gugin and St. Clair, *Governors of Indiana*, 112–22.

Stoler, Mildred C. "Insurgent Democrats of Indiana and Illinois in 1854." *Indiana Magazine of History* 33 (Mar. 1937): 1–31.

Stowell, Daniel. "Mobilizing Hoosiers: Abraham Lincoln's Indiana Appointments in 1861." Fourth Annual Civil War Study Group Symposium, Indianapolis, Indiana, Sept. 17, 2011.

Summers, Mark Wahlgren. *The Era of Good Stealings.* New York: Oxford Univ. Press, 1993.

———. *The Ordeal of the Reunion: A New History of Reconstruction.* Chapel Hill: Univ. of North Carolina Press, 2014.

———. *The Plundering Generation: Corruption and the Crisis of the Union, 1849–1861.* New York: Oxford Univ. Press, 1987.

———. *Railroads, Reconstruction, and the Gospel of Prosperity: Aid under the Radical Republicans, 1865–1877.* Princeton, NJ: Princeton Univ. Press, 1984.

Sylvester, Lorna Lutes. "Oliver P. Morton and Hoosier Politics During the Civil War." PhD diss., Indiana Univ., 1968.

Taylor, George Rogers. *The Transportation Revolution, 1815–1860.* New York: Holt, Rinehart, and Winston, Inc., 1951.

Tenney, Craig D. "To Suppress or Not to Suppress: Abraham Lincoln and the Chicago Times." *Civil War History* 27 (Sept. 1981): 248–59.

Thornbrough, Emma Lou. *Indiana in the Civil War Era.* Indianapolis: Indiana Historical Society, 1965.

———. *The Negro in Indiana Before 1900.* Bloomington: Indiana Univ. Press, 1985.

Towne, Stephen E. "Killing the Serpent Speedily: Governor Morton, General Hascall, and the Suppression of the Democratic Press in Indiana, 1863." *Civil War History* 52: 1 (Mar. 2006), 41–65.

———. "Scorched Earth or Fertile Ground? Indiana in the Civil War, 1861–1865." In *The State of Indiana History 2000: Papers Presented at the Indiana Historical Society's Grand Opening,* edited by Robert M. Taylor Jr., 397–415. Indianapolis: Indiana Historical Society, 2001.

———. *Surveillance and Spies in the Civil War: Exposing Confederate Conspiracies in America's Heartland.* Law, Society, and Politics in the Midwest Series. Athens: Ohio Univ. Press, 2015.

———. "Worse than Vallandigham: Governor Oliver P. Morton, Lambdin P. Milligan, and the Military Arrest and Trial of Indiana State Senator Alexander J. Douglas During the Civil War." *Indiana Magazine of History* 106, no. 1 (Mar. 2010): 1–39.

Treaster, Beth, et al. "Happy Birthday, Oliver P. Morton! August 4, 2013." Printed program. Centerville, IN: Centerville Public Library, 2013.

———. "Remembering Lincoln: Exactly 150 Years Later, April 19, 2015." Printed program. Centerville, IN: Centerville–Center Township Public Library, 2015.

Trefousse, Hans L. *Ben Butler: The South Called Him BEAST!* New York: Twayne, 1957.

———. *Benjamin Franklin Wade: Radical Republican from Ohio.* New York: Twayne, 1963.

———. *Carl Schurz: A Biography.* Knoxville: Univ. of Tennessee Press, 1982.

———. *Impeachment of a President: Andrew Johnson, the Blacks and Reconstruction.* Knoxville: Univ. of Tennessee Press, 1975.

———. *The Radical Republicans: Lincoln's Vanguard for Racial Justice.* New York: Alfred A. Knopf, 1969.

———. *Thaddeus Stevens: Nineteenth-Century Egalitarian.* Chapel Hill: Univ. of North Carolina Press, 1997.

Trelease, Allen W. *White Terror: The Ku Klux Klan Conspiracy and Southern Reconstruction.* Baton Rouge: Louisiana State Univ. Press, 1971.

Unger, Irwin. *The Greenback Era: A Social and Political History of American Finance, 1865–1879.* Princeton, NJ: Princeton Univ. Press, 1964.

Van Bolt, Roger H. "Rise of the Republican Party in Indiana, 1855–1856." *Indiana Magazine of History* 51 (Sept. 1955): 185–220.

Walsh, Justin E. *To Print the News and Raise Hell! A Biography of Wilbur F. Storey.* Chapel Hill: Univ. of North Carolina Press, 1968.

Wang, Xi. *The Trial of Democracy: Black Suffrage and Northern Republicans, 1860–1910.* Athens: Univ. of Georgia Press, 1996.

Watson, Harry L. *Liberty and Power: The Politics of Jacksonian America.* New York: Hill and Wang, 1990.

Waugh, John C. *Reelecting Lincoln: The Battle for the 1864 Presidency.* New York: Crown, 1997.

Weber, Jennifer L. *Copperheads: The Rise and Fall of Lincoln's Opponents in the North.* New York: Oxford Univ. Press, 2006.

Wertheim, Lewis J. "The Indianapolis Treason Trials." *Indiana Magazine of History* 85 (Sept. 1989): 236–60.

Whallon, Arthur. *Centerville, Indiana: A National Road Town.* Richmond, IN: Historic Centerville, n.d.

White, Jonathan W. *Emancipation, the Union Army, and the Reelection of Abraham Lincoln.* Baton Rouge: Louisiana State Univ. Press, 2014.

Wickre, John J. "Indiana's Southern Senator: Jesse Bright and the Hoosier Democracy." PhD dissertation, Univ. of Kentucky, 2013.

Wilentz, Sean. *The Rise of American Democracy: Jefferson to Lincoln.* New York: W. W. Norton, 2005.

Wilhelm, Hubert G. "The Road as a Corridor for Ideas." In *The National Road,* edited by Karl Raitz, 256–84. Road and American Culture Series. Baltimore: Johns Hopkins Univ. Press, 1996.

Wilson, Mark R. *The Business of Civil War: Military Mobilization and the State, 1861–1865.* Baltimore: Johns Hopkins Univ. Press, 2006.

Wilson, Oliver M. *Grand Army of the Republic.* Kansas City, MO: Franklin Hudson, 1905.

Wilson, William E. "Thunderbolt of the Confederacy or King of Horse Thieves?" *Indiana Magazine of History* 54, no. 2 (June 1958): 119–30.

Wood, Gordon. *Empire of Liberty: A History of the Early Republic, 1789–1815.* New York: Oxford Univ. Press, 2010.

Woodburn, James A. "Henry Smith Lane." *Indiana Magazine of History* 28 (Dec. 1931): 279–87.

Woodward, C. Vann. *Reunion and Reaction: The Compromise of 1877 and the End of Reconstruction.* Boston: Little, Brown, 1951.

Woollen, William Wesley. *Biographical and Historical Sketches of Early Indiana.* Indianapolis: Hammond, 1883.

Wyatt-Brown, Bertram. *Yankee Saints and Southern Sinners.* Baton Rouge: Louisiana State Univ. Press, 1985.

Zenor, Carl A., ed. *Indiana and the Civil War.* Indianapolis: Indiana Civil War Centennial Commission, 1961.

Zimmerman, Charles M. "The Origin and Rise of the Republican Party in Indiana from 1858 to 1860." Pt. 1. *Indiana Magazine of History* 13 (Sept. 1917): 211–68.

———. "The Origin and Rise of the Republican Party in Indiana from 1858 to 1860." Pt. 2. *Indiana Magazine of History* 13 (Dec. 1917): 349–412.

Index